SIKH SOLDIER

Mr Narinder Singh Dhesi in his latest Book on "Sikh Soldier: *At War* " places in proper perspective the chronicle of a class of men who rose from an insignificant socio-cultural background to rise in martial spirit and adopt the warrior ethos. In doing so they proved their merit and courage in various conflicts spanning a period of nearly four centuries. They amply proved that accidents of birth have no importance in the military tradition, where actions of merit and bravery are amply recognized and justly rewarded. The leap of faith in their enrolment into the brotherhood of arms was richly repaid by them in no small measure. Soldiering is not just about faith and reputation. It is the union of reason and intuition that cannot be defined but is only to be experienced. As, F. Yeats-Brown wrote in 'Martial India'; "A remarkable people, the Sikhs, with their ten prophets, five distinguishing marks, and their baptismal rite of water stirred with steel; a people who have made history, and will make it again." A must read book by all Military Historians.

Lieutenant General BS Dhaliwal (Retd) PVSM, AVSM, VSM
Indian Army

This is an excellent piece of work which makes an interesting reading for one and all. It is a tremendous effort to research, analyse and put the historic memorable facts for easy comprehension by the community and others. A saga of history, Wars, valour, bravery and Sikh leadership of a very high order in all spheres of soldiering has been brought out by Narindar Singh Dhesi in a very simple way that keeps the reader glued on to the book until the end. As one read the details of military actions and selfless devotion to the cause by Sikh soldiers and generals, one's heart swells up with pride. Of course one also wonders as to why we do not see such soldiers and generals these days. Where have they gone? This book deserves to be part of all libraries and households to ensure that we do not lose sight of our rich history and that we remain highly motivated for our cause in this ever expanding materialistic and artificial environment that confronts future generations. Thanks to Narindar Singh Dhesi for his untiring efforts to reflect on the historic bravery, courage and sacrifices of our community in the service of humanity.

Major General BS Dhillon, (Retd) VSM.
Indian Army

Sikh Soldier

Continuing the narrative of Sikh soldiery, this book is the fifth volume of the Sikh Soldier Series, written by Mr Dhesi. It is an extremely well researched book which covers a very wide canvas. The book starts with the Antecedents (or the predecessors) of the Sikhs, their Gurus and Church, birth of the Khalsa and the establishment of the Sikh Empire by Maharaja Ranjit Singh, and then goes on to describe the immense contribution of Sikh soldiers in the various wars of the past few centuries. He has also included snippets of acts of extreme valour of the Sikh officers and men who were awarded gallantry awards in the two world wars, as also the post-independence wars that India has fought with Pakistan and China, right up to the Kargil conflict of 1999. This was indeed a very herculean task, and Mr Dhesi needs to be commended for bringing out this scholarly work, which is a good reference point for those interested in Sikh religion and history.

Major General AJS Sandhu (Retd) VSM.
Indian Army

How can a people numbering a mere two percent of the Indian population have had such an inordinate amount of influence on the military fortunes of that country? How, what's more, can this same people have helped direct the fates of nations, wars and armies across the largest modern empire that the world has ever known? How is it that today representatives of this people can be found in the highest ranks of armed forces of countries in the Americas, Europe, Africa and Oceania, as well as Asia? It is the martial story of this people, the Sikhs that is depicted in these pages. It is the story of a people whose identity was forged in the martyrdom of its Gurus, tempered by nationhood under Ranjit Singh, and sharpened through the colonial wars of the British Empire. It is a story that in many ways reached its apogee in the supreme sacrifices of the Sikh soldier in the First and Second World Wars, when he laid down his life in the mud of Flanders, the shallows of Suvla, the jungles of Burma and the hills of Italy. And it is a story which carries on today across the world with outstanding military service in numerous armies, navies and air forces.

Narindar Singh Dhesi, whose own service in the British Army during the Cold War in Germany and Aden puts him in his own narrative, portrays the Sikh story from its earliest beginnings in the Indus Valley to the modern day. Whether with spear, lance, sabre, musket, rifle, machine gun, battleship or fighter jet, we see how the Sikh has fought valiantly and loyally to the colours. We are indebted to Mr Dhesi for this authoritative trove of information and we commend his work to anyone who has an interest in the feats of this remarkable people.

Lieutenant Colonel Gurcharan Singh Chana (Retd)
Kenya Army

Sikh Soldier

Narinder Singh Dhesi has done a great service in compiling Sikh Military history. He is showing the Sikh and broader community the gallantry and sacrifice of the Sikh soldiers who fought in many wars and conflicts around the globe. Even more important, Narinder Singh Dhesi reminds all Sikhs that there is no greater honour than to serve the nation you call home.

Lieutenant-Colonel Harjit Singh Sajjan, OMM, MSM, CD
Commanding Officer
The British Columbia Regiment
Canadian Army

As a Sikh, and a soldier at that, one believes that Sikhism and the warrior ethos are imbued in one's self. Sadly this ego and confidence can be misplaced as I discovered to my ego's cost when I was kindly asked by Narinder Singh Dhesi to review his book on the Sikh Soldier. I quickly discovered that the book has been extensively researched and covers all the battles the Sikhs have been involved in world wide. It articulates and brings to life the vista of the various campaigns and also the collective and individual bravery shown by the Sikh soldiers. Reading of the bravery awards one gets a clear sense of selfless sacrifice shown by the Sikhs. Anyone wishing to follow in the warrior footsteps of the Sikh soldiers past would be well advised to read this book to get an understanding of our ethos of selfless service. I congratulate Narinder Singh on this excellent work on the Sikh Soldier.

Lieutenant Colonel Tarlochan Singh Marwaha (Retd)
British Army

Narindar Singh Dhesi has laboured hard and long to produce the series of books on the Sikh Soldier. He has been able to extract the true nature of a Sikh: to be creative, productive and work in honest labour. In Sikh Soldier these virtues are amplified and in the battle field the warrior nature of a Sikh is naturally drawn. The bravery, courage and the sacrifices made by Sikhs are a credit to mankind. It is no wonder then that the Sikh Soldier was found in practically every war and campaign of the past, far away from his homeland. The battle scars can only be put into print and Narindar Singh Dhesi has amply done that. The Sikh Soldier is a must read for all Sikhs and should be made available in places of easy reach. Congratulations to Narindar Singh Dhesi for the hard work and the success that follows.

Lieutenant Colonel Baldev Singh Johl (Retd)
Malaysian Armed Forces

SIKH SOLDIER
VOLUME FIVE
At War!

Shaheed Baba Deep Singh Ji (1684-1757).

NARINDAR SINGH DHESI

Published by

The Naval & Military Press Ltd
Unit 10 Ridgewood Industrial Park,
Uckfield, East Sussex,
TN22 5QE England
Tel: + 44 (0) 1825 749494
Fax: + 44 (0) 1825 765701
www.naval-military-press.com
www.nmarchive.com

Copyright: Narindar Singh Dhesi

Maharajah Ranjit Singh
(1780-1839)

The Sikh Emperor

CONTENTS

Comments	1
Acknowledgements	8
Foreword	9
Introduction	10
Dedication	11
Punjab Antecedents	12
Sikh Ethos	21
Call to Arms	23
The Khalsa	34
Battles of the Khalsa	35
Sikh Misls	41
Afghan Invasions	51
Sikh Empire	58
Fall of the Sikh Empire	74
Northwest Frontier 1849-1857	83
Sepoy Mutiny	84
Northwest Frontier 1857-1878	85
Second Afghan War	86
Northwest Frontier 1881-1914	90
North East Frontier	96
Burma	97
Tibet	98
China	102
Malaya	105
Abyssinia	106
Egypt 1882	107
Sudan 1885	108
East Africa 1895	109
Jubaland	109
Uganda	110
Central Africa	111
Northern Rhodesia	112
Ashanti	113
Gambia	114
Somaliland	115
Indian Army WW1	117
Western Front	118
Aden	130
Suez Canal	131
Gallipoli	132
Senussi	133
Egypt, Palestine, Syria	135
Salonika Front	139
Mesopotamia	140

Contents

Persia	148
Bushire	152
Seistan	154
Trans-Caspia	155
East Africa 1914	158
Somaliland 1915	163
Burma 1914	164
Tsingtao	165
Third Afghan War	166
Waziristan	167
Iraq	170
Anatolia	175
Abyssinia 1934	177
East Africa 1940	178
Somaliland 1941	184
North Africa	185
Iraq 1941	195
Syria 1941	196
Iran 1941	200
Greece	201
Italy	202
Hong Kong	225
Malaya 1942	226
Singapore	232
Burma 1942	234
Java	268
Indo-Pak War 1947	269
Hyderabad	280
Goa	282
Indo-China War	284
Indo-Pak War 1965	287
Indo-Pak War 1971	294
Sri Lanka	318
Siachen	323
Kargil	325
American Sikh Soldiers	327
Malaysian Sikh Soldiers	330
Sikh Motor Muscle	334
Australian Sikh Soldiers	335
Canadian Sikh Soldiers	339
Appendix	347
Sources	368
Index	371

ACKNOWLEDGEMENTS

I must express my warmest thanks and respect to Vice Admiral Harindar Singh (Retd) PVSM, AVSMM of the Indian Navy, for writing the Foreword to this book and for invaluable help in writing my previous books. I salute you for that!

My sincere thanks to Major General Ardaman Jit Singh Sandhu (Retd) VSM of the Indian Army. I submitted a tome of a manuscript, yet to be published, of a detailed catalogue of 'Sikhs Soldier at War' to Major General Ardaman Jit Singh Sandhu, for his comments. What I received in return over various emails was a most comprehensible and invaluable corrections, suggestions and additions. Major General AJS Sandhu was actually very busy researching for his book on "The Battle of Chhamb 1971", and still found time to indulge me, with most valuable advice. Earlier on while I was constructing the volume four, 'Sikh Soldier; Warriors and Generals' Major General AJS Sandhu not only provided me with his own military profile but that also of his father Lieutenant General Jaswant Singh and that of Lieutenant General Prem Singh Gyani.

My Sincere thanks:
To Lieutenant Colonel Tarlochan Singh Marwaha (Tochi) (Retd), of UK armed forces, for most comprehensible and invaluable corrections, and suggestions for which I was able to make considerable changes to the text of the book.
To Lieutenant Colonel Baldev Singh Johl (Retd), Malaysian Armed Forces, inspite of his busy work schedule and tragic family circumstances, he still found time to edit the chapter on Malaya 1942 and write a review of the book.

To David R. Gray for invaluable information and penning the article about Canadian Sikh soldiers that served in France and Flanders during the WW1

To Major General Balli Singh Dhillon (Retd) VSM of Indian Army, for his kind encouragement, and writing the comments about this book.

To Lieutenant General (Retd) BS Dhaliwal PVSM, AVSM, VSM Indian Army, Lieutenant Colonel (Retd) Gurcharan Singh Chana (Chani), Kenya Army, and Lieutenant Colonel Harjit Singh Sajjan, Canadian Armed Forces, for writing most encouraging comments about the book.

To long suffering hon. Professor Graham Watkins for constructing the cover of this book and final help in submitting the text to the publishers.

To my son Jodh who composed the chapter 'About this Book' and valuable help in constructing the book.

To my son Jassa who constantly sorted out the incoming messages and texts.

To my daughters, Surindar and Sher who bore the brunt of my 'Sikh Attacks'.

And my final thanks to my wife Bev, who proofread and helped to make the manuscript ready for publication. Any mistakes in spelling and typos are attributed to her.!

FOREWORD

Indians have been particularly known to lack a sense of history and it was always the foreign powers who systematically recorded history but obviously from their point of view and leaving big voids. So where was the history of the Sikhs? No-one had really chronicled and documented the history, valour and sacrifice of the Sikhs in a consolidated form. In this book, and in four earlier ones, Mr Dhesi has admirably filled this so obvious void. This book makes compelling reading, dealing methodically, as it does, with the history of the Sikhs starting as the Punjabis of yore and morphing in to 'the Khalsa' and then on to the end of the last century. It brings out how, way back in 1710, Banda Singh Bahadur became perhaps the first to re-establish Indian rule after centuries of subjugation after a fierce battle. Sikhs led by their Gurus fought against Mughal tyranny, particularly their penchant for conversions, and finally in 1798 Ranjit Singh brought an end to the nightmare of eight centuries of foreign invasions and subjugation and allowed the rest of India to breathe in peace by setting up the first Sikh kingdom. The brave Sikhs did much in the twentieth century on battle fields around the world, during WW1, WW2 and the struggle for Indian Independence. To me, the 1897 Battle of Saragarhi is the ultimate in sacrifice and valour, where all 21 defenders were martyred, all given awards and medals for valour and Queen Victoria would go on to say "It is no exaggeration to record that the armies which possess the valiant Sikhs cannot face defeat in War." The book admirably chronicles the rise of the Sikhs and the constant universal theme of their valour and sacrifice in defence of their faith, around the world, in the armed forces of many countries they made their own and in the defence of many more. In fact their grit, determination and valour ensured many victories. Reading between the lines, the book brings out that Sikhs by nature are self-respecting, courageous and enterprising. Give a good look to their short history in the post war years and you will find that it is full of continuing sacrifices and that they have contributed immeasurably to nation-building in diverse nations, who valued them and accepted them. As far as India is concerned, if not for them, history may have been quite different. The gallant Sikhs have a record to be proud of and this book will go a long way. I came to know and had the privilege of knowing Mr. Dhesi in the course of my researching, helping him in writing some of his other books and developed the greatest admiration for him, particularly for his single minded devotion to seek the truth and record Sikh contributions for posterity. He has done all of us proud for surpassing the task at hand and bringing out this perfectly readable and well-chronicled record. This book is indeed a tribute to the author, a story born out of his love for the subject and for him this has been labour of love.

I am therefore honoured to be writing this Foreword for this book. Gur Fateh.

Vice Admiral Harinder Singh, (Retd) PVSM, AVSM
Indian Navy

INTRODUCTION

Many years ago I undertook a highly important task, very dear to my heart, to try and record the Sikh soldier's martial traditions. This volume is the final of five volumes in which I have endeavoured to cover all periods of war from 1500 BC to 1999 AD. It is a celebration of the Sikh Soldier's matchless courage in virtually every field of battle. This volume does not attempt to be a comprehensive history of the Sikh Soldier. The canvas of the Sikh Soldier's chivalry is so vast that if this final volume inspires someone to take up an exhaustive study and record the martial history of the Sikh Soldier; I shall consider my efforts well-rewarded. The gallantry awards of the Sikh Soldier and the actions fought, mentioned in this volume, are taken from the sister volumes of 'Sikh Soldier: Gallantry Awards' and 'Sikh Soldier: Policing the Empire'. Finally I reproduce the Introduction from the volume; 'Sikh Soldier, Battle Honours'.

Sat Sri Akal
N.S.Dhesi

'The annals of Sikh history are replete with examples of gallantry on the battlefield. One is always tempted to ask why this tiny community has made such disproportionate sacrifices. The Sikh soldier by nature seeks action, and the Punjabi tradition of the Saint-soldier began right from the very inception of the Sikh ethos.

The Punjabi soldier is imbued with the discipline of deeds - a primary concept for the path of virtuous deeds is the only discipline acceptable to God. He is inextricably tied to the world by the sword. This is the distinction that the Ten Masters deliberately and clearly demarcated as a departure from other Indian traditions.

For the Sikh soldier there is no other path than that which considers the good of all. For service for God is synonymous with service for man. Altruistic activities have the highest priority in the discipline of the Sikhs. The demands of moral life invite the greatest of sacrifices, even of life itself.

From this stems the Sikh battle anthem, "Oh God, grant me such a boon that I may never cease from doing righteous deeds. When time comes to end my life let me fall in mighty strife".

The Sikh soldier has fought on every major battlefield in the world: he fought and defeated the traditional conquerors of India – the Afghans and the Mughals - and established a Sikh Empire in Northern India. At the fall of the Sikh Kingdom he became a "Motor Muscle" of the British Empire, and fought from the trenches of France and Flanders to the sands of the African Sahara, from the deserts of Middle East to the steaming jungles of Burma, and the frozen tundra of China. After Independence in 1947 he was first in the field, and has the honour of having participated in all the battles to defend his Motherland since that time.'

DEDICATION

The Gurmukhi script with Gurcharan Singh 'Kulim'

ਸਿੱਖ ਸਿਪਾਹੀ ਦੀ ਪ੍ਰਾਰਥੱਨਾ ਹੁੰਦੀ ਐ, ਜਬ ਆਵ ਕੀ ਅਉਧ ਨਿਧਾਨ ਬਨੈ, ਅੱਤ ਹੀ ਰਨ ਮੈ ਤਬ ਜੂਝ ਮਰੋਂ
ਦੇਹ ਸਿਵਾ ਬਰ ਮੋਹਿ ਇਹੈ ਸੁਭ ਕਰਮਨ ਤੇ ਕਬਹੂੰ ਨ ਟਰੋਂ
ਨ ਡਰੋਂ ਅਰਿ ਸੋ ਜਬ ਜਾਇ ਲੜੋਂ ਨਿਸਚੈ ਕਰ ਆਪਨੀ ਜੀਤ ਕਰੋਂ
ਅਰੁ ਸਿਖ ਹੋਂ ਆਪਨੇ ਹੀ ਮਨ ਕੋ ਇਹ ਲਾਲਚ ਹਉ ਗੁਨ ਤਉ ਉਚਰੋਂ
ਜਬ ਆਵ ਕੀ ਅਉਧ ਨਿਧਾਨ ਬਨੈ ਅਤ ਹੀ ਰਨ ਮੈ ਤਬ ਜੂਝ ਮਰੋਂ

The Sikh soldier asked for no nobler end than a death on the battlefield:

O Lord, these boons of Thee I ask,

Let me never shun a righteous task,

Let me be fearless when I go to battle,

Give me faith that victory will be mine,

Give me power to sing Thy praise,

And when it comes the time to end my life,

Let me fall in mighty strife.

Sikh Warrior

PUNJAB ANTECEDENTS

Sikh homeland, the Punjab, is a very fertile region in the Northwest of India. The words punj (five) and ab (water), meaning the land of the five waters. The rivers are the Jhelum, the Chenab, the Ravi, the Beas and the Satluj. In 1947 the state of the Punjab was partitioned between British India's successor states, India and Pakistan. Today, three of the rivers run exclusively in Pakistani Punjab with the tributaries of the other two eventually draining there as well. Indian Punjab has the headwaters of the remaining two rivers which eventually drain over into Pakistan. The Pakistani Punjab now comprises the majority of the region. The Indian Punjab has been further sub-divided into the modern Indian states of the Punjab, Haryana, Himachal Pradesh and Delhi. Historically the Punjab embraced the entire plain between the rivers Jamuna and the Indus.

Stone Age, (70000 BC–3300 BC)

One of the earliest Stone Age cultures of South Asia was nourished in the Punjab. Oldest Homo sapiens lived here from 5–2 million years ago. Many articles of Stone Age are found from different Archaeological sites and are displayed at different museums of Pakistan.

Mehgarh Culture, (7000 BC–2600 BC)

Mehrgarh, one of the most important Neolithic sites in archaeology, lies on the Western edge of the Indus valley, where a large urban civilization emerged at the same time as those of Mesopotamia and the ancient Egyptian Empire. Early Mehrgarh residents lived in mud brick houses, stored their grain in granaries, fashioned tools with local copper ore and lined their large basket containers with bitumen. They cultivated six-row barley, einkorn and emmer wheat, jujubes and dates, and herded sheep, goats and cattle. The site was occupied continuously until about 2600 BC. Mehrgarh is now seen as a precursor to the Indus Valley Civilization.

Indus Valley Civilization, (3300 BC–1500 BC)

The Indus Valley civilization, flourished from about 3300 B.C. to about 1500 B.C. At its height, its geographical reach exceeded that of Egypt or Mesopotamia. The chief cities of the Indus civilization had large complex hill citadels, housing palaces, granaries and baths. Houses, often two-storied and spacious, lined the town streets; they had drainage systems that led into brick-lined sewers. The economy of the Indus Civilization was based on a highly organized agriculture, supplemented by an active commerce, probably connected to that of the ancient civilizations of Mesopotamia. The origin, rise and decline of the Indus valley civilization remain a mystery, but it seems most probable that the civilization fell (1500 B.C.) to invading Aryans.

Punjab Antecedents

Aryans, (1500 BC)

The Indo–Europeans, emerging from the Russian steppes in the region of the Caspian Sea, started spreading to Greece, Europe, and Asia Minor in search of pasture. By this time, they were known as Aryans. By 1500 B.C., a wave of them pushed through the passes of the Hindu Kush Mountains to the Punjab, where they destroyed an advanced Indus Valley Civilization. 'The coming of the Aryans was a backward step, since the Harappa culture had been far more advanced than that of the Aryans who were yet pre-urban.'(Khushwant Singh). The next thousand years' history of the Punjab is dominated by the Aryans. The primitive Aryans were not allowed to settle in the Punjab unmolested as long and bloody struggles were maintained in the wild. The life of the Aryans in the Punjab was martial and manly. Their warlike character developed and they adapted themselves to the conditions of tropical climate, very different to their cold, northern home. The Aryans spoke Sanskrit, which became the common language of the people.

It was in the Punjab that Vedic Hinduism was evolved and the four Vedas, the oldest living scriptures in the world, composed around 1500-1700 BC, supplies evidence concerning the life of the Aryans who settled in the Punjab. The Aryans were a spirit-drinking race and indulged freely in drinking beer, wine and spirit. Sages and saints drank alcohol and offered the fermented juice to the gods. The Aryans were tall and fair, and the people they subjugated were darker and of alien culture, of whom the Aryans were contemptuous. As they wanted to maintain the purity of their race, they developed a system of social exclusiveness, by breaking the society into separate Units: The Caste System. The caste system was enforced as law throughout the subcontinent until the adoption of the Indian Constitution in 1949, which outlawed the caste system. However, it remains a deeply ingrained social structure, particularly in rural India. There are four main castes into which everyone was categorized. At the very top were the Brahmins – (priests), scholars, and philosophers. The second highest caste was the Kshatriyas. These were the warriors, rulers, and those concerned with the defence and administration of the village or state. Third the Vaishyas, who were traders, merchants, and people involved in agricultural production. The lowest caste was the Shudras - the labourers and servants for the other castes. Each caste included many hierarchical sub castes divided by occupation. Below the Shudras were the Untouchables. These people had no caste at all. They performed the most menial of jobs, such as dealing with dead bodies and cleaning toilets. Higher-caste people believed that if they touched one of the casteless, they would be contaminated and would need to go through cleansing rituals. Caste was determined by birth - you fell into the same caste as your parents, and there was almost no way to change it. The caste system dictated your occupation, choice of spouse and many other aspects of your life. If you did something outside your caste, you could be excommunicated from your caste.

Punjab Antecedents

The Persians, (516 – 485 BC)

The Persians were also Indo–Europeans; they had left their homeland and settled in modern Iran. The foundation of classical Persian culture was the Achaemenid Empire. Created in 550 BC, Achaemenid Empire at its height extended from Egypt in North Africa to the Indus River in North-western India, making it one of the largest land empires in the world at that time. The location of the Punjab was on the outskirts of the Great Persian Empire. The emergence of the Achaemenid empire in Persia, founded by Hakhamaniš saw parts of the North-western subcontinent (modern day Pakistan) come under Persian rule. Indian emissaries were present at the courts of Cyrus the Great whose empire extended as far East as Gandhara and Sind. It is also believed that when Cyrus was threatened by Croesus of Lydia, he received military assistance from at least one Indian king. Under Darius, parts of India became the 24TH province of the Persian Empire. It was believed to be the richest in Darius's empire. Herodotus mentions the Indian contingent in the Persian armies consisting of Infantry, Cavalry and chariots. Later, elephants are also mentioned. Under Xerxes I, the successor of Darius, Indians fought alongside the Persian Army against the Greeks in the battlefields of Plataea and Marathon. The Persian Empire under the Achaemenid dynasty came to an end when Alexander defeated Darius in the battle of Arebala and paved the way for Alexander to penetrate the Punjab.

Porus

When Alexander occupied Gandhara, (Afghanistan) the Indian kingdoms had already regained their independence. While many clans and their chiefs were busy carving out principalities for themselves in the Punjab and the Northwest of India, a chief of the Paurava tribe, called Porus also set up an independent kingdom between the Jhelum and the Chenab. While the Persians influenced secularist and central theory of government, under the shadow of Achaemenid institutions at Taxila, the elements of anarchy, isolation and tribalism in the Punjab were being fought by Porus. At the same time, a scion of the Ambha family, who was called Ambhi, established himself at Taxila. Naturally, the relations between Porus and Ambhi were strained, for being neighbours they had a conflict of interests. Porus not only struck East and South but also exerted relentless pressure in the North and the West with the result that his next-door neighbour Ambhi was seriously menaced and profoundly perturbed by him. Hence, to cope with the menace, he had trained most of the husbandmen of his kingdom into soldiers. While these preparations were going on, Alexander appeared on the horizon. Ambhi took the occasion by the forelock and hastened to befriend him to secure his assistance against Porus and his ally.

Punjab Antecedents

Alexander of Macedon, (326 BC)

In 336 BC when Alexander succeeded to the Macedon throne, he inherited a strong kingdom and an experienced Army. In 334 BC he invaded Persian-ruled Asia Minor, and began a series of campaigns lasting ten years. He broke the power of Persia in a series of battles, most notably the decisive battle of Gaugamela where the Punjabis had fought alongside the Persians. Subsequently he overthrew the Persian king Darius III; this left him to campaign to the furthest limits of the Achaemenid Empire. Porus, the King of the Punjab, had come to the aid of Darius, but when he heard that Darius was slain, he returned to his country together with his troops. The fame of the might of Porus, his help to Darius with dispatch of his elephant corps and the view that it was not desirable to let a powerful king live and flourish across the frontier of an empire, compelled Alexander to gather his armies together, and command his soldiers to march against Porus. Alexander crossed the mountains at Attock and proceeded to Taxila, where he partook of the hospitality of its King Ambhi. From Taxila, he invited all the local rulers of the Punjab to submit to his authority. Some of the rulers did the same, but the ruler of the kingdom between the rivers Hydaspes (Jehlum) and Akesines (Chenab), the legendary king Porus, refused to submit to his authority. As a result, fierce battle took place. Both sides suffered heavy casualties. Porus lost his sons and got injured. In the end Alexander's forces took over the Punjab and they brought Porus to Alexander's court. Here the legendary conversation took place. Alexander asked Porus "How should I treat you?". Porus shot back "In the same way as a king treats another king". Alexander was struck by his genius and bravery. He not only returned the kingdom back to Porus but added to his original territory another of still greater extent. The battle of Jhelum ended in a treaty of peace between Porus and Alexander and the joint endeavour of both of them in reducing the independent tribes of the Punjab. The Greeks were involved in some very had fought battles across the five rivers of the Punjab. The resistance and fighting was so fierce that Alexander's soldiers mutinied, laid down their arms and refused to advance any further. Alexander, leaving garrisons and governors in the Punjab, marched away with the remnants of his armies in 326 BC to Persia and Susa. In a letter to his mother, Alexander had described his encounters with the trans-Indus tribes thus:

"I am involved in the land of a leonine and brave people, where every foot of the ground is like a well of steel, confronting my soldier. You have brought only one son into the world, but everyone in this land can be called an Alexander."

Alexander had conquered the whole of the then known world. He died in his palace in Babylon on June 10^{Tth} or 11TH, 323 B.C., in the 32ND year of his age. Within a few years of his death his vast empire divided among his generals, so that nothing remained of him but his name. Porus was recognised as the undisputed master of the Punjab to the East of Jhelum.

Punjab Antecedents

The Maurya Empire, (322 BC –185 BC)

Under Chandragupta, the Maurya Empire liberated the Trans-Indus, which was under Macedonian occupation. The Maurya dynasty was the largest and most powerful political and military empire of ancient India. At its greatest extent, the empire stretched to the North along the natural boundaries of the Himalayas, and to the East stretching into what is now Assam. To the West, it conquered beyond modern Pakistan, annexing Baluchistan, South Eastern parts of Iran and much of what is now Afghanistan, including the modern Herat and Kandahar provinces. Chandragupta's grandson Ashoka ruled 273-232 BC. As a young prince, Ashoka was a brilliant commander who crushed revolts in Ujjain and Taxila. As monarch he was ambitious and aggressive, re-asserting the Empire's superiority in Southern and Western India. However, when he personally witnessed the devastation and destruction of War, Ashoka embraced the teachings of Gautama Buddha, and renounced War and violence. Ashoka sponsored the spreading of Buddhist ideals into Sri Lanka, South East Asia, West Asia and Mediterranean Europe. The reign of Ashoka was followed for 50 years by a succession of weaker kings. Brhadrata, the last ruler of the Maurya dynasty, ruled territories that had shrunk considerably from the time of emperor Ashoka, but he was still upholding the Buddhist faith. He was assassinated in 185 B.C. during a military parade by the commander-in-chief of his guard. The fall of the Maurya Empire left the Khyber Pass unguarded, and waves of foreign invasions followed. The Greco-Bactrian king, Demetrius, capitalized on the break-up, conquered Southern Afghanistan and the Punjab around 180 BC, forming the Indo-Greek Kingdom

Indo-Bactrian kingdom, (189 BC)

The Indo-Greek Kingdom was a Hellenistic kingdom covering various parts of the Northwest regions of the Indian subcontinent during the last two centuries BC, and was ruled by more than 30 kings. The kingdom was founded when the Graeco-Bactrian king Demetrius invaded India early in the 2ND century BC. The Greeks in India were eventually divided from the Graeco-Bactrians centred in Bactria (now the border between Afghanistan and Uzbekistan). The most famous Indo-Greek ruler was Menander (Milinda). He had his capital at Sakala (modern Sialkot) in the Punjab, modern Pakistan, and he successfully invaded the Ganges-Yamuna Doab. During the two centuries of their rule, the Indo-Greek kings combined the Greek and Indian languages and symbols, as seen on their coins, and blended ancient Greek, Hindu and Buddhist religious practices, as seen in the archaeological remains of their cities and in the indications of their support of Buddhism, pointing to a rich fusion of Indian and Hellenistic influences. The Indo-Greeks ultimately disappeared as a political entity following the invasions of the Indo-Scythians. The kingdom of the last Indo-Greek king Strato was taken over by the Scythian ruler Rajuvula around 10 AD.

Punjab Antecedents

Scythians, (80 BC)
Scythians had their own kingdom North of the Black Sea. They had proved dangerous opponents for Persians, Macedonians and Bactrians. The Scythian tribes had poured into Persia. The Persians had fought desperately but were finally defeated. The Scythian hordes then continued their march towards India. They forced the Bolan Pass to conquer Sindh, and then swept up the Indus and occupied Taxila and Gandhara. The Scythian king Maues and his successor Azes in the process had destroyed any remaining Greek power in the Punjab. After the death of Azes, the rule of the Scythians in North-western India was shattered with the rise of the Parthian ruler Gondophares in the last years of the 1ST century BC.

Parthian Empire
After the death of Gondophares I, the Parthian empire started to fragment. The name or title Gondophares was adopted by Sarpedones, who become Gondophares II. The most important successor was Abdagases, Gondophares' nephew, who ruled in the Punjab. There were other minor kings but the Indo-Parthians never regained the position of Gondophares I, and from the middle of the 1ST century AD the Kushans under Kujula Khadphides began absorbing the Northern Indian part of the kingdom that was now expanding into India to create a Kushan Empire.

Kushans, (60 AD)
The nomadic tribes of central Asia, lead by the leading tribe the Kushans, were forced to migrate South. Their traditional raids into the Chinese empire were denied to them by the construction of the great wall. They cleared the Scythians from the lands surrounding the Aral Sea and occupied Bactria. The leading chief Kujula Khadphides then led them to the Punjab, destroying the Scythian kingdom of Gondophares. He also established himself in Kashmir by defeating the military governor Hermaues. Kanishka was the most famous of the Kushan kings. When Kanishka ascended the throne, his empire consisted of Afghanistan, Sind, Punjab, Kashmir, and most of the Genetic valley. He annexed three provinces of the Chinese empire, namely, Tashkent, Khotan and Yarkhand. He was the only king who ruled over these territories. He had two capitals, one at Purushpura (Peshawar now in Pakistan) and the other at Mathura in West Uttar Pradesh. Kanishka's immediate successor was Vashiska who was then succeeded by Huvishka. Mathura became the centre of the Kushans. Many monuments were erected during Huvishka's reign. The last great king of the Kushans was Vasudev I. The Kushans were overthrown by the Sassanians of Persia in the Northwest and the Guptas in the North.

Punjab Antecedents

Guptas Dynasty, (320 AD)
The Gupta Empire was one of the largest political and military empires in the world and covered most of Northern India. The time of the Gupta Empire is referred to as the Golden Age of India. Historians place the Gupta dynasty alongside the Han Dynasty, Tang Dynasty and Roman Empire as a model of a classical civilization. The Gupta dynasty was founded by a man known as Chandra Gupta I. During his reign Chandra Gupta extended his empire and controlled a substantial area of North India. There was renewed enthusiasm in religions like Hinduism and the world's first universities were established. The Guptas were able to check further invasions from central Asia for a considerable time, but the Huns overran the empire by 500 AD.

The Huns, (480 AD)
The Hephthalites, also known as the White Huns, were a nomadic confederation in Central Asia. A branch of them stormed upon Europe and devastated the Roman Empire. In Northern India, the Guptas put up fierce resistance to keep the Huns out. Eventually they broke through. The Hun king Tormana created an independent kingdom in Northern and central India. The Guptas continued to resist the Huns, and allied with the rulers of the neighboring Indian states. The Huns suffered a defeat by Yasodharman of Malwa in 528 AD, and by 542 AD Tormana's successor Mihirakula had been driven off the plains of Northern India, taking refuge in Kashmir, and he is thought to have died soon after. Mihirakula is remembered in contemporary Indian and Chinese histories for his cruelty and his destruction of temples and monasteries, with particular hostility towards Buddhism. After the end of the sixth century little is recorded in India about the Huns, and what happened to them is unclear; some historians surmise that the remaining Huns were assimilated into the South Indian population.

King Vardhana, (606 AD)
Harsha Vardhana commonly called Harsha, was an Indian emperor who ruled Northern India from 606 AD to 647 AD from his capital Kanauj. King Harsha blocked the mountain passes against future invasions. Harsha proved himself a great conqueror and an able administrator. After his accession, Harsha united the two kingdoms of Thanesar and Kanauj and transferred his capital from Thanesar to Kanauj. He was tolerant towards all other religions and supported them fully. Some time later in his life, he became a patron of Buddhism also. In 641 BC, he sent a mission to China, which helped in establishing the first diplomatic relations between China and India. At Harsha's death, apparently without any heirs, his empire died with him. The kingdom disintegrated rapidly into small states as the invaders once again forced open the Hindu Kush passes and poured into Northern India.

Punjab Antecedents

'In the name of God.'

Islamic Invasions, (712 AD)
At the advent of the Islamic invasions, the Punjabi people were a mixture of all the previous invaders. Over the centuries they had settled in the Punjab, married local women and were absorbed into the local communities. In the desert wastes of Arabia, the Prophet Mohammad established the religion of Islam. His followers at the sword point, furiously and with great enthusiasm, carried the Islamic banner to Syria, Egypt, Iran, Sudan, North Africa and Southern Spain. Mohammad Bin Qasim stormed the Islamic Khilafah Army through the Bolan Pass to Baluchistan. In 712-13 AD, he overran Sindh and captured Multan. The Punjab remained as a province of the Khilafah throughout the Delhi Sultanate and Mughal period.

Mahmud of Ghazni, (971-1030 AD)
Turkish nobleman Subuktgin, the ruler of Ghazni, a principality in Afghanistan, successfully defeated Jaipal, the rajah of the Punjab and extended the frontiers of his kingdom to Peshawar. His son and successor Mahmoud successfully defeated the flower of Indian princes lead by Anandpal. Until his death in 1030 AD, he savagely plundered the Punjab. His raids were essentially for the accumulated riches of the temples, which he destroyed, as was his custom. Added to which was the religious motive of killing the infidels. He massacred the Hindus by the thousands. He took thousands of prisoners, who were eventually sold as slaves in the markets of central Asia. The last years of his life he spent in fighting the Central Asian tribes threatening his empire.

The Delhi Sultanate, (1206-1526 AD)
Prince Mohammad of the Ghur dynasty invaded the Punjab in 1206. Taking Peshawar and Lahore and crossing the Satluj, he captured Bhatinda. He defeated and killed the rajah of Delhi at the battle of Tarain. He went on to conquer Delhi and establish the Sultanate. The Delhi Sultanate is a term used to cover five short-lived dynasties; Delhi based kingdoms or sultanates, mostly of Turkic and Pakhtun (Afghan) origin in medieval India. The sultanates ruled from Delhi between 1206 and 1526, when the last was replaced by the Mughal dynasty. The five dynasties were the Mamluk dynasty (1206–90); the Khilji dynasty (1290–1320); the Tughlaq dynasty (1320–1414); the Sayyid dynasty (1414–51); and the Afghan Lodi dynasty (1451–1526).This rule was essentially an armed occupation, sustained by a constant influx of Muslims from across the mountains and Central Asia. The Delhi Sultanate was founded in 1206 and lasted for 320 years.

Punjab Antecedents

Genghis Khan
From the establishment of Delhi Sultanate in 1206 AD for over 300 years, the Punjab bore the brunt of foreign attacks. In this painful process, the Punjab's population and prosperity diminished and its entire life was crippled. Because of constant Mongol raids, it remained depopulated and very little agriculture was carried on. After this period, the Punjab was almost an uninhabitable waste, except for a few walled cities. Despite the strenuous efforts of the Delhi Sultans to secure the Northern frontiers, Genghis Khan, through a series of battering raids between 1229 and 1241, took control of the Punjab. The Mongols remained in the Punjab until about 1270.

Tamerlan, (1398)
In 1398 came the visitation of Tamerlane, the Mongol descendant of Genghis Khan. With the excuse that Muslim rulers in India were being too tolerant toward Hindus, he led his Army there. With one of his grandsons taking Lahore and the other Multan, he fell on the plains and the cities. All the towns and cities were raised to the ground and one hundred thousand people were put to the sword. The same fate awaited the people of Delhi, where he created more carnage and devastation. He is described as having been pleased that he had penetrated India more deeply than had Alexander the Great or Genghis Khan. Leaving behind famine and decades of anarchy, he finally re-crossed the mountains and returned with Indian artists, craftsmen, and booty.

The Mughals, (1525)
Zahiruddin Babbar the Chaghatai Turk, the Mongol descendent of Genghis Khan and Tamerlane, had conquered Samarkand, the capital of his ancestors. He made his first advance upon India in 1519 and reached Bhera in the Punjab. The fort of Birhala, with all its treasures, fell into his hands. In 1520, he again marched into India and captured Sialkot and Syadpur, and massacred the inhabitants or carried them to slavery. In 1525, he plundered Lahore and defeated the Sultan's Army with great slaughter. As he advanced on Delhi, Sultan Ibrahim Lodhi offered him battle at Panipat. With his seasoned soldiers and strong Artillery, Babbar defeated and killed Ibrahim Lodhi and went on to lay the foundation of the Mughal Empire. Babbar died in Agra on December 26TH, 1530, having reigned thirty-eight years.

At the time the Mughals established their rule, the people of the Punjab were sharply divided into separate religious societies. One, the Muslim, was an occupational Army constantly sustained by fresh influx of Turkic and Afghan tribes, which practiced fanaticism and intolerance. The other, the Hindu, was rooted in idol worship, meaningless rituals and the degradation of caste. In this turbulent time a remarkable change started to take place in the Punjab.

SIKH ETHOS

Early Sikh tradition was founded and shaped by ten successive Sikh Gurus, between 1469 and 1708 in India. Sikhs reserve the title 'Guru' for these founders as well as the volume of sacred text which is today revered as 'Living Guru'. Central to its teaching is the opening statement Ik Onkar, proclaiming the oneness of the Creator and creation and calling upon humanity to recognize this unity, against a social backdrop of prejudice and intolerance between those of different faiths and social groupings. A popular three fold motto 'Meditate, work and share' (naam japo, kirat karo, vand ke chhako) is the basis of Sikh ethics, by which life is to be lived 'meditatively, industriously and generously'. Notions of spiritual development are thus grounded in daily life with commitments to work, family and wider society.

Guru Nanak Dev Ji, (1469-1539)

Meantime a remarkable people had emerged in the Punjab. They believed in the faith of Guru Nanak Dev Ji (Guru means a spiritual teacher and a guide). Nanak was born about 40 miles from Lahore (now in Pakistan) in 1469. He was one of the greatest religious innovators of all time and the founder of the Sikh religion. Nanak's religious ideas draw on both Hindu and Islamic thought, but are far more than just a synthesis. He was an original spiritual thinker and expressed his thoughts in extraordinary poetry that forms the basis of Sikh scripture. In 1496 Nanak set out on a set of spiritual journeys through India, Tibet and Arabia that lasted nearly 30 years. He studied and debated with learned men he met along the way and as his ideas took shape he began to teach a new route to spiritual fulfilment and the good life. The chief doctrines preached by Guru Nanak Dev Ji was " The Unity of God, Brotherhood of Man, Rejection of Caste and the futility of Idol Worship" Nanak was a strict, uncompromising monotheist. The most famous teachings attributed to Guru Nanak Dev Ji are that there is only one God, and that all human beings can have direct access to God with no need of rituals or priests. His most radical social teachings denounced the caste system and taught that everyone is equal, regardless of caste or gender.

The last part of his life was spent at Kartarpur in the Punjab, where many disciples attracted by his teachings joined him. When Guru Nanak Dev Ji saw that his last end was approaching, he named Lahna, one of his faithful disciples, his successor, who had proven his faith and devotion. Guru Nanak Dev Ji declared that his own spirit had gone into Lahna's body, and he changed from Lahna to Angi Khud, or Angad, meaning my own body. The belief common among Sikhs is that the spirit of Guru Nanak Dev Ji is inherited by each successive Guru. His followers became known as Sikhs. The word Sikh means a disciple and comes from the word shishya, which translates as a seeker of truth. The succeeding nine gurus nurtured Nanak's mission with great organizing ability, energy and devotion. They moulded the Sikhs into a distinct community, with its own language, literature, and its own religious beliefs and institutions.

Sikh Ethos

Guru Angad Dev, (1504 - 1552)
The Sikh religion would, in all probability, have gradually died out and sunk into oblivion, had it not been for the foresight and wisdom of its founder, in establishing an apostolic succession. Guru Angad Dev committed to writing much about his great predecessor and also recorded the results of his own devotional observations which became the nucleus of the sacred writing of the Sikhs. Angad also created Gurmukhi, the Punjabi script which gave the Sikhs a written language distinct from the written language of the Hindus or the Muslims and thus fostered a sense of their being a separate people. Guru Angad Dev passed away in 1552.

Guru Amar Das, (1479 - 1574)
Guru Amar Das, the third succeeding guru, showed great devotion in forwarding the work that Nanak and Guru Angad Dev had begun. He composed many beautiful verses, which have been incorporated in the Sikh scriptures. He disapproved of sati, a practice of burning widows, and encouraged the re-marriage of Hindu widows. Guru Amar Das was also a big proponent of the Langar, or community kitchen, in the Sikh temples. Amar Das died in Govindwal, on May 14TH, 1574.

Guru Ram Das, (1534 -1581)
Guru Ram Das was a man of considerable merit, well worthy of the choice of his master as the succeeding Guru. Like his predecessors he gave himself up to literary pursuits, in which he expounded his doctrines, which have been incorporated in the Sikh scriptures. Guru Ram Das moved from Govindwal to the neighbourhood of the tank and started building a town around it. The town, which was destined to become the religious capital of the Sikhs, came to be known as Amritsar. Guru Ram Das died in March, 1581

Guru Arjan, (1563-1606)
Guru Arjan became Guru in 1581. The most important work of Guru Arjan Dev was the compilation of Adi Granth. With a view to uniting the followers by one common religious tie; he gave a religious code, in which he incorporated the sayings and verses of Nanak, the compositions of his predecessors, and his own. This code he called the Granth, or the holy book. Guru Arjan completed the construction of Amritsar and founded other cities such as Taran Taran and Kartarpur. Emperor Jahangir was convinced of Guru Arjan's treason against the imperial authority. Eventually the Guru was thrown in prison and tortured; he died of heat apoplexy in prison. He had sent word to his son, who was only eleven years old, to assume the ministry of the community. Guru Arjan was a prolific writer, composed religious verses, which were incorporated in the Guru Granth. The martyrdom of Guru Arjan was a great turning point in the history of the Sikh nation; it changed the entire character of Sikhism radically from a passive people to courageous saint soldiers.

CALL TO ARMS

Guru Hargobind, (1595-1644)

Guru Hargobind, sixth Sikh Guru, developed a strong Army and gave the Sikh religion its military character. In accord with the instructions of his father, Guru Arjan (1563–1606), the first Sikh martyr, who had been executed on the order of the Mughal Emperor Jahangir. Up to the time of Hargobind, the Sikh religion had been passive. At his succession ceremony Hargobind is believed to have defiantly borne two swords, symbolizing his twin authority as temporal (Miri) and spiritual (piri) head of the community. He also devoted much time to military training and the martial arts, becoming an expert swordsman, wrestler, and rider. Guru Hargobind excelled in matters of state and his Darbar (court) was noted for its splendor. The arming and training of some of his devoted followers began. The Guru came to possess seven hundred horses, and his Risaldari (Army) grew to three hundred horsemen and sixty gunners in the due course of time. Additionally, five hundred men from the Majha area of the Punjab were recruited as Infantry. He had his own flag and War-drum which was beaten twice a day. Despite the Mughal opposition, Hargobind built up his Army and fortified his cities. In 1609 he built at Amritsar the 'Akal Takht' (Throne of God), a temple and assembly hall combined, where both spiritual and temporal matters pertaining to the Sikh nation could be resolved. He built a fort near Amritsar and named it Lohgarh. Deftly he instilled the will to fight and established high morale in his followers. Jahangir could not tolerate the armed policy of Guru Hargobind and consequently imprisoned him. The main reason for releasing him after years was that there were a lot of reports from across the length and width of the country that people were against the throne due to the popularity of the Guru, as well as the unjustified martyrdom of the fifth Guru. A lot of people were following Sikhism, and there was a possibility of a coup if the Guru was not released at the earliest opportunity. As it was, there were 52 Hindu kings in the Gwalior prison at that moment; the policies of Jahangir against the local majority people were oppressive in nature. Therefore, the situation compelled him to order the release of Guru Hargobind to save the throne. Guru Hargobind refused to leave the Gwalior fort alone and advocated for the release of the 52 other princes in captivity. For this reason, he is also known as Bandi Chhor – or the one who freed the convicts. Guru Hargobind followed his former militant course, recognizing that a clash with Mughal power was coming. After Jahangir's death (1627) the new Mughal emperor, Shah Jahan, persecuted the Sikh community in earnest. Shah Jahan revived the policy of oppression against non-Muslims and ordered the demolition of numerous Gurdwaras. This brought him into direct conflict with the Sikhs, who after the execution of Guru Arjan and imprisonment of Guru Hargobind were now determined to fight back. Both parties were primed for a clash at the slightest cause.

Call to Arms

Guru Hargobind, (Cont.)

In 1628, during one of his hunting trips to Lahore, Shah Jahan ran into the Sikhs, which led to a minor skirmish. As a result, Shah Jehan sent his governor, Mukhlis Khan to arrest the Guru. This was now the beginning of the Wars between the Sikhs and the Mughals. The Mughals attacked Lohgarh, the fortress surrounding Amritsar. This was a sudden and unexpected development. Guru Hargobind was already busy with the wedding preparations for his daughter Bibi Viro the next day. The Sikhs were reluctantly thrust into their first War and they fought bravely killing Mukhlis Khan. Victorious, and to avoid any further skirmish, Guru Hargobind retreated to a small village Jhabal, eight miles from Amritsar, where he was able to perform the marriage of his daughter. To avoid any further trouble, Guru Hargobind retreated to Kartarpur, near Jalandhar. However, in 1630, on the provocation of Bhagwan Das and his son Rattan Chand, another skirmish ensued between the Mughals and the Sikhs. After 3 days of hard fighting, Abdullah Khan, the governor of Jalandhar was killed and the Sikhs emerged victorious again. Then in 1632, Guru Hargobind's Sikhs were attacked by a powerful Army led by Lala Beg and Qamar Beg. A fierce battle ensued in the neighbourhood of the villages of Mehraj and Nathana, close to present day Bhatinda. More than 1200 Sikhs were wounded or killed, whereas many more Mughals, including the Mughal Commanders Lala and Qamar Beg were killed, leaving the Sikhs victorious in another fight.

After about another year, the Mughals regrouped, this time under the instigation of Painda Khan – once a loyal disciple of the Guru. The Guru's forces were encircled in Kartarpur, but were once again able to turn the tables on the Mughals. Fighting along with other Sikhs were Guru Hargobind's two sons, Baba Gurditta and Teg Bahadur. The Imperial Army was again routed and the renegade Painda Khan was killed. Guru Hargobind had won 4 battles with the Mughals. His purpose was always defensive and as a result he did not acquire even a small piece of territory in these victories. There was something far greater involved in this Warfare – A new heroism was rising in the Punjab, and the main aim was to create a will to resist the mighty power of the oppressive Mughal rulers. During the era of Guru Hargobind, the Sikhs increased greatly in number, and the fiscal policy of Guru Arjan and the armed system of Guru Hargobind had already formed the Sikhs into a kind of separate entity within the empire. Guru Hargobind's emphasis on martial arts to resist tyranny and oppression by despot rulers nearly completed the identity of Sikhs as a 'people.' The Sikhs under Hargobind defeated Shah Jahan's armies four times, crushing the myth of Mughal invincibility.* Guru Har Gobind breathed his last, peacefully, at Kiratpur Rup Nagar, Punjab, on 19TH March 1644.

- After this says Cunningham: "the Sikhs were in little danger of relapsing into the limited merit or utility of monks and mendicants"

Call to Arms

Guru Har Rai, (1630-1661)

Guru Har Rai, on succeeding Guru Hargobind, established himself at Kartarpur on the banks of the Satluj River. Guru Har Rai was a man of peace but he never disbanded or discharged the armed Sikh Warriors (Saint Soldiers), who earlier were maintained by his grandfather (Guru Hargobind Sahib). He otherwise further boosted the military spirit of the Sikhs but he never indulged in any direct political and armed controversy with the contemporary Mughal Empire. Once, Dara Shikoh (the eldest son of Emperor Shah Jahan), came to Guru Har Rai asking for help in the War of succession launched by his half-brother the murderous Aurangzeb. The Guru had promised his grandfather to use the Sikh Cavalry only in defense. He, nevertheless, helped him to escape safely from the bloody hands of Aurangzeb's armed forces. Once, while the Guru Har Rai was returning from a tour of the Malwa and Doaba regions, Mohammad Yarbeg Khan, (son of Mukhlis Khan, who had been killed by Guru Hargobind when he had led his forces against the Sikhs) attacked the kafla of the Guru with a force of one thousand armed men. The revengeful attack was repulsed by a few hundred 'Saint-Soldiers' of the Sikhs with great courage and bravery. The enemy suffered a heavy loss of life and fled the scene. This self-defense measure was a reply to the surprise attack of the Muslims overlords. Guru Har Rai often bestowed Sikh Warriors with robes of honor in reward. Guru Har Rai founded three missions and stressed the importance of Langar, insisting no one should ever be turned away hungry who visited them. He advised Sikhs to labour honestly and cheat no one. He stressed the importance of early morning worship and scripture, implying that whether or not words could be understood, hymns benefited the heart and soul. He admonished rulers to govern mercifully without oppression, attend only to their own spouses, abstain from drink, and be always available to their subjects. He suggested that they see to the people's needs, providing wells, bridges, schools, and religious ministry. Guru Har Rai learned the medicinal properties of herbs. He tended to injuries of animals which he found wounded and kept them in a zoo where he fed and cared for them. When appealed to for help by his enemy, Mughal Emperor Shah Jahan. Guru Har Rai provided a cure for his eldest son, Dara Shikoh, who had been poisoned with tiger whiskers. His most important contribution was the creation of a hospital where medicines and treatment were free for everyone. Guru Har Rai visited the Doaba and Malva regions of the Punjab where he preached to the Sikhs in huge numbers. He also visited Lahore, Sialkot, Pathankot, Samba, Ramgarh and many places in the Jammu and Kashmir region. Guru Har Rai established 360 Sikh 'missionary' seats called Manjis (after the small cot (*manjis*) used by the Guru's representatives.

Guru Har Rai passed away at Kiratpur on 6TH October 1661.

Call to Arms
Guru Tegh Bahadur, (1621-1675)

Guru Tegh Bahadur became the ninth Guru of the Sikh religion on March 20TH, 1665 after the untimely demise of his grand-nephew Guru Har Krishan. He is honored and remembered as the man who championed the right of religious freedom for all. He sacrificed his own life to save the Hindus from religious persecution from the Mughal Emperor Aurangzeb. He spent his early years mainly in meditation and spent his latter years as the Guru in spreading the teachings of Guru Nanak and spreading the joy of worship to God with humanity. Guru Tegh Bahadur can aptly be called the peerless martyr in the history of the world. He laid down his life for the protection of 'Tilak' or 'Sacred Thread' of the Hindus. He was a firm believer in the right of the people to freedom of worship. In the year 1674, the Hindu religious leaders of Kashmir, approached Guru Ji, to help them save Hindus from being forcefully converted to the Muslim faith by the Emperor Aurangzeb. **Guru Tegh Bahadur** agreed to protect their faith from the tyrant ruler. The Guru told the Pundits, "Go and tell the Emperor that you will agree to embrace Islam if he can persuade your Guru Tegh Bahadur to be converted to the Muslim faith". Aurangzeb on hearing this arrested Guru Tegh Bahadur and forcefully tried to convert him to Islamic faith. At his refusal to convert, **Guru Tegh Bahadur**, along with many of his devotees, was cruelly tortured. Bhai Mati Das, the devoted Sikh, was tied between two pillars and his body split in two by being sawn alive. Bhai Dyala was boiled alive in a cauldron of boiling water and Bhai Sati Das was wrapped in cotton wool and burnt alive. Determined not to renounce his faith, **Guru Tegh Bahadur** was even prepared to give up his life. By now, Aurangzeb had become very furious. He ordered that Guru Tegh Bahadur be executed publicly at Chandi Chowk, in Delhi. On November 11TH, 1675 Guru Tegh Bahadur took his early morning bath and recited the sacred Japji. Thereafter he was brought out of the Kotwali and seated on a platform. Guru Ji sat absorbed in deep meditation, while the executioner took his sword and at one stroke Guru Ji was beheaded. The Guru's body was left in the dust as no one dared to pick up the body for fear of the emperor's reprisal. Just then a severe storm swept through the city and under the cover of darkness a Sikh named Bhai Jaita managed to collect the Guru's head and carried it off to Anandpur Sahib to the Guru's son. Another Sikh Bhai Lakhi Shah who had a cart was able to smuggle the Gurus headless body to his house. Since a public funeral would be too dangerous, Bhai Lakhi Shah cremated the body by setting his house on fire. Meanwhile the head was taken to the grief stricken young **Guru Gobind Singh** and the widow Mata Gujari. On November 16TH, 1675 at Anandpur Sahib, a pyre of sandalwood was constructed, sprinkled with roses and the head of Guru Tegh Bahadur was cremated by young Gobind. Never in the annals of history has the religious leader of one religion sacrificed his life to save the freedom of another.

Call to Arms

Guru Gobind Singh, (1666-1708)

At the martyrdom of Tegh Bahadur, his son Gobind succeeded to the Guruship. To save the faith and the infant community from annihilation, he decided to transform the Sikhs into a fierce military brotherhood. In 1699, he created the Order of the Khalsa (the pure). He summoned the Sikhs to the city of Anandpur and baptised them to the fold of the Khalsa. The Guru administered *Khande-da–Amrit* (Baptism of the Sword). This symbolised their rebirth in the Order of the Khalsa. Henceforth their profession was to wield the sword in the cause of justice and defending the weak. They formed the nucleus of a fighting fraternity and were given new names with the surname Singh – Lion. They were to observe five Ks, Kesh (unshorn hair), to carry a Kangha (a comb in the hair), to wear Kacha (military pants), to wear a Kara (a steel bracelet) and always carry a Kirpan (a Sabre). The outward symbols of the Singhs, especially their beards and the turbans, were to set them apart, so they could not deny their faith, and to give them the courage to defend it. The orchard of the Sikh faith needed the thorny hedge of armed men for its protection. The Singhs of the Khalsa were the orchard and the hedge rolled into one, ever willing to wield the sword in righteous cause.

When Guru Gobind Singh created the Order of the Khalsa, he laid the foundations of the Sikh military might by setting up a tradition of reckless valour, which became the distinguishing feature of Sikh soldiery. They came to believe in the triumph of their cause as an article of faith, and like their Guru asked for no nobler end than a death on the battlefield.

> O Lord, with clasped hands this boon I crave,
> Let me never shun the righteous task,
> Let me be fearless when I go battle,
> Give me faith that victory will be mine,
> Give me power to sing Thy praise,
> And when time comes to end my life,
> Let me fall in mighty strife.

Guru Gobind Singh fought many desperate unequal battles against the Mughals. Two of his sons died in the fighting and Nawab Wazir Khan, the Mughal Governor of Sarhind, had executed the two younger ones. Wazir Khan later sent assassins to kill the Guru. They found the Guru in Nanded and attacked him after his evening prayer, stabbing him beneath his heart. Guru Gobind Singh fought and killed his assailant. Sikhs rushed to his aid and killed the second man. The wound began to heal but reopened several days later when the Guru attempted to use his bow. Realizing his end had come; Guru Gobind Singh assembled his Sikhs and instructed them that the scripture of the Granth should forever be their irreplaceable Guru and Guide. What Guru Gobind Singh had succeeded in doing was to "Teach the sparrow to hunt the hawk and one man to have the courage to fight a legion." (Khushwant Singh)

Call to Arms

The battles fought by Guru Gobind Singh

The Battle of Bhangani, The Battle of Nadaun, The Battle of Anandpur Sahib, The Battle of Nirmoh Garh, The Battle of Chamkaur and The Battle of Muktsar (1703).

Bhangani (1689)

At the age of twenty Guru Gobind Singh Ji fought his first battle. The battle took place in October 1686, in the small village of Bhangani on the right bank of the River Yamuna in Sirmur district of Himachal Pradesh. Encouraged by the Rajput chiefs of the hills, Guru Gobind Singh started organising his Army against the Mughals. The hill chieftains taking exception to Guru Gobind Singh`s teaching equalizing all castes, thought it highly dangerous to allow the Sikhs to continue their increase in power and number. They therefore, decided collectively to complain to the Delhi government against the Sikhs. The viceroy of Delhi sent General Din Beg and General Painda Khan each with five thousand men to resist the Guru's 'encroachments' on the rights of the hill Rajas. When the imperial forces reached Rupar, they were joined by the hill Rajas, with a force of 30,000 men and under the leadership of Raja Bhim Chand and Fateh Shah they rode towards Paonta Sahib. Guru Gobind Singh Ji's Army consisted of around 4,000 Sikhs. Forestalling the attack, Guru Gobind Singh advanced towards Bhangani with his Sikhs. The rajas, reinforced by a few hundred Pathans who had deserted the Guru's camp, were confident of their strength and had imprudently collected their force in the open ground on the river bed. The Guru established his base in a grove and kept his forward troops on a higher ground, and selected for himself a vantage point from where to direct the action. The Guru appointed the Five Beloved Ones as Generals of his Army. When the engagement began at Anandpur, the Turks were roasted by the continuous and deadly fire of the Sikhs. General Painda Khan, seeing the determined resistance of the Sikhs, shouted to his men to fight to the death against the infidels. He came forward to engage in single combat with the Guru and was instantly killed by Guru Gobind Singh. Din Beg assumed sole command of the troops. Maddened by Painda Khan's death they fought with great desperation but could not make any impression on the firm hold of the Sikhs. On the other hand, however, the Sikhs caused great havoc upon the enemy. The hill chiefs fled the field. In the meantime Din Beg was wounded and he beat a retreat but was pursued by the Sikhs as far as Rupar (upto the village of Khairabad near Chandigarh where there is a Gurdwara in that memory). The victory at Bhangani gave Guru Gobind Singh confidence to descend from the mountains to his ancestral home in Anandpur.

Call to Arms

Nadaun (1690)

The Battle of Nadaun was fought on 20TH March 1691 between an imperial expeditionary force aided by Raja Kirpal Chand of Kangra and Raja Dyal of Bijarwal in the Sivalik hills on the one hand and several other neighbouring chieftains who enjoyed the support of Guru Gobind Singh Ji on the other. The battle is also mentioned in the autobiography of Guru Gobind Singh called the Bachittar Natak. This was the second battle of Guru Gobind Singh after the Battle of Bhangani. The hill Rajas, taking advantage of Emperor Aurangzeb's preoccupation with the endless Maratha insurgency in the South, had neglected to pay their annual tributes into the imperial treasury for three years. Early in 1691 orders were issued to Hifzullah Khan, Governor of Jammu, to collect the revenue. Mian Khan dispatched a punitive force under Alif Khan. Two of the chieftains, Raja Kirpal Chand and Raja Dyal, submitted without opposition and in fact became Alif Khan's allies. Raja Bhim Chand of Kahlur (Bilaspur), the most powerful of the Chieftains rallied the rest of the rulers to resist the Mughal demands. Guru Gobind Singh, who did not cotton to the idea of anyone paying tribute to Aurangzeb and his religious Wars, was asked for help and joined in the combined effort to rout Alif Khan and his punitive force. Guru Gobind Singh came to his assistance with a force of his best Sikhs. The opposing armies met at Nadaun on the left bank of the River Beas, 32 km Southeast of Kangra and 12 km from the town of Javalamukhi with its Durga temple with the eternal flame, and joined in the combined effort to rout Alif Khan and his punitive force. Guru Gobind Singh's allies were Bhim Chand, Raj Singh, Ram Singh, Sukhdev Gaji of Jasrot, Prithi Chand of Dadhwar, where as in opposition there were Kirpal Chand of Kangra, Dyal Chand of Bijarwal, Rajputs of Nangal and panglua, soldiers of Jaswar and Guler and Alif Khan. Guru Sahib fought with Katochs. Guru Gobind Singh described in his autobiographical poem, Bachitra Natak the action that took place. As the enemy, he says, advanced with Dyal and Kirpal in the vanguard, a fierce battle commenced. It however did not take long to decide the issue. Bichitra Natak considered as being the autobiography of Guru Gobind Singh is one of the major sources of information about the battle, in which Guru Gobind Singh's poem; "The Almighty God hastened the end of the fight and the opposing host was pushed back into the river... Alif Khan fled in utter disarray leaving his camp to take care of itself..." Alif Khan fled his camp, leaving his belongings, along with all his Warriors.

Guru Gobind Singh Ji stayed in Himachal, remaining on the bank of the river for eight more days while he visited the palaces of all the chiefs. He then took leave and came home. The local rulers met at his camp to settle the terms of peace. Both sides came to an agreement and then Guru Ji returned to Anandpur.

Call to Arms

Anandpur Sahib (1700)

The Rajas of Jammu, Nurpur, Mandi, Bhutan, Kulu, Kionthal, Guler, Chamba, Srinagar, Dadhwal, Handur and others, assembled at Bilaspur to discuss the newly created situation. Raja Ajmer Chand of Kahlur (son of late Raja Bhim Chand) addressed them that if they overlooked the growing power of the Guru, he would one day drive them out from their territories. On the other hand if they were to seek assistance from Delhi again and again, they might be taken over by the Mughal Empire for ever. It was, therefore, decided that they must defend themselves. If the entire hill Rajas contributed reasonable contingents, they could muster a large Army which would be sufficient to annihilate the Guru and his Sikhs. Thus a simple and feasible measure was thought out to invest the Guru's capital, Anandpur, and starve its occupants into submission. Accordingly all the Rajas brought their contingents and marched towards Anandpur. It was now clear to the Rajas that the Guru would not surrender. Next morning they beat the drum of War. As anticipated a large number of Ranghars and Gujjars under the command of Jagatullah flocked to the side of the hill Rajas. Five hundred men from the Majha area arrived to join the Guru's forces. The hill Rajas opened fire with large guns on the Guru's fortress. Several brave Sikhs made a determined stand against the enemy and forced them to retreat. Raja Ghuman Chand of Kangra rallied his troops but failed to cause the Sikhs to retreat. Next morning the allied forces contented themselves with concentrating their attack on one particular part of the city but the Sikhs again offered valiant resistance. The allied forces rallied many times but could not overcome the brave Sikhs and so they decided to siege the city which lasted for a few weeks. As the blockade prolonged successfully, Raja Kesari Chand prepared to intoxicate an elephant and direct him against the city. The whole body of the elephant was encased in steel. A strong spear projected from his forehead for the purpose of assault. The intoxicated elephant was directed towards the gate of Lohgarh fort and the allied Army followed him. The Guru blessed his Sikh, Bachittar Singh to combat the elephant. Bachittar Singh took a lance to meet the furious animal. He raised his lance and drove it through the elephant's head armor. On this the animal turned around on the hill soldiers, and killed several of them. Meanwhile Ude Singh continued to advance against Kesari Chand, challenged him, and then with one blow cut off his head. Mohkam Singh, one of the Five Beloved Ones, cut off the mad elephant's trunk with one blow of his sword. What remained of the hill Army now fled the field. In the retreat the Raja of Handur was severely wounded by Sahib Singh. On the following day Ghuman Chand of Kangra directed the efforts of his troops against the city. Ghuman Chand's horse was killed by a bullet from the musket of Alim Singh. The battle lasted with varying success until evening, when Ghuman Chand, as he was proceeding to his tent in the evening, was mortally wounded by a chance bullet. All the hill chiefs now became disheartened and demoralized. Raja Ajmer Chand was the last to leave Anandpur and marched home in the dead of night.

Call to Arms

Nirmoh Garh (1701)

Ajmer Chand, in spite of the defeat of the allied forces, determined to oust the Guru. He sent an envoy to the Emperor's viceroy in Sirhind and another envoy to the viceroy of Delhi to complain against the Sikhs and sought their help to assist the hill chiefs in destroying the Guru's power and expelling him from Anandpur. Accordingly the imperial forces were directed to assist the hill chiefs. At the same time to save their faces, the hill chiefs proposed to the Guru through Pamma Brahman, that they would be friends with him for ever only if he left Anandpur for a while and come back later. The Guru agreed to the proposal and left for Nirmoh, a village situated about a mile from Kiratpur. After he reached Nirmoh, Raja Ajmer Chand and Raja of Kangra both thought that since he was now in the open and he had no fort around him for protection, it would be better to launch an attack. They attacked the Guru's Army without even waiting for the arrival of the imperial Army. A fierce battle ensued in which the Sikhs were ultimately victorious. The Army of Wazir Khan, the viceroy of Sirhind, arrived in due time. The Guru found himself in a very dangerous position between the hill Rajas on one hand, and the imperial Army on the other. But he resolved to defend himself in whatever way it was and his Sikhs stood faithfully and valiantly by him. Wazir Khan gave an order to his troops to make a sudden rush and seize the Guru. The Guru was successfully protected by his son Ajit Singh and his other brave Warriors. They stopped the advance of the imperial forces and cut them down in rows. The carnage continued until night. Next day the imperial Army and the hill chiefs made a furious assault when the Guru decided on retiring to Basoli, who's Raja had frequently invited him to his capital. Until the Guru's Army reached the river Satluj, fierce fighting continued in which brave Sahib Singh was slain. Biting his thumb Wazir Khan admitted that he had never before witnessed such desperate fighting. The Guru with his troops crossed over the river and reached Basoli. The hill chiefs were overjoyed and presented elephants to Wazir Khan and departed to their homes. Wazir Khan returned to Sirhind. This battle was fought at the end of 1701. Daya Singh and Ude Singh requested the Guru to return to Anandpur. After staying a few days at Basoli, he marched back to Anandpur and the inhabitants of the city were delighted to see him again among them. Finding the Guru again firmly established at Anandpur, Raja Ajmer Chand thought it most wise to pursue for peace. The Guru told Ajmer Chand that he was willing to come to terms with him, but he would punish him if he were again found guilty of treachery. Ajmer Chand was glad to find peace with the Guru and he sent his family priest with presents to him. The other hill Rajas also followed Ajmer Chand's example and made good relations with the Guru.

Call to Arms

Chamkaur (1703)

After leaving Anandpur and crossing the flooded Sarsa rivulet, and resting at Kot Nihang Khan for a few hours, Guru Gobind Singh reached Chamkaur. He was accompanied by not more than 40 Singhs, including two of his older sons, and the five Panj Piare, the original "Beloved Five". Their arms were mostly swords and spears, as their ammunition had exhausted during the eight-month defence of the besieged Anandpur. Halting in a small garden, they approached the local chief for permission to use his haveli for shelter during the night. The place belonged to two brothers. The elder brother Rai Jagat Singh refused, for fear of Imperial wrath. But his younger brother, Rup Chand, at his own risk, permitted them to stay in the small fortress like two-storey house, which had a moderate quantity of arms and ammunition inside. Despite promise of safe conduct given to Guru Gobind Singh, the Mughal and Rajput Commanders were in search of him, to catch him in person or get his head as a trophy. When they got information of his halt at Chamkaur, they came and laid siege to the haveli, which was like a small Garhi, or a fortress. The hordes of Rajput and Mughal Warriors rushed to join the manhunt. The arrows from the upper storey of the haveli kept many a soldier at bay. The battle lasted all day. When the ammunition and arrows in the Garhi almost ran out, the Singhs came out in batches of five, with swords and spears in their hands, to face the enemy that far outnumbered them. Their determination and fighting skill helped them kill many of the enemy, but odds were so heavy against them that they all fell in the field, one by one. They were followed by the next batch of five, charged with emotions of fighting a treacherous enemy. Determined to fight with all their vigour, they too were to lay down their lives the same way. Guru Gobind Singh's eldest son, 18-year old Sahibzada Ajit Singh went out to join the battle. After heroic confrontations with several of the enemy at a time, he fell in the field. After watching his brother being slaughtered, the younger Sahibzada, 15-year old Jujhar Singh, touched the feet of his father, gave him a hug, and bidding farewell sallied forth with the next and the last batch. With the setting of the sun that day, he too became a martyr. By nightfall, only six persons remained alive in the Garhi. The Singhs decided that Guru Gobind Singh must quit the haveli, so that he could rally his followers again. If he perished, loss to the community would be irreparable. Reluctantly, the Guru agreed to the proposal, which the Singhs presented as the 'Gurmatas' of five, which was binding. Bhai Sant Singh decided to stay back to guard the entrance, and thus gain some additional time, when the enemy barged in. In the middle of the night Guru Gobind Singh and three remaining Sikhs left the haveli, with a plan to go in different directions but meet in a garden outside Machhivara. The Mughals hastily chased after the Guru once they realised he had escaped. Guru Gobind Singh made a last stand against the Mughals at Muktsar. The battle of Muktsar was the last battle fought by Guru Gobind Singh.

Call to Arms

Khidrana, (Muktsar) (1703)

In late December of 1705, Guru Gobind Singh searched for an ideal location to engage the Mughal Army in Warfare. Accompanied by Sikhs who joined up with him along the way, the Guru eventually made his way to Malwa, near Khidrana. A delegation of Sikhs concerned by the likelihood of Warfare approached Guru Gobind Singh and offered to intercede on his behalf and negotiate with the Mughals. The Guru refused, reminding them of Mughal Emperor Aurangzeb's broken vows, deceitful ways and treacherous acts. Upon learning of the martyrdom of the guru's eldest sons at Chamkaur and his youngest sons and mother at Sirhind, Bhag Kaur (Mai Bhago), her brother Bhag Singh, and her husband Nidhan Singh, roused a band of 40 remorseful Sikhs from Majha who had returned home during the evacuation of Anandpur after renouncing Guru Gobind Singh in exchange for safe passage and deserting his Army. The Majha Sikhs expressed sincere repentance, sought permission to rejoin the Guru and readied themselves for battle. Upon reaching the Khidrana reservoir, Guru Gobind Singh positioned his Warriors. To confuse the enemy, the 40 Majha Sikhs spread tents of cloth over shrubs to give the appearance of an encampment and secreted themselves with weapons ready among Van trees and the surrounding Karir bushes. Charging into the trap they believed to be the Guru's camp, Mughal soldiers led by Wasir Khan suffered a relentless surprise attack. The Guru climbed high up the hill, or Tibbi, behind the cover of trees, where he shot arrows into the oncoming horde overwhelming the enemy. After expending their bullets, the Guru's Warriors clashed with the enemy face to face, courageously fighting hand to hand with swords and lances, both on horseback and on foot. One by one the 40 repentant Majha Sikhs sold their lives at a great cost to their Mughal adversaries. At the day's end, all 40 of the Majha Warriors had fallen. Their heroic sacrifice enabled the Guru to hold the valuable reservoir water so that exhausted enemy troupes had no recourse but to turn back or succumb to thirst. The Guru picked his way through the bodies of the defeated enemy looking for Sikh survivors. Of the 40 Majha Sikhs he found only Bhai Mahan Singh and Mai Bhago living. Bhai Mahan suffered a terrible infliction; Guru Gobind Singh knelt and lifted his beloved Warriors' mortally wounded body to his breast and bending close to his ear, thanked Bhai Mahan for his selfless act, and asked if he had a last request. Bhai Mahan replied that he lived and died only for his Guru's service and begged that the papers of renunciation the 40 had signed in Anandpur be destroyed and pleaded that the 40 be reinstated as the Guru's own. The Guru produced the paper and tore it into pieces casting it to wind.

At Nanded in Maharashtra, Guru Gobind Singh converted Madho Das to Sikhism and gave him the name of Gurbaksh Singh, although he became popularly known as Banda Singh Bahadur. Banda Singh and the Khalsa were sent by Guru Gobind Singh back to the Punjab with the objective to ending the unjust and tyrannical Mughal rule. Guru Sahib Ji ascended to the heavens on October 7TH 1708.

THE KHALSA

Neither the hill chiefs nor the Mughal government could tolerate the great revolution that the Sikh Gurus had effected with such tremendous success. Before and after the creation of the Khalsa, the imperial government had made many attempts at destroying the growing power of the Sikhs. But the Sikhs endured, suffered and survived. And the Sikh community thus created and reared by the indefatigable efforts of the ten Masters and blessed with noble traditions of intrepidity, bravery, sacrifice and virtuous conduct, took up the challenge of the Mughal high-handedness, persecution and injustice under the leadership of Banda Singh Bahadur. There was no let-up from either side for the next half a century till the Sikhs threw the Mughals and other contestants out of the Punjab. The Khalsa, as a combined body of the Sikhs, was made the supreme authority amongst the Sikhs in all matters. No leader, however great, could challenge the authority of the Khalsa and introduce any innovation in the rules of conduct of the Khalsa Panth. The guidance of the community lay with their collective wisdom and decisions. The rulers that we come across in the pageant of Sikh history may be regarded as the servants of the Khalsa Commonwealth, in whose name they functioned. Indeed, it was the Khalsa who led the community through its trials and ordeals and finally won political power, the victory being of the Khalsa, of the community as a whole and not of the few leaders, whatever their individual merit. However, the warlike Khalsa, produced leaders of pure military genius in the likes of Banda Bahadur.

Banda Bahadur, (1670–1716)

A hermit called Lachman Das, who had been renamed Gurbaksh Singh (popular name Banda Bahadur) by Guru Gobind Singh Ji, was given the task to lead the campaign in the Punjab against the Mughal administration. He was supplied with a standard, an arrow and a drum as symbols of temporal authority. He was given an advisory council of five devoted Khalsa. Twenty-five soldiers were given to him as his bodyguard. A prescript called Hukumnamah or a letter of authority in the handwriting of the Guru Gobind Singh Ji, instructing Sikhs to join Banda Bahadur in an expedition against Muslims to avenge the atrocities against Sikhs. As an insignia of his temporal authority invested in him, Guru Gobind Singh Ji gave Banda Bahadur his own sword, green bow and five arrows from his quiver. Banda Bahadur planted the Guru's standard near Delhi and called the Khalsa to arms and then proceeded towards the Punjab. He had approximately 500 men with him when he reached the borders of the Punjab. Here Banda Bahadur issued letters to Malwa Sikhs to join him in his crusade against Wazir Khan of Sarhind. Never perhaps in the history of The Punjab did the circumstances of the time offer so fair a field to the ambition of a leader, conscious of great talents, and called to the command of a Warlike people, only too eager to support him in any enterprise he might undertake. As he advanced towards Sarhind, Banda Bahadur seized a Government treasury, which was on its way from the Northern districts to Delhi, which was distributed amongst the rank and file of the Khalsa.

BATTLES OF THE KHALSA

Samana, (1709)
Samana was the native place of Jalal-ud-did Jallad, the professional executioner, who had beheaded Guru Tegh Bahadur, while his son had beheaded two younger sons of Guru Gobind Singh. It was an accursed place in the eyes of Sikhs. The entire peasantry of the neighbourhood was now up in arms, and Banda's following had risen to several thousand. Led by Banda, the Khalsa fell upon the town on November 26TH 1709. The inhabitants were massacred in cold blood and the town thoroughly plundered. Samana was the district town and had nine Parganahs attached to it. It was placed under the charge of Fateh Singh. Samana was the first territorial conquest and the first administrative Unit of the Khalsa. After the sack of Samana, the towns of Kunjpura, Ghuram, and Thaska, Shahbad Markanda, inhabited by Muslim Ranghars notorious for rape and rapine, were destroyed. Damla the village of Pathans, who had deserted Guru Gobind Singh in the battle of Bhangani, was reduced to rubble. The town of Kapuri, whose faujdar, Qadam ud Din, was notorious for his debaucheries and persecution of Hindus and Sikhs, was razed to the ground.

Sadhaura, (1709)
Usman Khan, the chief of Sadhaura had persecuted Sayyid Budhu Shah for helping Guru Gobind Singh in the battle of Bhangani. The Muslim population maltreated the local Hindus. On the approach of Banda the leading Muslims gathered in a big and strongly built mansion. They were all massacred. This building came to be known as Katal Garhi. Banda attacked the town and destroyed it. The contemporary historian Khafi Khan wrote: "In two or three month's time four to five thousands pony-riders, and seven to eight thousand Warlike footmen joined him. Day by day their number increased, and abundant money and material by pillage fell into their hands. Numerous villages were laid waste and he appointed his own police officers (thanedars) and collectors of revenue (Tahsil-dar-e-mal)"

Lohgarh, (1710)
The ultimate aim of Banda was to punish Wazir Khan and conquer Sarhind. He therefore established his headquarters, in the beginning of February 1710, at Mukhlispur situated in lower Shiwalik hills South of Nahan, about 20 km from Sadhaura. His fort stood on a hilltop. Two kuhls or water channels flowed at its base and supplied water to it. This fort was repaired and put in a state of defence. All the money, gold and costly materials acquired in these expeditions were deposited here. Banda struck coins and issued orders under his seal. The name of Mukhlispur was changed to Lohgarh, and it became the capital of the first Sikh state. Banda ruled over the region bounded on the North by Shiwalik hills, on the West by river Tangri, on the East by river Jamuna, and in the South by a line passing through Samana, Thanesar, Kaithal and Karnal.

Battles of the Khalsa

Lohgarh, (Cont.)

Banda Bahadur abolished the Zamindari System of land prevailing under the Mughals and declared the actual cultivators as the owners of land. Thus he established the peasant proprietorship, and won approbation and support of the overwhelming majority of the population. Khafi Khan says that Banda "issued orders to imperial officers and agents and big jagirdars to submit and give up their business." So Guru Gobind Singh's dream of political sovereignty was realized within a year of his death. Banda's name struck terror into the hearts of lawless people, and thefts and dacoity became a thing of the past. "In all the Parganahs occupied by the Sikhs," writes Irvine, "The reversal of previous customs was striking and complete. A low scavenger or leather dresser, the lowest of the low in Indian estimation, had only to leave home and join the Guru, when in a short time he would return to his birthplace as its ruler with his order of appointment in his hand. As soon as he set foot within the boundaries the wealthy and wellborn went out to greet him and with joined palms awaited his orders. Not a soul could disobey an order, and men who had often risked themselves in battlefields, became so cowed down that they were afraid even to remonstrate."

Battle of Sarhind, (1710)

The battle was fought at Chhappar Chiri, 20 kms from Sarhind. On the Mughal side Nawab of Malerkotla, Sher Muhammad Khan, was the leader of the right wing. Wazir Khan was in command of the centre. Sucha Nand, chief secretary of Nawab was put on the left. On the Sikh side, Baj Singh Bal headed the right wing. Binod Singh headed the left wing, while Banda commanded the centre facing Wazir Khan's Army. Shouts of Sachcha Padishah, Sat Sri Akal, Akal, Akal, and ya Ali, rent the sky. Sucha Nand could not withstand the ferocity of Baj Singh and soon fled away. The artillery fire of the Mughals told heavily on the plunderers in Banda's camp. The plunderers were equally divided between Baj Singh and Binod Singh's forces. Sher Mohammed Khan was about to overpower Binod Singh's wing when he was suddenly struck by a bullet and was instantly killed. His men immediately dispersed. Wazir Khan was rushing upon Banda, who stuck fast to his ground and discharged arrows relentlessly. Baj Singh and Binod Singh now joined Banda. Banda and the Sikh leaders now converged on Wazir Khan and killed him. Wazir Khan's head was stuck up on a spear and lifted high up by a Sikh who took his seat in the deceased's howdah. (A seat atop an elephant). The Sikhs with one voice and in wild excitement raised the sky-rending shouts of Sat-Sri-Akal. The Mughal soldiers on beholding the Nawab's head took alarm, and trembling fled helter skelter in dismay and despair. The Sikhs fell upon them and there was terrible carnage. The Sikhs reached Sarhind by nightfall. The gates of the city were closed. The guns mounted on the walls of the fort-commenced bombardment. The Sikhs laid siege to the place. Next day the Sikhs forced open the gates and fell upon the city.

Battles of the Khalsa

Battle of Sarhind, (Cont.)

The Government treasury and moveable property worth two crores fell into Banda's hand and was removed to Lohgarh. Several Muslims saved their lives by embracing Sikhism. Dindar Khan, son of Jalal Khan Rohilla, became Dindar Singh. The official news writer of Sarhind, Mir Nasir-ud-din, changed his name to Mir Nasir Singh. The entire province of Sarhind, consisting of twenty-eight Parganahs and extending from the Satluj to the Jamuna and from the Shiwalik hills to Kunjpura, Karnal to Kaithal, yielding 52 lakhs rupees annually, came into Banda's possession. Baj Singh was appointed governor of Sarhind. Ali Singh was made his deputy. Their chief responsibility was to be on guard against the Mughal troops from Lahore and Jammu. Fateh Singh retained charge of Samana. Ram Singh, brother of Baj Singh, became chief of Thanesar. Binod Singh in addition to his post of the revenue minister was entrusted with the administration of Karnal and Panipat. Banda retired to his capital at Lohgarh. The Zamindari system was abolished in the whole province at one stroke. Banda Singh's rule, though short-lived, had a far-reaching impact on the history of the Punjab. With it began the decay of Mughal authority and the demolition of the feudal system of the society it had created.

Lohgarh, (1710)

Imperial instructions were issued to the governors of Delhi and Oudh and other Mughal officers to march towards the Punjab. Emperor Bahadur Shah's order, issued on December 10TH 1710 was a general Warrant for the faujdars to "kill the worshippers of Nanak", wherever they are found. Banda was chased out of every corner of the Punjab and he took refuge in the Shivalik hills. He again started his campaigns against the Mughals and came out of the hills to the plains of the Punjab. The massive imperial force drove the Sikhs from Sarhind and other places to take shelter in the fort of Lohgarh in the hilly region. "It is impossible for me," says Khafi Khan a Muslim historian of that time, "to describe the fight which followed. The Sikhs in their Faqir's dress struck terror into the hearts of the royal troops. The number of casualties among the latter was so large that for a time it appeared as if they were going to lose." At Lohgarh Banda was closely invested by sixty thousand horse and foot. For want of provisions, Sikhs were reduced to rigorous straits. They killed their horses for food, and when they could stand up to the enemy no longer, they made a desperate bid to escape and hacked their way out of the imperial cordon. Banda was far from vanquished and, within a fortnight of his escape from Lohgarh, he began to send out *hukamnamas* exhorting the people to carry on the fight. Sikhs came out of their mountain haunts to recover their lost territories and once again occupied Sadhaura and Lohgarh. Farukh Siyar, who came to the throne of Delhi in 1713, launched against them the sternest proceedings that political authority stirred with a fanatical religious zeal could devise.

Battles of the Khalsa

Gurdas Nangal, (1713)

The Sikhs were hounded out of the plains of the Punjab and their main column, under Banda Singh of about 4,000 men, was subjected to most stringent siege at the village of Gurdas-Nangal, about six kilometres from Gurdaspur. Gurdas Nangal was an epic of purest heroism in the face of heavy odds. According to Muhammad Qasim, the Muslim author of Ibratnamah, who has given an eyewitness account of this campaign, the "brave and daring deeds (of the Sikhs) were amazing. Twice or thrice a day, some forty or fifty of them would come out of their enclosure to gather grass for their animals, and, when the combined forces of the emperor went to oppose them, they made short work of the Mughals with arrows, muskets and small swords, and then disappeared". For eight months the garrison resisted the siege of 100,000 Mughal troops under the gruesome conditions. Most of the Mughal Commanders were afraid of a face-to-face encounter with Banda, and were constantly pushing their Qazis and Mullas to the front to offer prayers to counter the spells of the enemy. Abdus Samad Khan openly prayed that Banda escaped from there, so that the whole business could be disposed off on any excuse. Only fresh orders from the Emperor to capture Banda dead or alive kept him at his task. He was taking new measures everyday to tighten the siege, to starve the defenders to submission. This siege dragged on for eight months.

Towards the end of November 1715, the defenders were running out of ammunition and food. They were trying to exist on boiled leaves and the bark of trees, and were gradually reduced to mere skeletons. Then on 17TH December 1715, Abdus Samad shouted across the separating moat, that he would not allow any killing by his men, if Banda opened the gate to the fortress. When Banda ordered the gate be opened, the Mughals rushed in to spear or stab as many as three hundred of the half-dead and helpless defenders. The rest, around 740 Sikhs, along with Banda Singh were taken to Lahore, and thence to Delhi. The cavalcade to the imperial capital was a grisly sight. Besides 740 prisoners in heavy chains, it comprised seven hundred cartloads of the heads of the Sikhs with another 2,000 stuck upon pikes. By the emperor's order Banda Bahadur and some two dozen leading Sikhs were imprisoned in the Fort, while the remaining 694 were made over to the *Kotwal*, Sarbrah Khan, to be executed at the Kotwali Chabutra at the rate of a hundred a day. Then Banda Bahadur was offered the choice between Islam and death. Upon his refusal to renounce his faith, his four-year-old son, Ajai Singh, was hacked to pieces before his eyes. He himself was subjected to the harshest treatments. His eyes were pulled out and his hands and feet chopped off. His flesh was torn with red-hot pincers and finally his body was cut up limb by limb. The ambassadors of the East India Company, John Surman and Edward Stephenson, who were in Delhi then and had witnessed some of these massacres, wrote to the governor of Fort William: "It is not a little remarkable with what patience Sikhs undergo their fate, and to the last it has not been found that one apostatised from his new formed religion."

Battles of the Khalsa

Dal Khalsa

After the brutal murder of Banda and his followers, the Khalsa faced a desperate struggle for survival. The Khalsa Jathas (fighting bands) left the plains and retreated to the hills and jungles 'The Sikhs, it was thought had been hammered out of existence. But the hammering did not reduce them to pulp, but hardened the remnants to tempered steel.'' Each *Jatha* grouped around a *Jathedar* or leader who came to occupy this position on account of his daring spirit. For every able-bodied Sikh who had undergone the vows of Khalsa, it became necessary to join one or the other *Jatha* to fight against the oppressors. Besides skill in the use of arms, he had to be a good horseman, because in guerrilla Warfare, such as Sikhs had to resort to against the superior might of the state, speed and mobility were of paramount importance. The weaponry, in the beginning, ranged from knobbed clubs, spears and battle axes, to bow and arrows and matchlocks. A long sword and a dagger were of course carried by every member of the Khalsa. Some of them wore Armour, but no helmets. During raids on Imperial columns and baggage trains, the booty most valued was good horses and matchlocks so that most of the *Jathas* were gradually equipped with firearms. The diverse Jathas voluntarily accepted the control of Sarbatt Khalsa, the assembly of all the Sikh Jathas at Amritsar, when the plans of action were formulated in the form of gurmatas or resolutions adopted in the presence of Guru Granth Sahib. The brief respite provided by a temporary détente with the government during 1733-35 enabled the Sikh Jathas to assemble and stay in strength at Amritsar with immunity. Under the guidance of Nawab Kapur Singh, their chosen leader, the Jathas were reorganized into twelve fighting Units. These Misls, meaning equal, operated independently of each other in the areas under their control, but facing common danger, merged under the banner of the Dal Khalsa (Sikh Army)

Nadir Shah

The Shah of Persia, Nadir Shah, took over Kandahar from the Afghans in March 1738, and went on to occupy the Mughal province of Kabul in June. In January 1739, he swept through the mountain passes to the Punjab, brushing aside the forces of the Mughal governor, Zakariya Khan, at Lahore, defeated the Imperial Army at Karnal and pushed on to the capital Delhi. In the summer of 1739 Nadir Shah turned homewards laden with enormous booty and thousands of slaves. The Dal Khalsa found Nadir's loot an easy prey. They began plundering the invader's baggage train and continued to do so all the way to the Indus. Nadir Shah is said to have questioned Zakariya Khan about the brigands who had been audacious enough to attack his troops. The governor replied: "They are fakirs who visit their Guru's tank twice a year and having bathed in it disappear." "Where do they live?" enquired the Shah. "Their homes are their saddles," replied Zakariya Khan. Nadir Shah is said to have prophesied, "Take care, the day is not far distant when these rebels will take possession of your country."

Battles of the Khalsa

Chhota Ghallughara, (Small Holocaust) (1746)

Chhota Ghallughara, minor holocaust or carnage, is how Sikh chronicles refer to a bloody action during the severe campaign of persecution launched by the Mughal government at Lahore against the Sikhs in 1746. Early in that year Jaspat Rai, the faujdar of Eminabad, was killed in an encounter with a roving band of Sikhs. Jaspat Rai's brother, Lakhpat Rai, who was a Diwan or revenue minister at Lahore, vowed revenge on the Sikhs. With the concurrence of the Mughal governor of Lahore, Yahiya Khan, Lakhpat Rai mobilized the Lahore troops, summoned reinforcements from Multan, Bahawalpur and Jalandhar, alerted the feudal hill chiefs, and roused the general population for jihad or crusade against the Sikhs. As an immediate first step, he had the Sikh inhabitants of Lahore rounded up and ordered their execution. Execution took place as ordered on 10TH March 1746. Lakhpat Rai then set out at the head of a large force, mostly Cavalry supported by cannon, in search of Sikhs who were reported to have concentrated in the swampy forest of Kahnuvan. He surrounded the forest and started a systematic search for his prey. The Sikhs held out for some time striking back whenever they could but, heavily outnumbered and under equipped, they at last decided to make a final sally and escape to the hills in the Northeast. They crossed the River Ravi and made for the heights of Basohli in the district of Jammu and Kashmir, only to find that the Hindu hill men in front were as hostile to them as the Muslim hordes following close upon their heels. Caught in this situation and bereft of provisions, they suffered heavy casualties in the area around Parol and Kathua. Yet making a last desperate bid, the survivors broke through the ring and succeeded in re-crossing the Ravi, though many were carried away in the torrent. With Lakhpat Rai still close behind, they crossed the Beas and the Satluj to find refuge in their old sanctuary, the Lakhi Jungle, deep into the Malva region. An estimated 7,000 Sikhs were killed and 3,000 captured in the action fought on 1ST and 2ND May 1746. Lakhpat Rai marched back in triumph to Lahore where he had the captives beheaded in batches in the Nakhas or site of the horse market outside the Delhi gate where, in later times, the Sikhs raised a memorial shrine known as the Shahidganj. Lakhpat Rai ordered Sikh places of worship to be destroyed and their holy books burnt. He even decreed that anyone uttering the word guru should be put to death. The nightmarish episode of March-May 1746 came to be known among the Sikhs as Chhota Ghallughara, as compared to a still greater killing that befell those 16 years later, the Vadda Ghallughara of 5TH February 1762. Lakhpat Rai's boast of a total annihilation of the Sikh people, however, was soon falsified. In about six month's time, the Sikhs were back on the scene converging upon Amritsar in small groups.

The civil war between the sons of Zakariya Khan, which commenced in the month of November 1746, resulted in the dislocation of the government machinery in the Punjab. During this respite the Sikhs quietly started recouping their strength.

SIKH MISLS

Sikh Misls

The period from 1716 to 1799 in the Punjab was a highly turbulent time politically and militarily. This was caused by the overall decline of the Mughal Empire, particularly in the Punjab, caused by Sikh military action against it. This left a power vacuum that was eventually filled by the Sikh Confederacy. This Confederacy was made up of individual Sikh kingdoms that were ruled by Sikh barons. Each of these barons has his own Army. Each individual Army had its own specific name, but the armies were referred to in general as Misls. Each Misl was made up of a number of soldiers, whose loyalty was given to the Misl's leader. A Misl could be composed of a few hundred to tens of thousands of soldiers. Every soldier was free to join any Misl he chose and free to cancel his membership of the Misl to whom he belonged. He could, if he wanted, cancel his membership of his old Misl and join another. The Barons would allow their armies to combine or coordinate their defences together against a hostile force if ordered by the Supreme Commander. (The Sikhs started the tradition of deciding the matters concerning the community at meetings which took place at Amritsar. These assemblies came to be known as the *Sarbat Khalsa* and a resolution passed by it became a gurmatas, *decree of the Guru*. The *Sarbat Khalsa* appointed the Supreme Commander and entrusted him to lead the Khalsa warriors in battle.) These orders were only issued in military matters affecting the whole Sikh community. These orders would normally be related to defence against external threats, such as Afghan military attacks. The profits of a fighting action were divided by the Misls to individuals based on the service rendered after the conflict using the Sardari system. (The centuries old Sardari system was established to promote the integrity and independence of the individual in a traditional society under a charismatic and paternalistic leadership).Sikh Confederacy is a description of the political structure, of how all the Barons' Kingdoms interacted with each other, (politically), in the Punjab. Although Misls varied in strength, the use of primarily light Cavalry with a smaller amount of heavy Cavalry was uniform throughout all the Sikh Misls. Cavalrymen (Ghorchurras) in a Misl were required to supply their own horses and equipment. A standard Cavalryman was armed with a spear, matchlock and scimitar. Prominent Sikh Misls: - Singhpuria, Ahluwalia, Dallewalia, Kanhaiya, Nishananvali, Ramgharia, Karora Singhia, Shahid, Nakai, Sukkarchakkia and Bhangi Misl. The twelfth, Phulkian Misl, was expelled from the Sikh Confederacy and Dal Khalsa for making alliances with the enemy (Afghans) and betraying and attacking other Sikh Misls.

On the following pages I include a brief history of each Misl including a short history of Phulkian Misls i.e. Patiala, Nabha, Jind, Kaithal, Kapurthala, Faridkot, Kalsia and Ladwa

Sikh Misls

Singhpuria Misl

Kapur Singh was the founder of this Misl. He commanded a force of 2500 Horse. "This force" says Latif "though small, was fiercest and most dreaded of all the Sikh soldiers." Kapur Singh attacked and occupied Faizullahpur. He changed the name of Faizullahpur to Singhpur, and the Misl began to be called Singhpuria Misl. Nawab Kapur Singh is considered one of the most revered, pivotal and legendary figures in Sikh history. Under his leadership, the then tiny Sikh community went through some of the darkest periods of its history. Nawab Kapur Singh proceeded to restructure the Sikh fighting force. He was one of the towering figures to establish Sikh power in the country. On his death in 1755, his nephew Khushal Singh succeeded him. He was a powerful Sardar who further expanded the Misl in power and territories. Khushal Singh died in 1795 and was succeeded by his son Budh Singh. In 1804, Maharajah Ranjit Singh annexed the Singhpuria Misl to the expanding Sikh Kingdom.

Ahluwalia Misl

Jassa Singh Ahluwalia was the founder of Ahluwalia Misl. Jassa Singh started seizing villages and towns in the Punjab and established the system of Rakhi or protection. In 1777, he defeated Rai Ibrahim, the Bhatti chief, and took from him the present town of Kapurthala, converting it into the capital of the Ahluwalia Misl. His successor Fateh Singh was the chosen companion of Maharaja Ranjit Singh, with whom he, in 1802, exchanged turbans in a permanent bond of brotherhood. In the majority of Ranjit Singh's campaigns Fateh Singh served him with his contingents. He fought at the battle of Haidru on July 13TH, 1813, when Fateh Khan, the Kabul minister, was utterly defeated. The Ahluwalia chief held a command in Bhimbar, Rajauri and Bahawalpur campaigns. In 1818, he participated in the siege of Multan when the whole province fell into the hands of Ranjit Singh. During the Kashmir campaign of 1819, Fateh Singh remained in charge of Lahore. In 1821, he assisted the Lahore Durbar in the reduction of the fort of Mankera. In 1823, when Ranjit Singh went to Khushab he left Lahore in the charge of Fateh Singh. The cordiality between the two chiefs was strained by Fateh Singh's direct communications with the British over the question of the Bhirog and Kotla chiefships, the construction by him of a strong citadel at Isru and his constant pleas for British protection. Feeling unsafe at Lahore, Fateh Singh fled across the river in 1825 to his Cis-Satluj territory and sought British protection. Ranjit Singh promptly seized his Trans-Satluj possessions. The rift between the Ahluwalia chief and the Maharaja of Lahore was, however, soon repaired. Fateh Singh returned to Lahore in 1827, and the Maharaja received him with honour restoring to him all his possessions. Later in his life, Fateh Singh lived at Kapurthala where he died in October 1836. On his death in 1837, Maharajah Ranjit Singh annexed his trans-Satluj territory except the Kapurthala state, to the expanding Sikh Kingdom. Kapurthala allied itself to the British and developed into a Sikh princely state of Kapurthala.

Sikh Misls

Bhangi Misl

In 1748 Hari Singh was acknowledged head of the Bhangi Misl. He vastly increased the power and influence of the Misl, which began to be ranked as the strongest among its peers. He created an Army of 20,000 dashing youths, captured Panjvar in the Tarn Taran Parganahs and established his headquarters first at Sohal and then at Gilvah. Hari Singh died in 1765. The Bhangi Misl reached the zenith of its power under his eldest son Jhanda Singh. Jhanda Singh marched on Multan in 1772 forcing the Nawab to flee. He next conquered Jhang, Kala Bagh and Mankera. He was killed in 1774 in a battle at Jammu. In 1765, Bhangi Sardars Lahina Singh, and Gujjar Singh had joined hands with Sardar Sobha Singh and occupied Lahore. On 7TH July 1799, Ranjit Singh arrived with 5,000 troops at the Shalimar Gardens. The Bhangi Sardars left the town hastily and Ranjit Singh became master of the capital of the Punjab, laying the foundation of Sikh monarchy. The last Bhangi chief to fall was Sahib Singh of Gujarat. Although Sahib Singh accepted the over lordship of Ranjit Singh, he exercised great influence in his territories which had strong forts at Jalalpur, Manawar and Islamgarh. About 1809, he developed strained relations with his son; Ranjit Singh availed himself of this opportunity and, occupied the whole of Gujrat including the towns of Gujrat, Islamgarh, Jalalpur, Manawar, Bajwat and Sodhra. In 1810 Ranjit Singh granted Sahib Singh Jagir of Bajwat. At Sahib Singh's death Ranjit Singh took two of his widows, Daya Kaur and Rattan Kaur, into his harem, marrying them by the ceremony of Chadar Pauna, Daya Kaur was the mother of Princes Pashaura Singh and Kashmira Singh and Rattan Kaur was the mother of Multana Singh. All Bhangi territories had merged with the Sikh kingdom of Ranjit Singh.

Dallewalia Misl

At the formation of the Dal Khalsa in 1748, Gulab Singh had bravely led the Dallewalia Jatha against Nadir Shah. Commanding a band of 400 horses, he plundered Panipat, Rohtak, Hansi and Hissar. In 1759, Gulab Singh fell fighting in the battle of Kalnaur. Tara Singh Ghaiba succeeded him as head of the Misl. One of his first exploits was to attack a detachment of Ahmad Shah Durrani's Army and rob it of its horses and arms. In 1760, he crossed the Satluj and seized the towns of Dharamkote and Fatehgarh. On his return to the Doab, he took Sarai Dakkani from Afghan chief Saif Ud-din of Jalandhar and marched eastwards seizing the country around Rahon. He made Rahon his headquarters. He next captured Nakodar from Manj Rajputs and several other villages on the right side of the Satluj, including Mahatpur and Kot Badal Khan. He joined other Sikh Sardars in laying siege to Sarhind and razing it to the ground after defeating its Faujdar Zain Khan. Tara Singh became a close friend and associate of Maharajah Ranjit Singh, and took part in his early Malwa campaigns. At his death in 1807 at the age of 90, Ranjit Singh annexed Dallewalia territories to the Sikh Kingdom.

Sikh Misls

Kanhaiya Misl

The Kanhaiya Misl was founded by Sardar Jai Singh, a Sandhu Jatt of the village of Kahna, 21 km South-West of Lahore. Jai Singh received the vows of the Khalsa at the hands of Nawab Kapur Singh and joined the Derah or Jatha of Sardar Amar Singh Kirigra. The Kanhaiya Misl under Jai Singh, seized part of Riloki comprising the district of Gurdaspur and upper portions of Amritsar. Jai Singh extended his territory to Parol and hill chiefs of Kangra, Nurpur, and Datarpur became his tributaries. In 1778 with the help of Mahan Singh Sukkarchakkia and Jassa Singh Ahluwalia, he banished Jassa Singh Ramgarhia to the desert region of Hansi and Hissar (Haryana Region). In 1781, Jai Singh and his associate Haqiqat Singh led an expedition to Jammu and received a sum of 3,000,000 rupees as tribute from its new ruler, Brij Raj Dev. On Jai Singh's death in 1793, control of the Kanhaiya clan passed into the hands of his daughter-in-law Sada Kaur. Sada Kaur, whose daughter Mehtab Kaur was married to Ranjit Singh, was mainly instrumental in the Sukkarchakkia chiefs rise to political power in the Punjab. In July 1799, Sada Kaur helped Ranjit Singh occupy Lahore. Supported by Sada Kaur, Ranjit Singh made further acquisitions and assumed the title of Maharajah in 1801. In the campaigns of Amritsar, Chiniot, Kasur and Kangra as well against the turbulent Pathan of Hazara and Attock; Sada Kaur led the armies side by side with Ranjit Singh. When Sada Kaur started secret negotiations with the British, to secure herself the status of an independent chief, Ranjit Singh annexed the Kanhaiya Misl to the expanding Sikh Kingdom.

Karora Singhia Misl

Baghel Singh, who succeeded as leader of the Misl, is celebrated in Sikh history as the conqueror of Mughal Delhi. In February 1764, Sikhs in a body of 40,000 under the command of Baghel Singh and other leading Warriors crossed the Yamuna and captured Saharanpur. In April 1775, Baghel Singh with two other Sardars, Rai Singh Bhangi and Tara Singh Ghaiba crossed the Yamuna to overrun the country then ruled by Zabita Khan. Zabita Khan in desperation proposed an alliance with Baghel Singh to jointly plunder the crown-lands. The combined forces of Sikhs and Rohillas captured villages around the present site of New Delhi. In March 1776; they defeated the imperial forces near Muzaffarnagar. The whole of the Yamuna-Gangetic Doab was now at their mercy. On 11TH March 1785, Sikhs entered the Red Fort in Delhi and occupied the Diwan-i-Am. The Mughal emperor, Shah Alam II, made a settlement with them, agreeing to allow Baghel Singh to raise Gurdwaras on Sikh historical sites and realize six annas in a rupee (37.5%) of all the duties in the capital. Baghel Singh stayed in an area called Sabzi Mandi, with 4,000 troops, and took charge of Chandni Chowk. He located seven sites sacred to the Sikhs and had shrines raised thereon within the space of eight months, from April to November 1783. Baghel Singh died in 1806 at Amritsar. His territories were annexed immediately after his death by Maharajah Ranjit Singh.

Sikh Misls

Nakai Misl

Nakai Misl was founded by Hira Singh, a Sandhu Jatt of the village of Bahirval. Hira Singh had taken to arms while still very young. He led a band of notoriously brave young men on great plundering raids. He was part of the Khalsa, when the Sikhs sacked Kasur in 1763 and conquered Sarhind in 1764. Hira Singh occupied Bahirval, Chunlan, Dlpalpur, Jambar, Jethupur, Kanganval and Khudian, establishing his headquarters at Chunian. In 1767, he led out an expedition to Pakpattan, but was killed in the action that took place. Ran Singh, who succeeded him, considerably increased the power and influence of the Nakais. Ran Singh had a force of 2,000 horsemen, with camel swivels and a few guns. Ran Singh died in 1781 and was succeeded by his eldest son Bhagvan Singh, whose sister, Raj Kaur, was married to Maharaja Ranjit Singh. His younger brother, Gian Singh, who died in 1807 leaving a son, Kahn Singh, succeeded Bhagvan Singh. Ranjit Singh granted Kahn Singh a Jagir of 15,000 rupees per annum and seized all the possessions of the family. The survivors of the Misl were pensioned off with an annual Jagir. Nakai became a prominent last name among several families. Many Nakai Sardars were converted to Islam lured by the women, power and money. A former Chief Minister of the Punjab, Arif Nakais grandfather was born as a Sikh but converted to Islam.

Nishananvali Misl

Nishananvali Misl owed its origin to Dasaundha Singh, whose Jatha was the standard-bearers of the Dal Khalsa. The Misl was originally based in Amritsar where it guarded the Holy Harimandar and also served as a reserve force of the Dal Khalsa. At the conquest of Sarhind by Sikhs in January 1764, Dasaundha Singh took possession of Singhanvala, Sahneval, Sarai Lashkari Khan, Amloh, Doraha, lirfi, and Ambala, establishing his headquarters at the last named station. On his and his younger brother Sangat Singh's death, his nephew Mohar Singh became the leader of the Misl. Among other leaders of the Misl, Naudh Singh, took possession of Khan close to Sarhind. Sudha Singh seized Machhivara East of Ludhiana, while Rai Singh secured 16 villages Southwest of Khanna. Jai Singh, another member of the Misl, captured 27 villages in Kharar. Karam Singh acquired the Parganahs of Shahabad and Ismailabad. Sawan Singh, a cousin of Dasaundha Singh and Sangat Singh, appropriated to himself several villages around Saunti. The military strength of the Nishananvali Misl had risen to 12,000 horses under Sangat Singh. Its territories included Ambala, Shahabad, Saunti, Kheri, Morinda, Amloh, Khanna, Doraha, Sahneval, Machhivara and Zira. Ambala was last ruled by Daya Kaur, widow of Gurbaksh Singh who had died in 1786. Nishananvali Misl's surviving ruler Daya Kaur allied to the British in 1809. Upon Daya Kaur's death in 1823, her estates and property lapsed to the British government.

Sikh Misls

Ramgharia Misl

Ramgarhia Misl took its name from Ram Rauni, an enclosure of unbaked bricks raised in Amritsar during the time of Jassa Singh. Jassa Singh became famous in Sikh history as Jassa Singh Ramgarhia. He gained reputation as a soldier of daring and skill. He, along with his brothers Jai Singh, Khushal Singh and Mali Singh, took up service under Adina Beg, faujdar of the Jalandhar Doab, which he quit when the Sikhs taunted him with betrayal of the Panth. To begin with, Jassa Singh joined hands with Jai Singh of the Kanhaiya Misl and seized large slices of territory in four out of the five Doabs. Within a decade Jassa Singh became one of the leading figures of the Dal Khalsa. In 1770, he led plundering expeditions into the hills. The local rajas sought safety in submission and Jassa Singh collected a tribute of 2,000,000 rupees from the Kangra hill states. Jassa Singh Ramgarhia, along with other Sikh Sardars, fought many pitched battles against Ahmad Shah Durrani, the Afghan invader.

As the Afghan threat receded, Sikh Sardars began fighting among themselves and Ramgarhia Sardar had to flee the Punjab. Driven out of the Punjab, Jassa Singh became a soldier of fortune. He took possession of Hissar and raised a large body of irregular horse, his depredations extending to the gates of Delhi and its suburbs, and into the Gangetic Doab. Once he penetrated into Delhi itself, and carried off four guns from the Mughal arsenal. The Nawab of Meerut agreed to pay him 10,000 rupees a year on his agreeing to leave his district unmolested. He soon, with a body of 30,000 horse and foot under him, and Karam Singh Shahid, crossed into Saharanpur district, ravaging it at will. On the death of Jassa Singh Ahluwalia in 1783, Jassa Singh Ramgarhia returned to the Punjab and recovered his lost possessions. He allied himself with the Sukkarchakkias, and their combined forces broke the power of the Kanhaiyas. At the height of its power, Ramgarhia Misl's territories in the Bari Doab included Batala, Kalanaur, Dinanagar, Sri Hargobindpur, Shahpur Kandi, Gurdaspur, Qadian, Ghuman, Matteval, and in the Jalandhar Doab, Urmur Tanda, Sanh, Miani, Garhdivala and Zahura. In the hills Kangra, Nurpur, Manndi and Chamba paid tribute to Jassa Singh.

Jassa Singh died in April 1803 at the ripe age of 80, leaving two sons, Jodh Singh and Vir Singh, the former of whom succeeded him. Jodh Singh was a deeply religious person. He built the Ramgarhia Bunga on the premises of the Harimandir at Amritsar and supplied blocks of perforated marble that served as parapets on both sides of the causeway leading to the sanctuary. In 1808, Ranjit Singh took possession of the territories of the Ramgarhia Misl. The same year he captured the fortress of Ramgarh, destroying all the Ramgarhia citadels. Adequate pensions were provided for Divan Singh and Jodh Singh, the leaders of the once powerful Ramgarhia Misl which had like many others collapsed under pressure of the new rising power in the Punjab.

Sikh Misls

Shahid Misl

The Misl headed by Dip Singh came to be known as Shahid Misl after he met with the death of a martyr (Shahid, in Punjabi). The Shahid Misl was mostly made up of Nihangs, a class of Warriors who owed their origin to Baba Fateh Singh, son of Guru Gobind Singh. The Shahids under Dip Singh had their headquarters at Talwandi Sabo. They also held control of the Harimandir at Amritsar. After Dip Singh's death, the leadership of the Misl passed on to Karam Singh, a Sandhu Jatt belonging to the village of Marahka in Sheikhupura district, now in Pakistan. In January 1764, at the conquest of the Sarhind province by the Sikhs, he seized a number of villages in the Parganahs of Kesari and Shahzadpur in Ambala district. In 1773, he overran a large tract of land belonging to Zabita Khan Rohilla in the upper Gangetic Doab. He captured a number of villages in Saharanpur district. After Karam Singh's death in 1784, his elder son, Gulab Singh, succeeded to the headship of the Misl. On Gulab Singh's death in 1844, his son Shiv Kirpal Singh succeeded to the family estate, the Misl having become extinct in 1809 after the Cis-Satluj Sikh states had accepted British protection.

Sukkarchakkia Misl

Buddha Singh laid the foundation of the Sukkarchakkia fortunes. His feats of endurance and daring in those days of adventure and plunder made him a legendary figure. When Buddha Singh died in 1718, there were scars of forty wounds by spear, sword and matchlock counted upon his body. Buddha Singh's son Naudh Singh was killed in a battle in 1752. Charhat Singh, the eldest son of Naudh Singh, moved his headquarters from Sukkarchakkia to Gujranwala and erected battlements round the town. The Afghan governor of Lahore came to apprehend Charhat Singh but was repulsed by the Sardar and forced to retreat, leaving behind his guns and stocks of grain. Charhat Singh extended his domains by capturing the towns of Wazirabad, Eminabad and Rohtas. Charhat Singh more than settled his account with the Afghans by chasing them on their return march and plundering their baggage trains. His last foray was into Jammu in 1770, where in one of the skirmishes he fell mortally wounded by the bursting of his own matchlock. Charhat Singh's young son, Mahan Singh, inherited his father's spirit and ambition. He increased the number of his horsemen to 6,000 and launched upon a career of conquest and expansion of his territory. He captured Rasulnagar from a Muslim tribe, the Chatthas, and took Pindi Bhattian, Sahival, 'Isa Khel and Jhang. In 1782, he proceeded to Jammu whose Dogra ruler fled leaving the rich city to the mercy of his men. With the loot of Jammu, Mahan Singh raised the Sukkarchakkia from a position of comparative obscurity to that of being one of the leaders of the Sikh Confederacy. At his death, his 10-year-old son, Ranjit Singh, became the head of the Sukkarchakkia house. Young Ranjit Singh had inherited from his ancestors a sizeable estate in Northwestern Punjab, a band of intrepid horse and matchlock men, and an ambition that knew no bounds. In due course, he became the powerful sovereign of the Punjab.

Sikh Misls

Phulkian Misls

Phulkian Misls of the Cis-Satluj territories did not serve under the banner of the Dal Khalsa. As they came to maturity at the decline of the Mughal power, they faced the ambitions of the Lion of the Punjab; Maharajah Ranjit Singh. They were saved from annihilation by the arrival of the British. They were familiar with the concept of Imperial authority and willingly accepted the British protection.

Patiala

Ala Singh laid the foundation of Phulkian fortunes by carving out the principality of Patiala. During his early career, he was engaged in Warfare with the Bhattals and the Afghans. By 1732, he had conquered a vast territory around Barmala, which served as his headquarters. In the forties and fifties during the Durrani-Mughal clashes in the Punjab, Ala Singh extended his hold over a number of villages in the Sarkar of Sarhind and occupied important towns such as Sunam, Samansa, Sanaur and Tohana. In 1753, he started building a fort around which grew the present city of Patiala and which became his capital. Baba Ala Singh died in August 1765 and was succeeded by his grandson, Amar Singh. His son Sahib Singh, like other Cis-Satluj Chiefs, accepted the British protection in 1809. Raja Sahib Singh died in 1813. After him a chain of Maharajahs ruled the Patiala state successively. The last ruler Maharajah Sir Yadvinder Singh signed the instrument of accession to independent India in 1947.

Nabha

Gurdit Singh laid the foundation of Nabha state. He had occupied large tracts of land during the struggle and expulsion of the Afghans from the Punjab. His grandson Hamir Singh was a brave and energetic chief and added largely to his possessions. He founded the town of Nabha in 1755. In 1764, he joined Ala Singh and the Dal Khalsa in the conquest of Sarhind, and received the Parganahs of Amioh as his share of spoils. On his death in December 1783, his son Jaswant Singh succeeded him. Jaswant Singh joined hands with the other Cis-Satluj states in 1809 and accepted British protection. The last Maharajah of Nabha state, Maharajah Pratap Singh signed the instrument of succession to the Indian Union in 1947.

Jind

Gajpat Singh took part in the attack of the Sikhs on the province of Sarhind in 1763. He occupied Jind and Sadiron as his share of the spoils. He made Jind his headquarters and built a large brick fort there. Raja Gajpat Singh died in 1786 and was succeeded by his son Bhag Singh. He was the first of all the Cis-Satluj princes to seek an alliance with the British. The British recognized in him a great friend and ally and showed him many marks of favour and regard. The Last Maharajah of Jind signed the instrument of succession to the Indian Union in 1947.

Sikh Misls

Kaithal

Gurbaksh Singh, the founder of the Chieftainship, was a fine soldier and an able man. He was a great friend of the Raja of Patiala, and they made many expeditions together, and he helped the Raja out of more than one difficulty. At his death his possessions were divided among his sons; but they soon increased the territories. Desu Singh captured Kaithal from the Afghans, Bikh Baksh Khan and Nihmat Khan, and, with his brother Budha Singh, seized Thanesar, though the town and fort were afterwards taken from them by Sardar Bhanga Singh, the most feared of all the Cis-Satluj chiefs. When Desu Singh died in 1781, Lal Singh was in confinement as a rebel against his father, and Behal Singh, the elder son, did all he could to keep his brother in prison; but he contrived to escape, killed his elder brother and took possession all the estates of his father, which he much enlarged by new acquisition. Lal Singh was, at the time of the British advance Northwards, in 1809, the most powerful Cis-Satluj chief, after the Raja of Patiala. He was a very able man, though utterly untrustworthy, and so violent and unscrupulous the English authorities had the greatest difficulty in persuading him to maintain anything like order. In 1819, the Government allowed him to succeed to the share of the estate held by Mai Bhagbari, the widow of his first cousin Karam Singh. Partab Singh the elder son and then the younger son, Udai succeeded, but on the death of the latter without issue in 1843, the whole of the Kaithal estate lapsed to the British government.

Kapurthala

The founder of the Kapurthala State was Jassa Singh Ahluwalia. He laid the foundations of an independent state in 1777, when he wrested Kapurthala from Rai Ibrahim Bhatti and expanded his territories to the river Jumna. His successor Sardar Fateh Singh had joined forces with Maharajah Ranjit Singh. He took part in almost all the early campaigns of the Maharajah: Kasur 1802, Malwa 1806, Kangra 1809, Haidru 1813, Multan 1818, Kashmir 1819 and Mankera 1821. He also held command in the Bhimber, Rajauri and Bahawalpur expeditions. As Ranjit Singh was subverting all the independent states, Fateh Singh placed himself under British protection at Jagraon. He died in October 1837. Raja Nihal Singh succeeded him. During the Anglo Sikh War of 1845, Raja Nihal Singh led his troops against the British at Badhowal and Aliwal. The British punished him by confiscating his territories South of the river Satluj. Nihal Singh died on 13TH September 1852. Raja-i-Raigan Raja Sir Randhir Singh succeeded him. Randhir Singh assisted the British during the Sepoy mutiny of 1857; by personally leading the Kapurthala contingent against the mutineers. He received vast lands for his distinguished service during the Sepoy mutiny. The house of Kapurthala provided a galaxy of senior Officers for the military service. Raja-i-Raigan Maharajah Jagjit Singh, honorary Colonel of 45th (Rattray's Sikhs), was promoted to be Brigadier in 1943. He signed the instrument of succession to the Indian Union in 1947.

Sikh Misls

Faridkot

The ancestor of the Faridkot principality, Bhallan, was an ardent follower of Sri Guru Har Gobind Ji. He helped the Guru in the Battle of Mehraj. He died issueless in 1643. Kapura, a nephew of Bhallan, succeeded him. Kapura founded the town of Kot Kapura in 1661 and was the Chaudhry of eighty-four villages. Although a Sikh he, not wanting to earn the enmity of the Mughals, did not help Guru Gobind Singh Ji in his fight with the Mughals. The famous last Battle of Muktsar happened after Nawab Kapura declined Sri Guru Gobind Singh's request to use his fort to fight the Mughal Army. Otherwise the last War between Mughals and Guru Gobind Singh Ji was destined to happen at Kot Kapura. Guru Ji moved from Kot Kapura to Dhilwan Kalan from there to Talwandi sabo via Guru Ki Dhab. However, later in the battle of Muktsar in 1705, Nawab Kapura helped Guru Gobind Singh Ji in an underhand manner. Kapura was slain by Isa Khan Manj in 1708. He had three sons named Sukhia, Sema and Mukhia. Mukhia killed Isa Khan and took control of the entire area. Sema was also killed in this battle in 1710. Kapura's elder son Sukhia again came into power in 1720. A dispute between the grandsons of Kapura (sons of Sukhia) led to the division of the state in 1763. The older brother, Sardar Jodh Singh Brar, retained control of Kot Kapura, and his younger brother, Sardar Hamir Singh Brar, was given Faridkot.

The state was captured in 1803 by Ranjit Singh, but was one of the Cis-Satluj states that came under British influence after the 1809 Treaty of Amritsar. During the Sikh Wars in 1845, Raja Pahar Singh aided the British, and was rewarded with an increase of territory. The state had an area of 642 square miles, and a population of 124,912 in 1901. It was bounded on the West and Northeast by the British district of Ferozepore and on the South by the state of Nabha. The last Ruler of Faridkot was Lt. HH Farzand-i-sadaat Nishan Hazrat-i-kaisar-i-hind Raja Sir Harindar Singh Brar Bans Bahadur.

Kalsia

Gurbaksh Singh Kalsia, a leading figure in the Karor Singhia Misl participated in several expeditions of the Dal Khalsa. At the time of the conquest of Sarhind in January 1764, he seized the parganah of Chhachhrauli, now in Jagadhari tahsll of Haryana, and founded an independent principality called Kalsia after the name of his native village. He went on to capture Bambeli parganah in Hoshiarpur district and collected immense wealth from different places in Haryana and Rajasthan. Gurbaksh Singh died in 1785. His successor and son Jodh Singh was an able person. Jodh Singh captured Dehra Bassi and also acquired territories of Lohal and Achrak. After his death, his son Sobha Singh assumed charge of Kalsia state and held it till his death in 1858. When his successor Lahna Singh assumed power, the Kalsia territory was intact as a British protectorate. The Kalsia Rajas held their estate till 1947 when it was merged with the Indian Union.

Sikh Misls

Ladwa

Sardars Sahib Singh and Gurdit Singh Ladwa were members of the Krora Singhia confederacy. After the defeat of Zin Khan, Governor of Sarhind in 1763, they seized Bahein, Shamghar and Ladwa. The last named district fell to the share of Gurdit Singh. In a skirmish with Agha Shafih, near Karnal, Sahib Singh was killed, and Gurdit Singh took the whole estate with the exception of Shamghar, which was given to the brother of Sahib Singh's widow, and twelve villages given to Bhagwan Singh, the adopted son of the deceased. Gurdit Singh was granted the district of Badhowal by Maharajah Ranjit Singh. He was succeeded by his son Ajit Singh, who built a bridge over the Saraswati at Thanesar, and obtained the title of Raja. During the first Anglo Sikh War Ajit Singh and Ranjodh Singh Majithia crossed the Satluj at Phillaur with a force of 8,000 men and 70 guns. In rapid marches they liberated the forts of Fatehgarh, Dharamkote, Gangrana, and Badhowal and stole into Ludhiana and set many barracks on fire. Sir Harry Smith was sent to relieve Ludhiana. The Sikhs harried Smith's column and when Smith tried to make a detour at Badhowal, attacked his rear with great vigour and captured his baggage train and stores. A few days later, Sir Harry Smith received reinforcements he was expecting and turned on the Sikhs. At Aliwal, Smith inflicted sharp defeat on the Sikhs and Ajit Singh of Ladwa was captured, his estates were confiscated and he was imprisoned at Allahabad. He contrived to escape, after killing his keeper. After long wanderings he is supposed to have died in Kashmir.

Let us now revert to the Afghan invasions of the Punjab. The Afghan invasions affected the history of India in several ways. Firstly, it accelerated the dismemberment of the tottering Mughal Empire. Secondly, it offered a serious check to the rapidly spreading Maratha imperialism. Thirdly, it indirectly helped the rise of the Sikh power. "His career in India," observes a modern writer, "is very intimately a part of the Sikh struggle for independence."

AFGHAN INVASIONS

Ahmed Shah Abdali

Ahmad Shah Abdali was a Cavalry General under the Persian emperor Nadir Shah. He had accompanied Nadir Shah to India when the Shah of Persia had sacked Delhi in 1739. At Delhi he had seen the weakness of the once great Mughal Empire and its powerless ruler Mohammad Shah. After Nadir Shah's assassination in 1747, Ahmad Shah, rose to power and established himself as the ruler of independent Afghanistan. Abdali once again traversed the mountainous passes into India seeking wealth, fame and glory. He invaded India eight times between the years 1748 and 1768. As the hammer blows of the Afghan invasions weakened the Mughal power, the Khalsa Misls started across the plains of the Punjab. Their enthusiasm was such, that against overwhelming odds, they confronted and defeated the Afghans and the imperial forces of the Mughal Empire.

Afghan Invasions

Ahmad Shah Abdali first attacked Peshawar driving out the Mughal governor, Nasir Khan, in October of 1747. On 11TH January he crushed the poorly trained forces of Lahore. Shah Nawaz, the Lahore governor fled to Delhi, abandoning all his baggage. Having occupied Lahore, Abdali then ordered a general massacre of the populace. After exacting a heavy tribute to put an end to the looting and slaughter, he advanced towards Sarhind to meet a Mughal Army. During the months that Abdali spent marching down from Lahore to the battle at Manupur, the Sikhs were busy taking control of the countryside, and chastising those Choudhries (hereditary title of honor, awarded by Mughal Emperors to persons of eminence) who had been rewarded by turning in the hunted Sikhs for execution. Whilst Abdali was engaged at Manupur, Jassa Singh Ramgarhia's band swooped upon Amritsar. When their Commander was slain the occupying forces fled, leaving the city and its holy tank once again in the hands of the Sikhs. Lacking Artillery and vastly outnumbered, Abdali was defeated at Manupur in March 1748 by Mu'in-ul-Mulk (Mughal governor of Lahore). He then crossed the Satluj at Ludhiana and hurriedly retraced his steps to Lahore. As he took his goods and property from Lahore and made a dash towards Afghanistan, Sikh bands under Jassa Singh, Charhat Singh and Karora Singh gave him a taste of the same guerilla raids that had plagued the rear of Nadir Shah's retreating columns. The Sikhs would swoop down on Abdali's camp late at night, and make away with stolen treasure, baggage, horses and rescue the prisoners, who were destined for slavery in Afghanistan.

Second Afghan Invasion, (1749)

Mu'in-ul-Mulk was appointed Mughal governor of the Punjab, but before he could consolidate his position, Abdali, in December 1749, again crossed the Indus. Receiving no reinforcements from Delhi, Mu'in-ul-Mulk was forced to make terms with Abdali. In accordance with instructions from Delhi, Abdali was promised the revenues of the Chahar Mahal (Gujrat, Aurangabad, Sialkot and Pasrur) which had been granted by the Mughal emperor Muhammad Shah to Nadir Shah in 1739. In short, Mu'in-ul-Mulk became a feudatory of the Afghan king as well as of the Mughal emperor. While Mu'in-ul-Mulk was facing Abdali on the Chenab he had left the city of Lahore unguarded. The Sikhs had swooped down on Lahore and for some hours Nawab Kapur Singh had the pleasure of having the capital at his mercy. He evacuated the city when he heard of the return of the governor. Mu'in-ul-Mulk returned to Lahore resolved to teach the Sikhs a lesson for their audacity in entering the capital in his absence. Miskin, a personal servant of Mu'in-ul-Mulk, gave the following account: "Muin appointed most of them (jezailcis) to the task of chastising the Sikhs. They ran after these wretches up to 28 Kos in a day and slew them wherever they stood up to oppose them. Everyone who brought Sikh heads to Muin received a reward of Rs. 10 per head. Anyone who brought a horse belonging to a Sikh could keep it as his own." Muin thus succeeded in executing thousands of Sikhs.

Afghan Invasions

Third Afghan Invasion, (1751)

The pretext for the third Abdali invasion was the nonpayment of the revenues of the Chahar Mahal by Mu'in-ul-Mulk. Lahore was besieged for four months and the surrounding country devastated. The supplies to the Lahore troops began to fail and thus Mu'in-ul-Mulk was compelled to leave his trenches to have a battle with the Afghans, in which he was defeated. Afterwards a treaty was signed by Mu'in-ul-Mulk, by the terms of which the provinces of Lahore and Multan were ceded to Afghanistan. On 13TH April the Emperor of Delhi put his seal on the treaty, thus losing the most important province of the Mughal Empire to the Afghans. Before leaving India, Abdali also conquered and annexed Kashmir to his kingdom.

Rakhi

The Sikhs had taken advantage of the conflict between the Afghans and the Mughals to spread out in the Bari Doab, Jalandhar Doab and across the Satluj as far as Jind, Thanesar, and beyond, coming within 50 miles of Delhi. Mu'in-ul-Mulk discovering how Sikhs had occupied large parts of his territory now resumed his policy of repression. To quote Miskin: "The persons, who brought Sikhs alive, or their heads or their horses, received prizes. Every Mughal who lost his own horse in battle was provided with another of a better quality at the expense of the government. The Sikhs who were captured alive were sent to hell by being beaten with wooden mallets. At times Adina Beg Khan sent 40 or 50 Sikh captives from Doab district (Jullunder); they were as a rule killed with strokes of wooden hammers." Prices were once again laid on their heads and strict orders were passed against giving refuge to them anywhere. Skirmishes between Sikh bands and Mu'in-ul-Mulk's roving columns took place in different parts of the province. Mannu's musketeers combed the villages for Sikhs. The able-bodied from among them were killed fighting; the non-combatants including women and children were brought in chains to Lahore and slaughtered at the horse market. The fighting and reprisals went on until the death of Mannu on 4TH November 1753. With Mu'in-ul-Mulk's death ended yet another attempt to quash the rising power of the Khalsa.

"With the passing of Mu'in-ul-Mulk the administration of the Punjab collapsed. The strongest force in the province was that of Dal Khalsa with its headquarters at Amritsar. Sikh leaders realized that the Punjab had neither government, nor the people any security of life or property. They took the first step towards becoming rulers of the country, and took people under their protection (Rakhi). Since the Sikhs were the only power which could fulfil its obligations, most of the Punjab readily accepted the offer of protection and for all practical purposes the country came to be administered by the Sikhs". (Khushwant Singh)

Afghan Invasions

Fourth Afghan Invasion, (1756)

During his fourth invasion Abdali ruthlessly plundered Delhi. Towards the end of March 1757, Abdali was forced to leave India. The Sikhs preyed upon him during his onward march and, when his son Prince Taimur was transporting the plundered wealth of Delhi to Lahore, Sikh Sardars barred his path at Sanaur, near Patiala, and robbed him of his treasures. They again attacked and plundered him at Malerkotla. The Prince gave vent to his chagrin by destroying Sikh shrines at Kartarpur, 15 km Northwest of Jalandhar, and subjecting its residents to indiscriminate massacre and plunder. The Sikhs again attacked Abdali several times between Delhi and the river Chenab. They easily succeeded in acquiring a part of the enormous booty he was carrying off. During his brief stay at Lahore, Abdali sent out troops who sacked Amritsar and desecrated the sacred pool, besides killing a large number of Sikhs. He left his son Taimur and his General Jahan Khan in charge of the Punjab and himself retired to Afghanistan.

Baba Deep Singh Shahid, (1757)

Baba Deep Singh, the leader of one of the Jathas entrusted with the care of the Temple, intercepted Jahan Khan's forces near the village of Goharwal, about five miles from Amritsar. Each Sikh fought with such great valor and courage that many of the enemy turned to flee in desperation. During the midst of battle, a large Army of reinforcements arrived for Jahan Khan's men, turning the odds against the Sikhs. Yet the Sikhs with Baba Deep Singh at their head continued fighting and advanced towards Amritsar. Baba Deep Singh was wounded very badly, with a deep cut in the neck. With one hand holding his neck, and the other a double edged sword, Baba Dip Singh made to the Parikarma (circumambulatory passage) of the Harimandir Sahib and thus fulfilled his pledge - of dying for the liberation of the holy shrines of Amritsar. After his victory Jahan Khan, from religious zeal, destroyed and polluted all the places of worship of the Sikhs at Amritsar and filled up the sacred tank.

Dal Khalsa, (1758)

The Dal Khalsa was mobilized by the Misldars to avenge the death of Deep Singh and the desecration of their shrines. They defeated Sa'dat Khan Afridi, plundered all the Jullunder Doab, and forced him to flee to the hills. Prince Taimur sent Khwaja Abed Khan from Lahore with twenty thousand horse and foot to fight the Sikhs. The Sikhs defeated Khwaja Abed Khan, many of his captains were slain, all of his camp and baggage were plundered and all the Artillery was captured. Miskin writes about the helplessness of the Afghans and the boldness of the Sikhs: "after this every force in whatever direction it was sent, came back defeated and vanquished. Even the environs of Lahore were not safe. Every night thousands of Sikhs used to fall upon the city and plunder the suburbs lying outside the walls of Lahore; but no force was sent to repel them and the city gates were closed one hour after nightfall. It brought extreme disgrace to the government and utter lawlessness prevailed."

Afghan Invasions

Fifth Afghan Invasion, (1759)
During Ahmad Shah's fifth invasion, the Sikhs gave him battle in the neighbourhood of Lahore in which he lost as many as 2,000 men. The Sikhs stayed in Lahore for seven days until the Afghan deputy appeased them with a present of Rs. 30,000 for sacramental **Karah Prasad (Karah Prasad is the holy pudding of the Sikhs)**. They went on to harass the Afghan chief of Chahar Mahal and sacked Jalandhar, Sarhind and Malerkotla. In March 1761 Abdali began his homeward march. As soon as he crossed the Satluj, the Sikhs closed in on him. The booty laden and battle weary Afghans were relieved of much of their spoils and the Sikhs liberated over two thousand Hindu women they were taking to stock Afghan harems and began systematic operations to expel Afghan officials from the Punjab.

Vadda Ghallughara, (Great Holocaust) (1762)
When Ahmad Shah returned for a sixth campaign the Sikh fighters retreated with a view to taking their families to the safety of the Hariana desert to the East before returning to confront the invader. When the Afghan leader came to know of the whereabouts of the Sikhs, he set out on a rapid march, and in the twilight of dawn, Ahmad Shah and his allies surprised the Sikhs, who numbered about 50,000, most of them noncombatants. Under these circumstances, the Sikhs could not engage in their favored hit-and-run tactics. Neither was a pitched battle advisable. It was decided that the Sikh fighters would form a cordon around the slow-moving baggage train consisting of women, children and old men. They would then make their way to the desert in the South-West by the town of Barnala, where they expected their ally Ala Singh of Patiala to come to their rescue.

An eye witness account describes the Sikhs. "Fighting while moving and moving while fighting, they kept the baggage train marching, covering it as a hen covers its chicks under its wings." More than once, the troops of the invader broke the cordon and mercilessly butchered the women, children and elderly inside, but each time the Sikh Warriors regrouped and managed to push back the attackers. The Afghan forces, which had inflicted terrible human losses on the Sikh nation, and had in turn suffered many killed and wounded, were exhausted, having not had any rest in two days. While the living remainder of the Sikhs proceeded into the semi-desert toward Barnala, Ahmad Shah's Army returned to the capital of Lahore with fifty cartloads of Sikh heads and hundreds of Sikhs in chains. From the capital, Durrani returned to Amritsar and blew up the Harimandir Sahib which since 1757 the Sikhs had rebuilt. As an act of intended sacrilege, the pool around it was filled with cow carcasses. It was estimated that 25,000 to 30,000 Sikhs were killed on that horrific day of 5TH February 1762. As it is doubtful their entire population would have numbered 100,000, it means one third to a half of all Sikhs perished.

Afghan Invasions

Seventh Afghan Invasion, (1764)

Ahmad Shah planned another crusade against the Sikhs and he invited this time his Baluch ally, Amir Nasir Khan, to join him in the adventure. He started from Afghanistan in October 1764 and reaching Lahore attacked Amritsar on 1ST December 1764. A small batch of thirty Sikhs, in the words of Qazi Nur Muhammad, the author of the Jangnamah, who happened to be in the imperial train accompanying the Baluch division, "grappled with the ghazis, spilt their blood and sacrificed their own lives for their Guru." Ahmad Shah came down to Sarhind without encountering anywhere the main body of the Khalsa. This time he went no farther than Sarhind. As he was marching homewards through the Jalandhar Doab, Sikh Sardars, including Jassa Singh Ahluwalia, Jassa Singh Ramgarhia, Charhat Singh Sukkarchakkia, Jhanda Singh Bhangi and Jai Singh Kanhaiya, kept a close trail constantly raiding the imperial caravan. Their depredations caused great annoyance to the Shah who lost much of his baggage to the Sikhs. The floods in the River Chenab took a further toll of his men and property, and he returned to Afghanistan mauled and considerably shaken.

Eighth Afghan Invasion, (1766)

The fear of his Indian empire falling to the Sikhs continued to obsess the Shah's mind and he led out yet another punitive campaign against them towards the close of 1766. The Sikhs had recourse to their old game of hide and seek. Vacating Lahore which they had wrested from Afghan nominees, they faced the Afghan General, Jahan Khan at Amritsar, forcing him to retreat, with 6,000 of the Afghan soldiers killed. Ahmad Shah offered the governorship of Lahore to Sikh Sardar, Lahina Singh Bhangi, but the latter declined the proposal. Jassa Singh Ahluwalia, with an Army of 30,000 Sikhs, roamed about the neighbourhood of the Afghan camp plundering it to his heart's content. Never before had Ahmad Shah felt so helpless. The outcome of the unequal, but bitter, contest now lay clearly in favour of the Sikhs. The Shah had realized that his Indian dominions were at the mercy of the Sikhs and he bowed to the inevitable. His own soldiers were getting restive and the summer heat of the Punjab was becoming unbearable. He, at last, decided to return home, but took a different route this time to avoid molestation by the Sikhs. As soon as Ahmad Shah retired, Sikhs reoccupied their territories.

Ninth Afghan Invasion, (1769)

The Shah led out his last expedition in the beginning of 1769. He crossed the Indus and the Jehlum and reached as far as the right bank of the Chenab and fixed his camp at Jukalian to the Northwest of Gujrat. By this time the Sikhs had established themselves more firmly in the country. Moreover, dissensions broke out among the Shah's followers and he was compelled to return to Afghanistan. He died at Qandahar on 23RD October 1772.

Afghan Invasions

Shah Zaman, (1796)

Shah Zaman, as soon as he succeeded his father Taimur, announced his intention of re-establishing the Afghan empire in India. He invaded India in 1793 and again in 1795 and 1796. By December 1796 he had occupied the Punjab as far as Jhelum. Ranjit Singh decided to call a meeting of all Sikh chiefs for Sarbat Khalsa at Amritsar. While some chiefs were in favour of abandoning the plains and going into the hills, the others felt that they should put up a united front under one supreme Commander. Finally Ranjit Singh was chosen as the supreme Commander of the Khalsa forces for the purpose of confronting Shah Zaman, who had occupied Lahore by January 1797. The advancing Sikh forces drove the Afghans and their Indian supporters out of Lahore and the countryside. The combined Sikh forces then drove Shah Zaman all the way across the Jhelum and took away much of his War material.

Shah Zaman, (1798)

Shah Zaman once again invaded India during the autumn of 1798. The Hindus and Sikhs began to leave their homes and seek safety in far off places. Sahib Singh Bhangi and Ranjit Singh Sukarchakia evacuated Gujrat and Gujranwala respectively. Once again chiefs of all Misls were called to Amritsar and Ranjit Singh was chosen the Commander of the combined Khalsa forces in order to defeat the forces of Shah Zaman. Once again Shah Zaman's forces were defeated by the Khalsa forces. After this the Afghans never dared to attack the Punjab.

Ranjit Singh

After the death of Jassa Singh Ahluwalia in the year 1783 there was no successor who could have been unanimously accepted as the supreme Commander of the Khalsa forces and Jathedar of the Khalsa Panth. In the absence of such a uniting force it was natural for the Commanders of the Sikh Misls to assert themselves in order to enlarge their territories and areas of influence. This not only caused conflicts between various Misls, but also weakened the overall strength of the Khalsa forces. Under such conditions it would have been a relatively easy task for the invading forces to defeat the Sikhs piecemeal and destroy them. Ranjit Singh decided to subdue the other Sikh Misls one by one and gradually annex their territories to make a United Punjab of which he would be the Maharaja.

SIKH EMPIRE

Maharajah Ranjit Singh

The Punjab presented a picture of chaos and confusion when Ranjit Singh took the reins of Sukarchakia Misl. The edifice of Ahmad Shah Abdali's empire in India had crumbled. Afghanistan was dismembered. Peshawar and Kashmir though under the suzerainty of Afghanistan had attained de facto independence. Barakzai were the masters of these places. Attock was ruled by Waziris-Khels and Jhang lay at the feet of Sials. Pathans were ruling Kasur. Multan had thrown off the Afghan yoke and Nawab Muzaffar Khan had taken its charge. The Sikh Misls had served their purpose, and had fallen prey to mutual rivalry and jealousy ending in anarchy. The time was ripe for the arrival of a strong monarch in the Punjab.

Lahore, (1799)

Lahore represented the symbol of prestige and power to any master of the Punjab. At this time Lahore was ruled by a Bhangi triumvirate. In 1765 a Bhangi-Sukarchakia combination had expelled Kabuli Mal, the rapacious Hindu governor of the Afghans. The capital of the Punjab remained in the hands of the Bhangis till 1796, when Shah Zaman occupied it. An Afghan Army of 20,000 under Muhammad Khan, the Shah's Vizier, having expelled the Bhangis, made a triumphant entry into the town and the Shah received the submission of the people. The Shah's stay at Lahore, however, proved to be short; the news of his brother Shah Mahmud's rebellion hastened his departure and the Bhangi Sirdars re-occupied it. However, on 25TH October 1798, Shah Zaman left Peshawar and advanced on Lahore. A Sukarchakia-Bhangi coalition with 10,000 horses attempted to hem in the Army of the Shah. The Khalsa drove a wedge between the main Afghan Army and cut off a force of 5,000 men commanded by the Shah's deputy near Jhelum. Shah Zaman had, however, little difficulty in occupying Lahore. The Shah made a hasty retreat towards Kabul on hearing the news that his rebellious brother had secured the support of the Persian King, Fateh Ali Shah, in his claim to the Kingdom of Kabul. He left his Indian possessions under the control of his general Shahanchi Khan. The Shah's retreat gave an opportunity to Ranjit Singh to expel his deputy Shahanchi Khan. He formed an alliance with Sahib Singh of Gujrat and Milkha Singh Pindiwala, and with an enormous Sikh force of 31,000 fell upon the Afghan garrison while Shah Zaman was still at Peshawar. Shahanchi Khan was killed, and with the dispersal of his forces, all semblance of Afghan authority between the Ravi and the Jhelum was obliterated. It seems that the Bhangi triumvirate had proved extremely weak and oppressive with the result that the citizens drew up a petition inviting Ranjit Singh to come and deliver them from the Bhangis. On 7TH July Ranjit Singh occupied Lahore. The Bhangi Sirdars, who had merely made a show of resistance, were allowed to leave the town unmolested. The occupation of Lahore by the youthful Sukarchakia chief is a landmark in the history of the Sikhs. It laid the foundation of a sovereign monarchy in the Punjab.

Sikh Empire

Jammu, (1800)

In late 1800, Ranjit Singh marched on Jammu, capturing Miroval and Narwhal on the way, and then laid siege to Jassarwal. On reaching Jammu, the Raja presented him nazranas (offerings, gifts or presents) thereby acknowledging his sovereignty. Ranjit Singh then moved on reducing Sialkot and then Dillawarth, and finally returned to Lahore. He now felt that the time had finally arrived for him to declare himself Maharajah, ruler of a sovereign state. This he did in 1801. On 1ST of Baisakhi, April $12^{TH,}$ Sahib Singh Bedi (tenth in direct descent from Guru Nanak) daubed Ranjit Singh's forehead with saffron paste and proclaimed him Maharajah of the Punjab. He was then twenty-one years old.

Khalsa Power, (1801)

Ranjit Singh's kingdom had by now become so large that he decided to restructure his Army and place troops at strategic locations throughout his kingdom. This was his first effort in this direction. Earlier, all moves to counter aggression were made by the force stationed with him at Lahore. With this decision he laid the foundations of what was to become a formidable Army. Desa Singh Majithia was given command of 400 Cavalry; Hari Singh Nalua was given 800 Cavalry and Infantry; Hukam Singh Chimni was appointed Superintendent of Artillery with 200 gunners; Ghausa Khan became the Commandant of Artillery with 2,000 troops; Baj Singh Moralliwala was the Commandant of 500 troops; Milkha Singh was positioned at Rawalpindi with 700 troops; Roushan Khan and Sheikh Abdullah were given 2,000 Najibs;(Muslims) Nodh Singh was to command 400 troops; Attar Singh Dhari received 500 Cavalry; Kurba Singh was given 1,000 troops; and Nihal Singh Attari was to command 500 troops. All the above were made Sirdars to give them additional authority,

Alongside the Units of the regular Army as listed above, a feudal Army or Jagirdari Fauj was created. Sirdars Jassa Singh and Bhag Singh Ahluwalia were ordered to equip and train 10,000 troops. The Kanhaiya Sirdars had to train 5,000 troops; the Nakais 4,000 troops; and the Sirdars of Doaba 7,000 troops. They had to do this from their own resources and were all made honorary Commanders. (Amarinder Singh)

Nihangs, (1802)

Ranjit Singh was keen to unite the political capital Lahore with Amritsar, the religious capital of the Sikhs. In the autumn of 1802 Ranjit Singh took possession of the city and acquired the services of Akali Phula Singh and his Nihangs. (Nihang is a famous and prestigious armed Sikh order). At times of War or major conflict, they allied themselves to the Khalsa, in four mounted Jathas called Changri; approximately four thousand strong. On these occasions, they were lead by Alkali Phula Singh and Alkali Sadhu Singh. They were a fanatic band of Warriors, who often formed the suicide squad of the Khalsa. Ranjit Singh owed many of his victories to the desperate valour of these Nihangs.

Sikh Empire

Kasur, (1802)

Kasur, situated South of Lahore, was a Pathan colony. In the nineties when Shah Zaman, King of Afghanistan, was trying to establish his rule in India, Nizam-ud-din had taken advantage of the situation and occupied Kankipura, Haveli, Atari, Nadian, Mahmonki, Khem Karan, Rukhanwala, and Chunian belonging to Tara Singh Chamiarivala and the Nakais. Maharajah Ranjit Singh sent Fateh Singh Kalianwala against him. The Afghan force opposed the Sikhs a few kilometres from Kasur. On being defeated, they took shelter in a fort inside the town. As Fateh Singh Kalianwala besieged the town, Nizam-ud-din sued for peace. He paid a large indemnity, accepted Ranjit Singh as his overlord and agreed to pay tribute and furnish troops whenever required. In 1802 when Ranjit Singh was busy reducing Chiniot, Nizam-ud-din carried his depredations up to the gates of Lahore and planned to seize the capital. Ranjit Singh sent Fateh Singh Ahluwalia to punish him for his treachery. In a pitched battle the Pathans were defeated and the town plundered. Nizam-ud-din submitted again on payment of a heavy fine and became tributary to Ranjit Singh.

Jhang, (1803)

Sials of Jhang were converted Muslim Rajputs. Ranjit Singh set out for Jhang at the head of his troops in 1803, attended by Fateh Singh Ahluwalia. The new Battalion, known as Najibwala, together with the Maharajah's own Artillery, formed part of the expedition. The battle commenced with a cannonade from both sides. When their gunpowder was exhausted, the Sial horsemen charged. The Sikh Infantry Battalions withstood the fierce onslaught and once the enemy had spent itself moved to the counter-attack. The Sials broke their ranks and galloped to safety behind the walls of their fortress town. The casualties on both sides were very great. Ranjit besieged the city by night, and cut off the communications of the besieged. The next day the fighting continued with the same pertinacity as before. Ahmad Khan superintended his Artillery personally. The siege lasted three days, when Ranjit's elephants crashed through the gates and compelled the citadel to lay down arms. Ahmad Shah slipped through the cordon and fled to Multan. The Maharajah entered the city and took possession of the immense wealth which the Sial chief had been accumulating for so many years. Ahmad Khan, having agreed to pay tribute to the Lahore Durbar, returned to Jhang. The Maharajah now crossed the Tirmu, attacked Uch, and exacted a large tribute from the chief of that place, Naga Sultan, a Bokhari Syed. The towns of Sahiwal and Garh Maharaja were then visited, and the Baluch Mussalman chiefs of those places were forced to satisfy the cupidity of the Maharajah with money and horses, with the alternative of having the Sikh Army let loose in their city to supply their own wants.

Sikh Empire

Multan, (1805)

Ranjit Singh's next expedition was into the districts which had been conquered by the Afghans in Hindustan. Ranjit Singh so impressed the Afghan governors of the districts that they, for the most part, elected to make their submission to him. He then led his Army into the Muhammadan country between the Chenab and the Indus, and the Nawab of Jhang was again pressed to settle an annual tribute, which was now raised to 1,200,000 rupees. A fresh attack on Multan was resolved upon; but when the Maharajah's advance guards had reached Mahatma, a village 20 miles North of Multan, the Nawab, who had no wish to fight the Sikhs, paid 70,000 rupees as ransom to Ranjit Singh, who then departed, after having bestowed a valuable Khilat (Robes of Honour) on the Nawab.

Anglo-Sikh Treaty, (1806)

Anglo-Sikh Treaty followed Jasvant Rao Holkar's (a Maratha Chief) crossing over into the Punjab in 1805 after he was defeated at Fatehgarh and Dig in December 1804 by the British. Accompanied by his Ruhila ally, Amir Khan, and a Maratha force estimated at 15,000, Holkar arrived at Patiala, but on hearing the news that the British general, Lake, was in hot pursuit, both the refugees fled Northwards, entered the Jalandhar Doab, and ultimately reached Amritsar.

Ranjit Singh, then camping near Multan, hastened to Amritsar to meet Holkar. He was hospitable and sympathetic towards the Maratha chief, but was shrewd enough not to espouse a forlorn cause and come into conflict with the British, especially when he was far from securely established on the throne. Through diplomatic negotiation, he brought about reconciliation between Holkar and the British Commander in Chief. A treaty of friendship and amity was entered into by Ranjit Singh along with Sardar Fateh Singh Ahluwalia of Kapurthala with the East India Company on 1ST January 1806 whereby it was agreed that, as long as these Sikh chiefs had no friendly connections with enemies of the British or committed no act of hostility, the British armies would never enter into the territories of the said chieftains, nor would the British government form any plan for the seizure or sequestration of their possessions or property.

The Anglo-Sikh treaty of 1806 brought the Sikh chief into direct contact with the British government. Ranjit Singh's reluctance to precipitate a clash with the British saved the infant State of Lahore from being overrun by Lake's armies. The Maharaja not only kept the Punjab from becoming a theatre of War between two foreign armies, but also saved the Maratha chief from utter ruin and had his territories beyond Delhi restored to him.

Sikh Empire

Kasur, (1807)

Ranjit Singh could not tolerate the independent principalities close to his capital. He had subdued the Pathans of Kasur in 1802. In 1807, well armed and augmented with fresh troops, the Pathans had declared independence. Its location and battlements afforded Kasur special protection. It contained fortified hamlets surrounded by a wall. A force commanded by Sardar Jodh Singh Ramgharia, with Akali Phula Singh at the head of his Nihangs in the forefront, compelled the Pathans to fall back in the fort. The fort was besieged and would not yield for a month. Eventually a breach was made, and the Nihangs, lead by Akali Phula Singh, took on the Afghans and occupied the fort. Kasur was annexed to the Sikh kingdom and was administered by Nihal Singh Attariwala. However, Qutab-ud-din was allowed to retain Mamdot territory and agreed to pay a nominal tribute and to serve at the head of 100 horsemen whenever called upon to do so.

In this battle the Sher Dil Regiment of young Hari Singh Nalua captured 200 soldiers of Kasur, for which deed they were presented before the Maharaja.

The Treaty of Amritsar, (1809)

The British, who fearing a French attack on the country through Afghanistan, decided to win the Sikhs over to their side and sent a young Officer, Charles Metcalfe, to Maharaja Ranjit Singh's court with an offer of friendship,. Ranjit Singh showed his willingness to co-operate with the British, provided the latter recognized his claim of paramount power over all the Majha and Malwa Sikhs. Ranjit Singh received a message from the Governor General that the British had taken the Sikh chiefs South of the Satluj under their protection. The British sent a force under the command of Colonel David Ochterlony who, passing through Buria and Patiala, came very close to the Satluj and stationed himself at Ludhiana. Ranjit Singh also started making Warlike preparations. Meanwhile, Metcalfe, who had followed Ranjit Singh to Lahore, presented a new treaty which was based on terms first offered by the British and the proposal made by Ranjit Singh. The treaty in this form was acceptable to the Sikh ruler. Although it stopped him from extending his influence beyond the Satluj, he was left master of the territories South of the rivers, which were in his possession before Metcalfe's visit. The treaty was signed at Amritsar on 25TH April 1809. It provided that the British government would count the Lahore Durbar among the most honourable powers and would in no way interfere with the Sikh ruler's dominions to the North of the Satluj. Both governments pledged friendship to each other. Although the treaty of 1809 halted Ranjit Singh's ambitions at the Satluj and prevented the unification of the Majha and Malwa Sikhs into a new commonwealth of the Khalsa, it gave the Sikh sovereign one clear advantage. Security on the Southern frontier allowed him freely to consolidate his power in the Punjab, evolve a centralized system of government, build up a powerful Army, and pursue unhampered his conquests in the North, Northwest and Southwest.

Sikh Empire

Gurkhas, (1809)

In 1752 the Hindu hill states came under the control of the Durrani Kings of Kabul, having been ceded along with the rest of the Punjab to Ahmad Shah Durrani by his namesake the Mughal Emperor, Ahmad Shah of Delhi. Under Ahmad Shah, Raja Ghamand Chand of Kangra was appointed governor of Jullunder and the hills between the Satluj and the Ravi. The Rajas of Chamba and Jammu seem also to have enjoyed the favour of the Durrani Kings.

The Sikh influence began to be felt in the hills about 1764. In 1770 Jassa Singh Ramgharia invaded Kangra and made several of the hill states tributary. His power was of brief duration, for in 1776, he was defeated by Jai Singh Kanhaiya, who then became the sovereign of most of the Kangra states. In 1785 Jai Singh in turn was defeated by Raja Sansar Chand. He abandoned to Sansar Chand the Kangra fort and the rich valley, along with the sovereignty of eleven hill states of the Kangra group.

In 1806 Gurkhas invaded Kangra and in 1809, unable to drive them out, Sansar Chand appealed to Maharajah Ranjit Singh for help. The Maharajah gladly accepted the invitation and advanced on Kangra at the head of a large Army. Once the Gurkhas fortified their hold over Kangra, the strategic advantage could post a permanent threat to the plains of the Punjab. Having taken nazranas from the hill chiefs of Jasrota and Nurpur, Maharajah Ranjit Singh marched his troops to the relief of the citadel of Kangra. The Sikhs took possession of the Kangra fort, and cut the Ghurkha's supply line with Nepal. The attack by the Rajputs on the Gurkhas was savagely repulsed. The Khalsa Infantry with their long curving *Kirpans* closed in on the Gurkhas. The Gurkhas were compelled to retreat in disorder. The stubborn fight put up by the Gurkhas greatly impressed Ranjit Singh. When the action was over, he not only allowed the Gurkha General, Amar Singh Thapa time to retire without further molestation, but also ordered his Sardars to help the Gurkhas in collecting their equipment. Some of the hill Rajas, who utilized the opportunity to plunder the vanquished foe, were severely reprimanded and made to restore the loot. The remnants of the Gurkha Army rested at Mandi for a short time and being pressed by the Khalsa troops, resumed their weary homeward march. The Gurkha menace to the Punjab was ended forever. Kangra was annexed to the kingdom and Desa Singh Majithia was appointed Subedar of the hill areas, with Pahar Singh Man Governor of Kangra. (Khushwant Singh)

Jammu, (1809)

Jammu was once the seat of Rajputs who ruled over a large territory in the hills as well as in the plains. Formerly Jammu had been tributary to the Sukarchakia Misl, but the tribute had not been paid for many years. In 1809, Ranjit Singh finally conquered Jammu and appointed Khushal Singh as its first Governor.

Sikh Empire

Sahiwal, (1810)
In the beginning of 1810, Ranjit Singh occupied himself in reducing the Muslim chiefs in the Chaj Doab. On 25TH January 1810, Fattah Khan, chief of Sahiwal, agreed to pay tribute to the Sikh Kingdom but did not implement it. Sahiwal was invested by the Khalsa on 7TH February and compelled Fattah Khan to surrender. He was taken prisoner and sent to Lahore with the whole of his family. Sahiwal was annexed to the Kingdom. In January 1811, Fattah Khan was set free with his family and was granted a Jagir.

Multan, (1810)
The Sikhs had attacked Multan multiple times in the past, the largest attack being in 1810. However, on the previous occasions the Sikh forces would defeat the defending force and seize the city only to have the Governor of Multan, Nawab Muzaffar Khan Sadozai, retreat into the Multan Fort. The fort was besieged but the soldiers inside blew up the Battery of General Attar Singh Dhari, killing him and his twelve men and severely wounding many more, among whom were Sardar Nihal Singh Attariwala and youthful Hari Singh Nalua. The valour, courage and bravery shown by Hari Singh Nalua in the battle of Multan raised his status in the eyes of the Maharaja as well the Army. However the Khalsa could not storm the formidable fort. At last, no alternative was left to the Maharaja but to accept the terms offered by the Nawab. During previous sieges the Sikhs had settled for large single payments of tribute, while the attack in 1810 resulted in Multan paying a yearly tribute. Muzaffar Khan paid nominal tribute to the Durbar, but the fort of Multan remained unconquered in his hands. Nawab Muzaffar Khan Sadozai ruled the province of Multan independently of the descendants of Ahmad Shah, the rulers of Kabul. Sardar Attar Singh Dhari's body was cremated with full military honours. The services of many brave soldiers were highly appreciated with the grant of Jagirs.

Bhimbar, (1812)
Ranjit Singh seized Gujrat from Sahib Singh Bhangi in 1810. Raja Sultan Khan of Bhimbar was Sahib Singh's tributary. Ranjit Singh invited Sultan Khan to attend his court at Lahore. The Raja feared imprisonment and evaded compliance. The Maharajah despatched two Battalions of Infantry under Faqir Aziz-ud-din to arrest Sultan Khan. Sultan Khan ambushed them and gunned down about 600 men and then fled away to higher mountains. The Faqir appointed Ismail Khan, a relative of Sultan Khan, as the head of the government and returned to Lahore. Sultan Khan came back to Bhimbar, slew Ismail Khan and resumed his authority. Ranjit Singh sent a larger force under Kharak Singh to punish Sultan Khan. Sultan Khan quietly submitted to Kharak Singh and accompanied him to Lahore at the head of a small force of his own. After sometime, the Sultan was escorted to Bhimbar and imprisoned, and his territory was annexed.

Sikh Empire

Kulu, (1812)

The beautiful Kulu valley is situated in the mountainous basin of the River Beas. Out of its total area of 6,607 square miles only 60 square miles was arable land, the rest of it was covered with forests. It is celebrated for its picturesque scenery, salubrious climate and delicious fruits. In 1809 the Raja of Kulu, named Ajit Singh, became feudatory of the Maharajah. In 1812 the Maharajah sent a force to chastise the Raja. He offered resistance and his fort was besieged. After three days hard battle the Raja submitted to the Khalsa.

Kashmir, (1812)

In 1793, Ahmed Shah's son Timur Shah died. Ahmed Shah's grandsons had a weak hold on the legacy left to them by their famous ancestor. This resulted in the deterioration of the Afghan hold over far flung territories, such as Attock and Kashmir. When Shah Mahmud dislodged his half-brother Shah Shuja, and blinded Shah Zaman, he became the ruling authority in Kabul in 1809. With the change of leadership in Kabul, the Afghan Governor of Kashmir, Atta Mohammed Khan Bamzai, declared his independence. Shah Shuja, was compelled to take refuge in flight, however, his person was seized by Jahandad, the Governor of Attock, who sent the royal prisoner to his brother, Atta Mohammed Khan, at Kashmir, where he was kept in close confinement. The blind Shah Zaman brought both the families to Lahore, seeking Ranjit Singh's help in obtaining the liberation of his brother, and replacing him on the Kashmir throne. The Sikh Sirdars and Generals had penetrated the various principalities in the hills South of Kashmir, and had, after repeated actions, rendered them tributary to the Lahore Kingdom. It only remained now to make a general advance into the valley itself; and the friendship professed for the ex-kings of Kabul, and the most humane duty of relieving the unhappy monarchs from their pending distress, was an ample excuse to justify an immediate advance. Meanwhile Fateh Khan Barakzai, Vizier of Shah Mahmud, appeared at the doorstep of the Sikhs with an offer of a joint expedition to Kashmir. Its purpose was to reclaim Kashmir from the errant Afghan Governor. The offer was necessitated because the passage to Kashmir now lay through territory tributary to the Sikhs. The estimation in which the Afghans in Kabul already held the Sikhs was evident from the fact that they actually sought their co-operation rather than risk confrontations. The Sikhs readily lent their assent to the proposal. The joint venture would not only give them first–hand knowledge of the passage into Kashmir, but a rich haul of booty was also promised to them. Most importantly Waffa Begum, Shah Shuja's wife, at this time refugee in the Punjab, had pledged to give Ranjit Singh the Kohinoor diamond for his assistance in securing her husband's release. The joint Sikh - Afghan venture was successful. The success of the Sikhs in the expedition was limited to securing the release of Shah Shuja, who then accompanied the Sikh Army back to Lahore.

Sikh Empire

Attock fort, (1813)

The fort at Attock, 'the Gateway to India', dominated the passage across the Indus to India. Attock fort was built at Attock Khurd during the reign of Akbar the Great from 1581 to 1583, under the supervision of Khwaja Shamsuddin Khawafi, to protect the passage of the Indus. Jahandad Khan, the Afghan Governor of Attock, whose ally Ata Mohamed had ejected from Kashmir and who was inimical to the Barakzai and fearing for his life, surrendered the fort to Ranjit Singh in a deal that gave him security against Kabul, and a handsome Jagir in the Punjab. With this fort under their control, Sikhs could successfully block the passage of invaders from the West.

Battle of Haidru, (1813)

Dial Singh occupied the Attock fort and the surrounding areas with a strong force, which included Cavalry and Artillery. Hari Singh Nalua also arrived with a detachment of Cavalry to secure the garrison. Accusing Ranjit Singh of treachery, Fateh Khan set off from Kashmir at the head of 15,000 Cavalry in April 1813 and invested the Attock Fort. At the same time Maharaja Ranjit Singh rushed from Burhan a force of Cavalry, Artillery, and a Battalion of Infantry to meet the Afghans. The Khalsa encamped at a position eight miles from the Afghan camp, unwilling to risk a decisive engagement, although both sides engaged in numerous skirmishes and took losses.

On July 12TH 1812, the Afghan supplies were exhausted and the Khalsa marched 8 kilometres from Attock to Haidaru, on the banks of the Indus River to offer battle. On July 13TH 1812 the Cavalry was split into four, command of one Division was given to Hari Singh Nalua .The lone Battalion of Infantry formed an Infantry square protecting the Artillery. The Afghans took up positions opposite the Sikhs, with a portion of their Cavalry under the command of Dost Mohammad Khan. Fateh Khan opened the battle by sending his Ghazis on a Cavalry charge, which was repulsed by heavy fire from the Sikh Artillery. The Afghans rallied under Dost Mohammad Khan who led the Ghazis on another Cavalry charge, which threw one wing of the Sikh Army into disarray and captured some Artillery. When it appeared the Sikhs had lost the battle, a Cavalry charge that repulsed the Afghans "at all points", routed the remaining Afghan troops. The Afghans broke and fled, leaving over two thousand of their comrades dead on the field and all their heavy guns and equipment to the victors. The victorious Sikh Army pursued the Afghans and drove them out of Khyrabad. This was the first victory of the Sikh Army over the Afghans in a pitched battle. Amritsar, Lahore, and other large cities across the Sikh Empire were illuminated for two months afterwards in rejoicing over the victory.

Sikh Empire

Kashmir, (1814)
After the victory at Attock, the Maharajah determined on making a complete conquest of Kashmir, and military operations were accordingly commenced. However, the expedition could not succeed as the rains had set in. Thus the whole expedition returned to Lahore, having lost its best Officers and men, and being shorn of everything that constituted its strength and utility as a military body. The failure of the Lahore expedition shook up the Sikh sway in the hill regions. Towards the close of the year, the Muslim chiefs of Bhimber and Rajauri broke out in open revolt, the Rajas of Poonch and Nurpur began assuming an independent tone. The reputation lost by the Sikhs could only be retrieved by successive punitive expeditions sent from Lahore during the next four years.

Hazara, (1814)
Ranjit Singh turned his attention to Hazara after his acquisition of the fort of Attock in 1813. It was difficult in fact to retain possession of Attock without the occupation of Hazara. The Sikhs annexed Hazara in two stages. Lower Hazara except Karlal country became tributary to the Sikhs, with the exception of the ongoing struggle against the Sikhs led by the likes of Sardar Muhammad Khan Tarin, Bostan Khan Tarin and others of this tribe, as soon as the Khalsa wrested the Fort of Attock from the Durranis. Hukma Singh Chimni was the first Governor of Hazara, in 1814, with his headquarters at Attock. In order to gain control over Karlal country Maharaja Ranjit Singh sent a large force under famous General Amar Singh Majithia which was defeated by Karlals with great slaughter. Amar Singh was also murdered by Karlals. Ranjit Singh himself then attacked Hazara and reduced all the Warring tribes into submission, carrying the Tarin chief Muhammad Khan with him, as prisoner. The Maharajah then summoned Sardar Hari Singh Nalua, Governor of Kashmir, to Hazara. Sardar Hari Singh Nalua marched by Muzaffarabad and Pakhli with 7,000 foot-soldiers. When he reached Mangal, he found that a large number of Jaduns and Tanaolis, estimated at not less than 25,000 men, had collected there to oppose his passage. Parleying having failed, he stormed their position and burnt the town. Some 2,000 of his opponents were killed, including many who perished in the flames or threw themselves from the walls. As a further punishment, Hari Singh levied a fine of between 5 and 6 rupees on every house inhabited by the Jaduns. He then built a fort at Nawanshahr, garrisoned it, and went on to Lower Hazara. Pleased with the treasure and presents brought from Kashmir, and with the victory won at Mangal, Ranjit Singh made him Governor of all Hazara. From 1822 to his death in 1837 Hari Singh, with brief intervals, ruled over Hazara, and in this period reduced the unruly tribes to submission by vigorous measures and consolidated the Sikh power. One of his first steps was to build the Haripur fort, which was known as Harkrishangarh, and was very strongly constructed.

Sikh Empire

Multan, (1818)

Multan was a commercial capital of the Punjab. There was a well-fortified massive fort inside the city, with an Afghan garrison of three thousand soldiers. The Khalsa had marched on Multan six times, from the years 1802-17. On every occasion the Afghan, Nawab Muzaffar Khan had submitted and paid tribute. Finally, in 1818 Maharajah Ranjit Singh dispatched Prince Kharak Singh with a very strong force to occupy the Multan fort. The Khalsa bombarded the well-defended city walls and took the city. The Afghan soldiers had fallen back to join the rest of the garrison in the fort. The Khalsa laid siege to the fort. Hundreds of Sikh soldiers lost their lives during the siege. Eventually Maharaja Ranjit Singh sent a large cannon named Zamzama* along with Akali Phula Singh's Nihangs. (Nihangs have been the standard bearers of the Sikh Warrior tradition). The Zamzama was fired with effect and the gates of the city were blown in. Once the breach was made, the first storming party was hurled back by the Afghans. Akali Phula Singh with Akali Sadhu Singh made a sudden rush and stormed the fort and destroyed the Afghan garrison. A special detachment under Jodh Singh Kalsia, Dal Singh Naherna and Deva Singh Doabia were left to garrison Multan.

Ghulam Jilani recorded the following soul-stirring incident in his work, *Jang-i-Multan*:

"During the bombardment of the fort walls, one of the Sikh guns lost one of its wheels at a time when another round of shots would have caused a breach therein. There was then no time for repairs, and any delay was extremely dangerous. The Sardar in charge of the gun saw no alternative other than to appeal to his comrades for the sacrifice of their lives for the honour of the Khalsa by laying their shoulders one by one under the axle on the broken side. Without doubt their lives would be lost under the enormous recoil, yet all the Sikhs jumped at the idea and readily agreed to do it. The Sardar, thereupon, ordered that they should come only in the order of seniority of rank, the senior-most man, meaning himself, going first. One by one, the brave gunners went forward to lay down their lives, and it was after the tenth or eleventh shot, when as many of them had been sacrificed under the pressure of the gun, that a breach was made in the wall, and Akali Sadhu Singh rushed to the spot and proclaimed victory of the Khalsa with shouts of Sat Sri Akal."

* Zamzama gun was cast in 1757 in Lahore which was at that time part of the Durrani Empire centered on Afghanistan. It was one of the largest guns ever made in the sub-continent. In 1762, the Bhangi chief, Hari Singh, attacked Lahore and took possession of the cannon. It then came to be known as Bhangian di Top. In 1802, when Maharaja Ranjit Singh occupied Amritsar, the cannon fell into his hands. Ranjit Singh employed it in his campaigns of Daska, Kasur, Sujanpur, Wazirabad and Multan.

Sikh Empire

Peshawar, (1818)

The commotions in Afghanistan were favourable to the views of Ranjit Singh, who perceived the time had come to put his designs on Peshawar, and the country beyond the Attock into execution, the more so as the Khattak Mohammedans had recently raised the standard of revolt and defeated a detachment of the Sikh troops. The troops were ordered to rendezvous across the Ravi, where the Maharajah was personally supervising the military arrangements. A detachment under Akali Phula Singh, Mehtab Singh Nakheria, and Gurmukh Singh was sent to chastise the Afghans, and an action was fought in which the Afghans were defeated. Firoz Khan and Najib-ulla-Khan, the Khattak chiefs, made their submission, and were pardoned, on payment of heavy nazranas. The Sikhs then reduced Khairabad, on the right bank of the Indus, and captured Jehangira, and the territory on the opposite bank of the river. At Naushera, Ranjit Singh ascertained from Dewan Sham Singh and others, who had been to Peshawar, that the Afghans had no organised force with which to oppose him in the field. He then directed an advance on Peshawar, which city he occupied on 26TH November.

Yar Muhammad, the Afghan Governor of Peshawar had evacuated the town on the approach of the Sikhs, and fled to Yuzufzai hills. The Maharajah saved the city from pillage, but set the Bala Hissar on fire. The Maharajah stayed at Peshawar with his Army, receiving the respects of the leading men of the tribes, and conferring dresses of honour upon them. He retired, placing his ally Jahandad Khan, brother of Ata Muhammad Khan, to whom he owed the possession of Attock, in charge of affairs at Peshawar. The Maharajah carried with him fourteen guns, which he had captured at Peshawar, and with them crossed the Attock, on his way back to his capital. Shortly afterwards, the Barakzai Sirdars, having come down to the plains with their mountain hosts, had taken possession of Peshawar, expelling the powerless Jahandad Khan, who had sought refuge at Hasht Nagar. Sardar Dal Singh at the head of 12,000 troops was despatched to Peshawar to replace the expelled Governor Jahandad Khan. The Barakzai Sirdars submitted to Sirdar Dal Singh, and paid tribute to the Lahore Durbar. The tribute was received, and the Sikh troops which were advancing on Peshawar recalled. (Muhammad Latif)

Anglo-Gurkha War, (1814-16)

According to the alliance between Britain and the Sikh Princely state of Patiala, the Patiala state force of Infantry and Cavalry served throughout the Anglo-Gurkha War, alongside the British forces under General Ochterlony, with great distinction.

Sikh Empire

Kashmir, (1819)

Maharajah Ranjit Singh had invaded Kashmir in 1814. The Khalsa forces were compelled to retreat, having lost men and materials. Finally in 1819, Ranjit Singh cut off Kashmir from Afghanistan by closing the North West Frontier passes. On April 20TH, 1819, the Maharaja marched from Lahore at the head of a 30,000 strong force. Sardar Hari Singh Nalua was commanding a division. These were followed by more troops under the command of Hukam Singh Chimni, Sardar Jawala Singh and Sardar Sham Singh Attari. The main battle was fought on July 5TH, 1819. For sometime the Afghans held the Sikh forces and were also able to capture two of their guns. But then the Sikhs rallied and regrouped their forces and made a severe attack on the Afghans who fled towards Shergarh. Jabber Khan was wounded and had a narrow escape. Kashmir was thus conquered and made part of the Sikh empire. The Maharaja's forces then made a triumphant entry into Srinagar.

Naushera, (1823)

The Battle of Naushera in 1823 was fought with the Pathan tribes of the Yuzufzai, Khattaks and Afridis. Prince Sher Singh and Hari Singh Nalua led the advance columns early in 1823. The Khattaks and Yuzufzai were pushed back and managed to entrench themselves on an eminence called Pir Sabak. The main Afghan force under Azim Khan's brother was separated from the tribal ghazis by a small but swift-running stream, the Landai. The Khalsa Artillery bypassed the tribesmen and reached the bank of the Landai, and trained its heavy guns on the opposite bank. Azim Khan made a dash from Peshawar and joined the Afghan forces on the opposite bank of the Landai. He could not cross the stream due to the heavy bombardment by the Khalsa forces from their side of the Landai. The Khalsa forces were heavily outnumbered by the Afghans, but they evened the odds by the tactics of their now well trained, disciplined Army. Then Akali Phula Singh and his Nihangs drove the Khattaks and Yuzufzai before them, leaving four thousand Afghans dead and dying on the field. It is said that they ran from their Nihang attackers saying:

> "Toba, toba-, Khuda Khud, Khalsa Shud"
> God forbid, it's as if, God himself has become a Khalsa

Mohammed Azim Khan retreated to Peshawar. He was too ashamed to face his people and thus he returned to Afghanistan and soon died. Even though the Khalsa had paid a heavy price with the death of a great Warrior Akali Phula Singh, it proved a crushing defeat for the Afghans, which convinced the Pathan tribesmen of the superiority of the Punjabi soldiers. Three days later the Maharaja entered Peshawar at the head of his victorious troops. The citizens welcomed him and paid homage with nazranas (monetary tributes).

Sikh Empire

Sayyid Ahmad, (1826)

Before his journey to the Peshawar region, Sayyid Ahmad had served in the Imperial Army of Amir Khan of Tonk in Northern India. He had performed the hajj (pilgrimage) to Mecca with many supporters and spent two years organizing popular and material support for his Peshawar campaign. A Muslim fanatic from India, he crossed into the tribal territories of the Frontier and proclaimed Jihad against the Sikhs. He asked the Muslims of Afghanistan and India to join his crusade. The bulk of the Muslim rulers in India and the leading Sardars in Afghanistan supported him, including the Mughal Emperor of Delhi. 100,000 crusaders answered his call. They swarmed in from the Pathan and Afghan territories to the Frontier. Thousands of well-trained and armed crusaders crossed over from India through Sindh to the North West Frontier to destroy the Sikhs. Akora, the home of the Khattak Afghans, was an important place in the tribal territories. Budh Singh Sindhanwalia was stationed there with the garrison of 4,000 men. In December, the crusaders attacked the garrison in the early hours of the morning inflicting heavy casualties on the Sikhs. The Khalsa rallied and repulsed the Fanatics, who fled towards the hills. The cost of the victory was heavy, the Khalsa having 500 men killed.

Sayyid's call went out for more volunteers and in March, he attacked a garrison of 10,000 men and 12 guns at the village of Pirpai. The Khalsa let the crusaders exhaust their ammunition for three days, then bombarded and charged them. The Sikh Cavalry in hot pursuit decimated their ranks. Sayyid and the remnants took to the hills, leaving 6,000 of their brethren dead on the field. Sayyid's plan to capture Attock was foiled with the arrival of General Hari Singh. In the clash, the crusaders broke ranks and fled, the ones who were slow in fleeing were massacred by the Khalsa. There were further clashes at Ashra, Amb and Phulra. In all these clashes the crusaders lost heavily. The clashes with the crusader carried on for a few years.

In 1829 at the peak of his local influence, Sayyid Ahmad obtained agreement that the Khans and general public on the frontier would administer their principalities according to the laws of the Shariat. The decisive moment for Sayyid Ahmad came in 1830. In addition to the stated social agenda, Sayyid Ahmad also attempted to collect the Islamic tithe (usher) of ten per cent of crop yields. In coercing the reluctant Khans to pay, Sayyid Ahmad antagonized the chief of Hoti, Mardan and who then formed a power alliance with Sultan Muhammad, Governor of Peshawar. The union was defeated and the Islamic reformers finally occupied Peshawar. Over several months during 1830 Sayyid Ahmad tried to conciliate established power hierarchies. But before the end of 1830 an organized uprising occurred and the agents of Sayyid Ahmad in Peshawar and the plains villages were murdered and the movement retreated to the hills. Finally the Khalsa, at a place called Balakot, cornered Sayyid and his fanatic crusaders. The Khalsa killed Sayyid and 500 of the crusaders.

Sikh Empire

Jamrud, (1837)

General Hari Singh Nalua had built a chain of forts to secure the North West Frontier and to keep the Afghans out. The Afghans took these measures to be a threat to Afghanistan and were constantly waiting for an opportunity to eject the Sikhs from their territories. The opportunity arrived on the preparations of Prince Nau Nihal Singh's wedding at Lahore. Maharajah Ranjit Singh had recalled the cream of the Khalsa forces to the wedding, only a token force was retained to guard the passes. General Hari Singh Nalua was sick and bedridden at Peshawar. Sardar Maha Singh, with a garrison of 600 manned the fort at Jamrud. Dost Muhammad despatched twenty five thousand Afghans and Pathans with 18 heavy guns to reduce the Jamrud fort. The Afghans laid siege and started pounding the fort with heavy Artillery. As the walls were being reduced to rubble, the Khalsa returned the fire, killing about 500 Afghans. Urgent appeals were made to General Hari Singh Nalua at Peshawar for assistance. Nalua rose from his sick bed and advanced on Jamrud with 6,000 foot, 1,000 regular Cavalry, 3,000 irregulars and 20 pieces of cannon. The Khalsa bombarded and drove the Afghan Army into the plains, then charged them and compelled them to retreat. At their retreat, the Khalsa started plundering the Afghans and were in turn charged by a fresh Afghan force, suffering heavy casualties. As Nalua led by the front, he was fatally wounded. He asked his death to be kept secret until the arrival of the Maharajah. Sardar Maha Singh took charge of the Khalsa and drove the Afghans back. This was followed by another engagement, when Akbar Khan engaged the Sikhs with a fresh force. The Afghans were driven back to the hills, abandoning their guns. The Sikhs pursued them through the Khaibar Pass and decimated them. The remnants and Akbar Khan fled away to Kabul.

There was a heavy price to pay that day. The Khalsa lost 6,000 men and the Afghans who outnumbered them, left about 11,000 dead on the blood-drenched fields. The greatest loss was the death of Nalua. General Hari Singh Nalua was the Murat - The Face - of the Khalsa. The most dashing of the Khalsa Generals, he was a legend in his own lifetime.

The Tripartite Treaty, (1838)

In 1838, a Tripartite was made between Ranjit Singh, Shah Shuja and the British government. Shah Shuja was to be restored to the Afghan throne by the British and the Khalsa bayonets. It confirmed to the Sikh Kingdom in perpetuity, Kashmir, Attock and Hazara; Peshawar and the Yuzufzai dependencies up to the Khyber; Bannu, Tank, Kala Bagh, the Derajat and the rich province of Multan. The Afghans agreed to these territories as forming part of the Sikh Kingdom. Finally, both the British and the Sikh governments would jointly control the foreign relations of Afghanistan. In practice, the plan replaced Dost Mohammad with a British figurehead whose autonomy would be as limited as that of other Indian princes

Sikh Empire

Death of Maharajah Ranjit Singh, (1839)

Maharajah Ranjit Singh died on 27TH June 1839. He rose from the status of a petty chieftain of a few villages and by welding together the rude Barons of the Sikh Confederacy became a King of an Empire extending from Tibet to the deserts of Sindh and from the Khyber Pass to the Satluj. His Army was one of the most powerful at that time in Asia He was a benevolent King. Even though the Government of the Punjab was called Sarkar Khalsa, no laws were imposed on any other religious community. Sikhs at this time were about 15% of the whole population; Hindus around 25%, the rest were Muslims. Ranjit Singh governed for forty years from Lahore with secular ideals. He would fast with Muslims during Ramadan and play Holi with Hindus, yet he would be at Amritsar almost every month to take a bath. Ranjit Singh would often roam in the streets of Lahore in disguise to check his rule; whether people were happy or not. Although he was a devout Sikh, he cannot be called a strict Khalsa Sikh adhering to all the principles of Sikhism. He was a very well disciplined soldier of the Khalsa, who was also secular, as well as enjoying his life, like drinking, etc. The spirit of stern religious discipline and sacrifice which had supported Sikhs through a critical period of their history and led them to power and glory was not dimmed in the pomp and splendour of his sovereignty. Ranjit Singh's death on June 27TH, 1839, left a deep hiatus. The Khalsa lost a leader who had, by commanding personality, foresight and skill, become their *beau ideal* and secured them the status of sovereign people.

Khalsa Banner at Kabul, (1839)

Prince Kharak Singh, who succeeded to the throne, was an irresolute weakling. Prince Nau Nihal Singh, son of Kharak Singh, who possessed the qualities of his grandfather, decided to intervene and take the matters of state in his own hands. The Prince energetically dispatched the Khalsa to bring the provinces to heel. He honoured the tripartite treaty and ordered the Khalsa to cross the Indus and assemble at Peshawar. The Durbar's Najib Battalions of 6,140 men with 16 guns and 140 pieces of Artillery forced the passes, suffering heavy casualties and occupied Ali Masjid. Meantime Kabul had fallen to the British. Colonel Sheikh Bassawan carried the Khalsa banner at the victory parade in Kabul. The Governor General recognized the gallantry of the Durbar's troops by the presentation of a Sword of Honour to the gallant Colonel. Maharajah Kharak Singh died on 5TH November 1840. After the funeral, as Prince Nau Nihal Singh was passing under a gateway, the arch gave way, the falling masonry crushed his head, and he died a few hours later. The only hand, which could have kept the Kingdom together, was taken away.

FALL OF THE SIKH EMPIRE

Maharajah Sher Singh, (1841)

At the death of Kharak Singh and Nau Nihal Singh, the widow of Kharak Singh, Chand Kaur, had assumed the powers of a regent. Prince Sher Singh sought the help of the Khalsa Army. The Khalsa declared for Sher Singh and proclaimed him the Maharajah. Chand Kaur was pensioned off and her backers, the Sandhawalia Sardars, fled across to British territory. The British asked Sher Singh to allow the Sandhawalia Sardars back to the Punjab and their estates. They were allowed back into the kingdom, and welcomed by Maharajah Sher Singh. As Maharajah Sher Singh was taking a salute at a march past by the Sandhawalia contingent, Ajit Singh Sandhawalia assassinated him and his son. The Khalsa in their fury killed Ajit Singh and his escort of 600 soldiers.

The Army Panchas, (1843)

At the death of Sher Singh, Maharajah Ranjit Singh's youngest son Dalip Singh was proclaimed Maharajah. At the ensuing bloodletting between various factions, the Khalsa Army took control of the state. They were the people's Army. They had created the state and the Sikh Kingdom. They were the state's defenders and preservers, and became an executive sovereign of the state. They ruled through the congregation of the Panchas, the five selected members from each Unit. They faced a corrupt government, the Sardars and the Sovereign, who were seeking British interference to safeguard their estates and privileges. The Khalsa proceeded to punish the traitors. It brought the Jammu Rajas to heel, wiped out the Sandhawalia faction and expelled the foreigners from the state. The court and the leading Sardars frantically sought British intervention for the destruction of the Khalsa Army.

First Anglo – Sikh War, (1845)

After the fall of Delhi, the British had a stand off against Maharajah Ranjit Singh. However, they checked the expansion of the Sikh Kingdom by taking the Cis Satluj territories under their protection. They also checked the state's expansion towards Sindh and the sea, by taking the Amirs of Sindh under their protection. They had made no secret about the destruction of the Sikh Kingdom and annexation of the Punjab to the British Empire. With the turmoil in the Punjab, and their under estimation of the fighting qualities of the Sikh soldier, the British started massing their armies; the largest force ever assembled in India, on the Kingdom's borders. The most experienced senior Officers led the force consisting of 10,472 men and 24 guns at Ferozepore, 7,235 men and 22 guns at Ludhiana, 12,972 men and 32 guns at Ambala, 9,844 men and 24 guns at Meerut. The strength of the British forces, including those at the hill stations, was 40,523 men and 98 guns. The British also had the understanding of co-operation with Gulab Singh Dogra, the Raja of Jammu, the Chief Minister Lal Singh and the Commander in Chief Tej Singh. Their intention was to shatter the Khalsa on the British Bayonets.

Fall of the Sikh Empire

The Khalsa Army

The morale of the Khalsa was extremely high. The Sikh soldier was extremely brave and had always carried everything before him. The weakness lay in the Officer Corps, who merely became the figureheads, as the Panchas made all the decisions. "The Sikh Regimental Officers were mostly illiterate and, brave that they might be, were not worthy of the men they commanded." "Neither of the two principal Generals, Lal Singh and Tej Singh, were Sikhs, but Brahmins, and were not committed to the cause for which they were fighting." A powerful, well-trained, and confident Sikh Army prepared for War under the leadership of a Commander in Chief under orders from a Vizier, and watched from the sidelines by a powerful and clever Chieftain. All three men dedicated to the defeat of the Army they led, and secretly informing their British opponents of that fact! The Khalsa decided to be the first in the field and crossed the Satluj on 12TH December 1845.

Battle of Mudki, (1845)

As soon as Lal Singh crossed the Satluj, he waited for instructions from Captain Nicholson. He was told not to attack the weak garrison of Ferozepore, delay his march, and then march towards the Governor General. Lal Singh followed the instructions and split the Khalsa Army in two parts. The smaller force under Tej Singh was sent to threaten but not attack Ferozepore! Tej Singh with his overwhelming force could have easily defeated the Ferozepore garrison, but that was not a part of the plan. Lal Singh marched the main force and entrenched it near the village of Ferozeshah. He then took a detachment from the main force of 3,500 Cavalry, 2,000 Infantry and 20 guns and advanced to confront the British force of 12,000 men with 48 guns and four troops of horse Artillery. They sighted the British forces on 18TH December 1845, near the village of Mudki, and attacked immediately. As soon as the attack started, Lal Singh promptly deserted his men and retreated to the camp at Ferozeshah. Though outnumbered, the Sikhs fought the enemy to a standstill. General Wheeler's Brigade was so terrified at the sight of the Sikh Cavalry, it formed squares, and would not obey orders to reform and advance. In the fierce encounter, the Sikh gunners nobly served their beloved guns and the Khalsa took on the numerous enemies in grim hand-to-hand fighting. Having lost almost half of their force and fifteen guns, the leaderless Khalsa withdrew back to the main force at Ferozeshah. The British had lost 872 dead and wounded. The dead included Quartermaster-General Sir Robert Sale, Sir John McGaskil and Brigadier Bolton. The British were shaken by the fighting qualities of the Khalsa, the likes of which they had never encountered in India. The Commander in Chief Lord Gough, warned General Littler at Ferozepore, not to be drawn into action against the Khalsa, but evade the Khalsa and join the main force. The British licked their wounds and frantically waited for reinforcements to arrive from Ambala, Meerut and Delhi.

Fall of the Sikh Empire

Battle of Ferozeshah, (1845)

Ferozeshah was the most terrible British defeat in the annals of British Indian history. The British forces were saved from annihilation by the treachery of the Sikh Commander in Chief. The Sikh Artillery opened up a heavy cannonade on the British attacking force. The British batteries were no match against the Sikh guns and suffered severely. Litter's Divisional attack was repulsed with terrible slaughter. The whole Division retreated and stayed out of action for the rest of the day.

General Gough in desperation poured all of his Cavalry, Infantry and Artillery into the jaws of death. The Khalsa repulsed every British charge and decimated the parties which had penetrated their lines. On that night the British were a spent force. Here are some of the quotes from the leading Officers: General Sir Hope Grant, "Truly that night was one of gloom and never perhaps in our annals of Indian Warfare has a British Army on so large a scale been nearer to defeat which could have involved annihilation. The Sikhs had practically recovered the whole of their entrenchment camp: our exhausted and decimated divisions bivouacked without mutual cohesion over a wide area..." Capt. Cunningham, who was an eye-witness wrote; "...men of all Regiments were mixed together; Generals were doubtful of the fact or of the extent of their own success, and the Colonels knew not what had become of the Regiments commanded, or of the Army which they formed part." and about the Khalsa; "The resistance met with was wholly unexpected, and all started with astonishment. Guns were dismounted, and their ammunition was blown into the air; Squadrons were checked in mid career; Battalion after Battalion were hurled back with shattered ranks, and it was not until after sunset that portions of enemy position were finally carried." The Governor General was convinced that the British Army would be cut to pieces the next day. He sent away his son to Mudki with Napoleon's sword that he had received from the Duke of Wellington, for safety and gave instructions for all his private papers to be destroyed. His secretary Fredrick Currie wrote in his dairy; "December 22ND: News came from the Governor General that our attack of yesterday had failed, that affairs were desperate, that all the state papers were to be destroyed, and if the morning attack failed, all would be over: this was kept secret by Mr. Currie and we were concerning measure to make an unconditional surrender to save the wounded, part of the news that grieved me the most" The British had suffered 2415 casualties, the bulk of the Artillery was out of action without any ammunition, the men were cold, tired and hungry with no reserves and reinforcements. The next morning, as the battered British force gathered itself, Battalions and Battalions of Khalsa Army with heavy guns appeared on the battlefield. The Sikh guns opened fire; there was no reply from the British Artillery. As the British steeled themselves to be slaughtered, Tej Singh wheeled away the Sikh Army and abandoned the battlefield. The shattered British ranks immediately retreated to Ferozepore. At the conclusion of the 1845 War, the British rewarded Tej Singh by making him a Raja of Sialkot.

Fall of the Sikh Empire

Skirmish at Badhowal, (1846)

After the battle of Ferozeshah the British force had been considerably weakened and did not intend to engage the Sikhs. The British were seeking reinforcements from all quarters and troops with heavy guns were on their way from Meerut, Ambala and Delhi. The Sikh Commander Ranjodh Singh Majithia, with a force of 8,000 men and 70 guns, crossed the River Satluj, sacked the forts of Fatehgarh, Dharamkote, Gangrana and Badhowal and raided Ludhiana. Gough immediately ordered General Harry Smith's Division to Ludhiana. Harry Smith's force collided with the moving column of the Khalsa. The British force would not give battle and hastily retreated. The Sikhs closed in on the retreating force, captured their baggage train and stores, inflicting 137 casualties and taking 77 prisoners. Ranjodh Singh re-crossed the Satluj, as there was a danger of being trapped between Gough and the advancing reinforcements. Nevertheless, Smith succeeded in reaching Ludhiana, with his troops exhausted. A Brigade of troops from Delhi, including two Gurkha Battalions, reinforced him. After resting his troops, Smith once again advanced to Badhowal. The Sikhs had withdrawn to Aliwal on the Satluj awaiting reinforcements.

Battle of Aliwal, (1846)

This battle was fought in January 1846 between a British force detached from the main Army, under Sir Harry Smith and a portion of the Sikh Army, under Ranjodh Singh, which had been threatening Ludhiana. The Sikhs had occupied a position 4 miles (6.4 km) long, which ran along a ridge between the villages of Aliwal, on the Satluj, and Bhundri. The Satluj ran close to their rear for the entire length of their line, making it difficult for them to maneuver and also potentially disastrous if they were forced to retreat. After the initial Artillery salvoes, Smith determined that Aliwal was the Sikh weak point. He sent two of his four Infantry Brigades to capture the village, from where they could enfilade the Sikh centre. They seized the village, and began pressing forwards to threaten the fords across the Satluj. As Smith attacked the Sikhs and carried their entrenchments, Ranjodh Singh and his Officers deserted the troops. At the repeated Cavalry charges, the leaderless men refused to retreat. 3,500 were killed and 54 guns were lost. Eventually they abandoned all their posts South of the River Satluj, except for the bridgehead at Sobraon.

Humbley wrote, "although their leader, Ranjodh Singh, was the first to fly and basely quit the field leaving his brave followers to conquer or lose, their courage never quailed," and "Again they rallied and made one last vigorous effort. Though defeat made them desperate, they fought like men who jeopardized all." The Sikhs abandoned all their posts South of the river Satluj, except for the bridgehead at Sobraon.

Fall of the Sikh Empire

Battle of Sobraon, (1846)

Gulab Singh was a feudal chieftain of the Sikh Government, and commanded two Divisions of the Sikh Army. He had been in direct communications with the British, "A secret understanding was arrived between Gulab Singh and the British that Maharajah Dalip Singh would be allowed to retain his nominal sovereignty, provided the British forces were allowed to occupy the capital of the Sikhs unopposed." Thus with ignominious treachery and deceit were sold the lives of the valiant soldiers of the Khalsa by their Vizier.

The Khalsa had constructed formidable entrenchments with 70 heavy guns and Battalions of Infantry in treble trenches. On 18TH February, General Gough received his reinforcements of men, ammunition, stores and heavy guns and Sir Harry Smith's Division. Gough took two days to prepare for battle and then launched frontal attack on the Sikh entrenchments. The first attack by Stacey's Brigade was repulsed, as was the next Brigade attack. Then the British heavy Artillery in two hours cannonade put the Sikh Artillery out of action. As the Sikh guns silenced for the lack of powder and shell, Gough threw the full weight of the three Divisions and field guns on the entrenchments.

Tej Singh fled from the battlefield, destroying the pontoon bridge, and cut off the Sikh retreat. Lal Singh had decamped soon after the first assault. Sardar Sham Singh Attariwala organized a last stand but gallantly as they fought, they were overwhelmed. The British casualties were 2,403. The Sikhs had 3,125 killed. The British Generals, although they had the cooperation of the Sikh Commanders, had won the War at enormous cost. They duly paid tribute to the Khalsa soldiery. Harding wrote: "the republican Army had more vigour and resolution in it than any in which we have yet had to contend" "the Sikh soldiers are the finest men I have seen in Asia, bold and daring republicans." Gough paid tribute to the gallantry of the Sikhs "Policy precluded me publicly recording my sentiments on the splendid gallantry of our fallen foe, or record the acts of heroism displayed, not only individually, but almost collectively, by Sikh Sardars and the Army.'

Between the Wars

After the victory at Sobraon, the British crossed over and occupied the fort at Kasur. Gulab Singh and the Durbar's courtiers arrived the same day, to accept any terms dictated by the Governor General by the treaty of Lahore, imposed on the Durbar. The kingdom surrendered to the British all its Cis-Satluj estates. The territories of Jalandhar Doab, the territories lying between Satluj and Beas, and the provinces of Kashmir and Hazara were ceded to the British. The Khalsa Army was restricted to 20,000 Infantry and 12,000 Cavalry, and were crushed as a military power. The British government became the guardian of the young Maharajah Dalip Singh. The Punjab became a British protectorate. The British resident in effect became the successor to Ranjit Singh.

Fall of the Sikh Empire

Revolt at Multan (1948)

The district of Multan was a tributary of the Sikh Kingdom. At the death of his father, Mulraj had taken over the governorship of Multan. As he was unable to pay the accession fee and the increased tribute to the central government, he submitted his resignation. His resignation was accepted. Sardar Kahan Singh was appointed as the new Governor. Two British Officers, Vans Agnew and Anderson would accompany him to Multan. Kahan Singh was to be a nominal figurehead; the British Officers would conduct the administration. Sardar Kahan Singh, along with the British Officers and an escort of 1500 troops, including a Regiment of Gurkhas in Sikh service reached Multan on 14TH April. As the Multan troops were going to be set free, losing their livelihood and replaced, they mutinied and killed the two British Officers. They took Mulraj prisoner, and compelled him to be their leader. They appealed to the people to join the rebellion. The Lahore escort deserted and went over to join the Multani soldiers. The rebellion was allowed to spread for five months, despite the leading British Officers straining at the leash for instant action, which would have forestalled any Sikh insurrection. The British were warned about the despatch of Sikh troops to Multan, that they would prove mutinous. The British deliberately despatched all the available Sikh forces to Multan, including the main force led by Sher Singh. All forces converged on Multan and laid siege to the massive Multan fort in preparation for the final annexation of the Punjab to British India.

Sardar Chattar Singh Attariwala

Sardar Chattar Singh Attariwala was the Governor of the Northwest Frontier districts. His daughter was engaged to Maharajah Dalip Singh. He ardently supported the British in all measures they wished to take, as did his son Sher Singh Attariwala, who was energetically co-operating with the British at the siege of Multan. Since the Multan outbreak, which was allowed to spread, the British started inciting the tribesmen on the Frontier against the Sikh garrison. Captain James Abbot sought the help of Hazara chiefs and their Levies and advanced to expel the Sikh Governor. Chattar Singh, for his own safety moved into the fort of Hajipur. His guns were in the charge of an American, Colonel Canora, who was in the Durbar's service. Canora refused to hand over the guns without orders from Abbot; he was instantly killed for insubordination. At the court of enquiry, it was established that as Governor of the province, he had acted to defend the besieged capital of Hazara from Abbot's Muslim mercenaries. Not withstanding the findings, Chattar Singh's estates were confiscated and he was dismissed from his post. The actions of the British Officers on the Frontier, raising Muslim Levies to attack the Sikh garrisons and humiliation and dismissal of the Durbar Governor of the North West Frontier, and the measures taken by the Governor General, moving a force of 10,000 to Lahore, the occupation of the Lahore citadel and putting leading Sikh Sardars under guard, convinced Chattar Singh that the British were preparing for the final annexation of the Punjab.

Fall of the Sikh Empire

Second Anglo – Sikh War, (1848)

The old Sardar decided to fight the British and wrote to his son Sher Singh to join him. Sher Singh realized that the die was cast, and reluctantly left the British camp to join his father. The Governor General declared, "The die is cast; this is a national rebellion to expel us. It is a religious War for the Khalsa. Consequently, after anxious and grave deliberation we have without hesitation resolved that the Punjab can no longer be allowed to exist as a power and must be destroyed." The British were the rulers of the Punjab and the guardians of the young Maharajah. The rebellion of the Attariwala Sardars was against the authority of the Durbar. The Guardian was set to punish and destroy the Ward, which he was bound to protect by the Treaty of Bhayirowal! Even the Commander in Chief, General Gough appears to have been in some doubt whether he was carrying out operations to suppress a rebellion on behalf of the Durbar or whether the Durbar in Lahore was itself to be regarded as an enemy. The British invading force deployed at various points in the Punjab was a staggering total of 104,666 men, 61,366, Regular British Army; 5,300, Lahore Army; 38,000, Irregular troops; 13,542, Cavalry; 123 Field guns, and 22 Heavy guns. At the conclusion of the First Anglo-Sikh War, the British had methodically destroyed the military power of the Sikhs. The soldiers had been disarmed, disbanded and dispersed. The pride of the Khalsa, the guns, were dismantled and taken away. What remained was but a shadow of the colossal military machine of Maharajah Ranjit Singh. The remnants of the Khalsa permitted were 20,000 men and 12,000 Cavalry. The total force the Attariwala Sardars could muster was 23,000; these were the various contingents from Hazara, Peshawar, Tank, Bannu, Kohat and Attock including 10,000 Irregulars.

The Battle of Ramnagar, (1848)

Sher Singh had withdrawn across the river Chenab, to the village of Ramnagar, which lay about two miles from the river. Brigadier General Campbell, with an Infantry Division accompanied by a Cavalry Division with Horse Artillery under Brigadier General Cureton, was ordered to attack the Sikhs. On arrival at Ramnagar, Campbell ordered a Squadron of Light Dragoons, 8TH Light Infantry and the Horse Artillery to attack the parties of Sikh soldiers who were marching towards their main encampment. Their attack met with disaster. The withering cannonade from the Sikh guns compelled the attacker to make a hasty retreat, abandoning a heavy gun and wagons of ammunition. The Sikh Cavalry crossed the Chenab, checked, and routed the attack of 14TH Light Dragoons and 5TH Light Cavalry. Another concentrated attack by the Commander of the Cavalry was repulsed with a loss. The whole British attacking force retreated from the field. Ninety British Officers and men were killed in the attack, including Lieutenant Colonel Havelock and Brigadier General Cureton. The Commander of 14TH Dragoons was reported missing presumed dead.

Fall of the Sikh Empire

Battle of Chillianwala, (1849)

As Gough waited for re-enforcements, he allowed the Sikhs ample time to prepare defensive positions. The main Sikh force moved to Lollianwala on the river Jhelum, and entrenched in a strong position commanded by the Artillery and had established strong picket lines in the surrounding villages. The Sikhs deployed one Regiment of Cavalry, four Regiments of Infantry and seventeen guns on the right under Sardar Ram Singh. Then came two Regiments of Cavalry, ten Regiments of Infantry, of which four were newly raised and seventeen guns under Sardar Lal Singh and Sardar Atar Singh. On the left under personal command of Sher Singh was a Regiment of Cavalry, nine Regiments of Infantry of which five were newly raised. Various strengths of Irregular Horse were stationed at Russool and Moong. The total Sikh strength was about 10,000 and 54 guns. The British deployments, on the left were White's Cavalry Brigade with Horse Artillery Battery, then Campbell's Division with two Brigades, which were supported by Robertson's Field Artillery Battery. The heavy guns were in the front of the dispositions. The total strength of the invading force was about 12,000.

The British troops were better trained and battle hardened than the majority of the Sikhs. On 13TH January, the British approached the village of Chillianwala, and came under sharp Artillery fire. The British heavy guns and field batteries opened up and belched their cannonade for about an hour. Then they launched both Divisions simultaneously on the Sikh positions with disastrous results. The British Divisions completely lost their formations in the dense jungle. The Sikh Infantry and Artillery took heavy toll on the disorganised Regiments. The Sikh Infantry and Cavalry fell on Campbell's Brigade, decimated their ranks and drove them back at bayonet point. The dreaded Sikh Irregular Light Cavalry charged Pope's Cavalry Brigade. The entire British Cavalry Brigade fled against the Khalsa attack and disappeared from the field, abandoning four of their guns and leaving their comrades at the mercy of the Sikhs. The Governor General Dalhousie records: "the Cavalry on the right disgraced their name and the colours they carry. They galloped into the Field Hospital, among the wounded and never stopped till they were brought up by the Chaplain, who was administering the wounded, and who, pistol in hand, declared he would shoot at the first man who passed him." In another direction Pennyquik's Brigade advancing through the thick forest was trapped and shattered by the Sikh Artillery. The shattered ranks of the Brigade fled the deadly destruction of the Sikh Artillery, leaving behind their Commander and Field Officers dead on the field. The panicked retreats and the reverses left the second Infantry Brigade with no cover of Cavalry or Artillery. The Khalsa surrounded the Brigade and drove it back with heavy loss. When darkness fell the British left the battlefield and fell back on the village of Chillianwala. The British casualties amounted to 2,446 men, with 132 Officers killed and 4 guns lost. Chillianwala was the worst defeat the British had suffered in their annals of Indian Warfare.

Fall of the Sikh Empire

The Battle of Gujrat, (1849)

The Muhammadan element of the Sikh armies did not have commitment to the Honour of the Khalsa and deserted to the British. The Leading Muslim Officers, General Imam Ud Din, General Illahi Baksh the Artillery Commander and Amir Khan the Cavalry Commander, all went over to the British, taking their forces with them. The Guides and the Sikh Local Infantry, raised at the conclusion of the first Anglo-Sikh War, also fought against the Khalsa, as did some leading Sikh Sardars including Sardar Shamsher Singh and Sardar Attar Singh. The total strength of the entire Khalsa force was about 23,000. The total British Army, inclusive of the Lahore force, amounted to 56,000 men of all arms, 11,569 Cavalry, 96 field guns and 67 siege guns. Thus assured of an overwhelming superiority of men and heavy Artillery, Gough ordered the entire force forward. The British opened up with a cannonade of 100 guns for two hours, decimated the Sikh ranks and silenced their Artillery. As the guns fell silent, the British swarmed over the Sikh positions and within an hour, the battle was over. On 14TH March, the Attariwala Sardars surrendered their swords to General Gilbert. "Observers who watched the surrender greatly admired the bearing of the Sikh soldiers, who still carried themselves with pride. They were tired and hungry, but their spirit was in no means broken. It was noticed that many of the older men threw down their Tulwars with a gesture of disgust. The Punjab was annexed to British India and Maharajah Dalip Singh pensioned off to England. Gradually the Sikh soldier went soldiering to the far corners of the British Empire under British colours.

Sikh Soldier

In 1846, the British had raised two Regiments of Sikh Infantry from the protected Sikh princely states of Malwa. The Sikhs were considered the finest soldiers in the East. "If I had anything to say to annexation," Harding commented "I should enlist whole Regiments of Sikhs into our service". At the conclusion of the First Sikh War, the British inherited the Sikh Kingdom's borders to the North West Frontier. In 1846 a Frontier Brigade consisting of a Corps of Guides, four Regiments of Sikh Local Infantry, five Regiments of the Punjab Infantry, five Regiments of the Punjab Cavalry, and a Light Battery of Artillery was formed to guard the frontier and to police the truculent mountain tribes. All of the volunteers were soldiers and gunners of the disbanded Sikh Army .The expansion of the force was delayed because of the commencement of the Second Sikh War. After the terrifically hard fought battles and the annexation of the Punjab, the Frontier Brigade was strengthened in 1849. The new establishment included three Light Batteries of Artillery, which were bodily transferred from the disbanded Sikh Horse Artillery. The disbanded Sikh soldiery was welcomed into all arms of the East India Company's armies, thus joining the British Imperial Forces. They were keenly recruited for their unsurpassed fighting qualities, and came to be known as 'The Sword Arm of the Empire'.

NORTH – WEST FRONTIER, 1849-1857

North West Frontier

The greatest legacy of the Sikhs is the conquest of Hazara and Peshawar and consolidation of the Northwest frontier. If it were not for this achievement all the regions, along with the entire trans-Indus territories, would have been lost to India forever and in that case these territories would not have been part of the British Empire. The stability of the Frontier became cornerstones of defensive strategy for British India. Military history of guarding the frontier of this region of the British Empire had been a succession of punitive expeditions against offending Pakhtun (or *Pathan*) tribes, punctuated by three Wars against Afghanistan. The bulk of the soldiers fighting on the frontier and Afghanistan in a succession of punitive expeditions were veterans of the Sikh armies of Maharajah Ranjit Singh.

The basic characteristics of Frontier fighting had long been known to the Sikh soldier. Following the annexation of the Punjab in 1849 he served under the British colours against the heavily-armed trans-border Pathan tribes, who repeatedly raided areas now under direct British administration, and attacked trading caravans. The localized armed forces raised specifically to protect the trans-Indus areas - the Punjab Irregular Force (PIF) - quickly learnt that fighting in mountainous terrain against tribal lashkars (War parties) posed a range of difficulties very different from those encountered in conventional Warfare. When operating in tribal territory Indian troops were tied to protecting long, vulnerable and cumbersome columns of pack transport, carrying food, water and ammunition, on which they depended in the barren hills. Freedom of movement was restricted to the valley floors while lightly-equipped opposing tribesmen operated with comparative freedom on the hill sides. A lack of reliable maps made it difficult to select suitable objectives, while the difficult climate and endemic diseases in tribal territory often inflicted heavier casualties than the opposing tribesmen. On the other hand, tribesmen were well acquainted with fighting in their native mountains, matching their relative strengths of mobility, flexibility and superior marksmanship, in elusive guerrilla warfare against cumbrous British columns.

Between 1849 and 1857, the British had mounted seventeen major military expeditions all along the Frontier, from the Bazai of the Swat Valley and the Cis-Indus Yuzufzai of the Black Mountain in the North, down through Mohmand and Afridi country, to the Wazirs and Shiranis round Dera Ghazi Khan in the South.

Subedar Kor Singh and Sowar Dul Singh of the Corps of Guides, were awarded the Indian Order of Merit in consideration of their conspicuous gallantry during the action against the Afridis in 1853, and Sepoys Bux Singh and Jawahir Singh of 2ND Punjab Infantry, were awarded the Indian Order of Merit in consideration of their conspicuous gallantry against the Bozdar tribe in 1857.

SEPOY MUTINY

Sepoy Mutiny, (1857–58)

The Bengal Army mutinied at the Meerut cantonment near Delhi on 10TH May 1857. The Mutiny spread to Delhi, Agra, Cawnpore and Lucknow, starting a year-long insurrection against the British. The Indian soldiers were dissatisfied with their pay, as well as with certain changes in regulations, which they interpreted as part of a plot to force them to adopt Christianity. This belief was strengthened when the British furnished the soldiers with cartridges coated with grease made from the fat of cows (sacred to Hindus) and of pigs (anathema to Muslims). They replaced the cartridges when the mistake was realized; but suspicion persisted and in February 1857, began a series of incidents in which Sepoys refused to use the cartridges.

'The Sikhs in the background of their rule in the Punjab and egalitarian tradition could hardly be expected to side with Muslim and Hindu princes to regain their kingdoms, nor could religious taboos which affected Hindu and Muslim sentiments, against many of which the Sikh Gurus had led a crusade, in any measure inflame Sikh sentiments. The Cis-Satluj chiefs of Patiala, Malerkotla, Kalsia, Nabha, Faridkot and Jind, along with their mercenary forces, rendered full help to the British in suppressing the rebellion. These chiefs owed their existence to the British, who had protected them from the conquests of Maharajah Ranjit Singh. They still remembered with gratitude the support extended to them by the British against Maharaja Ranjit Singh. But for the British protection, Ranjit Singh would surely have sought to annex their kingdoms long ago.

All the Sikh Battalions participated in suppressing the Sepoy Mutiny including the newly raised Sikh Pioneer Regiments that were prominent in the siege, attack and capture of Delhi. The Regiment of Ferozepore fought a series of actions during the relief of Lucknow, in which the attack on the Little Imambara in March 1858 was noteworthy. It was after this, that the Battalion was permitted to wear the red *pugree (turban)* as a mark distinction. This is now the headdress of the Sikh Regiment. Another reward for gallantry, unique by its very nature, was a grant of one rank higher for all ranks. All the Subedars were awarded Indian Order of Merit for gallantry. The Regiment of Ludhiana was at Banares when the Mutiny started and performed many acts of gallantry against the mutineers. Sepoy Chur Singh was promoted to the rank of Jemadar for gallantry. The Defence made by the Sikh Military Police Battalion at a house at Arrah by a detachment of sixty men for ten days against three disciplined Regiments is the most extraordinary on record. The Battalion faced about 3,000 men, and held them at bay till help arrived. In 1864 the Battalion became a Regular Unit as the famous 45TH Rattray's Sikhs. 231, Indian Order of Merit gallantry awards were awarded to the Sikh soldiers during the Mutiny. The soldiers belonged to all the teeth arms of the Indian Army.

NORTH WEST FRONTIER, 1857-1878

Between 1857 and 1878, the British had mounted thirteen major military expeditions along the Frontier, when the Second Afghan War broke out in 1878. The Sikh soldier was in the vanguard of all these expeditions.

Ambela, (1863)

Towards the end of 1863, 14TH Ferozepore Sikhs were the first to carry out punitive operations against Hindustani Fanatics at Malka. They took part in a series of fierce battles around an important post, the Crag Piquet. On 18TH November, the tribesmen advanced in great strength and attacked the defences of a camp, held by one hundred and thirty men of 14TH Ferozepore Sikhs. The enemy attacked with great ferocity, but the Sikhs, although completely outnumbered, held out with great determination until reinforcements arrived and the tribesmen were driven back. The night of 16TH December 1863 was a memorable one for both 23RD and 32ND Sikh Pioneers.

Lieutenant J. Campbell of 93RD Highlanders has communicated this interesting account of the Ghazis charge to the Sikh Pioneers' history. 'I happened to be looking when the 200 Ghazis made their splendid charge on the two Muzbee Regiments, and I shall never forget the scene. The Ghazis came down the front of the two Regiments, cutting and slashing with their Tulwars and every one of them was killed. They came out to die, and die they did. Thus terminated the first important combined action of the sister Regiments, in which they had but gloriously upheld the honour of the Muzbee, their Regiments, and the Khalsa and the crown. As in the days of old in the Khalsa armies the Muzbee were in the front of the fight and bore the first onslaught of the enemy. Pushed back at first by weight of numbers and the suddenness of the attack, they soon rallied, and killed every Hindustani Fanatic of those two hundred, not allowing one to escape.' (Macmunn)

Jowaki Afridis, (1877-1878)

In the autumn of 1877, 14TH Ferozepore Sikhs formed part of a column under Brigadier General Ross, and moved into the Jowaki district, for a punitive operation against the Afridis. They had attacked police posts, plundered and burnt villages, and finally burnt a bridge on the Khushalgarh road. The Afridis opposed the Column on the Shergasha Heights and the Sikhs were detailed to assault the position. The fighting was, however, not severe and the Afridis withdrew without offering much resistance. The force moved into the Boris valley and destroyed the offending villages with stout resistance from the tribesmen. It then withdrew to Peshawar in 1878 without incident. Havildar Dharum Singh of 14TH Ferozepore Sikhs was awarded the Indian Order of Merit for conspicuous gallantry in action against the Afridis. He was the only soldier to be awarded a gallantry award during these operations.

North West Frontier, 1857-1878

Utman Khel, (1878)

In December 1876, a dastardly attack was made by the Utman Khel tribe on the camp of a number of unarmed coolies employed in the construction of the Swat Canal near Abazai. Several of the unfortunate men were killed or wounded and their camp was then plundered. On February 14TH 1878, a force consisting of 280 men of the Guides left Mardan under Captain Wigram Battye and Jemadar Jewand Singh, to exact punishment for the outrage. In addition to coercing the Utman Khel, the Guides had another little brush with the Ranizais. The Guides surrounded the Ranizais village of Shalkot at dawn on March 14TH 1878, and the unconditional surrender of the tribesmen was received at once. The Guides had seven wounded in this affair, including Jemadar Jaggat Singh, who received the Indian Order of Merit for gallantry in action.

SECOND AFGHAN WAR

The British had always been worried about the Russians and their expanding empire encroaching onto their Northwest Indian border. With Afghanistan acting as a buffer zone, and existing as the open route from Russian to British territory, it was felt that control of Afghanistan - in the form of a friendly Amir - would solve this perceived threat. When the Amir, Sher Ali Khan, was not quick enough to accept British influence they invaded Afghanistan. The Second Afghan War was split into two campaigns, November 1878 - May 1879, and September 1879 - September 1880. The first campaign began in November 1878 with the British invasion of Afghanistan in three columns and the battle of Ali Masjid, and ended with the Treaty of Gandamak on 26TH May 1879, and a new Amir (Yakub Khan). As part of the terms of that treaty the British sent an envoy (Sir Louis Cavignari) and a small military escort to Kabul. On 3RD September 1879 this mission was attacked and the conflict was reignited. It ended in September 1880 after a new Amir had been found (Abdurrahman) and another candidate, Ayub Khan, had been defeated.

Ali Masjid, (1878)

The Afghans were known to be holding a position at Ali Masjid in the Khyber Pass and were supported by the local frontier tribesmen. The British Commander, Sir Sam Browne decided to capture the Ali Masjid position. A Company of the 14TH Ferozepore Sikhs advanced against strong opposition, and were at close grips with the enemy under very heavy fire. However, there was no sign of the British turning columns, so Sir Sam Browne decided to break off this attack to avoid unnecessary casualties. The Sikhs, with 27TH Punjabis in support, were in very close contact with the enemy when they were ordered to withdraw. It was a very difficult operation, but the Sikhs, displaying great gallantry and determination, managed to break contact after dark and withdraw. Six Sikh soldiers of 14TH Ferozepore Sikhs, and six Sikh soldiers of 27TH Punjabis, were awarded the Indian Order of Merit for gallantry in the action at Ali Masjid.

Second Afghan War

Peiwar Kotal, (1878)

On 21ST November 1878, Major General Roberts and his Kurram Field Force moved up the Kurrum valley. The Afghans, 1,800 in number with 12 guns, retreated before them until they reached Peiwar Kotal, joining the existing garrison, so that 4,000 Afghans with 23 guns held the 4-mile long fortified position centred on Peiwar Kotal. Early on 28TH November 1878 the attacking force moved off to attack Peiwar Kotal. Heavy fighting developed as the troops continued to attack, making their way up the Northern side of the valley until close to the Peiwar Kotal itself. The mountain Battery followed the Infantry and opened fire on the Afghan camp and positions. The Afghan troops fled down the valley, pursued by 12TH Bengal Cavalry, while the tribesmen ran for the hills.

Six Sikh Officers and soldiers were awarded the Indian Order of Merit for their conspicuous gallantry at Peiwar Kotal.

Kabul Residency, (1879)

The British Residency was in the Bala Hissar, an ancient fortress located at Kabul, the capital of Afghanistan. On 3RD September 1879, without warning, Afghan soldiers attacked the Residency and were joined by the civilian population. British Officers and Indian troops were attacked by countless thousands of Afghan soldiers and civilians. Soon all the British Officers were dead. The Guides fought desperately, even charging out of the Residency to bayonet the crews of Artillery brought against them. The Afghans set the Residency on fire and the buildings started to collapse. All day the Afghans called upon the Guides to surrender, promising them their lives. The Guides rejected this offer and after 12 hours of fighting the few remaining men commanded by a Sikh Jemadar, Jewand Singh, fixed bayonets and charged out to their deaths. Thirty Sikh soldiers of Guides Cavalry and Infantry sacrificed their lives, and by their deeds they conferred undying honours on the Sikh nation. Over 600 Afghan dead bore witness to the heroic sacrifice of this small force.

Charasia, (1879)

The death of the British resident Sir Cavignari, resolved the government for a full invasion of the country, and punitive action against the killers of Cavignari's party. On 3RD October 1879, the Kabul Field Force began the final 36-mile march to Kabul. On the morning of 6TH October 1879 a force comprising 23RD Sikh Pioneers and 92ND Highlanders with Cavalry and 2 guns made an immediate attack on the Afghan Army blocking its road to Kabul. During the attack, it was a charge by 23RD Sikh Pioneers, which finally caused the Afghans to break. The brilliant victory of Charasia threw open the road to Kabul, gained over thirteen regular Afghan Battalions and a host of tribesmen. The courage and resource of the Sikh soldiers won the battle against great odds. Eight Sikh soldiers of 23RD Sikh Pioneers were awarded the Indian Order of Merit for gallantry at Charasiah.

Second Afghan War

Sherpur, (1879)

The British found restoring order to the Kabul region to be a difficult and dangerous task: the Afghan tribes were outraged and the Afghan forces elusive, harassing the marching British columns with long-range sniper fire. Following four days of fierce, protracted fighting around Kabul itself, Roberts took refuge in Sherpur cantonments on 14TH December, requesting reinforcements. Brigadier General Charles Gough was ordered to relieve Roberts as the siege began. Subedar Dewa Singh of 23RD Sikh Pioneers was awarded the Indian Order of Merit for conspicuous gallantry in action near Kabul on 1ST September 1879, on which occasion he led the way in a charge on one of the enemy's Sangars, which he was the first to enter, and in which two guns were captured.

Siege of Sherpur, (1879)

Sherpur was a vast rectangular enclave that enclosed a space of some five miles. It defended access to the Khyber Pass to the East. Roberts spent the first few days of the siege strengthening his defences. On 23RD December, as the British forces manned their snow-shrouded defences (heavy snowfalls had commenced on the 18TH) the Afghans began streaming toward the cantonment in their thousands, their vanguard composed mainly of ghazis (religious zealots). The Artillery fired star shell to illuminate the scene, and thousands of muzzle-flashes began to ripple along the perimeter as the defenders commenced volley fire. The Afghans attacked all four faces of the perimeter but failed to penetrate the defences. The assault slackened at about 9:30 and petered out altogether by midday. Roberts dispatched a mixed force of Infantry, Cavalry and 2 guns to sweep the area to the South and East and secure the roads leading to Kohistan and Kabul. Nearby villages and forts were destroyed, and straggling fugitive tribesmen were ferreted out of their hiding places and shot without quarter. Charles Gough arrived the following morning, after an epic and dangerous march. Roberts estimated Afghan losses at some 3,000 killed. The British suffered 5 dead and 28 wounded. The power of the tribal coalition was smashed.

Five Sikh Officers and men of 5TH Punjab Cavalry were awarded a collective Indian Order of Merit for their conspicuous gallantry in action at Latabad Pass on 2ND April 1879.

Six Sikh Officers and men of the Guides Cavalry were awarded a collective Indian Order of Merit for their conspicuous gallantry in a Cavalry charge against a large body of fanatical Khugiani Ghazis near Fatehbad on 2ND April 1879.

A Subedar Major Gurbux Singh and Sepoy Ala Singh of 2ND Sikh Infantry were awarded the Indian Order of Merit for their conspicuous gallantry in charging a band of Ghazis while under continuous enemy rifle fire, in which the Sepoy single handedly attacked several Ghazis, killing two of them.

Second Afghan War

Latabad, (1879)

Hundreds of Ghilzais surrounded a small garrison manned by 23RD Sikh Pioneers at Latabad and established a piquet within close range. Subedar Mehtab Singh led forth forty Sikh Pioneers from this piquet against the Ghilzais with great success. Subedar Mehtab Singh and Havildar Ghulab Singh were awarded the Indian Order of Merit, for their gallantry in this action.

Ahmed Khel, (1880)

On 19TH April 1880, a column commanded by Lieutenant General Sir Donald Stewart, marching from Kandahar to Kabul to help pacify the area, was attacked by Ghazi and Hazara religious fanatics about 20 miles West of Ghazni. The musketry fire of the Infantry, particularly of 2ND Sikhs, inflicted heavy casualties on the Afghan tribesmen who finally turned and fled, pursued by the Lancers. Having won the battle, the troops then attacked and occupied Ghazni. They also broke up another concentration of tribesmen at Arzu, and then, the area being relatively pacified, returned to Kabul. Nine Sikh Officers and soldiers of 19TH Bengal Lancers were awarded the Indian Order of Merit in consideration of their conspicuous gallantry at Ahmed Khel.

Maiwand, (1880)

The battle of Maiwand was one of the principal battles of the Second Afghan War. In order to prevent Ayub Khan capturing Ghazni, the British advanced to Maiwand on 27TH July, and attacked Ayub Khan. The Afghans, who numbered 25,000, outflanked and attacked the British. The British were completely routed, and were forced to fall back on Kandahar with the loss of over 1000 men. Five Sikh soldiers of 3RD Horse were awarded the Indian Order of Merit in consideration of their conspicuous gallantry in keeping off parties of the enemy's Cavalry, who were in pursuit, thus saving the lives of many wounded and exhausted men.

Kandahar, (1880)

After the disastrous defeat at Maiwand, the remnants of battle-wearied Army was forced to fall back on Kandahar with the loss of over 1000 men. Ayub Khan then laid siege to Kandahar. As soon as news of the defeat and siege reached Kabul, a force left for Kandahar on 8TH August. It attacked the Afghan Army and defeated the Afghans after fierce hand-to-hand fighting. Ayub Khan fled, leaving his Army to disperse, pursued by the British Cavalry. The Battle of Kandahar ended the Second Anglo-Afghan War. Ayub Khan had been decisively beaten. The British appointee Abdur Rahman was thus securely established, under British protection, as Emir of Afghanistan. Twenty four Sikh Officers and men of 45TH Sikhs, 1ST Punjab Cavalry, 4TH Punjab Cavalry, Guides Infantry, 2ND Sikh Infantry, 3RD Sikh Infantry, 4TH Sikh Infantry, 5TH Punjab Infantry and 4TH Royal Artillery were awarded the Indian Order of Merit in consideration of their conspicuous gallantry during the Second Afghan War.

NORTH WEST FRONTIER, 1881-1914

Between 1881 and 1914, the British had mounted twenty-two major military expeditions along the Frontier, when the First World War broke out in 1914. The Sikh soldier was not only present in the Infantry, Cavalry and the Artillery Regiments of the Imperial forces, but also in the formed Regiments of the Sikh Princely States of Patiala, Jind, Nabha, and Kapurthala. 1ST Patiala Infantry (Sikhs), Jind Regiment (Sikhs), Nabha Regiment (Sikhs), Kapurthala Regiment (Sikhs),

Hazara, (1891)

The objectives of the British operations were to assert their right to move along the crest of the Black Mountain; to inflict punishment on the clans that had recently shown hostility to a force under Sir John McQueen; and to occupy the country until complete submission had been made. The advance Northward to the Black Mountain along the Indus River from Darband commenced on 12TH March 1891 for the purpose of attacking the more important Hassanzai and Akazai villages. On 19TH March a determined attack was made on an advanced post at Ghazilot, which was held by a Company of 4TH Sikh Infantry. The Sikhs, however, defended themselves with Great Spirit till dawn, when they were able to take the offensive and give their assailants a rough handling. The brief campaign came to an end on 17TH April 1891 and within the next fortnight the tribesmen made their submission and accepted the terms imposed on them. Naik Gian Singh of 4TH Sikh Infantry was awarded the Indian Order of Merit for conspicuous gallantry during these operations.

Hunza and Nagar, (1891)

The Hunza-Nagar Expedition was ostensibly due to the defiant attitude of the Hunza and Nagar chiefs towards the British agent at Gilgit. Towards the end of the 19TH century just as Imperial troops began consolidating territory in tribal areas - these tribes began to acquire rifles and ammunition. The British suspected Russian involvement with the Rulers of the petty States on the Northern boundary of Jammu and Kashmir. The British gained control of Nagar during a battle at Nilt Nagar in 1891. Sapper Hazara Singh of Bengal Sappers and Miners, with a storming party, blew open the inner gate with gun cotton which he had placed and ignited. This point was under heavy fire from the towers flanking the gateway and from loopholes in the gate itself. Sapper Hazara Singh was awarded the Indian Order of Merit for conspicuous gallantry in this action. However his comrade in the same action, Captain Aylmer was awarded the Victoria Cross. After a fortnight's delay the cliffs beyond it were also carried by assault. Hunza and Nagar were occupied, the chief of Nagar was reinstated on making his submission, and the half-brother of the Raja of Hunza was installed as chief in place of his brother.

North - West Frontier 1881-1900

Gulistan, (1891)
The enemy were busy destroying the roads that had been recently under construction on the Samana Ridge, and constructing Sangars for the defence of the position. By April an expeditionary force was ordered to concentrate against the tribesmen. A short but fierce action was fought against the Orakzais tribe at Gulistan on 20TH April 1891, resulting in British victory with one man killed and four wounded. The Orakzais lost about 200 men and the remainder took flight. During the remainder of April and the first week of May, Orakzais territory was scoured in all directions by various detachments; the enemy was given no rest; and all opposition speedily came to an end. Sepoys Diwan Singh and Jaimal Singh of 29TH Punjabis were awarded the Indian Order of Merit for conspicuous gallantry during these operations.

Wana, (1894)
A strong military escort was allocated to the Border Commission at Wana. On 3rd November 1894, in the pitch dark, the camp at Wana was attacked by around 2,000 tribesmen. Many encountered the charging tribesmen as they came out of their tents, fighting in the dark, bayonet against sword and shield. With full daylight the General ordered out the Squadron of 1ST Punjab Cavalry in pursuit of the tribesmen. The pursuit followed the tribesmen to the Inzari Pass, leading into Mahsud country. The Cavalry were able to catch and kill some 50 tribesmen over a distance of around 11 miles. The pursuit was abandoned once it was clear that the Mahsud lashkar had dispersed leaving no worthwhile force to pursue. Daffadar Thakur Singh and Sowars Man Singh and Khanda Singh of 1ST Punjab Cavalry were awarded the Indian Order of Merit for their conspicuous gallantry at Wana.

Defence of Chitral, (1895)
In early 1895, following the death of a chieftain and conflict over the succession, a British force ended up besieged in Chitral fort. The small British garrison of the fort, which included a detachment of 88 men of 14TH Ferozepore Sikhs, was responsible for the defence of the fort for 46 days. Captain Townsend, in his report on the siege, wrote: "The spirit of 14TH Ferozepore Sikhs was our admiration; the longer the siege lasted the more eager they became to teach the enemy a lesson. There could not be finer soldiers than these men of 14TH Ferozepore Sikhs and they were our sheet anchor in the siege". In recognition of the gallant and successful defence of the fort at Chitral, His Excellency the Viceroy sanctioned a grant of six months pay to all ranks. Subedar Gurmukh Singh was appointed to the Order of British India and Subadar Major Atar Singh, Subedar Partab Singh, Naik Atar Singh and Sepoys Bhola Singh, Partab Singh and Mal Singh of 14TH Ferozepore Sikhs were awarded the Indian Order of Merit for gallantry in the defence of Chitral fort.

North - West Frontier 1881-1900

Relief of Chitral, (1895)
32ND Sikh Pioneers set out from Gilgit to cover 220 miles of very poor road to Chitral. The importance of the Sikh Pioneer's epic march was never fully recognized, most of the publicity and fame for the relief being lavished on the well-known British Regiments. The following Sikh Officers of 32ND Sikh Pioneers were awarded the Indian Order of Merit for their conspicuous gallantry in the relief of the Chitral Fort; Jemadar Sher Singh, Havildars Wadhawa Singh, Wasawa Singh, and Subedars Bhag Singh and Prem Singh.

Koragh, (1895)
Captain C. R. Ross, with Lieutenant H. J. Jones and a party of some 60 Sikhs became entrapped at Koragh on 8TH March 1895. Starting at two o'clock in the morning they rushed along, losing heavily. Ross behaved with astounding gallantry. It is related that he charged a Sangar a little off the track by himself, and killed two or three of its inmates with his revolver at close quarters. Then a stone partially stunned him and he was shot dead. Jones and seventeen Sepoys got through to the plain on the Koragh side of the defile, where two consecutive masses of charging swordsmen withered up and melted before them, teaching the Chitralis their bitter mistake in attacking Sikhs on open ground. But three more were killed, and the remaining fourteen, ten of whom, including Jones, were grievously wounded, crawled painfully into Buni at six o'clock in the morning. These fourteen men and one other were the sole survivors of the sixty soldiers who entered the Koragh defile. Lieutenant Jones was subsequently awarded the D.S.O. and each of the 14 surviving Sikhs received the Indian Order of Merit.

Maizar, (1897)
A political agent with a military escort of British Officers and Indian Sepoys rode out to Maizar, to settle a dispute between the tribal Maliks. As the escort rested under some trees, the tribals suddenly attacked them. All of the British Officers were soon wounded but the Sikh Officers nobly rose to the occasion. Subedars Naryan Singh and Sundar Singh gallantly covered their retreat, in the course of which the latter and ten of his Sepoys sacrificed their lives to enable the remainder to get clear of the village. Ten Sikh Officers and men of the Mountain Batteries were awarded the Indian Order of Merit for their conspicuous gallantry in this action. Seven Sikh Officers and men of 1ST Sikh Infantry Regiment, two Sikh Officers and men of 51ST Sikhs and two Sikh Officers and men of 55TH Rifles, who had sacrificed their lives, were awarded the posthumous Indian Order of Merit and their widows granted pensions.

North - West Frontier 1881-1900

Malakand, (1897)

In July 1897 the garrison in Malakand was alerted to a mass attack led by the 'Mad Mullah'. Although there was a fort at Malakand, many of the men were in camps outside the fort. When the alarm sounded the British Officers McRae and Taylor ran out with some Sikhs and engaged the attackers in a narrow defile, in which Taylor was killed. This action prevented the enemy from encircling the camp and cutting it off from the fort. The Sikhs held the right of the position against repeated day and night attacks between 26TH and 30TH July. A detachment of 45TH Rattray's Sikhs clashed with a fanatical tribal horde advancing on the garrison. Outnumbered by swarms of tribesmen, the Sikhs disputed every yard as they retreated back to the rest of their Regiment. They were required to make a desperate bayonet charge during the storm-laden night of 30TH, which scattered the tribesmen. It was all over by the time reinforcements arrived the next day; the tribesmen had fled back to the hills. Three Sikh Officers and men of 24TH Punjabis, two Sikh Officers and men of 35TH Sikhs, twelve Sikh Officers and men of 45TH Rattray's Sikhs, and five Sikh Officers and men of the Guides Cavalry, were awarded the Indian Order of Merit for their conspicuous gallantry in these operations.

Sargarhi, (1897)

On 12TH September 1897, a detachment of 22 men of 36TH Sikhs manned a detached, fortified, signaling post of Sargarhi. The post was surrounded by some 10,000 Afridis and Orakzais who promised the detachment safe conduct if they surrendered. The Sikhs chose to fight instead and repulsed repeated attacks for three days. The tribals set fire to the post, while the brave garrison lay dead or dying with their ammunition exhausted. Next morning the relief column reached the post and the tell tale marks of the epic fight were there for all to see. The tribals later admitted to a figure of 180 dead and many more wounded. This episode, when narrated in the British Parliament, drew from the members a standing ovation in the memory of the defenders of Saragarhi. All the 21 valiant men of this epic battle were awarded the Indian Order of Merit (posthumously) which at the time was one of the highest gallantry awards given to Indian troops. The dependants of the Saragarhi heroes were awarded 50 acres of land and 500 Rupees. Never before or since has a body of troops, that is all of them, won gallantry awards in a single action. It is indeed a singularly unique action in the annals of Indian military history. The Sikh Regiment celebrates 12TH September annually as "Sargarhi Day". The story of this battle of epic dimensions is taught to school children in France and is one of the eight stories of collective bravery published by UNESCO.

North - West Frontier 1881-1900

Chakdara Fort, (1897)

Defence of Chakdara Fort by six British Officers and 240 Indian soldiers of the 45TH Sikhs and 11TH Bengal Lancers against 14,000 Pathan tribesmen, must rank as one of the greatest feats of arms in military history. Eventually there was tremendous execution of the tribals at Chakdara Fort. Naik Channan Singh of 45TH Sikhs and Naik Arjan Singh of 11TH Bengal Lancers were awarded Indian Order of Merit for their conspicuous gallantry at the Chakdara Fort.

Fort Gulistan, (1897)

At the time of the Afridi incursion into the Khyber and Samana ranges, 165 men of 36TH Sikhs occupied the Fort. The attackers had got up to within 20 yards of the walls and had built stone Sangars for cover during the night. Havildar Kala Singh volunteered to take 16 men to attack a Sangar. As they charged towards the Sangar, heavy fire forced them to the ground. Havildar Sunder Singh, without waiting for orders, took 11 men to help them. A concerted effort was made and the Sangar was reached. They drove out the tribesmen capturing three enemy standards in the process, and it is said that the three sections of the tribesmen represented by these standards went off to their homes. Of the 29 men who had taken part in this action, 14 were wounded, three of them fatally. One of these three was Havildar Kala Singh, the original volunteer, who died on 15TH September. Gulistan was continuously under attack from about 8000 Pathans. The relieving force reached Gulistan at 1 pm on 14TH September 1897, thus ending the siege. The 36TH Sikhs had been under continuous fire since 9 am on 12TH, a total of 52 hours, suffering 44 men killed or wounded. For their stout-hearted defence of these posts 36TH Sikhs were later awarded the Battle Honour 'Samana', a distinction held by no other Regiment, British or Indian. Twenty-nine Sikh Officers and men of 36TH Sikhs were awarded the Indian Order of Merit for their conspicuous gallantry at Ft.Cavagnari.

Shabkadr, (1897)

In August 1897, the Mohmands, inspired by the Mullah of Hadda, Najib-ud-din, attacked the village of Shankargarh some 18 miles North of Peshawar. Most of the villagers had taken refuge in the Shabkadr fort and the Mohmands, who numbered about four to five thousand, made a planned assault on the fort. The fort stood on a mound and had 50 ft. high walls. It was held by a detachment of Border Police, who managed to repel that first attack. The 13TH Bengal Lancers went to the relief of Shabkadr fort and chased the Mohmands back to the hills. Daffadar Sewa Singh and Sowar Hira Singh of 13TH Bengal Lancers were awarded the Indian Order of Merit for their conspicuous gallantry against the Mohmands.

North - West Frontier 1881-1900

Bajaur, (1897)

Afghanistan's Kunar Province bordered the district of Bajaur on the North West Frontier of India. The district was of strategic importance to British India. The Army constantly patrolled the district to stem cross-border raids by the tribals at Badmani, Bilot, Inyat Killa, and Darbur. Three Sikh Officers and men of 11TH Bengal Lancers, two Sikh Officers and men of 8TH Mountain Battery, and three Sikh Officers and men of 35TH Sikhs were awarded the Indian Order of Merit for their conspicuous gallantry against the raiders.

Dargai, (1897)

There were some 12,000 Afridis on the heights of Dargai in strongly built Sangars, their standards bravely mocking the troops far below. Covered by the divisional Artillery and despite heroic efforts, the attackers had to take cover in dead ground. The Gurkhas were the first to attack but were pinned down at the base of the cliffs. The Dorset Regiment followed a couple of hours later and was also pinned down. Then occurred one of the most famous attacks on the Frontier. The Gordon Highlanders and 3RD Sikhs stormed the Dargai Heights. With bayonets glinting in the bright sunlight, they charged across the glacis, past the trapped Gurkhas and Dorsets, and on, up the narrow twisting path, scrambling ever higher towards the muzzle flashes in the Sangars, while all the way, above the shouts and yells, the crash and the rattle of musketry, the pipes screamed their ancient rant with the Sikh cries of "Khalsa! Khalsa! Sat Siri Akal" The Afridis knew it was time to go and everywhere gave way and ran. Soon the Highlanders and the Sikhs crowned the heights and Dargai was won.

Subedar Lehna Singh, Jemadar Mit Singh, Lance Naik Jai Singh, Sepoy Davi Singh, Sepoy Magar Singh of 3RD Sikh Infantry with Havildar Bogga Singh, Jemadar Kaka Singh of 14TH Ferozepore Sikhs and Jemadar Waryam Singh, Havildar Bela Singh, Sepoys Bhola Singh, Kishan Singh, Amar Singh and Bishan Singh of 15TH Ludhiana Sikhs were awarded Indian Order of Merit for conspicuous gallantry at Dargai.

Tirah, (1897)

During the summer of 1897, along the Northwest Frontier of India, various tribes fielded a force of close to fifty thousand men to harass and destroy British forts and villages. When they captured the Khyber Pass in August, the British Government decided they must be removed. The Army immediately fielded two Divisions to engage them. The campaign in Tirah employed by far the largest force in a Frontier Expedition. There was some hard fighting at the Khaibar Pass, Tseri Kando, Maidan, and Arhanga Pass. Naik Ganga Singh, Gunner Hira Singh, Driver Mehtab Singh of 2ND Mountain Battery and Hon. Lt. Phuman Singh, Subedar Hira Singh, Naik Gulab Singh, Naik Kirpal Singh of 15TH Ludhiana Sikhs was awarded the Indian Order of Merit for their conspicuous gallantry at Tirah in 1897.

NORTH-EAST FRONTIER

North-East India had been added to India during the British Raj, when British colonial authorities annexed traditionally separate Border States into Indian Territory, to form a buffer between their dominion and external powers. The annexation of the Border States was carried out by the formed Regiments of the Indian Army that included 5TH Regiment Native Infantry, 14TH Bengal Cavalry, 19TH Punjabis and 44TH Regiment of Light Infantry. The defence was entrusted to locally raised para military police forces that recruited Sikhs and other Punjabis in considerable numbers.

According to tradition, Sikhs came to Assam on an invitation from the Ahom (king) to defend Assamese liberty against the Burmese. King Viswanarayan sought Maharaja Ranjit Singh's help against the Burmese Army. Accordingly, Maharaja Ranjit Singh dispatched 500 Sikh soldiers under the leadership of General Chetan Singh to Assam. The Sikhs fought in a pitched engagement at Hadirachaki and many paid the supreme sacrifice. After defeating the Burmese, those who survived did not return to the Punjab. They married Assamese women and identified themselves as Assamese Sikhs.

During the Anglo-Burma War of 1824-26, the British conquered lower Assam and formally annexed it to British India. The following year they defeated the Burmese in upper Assam, leading to the Treaty of Yandaboo. In March 1828, at the death of King Govinda Chandra, the British annexed the Kachari kingdom under the Doctrine of Lapse. In 1832, they occupied the territories of the Khasi king and increased their influence over the Jaintia ruler. In 1833, upper Assam became a British protectorate under the erstwhile ruler of the kingdom, Purandhar Singh, but in 1838, the region was formally annexed to the British Empire. The growth of industry and other commercial interests prompted the adoption of a more acquisitive policy, leading in time to the annexation of Naga, Lushai and Chin territory in particular. Tribal feuds, murders and minor raids, as well as attacks on Army and Frontier Police outposts, were almost continuous throughout the British stay. The expeditions against the hill tribes are too numerous to be listed here except to say that there were at least 37 expeditions from 1862 to 1900, and the Sikh soldier was in the vanguard of these operations.

North East Frontier, (1865-1891)

Risaldar Charan Singh, Sowar Darshan Singh, Sowar Bhurt Singh of 14^{Th} Bengal Cavalry and Havildar Prem Singh and Naik Hira Singh of 19TH Punjabis were awarded the Indian Order of Merit in consideration of their conspicuous gallantry during the Bhutan expedition of 1865. Sepoy Narian Singh of 5TH Native Infantry was awarded the Order of Merit during the Manipur expedition of 1866. Naik Bughet Singh of 44TH Light Infantry was awarded the Order of Merit during the Lushai expedition of 1871. Subedar Amar Singh of YEU Battalion was awarded the Order of Merit in action at Mona on 27TH April 1891 during the Anglo-Manipur War.

BURMA

The First Anglo-Burmese War, (1824)

The First Anglo-Burmese War ended in a British East India Company victory, and by the Treaty of Yandaboo, Burma lost territory previously conquered in Assam, Manipur, Tenasserim, and Arakan. As the century wore on, the British East India Company began to covet the resources and main part of Burma during an era of great territorial expansion.

Second Anglo-Burmese War, (1852)

In 1852, the Viceroy of India, Lord Dalhousie, dispatched Commodore Lambert to Burma to deal with a number of minor issues related to the previous treaty. Lambert eventually provoked a naval confrontation in extremely questionable circumstances and thus started the Second Anglo-Burmese War in 1852. The invading force detailed for the invasion included a Regiment of Ludhiana Sikhs and 4TH Sikh Local Infantry; they were extensively employed in the operations.

Third Anglo-Burmese War, (1885)

As a consequence of the Second Anglo-Burmese War, Burma's foreign policy was effectively determined by the British Resident. The Burmese, highly uncomfortable with this situation, entered into communication with the Italians and the French and provided the excuse for the British to act. Sikh soldiers of the Punjab Mountain Battery, Bombay Mountain Battery, 4TH Bengal Infantry, 27TH Bengal Infantry, Bengal Sappers and Miners, and 15TH Sikhs had taken a prominent part during the War.

Unrest continued in the Northern tribal areas and the British had to mount constant expeditions in the tribal areas including; Chin Lushai Expedition 1889, Chin Hills Expedition 1892, Kachin Hills Expedition 1892, and Kachin Hills Expedition 1895.

Havildar Sripal Singh, Havildar Mohan Singh, of 4TH Bengal Infantry, Sapper Kala of Bengal Sappers and Miners and Havildar Mangal Singh of 27TH Bengal Infantry were awarded the Indian Order of Merit in consideration of their conspicuous gallantry during the Third Anglo-Burmese War.

Subedar Ratan Singh, Subedar Amar Singh, of 8TH Bengal Infantry, Havildar Kirpal Singh, Jemadar Kahan Singh of 5TH Punjab Cavalry and Jemadar Mangal Singh of 21ST Bengal Infantry were awarded the Indian Order of Merit in consideration of their conspicuous gallantry during the Chin Lushai Expedition of 1889.

Burma Military Police at the end of 1888 included 3,937 Sikhs. The Military Police Battalions were organized like regular Army Regiments and their duties were entirely military. In 1893, nine Sikhs of the Burma Military Police were awarded the Indian Order of Merit in consideration of their conspicuous gallantry in the defence of Sima Post at Palap.

TIBET

In May 1841, the 5000 strong Dogra Army in service of the Sikh Kingdom, advanced Eastwards in three Divisions. Overcoming all the Tibetan and Chinese opposition it set up base at Taklakot in September 1841, after traversing a distance of 450 miles from the Indian frontier. With the onset of severe winter and the lack of provisions, they were overcome by a Sino-Tibetan force on 12TH December 1841. The Tibetans and their Chinese allies then invaded Ladakh but were defeated at the Battle of Chushul. The boundary between Ladakh and Tibet was finally settled by the Treaty of Chushul. At the fall of the Sikh Kingdom, when Britain sold Kashmir to Gulab Singh, they informed the Chinese of their suzerainty over Kashmir and suggested that the Sino - Sikh treaty be amended. The Sino - Sikh treaty was consequently redrafted in August 1846 as desired by the British. Tibet was a vital geographic location; it had served as a springboard for the invasion of Nepal and a threat as a base for attacking India. In 1793 a Chinese Army of over 70,000 men had crossed the Himalaya Mountains from Tibet into Nepal on the Indian side, via the Kirong Pass and had dealt a crushing defeat on the Nepalese near their capital. With this understanding the British knew Tibet could be used as a penetrable frontier to attack India and so it could not allow Tibet to be acquired by any hostile power. If Britain's great rival, Russia, was allowed to establish herself in the rich valley of Lhasa or exert influence in the region, then it would have far-reaching political effects all along the British Eastern frontier for over a thousand miles, in the North from Ladakh to Kashmir and in the South from Nepal to Assam. This could have also possibly led to a combination of Himalayan states siding with Russia against British India. It could prove militarily costly for Britain, who would have to go to enormous lengths to ensure that the Eastern frontier was fortified and that the standing Army would have to be substantially increased.

In December 1903 the British marched over the Himalayas to Tibet to counter a non-existent Russian threat. A medieval Tibetan Army confronted them. It was a clash between the mightiest political power in the world at that time, armed with Maxim guns and Lee Enfield rifles, and one of the weakest. 23RD Sikh Pioneers Regiment supplied the main fighting force, supported by Units of 32ND Sikh Pioneers. Both Regiments were veterans of frontier Warfare but unusual in that they fought with a pick-axe in one hand and a rifle in the other, a dual role combining the duties of a Pioneer Regiment with that of Fighting Infantry. The Sikh Pioneers endured terrible weather conditions, including crossing the Kangra-La Mountain at 17,500 feet. The world record of high altitude Warfare established by the Sikh Pioneers at the battles of Karo lasted for the best part for ninety years. It has certainly been broken by 15TH Punjab (Patiala) Battalion, at the unique, high altitude battle of Zojila, against Pakistan.

Tibet

The Sikh Pioneers

The two Sikh Pioneer Regiments that played a prominent role in the Tibet Mission, were veterans of frontier Warfare but unusual in that they fought with a pick-axe in one hand and a rifle in the other, having been raised to take on a dual role combining the duties of a Pioneer Regiment with that of Fighting Infantry. The present mission was the third 'show' on which 23RD and 32ND had been together during the last nine years. In Chitral and Waziristan, they fought side by side. It is no exaggeration to say that these Regiments had been on active service three years out of five since they were raised in 1857. The original draft of the 32ND, it will be remembered, was the unarmed volunteer corps of Mazbi Sikhs, who offered themselves as an escort to the convoy from Lahore to Delhi during the siege. The Mazbis were the most lawless and refractory folk in the Punjab, and had long been the despair of the Government. On arrival at Delhi, they were employed in the trenches, rushing in to fill up the places of the killed and wounded as fast as they fell. A detachment of them carried out and laid the powder-bags to blow in the Kashmir Gate, which led to the fall of the city. The whole detachment of nineteen men, were killed or wounded. A hundred and fifty-seven of them were killed during the siege. With this brilliant opening it is no wonder that they had been on active service almost continually since.

A frontier campaign would be incomplete without 32ND or 23RD. It was 32ND who made a great name for themselves in 1895 at the lifting of the siege of Chitral, when they forced a path through five feet of snow over the Shandur Pass to bring the guns through. The 23RD Pioneers were also raised from the Mazbi Sikhs in the same year of the Mutiny, 1857. The history of the two Regiments is very similar. The 23RD distinguished themselves in China, Abyssinia, Afghanistan, and numerous frontier campaigns. They had distinguished themselves in recent frontier operations against the Utman Khel, the Afridis, the Wazirs, and the Mahsuds. One of the most brilliant exploits was when, with the Gordon Highlanders under Major (later Sir George) White, they captured the Afghan guns at Kandahar. Both these Regiments had been employed on every kind of military duty as Pioneers, Engineers, Infantry soldiers, Artillerymen, and now they had added one more branch of the service to their long list of experiences, and proved themselves as good mounted Infantrymen as they were Pioneers.

The men of the two Regiments met again as members of the same corps on the Lingmathang Plain. Naturally, the most cordial relations existed between the men, and one could hear the veterans discussing old campaigns as they sat round their pinewood fires in the evenings.

Tibet

Military Force

Younghusband's mission was expanded into a full scale military force consisting of 23RD and 32ND Sikh Pioneers and 8TH Gurkhas with sixty-five Mounted Infantry, formed from the above Regiments. Soon the Mounted Infantry was to be raised to one hundred strong, with ten more men from 23RD Pioneers and sixteen from 32ND under the command of Jemadar Prem Singh. Three more Sikh Officers were sent for from India i.e. Subedar Sangat Singh, Jemadar Hazara Singh and Jemadar Thakur Singh. By early December, it was poised at the Jelap La Pass, the 14,000 foot entrance into Tibet, the "roof of the world". To the hazards of travel over some of the roughest and highest terrain in the world, was added sub-zero winter cold. Conditions were frightful. Rifle-bolts froze into the breaches and subalterns kept the Maxims' bolts warm in their own beds. The troops' clothing, though lavish by the standards of those days, offered no real protection and was, in addition, too bulky to allow free movement for firing.

"The Mounted Infantry – a jolly, swashbuckling crew who regarded themselves as a *corps d'elite* – were to prove invaluable in reconnaissance and demoralizing pursuit." (Fleming)

Guru, March, (1904)

On March 31ST, 1904, the British reached the Tibetan fortifications and presently 23RD Pioneers and 8TH Gurkhas now proceeded to clear the Sangars. It was, however, impossible for the British column to advance with a large armed force encamped right across the road. The Tibetans were accordingly informed that they must either retire or give up their arms. They showed no intention of doing either, and Younghusband ordered the Sikhs to disarm the Tibetans. As Sikhs disarmed the Tibetans, a Tibetan General, who in a sudden impulse of anger at seeing the Tibetans being disarmed, drew his pistol and blew off the jaw of the Sikh Sepoy who was taking the arms. Fighting broke out instantly. Volley after volley of British bullets crashed into the solid mass of Tibetans. There were certainly 1,500 Tibetans and had they not been fired on promptly, they would have rushed on and easily cut up the 150 Sikh Sepoys confronting them. On the outbreak of the firing, the Tibetans in the Sangars on the hill began throwing stones and firing on the Sikhs and 2ND Mounted Infantry, and then the fight became general. Suddenly the Tibetans turned and fled with the Sikhs, with the two Companies of Mounted Infantry, in hot pursuit. Guru village was rushed and cleared and as they retreated along the Gyantse road, they were pursued for twelve miles and thoroughly dispersed. The Tibetans numbered 2,000; half of them were regular soldiers, armed with matchlocks. They left 628 killed and wounded on the field, and 222 prisoners.

Tibet

Karola, May, (1904)

On May 3RD, a column that included 32ND Pioneers, and a detachment of Mounted Infantry, marched up the pass and encamped about two miles from where the Tibetans had built their wall. A reconnaissance that afternoon estimated the enemy at 2,000, and they were holding the strongest position on the road to Lhasa. They had built a wall the whole length of a narrow spur and up the hill on the other side of the stream, and in addition held detached Sangars high up the steep hills. Their flanks rested on very high and nearly precipitous rocks. The fire from the wall was very heavy and the advance of Cullen's and Bethune's Companies was checked. Then compelled by some fatal impulse, Bethune with half a Company, left the cover of the riverbed and rushed out into the open, within forty yards of the main wall, exposed to a withering fire from three sides. Bethune fell, shot through the head. It was a gallant, reckless charge against uncounted odds. The frontal and flanking attacks had failed.

Bethune and seventeen men were killed. The guns had made no impression on their wall and a large reinforcement of at least 500 men came up to join the enemy. The situation was critical. When the front attack had failed, fifteen men of 32ND were sent up the hill. The party, led by Subedar Wasant Singh, scaled the 'almost perpendicular face of the 1,500-foot Southern scarp'. Subedar Wasant Singh's gallant section poured down deadly rifle fire on the Sangar. Twice the Tibetans rushed out, and, coming under a heavy Maxim fire, bolted back again. The third time they fled in mass, while the Maxims mowed down about thirty. The capture of the Sangars was a signal for a general stampede of the Tibetans. From the position they had won the Sikhs could enfilade the main wall itself. The Tibetans on the wall turned and fled in three huge bodies down the valley. Thus, the fifteen Sikhs on the right saved the situation and Subedar Wasant Singh and Sepoy Bhagwan Singh were awarded the Indian Order of Merit for their conspicuous gallantry. Directly the flight began, the Mounted Infantry poured into the valley and harassed the flying masses, riding on their flanks and pursuing them for ten miles to within sight of the Yamdok Tso. It showed extraordinary courage on the part of this little band of Sikhs and Gurkhas. They did not hesitate to hurl themselves on the flanks of the enormous body of men, like terriers on the heels of a flock of sheep, though they had had experience of their stubborn resistance the whole day long. They rode through the bodies of their fallen comrades. Not a man drew rein. The Tibetans were caught in a trap. The hills that sloped down to the valley afforded them little cover. Their fate was only a question of time and ammunition. The mounted Infantry returned at night with only three casualties, having killed over 300 men. The sortie to the Karo La was one of the most brilliant episodes of the campaign. On 23RD, the force marched out for India.

Twelve Sikh soldiers were awarded the Indian Order of Merit in consideration of their conspicuous gallantry during the Tibetan operations.

CHINA

First Anglo-Chinese War, (1842)

Until the 18TH century, opium use in China had consisted mostly of medicinal purposes. By the early 1800s, however, millions of Chinese had become addicted to opium and the illegal drug thrived through black market trade. The main purveyors of opium were the British. In Canton in March, 1839, the Emperor's special emissary, Lin Zexu, took swift action against the foreign merchants and their Chinese accomplices, making some 1,600 arrests and confiscating 11,000 pounds of opium. Despite attempts by the British to negotiate a compromise, in June, Lin ordered the seizure another 2,000 crates of opium from foreign-controlled factories, holding all foreign merchants under arrest until they surrendered nine million dollars worth of opium, which he then burned publicly. Finally, he ordered the port of Canton closed to all foreign merchants. The situation escalated until the British declared War on China in November 1839.

In August 1842, the Treaty of Nanjing officially ended the brutal War. Under the terms of the Treaty China ceded the island of Hong Kong to Great Britain, and opened five "Treaty" ports (Canton, Amoy, Foochow, Shanghai, and Ningbo) to Western trade.

Second Anglo-Chinese War, (1860)

In the 1850s the Western Powers sought to renegotiate their commercial treaties with China. The British wanted the opening of all of China to merchants, legalization of the opium trade and exemption of import tariffs. The Qing Government refused and relations deteriorated when a Hong Kong vessel "Arrow" was boarded by the Chinese, and there was an attempt to poison Europeans in Hong Kong. The French were drawn in following the execution of a missionary and the Russians and Americans also made representations. Finally a combined British and French force was despatched against the Chinese.

The British attacking force gathered in Hong Kong, under Lieutenant General Sir J. Hope Grant, consisting of 4 Infantry Brigades of British and Indian troops that included the Sikh soldiers of 15TH Ludhiana Sikhs, 23RD Sikh Pioneers, 20TH Punjab Regiment and 27TH Punjab Infantry. The Cavalry Brigade included Probyn's Horse and Fane's Horse. Both Regiments were raised during the Sepoy mutiny from the disbanded soldiers of the Khalsa armies of the Sikh Kingdom. In all, there were 11,000 British and Indian troops, plus 6,000 French troops. 1ST Sikh Cavalry (Probyn's Horse) consisted of 446 men and Fane's Horse 352 men. The British expedition landed at Odin Bay on 1ST August, 1860, and went into action against the Chinese more or less straightaway.

China

Sinho, (1860)
The Chinese forces encountered during this campaign were, with the exception of the troops holding Taku Forts, composed almost entirely of Tartar Cavalry, mounted on small hardy horses. They were very fast and capable of great endurance. The Tartar horsemen were nearly all Mongols of fine appearance, especially enrolled for the service of their clansman the Emperor. On 14TH August Probyn's Horse armed with the lance for the first time, fought an action around Sinho, against Tartar Cavalry. Probyn's casualties at this stage were two Officers, two Sergeants and two rank and file wounded. Sowar Muttah Singh was wounded in the chest and later died.

Peking, (1860)
When the Anglo-French forces, entered Peking on 6TH October, the Emperor Xianfeng fled the capital, leaving his brother, Prince Gong, to be in charge of negotiations. After Parkes and the surviving diplomatic prisoners were freed, Lord Elgin ordered the Summer Palaces destroyed, starting on 18TH October. Peking was not occupied; the Anglo-French Army remained outside the city. The destruction of the Forbidden City was discussed, as proposed by Lord Elgin, to discourage the Chinese from using kidnapping as a bargaining tool, and to exact revenge on the mistreatment of their prisoners. Elgin's decision was motivated by the torture and murder of almost twenty Western prisoners, including two British envoys and a journalist for The Times. The Russian envoy Count Ignatiev and the French diplomat Baron Gros settled on the burning of the Summer Palaces instead, since it was "least objectionable" and would not jeopardize the treaty signing. After emperor Xianfeng and his entourage had fled Peking, the emperor's brother, Prince Yixin, ratified the Treaty of Tianjin in the Convention of Peking on 18TH October 1860, ending the Second Chinese War. China not only had to pay further reparations to France and Britain but also cede the port of Kowloon to Great Britain.

What had begun as a conflict of interests between English desire for profits from the trade in silk, porcelain, and tea and the Confucian ideal of self-sufficiency and exclusion of corrupting influences resulted in the partitioning of China by the Western powers (including the ceding of Hong Kong to Great Britain), humiliating defeats on land and sea by technologically and logistically superior Western forces, and the traditional values of an entire culture undermined by Christian missionaries and rampant trading in Turkish and Indian opium. No wonder the Boxer rebels' chief goal was to purify and reinvigorate their nation by the utter annihilation of all "foreign devils."

China

Boxer Rebellion, (1900)

In 1900, the Boxers, a xenophobic movement in China, carried out a series of attacks on foreign missionaries, merchants and property. The Chinese government did little to remedy the situation, and in June 1900 issued an edict, which amounted to support for the Boxers. The foreign legations in the Imperial capital Peking (Beijing) were besieged by the Boxers, and held out for three months despite having a small garrison. An international relief force was organised by eight nations, and in June 1900 the Taku Forts were captured. The force then moved on Peking, which was captured in August. Eventually peace was concluded in January 1901.

The only Cavalry that was of any use was that from the Indian Army; the Japanese had only a Cavalry Régiment, so poor in quality that only 60 horses out of 400 reached Peking! All the work was carried out by the Indian troops. Upon arriving at Yang Tsun, the allies were attacked by the rebels. In the Battle of Yang Tsun, the post of honor in the fighting was taken by a Company of Sikhs (24TH Punjab Infantry) and a Regiment of Americans, who raced each other over a plateau of 5000 yards, exposed to a fierce hail of shell and rifle fire, to occupy a formidable entrenched position. Then the order was given to fix bayonets, and a simultaneous charge was made, immense slaughter being inflicted upon the Chinese. The battle culminated in a brilliant charge of the Sikhs and American forces. Simultaneously the Sikhs and 14TH American Regiment occupied Yang Tsun. Finally the relief force of more than 3000 soldiers from Sikh Regiments advanced to the legations, lifting the siege, which eventually paved the way for the occupation of Beijing. The siege was over after 55 days. The Boxer Protocol of 7TH September 1901 ended the uprising and provided for severe punishments, including an indemnity of 67 million pounds, more than the government's annual tax revenue, to be paid over a course of thirty-nine years to the eight nations involved. Over 200 people had been killed and wounded in the legations; in the country itself 30,000 Christian Chinese were killed by the Boxers. Two weeks after, a siege victory parade was held, marching through the city. Later some of the Boxers who had been captured were beheaded in public. The Ch, I Nien, hall of annual prayers, was at the Temple of Heaven, where the Chinese Emperor would pray for a good harvest. After the siege, Sikh Infantry posed here with their British Officers.

Lance Naik Lehna Singh and Naik Dial Singh of 24TH Punjab Infantry were awarded the Indian Order of Merit for their conspicuous gallantry during the boxer rebellion.

MALAYA

Sikh Police

The 'proud Sikh soldier' and his various attributes prompted British administrators of Malaya and the Straits Settlements to consider the Sikhs as an appropriate racial category to recruit from for the para - military policing needs of the Malayan Native States and the Straits Settlements. In 1873, Captain Speedy recruited 110 Sikhs from the Patiala, Ludhiana and Ferozepur districts of the Punjab for service in Perak (in Malaysia). This band was known as the Perak Armed Police and by 1888, under one Captain Walker, the group had grown and came to be known as 1ST Perak Sikhs. The success of these early recruits prompted the British to recruit more Sikhs for service in Selangor, Negri Sembilan and Pahang, where the original police forces were largely Sikhs. They came as the lawmen to guard the mines and keep law and order during the intense gang fights between the various Chinese mining clans.

Malay States Guides*

The need for Malay States force to deal with bushfire Wars in the Peninsula, clearly demanded unification under a purely military command, and separation from the ordinary police, and this was affected in 1896. The new force, The Malay States Guides, was raised by Walker from the Sikh forces of the four states, between July and October 1896; in November it consisted of 9000 NCO'S and men, with Walker as their first Colonel. At the same time, the police forces of the states, consisting of Malays and the remaining Sikhs, were placed under a Federal Commission of Police, with Deputy Commissioners or Superintendents in the states. The dual organisation of the police had resulted in Units not fully effective as either police or soldiers, and thus came to an end. It is to be noted the Perak Sikhs were the core of the Malay States Guides, and were earlier established and best trained for a military role.

Upto 1900, fourteen Sikh soldiers had lost their lives fighting during the various punitive actions in Malaya.

In 1894 Ram Singh was awarded the Imperial Service Medal for his bravery during the desperate fighting at Kuala Tembling. The Malays had attacked the stockade at Kuala Tembling, which was manned by 11 Sikh Police Officers, killing five Sikh Police Officers. Ram Singh suffered more than thirty wounds and yet had managed to fight his way out to reach Pulau Tawar for reinforcements.

*During the First World War the Malay States Guides joined the Aden Defence Force in 1915. They were almost continuously in contact with the Turks, with frequent engagements. The Regiment was disbanded in late 1919.

ABYSSINIA 1868

The British 1868 Expedition to Abyssinia was a punitive expedition carried out by armed forces of the British Empire against the Ethiopian Empire. Emperor Tewodros II of Ethiopia, also known as "Theodore," imprisoned several missionaries and two representatives of the British government in an attempt to get the attention of the British government, which had been ignoring his requests for military assistance. The British despatched 13,000 well-equipped United Kingdom and Indian troops from Bombay, led by Sir Robert Napier.

The advance force landed at Annesley Bay, on 21ST October 1867, and the main force on 2ND January 1868. With the co-operation of the local ruler of Tegray, it proceeded inland, across 250 miles (402 km) of mountainous country, toward the emperor's fortress of Magdala. At the decisive battle of Aroge (Apogee), a detachment of 23RD Sikh Pioneers charged forward and met the enemy in close combat. The Abyssinian courage could not stand up to the Sikh bayonets and they were beaten off with very heavy losses.

The battle had been all along the Apogee Valley. The Abyssinians were in rapid retreat, and the blood of the Sikhs was fairly up. They fixed Bayonets and charged with cold steel, with which they were doing fearful execution, having penned their antagonists into one of the ravines running down from the heights of Selassie and Fahla.

After the crushing defeat at Apogee, the British, using cannon, breech-loading rifles, and rockets, inflicted immense casualties on Tewodros poorly equipped forces. Their dead included the emperor's childhood friend Fitawrari Gabreye. Tewodros then released his European prisoners, and sued, unsuccessfully, for peace. British forces thereupon stormed Magdala on 13TH April. After an opening bombardment by British mountain guns, the Infantry provided covering fire for the Engineers to approach the gates. A storming party of Engineers arrived at the gate under fire, only to realize that they had forgotten their explosives. In the confusion, a soldier of 33RD Regiment found an alternative entrance. Enough soldiers managed to climb over a wall that they were able to overpower the defenders at the gate and allow the main assault force into the fortress and found that Tewodros had committed suicide. The remainder of King Theodore's forces were rounded up and the fortress was cleared out. A few days later, the Engineers destroyed the gates; the remainder of any ammunition and the city was torched and looted, before leaving the country.

Subedar Major Natha Singh, Subedar Kharak Singh and Sepoys Futteh Singh, Jowala Singh and Khushal Singh of 23RD Sikh Pioneers were awarded the Indian Order of Merit in consideration of their conspicuous gallantry. They were the only gallantry awards made to the Indian soldiers in this expedition.

EGYPT 1882

The importance of Egypt to Britain rose dramatically after the opening of the Suez Canal in 1869. At a stroke, there was a new route from Europe to the Far East that halved the journey time between Britain and India. Egypt passed through various phases of fortune until the year 1876. In this year the extravagance of the Khedive, Ismail Pasha, had brought the country to the verge of bankruptcy and the unfortunate inhabitants were the victims of an extortionate taxation and corrupt system of justice. Pressure was accordingly brought to bear on the Khedive by the two Powers most interested in the country, England and France, and a dual control was established. In 1879 Ismail was deposed by the Sultan at the request of the above Powers, and Tawfiq appointed the Khedive in his stead. In 1881 as a protest against the way in which all the higher appointments in the Army were given to Turks instead of native Egyptian Officers, a military revolt broke out in Cairo, headed by Colonel Ahmed Bey Arabi. In consequence of the military revolt it was decided in July 1882 to despatch a British expedition to that country that included an Indian contingent of 7,000.

At Tel-el-Kebir, the Egyptian Army had prepared defences consisting of a number of deep ditches and embankments constructed out of the desert sand. The British attacked the Egyptian entrenchments at the first gleam of dawn. As the Mountain Battery came into action the Infantry advanced by rushes, drove the enemy from their entrenchments on the South bank, and captured four guns. The whole line now advanced, driving the enemy before it and capturing his guns. The Cavalry were pushed forward to cut off the fugitives who were soon pouring into the village of Tel-el-Kebir from the Northern side. Once Tel-el-Kebir was in British hands, a number of Infantry and Cavalry Divisions moved off to secure other positions. These included a triumphant march on Cairo on 14TH September. It was soon seen that the Egyptians had decided to capitulate. A small party of Cavalry occupied the citadel; 10,000 of the enemy had surrendered their arms and started for their own homes. Arabi and his associates were taken prisoner, court-martialed, and exiled to Sri Lanka; Khedive Tawfiq was restored to power. The War was effectively over and Egypt became a British protectorate.

During these operations, Sepoy Surain Singh earned the Indian Order of Merit for conspicuous gallantry against the enemy while Lance Daffadar Aussan Singh was specially brought to notice for his gallant conduct.

SUDAN 1885

The Sudan Campaign was fought between a radical group of Moslem dervishes, called Mahdists, who had over-run much of Sudan, and the British and Egyptian forces who nominally controlled the government of the region. They had long held most of the population in subjugation, and now either made alliances with or massacred the native tribes in the region. In a short time, the Mahdists, who opposed not only the infidel British, but also the secular Egyptian government, controlled much of Sudan. The Mahdist Warriors were fanatical, brutal, and nearly fearless, and much of Sudan fell under their influence out of sheer terror. The British Government placed General Sir G. Graham in command of a strong force collected at Suakin, with instructions to destroy the power of the Osman Digna and to occupy the Hadendowa territory.

The Indian contingent of 3,000 men included Sikh soldiers of the following Regiments; 15TH Ludhiana Sikhs, and 9TH Bengal Cavalry,

Battle of Tofrek, (1885)

The British force and Indian Contingent marched from Suakin towards Tamai, to build three Zaribas at Tofrek. While still unfinished, they were heavily attacked by Arabs of the Hadendoa tribe. In one action 17TH Bengal Infantry broke and retreated. On the retreat of 17TH Bengal Infantry, the Arabs stampeded the animals collected to the left of that Regiment and swarmed into the Berkshire Regiments *Zareba*, stabbing and cutting everywhere. Large bodies of the enemy rushed round in every direction, charging on the fence with the utmost courage, and intervening between *Zarebas* and the transport animals. They destroyed an enormous number of the latter. The Berkshires were pursued by the yelling Arabs. Fortunately the Sikh outposts kept their heads and retired steadily and in good order, which just gave the Berkshires time to reach safety. Even so, a few of the slower ones would have been overtaken, had not a very gallant Sikh Subedar turned back single handed, and killed several of their pursuers with his sword.

"Two soldiers of the Berkshires were saved from certain death by the magnificent daring of Subedar Gurdit Singh of 15TH Ludhiana Sikhs, who, placing himself between the pursuers and their prey, killed three Arabs in |succession by rapid sword cuts." (*Frontier and Overseas Expeditions*)

Resaidar Hookum Singh, Lance Daffadar Indhur Singh, Lance Daffadar Poourn Singh, and Trumpeter Kaiser Singh of 9TH Bengal Cavalry were awarded the Indian Order of Merit in consideration of their conspicuous gallantry during the operations.

For political reasons the withdrawal of the troops from Sudan was ordered on 11TH May 1885; and nothing was achieved!

EAST AFRICA 1895

The Imperial British East Africa Company (IBEAC) received a royal charter in 1888 to exploit the region of the Great Lakes in Central Africa and take over the British concessions negotiated with the Sultan of Zanzibar. The British also occupied Kismayu in Jubaland. When the Company collapsed in 1895, Britain declared a Protectorate over the Company's East African territories. It covered present day Kenya and the land west of the Juba River. The Protectorate's soldiers, consisting of Sudanese, Sikhs and locally recruited tribesmen in equal number, were formed as the East African Rifles. The first commandant of East African Rifles was Major Hatch, with headquarters at Fort Jesus, Mombasa. Major Hatch suggested that in view of the troubled state of the coast, 300 trained troops from a Punjab Regiment be recruited for East Africa. The establishment authorised in 1895 allowed for 300 Sikhs, 250 Sudanese, 300 Swahilis, and 200 'mixed' men. The force included fifteen Sikh gunners and some hospital attendants recruited in India. With the continuous activities by the rebels the Government decided to send troops from India to supplement the 300 men of the newly arrived Indian contingent. The troops from India consisted of 24TH Bombay Infantry, with a Company of Sikhs to stiffen the Regiment. The rebellion was suppressed by the constant pursuit of the insurgents.

The East African Rifles with their Sikh contingent carried out five expeditions against the Nandi tribe in Kenya, from 1895, for their constant attacks on the caravans bound for Uganda. The final campaign against them was in December 1905. The Nandi had 750 killed and were moved into a smaller reserve and thereafter no further trouble occurred.

JUBALAND 1898

The Ogaden Somalis are a group of fierce and warlike tribesmen. In 1898, it became necessary to coerce the Ogadens and punish them for raiding in the Kismayu district. Major W. Quentin commanded the expedition. The expedition force included 4TH Bombay Rifles (with a Sikh Company), East African Rifles and Uganda Rifles (with their Sikh contingents). On 22ND of June 1898 a patrol of 41 Sikhs, including Rifleman Butta Singh, under Jemadar Radha Singh, was sent out on reconnaissance from Helishid. They were ambushed by a large force of Somalis and suffered very heavy losses, with 27 killed, including the Jemadar, and 4 wounded. Naik Butta Singh was granted the Indian Order of Merit for conspicuous gallantry in this action.

Rifleman Butta Singh richly deserved the only gallantry decoration granted for this campaign. It is not known how long Butta Singh had served with 4TH Bombay Rifles, but it is certainly a significant feat of arms that, as a rifleman, he had the composure, the leadership skills, and enough understanding of field tactics to execute this withdrawal against such overwhelming odds with such few men.

UGANDA 1897

The Republic of Uganda is a landlocked country in East Africa. It is bordered on the East by Kenya, on the North by Sudan, on the West by Congo, on the Southwest by Rwanda, and on the South by German East Africa. The Southern part of the country includes a substantial portion of Lake Victoria, which is also bordered by Kenya and Tanzania. Uganda takes its name from the Buganda kingdom, which encompassed a portion of the South of the country including the capital Kampala. Roughly, 10,000 Ugandans of Sudanese descent are classified as Nubians, referring to their origin in the area of the Nuba Mountains in Sudan. They are descendants of Sudanese military recruits who entered Uganda in the late nineteenth century as part of the colonial Army and were employed to quell popular revolts. In 1890, Captain Lugard arrived with a few soldiers to impose the Imperial British East Africa Company's rule (IBEAC) on Uganda. In 1893, the IBEAC transferred its rights to the British Government, and a Protectorate was proclaimed, to which effect a treaty was signed in 1893. A mutiny in 1897 of the Sudanese troops used by the colonial government led Britain to take a more active interest in the Uganda Protectorate. A party consisting of Lieutenant Macdonald, Jemadar Bhagwan Singh and thirty men of 14TH and 15TH Sikh Regiments with half-trained Swahili soldiers joined an expedition formed under Major J. R. L. Macdonald to fight mutineers and other hostile elements in Uganda. A small force under Major Macdonald arrived at Lubwa Fort on Lake Victoria on 18TH October 1897, where they found it occupied by mutinous Sudanese troops. On the following day, the mutineers attacked Major MacDonald's force for five hours, but were defeated and driven back into the fort. This was a remarkable feat by the Sikhs, who with their Maxim guns had performed prodigious acts of valour with the half-trained Swahilis and by the fact the mutineers were led by experienced native Officers. On 11TH December, Lieutenant Macdonald and his small party were covering the activities of men delegated to destroy the rebels' plantations and gardens, when the enemy made a desperate flank attack on the working parties. Lieutenant Macdonald was shot and mortally wounded. Sepoy Sahib Singh, with the help of Sepoy Phuman Singh, defended Lieutenant Macdonald against overwhelming odds and carried him to a more secure position. Another force, crossing a swamp supposed to be impassable, attacked the rebel stockade at Kabagambi and carried it with great gallantry.

Writing about the Sikhs, Major Macdonald stated. 'This detachment fully maintained the great reputation of the Sikhs, and fought with such gallantry that they secured the admiration of all' and 'The detachment of Sikhs, men selected from 14TH and 15TH Sikhs, fought with such determined and conspicuous gallantry as to add to the already high reputation of these Regiments.'

Four Sikh soldiers of 14TH Ferozepur Sikhs and Six Sikh soldiers of 15TH Ludhiana Sikhs were awarded the Indian Order of Merit for conspicuous gallantry in action at Kabagambi and Lubwa Hill.

CENTRAL AFRICA 1884

A.J. Swann, a contemporary writer, describes the situation in Central Africa thus: 'The whole of the East African Coast and the Interior was either in the hands of native chiefs, Arabs, or marina half castes. They all had one objective. Their ambition was to sell and transport to the coast as many of the inhabitants as they could possibly capture. Besides those actually captured, thousands were killed or died of their wounds and famine, driven from their homes by the slave raiders. Thousands perished in internecine Wars, waged for slaves, with their own clansmen or neighbours, slain by the lust for gain, which was stimulated by the slave purchasers. The many skeletons that have been found amongst the rocks and woods all testify to the awful sacrifice of human life which must be attributed directly or indirectly to this trade of hell.'(Swann)

On establishment of the British protectorate over the territory later known as Nyasaland, the administrator H.H. Johnston obtained Sikh volunteers from the Indian Army to fight the Slavers. The Sikh contingent was to form the first armed force of the new Protectorate, the Central African Rifles. For nigh on ten years the Sikh soldiers fought the slave hunters in the steamy jungles of Central Africa and prevailed in stopping the 'trade of hell.

'At this time slave trading was the main and flourishing Industry of Africa and it has been estimated that up to 100,000 East African natives were killed or captured each year. The entrepreneurs of this trade were Arabs and half-breeds with the enthusiastic co-operation of the local African chiefs.' (Magor)

'During the initial period of pacification, the Sikhs performed the role of shock troops, leading attacks against various chieftains. By 1895, as the country became more settled, the Sikhs undertook garrison duty at a half dozen forts scattered across the protectorate.' (Metcalf),

"Guardian over all stands the Sikh, who being immune to local influence of all kinds, constitutes the 'motor muscle' of Imperial Authority as he stands erect beside his rifle on guard over British Interests 6,000 miles from the Punjab. He is a picked volunteer from all the Sikh Regiments. If at any time considerations of expense or desire to obtain homogeneity in the military forces of the Protectorate should lead to the disbandment of these Companies, those who take the decision will have incurred responsibility which few would care to share with them.' (Churchill)."

The Sikhs also trained and put together a native force, which in due course met all the requirements of the Protectorate. Subsequently, because of the cost factor the Sikh contingent was phased out.

During this period six Sikh soldiers made the supreme sacrifice, they were killed in action. Altogether eighteen Sikh soldiers were awarded the Indian Order of Merit for their conspicuous gallantry against the Slave traders.

NORTHERN RHODESIA

Northern Rhodesia was a territory in Central Africa initially administered under charter by the British South Africa Company and formed by it in 1911 by amalgamating Northwest Rhodesia and North Eastern Rhodesia. Although it had features of a charter colony, the territory's treaties and charter gave it Protectorate status. From 1924, the United Kingdom government administered it as a British Protectorate. Northern Rhodesia became independent in 1964 as Zambia.

The Angoni people who feature in this work are descended from the Ngoni tribe in South Africa. They had adopted the fighting tactics of Shaka Zulu. They conquered indigenous tribes with ease as they wandered as far North as Lake Tanganyika, and subsequently settled on the plateau of Eastern Zambia and adjoining areas of Nyasaland, between 1850 and 1870.The Angoni ruled this area until the British, with the Sikh troops coming in from Nyasaland, conquered it in 1897.

Angoni Rebellion. (1898)

Across the Northern Rhodesian border, the Angoni tribe were living around the area of Fort Jameson where a trading Company tried to expropriate a large tract of Angoni land by a fraudulent concession. Consequently, the Angoni threatened the Company. The Company frantically appealed for help. British Central Africa Protectorate had undertaken to provide military support for Northern Rhodesia when that was requested.

A military force was despatched across the border to reach Fort Jameson. Captain H. E. J. Brake was in command and he had with him six rifle Companies of Africans, 118 Sikhs, Maxim Guns and two 7-pounder field guns. A British Officer assisted by a Sikh Colour Sergeant and three Sikh Sergeants commanded each African Company. The African gun crews were commanded by Sikh instructors. The remainder of the Sikhs formed their own Rifle Company.

Operations against the Angoni, (1900)

In November, renewed operations took place in Central Agoniland. During these operations, over 300 villages were destroyed and twenty tribesmen killed. In spite of these reprisals, a mail runner was murdered and a strong force was, therefore, sent out to avenge his death. More villages and stockades were destroyed and Chief Tambola, who had escaped in 1896, was captured.

ASHANTI 1900

The Ashanti Campaign, (1900)

The Ashanti were a powerful and highly organized group of tribes living in the North of the Gold Coast Colony. (Ghana) The consciousness that the Ashanti were a great people was aroused by their wise man Anoky, who affirmed that the spirit and the strength of the nation were enshrined in the Golden Stool. All chiefs were 'enstooled', not crowned, for in Ashanti it was the symbol of royal authority.

The British had conducted operations against the Ashanti in 1873-74 and in 1895-96. After the last occasion, King Prempeh was deported and a treaty was drawn up with the remaining chiefs. In March 1900, the British Governor visited Kumasi, held a meeting of the chiefs, and asked why, as representative of the paramount power, the Golden Stool had not been brought from its hiding place for his use. This demand was a serious blunder and precipitated a rebellion among Kumasi, Ofinsu, Ejisu and Adansi sections of the tribe. To put down the rebellion, troops were ordered to the Gold Coast, which included 1ST Battalion, Central African Rifles with four British Officers, seventy-three Sikhs, 276 African Askaris and a Machine Gun detachment. They left Zomba for the Gold Coast, under the command of Major Cobbe, with half of 2ND Battalion to follow from Berbera. Cobbe and his men were in action in August and suffered heavy casualties in thick bush. 'All ranks, especially the fine soldiers the Sikhs, behaved admirably' wrote Colonel Wilcocks, the Commandant of the West African Frontier Force in his despatch, 'and if it were not for this impossible bush we should soon wipe out most of the Ashantis'. Lieutenant Colonel Brake and four Companies of 2ND Battalion arrived on 13TH August and were in action a week later. At the battle of Obassa on 30TH September, the Ashanti held firm and continued to fire volley after volley at close range so the assault could not be pressed. It was plain that the undertaking was beyond the capacity of the advance guard and its supporting troops. Colonel Wilcocks himself came forward. As a former Officer of the Indian Army, he placed great reliance on the Sikhs and telling them that he would watch the charge, he ordered them to attack the centre of the stockade in the teeth of the Ashanti fire. As the bugles sounded, the Sikhs dashed down the slope followed by the rest of the line. This charge decided the issue of 'a somewhat doubtful day.' The Ashantis still fought on but gave way before the Sikhs, as they came under devastating enfilading fire that rapidly spread panic and completed the rout. Obassa was a hard fought victory over a most courageous enemy.

The Sikhs fought several actions in conjunction with the West African Frontier Force. When the campaign ended, they earned high praise from Colonel Wilcocks for their discipline, drill, and shooting. They returned to Nyasaland via the Mediterranean, having gone around the cape, so they circumnavigated Africa.

Naik Hira Singh, a volunteer attached to the Central African Rifles, was awarded the Indian Order of Merit for conspicuous gallantry in action. He was foremost in the attack as the Ashanti fled to the bush.

GAMBIA

Gambia is a country in Western Africa. It is the smallest country on mainland Africa. It is bordered to the North, East, and South by Senegal, and has a small coast on the Atlantic Ocean in the West. On 18TH February 1965, Gambia was granted independence from the United Kingdom.

The West African coastline had been an important source of slaves for European and American traders, but during the 19TH Century, the trading emphasis moved towards obtaining African agricultural and mineral commodities in exchange for European manufactured goods. This led to European expeditions methodically exploring the hinterland of the West African coast. Both France and Britain were interested in the territory now known as The Gambia, and eventually an amicable agreement was reached by which Britain controlled a strip of land on each side of the navigable course of the River Gambia, whilst France controlled the land surrounding the strip.

Britain established a capital at Bathurst (now named Banjul) on the coast, built Fort Bullen at Barra Point on the North side of the river mouth and Fort James 19 miles further upstream on James Island. The British suppressed slavery and administered Gambia from a headquarters in Sierra Leone. The agreement with the French had settled the boundaries of Gambia in 1889, but this meant little to the native slave raiding chiefs, who were accustomed to operate indiscriminately on both sides of the frontier. One of these chiefs, Fodi Kabba, had been driven out of the colony in 1892 and had settled at Medina, beyond the frontier in French territory, whence he raided impartially in all directions. On 14TH June 1900, two travelling commissioners were murdered with their police escort of six constables, as many chiefs refused to recognize British authority. In 1901, a military expedition was authorized against the rebellious chiefs, and afterwards prolonged to settle matters with the slavers. As Gambia possessed an armed police force of only 100 men, it was decided to employ four Companies of 2ND Battalion, Central African Rifles (with a detachment of Sikh soldiers) and four Companies of West India Regiment from Sierra Leone. Their objective was the stockaded town of Dumbutu, which they reached after a three-hour advance through long grass. Two Companies of 2ND Battalion, Central African Rifles, under Major Plunket, moved round to the left flank to get between the village and the French border. Surprise was complete and when the defenders finally surrendered, more than forty were dead and over 200 men and women were captured. Losses on the British side were one carrier killed and four men wounded. There were some sweeping–up operations, including tax collection and capture of over 200 rifles. The Sikhs then went to the Gold Coast, to put down a mutiny in the West India Regiment.

On 3RD June a detachment of Central African Rifles, including a Sikh Havildar Jaimal Singh embarked for England. On 26TH June King Edward V11 inspected them at Marlborough House and presented medals for both the Ashanti and the Gambia campaigns.

SOMALILAND

The British and Egyptian navies cooperated in the suppression of the Slave trade in the Red Sea until the Egyptians abandoned Somalia in 1884. The British, French, Italians and the Ethiopians then divided the whole area into spheres of influence. The British occupied Berbera, where four Somali tribes placed themselves under their administration for protection against the Ethiopians. In 1905 generally the British did not have much interest in the resource-barren region. They principally viewed the protectorate as a source for supplies of meat for their British Indian outpost in Aden. Hence, the region's nickname of "Aden's Butcher's shop". From 1899, the British were forced to expend considerable human and military capital in a bloody struggle to contain a decades-long resistance movement led by the Somali religious leader Sayyid Mohammed Abdullah Hassan, referred to colloquially by the British as the 'Mad Mullah'. Opposing them were the Sikhs with their courage and self-sacrifice, thousands of miles away from their homeland. The Mullah died on 23RD November 1920, sounding the death knell of the dervish movement. Disintegration soon followed and the Mullah's followers returned to their tribal areas and the Sikhs back to the Punjab.

Sikh Soldier

Somali Levy with fifty Sikh instructors, Somaliland Camel Corps (formed from the Sikh element of the disbanded 6TH Battalion Kings African Rifles.) The Sikh Cameleers were eventually increased to 350 and operated as an integral part of the corps, The Camel Battery, also operated as an integral part of the corps, and was entirely manned by Sikhs. Two Regiments of Central African Rifles (All Sikhs), 5TH Kings African Rifles (All Sikhs), 6TH Battalion Kings African Rifles (Contingent of Sikhs), The Sikh soldier was also present in the regular Indian Regiments operating in Somaliland. These were; Aden Troop, 2ND Sikhs, Punjab Mounted Infantry, 27TH Punjabis, 7TH Bombay Pioneers, 17TH Bombay Infantry, and Lahore Mountain Battery.

From 1905 the defence of the protectorate was entrusted to the local forces supported by special corps of 600 mainly Sikhs, recruited in the Punjab. The Corps was constantly engaged in the pursuit and destruction of the dervish bands right upto the death of the Mullah in 1920. The last of the time expired Sikhs left the Corps in 1922.

Subedar Jaimal Singh of 17TH Regiment of Bombay Infantry was awarded Indian Order of Merit for conspicuous gallantry in the repulse of the enemy at Hussain on the 29TH January 1890.

The Return of the Mullah is listed separately in the chapter on First World War.

Somaliland

Battle of Gamburu, (1903)

On 17TH April Lieutenant Colonel Cobbe was commanding a Flying Column ahead of the main body moving against the Mullah. Having established a *Zariba* (a camp fortified with a thorn hedge) near Gumburu, he had cause to send forward 'A' Company 2ND Battalion Kings African Rifles, 48 men of 2ND Sikh Regiment and two maxim guns under Lieutenant Colonel Plunkett to secure the return of a small scouting party. Colonel Plunkett, in his eagerness to engage the enemy, was drawn on to a distance of four miles from the *Zariba* where he was attacked by the whole of the Mullah's force, numbering perhaps some 14,000 men. The British column of 224 of all ranks had apparently formed three sides of a square in single rank on the march out, with the Sikhs in the front face. Afterwards a half Company was thrown across the rear face. The troops were attacked by about 4,000 horsemen and 10,000 Warriors, apparently commanded by the Mullah in person. With the fanatical contempt for death that they always showed in his presence, the dervishes swept from all sides upon the square, first horsemen, then riflemen on foot, and finally hordes of spearmen who broke into the square with the weight of their headlong rush, heedless of the devastating fire of maxims and rifles. All were successfully repelled until the ammunition ran out. The Sikhs had taken with them 100 rounds per rifle in their pouches. There was no reserve ammunition. Moreover, the Sikhs used solid bullets not suited to stop a charging savage. When the ammunition started to run out the order was given to breakout with the bayonet and charge back to the *Zariba*. Plunket was killed and the little force was borne down and overwhelmed. No European or Sikh survived the fight.

Battle of Jidbali, (1904)

In January 1904, the British employed more than 8,000 troops, in the hope that the Mullah's power would be permanently shattered. The enemy's force, which numbered between 6,000 and 8,000, was concentrated at Jidbali, where the Mullah, deciding to make a stand, received a most crushing defeat. His casualties in the actual fight at Jidbali must have been very large, but far greater were his losses during the course of his subsequent flight Northwards to Jidbali, and thence Eastward into Italian territory. Thus, this expedition was completely successful in all but bringing the Mullah himself to bay, and so putting an end to his movement. The morale of his Dervishes as a fighting body had been utterly destroyed; and their numbers, estimated at 6,000 to 8,000 before Jidbali, could not have exceeded 800 on the conclusion of the campaign. Above all, the Mullah's personal prestige was temporarily shattered. In March 1905, the Illig or Pestalozza Agreement was concluded between the Italian Government and the Mullah, whereby peace was declared between the Dervishes on the one hand and the British and Italian Governments on the other. The Mullah was assigned a port and certain territories in Italian Somaliland, beyond which he and his Dervishes undertook not to encroach.

INDIAN ARMY WW1

In 1914, the Indian Army was the largest volunteer Army in the world with a total strength of 240,000 men and by November 1918 it contained 548,311 men, being considered the Imperial Strategic Reserve. It was regularly called upon to deal with incursions and raids on the North West Frontier and to provide garrison forces for the British Empire in Egypt, Singapore and China. This field force was divided into two armies: The Northern Army, which stretched from the Northwest Frontier to Bengal with five Divisions and three Brigades under command and the Southern Army, which stretched from Baluchistan to Southern India and it in turn, had four Divisions under command and two formations outside the subcontinent. The two armies contained 39 Cavalry Regiments, 138 Infantry Battalions, a joint Cavalry-Infantry Unit the Corps of Guides, three Sapper Regiments and 12 Mountain Artillery Batteries and Pioneer Regiments. The Pioneer Regiments were unique because in addition to producing skilled technical troops, capable of carrying out the most complex engineering assignments, they were at the same time trained Infantry Battalions, armed with machine guns and mortars and embodying such ancillary troops as Signallers and Medical Orderlies.

In addition to the regular Indian Army, the armies of the Princely States could also be called upon to assist in an emergency. The Princely States formed the Imperial Service Brigades and in 1914, had 22,613 men in 20 Cavalry Regiments and 14 Infantry Battalions. By the end of the War 26,000 men had served overseas on Imperial Service. The Sikh Princely States forces had seen extensive service on the North West Frontier of India with great distinction. Also available were the Frontier Militia and the Military Police, which could field 34,000 men between them. In World War One the Indian Army fought against the German Empire in German East Africa and on the Western Front. Indian Divisions were also sent to Egypt, Gallipoli, Mesopotamia, and in Russia against the Bolsheviks. While some Divisions were sent overseas others had to remain in India guarding the North West Frontier and on internal security and training duties. The normal annual recruitment for the Indian Army was 15,000 men. During the course of the War over 800,000 men volunteered for the Army and more than 400,000 volunteered for non-combatant roles. In total almost 1.3 million men had volunteered for service by 1918. One million Indian troops served overseas during the War, of these 62,000 died in combat and another 67,000 were wounded.

The number of Sikhs who fought rose from 35,000 in 1915 to more than 100,000 by the War's end. The Sikhs formed 20% of the British Indian Army in action, despite being only 2% of the Indian population.

During the First World War 27 Sikh Officers were awarded the Military Cross and 288 Sikhs of all Armed Services in all theatres of War, were awarded the Indian Order of Merit in consideration of their conspicuous gallantry.

WESTERN FRONT

The Indian Army contingent - the Indian Corps - that served on the Western Front consisted of two Divisions of Infantry, namely 3RD (Lahore) Division, and 7TH (Meerut) Division, along with their support troops of Pioneers, Artillery, and one Brigade of Cavalry, 4TH (Secunderbad) Cavalry Brigade.

Three class Regiments of Sikhs Infantry formed part of the Indian Corps in France, 15TH Ludhiana Sikhs, 47TH Sikhs, and 34TH Sikh Pioneers. The Sikhs were, however, largely represented also in 27TH, 33RD, 69TH, and 89TH Punjabis, 57TH, 58TH, 59TH Rifles and 107TH Pioneers in which Sikh Companies varied from one to four. All the Cavalry Regiments present in the Indian Corps in France contained Sikh Companies: 2ND Lancers-1 Squadron, 3RD Skinner's Horse-1 Squadron, 4TH Cavalry-1 Squadron, 6TH King Edward's Own Cavalry-2 Squadrons, 9TH Hodson's Horse-1 Squadron, 18TH King George's Own Lancers-1 Squadron, 19TH Lancers-2 Squadrons, 20TH Deccan Horse-1 Squadron, 29TH Lancers-1 Squadron, 30TH Lancers-2 Squadrons, 36TH Jacob's Horse-1 Squadron, 38TH King George's Own Central India Horse-2 Squadrons, and 39TH King George's Own Central India Horse-2 Squadrons.

When the Indian Corps was withdrawn from the Western Front, the two Indian Cavalry Divisions remained in France until 1918. Before being withdrawn they took part in the Battle of the Somme, the Battle of Bazentin, the Battle of Flers-Courcelette, the advance to the Hindenburg Line and finally the Battle of Cambrai. The Meerut Cavalry Brigade was finally transferred to Mesopotamia and the remainder of the Cavalry left for Egypt in February 1918.

The Sikhs landed in France, clad only in tropical uniforms. These uniforms were totally inadequate for the bitterest winter Europe had known. The thick serge Khaki uniforms as issued to the British Army would not be available to the Sikhs until December.

'It was dark days of 1914 when our men had to face mortars, hand grenades, high explosive shells for which they themselves were not provided. They could reply only with their valour, their rifles and two machine guns per battalion. And yet they did it. (Lt. Gen. Sir James Wilcox, Commander of the Indian Corps.)

'We have claimed in an earlier passage that the Indian Corps saved the Empire. The proposition to those who know the facts is almost self-evident. The original Expeditionary Force, with the supplementary Divisions, had gone through the Retreat, the Marne, the Aisne, and the bloody hand-to-hand fighting which at every step marked the race to the sea. At the time when the Indians landed, the resistant power of the British Army, cruelly outnumbered, and exhausted by constant fighting against superior Artillery and a more numerous equipment of Machine Guns, was almost overcome. And except for the Indian Army there were no trained regular soldiers in the Empire at that moment for service. They played a glorious part in the battle of Neuve Chapelle. The second battle of Ypres, the struggle for the Aubers ridge, and the desperate assaults of Loos – all claimed a toll of blood of this devoted Corps'. (Merewether and Bart)

Western Front

Ypres, (1914)

The Battle of Ypres was a battle between British and German forces in Northern France in October 1914, and was part of the Race to the Sea. The German 6TH Army took Lille before the British force could secure the town, while 4TH Army arrived and attacked the exposed British flank at Ypres. The British were driven back; the German Army occupied La Bassée and Neuve Chapelle. Around 15TH October, the British took over initiative and recaptured Givenchy. However, they failed to reach La Bassée. Meanwhile, the German troops got reinforcements, and retook the initiative. On 21ST October the Germans commenced an offensive along the whole front line from La Bassée in the South to Menim in the North and the British were pinned down to the defensive. The position was critical, for the allies were outnumbered and out gunned.

The same period also saw the arrival of the Lahore Division of the Indian Corps to the rear of the line. During the rest of the battle Indian troops would play an increasingly important role in the fighting at La Bassée. 57TH Rifles were the first Battalion of the Indian Corps to enter the trenches. 57TH Rifles was one of the five Battalions raised in 1849 by Sir Henry Lawrence to form part of the Trans-Frontier Brigade, and most of the personnel were Sikh soldiers of the disbanded Regiments of the Khalsa Durbar.

The 57TH Wilde's Rifles moved up to Wulverghem, about seven miles South-West of Ypres, and were attached to 2ND Cavalry Division. Half the Battalion was then placed under 4TH Cavalry Brigade and half with 5TH Cavalry Brigade, both Brigades being in the vicinity of Wytschaete. The Sikh and the Punjabi Mussalman Companies were ordered to improve the second line trenches East and South East of Wytschaete. On 23RD October the Sikh Company was ordered to relieve the Household Cavalry Regiment on the Northern end of the Cavalry Corps' area. On 26TH October orders were issued for an attack on that portion of the German lines which formed a wedge from Gapaard running North East to Wambeek. 'The Indian Corps first taste of offensive action it was significant. They suffered very few casualties and showed that they were able to operate in conjunction with the British Units and formations. Most important of all they showed the British Army that their vaunted fighting spirit was not just legend; they had gone forward with alacrity, had come under enemy Artillery and machine-gun fire and they had stood it well'.(Corrigan)

'The situation was desperate and these Units were at once fiercely engaged, distinguished themselves greatly and lost very heavily. The story of their attack intermingled with the Cavalry, and their holding of the feeble and flooded trenches against German attacks, is an epic in itself.'(Macmunn)

The confused fighting around Ypres in that last week of October 1914 cost 57TH Wilde's Rifles three British Officers, two Indian Officers and 80 Indian Other Ranks killed, and three British Officers, two Indian Officers and 196 Indian Other Ranks wounded. Of the 750 all ranks that had entered the Salient, only 460 remained.

Western Front

La Bassée, (1914)

La Bassée was held by the Germans under the Crown Prince of Bavaria, also the La Bassée–Lille canal and country immediately to the South and East. The British 2ND Corps had been facing the German onslaught for 10 days, and after continuous fighting, was wilting under the strain. The Jullunder Brigade was at once utilized on the left of the French Cavalry. The 15TH Sikhs, 34TH Sikh Pioneers, and 59TH Rifles were pushed to support the French Cavalry, with orders to counter attack if the French were driven out that day. The 15TH Sikhs were on the right of the line; 59TH Rifles carried on the line on the left, where one Company of 34TH Sikh Pioneers took over the advanced post from the French. This detachment was attacked within an hour of its relieving the French, and during the night the British Officers were severely wounded. The defence was very ably carried on by Subedars Sher Singh and Natha Singh till the evening of 26TH October. Subadar Sher Singh received the Indian Distinguished Service Medal for his gallant leadership. Throughout the day 15TH Sikhs were subjected to very heavy shell fire, but held their own till the attack ceased. The remainder of 34TH Sikhs reinforced the firing line when half of 47TH Sikhs arrived, a very welcome addition, as the situation was rapidly becoming critical. The night was a trying one, wet and cold, and the men, who had now been fighting without food and with little or no sleep for two days, were soaked to the skin. On 27^{TH,} 59TH Rifles were heavily attacked, a vigorous fire fight followed in which the enemy was beaten back to his trenches all along the line.

The casualties during the period 24TH October to 1ST November were very severe:
15TH Sikhs lost 3 British and 3 Indian Officers wounded; Other Ranks, 11 killed, 240 wounded, and 12 missing presumed dead.
34TH Sikh Pioneers lost 1 British Officer killed 2 British and 3 Indian Officers wounded, 15 Other Ranks killed and 89 wounded.
47TH Sikhs had 2 British Officers and 118 Other Ranks killed.
59Th Rifles had 1 British Officer killed. 1 British and 2 Indian Officers wounded, 13 Other Ranks killed and 189 wounded.
(The class composition of 59TH Rifles was Sikhs, Dogras, Pathans, and the Punjabi Mussalmans consisting of two Companies each.)

Armentieres, (1914)

On 15TH October III Corps was ordered to capture Armentieres. The town was captured on 17TH October, Armentieres remained in British hands throughout the fighting, although the front line was pushed back slightly the fighting continued on this front throughout November, involving 47TH Sikhs, 34TH Sikh Pioneers, 27TH Punjabis and 58TH Rifles (Frontier Force).

Western Front

Neuve Chapelle, (1914)

The British Indian Army saw a significant amount of combat around Neuve-Chapelle. First their attempt was to seal the breach that the Germans had created in the British Line just South of Neuve-Chapelle. On 28TH October 1914, a portion of 9TH Bhopal Infantry and 47TH Sikhs advanced on the village with 20TH and 21ST Companies Sappers and Miners. When they were yards from the outskirts of the village, the Germans in the front trenches began to bolt, pursued by the Sikhs and Sappers with the bayonet, a few being killed and some captured. They then tore on into the village; Sikhs and Sappers mixed together, and worked in parties up the streets, under furious fire from the roofs of buildings. By degrees the houses were cleared after desperate hand-to-hand fighting, in which a man of 47TH Sikhs is reported to have captured three Germans out of eight, having previously killed the other five. The fighting went on; counter-attack following counter-attack. Without immediate reinforcements, the position of 47TH Sikhs was now quite untenable, as their losses had been very heavy. They were compelled to give up all they had won at such fearful cost and retire. The British Officer was severely wounded directly he came into the open, and Subedar Thakur Singh took command of the Company and led it with skill and gallantry till he was also hit. He subsequently received the Military Cross for his conduct in this action.

The line of the retreat lay over about 500 yards of open ground, exposed to a tornado of shell and machine gun fire, and the bodies of Sikhs soon lay thick on the ground, but eventually the remains of the half Battalion got back to comparative safety, only 68 out of 289 actually collecting on the La Bassée road. Throughout its service in France, this magnificent Regiment never failed to answer all calls; its reputation would be secure, and its right to fight shoulder to shoulder with the best troops would be established, if based only on the record of Neuve Chapelle; but this action was only one of many in which 47TH Sikhs distinguished themselves. In the meantime, in the late afternoon of a cold, wet late autumn day, the Bhopal's went to the aid of the remnants of a British Battalion near Neuve Chapelle.

Still in cotton-drill, they had their first encounter with trenches and barbed wire and stayed locked in battle for three days without food. While early on the morning of 24TH affairs began to look critical, all the British Officers had been killed. Havildar Indar Singh then took command of the Company and held the position against heavy attacks until relieved next morning, for which he was promoted to Jemadar and awarded the Military Cross. Their losses were 11 Officers and 262 men.

On one occasion – a feat almost incredible, though well established, Sapper Dalip Singh of 3RD Sappers and Miners was attacked by as many as twenty of the enemy, but beat them off, and got the injured British Officer Lieutenant Rait-Kerr away. For his signal act of bravery and devotion to duty, Sapper Dalip Singh was awarded the Indian Order of Merit.

Western Front

Neuve Chapelle, (1914) (Cont.)

Subadar Malla Singh too fought with supreme disregard of danger and when retreat was inevitable, he conducted his small party with the greatest skill and coolness. For his gallantry throughout the action he received the Military Cross. For his gallantry Captain G.D. Martin received the Military Cross, while Subadar Major Bhure Singh and Havildar Amar Singh were awarded the Indian Distinguished Service Medal.

The magnificent conduct of the troops was recognized by Field-Marshal Sir John French, who in his dispatch, dated 20TH November, 1914, remarked as follows:-
"On 28TH October especially 47TH Sikhs and 20TH and 21ST Companies of the Sappers and Miners distinguished themselves by their gallant conduct in the attack on Neuve Chapelle, losing heavily in Officers and men." Neuve Chapelle had been a dearly bought victory, 12,811 casualties with 190 Officers and 2,337 Other Ranks dead, of which Indian Corps had over 4,000.

Festubert, (1914)

During the night of 23RD November, the enemy pushed up his sap to within five yards of the trenches of 34TH Sikh Pioneers, and as dawn broke; he commenced a storm of hand grenades from his nearest sapheads, to the junction of 34TH, where the maxim of 34TH was in position. Subadar Natha Singh was near the machine gun, around which bombs fell fast, killing a number of men. He at once took charge and held his position against the enemy, who had broken in, until he was forced to retire. This Officer previously distinguished himself on several occasions and received the Indian Order of Merit.

Havildar Nika Singh, when all the men of the machine gun team had been killed or wounded, carried the gun by himself under a withering fire back to the support trenches, for which act of bravery he also received the Indian Order of Merit. Captain McCain was in command of the Company next to Subadar Natha Singh. Although already wounded in the head, he fought to stem the German charge and was mortally wounded. Sepoys Ishar Singh, Bachittar Singh and Kanhaiya Singh at once carried him through the bursting bombs to a shelter. Lance Naik Tota Singh was killed beside Captain McCain and was awarded the Indian Order of Merit for his fidelity and valour. Colour-Havildar Chanda Singh, Havildar Naryan Singh and Sepoy Teja Singh held on to their position. When the enemy entered the trench, they blocked up the traverse and fired through loopholes in it, until after Naryan Singh had been wounded, they were ordered to retire. Naryan Singh was again wounded, this time mortally, while being carried to the aid post; his bravery was recognized by the award of the Indian Distinguished Service Medal. Subadar Sant Singh rallied his half Company and held them in position when the enemy broke in. He received the Military Cross.

Western Front

Festubert, (Cont.)

During this attack, the building in which the Regimental aid post was established came under heavy shell fire, the house being repeatedly struck. Sub-Assistant Surgeon Harnam Singh and Havildar Pala Singh, who was hospital Havildar, removed all the wounded, the stretcher-bearers being away near the firing line, and carried them into safety along the road, which was being shelled. These two men showed absolute disregard of danger, and were awarded the Indian Order of Merit. The 34TH Sikh Pioneers were overpowered by numbers and bombs, and their left was pushed out into the Connaught Ranger's trench, while the Germans continued to clear each traverse with grenades as they advanced. The Cannaught's fought them traverse by traverse, but owing to the want of bombs they suffered considerable loss and could do little injury to the enemy. Step by step they retreated until, to avoid being taken both in flank and rear, they had to seek cover in the trench on the right of 57TH Rifles, where they built a rough barricade and defied all the efforts of the enemy to move them. A counter attack was immediately organized and carried out by 34TH Sikhs with the portions of 6TH Jats and 9TH Bhopals, but they were at once held up by machine gun fire. Subedar Natha Singh distinguished himself by getting into the enemy's trench on the left with only twenty-six men. The Commanding Officer reported that his conduct during the whole of these operations was an exceptional example of the highest courage and coolness. He well merited the Indian Order of Merit bestowed on him, to be followed later by the Order of British India.

The 34TH Sikhs had suffered heavy losses, among the killed were Subedars Natha Singh and Ram Singh, with Subedar Sant Singh and Jemadars Pala Singh and Mit Singh wounded. Of the Other Ranks, 161 were killed and 105 wounded. Captain Baldwin was killed in a counter attack and the command of the Company was then taken by Havildar Indar Singh, who held the position against heavy assaults until relieved the next morning, for which he was promoted to Jemadar and received the Military Cross. The losses of 58TH during the action were: Jemadar Wazir Singh and 42 Other Ranks killed, Subedar Gujar Singh and 61 Other Ranks wounded, while eleven men were missing presumed dead. The 57TH Rifles and 129 Baluchis suffered a great loss by the death of their Medical Officers, Captain Inderjit Singh and Major Atal. The enemy shells blew up their combined dressing stations. Captain Inderjit Singh had been awarded the Military Cross for his services at Wytschaete, Messines and Levantine. The notification did not arrive until after his death, and he therefore did not know the honour he had gained. The losses of 34TH Sikh Pioneers were heavy, bearing eloquent testimony to the struggles that they had led. (Macmunn)

Western Front

Givenchy, (1914)

On 19TH December, Sharp fighting broke out, when Indian troops launched an attack and successfully captured two lines of German trenches. A prompt aggressive counter-action pushed Indian troops back again. The force of the German attack was clearly focused against the trenches held by the same Indian troops who had initiated operations on the previous day. The 59TH Rifles had been going through a very trying experience at Givenchy. They moved up into the trenches of 129TH Baluchis, and as soon as bombardment ceased they climbed out and advanced. On the right as the Sikh Platoon reached the wire, it was wiped out by German machine gun fire. Jemadar Mangal Singh and another Sikh Platoon were ordered to take the German sap on the right, which they accomplished with a rush. They continued to hold this sap against every effort of the enemy, for twenty four hours, and in spite of heavy losses, had killed a number of Germans and captured a wounded Officer. There were many instances of individual gallantry.

The losses of 59TH Rifles in this gallant action were heavy:-Four British Officers and 22 men were killed and one British Officer and 85 Other Ranks wounded. On 19TH December 34TH Sikh Pioneers were detailed to accompany the Sarhind and Ferozepore Divisions in an attack on the trenches to the front and connect up the trenches with those carried. During this attack fourteen Other Ranks were killed or wounded. On 20TH December Captain Padday, 47TH Sikhs, with a bombing party of his Regiment, made a gallant attempt to clear the enemy out, but the machine guns were merciless and many of the party were killed. Captain Padday and 7 men were killed while 120 Other Ranks were wounded or missing.

Under the orders of Lieutenant Colonel Hill, working parties of 15TH Sikhs, ten in each party, had followed up 129TH Baluchis, and had at once commenced to dig back from the saphead to the Sikh trench. It was necessary to keep Colonel Hill informed of the events, and Havildar Mastan Singh of 15TH Sikhs made two perilous journeys under a torrent of lead between the sap and the Sikh trench. He tried to get across a third time, but was shot dead.

On one occasion a party of Sappers and Miners were employed in making a gallery towards a German saphead. A charge had been placed in position and was being tamped, when the enemy began bombarding the place with a medium trench mortar. Havildar Sucha Singh of the Sappers was in charge of the work in the mine shaft. He temporarily withdrew his party to assist in getting out those who had been buried. Having done this, he again went down the shaft to finish off the tamping and to complete the preparations for blowing up the mine, in spite of the fact that two trench-mortar bombs had fallen directly on the roof of the gallery, breaking two of the supporting frames, and that his party was isolated as the trench had been evacuated. Havildar Sucha Singh finished his work unperturbed and withdrew his men, afterwards receiving the Indian Distinguished Service Medal.

Western Front

Neuve Chapelle, (1915)

The British Indian Army saw a significant amount of combat around Neuve-Chapelle. First they attempted to seal the breach that the Germans (under General Erich van Falkenhayn) had created in the British Line just South of Neuve-Chapelle. On 28TH October 1914, the Indian Corps initially succeeded in entering the village of Neuve Chapelle but were forced to retreat after a strong German counter attack. Further fighting continued for a week with the additional loss of 25 British and more than 500 Indians killed, with 1,450 wounded. In December 1914, the Indian Corps moved to the Givenchy area South of Neuve-Chapelle. On 16TH December 1914, they attempted to capture a German front trench line without success losing 54 men. This raised the total number killed to that date to over 2,000.

The Indian Corps provided half the attacking force at the Battle of Neuve Chapelle which started on 10TH March 1915. It was one of the major engagements for the Indian Army on the Western Front. Elements of the Indian Corps participated in an attempt to break the German lines at Neuve Chapelle and went on to capture Aubers. However, a logistical failure in moving British guns within range to cover the advance saw the Indian troops go in without covering fire. The battle ended with the British in control of the village of Neuve-Chapelle but the Germans occupied the ridge to the East. The 47TH Sikhs, who had so greatly distinguished themselves at Neuve Chapelle in October 1914, had scarcely advanced when Subadar Harnam Singh was killed while leading his half-Company. His bravery had been most conspicuous throughout the campaign, and had won him the Indian Order of Merit at Festubert in December 1914, in which action his only son was killed. The Subadar, after his death, was granted the Order of British India.

Following on from an intensive 30-minute barrage by 345 guns, ranged by British reconnaissance aircraft, the British and Indians attacked along three kilometres of front. The water table was so high here that the Germans had partially resorted to above ground fortifications. Neuve Chapelle fell, as did four lines of the German trenches. However, due to a transportation failure in getting the British guns moved in time to cover the advance on the Aubers sector, the troops there went in without covering fire and almost 1,000 were completely wiped out. Other equally futile attacks were ordered that day by the British 1st Army Commander, General Sir Douglas Haig, with similar tragic results. On 12TH March the British and Indians repelled a German attack and almost immediately followed it with a counter attack. The attack fizzled out with very heavy losses and with it the Battle of Neuve Chapelle. **During the fighting, Havildar Gajjan Singh and Sepoy Rur Singh volunteered to bring in a wounded comrade. This conspicuous act of bravery was performed in a most exposed position, when any movement drew heavy machine-gun fire from both flanks. Havildar Gajjan Singh and Sepoy Rur Singh were awarded the Indian Order of Merit.**

Western Front

Ypres, (1915)

On 22ND April 1915 the German forces around Ypres launched an attack on the salient with the first use of poison gas. This action became the Second Battle of Ypres. On 22ND April 1915 at 5 p.m. the second Battle of Ypres began with the first successful gas attack in history. Again the British Indian Corps - not yet recovered from the terrible Battle of Neuve-Chapelle - was called upon to fill a gap in the line. When the gas reached the Indian troops, an Indian Havildar was heard shouting: "Khabardar, Jehannam pahunche", which means, "watch out, we have arrived in Hell". After the gas attack, the Germans had gained a considerable portion of the Northern part of the Ypres Salient. Now the British, together with the French troops, wanted to make a counter-attack in order to force the Germans to withdraw from this new position. On the morning of 26TH April 1915, the Lahore Division assembled between the Ieper-Langemark road on the left and Wieltje on the right, some 600 yards north of la Brique. The Ferozepore Brigade moved to its position through Vlamertinge, but the Jullunder Brigade went to Wieltje by the road winding along the Ypres ramparts. There they were caught in a heavy bombardment. As soon as the Division was deployed in the fields near Wieltje, they were shelled with tear gas. After the first gentle slope, they arrived in an inferno of gunfire, machine gunfire and shells, among which were also tear gas shells. The men fell by the dozen.

The 47TH Sikhs, which was in the first line of attack, was almost annihilated as soon as the Regiment advanced. The losses of 47TH reduced the Regiment to a mere shadow of its former self. Its strength going into action was 11 British, 10 Indian Officers and 423 ranks. On the morning of 27TH April, when muster was taken, the Regiment numbered 2 British, 2 Indian Officers and 92 others, its losses being 9 British, 8 Indian Officers and 331 Other Ranks or 78 per cent. No Regiment could wish, and none in the Army possesses, a prouder record than that of 47TH Sikhs at the attack on Neuve Chapelle in October, 1914, the battle of Neuve Chapelle in March, 1915 and the second battle of Ypres. As 57TH Rifles advanced it came into an absolute inferno, and from there onwards Officers and men fell fast. The Regiment swept on, in spite of their losses, and the remnant succeeded in reaching a point about 80 yards from the German line. Naik Atma Singh, a member of the machine gun detachment, helped to bring a gun up to near the firing line, and got it into position under a hot fire. Here he held on until the front line was driven out by gas, but he himself declined to budge until ordered to retire. For his conspicuous gallantry Naik Atma Singh received the Indian Order of Merit. Here Subadar Badawa Singh and Jemadar Kirpal Singh were killed and four other Indian Officers were wounded. Bhan Singh was wounded in the face early during the attack. Nevertheless, he stayed near his Officer, Captain Banks. When Banks fell, Bhan Singh thought just of one thing, bringing Banks back, dead or alive. Weakened as he was, he stumbled on with Banks' body under heavy fire until he was completely exhausted. However, he did not return without first saving Banks' personal belongings.

Western Front

Ypres, (1915) (Cont.)

For his signal act of devotion and bravery Sepoy Bhan Singh was awarded the Indian Distinguished Service Medal, and eventually received the Russian Medal of St. George. During the latter part of the attack, Jemadar Lehna Singh displayed great coolness and courage in bringing his support up through the front line. He then occupied and held a position with wonderful tenacity under heavy fire at close range. For his conspicuous bravery he received the Indian Order of Merit. But let's get back to the night of 26TH–27TH April 1915, when the chlorine gas was to be smelt the whole night. Men of 34TH Sikh Pioneers did try to consolidate the difficult position and did manage to keep a stand. Later, two men of that Unit, Sappers Jai Singh and Gujar Singh, were awarded the Indian Distinguished Service Medal because they had established communication lines under constant fire. Among the many stories of daring is the following. During an attack, shells had cut communications and it was urgently necessary to get a message through. It had to be carried by hand. Sepoy Bakshi Singh twice volunteered to take messages over a space of some 1500 yards, which was literally swept by fire. On both occasions he was successful and returned with the replies. On 1ST May he again distinguished himself by going several times to repair telephone wires, which had been cut by shells. For his gallant conduct he was awarded the Indian Order of Merit.

Festubert, (1915)

The battle of Festubert, 15-27TH May 1915, was the second British contribution to the second battle of Artois, the major Allied Spring offensive of 1915. Festubert marked a significant step on the journey from the search for a breakthrough to the War of attrition. The attack went in early on 15TH May, with some British Units reaching and capturing the German front line. Over the first few days of the battle, the British were able to capture more segments of the German front lines. After a series of failed attacks on 18TH May the British rested and replaced some Units in the front line. The battle ended with a series of unsuccessful German counterattacks, aimed at recapturing their original front lines.

On the night of 17TH May a Company of 15TH Sikhs relieved 2ND Highland Light Infantry in a section of the captured trench known as the "Glory Hole" on account of its dangerous position and the number of casualties which had occurred there. Towards dawn on 18TH it was observed that swarms of Germans were seen rushing towards the further extremity of the trench and when day broke, it was found that the hostile trench was packed with men and an attack seemed certain. Shortly afterwards the Germans commenced heavy bombing, to which 15TH Sikhs replied vigorously, and succeeded in holding their own till noon when all dry bombs had been expended, the remainder having been rendered useless by the incessant rain and the mud. The situation at once became very critical, as without bombs the position could hardly be held.

Western Front

Festubert, (Cont.)

Lieutenant Smyth, 15TH Sikhs, was ordered to attempt to take bombs and a bombing party from the support trench to Captain Hyde-Cates. The distance to be covered was about 250 yards over open ground. The only means of communication was a shallow trench half full of mud and water, and in many places exposed to the fire of the enemy's snipers and machine guns. The trench was crammed with the dead bodies of British and Indian soldiers, as well as Germans. Lieutenant Smyth took ten bombers from No. 4 Company, selected from the crowd of volunteers who at once responded to the call.

The names of these heroes deserve to be remembered. They were Lance Naik Mangal Singh, Sepoys Sucha Singh, Sapuran Singh, Surain Singh, Sunder Singh, Ganda Singh, Harnam Singh (the last four being all of 19TH Punjabis), Fateh Singh and Ujagar Singh, both of 45TH Sikhs. The party took with them two boxes of bombs containing 48 each. For the first 50 yards the trench gave cover from the enemy's view, but on emerging from this portion the men came under enfilade shrapnel fire from the German field guns. This was so severe as to force them to crawl off to the right and take refuge in a small stream where the water reached chest high. They painfully wriggled their way through the mud, pulling and pushing the boxes along till they reached the scanty shelter afforded by the old trench. By means of Pagris attached to the boxes, the men in front pulled along, over and through the dead bodies that encumbered the trench, while those behind pushed with all their might. If a single bullet or a single shell fragment had penetrated one of the boxes of explosives, the men propelling it would have been blown to pieces. Before they progressed a few yards, Fateh Singh fell severely wounded; in another hundred yards, Sucha Singh, Ujagar Singh and Sundar Singh were shot down, leaving only Lieutenant Smyth and six men to get the boxes along. However, in quick succession, Surain Singh and Sapuran Singh were shot dead, while Ganda Singh, Harnam Singh and Naik Mangal Singh were wounded. The second box of bombs had, therefore, to be abandoned and Lieutenant Smyth and the remaining Sepoy, Lal Singh, wriggled their way ahead yard by yard, emerging from the comparative shelter of the trench, until they found themselves confronted by a small stream, which at this point was too deep to wade. They had therefore to turn aside and crawl along the bank of the stream until they came to a place which was just fordable. They struggled across, the water churned up by a hail of bullets, clambered up the further bank and in a minute or two were amongst their cheering comrades. Both were unhurt, though their clothes were perforated by bullet holes. However, shortly afterwards Lal Singh was struck by a bullet and killed instantly.

So ended one of the most gallant episodes of the War. For his most conspicuous bravery Lieutenant Smyth was awarded the Victoria Cross, and later Order of St. George. (Russia) Lance Naik Mangal Singh received Indian Order of Merit, while the Indian Distinguished Service Medal was conferred on all the Sepoys of the party.

Western Front

Loos, (1915)

On September 25TH the Corps took part in the battle of Loos. The attack, the signal for which was the explosion of a big mine under the German salient, was at first a great success, 58TH Rifles penetrating a long way to the Aubers Ridge. Jemadar Sehel Singh lost his life at Aubers Ridge and was awarded the Indian Order of Merit posthumously for his conspicuous gallantry. The 58TH Rifles and 33RD Punjabis who had started the battle in reserve, lost heavily, to the extent of 262 and 258 respectively. Subadar Major Maluk Singh of 33RD Punjabis was awarded the Indian Order of Merit for gallantry in this battle.

The 69TH Punjabis lost 348 men out of 663. Subedar Major Jogindar Singh and Lance Naik Nidham Singh both of 69TH Punjabis were awarded the Indian Order of Merit for their conspicuous gallantry in this battle. Sepoy Nihal Singh of 62ND Punjabis was awarded the Indian Order of Merit and the French Croix de Guerre for his gallantry in this battle, as was Sepoy Indar Singh of 89TH Punjabis who was awarded the Indian Order of Merit. The total Indian loss in the battle of Loos was 1,926 men. The battle of Loos was the last big fight in which the Indian Corps took part in France. They were to undergo fresh trials and win fresh honours in other theatres of the First World War.

"Of the Indian Corps it may be said that as much was asked of them as has been asked of any troops at any period or in any theatre of this War. They stemmed the first German onslaught through the late autumn of 1914, which ended in bitter fighting at Givenchy. They played a glorious part in the battle of Neuve Chapelle. The second battle of Ypres, the struggle for the Auburs Ridge, and the desperate assaults of Loos- all claimed a toll of blood from this devoted Corps. They were asked to do much, and they tried to do everything they were asked." (Merewether and Bart)

Indian Cavalry

The departure of the bulk of the Indian Corps in France in December 1915 was not quite the end of the story of Indian participation in the War on the Western Front. Two Indian Cavalry Divisions remained in France until 1918 and took part in the Battle of the Somme, the Battle of Bazentin, the Battle of Flers-Courcelette, the advance to the Hindenburg Line and finally the Battle of Cambrai. The Meerut Cavalry Brigade was finally transferred to Mesopotamia and the remainder of the Cavalry left for Egypt in February 1918.

Risaldar Mukand Singh of 2ND Lancers was awarded the Military Cross in 1917, and Resaidar Bur Singh of 16TH Lancers was awarded the Military Cross in 1918. During the battles on the Western Front seven Sikh Officers were awarded the Military Cross and 58 Sikhs of all Armed Services, were awarded the Indian Order of Merit in consideration of their conspicuous gallantry against the Germans.

In 14 months the Indian Corps had lost 34,252 men (dead, wounded, ill, or prisoners of war) on the Western Front.

ADEN

Shaikh Sa'id, (1914)

Shortly after the outbreak of War with Turkey, on October 31ST, 1914, it became clear that the Turks, in co-operation with a number of the Arab tribes, were preparing an advance against the Aden Protectorate. The Turks had gathered in some strength on the Shaikh Sa'id Peninsula, which runs out to the South of the Red Sea towards the Isle of Perim. The 29TH Indian Infantry Brigade, then on its way from India to Suez, was ordered to interrupt its voyage to capture Shaikh Sa'id and destroy the Turkish works, armaments, and wells there. On November 10TH, 23RD Sikhs stormed the Turkish positions and compelled the enemy to retreat, leaving his field guns behind. The Sikh Pioneers carried out demolitions at Turbah Fort and guardhouses, which included the destruction of two 6-inch guns, and four field guns of sorts, large quantities of shells and cordite. Having accomplished its task, the Pioneers re-embarked and sailed for Aden, after receiving a message of hearty thanks from General Cox, who was proceeding to Egypt with a Brigade. It was not considered advisable at this time to push an expedition into the country to attack the Turks there. The Turks, consequently, remained in some force on the Northern boundary of the Aden Protectorate.

Perim, (1915)

When the Sikh Pioneers arrived at Aden from Shaikh Sa'id, a Company was sent to Perim, which was threatened by the Turkish activity on the mainland. The Turks had reoccupied Shaikh Sa'id and endeavoured from there to effect a landing on the North coast of the Isle of Perim. The garrison of the island, a Company of the Pioneers, successfully repulsed this attack. As the Turks had put out the lights in the Red Sea, the British took these over and the Pioneers put guards on the lighthouses. Havildar Kehar Singh captured a dhow bringing an angry letter from the Turkish authority wanting to know why a light was burning (the British occupation not having been realised!!).

Lahaj, (1915)

In 1915, the Aden Movable Column was re-inforced with the Malay States Guides. The force composed entirely of Sikh Infantry and Gunners. The most serious engagement began on 4TH July 1915, when the Aden Movable Column and Aden Troop advanced against Lahej, which was threatened by the Turks. The Turks were defeated in a skirmish in which Havildar Kehan Singh and Sepoy Sarwan Singh won the Indian Order of Merit. The Turks were defeated at Jabir and Mahat. The vital port of Aden remained safely in British hands and was never seriously threatened by an enemy which simply could not pierce its defensive cordon. Sepoy Sohan Singh 23RD Sikh Pioneers, Jemadar Gurdit Singh and Havildar Kehan of Malay States Guides and Subadar Molar Singh of 53RD Sikhs were awarded the Indian Order of Merit for conspicuous gallantry and devotion to duty during the Aden operations.

SUEZ CANAL

Great Britain and France declared War against Turkey on 5TH November 1914. At that time Egypt was theoretically still a province of the Turkish Empire but for practical purposes the country had been occupied and controlled by Britain since 1882. Egypt's strategic importance lay in its possession of the Suez Canal, a waterway regarded with good reason by the Turks as the jugular vein of the British Empire. The Turks needed to close the Canal. The Turks began to build up a force of 20,000 men under the command of Fourth Turkish Army. Djemal Pasha was both Commander in Chief of this Army and Governor of the Ottoman Empire in Palestine. Indian Army Battalions were to play a vital role in the forthcoming struggle. The Indian Army now took over the first-line defence of the Suez Canal, supported by Allied Warships. The 100 miles (160 km) long canal had a railway running along its whole length and was supplied with water behind it, with only brackish wells in front. The length of the canal included about 29 miles (47 km) of the Great and Little Bitter Lakes and Lake Timsah, which divided the three sectors organised for the defence. These troops were deployed at the Esh Shat, El Kubri, Gurkha, Shallufa, Geneffe, Suez posts, Deversoir, Serapeum East, Serapeum West, Tussum, Gebel Mariam, Ismailia Ferry and Ismailia Old Camp posts, Ballah, Qantara East, Qantara West, El Kab, Tina, Ras El Esh, Salt Works, New Canal Works and Port Said posts.

Bir-en-Nuss (1914)

A Sikh Princely States Unit, Patiala Lancers, extensively patrolled the vicinity of the Suez Canal. Their first clash came in North Sinai when they encountered a force of some 200 Bedouins and Turks near Bir-el-Nuss. The Patrol lost one Indian Officer, twelve Other Ranks killed, and three Sepoys wounded but inflicted some sixty casualties on the enemy.

Serapeum (1915)

92ND Punjabis were given the task of defending the Serapeum section of the Suez Canal. Early in January, the Turks raided Kantara. Supported by rifle and machine gun fire, they succeeded in approaching Serapeum. 92ND successfully charged the attackers, taking many prisoners. On the morning of 4TH February the Turks were still in strength, entrenched on the East Bank of the Canal. 92ND Punjabis were ordered to attack and round up the Turks in this position. The Punjabis stormed the entrenchments and compelled all the Turks to surrender.

Havildar Suba Singh of 92ND Punjabis, Naik Nihan Singh of 92ND Punjabis and Sepoy Dasunda Singh of 89TH Punjabis were awarded the Indian Order of Merit for conspicuous gallantry in the operations on the Suez Canal.

1ST Patiala Rajindra Infantry defended the portion of the Suez Canal from Tinch to Port Said during the Turkish attacks on the canal during 1915.

Captain Bhagwan Singh and Subedar Dharm Singh of Patiala Infantry were awarded Indian Order of Merit for conspicuous gallantry in the operations on the Suez Canal.

GALLIPOLI

The Gallipoli Campaign took place at the Gallipoli peninsula in Turkey from 25TH April 1915 to 9TH January 1916. The attempt to capture the Ottoman capital of Constantinople (Istanbul) failed. The campaign was considered one of the greatest victories of the Turks and was reflected on as a major failure by the Allies.

Geba Tepe (1915)

The landings on Gallipoli began on 25TH April 1915. Among the first invasion force were 21ST (Kohat) and 26TH (Jacob's) Mountain Batteries. The landing was fiercely contested for the next two days. Both sides lost heavily, but the Turks had the worst of it, and the position was held and improved. The first Indian Order of Merit of this campaign was won only a day later on 26TH April by Havildar Gurdit Singh of 26TH Mountain Battery, followed by the Indian Order of Merit to Naik Karam Singh of 21ST Mountain Battery.

Krithia (1915)

Never has any Battalion displayed such courage and devotion to duty as was displayed by 14TH Sikhs in the Third Battle of Krithia. They were highly praised for their gallantry and determination in a series of bitter hand-to-hand encounters. Writing to the Commander in Chief in India, General Sir Ian Hamilton paid noble tribute to the heroism of all ranks. The following are some of the passages from his letter: "In the highest sense of the word extreme gallantry has been shown by this fine Battalion. In spite of these tremendous losses there was not a sign of wavering all day. Not an inch of ground gained was given up and not a single straggler came back. The ends of the enemy's trenches leading into the ravine were found to be blocked with the bodies of Sikhs and of the enemy who died fighting at close quarters, and the glacis slope is thickly dotted with the bodies of these fine soldiers all lying on their faces as they fell in their steady advance on the enemy. The history of the Sikhs affords many instances of their value as soldiers, but it may be safely asserted that nothing finer than the grim valour and steady discipline displayed by them on 4TH June has ever been done by soldiers of the Khalsa. Their devotion to duty and their splendid loyalty to their orders and to their leaders make a record their nation should look back upon with pride for many generations." The Sikh soldiers left Gallipoli with a great reputation and their gallantry and devotion to duty had added further laurels to their already high reputation and good name.

Lance Naik Karam Singh of 21ST Mountain Battery, Havildar Indar Singh, Havildar Gurdit Singh and Gunner Naik Bir Singh of 26TH Mountain Battery, Lance Naik Hazara Singh of 14TH Ferozepore Sikhs, Subedar Kala Singh of 1ST Patiala Infantry and Sub Assistant Surgeons Bhagwan Singh, Ishar Singh, Narain Singh, and Daulat Singh were awarded the Indian Order of Merit for great gallantry during the Gallipoli campaign.

SENUSSI

In 1914, 15TH Ludhiana Sikhs went to fight in France with 3RD Lahore Division, but in late 1915 the Regiment was posted to Egypt where it operated against a much more traditional and tribal enemy.

Working from Eastern Libya, Sayed Ahmed, known as the Senussi, was the leader of a sect of devout Muslims. His men had been fighting the Italian occupiers of Libya with considerable success. They were trained and assisted by a group of Turkish military Officers led by Nuri Bey, half-brother of the Turkish War Minister, Enver Pasha. During 1915 German submarines began supporting the Turkish effort with the Senussi's Army by transporting Turks and weapons to Eastern Libya and attacking shipping along the Egyptian coast. The Senussi was at first reluctant to fight Britain, but in the end Nuri Bey persuaded him to join the Turkish Holy War and to invade Egypt. The Allied reverses at Gallipoli doubtless influenced the Senussi's thoughts and actions.

Wadi Senab (1915)

On 20TH November 1915, the British formed the Western Frontier Force (WFF). The WFF contained an Infantry Brigade composed of three partially-trained British Battalions, 6TH Royal Scots, 2ND and 7TH Battalion, 8TH Middlesex Regiment, plus 15TH Sikhs. The 15TH Sikhs was the only regular major Unit. On 11TH December, General Wallace sent out a Column to disperse a group of enemy reported to be at Duwwar Hussein, sixteen miles West of Matruh. Lieutenant-Colonel J.L.R. Gordon was appointed Column Commander. The Column included 15TH Sikhs. As the British Column approached the Wadi Hasheifat from the East, the Cavalry was forward and dispersed, No. 2 Company of 15TH Sikhs was the advanced guard, and two Platoons of the Royal Scots formed the left flank guard. Lieutenant-Colonel Gordon heard heavy firing on his left and observed his left flank guard running very swiftly towards the shore, pursued by an equal number of uniformed and well-drilled soldiers who used formations and cover as they followed up the fleeing Royal Scots. The British soldiers were making no attempt to engage the enemy, who were troops of the Muhafizia, the Senussi's regular Army trained by the Turks. The Sikhs' two machine guns came into action to halt the enemy advance. Knowing he could not achieve a decisive result and aware of the fatigue felt by his men, Lieut.-Colonel Gordon withdrew his men to their camp and on the next day the Column returned to Matruh. British casualties amounted to nine killed and fifty-six wounded whilst enemy casualties were around 100 killed and wounded. The Official History comments:

'The enemy had been driven off, but had been able to retire unmolested, and must be given credit for the surprise and the vigour of his attack. Had the standard of training and the experience of the whole column been equal to those of 15TH Sikhs, the Senussi might have been heavily defeated.'

Senussi

Wadi Majid, (1915)

The enemy was concentrating 900 Muhafizia in three Battalions, plus four mountain guns and two machine guns, six miles South-West of Matruh. General Wallace hoped to surprise the enemy force, and on 25th December two columns moved out from Matruh. Observing that Jebel Medwa was not occupied, Gordon sent one of the two 15th Sikh Companies forming the advanced guard to seize the Jebel, and this was achieved without opposition. The 15th Sikhs now advanced on the enemy ridge on a frontage of 200 yards. As the British troops moved onto the ridge the enemy broke and fled into Wadi Majid followed by the Sikhs and New Zealanders. The enemy camp in the wadi was set alight and the Muhafizia rearguard, demoralized but still fighting effectively, was driven onto the beach. Some of the enemy feigned death or wounds, but then opened fire at close range. This so enraged the Sikhs that any of these men taken alive were thrown into the burning tents. British losses had been thirteen killed and fifty-one wounded. The Senussi's force lost between 300 and 400 dead, and eighty prisoners were taken.

Halazin, (1916)

On 19th January an aeroplane located the main enemy camp at Halazin, twenty-two miles South-West of Matruh. As 15th Sikhs attacked, the enemy displayed considerable skill in withdrawing to prepared defences and made good use of mountain guns and machine guns. The shape of the British advance now resembled a horse shoe with the Sikhs in the centre of the curve. The Sikhs, New Zealanders and South Africans were through the enemy camp and into the entrenchments. The enemy defenders broke and retreated into the desert, abandoning their position. The 15th Sikhs suffered eighteen men killed and two British and three Indian Officers and 115 men wounded. The Senussi escaped, but he had lost around 200 men killed, including Turkish troops, and up to 500 wounded.

The Senussi and his followers continued to present a security threat in the Western Desert for a further twelve months. But the participation of 15th Sikhs in the campaign was over, as the Regiment now received orders to proceed to India. The 15th Sikhs had borne the brunt of the fighting so far, and had provided the backbone for a very untrained, inexperienced and under-staffed Western Frontier Force. The Regiment had acquitted itself with distinction, and for its services in this theatre it received the honour 'Egypt 1915-17.' As a result of the post-War reforms of the Indian Army, it became 2nd Battalion, 11th Sikh Regiment.

Jemadar Basant Singh of 15th Sikhs, received the Indian Order of Merit for gallantry at Halazin, the only Indian Order of Merit granted for this campaign.

EGYPT, PALESTINE, and SYRIA

The Turks sought to strike across Sinai and surprise the British and seize the Canal before the British had fully prepared their defences. The attack across Sinai failed and the small British force in Egypt repulsed the Ottomans (1915). The British began mobilising up forces in Egypt, of which the Commonwealth and Indian troops were in majority and went on to defeat the Turks with great dash and gallantry.

Romani, (1916)
The battle of Romani, August 1916, saw the defeat of a Turkish Army 16,000 strong that was attempting to come within Artillery range of the Suez Canal. The Turkish attack was repulsed, and the Turks escaped back across the Sinai. Even so, Turkish losses were heavy. The British captured 4,000 prisoners, four guns and nine machine guns, and overall losses were much higher, probably between 6,000 and 8,000. The victory at Romani ended Turkish attempts to attack towards Egypt.

Magdhaba, (1916)
As the British advanced on El Arish, the Turks abandoned the place. Some of the troops from El Arish moved to Rafah, others to Magdhaba. The British then decided to attack the Turkish position at Magdhaba, which threatened the right flank of the British advance. The Turks were in a strong position at Magdhaba. The 80th Turkish Regiment, 1,400 strong, occupied a strong position in a circle of redoubts. The Turks were outnumbered, but put up a strong resistance but finally surrendered to the British. With the fall of Magdhaba, the only Turkish position left in Egypt was at Rafah.

Rafah, (1917)
The fall of Magdhaba left a 2,000 strong Turkish force at Rafah. The British dispatched a mobile column to attack Rafah. The battle of Rafah cost the British 71 dead and 415 wounded. The Turks lost 200 dead and 1,635 captured. The British position at El Arish was now secure, and attention could turn towards a possible invasion of Palestine. The British Commander in Egypt, General Murray, soon decided to make an attempt to capture Gaza, to clear the way for the main invasion.

First Battle of Gaza, (1917)
The first of three battles fought in the Allied attempt to defeat Turkish forces took place in and around the Palestinian city of Gaza. After confronting a renewed Turkish counterattack, the British were forced to call off the attack. British forces had suffered 4,000 casualties during the First Battle of Gaza, compared with only 2,400 on the Turkish side. Where Turkey had previously been demoralised by the retreat through the Sinai, this victory encouraged the Turks to defend the Gaza-Beersheba line with more determination.

Egypt, Palestine and Syria

Second Battle of Gaza, (1917)
The second battle of Gaza, 17TH-19TH April 1917, was the second British attempt to capture Gaza in under a week. Unable to extract anything more than minor gains in spite of a two-to-one manpower advantage, the British called off the patently unsuccessful attack on the third day. British casualties were heavy: 6,444 men, with Turkish losses under a third of that figure. Shocked officials in London took the opportunity to purge the high command with General Murray being recalled to London. In his stead was sent General Sir Edmund Allenby, who engineered a spectacular revival of his and his Army's fortunes in a series of comprehensive British victories in Palestine.

Battle of Beersheba, (1917)
The main problem faced by General Allenby was the strength of the Turkish positions around Gaza. At that time the Turks held a strong position from the sea at Gaza to Beersheba. The Turkish defences of Beersheba were strongest. The town was defended by 3,500-4,000 Infantry, 1,000 Cavalry with four batteries of Artillery and fifty machine guns. Over the course of the day the Turks were slowly forced out of their strong defensive positions and eventually the Turks were forced out of the entire position.

Third Battle of Gaza, (1917)
The plan now required an attack at Gaza, while the forces at Beersheba prepared for their next attack. Accordingly the attack at Gaza was launched on the night of 1/2ND November. Fighting continued until the Turks were forced to pull back by the general retreat further west. The British captured Hareira and Sheria itself fell early on 7TH November. With their left broken, the Turks pulled out of Gaza.

Jerusalem, (1917)
On 19TH November, the Infantry advanced and Kuryet – el – Enab was attacked and captured after a stiff fight. The 58TH Sikhs distinguished themselves on this occasion with Lance Naik Diwan Singh and Sepoy Bhola Singh winning the Indian Distinguished Service Medal. On 21ST November the Nabi Samwil Ridge was taken. During the next month, the Turks launched a series of counter-attacks against Allenby's line but were repulsed each time with heavy losses. Finally, after four days of fighting against the defence line around Jerusalem, the city itself was taken without a shot being fired against it on 9TH December. In his Despatch recording this historic achievement, General Allenby wrote: "All ranks and services in the Force under my command have acquitted themselves in a manner beyond praise. Fatigue, heat, thirst and cold have been endured uncomplainingly. The co-operation of all arms has been admirable, and had enabled success in battle to be consummated by irresistible and victorious pursuit."

Egypt, Palestine and Syria

Judean Hills, (1918)

Allenby next turned his forces against the Judean Hills, to push back the Turks to the line between Jerusalem and Jaffa; there was fighting North of Budrus on 15TH December and between 25TH December and 1ST January, Turkish attempts to regain Jerusalem were decisively defeated. In February, the Turks were driven from the area between Jerusalem and the mouth of the Jordan River and in March they were pushed Northwards. There was very severe fighting in some of these operations. Allenby then struck against Turkish lines of communication with the Hedjaz region, also aiming to help King Faisal by deflecting Turkish forces from the Dead Sea area. The Jordan was crossed in the face of stiff resistance on March 21ST and raids against Es Salt and Amman, with pressure on the Judean front being maintained with attacks on El Kefr and Deir Ballut in April.

Jordan Valley, (1918)

Between Christmas and New Year's Day, the Turks made a desperate attempt to recover Jerusalem. At the end of it they were from three to six miles further from it than before and had lost 1,000 dead, 750 prisoners and 24 machine guns.

January 1918, was devoted to improving communications, February to driving the enemy out of the tract between Jerusalem and the mouth of the Jordan, and the first half of March to pushing him Northwards and denying him all the lower fords of the Jordan. Large numbers of Indian soldiers were brought in, mainly from Mesopotamia, to replace the losses, with strong reinforcements of all arms also coming from India itself. It took the summer of 1918 to re-organise and acclimatise the new forces, so that the offensive operations were reduced to a series of minor actions and raids. A particularly brilliant and successful raid was by the Sikh Squadron of the Hodson's Horse on the night of 23RD May, for which the Regiment was congratulated by the Corps Commander: - "The Turks were met in considerable strength in an entrenched position with a good field of fire, and it is only due to the determined leading and the soldierly spirit and dash of leaders and men that success was obtained."

The Lightening Advance, (1918)

The first blow in what was to become an amazingly successful advance was seizing Wadi Samieh. An intense bombardment of the coastal sector of the Turkish line was followed by a massive Infantry attack; Regiment after Regiment of the Indian Army distinguished itself in attacks on specific targets, taking Kefr Kasim, Jiljulieh, Kefr Saba, Kalkilieh, Tabsor and El Tireh. In what was from now on becoming largely a Cavalry campaign, mounted forces were able to penetrate the gap in Turkish lines along the coast and the important town of Tulkeram was attacked. Village after village was taken in a series of swift Cavalry advances. By 21ST September, all organised resistance in the coastal sector had ended and the Turks were pouring Northwards and Eastwards, relentlessly pursued by Cavalry and aircraft.

Egypt, Palestine and Syria

Armistice, (1918)

On 22ND September, a part of the Haifa garrison was attacked and defeated by Indian Cavalry as it tried to flee by night across the desert and the next day, Haifa was captured and Acre fell without opposition. Mann and Es Salt were also taken on 23RD, Tiberias and Amman on 25TH. At the same time, and co-operating with Arab forces, which had captured Deraa, the Desert Mounted Column started for Damascus. Although they faced some opposition, they broke up retreating Turkish Units and drove them into the arms of the Cavalry at Sahnaya on 30TH September. By the evening of 30TH, Damascus was isolated and it fell on 1ST October. Pushing forward quickly, mounted troops passed via Tyre and Sidon to Beirut, which they reached on 8TH October and Holms and Tripoli fell on the 12TH and 13TH. Aleppo fell to the Arabs on 25TH October. What was probably the last Cavalry charge of the War took place near Haritan on 26TH October but general armistice with Turkey brought it to a halt on 31ST October 1918. Allenby's campaign in Northern Palestine and Syria was an amazing success.

Indian Cavalry

The Desert Mounted Corps, during its final offensive from 19TH September to 26TH October, destroyed three Turkish Armies and took 46,000 prisoners out of 83,000 captured by the whole force. It had a total of five Australian Regiments and one French Cavalry Regiment in the Australian Division and five British Yeomanry and 13 Indian Cavalry Regiments including three Indian State Force Regiments. Thus the majority of the troops in the Corps were Indian Cavalry and although there is no desire to decry the contribution of other troops, yet the fact that the backbone of the Corps was composed of the Indian Cavalry must not be forgotten.

Eight Sikh Officers of various Infantry and Cavalry Regiments were awarded the Military Cross in consideration of their conspicuous gallantry during the Egypt, Palestine and Syria campaign.

Thirty five Sikh Officers and men of various Infantry and Cavalry Regiments were awarded the Indian Order of Merit in consideration of their conspicuous gallantry during the Egypt, Palestine and Syria campaign.

The Sikh gunners of Hong Kong and Singapore Royal Garrison Artillery after a tour of duty in the Suez Canal defences then took part in the battles of Maghdada and Rafah including the three battles of Gaza, the action at Nebi Samil, the capture of Jerusalem and the attacks on Ammaw, Es Salt, Abu Tehnib and Megiddo. The following Sikh Officers were the only Indian soldiers ever to be awarded 'The Distinguished Conduct Medal' for services in the field.

Havildar Fateh Singh (April 1917) Havildar Kishen Singh (Sept. 1918) Havildar Chajja Singh (May 1918) Havildar Rur Singh (Oct. 1918).

The DCM is regarded as second only to the Victoria Cross in prestige.

SALONIKA FRONT

The Salonika Front was opened in 1915 to assist Serbia against the central powers, Germany, Austria-Hungary and Bulgaria. The British Salonika Force was one element in an Allied Army, which contained also Greek, Serbian, Montenegrin, and Yugoslav, French, Italian, Russian and Indian troops.

The following Regiments in Salonika were partly recruited or were re-inforced from the Sikhs: -
No 2 Mountain Battery R.G.A., No. 5 Mountain Battery R.G.A., No. 7 Mountain Battery R.G.A., 2ND Lancers (Gardner's Horse), 24TH Punjabis, 25TH Punjabis, 31ST Punjabis, 66TH Punjabis, 67TH Punjabis, 76TH Punjabis, 84TH Punjabis, and 89TH Punjabis.

After the landing in October 1915, Allied forces pushed along the Vardar valley into Serbia but were then compelled to retire to Salonika, which was held as a fortified camp for a year. An Allied offensive in the second half of 1916 established a line running from Monastir to the gulf of Strymonikos, the British Force holding the sector Eastward from Doiran. It was not till towards the end of the War that India began to take a large share in the operations on the Salonika front. In May 1918 a siege Battery and in October 12 Indian Battalions were sent thither from Mesopotamia, together with two agricultural Labour Corps and the personnel of four Indian Hospitals. This was to remain the Allied line until September 15TH 1918 when the decisive breakout to the North led to the surrender of Bulgaria a fortnight later. In the three years of its existence, the British Salonika Force suffered 10,000 casualties, of which nearly half were due to the high incidence of malaria in this campaign. At the time of the Armistice, there were 15,000 Indian fighting men and 3,000 followers on this front, but the Bulgarian Army had already been disposed of in September and Turkey threw down her arms before General Mine had actually launched an attack on Constantinople from the West.

In the Indian cemetery of Thessalonica there are about 26 Sikhs, all buried together. The 26 Sikhs who died in Thessalonica were mostly soldiers or drivers in the Punjabi Units. On a few Sikh graves, there is an inscription in Gurmukhi: Ek Om kára Shri wahe Guru Ji ki Fateh. (Victory to One Almighty God).

MESOPOTAMIA

On 6TH November 1914, a force of Indian and British Infantry landed at the head of the Persian Gulf, ostensibly to protect imperial oil interests now threatened by Turkey, who had joined the Central Powers on 28TH October and to prevent Turkish agents from stirring up trouble amongst India's Muslims. The force fighting in Mesopotamia was principally one of the Indian Army, 6TH (Poona) Division, 12TH Indian Division, 3RD (Lahore) Division, 7TH (Meerut) Division, 14TH Indian Division, 15TH Indian Division, 17TH Indian Division, and 18TH Indian Division, with only one solely British formation, 13TH (Western) Division.

Fao, (1914)

On 6TH November 1914, the British offensive began with the Naval Force bombarding the old fort at Fao, which was located at the point where the Shatt-al-Arab meets the Persian Gulf. The port of Fao was captured on November 6TH, and here the first military distinction was won on the front by Bugler Surain Singh of 20TH Punjabis, who very bravely set fire to a village held by the enemy. The main force of the enemy was concentrated at Sahil, close to the river. While under fire from an old fort, lying on the edge of a palm grove on the enemy's flank, Subadar Sebal Singh and Lance-Naik Net Singh, of 104TH Wellesleys Rifles, gallantly stormed the outer wall of the fort, at the head of some twenty or thirty men of various Units. They were the first in this part of the line to enter the enemy's position, and Subadar Sabal Singh and Lance-Naik Net Singh were rewarded with the Indian Order of Merit for their conspicuous gallantry. In the same action Naik Dalip Singh of 3RD Sappers and Miners, led his squad with great determination into the enemy's trenches and won for himself the Indian Order of Merit. Bugler Surain Singh of 20TH Punjabis was awarded the Indian Order of Merit for his conspicuous gallantry at Saihan on 13TH November 1914.

Basra, (1914)

After the capture of Fao by the British, the Army began to converge on Basra. The Ottomans prepared defensive positions at Saihan, and on November 15TH the British attacked. The Ottomans were beaten, suffering 250 casualties and the British continued to advance. The main Ottoman position was at a place the British called Sahil. The Ottomans had 4,500 soldiers dug in near some palm groves and an old mud walled fort. The British and Indian troops pressed on and when they came close the British Artillery finally found the range, bringing fire directly upon the Ottoman trenches. The mud walled fort fell, and with that the entire Ottoman force got up and ran. Ottoman losses were maybe 1,000; the British and Indian troops lost 350. On November 21ST, the Indian troops occupied Basra.

Mesopotamia

Qurna, (1914)

A small force of two and a half Indian Infantry Battalions found themselves in a fire-fight against the Turkish defences as they advanced on Qurna. The British were forced to retire, until reinforcements arrived. In the interim, the Turks had advanced across the Tigris and occupied Qurna. Before the Turks in Qurna knew what was happening, the Infantry had encircled the town and captured the Turkish garrison of 42 Turkish Officers and over 1000 men. Naik Guman Singh of 104TH Rifles was awarded the Indian Order of Merit for his conspicuous gallantry at Qurna.

Shaiba, (1915)

The Ottoman Commander Suleiman Askeri had about 4,000 regular soldiers, including a large number of irregular Arabs and Kurds, numbering maybe 14,000, for a total of 18,000 personnel. He chose to attack the British positions around Shaiba, Southwest of Basra. The British garrison at Shaiba consisted of about 7,000 men in a fortified camp. On 12TH April, the Turkish attack on the British camp was repulsed. Next day 2ND Dorsets and 24TH Punjabis routed the Arab irregulars, capturing 400 and dispersing the rest. Sulaimann Askari had his Ottoman regular troops fall back on Barjisiya Wood. The Dorsets and the Punjabis then launched a bayonet charge that overwhelmed the rest of the Turks. The enemy was forced to retire on Nasiriyah, with a loss of 3,000 killed and wounded and 700 prisoners. The losses on the British side were about 1,000 killed and wounded, especially among 24TH Punjabis. Askari would end up committing suicide over the loss, which he blamed on the Arab irregulars and their failure to support him. Lance Daffadar Arjan Singh of 33RD Cavalry was awarded the Indian Order of Merit for his conspicuous gallantry at Shaiba.

Barjisiya, (1915)

On 14TH April the Turks started to withdraw from Bajisiya wood towards Nukhaila. The Cavalry Brigade was deployed and ordered to threaten the Turkish line of retreat across the Nukhaila mud flats. The plan by the Cavalry was abandoned, when it was discovered that they had well entrenched Infantry and guns covering the wood. The Infantry launched a general assault and the Cavalry supported them by dismounted fire from the right flank. The front line of the trenches was captured by 5 p.m. and the bulk of the defenders killed. The enemy evacuated Bajisiya wood during the night and withdrew nearly 140 km across the desert. Following this success, troops were dispatched to the Karun River to deal with Turkish forces, which had harassed Ahwaz. The hostile Arab stronghold of Khafajiya was reduced to submission. The 24TH Punjabis, 76TH Punjabis with 66TH Punjabis and 33RD Cavalry were very forward in these operations, which had the further advantage of preventing the forces engaged from reinforcing Amara, which was the next object of attention.

Mesopotamia

Amara, (1915)

The capture of the important Turkish administrative base of Amara in late May 1915 was a remarkable triumph for the Indian troops. Commencing on 31ST May 1915 the operation quickly secured Turkish outposts. News from reconnaissance aircraft reached the British Commander Sir Charles Townshend the following day indicating that the main Turkish force at Ruta had opted to move North towards Amara. On 31ST May, 6TH Division, advanced up the Tigres, and 17TH Brigade in an amphibious battle drove the Turks out of their advanced position by noon. Following up his success at full speed, General Townsend reached Amara on a gunboat and bluffed the town into surrender on 3RD June. Here he was joined by 12TH Division, which had made a historic desert march from Ahwaz.

Nasiriyah, (1915)

On the Euphrates front, 12TH Division began operations against the Turkish garrison at Nasiriyah. On 5TH July was fought the battle of Hadqiqa, in which the enemy's position was carried at a cost of 26 killed and 85 wounded. Then the enemy entrenched just below Nasiriyah, which was occupied on July 25TH, the taking of it having cost 600 killed and wounded. The Turks lost 3,000 men and all their guns and ammunition and over 1,000 prisoners. The victory had tremendous influence on the Arabs; because Nasiriyah was the capital of the Muntafik Arabs, the most powerful of all the tribes on the Euphrates. During these operations on the Euphrates, 30TH Mountain Battery again distinguished itself, as did 17TH Company of Sappers and Miners, 24TH Punjabis, 48TH Pioneers, 67TH, 78TH, and 90TH Punjabis, 33RD Cavalry and the Signal Company. Sikh soldiers of various Regiments won a galaxy of Indian Order of Merits for their conspicuous gallantry at Nasiriyah.

Kut – al – Amara, (1915)

Following the successive defeats of their forces and their continued withdrawal further up country, the Turks concentrated around the town of Kut-al-Amara, with extensive defence lines on both sides of the Tigres around Es Sinn. The battle to take Kut from the Turks began on 27TH September and lasted for two full days, and successively drove them out their positions, forcing them back on Ctesiphon. British casualties amounted to 1,233 men, including many slightly wounded, while the Turks lost over 4,000, including 1,153 prisoners. Distinctions were won by the Sikh soldiers of 20TH, 22ND, 24TH, 76TH Punjabis, 7TH Hariana Lancers, 16TH Cavalry, the Sappers and Miners, and 34TH Signal Company. "The battle of Kut-al-Amara will be remembered as one of the most brilliant actions, possibly the most brilliant fought by the Indian Army." (Chandler: *Long Road to Baghdad.*)

Mesopotamia

Ctesiphon, (1915)

General Townshend advanced to Azizieh on 5TH October and the Turks fell on Ctesiphon. Here on 22ND November, General Townshend attacked them: the troops engaged were the same as those who had taken Kut; the brunt of the attack was entrusted to the men of 30TH Brigade, they and 6TH Division all fought brilliantly. The enemy was driven back across the Diala and General Townshend bivouacked on the ground he had won, but at a very heavy cost. The Infantry lost 4,000 out of the 8,500 men engaged, and even the Cavalry lost 200 out 1,200; 76TH Punjabis in particular suffered severe casualties. The enemy, who had been strongly re-inforced, counter attacked strenuously on the night of $23^{RD,}$ but was resolutely repulsed with heavy loss. On 1ST December the Turkish advance guard attacked Umm-el–Tubul, but was brilliantly repulsed. Exhausted and outnumbered the British retreated to Kut-al-Amara on 2ND December, and it was obviously important to hold it. The Turks closed round the Kut-al-Amara on 5TH December. Thus began the siege of Kut-al-Amara.

Sheikh Saad, (1916)

At the siege of Kut a relief expedition was organized under Aylmer and concentrated at Ali-el-Gherbi. On January 4TH, Aylmer ordered an attack on Sheikh Saad. The Turks had effectively blocked Aylmer's path by placing approximately 22,500 troops and 72 guns on both banks of the Tigris. The 28TH Brigade and 92ND Punjabis on the South bank captured the enemy's trenches, killed over 350 Turks and captured 600 prisoners and two guns. Exhausted and dispirited, the British force had suffered around 4,000 casualties during the engagement for no significant gain. The operation to relieve Townshend at Kut had not been notably advanced. Six Sikh Infantry-men and Sub Assistant Surgeon Pargan Singh of I.S.M.D. were awarded the Indian Order of Merit for their conspicuous gallantry in the battle of Sheikh Saad.

Wadi, (Fort Chibibat) (1916)

The first attempt to relieve Townshend's beleaguered force under siege had ended in failure. The British Commander believed that Aylmer's force of 10,000 men, added to Townshend's 10,000 in Kut, would prove sufficient to break the ill-disciplined Turkish Army. The local Turkish Commander led 20,000 troops in the area but could also call upon a further 30,000 stationed in nearby Baghdad. Aylmer began operations on 13TH January 1916, quickly becoming bogged down, as the element of surprise was lost. The 28th Brigade's frontal attack was entirely repulsed, 56TH Sikhs losing heavily, and the attack was called off by Aylmer as the day closed.

Mesopotamia

Hannah, (1916)

On 21ST January Umm-el-Hannah's very strong positions were assaulted from El Orah, with the Indian Units suffering appalling losses in frontal attacks. The 62ND Punjabis, for example, were reduced from nearly 1,000 men at the start of the action to 160 by the end and in 35TH Brigade every Field Officer suffered injury. During February, despite repeatedly shelling the Umm-el-Hanna lines, the relief force was brought to a standstill.

Dujailah, (1916)

The next attempt to force the Turks to abandon their position was made against their lines on the South bank of the Tigres at Dujailah. The Turks had reinforced the Dujailah positions in time to fight off the Indian assault. Again there were terrible losses. The 8TH Brigade lost nearly fifty percent of its men. On the early morning of 10TH, 89TH Punjabis assisted in an unpremeditated fight in the open with the Turks at Abu Roman; they killed a large number of Turks but lost 200 men in the process. 10 Sikh soldiers were awarded the Indian Order of Merit for their conspicuous gallantry at Dujailah, Butaniyeh and Nasariyah.

Sannaiyat, (1916)

The next enemy position to be attacked was at Sannaiyat. The casualty figure was appalling; 19TH and 28TH Brigades lost sixty percent of their men in a matter of minutes. Attacks continued but though the Turkish trenches were often gained, weakened Units simply could not hold them. Once more, the attempt to reach Kut ground to a halt. Attention was shifted to the South bank of the Tigres with 3RD Division brilliantly taking Bait Aiessa on 12TH April and holding on to its gains in the face of repeated Turkish counter-attacks. The last raid on the Sannaiyat position involved two Officers and 30 men each of 53RD Sikhs and 56TH Rifles devoting themselves to practically certain death.

Kut – al – Amara, (1916)

The failure of the attempt to break through the Sannaiyat position and reach Kut spelled the end for Townsend's garrison, strained to the limits of its endurance by hunger and disease. The town surrendered on 29TH of April 1916 after a siege of 147 days. The following day 277 British and 204 Indian Officers, together with 2,592 British and 6,988 Indian Other Ranks were taken into captivity, together with 3,248 Indian non-combatants. Approximately 345 badly wounded or sick men (mainly Indians) were exchanged for Turkish prisoners and sent down to Basra. For the remainder, the chances of survival were low. Of the 2,592 British troops captured at Kut, about 1,750 died on the march or later in the camps, and of the 6,988 Indian troops, about 2,500 died in similar fashion.

Mesopotamia

Hai Bridge – Head, (1917)

On January 26TH, 26TH and 82ND Punjabis gave very good account of themselves, capturing the enemy's trenches though they lost nearly half of their effectives. On February 1ST, 36TH and 45TH Sikhs bore the brunt of a desperate counter attack. About 1,200 Turks held this position in very well prepared entrenchments. Both of them assaulted shoulder to shoulder in the face of heavy machine gun fire. Although the first three trench lines were captured, casualties were very heavy during the course of the day. At one time, 45TH was more or less isolated as the Turks launched enveloping counter-attacks. These were eventually pushed back. The fierceness of the fighting can be judged by the fact that at the end of the day, 45TH Sikhs was left with just three British and three Indian Officers and 200 men. Of the 22 British and Indian Officers, who had become casualties, two-thirds, including the Commanding Officer, were killed. The other Battalion also suffered heavily, and was led out of action by the Subedar Major, the lone survivor of the British and Indian Officers who had taken part in the battle. On February 3RD, 62ND Punjabis helped to capture the enemy's second line. By the next day more than 2,000 prisoners had been captured. However, the enemy were still strongly entrenched in their old lines at Sannaiyat.

Sannaiyat, (1917)

Further frontal assaults on the trench systems on 17TH February again failed to gain foothold and it was not until 22ND February, 92ND Punjabis, 125TH Sikhs and the Seaforths returned to the charge and with the aid of 51ST and 53RD Sikhs captured and held the first and second lines, and held them against a series of dogged counter-attacks. On 23RD and 24TH of February, in the teeth of fierce resistance, the successive Turkish lines of the Sannaiyat system were taken and successfully held. On 23RD February, forces on the South of the Tigres crossed the river at the Shumran Bend, and made a feint attack at Magasis. By nightfall the Turks began to withdraw from the Sannaiyat positions.

Baghdad, (1917)

The Turks had now to flee for their lives. On 27TH February, the Cavalry captured Azizeh and drove the Turks out of Lajj. Baghdad railway station was taken on 11TH March and on the same day the Tel Muhammad position across the Diala captured. Soon afterwards, Cavalry forces marched into Baghdad. The Capture of Baghdad itself was somewhat of an anticlimax. The British troops had feared fierce resistance; instead the Turkish Commander ordered a general retreat. By the time the British entered the city there were only 9000 Turkish troops remaining. They surrendered rather than put up a fight.

Mesopotamia

Jebel Hamlin, (1917)

The Battle of Jebel Hamlin saw a British-led force attempt to encircle 15,000 Turkish troops led by Ali Ishan Bey. Led by General Keary, the Anglo-Indian force shifted towards the Turkish position at the foot of the Jebel Hamlin Mountains. Meanwhile 4,500 men of Ishan's force proceeded to dig secure lines on high ground behind two canals among the mountains. Keary's consequent preparations to storm the Turkish lines were not undertaken in secrecy, with the result that when the British attack finally began on 25TH March, they found the Turkish defence well prepared. The attack was a failure, some 1,200 British casualties were suffered while Ishan's force managed to escape Southwest, headed for Turkish forces sited on the River Tigris.

Khan Baghdadi, (1917)

The next significant advance was made on the South side of the Tigres, where Beled Station was captured on 8TH April and Harbe occupied next day. Renewed attempts by the Turks to combine forces were frustrated later in the same week. On 18TH April, the passage of the Shatt-el-Adhaim on the left bank of the Tigres was forced and a further advance on the right bank pushed the Turks out of Istabulat on 21ST. The fighting here was severe, with 9TH Bhopals losing in ten minutes 200 men and all their Officers bar one.

On 3RD December, the British forced the Turks out of the Sakal Tutan Pass and defeated them on 5TH at kára Tappah. 1918 began with further advance along the Euphrates, with the towns of Uqbah, Hit and Salahiyeh being occupied between 9TH February and 10TH March. The Turks fell back to Khan Baghdadi, where they were decisively beaten on March 26TH. Turkish power on the Euphrates had more or less ceased to exist and the remnants of their Army were pursued for seventy miles towards Aleppo.

Mosul, (1918)

After a union with the Russians had been made by the occupation of Bakuba, and when Feludjah had been captured and the Euphrates made secure as far as Hit, the English continued their march toward Mosul. By a simultaneous advance of the principal columns along both banks of the Tigris and the victorious battle at Istabulat (April 21ST, 1917) Samara was reached, the two defeated Turkish corps being compelled to fall back to Mosul. After a long pause, necessitated by the climatic conditions, the British succeeded in nipping in the bud a design on the part of the Turks to deliver a blow against his left flank, in order to sever his rear communications. The powerful Turkish position on the Euphrates near Ramadieh was successfully attacked on September 28TH, with sufficient forces (a former attempt had failed), was surrounded by the Cavalry and forced to surrender, whereby the Turkish Commander Achmed Bey and 3,500 men were taken prisoners.

Mesopotamia

Kurdistan, (1918)

Operations continued in Southern Kurdistan in April and May 1918 with the Turks losing heavily in their flight. Towns successfully occupied by British forces included Kifri, Kulawand, Tuz Kharmatli, Kirkuk and Altun Kupri. The lesser Zab was to be the final battle area of the Mesopotamian campaign during the Great War. The Turks were defeated at Fathah on 24TH October, the Zab being crossed next day and the Turks forced onto the West bank of the Tigres. On 29TH October 1918 after four days of heavy fighting, the Turks were surrounded at Sherqat, where on 30TH they surrendered. Within two days, the Armistice with Turkey had been announced and the Mesopotamian campaign came to an end. In four years, the Indian Expeditionary Force had grown to over 400,000 men. It had suffered 100, 000 casualties, of which 30,000 were fatal.

Altogether 132 Indian Order of Merit gallantry awards were made to the Sikh Officers and men of all services for their conspicuous gallantry during the Mesopotamia Campaign.

The following Sikh Officers were awarded the Military Cross in Mesopotamia; Subedar Mit Singh of 47TH Sikhs, Jemadar Sohan Singh of 24TH Punjabis, Jemadar Kehar Singh of 28TH Punjabis, Subedar Kehar, Singh Subedar Narain Singh, and Subedar Jaimal Singh of 45TH Sikhs.

Jemadar Puran Singh of 21ST Mountain Battery, Havildar Kishan Singh of Guides Infantry, Subedar Badan Singh of 22ND Punjabis, Havildar Dewa Singh of 47TH Sikhs and Sowar Kaka Singh of Burma Military Police were awarded the highest French gallantry award of 'Croix De Guerre' for their conspicuous gallantry during the Mesopotamia Campaign.

Havildar Hardit Singh of Sappers and Miners, Naik Sham Singh of 45TH Sikhs, Havildar Sawan Singh of 52ND Sikhs (FF) were awarded the French gallantry award of 'Medaille Militaire' for their conspicuous gallantry during the Mesopotamia Campaign.

Naik Kala Singh of 36TH Sikhs, Naik Fateh Singh of 45TH Sikhs, Havildar Mal Singh of 47TH Sikhs, Havildar Bhagwan Singh of 57TH Rifles, and Havildar Sundar Singh of 90TH Punjabis were awarded Italian 'Medal for Military Valour' for their conspicuous gallantry during the Mesopotamia Campaign.

PERSIA

The story of the operations undertaken in Persia by the Indian Army during the period of the Great War is rather complicated, involving a number of different regions, local tribal disturbances, and a Persian mutiny and in the end activities against Bolsheviks during the Russian Civil War. Detailed account of all these operations are beyond the scope of this book. However I have endeavoured to record the participation of Sikh soldiers in some of the operations carried out by the Indian Army in Persia.

Southern Persia

Southern Persia was in the British sphere under the terms of the Anglo-Russian Convention of 1907. British officials were increasingly concerned about the security of the trade routes from the Persian Gulf to the hinterland because of the value of the trade to the Indian government and the strategic importance of maintaining Britain's ascendancy over the Persian Gulf. In the years leading up to World War I, banditry, armed robbery on the roads, and attacks on foreign residents increased in proportion to the government's loss of control over the provinces. A British-controlled force had become more pressing, given the interest in the nascent Anglo-Persian Oil Company. The British proposed to mend matters by undertaking punitive operations against the offenders, in the first place against those in the vicinity of the main trade routes. This work had to be carried out mainly by the Indian troops.

Burma Mounted Rifles

The Burma Military Police Battalions (Composed of Sikhs and the Punjabi Mussalmans recruited in the Punjab) were organized like regular Army Regiments, and their duties were entirely military. In 1916, the Burma Police Battalions were bodily formed into Squadrons of the Burma Mounted Infantry for service in Persia. Eventually the Squadrons were renamed the Burma Mounted Rifles.

Dehbid, (1917)

On 1ST June, a Squadron of the Burma Mounted Infantry on their way to Dehbid came into collision with a band of robbers belonging to a Khamseh tribe and pursued them for some miles, inflicting casualties without loss to them. On the 18TH and 19TH June part of the Burma Mounted Infantry detachment at Dehbid were engaged in that vicinity with a robber band that had looted a donkey caravan. The action was most effective, nine of the robbers being killed or wounded and eighteen captured, while part of the lost property was recovered. This affair had an excellent effect in the neighbourhood.

Persia

Qashqais, (1917)

On 4TH July a column of the Burma Mounted Infantry had to deal with a band of Qashqais robbers. The column under Jemadar Partab Singh had been under arms for over fifteen hours and had covered distances varying from thirty-three to forty-six miles. It was by this time very tired and hungry, but they responded with spirit to the order to assault the fort. The tribesmen in the fort, discouraged by the steady determination of the advancing Indian Infantry, started to flee when these arrived within one hundred yards and fixed bayonets. On 5TH of July 1917 a troop under Jemadar Partab Singh encountered heavy fire but charged ahead to join a detachment engaged in a fire-fight against 500 robber-tribesmen. They killed 23 and the rest fled to the hills.

Khwaja Jamali, (1917)

Sir Percy Sykes urged the necessity for punishing the robber tribes who had been guilty of a long series of depredations on the Kerman – Yezd, Shiraz – Isfahan, and Shiraz – Saidabad roads. A small column with one Squadron of the Burma Mounted Infantry, marched off from Qawwamabad on 20TH September. Having destroyed several forts and having captured or destroyed a considerable amount of forage, the column halted at Abadeh Kaleh on 25TH to destroy several more forts. Starting on its march again on the same day, the column found its way blocked by a body of some five or six hundred Lashanis, who were holding a position round the village of Khwaja Jamali. Two Troops of the Burma Mounted Infantry were sent to attack and turn the enemy's left flank, which they did, compelling the tribesmen to flee northwards.

Gumun, (1918)

On 25TH January, the Burma Mounted Infantry encountered about 200 raiders in the vicinity of Gumun and attacked and killed 25 and wounded about 80, destroyed two of their camps, and recovered a considerable number of plundered animals. They completely routed the raiders, burning their remaining camp and recovering many more animals they had plundered.

South Persia, (1918)

The performance of the Sikh soldier for gallantry was so high that the authorities sought for another Squadron of the Burma Mounted Infantry for service in Persia. On arrival of the third Squadron the title of the contingent was changed to the Burma Mounted Rifles.

Northern Fars, (1918)

The operations against the Chah Haqis and the Labu Muhammadis included two Squadrons of the Burma Mounted Rifles. Boldly advancing with bayonets fixed, they drove the tribesmen into the high hills to the West and pursued them for some distance, which coming after sixteen hour's fighting and having covered about fifty miles was a fine effort.

Persia

Ziarat May, (1918)

Colonel Grant, receiving information that a well-known robber chief, Mullah Qurban, with a strong following, was near Ziarat, decided to take action against him. One Squadron of the Burma Mounted Rifles, reinforced by another half Squadron, gradually drove the enemy, who fought hard, first off the hill immediately behind Ziarat and then up the rocky slopes as far as the snow-line. During the day Colonel Grant received information that many of the Chehar Rahis, abandoning their forts had betaken themselves to the main tribal stronghold on the Kuh-I-Khan, which was about twelve miles West of Ziarat. Here, in a position which they deemed impregnable, they were said to be prepared to fight. The attack on the Kuh-I-Khan stronghold started with the Infantry capturing the enemy's main position. With the fire from Lewis guns of the Burma Mounted Riles very few of the enemy escaped. Colonel Grant attributed his success to the accuracy of his intelligence, the brilliant tactics of the Burma Mounted Rifles, and the presence of Lewis guns.

Khan -I-Zinian, (1918)

It is estimated that 3,000 Qashqais had invested Khan-I-Zinian, a military post held by the South Persia Rifles. On 24TH May three Squadrons of the Burma Mounted Rifles marched out to attack the tribesmen besieging the garrison. They engaged the enemy in some very stiff actions. It was calculated that the enemy strength in action had been about 4,500 Qashqais and 300 Khamseh men. They had been well armed with two machine guns, rifles and plenty of ammunition; and they had fought bravely and estimated to have sustained between 600 and 700 casualties.

Ahmadabad, (1918)

Learning that there were about thirteen hundred tribesmen at Ahmadabad, another three or four hundred at Chenar and between two and three thousand Qashqais at Deh Shaikh, Colonel Orton decided to take the offensive and during the fighting that ensued the Qashqais displayed great bravery and in places got within two hundred yards of the Burma Mounted Rifles, but the increasing volume of fire they encountered was too much for them and they had fallen back, having sustained heavy losses. Colonel Orton had achieved his objective most successfully, it being estimated that of about 3,200 tribesmen engaged, 200 had been killed and 300 wounded; the total British losses being 5 killed and 24 wounded. Next day Sir Percy Sykes telegraphed India expressing his high appreciation of the discipline, gallantry and soldierly spirits of the Burma Mounted Rifles.

Persia

Firuzabad, (1918)

A force, commanded by Colonel Orton, left Shiraz on 20TH October with a column composed of three Squadrons of the Burma Mounted Rifles, two sections of 36TH Mountain Battery and 124TH Baluchis to take action against the Qashqais at Firuzabad. On 24TH October, it was evident that the enemy intended to stand and fight and about 2.50pm they were seen in occupation of a ridge Westward of Ibrahimabad village. Meanwhile Colonel Dyer, with two Squadrons of the Burma Mounted Rifles, their advance supported by the fire of the mountain guns, had secured a minor ridge some 1,200 yards North of the enemy's main position. The Baluchis were sent forward to secure the left flank about Ibrahimabad and to attack this position. The remaining Burma Squadron and a Baluchi Company were retained as a reserve. Two of the Baluchi Companies gained a knoll about 1,000 yards Northwest of the enemy's position without difficulty; the third Company, securing the left flank about Ibrahimabad. These movements had brought the enemy's main position under accurate gun fire and a cross fire from the Lewis guns and rifles of the Burma Mounted Rifles, with a result when an attack was launched it attained complete success within twenty minutes. So far, the Indian casualties had been only seven, all among the Baluchis, but the enemy, had lost about eighty killed and wounded.

In the meantime a Squadron of the Burma Mounted Rifles had inflicted severe loss on the Qashqais. The Squadron had reached Deh-I-Barm unobserved and taken up a concealed position in front and in the village, while sending some scouts towards the enemy's camp. These scouts afterwards came galloping back to the village pursed by some five to six hundred Qashqais horsemen. The Burma Mounted Rifles then opened fire with their Lewis guns and rifles with devastating effect before the Qashqais could wheel off and get out of range. Nevertheless, and in the face of this heavy fire, the tribesmen made two or three gallant attempts to gallop in again, so as to recover their wounded men and rifles. But as they only sustained further casualties without succeeding they finally abstained, and at dusk the Burma Mounted Rifles withdrew to Gilak without molestation. After dark the Qashqais returned and carried off their wounded, subsequently estimated at 100, leaving 103 dead where they had fallen.

The Burma Mounted Rifles evacuated South Persia in May 1919, leaving behind them a reputation for discipline and gallantry.

For displaying gallantry near Gumun Sowar Uttam Singh of the Burma Mounted Rifles, was recommended for the award of the Victoria Cross but was reduced to the Indian Order of Merit. Risaldar Gulzar Singh and Jemadar Kishan Singh of the Burma Mounted Rifles were awarded the Indian Order of Merit for their conspicuous gallantry against the enemy in South Persia.

Four Sikh soldiers of the Burma Mounted Rifles were recommended for the award of the Indian Order of Merit; however, their rewards were reduced to the award of the Indian Distinguished Service Medal.

BUSHIRE

As Bushire was the principal Persian port, a British political Residency and a telegraph station were located there, with the garrison which by 1916 included the Sikh soldiers of 15TH Lancers, 14TH Sikhs, and 22ND Punjabis. The tribal area of Tangistan was located South-East of Bushire and the Tangistani were a ferocious and predatory people. Inflaming these tribesmen against the British was Doctor Listermann, the German consul in Bushire. Listermann incited Rais Ali, the tribal Chief of Dilwar, to attack the British Residency. In May 1915, the Persian Governor of Bushire, aware of a village chieftain's plot to attack the British residency and needing support because his own gendarmes were defecting, asked for British help.

Action at Bushire, (1915)

In 1915, Wilhelm Wassmuss, a former German Bushire Consul, urged the Dilwar Tangistanis to attack Bushire and kill all the British there before Ramadan started, and some of them obliged him. A two-pronged insurgent attack was planned from the South and from the East. On 12TH July Major H E Oliphant, Commander of the British outposts, rode out on reconnaissance with the Assistant Political Officer, Captain G J L Ranking, accompanying the two Officers were five mounted Sowars of the Residency escort and 27 rifles of Indian Infantry. Unfortunately Oliphant's mounted party rode too far ahead of its supporting riflemen and was surprised by the insurgents; Oliphant and Ranking were killed and three Sowars were killed or wounded. As dusk fell that evening the insurgents attacked the outposts but were repulsed. Another attack early next day was also defeated and the Tangistanis then disappeared.

Attack of Dilwar, (1915)

Britain determined to occupy Bushire and to attack Dilwar to punish the insurgents. A Naval force, that included one Squadron from 16th Cavalry, proceeded to Bushire. On 10TH August 1915 a British expedition left Bushire to carry out punitive measures against Dilwar. Once the marines landed, the tribesmen hastily withdrew about two kilometres inland. A base was established and entrenched near the beach and Major Wintle took command. Major Wintle decided to advance 2,000 metres to a palm grove, known to be occupied by the Tangistanis that lay in front of the village of Old Dilwar. The British silent advance began at 0330 hours on 14TH August, led by the Marines and a Company of Sepoys. The palm grove was rushed quietly without use of covering fire and its inhabitants sprinted away into the darkness. As day broke New Dilwar could be observed 1,300 metres away.

Bushire

Attack of Dilwar, (1915)

The Dilwar fort had walls 10 metres high with a strong garrison of 400 Riflemen. Major Wintle led his men towards New Dilwar on 15TH August. He ordered the demolition party to run forward and breach the wall, which it successfully did, allowing the fort to be immediately rushed and occupied. Once in the fort the British destroyed it and New Dilwar. Wintle then commanded a fighting withdrawal. The Tangistanis were believed to have lost a considerable number of men during the action.

Tangistani attack on Bushire, (1915)

During July and August tribesmen regularly infiltrated through the British outposts around Bushire and mounted four serious raids, causing eleven casualties. The Tangistanis killed or captured around 40 horses and mules and only suffered minor casualties themselves. However, the Squadron of 16TH Cavalry had more success in closing with the Tangistanis and inflicting casualties on them. On 3RD September Tangistanis attacked the Bushire outposts but were driven back; amongst the enemy dead was Rais Ali, the hostile Khan of Dilwar.

Mashileh, (1915)

A sizeable enemy force attacked Bushire and the South-Eastern outposts engaged the Tangistanis. Then Major William Herbert Pennington, commanding a Squadron of 16TH Cavalry, was ordered to close in on the enemy. Immediately the Squadron charged straight into the mass of the enemy. Very savage fighting followed in which the Squadron lost a third of its strength, Major Pennington, 2ND Lieutenant Leslie Irvine Lumsden Thornton, Indian Army Reserve of Officers, two Indian Officers and 11 rank and file being killed or dying of wounds whilst 10 rank and file were wounded. After the charge the Squadron needed time to reorganise its troops and evacuate casualties. This gave the Tangistanis a breathing space to break contact with the pursuing Infantry, although the British guns continued to inflict casualties. Soon the fleet-footed tribesmen were across the Mashileh and hidden in the broken ground on the mainland; they had left 43 dead, 14 wounded and 4 unwounded prisoners behind on the sand, but they were believed to have taken many wounded men with them. However the Tangistanis had been defeated without having captured one British outpost and, brave men though they were, they did not mount further attacks on Bushire. On 13TH September General Brooking, his task of defending Bushire successfully completed, left for Mesopotamia and handed over to Colonel S.M. Edwardes DSO, Indian Army.

Jemadar Gopal Singh and Risaldar Prem Singh of 16TH Cavalry, and Subadar Dhan Singh and Sepoy Mehar Singh of 96TH Infantry, were awarded the Indian Order of Merit for their conspicuous gallantry against the enemy in Bushire.

SEISTAN

At the beginning of January the British force in East Persia under Colonel Wikely also consisted of the Sikhs of 28TH Light Cavalry, 36TH Mountain Battery and 19TH Punjabis. It was decided to appoint a more senior Officer to command in East Persia and on 17TH February Brigadier General Dyer * was appointed to command the force, which became the Seistan Force and was to ensure the tranquillity of the region and frustrate the activity of German agents.

Raids on the lines of communication of the force were made by certain tribes of Persian Baluchistan, notably the Damanis of Sarhad. In order to prevent these, and to control the Damanis, Brig.-Gen. R. E. Dyer, moved a part of his force to Khwash in May, 1916. In July the hostile attitude of the Damanis necessitated punitive measures. The Damanis are divided into two main sections, the Yarmahomedzais and the Gamshadzais. Brig.-Gen. Dyer determined to move to Gusht in order to intervene between these two sections, and to deal with each in detail. Operations in the vicinity of Gusht from 12TH July to 29TH July resulted in the capture of the bulk of the Yarmahomedzais flocks and herds, the infliction of considerable loss, and the separation of the two Damani sections.

During this period several small actions were fought under trying conditions of climate and terrain, the chief engagement being one at Kalag, near Gusht, on 21ST July. During August, General Dyer traversed without opposition a large part of the Gamshadzais country, returning to Khwash on 24TH August. As a result of the above operations agreements were arrived at with the chiefs of the Damanis, by which they promised to pay certain fines and to refrain from future hostility.

The troops maintaining a cordon in Seistan were engaged with hostile bodies on three occasions; At Lirudik on 13TH April, 1916, a force of 70 men of the Punjabis inflicted considerable loss on a lashkar estimated at 700 men. At Kalamas, on 26TH September, a party of 23 men of the Light Cavalry defeated a party of gunrunners, capturing a large number of rifles, ammunition, and camels. Near Chorab, on 24TH March, 1917, a party consisting of 16 men of the Light Cavalry and 25 men of the Punjabis attacked a gunrunner's caravan. The whole of the transport of 20 camels, as well as 447 rifles and some 23,600 rounds of ammunition were captured.

Subedar Karam Singh of 36TH Mountain Battery was awarded the Indian Order of Merit for conspicuous gallantry during the action on 16TH June 1918.

Following the Revolution in Russia, the Malleson Mission was sent to Trans-Caspia. With the withdrawal of the force from Trans-Caspia, the troops in Persia were withdrawn and the last elements left in November 1920.

* 'The Butcher of Amritsar'
On 13TH April 1919, General Reginald Dyer marched a squad of Indian soldiers into the Jallianwala Bagh, a large enclosed public space in the holy city of Amritsar, and opened fire without warning on a crowd gathered to hear political speeches, leaving over 200 dead.

TRANS-CASPIA

Intervention by British-Indian troops in Transcaspia in 1918, were actions primarily undertaken against Turco-German arms as part of a plan to block an enemy advance through the Caucasus towards India and Afghanistan. The Intervention brought British troops into conflict with Soviet Russian military forces on the Caspian and in Transcaspia. The British force was to be led by General Wilfred Malleson and included the Sikh soldiers of 19TH Punjabis and 28TH Light Cavalry.

Bairam Ali, (1918)

The detachment from Meshed, consisting of 25 sabres 28TH Light Cavalry and 175 rifles and two machine guns 19TH Punjabis, reached Muhammadabad (near the Perso-Russian frontier) on 2ND August 1918. On 8TH August General Malleson learnt the Trans-Caspian force had been driven back by the Bolsheviks to Bairam Ali, on the Eastern edge of the Merv oasis. The two machine guns of 19TH Punjabis left Muhammadabad on 11TH August and reached Bairam Ali on 12TH. Next day the Bolsheviks attacked. The Trans-Caspian force consisting of about 1,000 men, largely Turkomans, was defeated by the Bolshevik attacking force. The Trans – Caspian force's retirement would have resulted in a decisive disaster, but for the gallant behaviour of the Punjabi Machine Gun Detachment. These men fired their guns till they became too hot to handle and, inflicted 350 casualties on the enemy. Two of the Punjabi Detachment were wounded and one of its machine guns had to be abandoned after two men had been burnt in trying to carry it out of action. The Trans-Caspian force, thoroughly demoralised, fell back to Merv on 14TH August, after damaging the bridge over the Murghab River. They retreated before a Bolshevik advance without attempting resistance past Tejend to Dushak. The Punjabi detachment, returned to Muhammadabad.

Kaahka, (1918)

There was further action at Kaahka on 28TH August, 11TH and 18TH September. The village of Kaahka was grouped round the railway station. On 28TH September, the Bolshevik's opened with an Artillery bombardment, and the Infantry advanced forward till they reached the orchards immediately North of the station. Here they were checked for some time by the gallant resistance offered by a few Punjabis, who had been left in camp on various fatigue duties. Meanwhile, a Company of Punjabis, arriving almost simultaneously with the enemy, charged with the bayonet and drove Bolshevik's back, eventually putting him to flight and capturing five of his machine guns. This ended the fighting – which had been confined to the area North of the station – for the Bolshevik force all withdrew.

Trans-Caspia

Dushak, (1918)

The British detachment at Kaahka was composed of about 180 sabres, 28TH Light Cavalry, two guns of 44TH Field Battery, 120 rifles 4TH Hampshire Regiment and 330 rifles 19TH Punjabis. The Bolshevik force was at Dushak, some twenty five miles to the East. The British detachment on 14TH found the main body some distance to the North of Dushak; it was met by a heavy gun and machine gun fire. The Punjabis pushed on with speed and determination, but suffered heavy casualties. The British guns, firing with great accuracy, did much damage to the enemy trains and to the station, which just as the Punjabis reached it, was totally wrecked by an explosion of some trucks full of munitions. The enemy had lost the station, but started a counter-attack, at the same time as reinforcements from the Tejend direction commenced an attack from the East. The enemy attacks had been met by about 150 Punjabis and 120 dismounted Indian Cavalry. A retirement became necessary and withdrawal was ordered. The British casualties had been considerable. Those in 28TH Light Cavalry amounted to 6 killed and 12 wounded, while the Punjabis, with 47 killed and 139 wounded, and had lost about 50 percent of their strength. The Battalion was led by Subedar Bal Singh. As the Chief of Staff said in his official report, only the disgraceful action of their own troops had prevented them from obtaining a decisive victory, and only the heroic conduct of the Indian troops had saved them from complete disaster. General Malleson also reported that Russian circles were filled with the greatest admiration for the part played by the Indian troops, whom they regarded as being equal to ten times their own number of any of the other combatants.

Annenkovo, (1919)

On 16TH January a Bolshevik force made a sudden attack on the Trans-Caspian position at Annenkovo. Besides the Trans-Caspian force, there were at Annenkovo a half-Squadron 28TH Light Cavalry and a Company (150 rifles) 19TH Punjabis. The Punjabis experienced little difficulty in maintaining their position, but the Armenians were greatly outnumbered and had to be reinforced by a Punjabi Platoon. The enemy, however, continued to push in fresh troops and, under a heavy enfilading machine gun fire, the Armenians broke and fled. Fortunately, at this critical juncture, the train carrying a Company of Punjabis from Bairam Ali steamed up and came on right into the hail of bullets. The Bolsheviks held their ground till the Punjabis were within 50 yards and then broke and fled in disorder, losing heavily as they crossed the front of the other Punjabi Company. In the meantime about three Squadrons of Bolshevik Cavalry and 1,500 Bolshevik Infantry had started to attack 28TH Light Cavalry just as a Platoon of Punjabis came up to their assistance, and brought the Bolshevik attack to a standstill. By this time the main Bolshevik force was in full flight across the desert and, seeing this, those attacking the Trans-Caspian right also broke and fled.

Trans-Caspia

Annenkovo (Cont.)

The Bolshevik casualties had been severe, nearly 200 corpses being found next morning, his total losses being subsequently estimated at 600. In addition, it was said, the bitter cold had caused the Bolshevik about 500 cases of frost-bite. However, the Bolshevik had inflicted 70 casualties on the Trans-Caspian force and 46 among the Punjabis. It was subsequently ascertained that the Bolshevik plan had been to cut the railway and telegraph communications and then immediately surprise and overwhelm the Annenkovo detachment by simultaneous attacks against both flanks; that against the left being carried out by 2,500 Infantry and the one against the other flank by 1,500 Infantry. This affair enhanced greatly the already high reputation locally of the Indian troops.

Trans-Caspia, (1919)

At this time the total strength of the British force (or perhaps it should be described as an Indian force with added Brits) in Trans-Caspia was well under 1,000,226. General Milne arrived at Ashkhabad on 21ST January 1919, meeting General Malleson there and visiting the front. His view of the military situation was that it would be ludicrous if it were not so unsound. "We should either assume the burden of complete control and of support, involving time, money and labour in an almost hopeless task, or we should leave the country to its fate with the accompanying anarchy and bloodshed." The British government, with the Indian government concurring, decided that enough was enough and on 15TH February orders were issued to General Milne for the withdrawal of General Malleson's force. The process of withdrawal of the British force, which numbered some 950,243, began early in March; the last remaining British troops left in the early hours of 14TH April 1919. The Indian troops evacuated Trans-Caspia, leaving behind them a reputation for discipline and gallantry which any troops might be proud of and which they well deserved. One of their last exploits at the beginning of March, though of little material importance, is worthy of narration as exemplifying the fighting spirit with which they were imbued. A reconnoitring patrol of 28TH Light Cavalry, fourteen strong, finding itself cut off by a body of about 150 Bolshevik Cavalry, had charged through them and had then turned and charged through them again, killing or wounding 21 of the Bolsheviks, at a loss to itself of one wounded and two made prisoner.

Subedar Bala Singh, Sepoy Dalel Singh and Subedar Hukam Singh (Posthumous award) of 19TH Punjabis, were awarded the Indian Order of Merit for their conspicuous gallantry in the fighting at Dushak.

EAST AFRICA

At the outbreak of the First World War, the Germans in East Africa not only cut the vital line of British communication from the Cape to Cairo but also provided Germany with a Naval base from where the German ships could operate in the Indian Ocean and destroy British ships en route to and from India. Consequently the British Government decided to capture German East Africa. The Indian Government was given responsibility for this. India despatched its Army to East Africa and so began the East African campaign. Other British Imperial, Colonial and South African troops also came to join the campaign in East Africa. However, the Indian Army maintained a force to at least Brigade strength throughout the fighting, and a total of 17,500 Indian soldiers served in East Africa during the War.

The following Units with Sikh soldiers saw action with the East African Expeditionary Force; Faridkot Sappers and Miners, Kapurthala Infantry, Jind Infantry, 25TH Cavalry (Frontier Force), 24TH Hazara Mountain Battery (Frontier Force), 27TH Mountain Battery, 20TH Punjabis, 29TH Punjabis, 30TH Punjabis, and 33RD Punjabis.

The main actions took place over a stretch of East Africa then known as Kenya, Tanganyika and Uganda. At one time the Germans were operating South of the present Mozambique border. At most, the German forces numbered approximately 3,000 white troops and 11,000 Askari.

Tsavo River, (1914)

On August 15TH, Taveta, a place situated at the South-Eastern foot of Kilimanjaro in British East Africa, which was weakly held by the British, was taken by German force under Captain Von Prince. The first Indian contingent to see action in East Africa was 29TH Punjabis. The Regiment had disembarked at Mombasa and was at once sent up the country by rail. On September 4TH the British received information that a German force was advancing on Tsavo. This German force had compelled a small British detachment on upper Tsavo to withdraw, after an encounter near Mzima. Two Companies of 29TH Punjabis were ordered to attack the German force in the flank and rear, driving it to the other two Companies of Punjabis, who were in a position astride Tsavo River, five miles West of Tsavo. However, the German force of 300 men with two Pompoms and three Maxim Guns, took the rear guard unawares with heavy fire. After the encounter, the German force retired, receiving a severe mauling.

East Africa

Gazi, (1914)
On 7TH October, 29TH Punjabis and the Jind Infantry defended Gazi area against a German force about 300 strong. In the counter-attack, one Company of 29TH Punjabis hit the German force's right flank, while one Company of Jind Infantry attacked the left flank successfully, and two Companies of Jind Infantry attacked the front of the German force. This double enveloping movement, combined with the frontal attack by the Indian Units, compelled the Germans to retreat.

Tanga, (1914)
The most famous and tragic action of the East African campaign was the attack on the German port of Tanga. The battle was a disaster for the Indian force engaged, and led to humiliating withdrawal and the unnecessary loss of huge quantities of equipment, which was of great value to the German forces. The plan of attack had been over-ambitious, in trying to cut off the enemy's retreat by railway with so small a force.

Longido, (1914)
Longido is an isolated hill situated to the Northwest of Kilimanjaro Mountain. About 800 to 1,200 German soldiers garrisoned Longido. On November 3RD an attack was made on Longido, in which 29TH Punjabis captured three enemy positions in succession. The Kapurthala Infantry, (Sikh Princely State Unit) who had arrived on 3RD October and been employed at Kajiado, Bisal, and Menga Hills, also took part in the fight. However, the British forces retired without achieving their object. The total loss of the British force was 19 killed, 33 wounded, while the German losses were 118 killed and wounded.

Jassin, (1915)
On 16TH December, a general advance from British East Africa pushed the Germans back across their frontier in the Umba Valley. Jassin was occupied on 2ND January 1915, and the Jind Infantry took up an advanced entrenched position. A German counter-attack was made on 12TH January but was successfully driven off. On 18TH, however, the enemy made a more determined effort on Jassin. The Jind Infantry made a very plucky effort to support the Garrison, but were driven back by vastly superior numbers and had to retire. Major-General Natha Singh was wounded and it would have gone harder with the Regiment but for a gallant counter-attack by Subedar Harnam Singh, who was taken prisoner after all his men were killed.

East Africa

Bukoba, (1915)

In June 1915, it was decided to take action against Bukoba town, situated on the Western shore of Lake Victoria. This town had a powerful wireless station and it was thought that its capture would dislocate the German line of communication. The attacking force included 28TH Mountain Battery, escorted by 29TH Punjabis, The Faridkot Sappers and Miners (Sikh Princely State Unit) and the British section of 25TH Fusiliers. The German force, consisting of 200 rifles and Maxim guns, was holding a very strong position. On June 22ND, the guns of 28TH Mountain Battery started firing on men seen digging entrenchments around the Rest House. The German force replied to this fire from a position at Bukoba where they had a gun. The 28TH Mountain Battery soon knocked out this gun. The German force had to retire under pressure of the fire of 28TH Mountain Battery. The victory in this engagement was due to the accurate fire of the Mountain Battery.

Mbuyuni, (1916)

Early in 1916, the enemy was driven out of Serengeti and Mbuyuni and had to withdraw their garrison at Kasigau. South African General Smuts took command of the forces in East Africa and began operations against German forces around Kilimanjaro Mountain.

Kilimanjaro, (1916)

The 1ST Division started from Longido Hill towards its first destination, Vie Bomaja Ngombe on March 5TH, 1916. The following morning, a German detachment met this force at Ngaserai and was driven off by the two Companies of 29TH Punjabis and a section of 27TH Mountain Battery. On 8TH March, 1ST Divison reached Gerarague from where it advanced and took Ngombe by the night of March 12$^{TH.}$ While 1ST Divison was thus engaged, 2ND Division advanced towards Salatia Hill. A frontal attack was delivered on March 8TH at Salatia, which drove away the Germans and the next day the Salatia Hill was occupied by 2ND Division. The British advance, under pressure of the heavy fire of the Germans, had to retire. Later they decided to push forward and endeavour to clear the Ridge with a bayonet charge. In the fight which ensued, the German forces were driven back. The following morning, the Germans evacuated their position at the Latema Hills. Consequently, the British forces occupied these positions on Mach 13TH. "Thus the conquest of the Kilimanjaro-Meru area, probably the richest and most desirable district of German East Africa, was satisfactorily accomplished." General Smuts wrote enthusiastically about the conduct of the British troops, "All these hardships were endured with unfailing cheerfulness and a chance of dealing a blow at the enemy seemed to be the only recompense required."

East Africa

The attack on Kisangire, (1916)
Fearing that the Germans might be tasked with operating against the Central Railway, the British decided to attack Kisangire. Major General Natha Singh, the Commander of the 240-man strong Jind Infantry, was ordered to march from Dar es Salaam with his Sepoys and his two machine guns. The Ruler of the Sikh Princely State of Jind had supplied the Jind Infantry to the War effort as part of the Indian Imperial Service Scheme. The Jind Infantry had been fighting in East Africa since 1914 and had gained a reputation for professionalism and bravery in action. Already operating around Kisangire and observing the enemy's movements were 40 Scouts under the command of Lieutenant G. D. Howarth of the Intelligence Department. Howarth reported that the German post was in a building on top of a steep conical hill, around which two lines of trenches had been dug. The easiest line of approach was from the West and South-West. Moving off before dawn on 9TH October 1916, the Sikhs marched around the rear of the conical hill, and at 0930 hours, they were ready to attack. Nathan Singh placed three of his Companies and the machine guns in the first line and kept his fourth Company as a reserve in a second line. He had 183 Sepoys deployed. The Sikhs worked through the bush towards the hill until enemy outposts engaged them and then they rushed forward and captured the first trench line. From there a bayonet attack was mounted that captured the inner trench line. But now problems arose because of the lack of Artillery support for the Jind troops. The building was engaged with machine gun and rifle fire but these rounds had no effect on the strong stonewalls of the post. In retaliation, the enemy shot down both Sikh Machine Gun Crews. After losing 13 men dead or mortally wounded, 27 others wounded, and eight wounded and missing, Nathan Singh broke off the action, and withdrew to Maneromango and re-grouped.

Behobeho Chogwali, (1917)
During 3RD January, 1ST East African Brigade made an exhausting cross-country march culminating in a 60-metre descent over a field of huge boulders. The Brigade Commander halted his exhausted men for the night a few kilometres short of the destination. The following morning, Behobeho Chogwali was reached without incident and the advance turned North to Behobeho Kwa Mahinda. At about 1030 hours, contact was made with the enemy and two Companies of 30TH Punjabis came up in support, as the Kashmiris extended the left flank. Ninety minutes later Wangoni Company came into view from the North. The Wangoni Askaris, relatives of the Zulus, immediately attacked the British-held ridge. A lively and lengthy action then developed but the Punjabis held their ground, efficiently using their two Maxim machine guns and two Rexer light machine guns. The Punjabis lost Naik Gurdit Singh killed and three Sepoys wounded in the desperately fought action.

East Africa

The Last Push, (1917)

Advancing from Kilwa on 5TH July, one column pushed the Germans back on Narungomba, from where they were driven by 33RD Punjabis and 40TH Pathans after fierce fighting on 19TH. Perhaps the hardest and the most costly action of the campaign was fought from 16TH to 19TH October 1917 at Nyangao, where four days solid fighting were necessary to defeat the Germans and force them Southwards once more. The German troops exhausted and short of supplies of all kinds, surrendered at the end of 1917. At the fall of German East Africa, mainland Tanganyika was placed under the control of the British Colonial authority in 1919. On 9TH December 1961, Tanganyika gained independence from Great Britain. In 1964, Tanganyika United with several islands in the Indian Ocean, including Zanzibar and Pemba, to form the United Republic of Tanzania.

Faridkot Sappers and Miners (Sikh Princely States troops)

The Faridkot Sappers were in Africa from November 1914 to February 1918. In February, they returned to India. Lieutenant Colonel Nand Singh was awarded the O.B.I. and the Indian Order of Merit and Lieutenant Colonel Bishan Singh was awarded the O.B.I. and Jemadar Moti Singh the French gallantry award of Croix de Guerre.

Kapurthala Infantry (Sikh Princely States troops)

The Kapurthala Infantry were in Africa from October 1914 to December 1917. Major General Sardar Puran Singh was awarded the O.B.I., as well as C.I.E. Lieutenant Colonels Nihal Singh and Moti Singh and Major Maya Singh and Captain Rur Singh were awarded the O.B.I.

Jind Infantry (Sikh Princely States troops)

The Jind Infantry were in Africa from October 1914 to December 1917. They earned the highest opinions of all the Generals under whom they served, especially their fighting at Jassin. Major General Natha Singh, who commanded with great gallantry, was awarded the O.B.I., as well as C.I.E. Lieutenant Colonel Baldev Singh was awarded the O.B.I. and Captain Sundar Singh the French gallantry awards of Croix de Guerre and Naik Such Singh the Russian Cross of St. George.

Subedar Harnam Singh, Subedar Bhagwan Singh and Sepoy Sada Singh of Jind Infantry, Gunner Havildar Bhan Singh and Lance Naik Natha Singh of 27TH Mountain Battery, Jemadar Sundar Singh and Subadar Labh Singh of 30TH Punjabis, Sub Assistant Surgeon Hukam Singh and Sub Assistant Surgeon of Indian Subordinate Medical Department, were awarded the Indian Order of Merit for their conspicuous gallantry in East Africa.

Subedar Major Bishan Singh of 66TH Punjabis was awarded the gallantry award of Croix de Guerre for the East African Campaign.

SOMALILAND

Shimber Berris, (1914-15)

Operations were undertaken in Somaliland from November 1914 and February 1915. These operations though part of the First World War, were less directly connected with the struggle against the Central Powers, but involved some Sikhs who were fighting in the other theatre of War, also the Sikhs who formed part of the local contingents.

So-called 'Mad Mullah', Muhammad ibn Abdullah Hassan, had built a series of forts on the plateau of the Burao range, each capable of holding 50 men. Fields of fire had been cleared around the forts and the area was full of caves. The forts were remarkably well sited and very strong. The walls were 9 to 12 feet thick at the base, 16 to 20 feet high, and 24 feet wide, provided with well made machicouli galleries. The sides of the cliffs were honeycombed with caves, some of which were capable of containing 100 men and animals. On 19TH and 23RD November 1914, a mounted column from Burao, composed of Indian troops and Camel Constabulary, attacked the Mullah's forts at Shimber Berris. The operation was not entirely successful. It was renewed in February 1916, with the help of a detachment of 23rd Sikh Pioneers from Aden. Explosives were obtained from Aden and India. A force, partly mounted and partly dismounted, of 15 Officers, 570 rank and file, (Sikhs and Somalis), six machine guns and two guns advanced to the neighbourhood of Shimber Berris on 2ND February. On 3RD February, two columns advanced against the forts of the Burao. Although the Dervishes had commenced construction of new forts, the hilltop was unoccupied and the Sikh Pioneers blew up the forts. The following morning, 4TH February, the column was transferred from South to North of the Burao by a pass seven miles West of Shimber Berris and was concentrated on the plain close to that place by noon. The enemy were holding two forts overlooking and flanking a deep Nullah and a fort at the far end of the Nullah. They were also in occupation of the numerous caves in the hillsides. The two flanking forts were captured after two hours fighting, but the enemy developed a heavy fire from the caves, from the middle fort and from the vicinity of the fort. The guns were brought forward and with machine guns engaged the middle fort and the caves at close range. The enemy's fire slackened, and the Dervishes were observed to be evacuating the fort and retiring Southwards up the ravine. A Company was despatched against this fort, but, although unable to affect an entrance, the Company remained round the fort and enabled the Pioneers to place a charge of guncotton against the door, under a hot fire from the occupants inside. The fort and its defenders were blown up, hand grenades were thrown into caves, known still to be occupied and the two flanking forts were also blown up. A certain amount of raiding continued until 1920, when the Mullah and his followers were finally crushed.

Havildar Teja Singh and Naik Sher Singh of 23RD Sikh Pioneers were awarded the Indian Order of Merit for their conspicuous gallantry in action on 4TH February at Shimber Berris

BURMA 1914

Burma was made a Province of British India 1885. There were many ethnic minorities in the country; the Kachins were one of these minorities. The Kachin inhabited the mountainous North-Eastern corner of Burma that is adjacent to China. The Kachin were Warriors and disciplined fighters, using advanced jungle Warfare and survival skills. They had firearms obtained through cross-border trade that were replacing their traditional cross-bows and spears. Every tribesman carried a curved sword named a Dha that was a useful decapitator. In December 1914 it appears that four Shan tribesmen had gained influence amongst the Kachins in the Hukawng Valley by preaching sedition against British rule. It is quite possible that the four Shans were in the employ of Germany, as that country had definite plans to destabilise India and Burma.

The Germans had developed strong links with the expatriate revolutionary Indian Ghadar Movement and German money was being used to ship arms to India and Burma to be used by revolutionaries.

The pre-War military garrison included the Burma Military Police Battalions. The Burma Military Police (BMP) was a Regiment that had been raised in 1886. Initially recruits for the BMP came from the Punjab area of Northwest India. The Burma Military Police, at the end of 1888, included 3,937 Sikh militiamen. Each BMP Battalion had a mounted detachment and some had obsolescent muzzle-loading Artillery pieces. The BMP maintained law and order in remote regions of Burma but it was more similar to a Light Infantry Regiment than a Police Unit. The Burma Military Police columns marched into rebel areas and started punishing the inhabitants by shooting armed belligerents, burning down stockades and huts and by confiscating domestic animals. They experienced some stiff fighting over very rugged and jungle-covered ground.

The Kachins had had enough and ceased hostilities; they were resentful of the failed guarantee made by the Shans that their mystical powers would protect the Kachins. The four Shans had fled Eastwards into the Triangle, an area bounded by the Malikha and Nmaikha Rivers; this territory was similar to the Tribal Territory on the Indian Northwest Frontier, in that the British chose not to administer it. Kachins from Nkraun village in the Triangle seized the Shans and handed them over to the British. In September 1915 the Shans pleaded in court that they were only in the Kachin Hills to buy drugs and were not connected with the rebellion, but the Mandalay Sessions Judge sentenced them to death and they were hanged.

One Burma Military Police Sowar (mounted soldier), Kala Singh, received the award of the Indian Order of Merit for conspicuous gallantry, coolness and resource on 24TH February 1915.

TSINGTAO

Tsingtao, (1914)

Tsingtao was the most important German possession in China. At the end of the nineteenth century Germany had gained control of part of the Shandong peninsula, and founded a port at Tsingtao. The port then became the headquarters of the German Far East Squadron. At the start of the First World War that Squadron was under the command of Admiral Graf von Spee. His Squadron inflicted an early defeat on the British at the battle of Coronel (1ST November 1914), before being destroyed at the battle of the Falkland Islands on 8TH December 1914.

The Germans had a 4,000 strong garrison in Tsingtao. This may have been enough to deter an early British attack, but at the end of August 1914 Japan joined the War on the Allied side, hoping to gain control of the German empire in the Far East. The attack on Tsingtao began on 18TH September 1914 when 23,000 Japanese troops landed above the city and began to prepare for a formal siege, digging siege parallels that slowly approached the city. At the same time a Japanese fleet prepared to bombard the port. The Japanese were joined by a small force of British troops; 2ND Battalion South Wales Borderers, 36TH Sikhs, personnel of Royal Army Medical Corps and Army Service Corps (1,500 strong) as well as a Squadron of British Warships. Tsingtao came under bombardment from land and sea while the siege works approached the city. The final assault came on the night of 6-7TH November. The allies fought their way into the main line of defence, capturing most of the important strong points. The Japanese suffered 1,800 casualties, the Germans around 700 and the British only 70. Many of the Japanese casualties came when a cruiser was sunk by a mine. The next morning (7TH November) the German garrison surrendered. The Japanese would go on to capture Germany's island possessions in the Pacific.

On night of 4TH November, 36TH Sikhs lost two Sepoys killed and two Officers wounded during heavy Artillery fire directed on the Sikh trenches.

Ten Sikh Officers and men were mentioned in the despatch of Brigadier General N.W. Barnardiston on 13TH November, 1914, including Subadar Gurmukh Singh, I.O.M.

At the end of the War 36TH Sikhs was awarded the Battle Honour 'Tsingtao', becoming the only Indian Battalion to gain the distinction.

THIRD AFGHAN WAR

The Third Anglo-Afghan War began on 6TH May 1919 and ended with an armistice on 8TH August 1919. It was essentially a minor tactical victory for the British in so much as they were able to repel the regular Afghan forces. For the British, the Durand Line was reaffirmed as the political boundary between Afghanistan and British India and the Afghans agreed not to foment trouble on the British side. The end of the Second Afghan War in 1880 marked the beginning of almost forty years of reasonably good relations between Britain and Afghanistan under the leadership of Abdurrahman and Habibullah, during which time the British attempted to manage Afghan foreign policy through the payment of a large subsidy. Ostensibly, the country remained independent, however, under the Treaty of Gandamak (1879) it was accepted that in regards to external matters it would "have no windows looking on the outside world, except towards India". The death in 1901 of Amir Abdurrahman led indirectly to the War that began eighteen years later. His successor, Habibullah, was an unreliable and unstable leader who alternately sided with Britain and Russia according to whoever paid the highest price.

Despite feeling considerable resentment over not being consulted over the Anglo-Russian Convention of 1907 (Convention of St. Petersburg), Afghanistan remained neutral during the First World War (1914–1918), resisting considerable pressure from the Ottoman Empire when it entered the conflict on the side of Imperial Germany and the Sultan (the titular leader of Islam), called for a jihad against the Allies. Upon seizing the throne, Amanullah had his brother Nasrulla arrested for their father's murder and had him sentenced to life imprisonment. Nasrulla had been the leader of a more conservative element in Afghanistan and his treatment rendered Amanullah's position as Amir somewhat tenuous. By April 1919 he realised that if he could not find a way to placate the conservatives he would be unlikely to maintain his hold on power. Looking for a diversion from the internal strife in the Afghan court and sensing advantage in the rising civil unrest in India, following the Amritsar massacre, Amanullah decided to invade British India. The military skirmishes ranged along much of the border area. Fighting occurred in Chitral, in the Khyber Pass, through the Kurram Valley, in the Tochi Valley, in Waziristan, and Baluchistan.

The War did not last long, however, because both sides were soon ready to sue for peace. The Afghans were unwilling to sustain continued British air attacks on Kabul and Jalalabad, and the British were unwilling to take on an Afghan land War so soon after the bloodletting of First World War. Amanullah sued for peace on 31ST May, and peace was restored by the treaty of Rawalpindi on 8TH August 1919.

Six Sikh soldiers won the Indian Order of Merit for their conspicuous gallantry during the Third Afghan War. They belonged to the Regiments of; 3RD Horse, 31ST Lancers, 34TH Sikh, and 66TH Punjabis.

WAZIRISTAN

The Afghan War ended but this did not improve the situation in Waziristan. A British Officer wrote: "At no time in their history had the Mahsuds and Wazirs been so well armed as at this juncture, since in additon to their normal armament, considerable quantities of government rifle and ammunition had fallen recently into their hands. To supplement their stocks the tribesmen had received large supplies of ammunition through the agency of anti-British Afghan officials in Khost. These tribesmen have long been remarkable for their courage, activity and hardihood, and when the mountainous and difficult nature of their country is considered, together with the fact that their numbners included about 1,800 Army deserters and so highly trained in our tactics and methods of fighting, it will be realized that they constituted a formidable enemy."

During the Third Afghan War, certain tribes of Waziristan made common cause with the Afghans, but at the time, the government of India had not found it convenient to punish them in the manner deserved. The Afghan menace being checked, the offending tribesmen were summoned to attend meetings to hear the terms, which the Government intended to impose upon them. The offending tribesmen refused to agree to the terms offered them. Consequently, a force was assembled at Tank to deal with them. This was the beginning of some of the most difficult and costly operations ever undertaken on the frontier. The morale of the Mahsuds at this time stood at a high level. This was due to their success in several encounters against the British troops during the summer. It was their fervent hope that their actions would compel the British government to discontinue punitive measures against them. That, as in the past, they would succeed in gaining a reduction, if not abrogation of the Government's terms, by adopting a threatening attitude. Added to this was their belief that the Great War had reduced the Army so greatly in numbers and training, that the Mahsuds could defeat any force which could be brought against them.

Jandola Fort, (1919)

More than 6,000 Mahsuds and Bhittanis surrounded Jandola fort in the tribal area of South Waziristan, on May 28TH. The tribesmen cut off the fort's water supply, a mile distant from the fort. On the first day of the siege, water was rationed to one water bottle a man a day. The weather was extremely hot and discipline was severely tested by this scarcity of water. On 7TH June a party from the fort rushed out to obtain water, bringing back with them three day's supply. It was during this operation that *Bhishti* (water carrier) Gurdit Singh earned the Indian Order of Merit. He went backwards and forwards continually to carry water. Even after he was wounded, he went out again. On his final trip, his *mashk* (leather water-container) being punctured by bullets in two places, he plugged the holes with his hands, although he was again wounded on his way back. Fortunately, his wounds did not prove fatal and he lived to serve the Battalion for many years.

Waziristan

Spinkai Ghash, (1919)

On December 18TH 1919, a military column moved out to take Spinkai Ghash, with the idea of covering the occupation of a camp on Palosina plain, three miles North of Jandola. A Mahsud lashkar about 2,000 strong and about 1,000 Wana Wazirs were on their way to oppose the advance of the column. On 19TH and 20TH two abortive but costly attempts were made to establish a permanent piquet on Mandanna Hill, which was rushed and captured by the Mahsuds. That evening it was decided to establish a permanent piquet on Black Hill. The Units detailed for the task were 82ND Punjabis, 109TH Infantry, and 34TH Sikh Pioneers, supported by some Artillery. On 21ST as the Units occupied Black Hill unopposed, the Mahsuds rushed the hill from three directions. They drove in the Companies of 109TH Infantry and 82ND Punjabis and killed the Company Commander and the Havildar. At this juncture Havildar Maghar Singh took charge and the Sikh Pioneers beat off four attacks and forced the Mahsuds to retire. Havildar Maghar Singh was awarded the well-deserved Indian Order of Merit.

Tarakai, (1919)

Two Companies of 34TH Sikh Pioneers started constructing the piquet position at Tarakai, building walls and putting up wire, under the protection of 82ND Punjabis. The Pioneers were Infantry trained and also performed simple engineering tasks. They had built up a reputation as dour, dogged fighters. They had piled arms fifty yards below the work-site, rolled up their sleeves and started collecting boulders for the Sangar-wall. Suddenly a solid mass of several hundred tribesmen emerged from dead ground and dashed towards the piquet, yelling, shooting and brandishing swords and knives. The covering parties lost their nerve and fled. The Pioneers also ran – but only as far as their piled rifles. Grabbing these, they dashed back to the Sangar, just in time. The walls were only two feet high and there was but one strand of barbed wire stretched across the front. Charge after charge of the tribesmen was checked by the puny strand of wire. Their onslaught withered away under fire from Lewis guns and the Pioneers' rifles. With ammunition running low, a Jemadar and a seventeen-year old bugler, Sangat Singh, who had no rifle, went down to organize a working party to bring more ammunition from a dump at the bottom of the hill. On their way back, a tribesman in ambush fired at the Jemadar at point blank range, and missed; the Jemadar fired back and missed. Sangat Singh then went for him with a pickaxe and did not miss. He arrived back at the Sangar gleefully carrying his victim's rifle and ammunition. There they found the most savage hand-to-hand fight raging. The post was designed to hold 120 men, and there must have been at least 300 packed into it, hacking and thrusting, slashing and stabbing as a century's hatred between Pathan and Sikh exploded. Then the Regimental Havildar Major roared out with a drill instructor's voice the Sikh War cry of 'Jo Bole So Nihal, Sat Sri Akal' they all took up the War cry and with a concerted effort expelled the Mahsuds from the Sangar. Of the 250 Sikh Pioneers in that action, 189 were either killed or wounded.

Waziristan

Islam Bibi, (1936)
In 1936, a Hindu girl eloped with a young Muslim student. The girl's relatives recovered the girl. The Muslims alleged that she had been converted to Islam, taking the name of Islam Bibi. The decision of the Court at the trial was that the Hindu community be made her custodians. The Faqir of Ipi took up the issue of Islam Bibi. The quiet Mullah, turned fanatic, led the Duars, a fanatically minded tribe, on Bannu, where the case was to come up again. Action was taken against the tribe, their Lashkar dispersed and their leaders arrested, all save the Faqir, who escaped. The Faqir skilfully intensified his propaganda and managed to unite the tribes of Tori Khel Wazirs, the Mahsuds, and Bhittanis, against the British. The rising hostility manifested itself in early February 1937, when two British Officers were murdered, one in Mahsud and the other in Wazir territory. These outrages were followed by many other hostile acts, which created an alarming situation.

Tori Khel, (1936)
In May 1937, two Brigades advanced against Arsal Kot, a village where the Faqir had a stronghold. One Brigade advanced against the high ground, held by 4,000 tribesmen, while the other Brigade made a daring and hazardous night march up the Iblanke spur to the East. The Mountain Battery Gunners and Machine Gunners of the Infantry destroyed towers beyond Dakai Kalai, where considerable resistance was experienced. The Punjabis had to be extricated by the Artillery and 11TH Sikhs from a nasty position, in which assistance from the air had to be called in. The Faqir fled to Arsal Kot, which was subjected to constant air bombing. By 14TH both Brigades were back in their stations, having for the time being completely destroyed Faqir's supporters.

Shahur Tangi, (1937)
In April 1937, as a convoy entered the Shahur Tangi, a murderous fire was opened on it. Drivers were killed, lorries splayed all over the road, which was blocked and as Officers and men jumped out, they were shot down. The convoy escort, in close combat beat off all the attacks throughout a very long day. They sustained heavy casualties in their magnificent stand, eight killed, and 13 wounded. Not a rifle, bayonet, or round of ammunition fell into the hands of the tribesmen. The tribesmen also suffered severely. The Faqir was never captured but largely Waziristan quietened down and was to remain so for the next eight years. This was just as well, for from 1939 onwards larger and more pressing tasks claimed the attention of the British and Indian armies.

IRAQ

15TH Ludhiana Sikhs

The tribesmen in Kurdistan, under the leadership of Shaikh Mahmud, were actively hostile to the British administration and had taken up arms against it. Following are details of the Rania incident:-

On 29TH August, 1922, a section of the Pack Artillery Battery and a Company of 15TH Sikhs, with Lieut.-Colonel Hughes and his Staff, arrived at Darband. At 0400 hours, 31ST August, a Sikh picket South of Darband on the left bank of the Zab was overwhelmed. During 31ST August Darband was reinforced by Hughes with the whole of the Kurdish levies from Rania. The column at Darband was then composed of, 1 section of Pack Artillery Battery, "C "Company, 4TH Battalion, 15TH Sikhs, Kurdish Levies, less 1 Company, an Assyrian Machine Gun Platoon and wireless pack set. That night Hughes advanced on Rania by moonlight and the column came under hostile fire. The Kurdish levies then got entirely out of hand, with the result that there was considerable confusion. Some order was established by daybreak on 1ST September and the column moved on Rania, but found the enemy holding it. Hughes then decided to go straight across country to Koi Sanjak with the regrettable result that in the rice fields his mules became badly bogged down. There was practically a stampede on the part of the Kurdish levies, and nearly the whole burden of withdrawal was borne by the Sikhs who gave a fine display of steadfastness, and on more than one occasion used the bayonet.

During the morning of 1ST September, the enemy attacked from all sides with vigour, riding close up to the column. Later, great assistance was rendered by aeroplanes in covering the withdrawal and the enemy appeared to have stopped as soon as he saw he had definitely failed in his attempt to surround the column. The column reached a ridge immediately North-East of Koi Sanjak on 2ND September. Lieut.-Colonel Hughes reported that heavy casualties were inflicted on the enemy. One Company and a Machine Gun Section of 15TH Sikhs from Baiji reached Koi Saniak on 1ST September. The morale of the Sikhs was very high; however, the Kurdish levies were quite unreliable. Aeroplanes had daily bombed the enemy, who, however, offered few targets and showed no sign of activity. At Rania the Turkish flag was flying.

The Rania uprising compelled the British withdrawal from Sulaimanieh and Halebja to the Tigres. The Tigris line of communications not only gave the covering troops sufficient depth in which to fight, but also early information of hostile concentrations and movements of the Kurdish tribesmen. The withdrawal removed any influence the British had exerted over the tribes East of the line Kirkuk—Erbil—Kifri, and it was assumed that they would throw in their lot with any hostile bodies which may advance from the East. Knowing the importance of prestige in the East, the immediate re-taking of Rania would have been advisable, but, as this was out of the question, as there was a distinct possibility of the outbreak of a serious uprising in Kurdistan at any time, the British considered that there was no alternative but to withdraw from the Vilayet of Mosul.

Iraq

32ND Sikh Pioneers

The Great War had ended in Mesopotamia with the signing of an armistice on 31ST October 1918, and the surrender of the remnants of the Turkish 6TH Army at Mosul. However, the country actually remained a theatre of Warfare until a peace treaty was ratified in 1924. Britain had de-mobilised and run-down its forces in Mesopotamia and was totally unprepared when conflict started. The Arabs, encouraged by Turkish and Syrian intriguers, organised themselves and formed bands of armed horsemen that could move extremely quickly and fight very brutally and ferociously. In May a train was ambushed by insurgents near Sherqat, the terminus of the rail line running North from Baghdad, and armed Arabs searched the train for non-Muslim soldiers, whom they wished to pull out and kill.

On 4TH June 1920 the people in Tel Afar, 30 miles West of Mosul, rose up against the British-Officered local Arab levies and killed the levy Commander, the Assistant Political Officer and other locally employed British personnel. A section of two British Armoured cars from 14TH Light Armoured Motor Battery, Machine Gun Corps, was sent to Tel Afar to provide fire support. The cars were surrounded in the narrow streets of the town and the nine men of their crews killed. A British column of 1,000 men composed of Cavalry, Artillery and Infantry was then sent. The column skirmished with around 1,200 Arab horsemen before it entered Tel Afar and applied heavy punitive measures on the townsfolk. Punitive measures included destroying selected buildings, burning down entire villages, seizing weapons, crops and livestock, hanging known killers and levying fines. This was followed by the siege of a British detachment at Rumeitha on the rail line between Basra and Baghdad.

A strong British relief column containing six Infantry Battalions with supporting arms had to fight fiercely to lift the siege. The British defenders of the town lost 145 men killed, wounded or missing before they were relieved. A situation now developed in the Kifl – Kufa area on the Euphrates River South of Baghdad. The local Political Officer requested a show of force in the area and the British Commander at Hillah sent a column that contained a Company of 32ND Sikh Pioneers. As the column marched towards Diwaniyia it was heavily attacked at night, the Commander was foolish enough to listen to the advice of his Political Officer and endeavoured to retire in the dark to Hillah. The confusion and disaster that followed was considerable. The Company of 32ND Sikh Pioneers lost thirty pioneers. The Battalion received unmeasured praise for its long service in Iraq, and above all in the holding of the Hillah- Diwaniyia section of the railway and the defence of Jearboyah. It proceeded to India on 21ST April 1921.

'The Regiment whose principal role had been Pioneering rather than Infantry work, had lost thirty four killed, fifteen missing, ten prisoners, 187 wounded.'

Iraq

45TH Rattray's Sikhs

In the mid 1920's violent fighting erupted in Mesopotamia, between certain tribal groupings and the British forces, who were occupying the region. On 25TH June 1920 the Assistant Political Officer at Rumeitha, Lieutenant P.T. Hyatt, urgently requested reinforcements. Captain Bragg arrived with the reinforcements and took command of the Rumeitha garrison. There were now four British Officers and 308 Sepoys in Rumeitha, along with two other British Railway Officers, 153 railway personnel and 60 Indian civilians.

Lieutenant Hyatt learned that inhabitants of the village of Abu Hassan were coming into Rumeitha and looting the bazaar and terrorising the townsfolk. Hyatt took out two Platoons of 99TH Infantry under Lieutenant J.R. Marriott to punish the village. Marriott's advance was delayed and this gave the Dhawalim time to concentrate a large force. Hyatt then rashly urged Marriott not to withdraw until Abu Hassan village had been burned down. This advice was fatal as over 1,500 tribesmen suddenly attacked and overwhelmed the two Platoons, killing 43 Sepoys and wounding a further 16 Officers and men; the survivors retreated rapidly to Rumeitha.

This British defeat led to the inhabitants of Rumeitha openly siding with the insurgents and a further six Sepoys were killed by snipers and 14 others were wounded. A small column was formed to march into Rumeitha, to relieve the garrison and it included a Battalion of 45TH Rattray's Sikhs. The column Commander was Lieutenant Colonel McVean DSO, the Commanding Officer of 45TH Rattray's Sikhs. By 6TH July the column, with an accompanying train carrying supplies and water, was ten kilometres north of Rumeitha. McVean advanced tactically and his Sikh advance guard of 'B' Company under Captain J.A. Finlay was heavily fired on from the left flank. McVean's casualties that day, all of them Sikhs, were one Sepoy killed and 13 others and one mule driver wounded. On 7TH July the advance continued with the Sikhs' 'A' Company under Lieutenant R.V. Fox leading. After progressing for 1,500 metres, heavy fire was received from an embankment to the front, and 'B' Company moved to support 'A' Company whilst 'C' Company under Captain A.L. Butcher advanced on the right of 'A' Company. A direct assault was mounted but the weight of fire from the embankment, combined with the marshy ground in front of it, halted the attackers 200 metres from their enemy. The Sepoys took what cover they could on the ground and returned fire under a very hot sun. All the men were now suffering from thirst and Regimental Bhisti (water carrier) Dhunni, from Lohar Village in Ludhiana District, repeatedly carried his water bag from the train, 700 metres to the rear, up to the firing line to supply the troops. Eventually he was shot dead and although he was recommended for an Indian Order of Merit this was not approved; however he was later mentioned in Despatches.

Iraq

However 45TH Sikhs did receive four Indian Orders of Merit that day for conspicuous gallantry and devotion to duty. All these awards are examples of how specialists and trained soldiers in a good Infantry Battalion react on the battlefield.

The 45TH Sikhs were still at Imam Hamzah and so the railway line from there back to Hillah was protected by double-Platoon posts and block-houses three to six kilometres apart; these detachments used-up the rifle strength of two Battalions and were regularly but unsuccessfully attacked. An attempt in the town by Hyatt to obtain a political settlement failed and Cunningham's column reached the ten kilometres from Rumeitha point on 19TH July. The insurgents, led by former Officers in the Turkish Army, had strengthened their defensive positions around the embankment where the previous action had been fought by digging well-sited parallel lines of trenches. The embankment was in fact the second line of defence as a concealed trench had been dug 200 metres to the front.

An immediate attack was ordered with 45TH Sikhs and 116TH Mahrattas leading, whilst 87TH Punjabis secured the river bank to the left and minimised sniping from across the river. The two Field Artillery Batteries registered on the embankment and put down a barrage at 1745 hours when the Infantry advanced. Initially the advance was steady, although heavy enemy fire was received, and a re-organisation halt was made about 400 metres away from the embankment. Then the Sikhs observed the Mahrattas on the right rapidly retreating; the Mahrattas Commanding Officer was the only British Officer still standing and he alone could not prevent the flight of his Sepoys. The enemy immediately took advantage of the situation and counter-attacked, consequently the Sikhs had to 'right-form' two Platoons of 'B' Company to protect the right flank; this was successful and the Arabs quickly retreated before this firepower, to the cover of their trenches, having lost many men.

During these operations Havildar Tara Singh, Havildar Hardit Singh, Sepoy Ram Singh, Sepoy Chanan Singh (died of wounds) Sepoy Gurdit Singh and Havildar Ganga Singh were awarded the Indian Order of Merit.

The citation of Havildar Ganga Singh reads;

"For conspicuous gallantry and devotion to duty on July 22^{ND,} 1920. When the rear guard was heavily attacked and driven back, on his own initiative he took up a position, and brought such a defective fire to bear on the enemy that the latter was unable to advance. By his bravery and coolness, he inspired the men under his command, that the line was restored and the enemy driven back."

Iraq

14TH Ludhiana Sikhs

The 14TH Sikhs left Jullunder on 20TH February for Iraq and proceeded to Baghdad, where they were detailed for garrison duty. Later in the year 14TH Sikhs moved to Kut al Amara, where they were employed in closing down the military cantonment and demolishing the post. Early in 1923, 15TH Sikhs were back again in Baghdad and were responsible for the protection of the Royal Air Force aerodrome.

At this time tribesmen in Kurdistan, under the leadership of Shaikh Mahmud, were actively hostile to the British administration. They had met with considerable success in the autumn of 1922 and the British forces had not been able to deal with them during the winter, on account of the bad weather. In February troops were urgently required in Kirkuk and, 'A' and 'B' Companies, under Captains Maclaren and Spankie, were detailed for this role. The two Companies were transported there by air on 21ST February. This was the first occasion in history on which a large body of troops had been carried by air for military operations. The two Companies, in full fighting equipment, were moved in nine troop-carrying airplanes and the actual journey in the air took less than an hour, whereas by march route; Kirkuk could not have been reached in less than a week.

The 14TH Sikhs took part in the punitive operations directed by the Commander of the Royal Air Force in Iraq against Shaikh Mahmud and his forces in May and June, 1923. They joined a column under Colonel B. Vincent and concentrated in Kirkuk. The column marched from Kirkuk on 12TH May and for a fortnight traversed the Kurdistan country, making many long marches. However, no serious fighting took place, and no casualties were suffered. The column returned to Kirkuk in June and then dispersed, although 14TH Sikhs remained at Kirkuk until the end of September. For their services in Kurdistan, Major Story received brevet promotion to Lieutenant-Colonel and Subadar Bogh Singh was awarded the Military Cross. The Regiment arrived back in Baghdad in October and remained there until its return to India at the beginning of 1924.

Anglo-Iraqi Treaty of 1922

The Anglo-Iraqi treaty of 1922, gave Iraq partial independence, but left Britain with economic and military control over the country. Britain had in 1921 installed Faisal bin Hussein as King of Iraq, and wanted a formal agreement after years of being the country's mandate power. The treaty was signed in October 1922, but not ratified until March 1924. The constituent assembly did not vote in favour of the agreement until the British High Commissioner had threatened to suspend the constitution drafted by the assembly. While the treaty was humiliating for many Iraqis, it still had in it the seed for independence. Actual independence came 10 years later. The 1922 treaty was superseded by a new treaty in 1930. On October 3RD, 1932, Iraq was admitted to the League of Nations as an Independent State.

ANATOLIA

The British Army of The Black Sea was tasked with ensuring that Turkey complied with the terms of the Armistice. Important terms were the Turkish evacuation of territories outside Anatolia such as the Caucasus region, and the demobilisation and disarming of the Turkish Forces. The 24TH Punjabis were deployed around Batum, an important port on the East coast of the Black Sea and a main access point to the Caucasus. Detachments occupied posts in villages and on the main routes to Kars and to Tiflis in Georgia. In September 1919, 24TH Punjabis were re-deployed to Bostanjik in Anatolia, on the coast of the Sea of Marmora, South of Constantinople.

In Anatolia a Turkish National Movement was developing under the strong and effective leadership of Mustafa Kemal Ataturk, the successful Turkish front-line Commander at Gallipoli. The Nationalists were extremely resentful of the Armistice of Mudros, signed on 30TH October 1918 that had brought an end to the hostilities between Turkey and the Allies. It not only heralded the dismemberment of the Ottoman Empire, but granted the Allies the right to occupy forts controlling the Dardanelles and the Bosporus, and any other Turkish territory in the event of an outbreak of disorder that threatened the integrity of the armistice. Nationalist supporters armed themselves and prepared to fight a War of Independence. Attacks on Allied Units began. The Punjabis arrived at Bostanjik to find that the most distant post occupied by British troops was at Ismid, 60 miles away. Nationalist pressure had led to the withdrawal of two more distant British posts. The Battalion moved to Derinje on 19TH May 1920 to relieve 25TH Punjabis. The 24TH Punjabis were now employed on posts securing the rail link to Bostanjik. However on 11TH June "C" Company was deployed two miles North of Ismid. The Turks moved in small parties towards Ismid. They cut the British telephone line and posted a strong Turkish piquet 200 yards from the British perimeter in a dominating position above the road to Ismid. The Turkish troops became openly hostile and abusive towards the Sepoys. Lieutenant Mattox went out to ascertain the Turkish intentions but he was threatened and temporarily detained. Again a Turkish Officer approached the post and demanded a British evacuation to avoid bloodshed, stating that his men were fanatical and could not be controlled. He advised that a message be sent to the British GOC stating that the post would be attacked during the night if it was not evacuated. When this advice was rejected the Officer departed stating that no one would now be allowed to leave the post. The British orders were that fire was not to be opened unless the Turks actually fired into or advanced upon the post. Neither of those actions happened and they decided to evacuate the post. Tents were struck and dumped in a hollow along with kits, stores, rations and bombs and kerosene oil was poured on. The perimeter was evacuated and the dump fired to prevent looting. "C" Company moved off in three parties. The advance guard was a Sikh Platoon commanded by Havildar Harnam Singh. The remaining Sikh Platoon under Subadar Kehr Singh initially stayed on Point 325 with its Lewis Guns ready to provide covering fire.

Anatolia

As the advance guard arrived below the Turkish piquet, the Sikhs were ordered back to the post. Havildar Harman Singh responded by doubling his men forward down the road to Ismid. A Turkish whistle was now blown as a signal and the Nationalists opened fire at close range, supported by several machine guns deployed in various locations along the road. The enemy then swarmed down onto the road and engaged in hand-to-hand fighting with the main body. Subadar Kehr Singh's Lewis gunners could not give effective support because of the confusion between friend and foe. Lieutenant Mattox and Company Havildar-Major Kesar Singh were both shot down at point-blank range, as was the Greek interpreter, the Sub-Assistant Surgeon and several Sepoys. Further casualties were only avoided by Subedar Ram Singh deploying his men into a deep watercourse. The withdrawal was ordered to continue. Further up the road the advance guard had become scattered and of eight men who had taken up position on the road with a Lewis gun, four had been hit and the gun had jammed after firing two short bursts. Annihilation of the British detachment was avoided by both the poor shooting of the Turks and the surrounding broken ground, which allowed "C" Company to disperse into cover and to move to Ismid in small parties. When the Company concentrated again at Ismid the casualty figures were found to be, 18 Sepoys killed in action and 16 Sepoys wounded in action. On 29TH June 1920 the British evacuated Derinje and 24TH Punjabis moved to Beikos on the Asiatic side of the Bosporus, and the Battalion operated with the Greek Archipelago Regiment in an attempt to surprise and capture the Nationalists. Then the Punjabis moved to Shileh on the Black Sea coast. From there patrols reconnoitred villages in the interior. At the end of September orders were received for 24TH Punjabis to return to India and the Battalion disembarked at Karachi on 21ST October 1920. .

Gallantry awards made for the Ismid action and Meritorious Service awards made for service with the Army of the Black Sea:

Naik Bhag Singh IOM
"Naik Bhag Singh was awarded the Indian Order of Merit for conspicuous gallantry and devotion to duty on 15TH June 1920. Although severely wounded, he continued to lead his section and direct his Lewis guns under heavy machine gun fire. He set a splendid example to his men."

Lance Naik Kehr Singh IOM
"Lance Naik Kehr Singh was awarded the Indian Order of Merit for conspicuous gallantry and devotion to duty on 15TH June 1920. Although severely wounded he continued to fire his Lewis gun under heavy machine gun fire from three directions. He was afterwards carried back, but retained his Lewis gun which he brought into action in another position."

ABYSSINIA

Like Britain and France, Italy had joined in the so-called "Scramble for Africa. However, the prize territories had been conquered by others and Italy was left with unimportant areas such as Eritrea and Somaliland. The Italians had attempted to expand in Eastern Africa by joining Abyssinia to her conquests, but in 1896, the Italians were heavily defeated by the Abyssinians at the Battle of Adowa. This defeat had an enormous impact on Italian pride. The loss of 6000 men against a backward Army from Abyssinia was difficult for the Italian people to comprehend. However, this defeat did not stop politicians in Italy planning for a new attempt to take over Abyssinia. The desire to show the world how powerful Italy was became the prime motivation of Mussolini. He saw himself as a modern day Julius Caesar who would one day be in charge of a vast Italian empire, as had existed in the days of Caesar.

In 1928, Italy signed a treaty of friendship with Haile Selassie, the leader of Abyssinia but an invasion of the country was already being planned. In December 1934, Mussolini accused the Abyssinians of aggression at an oasis called Wal Wal. He ordered Italian troops stationed in Somaliland and Eritrea to attack Abyssinia. Large quantities of ammunition and supplies had been stockpiled there. In October 1935, the Italian Army invaded Abyssinia. The Abyssinians could not hope to stand up to a modern Army - they were equipped with pre-World War One rifles and little else. The Italians used armoured vehicles and even mustard gas in their attack. The capital, Addis Ababa, fell in May 1936 and Haile Selassie was removed from the throne and replaced by the King of Italy, Victor Emmanuel. Somaliland, Eritrea and Abyssinia were all united under the name Italian East Africa.

When it became apparent 1934 that Mussolini was about to launch his legions against Abyssinia, the British Minister sought military aid to defend British interests in the event of a defeat sparking off anti-foreign riots and attacks in the capital. It arrived in the shape of the Sikh Company of 14TH Punjabis. When in 1936 the Emperor's Army was routed, looting in the city was universal, fires blazed everywhere. But lorry patrols of the Sikhs kept touch between foreign legations; issued rifles to the Americans, Japanese, Italians and Germans; escorted 1,770 refugees of thirty nationalities to the British Legation and defended them there. They fought pitched battles with the Imperial Guard who were attacking the British legation; and evacuated the American diplomats as their Legation went up in flames. After five days of mayhem, the Italian Army arrived and restored order with a heavy hand.

Watched by Carabineers and black shirt militia, the Sikh Company paraded to celebrate the King's birthday and was formally thanked for their services by the new Italian Viceroy, the Duke of Acosta

However, the Sikhs would be back in Abyssinian during the Second World War to fight and defeat the same Italians.

EAST AFRICA 1940

Sikh soldiers of the Fourth Indian Divison and the following Units of the Fifth Indian Division, participated in the East African Campaign; 1ST Punjab Regiment, 2ND Punjab Regiment, 12TH Frontier Force Regiment, 13TH Frontier Force Rifles, 14TH Punjab Regiment, Indian Armoured Corps, Indian Engineers, Indian Signals, and Indian Transport Corps.

Italian Army

On 10TH June 1940, when Mussolini led Italy into World War II against the British and the French, the Italian forces in Africa became a potential threat to British supply routes along the Red Sea and through the Suez Canal. While Egypt and the Suez Canal were Mussolini's obvious primary targets, an Italian invasion of either French Somaliland or British Somaliland were reasonable choices too. But Mussolini initially looked past both of these small, isolated colonies and instead looked forward to propaganda triumphs in the Sudan and British East Africa. In Eritrea and Abyssinia were a quarter of a million Italian and colonial troops, many of excellent quality, two hundred military aircraft, sixty tanks, a hundred Armoured cars, ten Regiments of Field Artillery which in the Italian Army was very good and fifty-eight batteries of pack-Artillery.

Sudan (1940)

On July 4TH, Italian forces in Eritrea crossed the Sudanese border and forced the small British garrison holding the railway junction at Kassala to withdraw. The defenders lost 10 men, the attackers 117. The Italians also seized the small British forts at Gallabat, just over the border from Metemma, some 200 miles from Kassala. Even the villages of Qaysan, Kurmuk, and Dumbode on the Blue Nile were conquered. Having taken Kassala and Gallabat, however, the Italians were then bogged down as the seasonal rains had turned most of Eastern Sudan into quagmire. General Platt had a 1200-mile frontier with Abyssinia to watch with his meagre forces. But the arrival at Port Sudan in September of 5TH Indian Divison, transformed his position. The Division's two Brigades were made up to three, 9TH, 10TH and 29TH, each of one British and two Indian Battalions. It also provided most of 'Gazelle Force', one of those piratical semi-private armies that consisted of the motor-machine-gun batteries of the Sudan Defence Force, a 5TH Indian Divisional Cavalry Regiment mounted in 15cwt trucks, a Field Regiment, and one or two Companies of Infantry whenever they could be spared. At the end of December the leading Brigade of 4TH Indian Division, 11TH Brigade, arrived straight from its victory at Sidi Barani.

Gallabat (1940)

On November 6TH, a small mixed force attacked the enemy position at Gallabat, and had the privilege of instituting the first British offensive in Africa. The fort was thoroughly bombed, while the Artillery put down a heavy concentration on it. The Infantry followed up tanks in a direct assault. The fort was reached and fierce hand-to-hand fighting ensued. The enemy fought well. Some very stout hearted Italians and Eritrean, who had remained to fight in spite of the severe bombing and shelling, took a deal of evicting. After this action constant offensive patrolling was maintained, shaking the enemy's morale and inflicting further casualties. British Gunners forced the Italians to evacuate the town and fort of Metemma. The troops which took part had been blooded and in their patrolling were so fierce, the enemy feared to stir out of their trenches behind barbed wire. In addition to the daily bag of prisoners, a steady stream of deserters began to come in.

Keren (1941)

On the arrival of 4TH Indian Division in the Sudan, it was intended to attack the enemy in the Kassala and Tessenei area, thus driving the Italians out of the Sudan. The mobile 'Gazelle Force' was placed under 4TH Indian Division, some Artillery and part of a Brigade. The 4TH Battalion, 11TH Sikh Regiment joined Gazelle and was supplied with Lorries, to make them as mobile as the remainder of this little force. On January 19TH, the advance began. The enemy was found to have evacuated both Kassala and Tessenei, and both forces set off in pursuit. The 5TH Division pushed along the fine road to Aicota, while 4TH Division advanced along the dry weather track towards Keru. Both columns were delayed by road mines, obstructions and demolitions prepared by the Italians, and the Sappers and Miners had their first taste of the dangerous and trying work of clearing the roads. By the afternoon Gazelle caught up with the enemy at Wachai, some 40 miles from Kassala, and at once engaged them, the Sikhs having their first taste of fighting. During the night and early morning the enemy, who had suffered a number of casualties, abandoned Wachai, retiring towards Keru. Gazelle Force having advanced against opposition nearly 70 miles in 48 hours, made contact with the enemy in the Keru defences. During the early hours of 22ND, the Sikhs climbed the mountains just to the South of Keru Gorge and by daylight were on top, after hard fighting. Fighting continued on the hill throughout the day. By nightfall the enemy's defences had been driven back and severe losses inflicted. During that night patrols kept touch, and by the morning it was found that the enemy had abandoned this almost impregnable position. On January 24TH the first major defeat of the Italian forces in Eritrea took place, when the five Colonial Battalions cut off in the Keru hills were smashed and captured 700 prisoners including the Brigade Commander and all his staff.

East Africa

Agordat (1941)

The two battles, 4TH Division at Agordat and 5TH Division at Barentu, were fought simultaneously. For the sake of clarity they are recounted separately.

The 4TH Indian Division, in a frontal attack captured the four hills astride the road just outside Agordat, which were fortified with concrete emplacements, trenches and wire. Resistance died away in the face of this attack and the Italians bolted away before they were captured. Next day the Division went into town, which was found to be abandoned and the enemy had slipped away, leaving his guns, vehicles, and huge quantities of stores. About a thousand prisoners had been taken and this number was doubled when the pursuing forces overtook stragglers.

Barentu (1941)

Barentu is another town similar to Agordat, lying on a small plain surrounded by steep, scrub-covered hills. One Brigade of 5TH Division was advancing from Aicota, the other from Agordat; the only possible line of retreat left to the Italians was by a road running Westward. But this road fades out 25 miles from Barentu, and there is no way up the escarpment except for men and animals. Retirement would mean the loss of all guns, vehicles and stores, so the Italians had no alternative but to stand and fight it out. Fighting round Barentu was a grim soldier's battle in which the better men won by sheer fighting ability. The commanding heights and the lower features were well held by the enemy. On subsequent days of stiff fighting the enemy would be cleared from one feature, but there were always other positions in this hilly intricate country. On the morning of February 2ND the Italians abandoned their defences and Barentu fell. In Barentu only the wounded in the hospitals abandoned by the Italians were taken prisoner, but in following up along the road to the East, a Motor Machine Gun Company of the Sudan Defence Force picked up many exhausted stragglers, both Italian and Eritrean. Some guns, vehicles and considerable quantities of stores were found in the town, and the booty was greatly increased when the pursuing troops reached the mountains. Below the precipitous wall lay all the guns, ammunition and stores, for, unable to get anything except men and animals up the mountains, the enemy had to abandon everything else. Chased by the armoured cars and mobile troops, continually bombed from the air, this enemy force was utterly disorganised. Over 3,000 prisoners were taken. Many of the native troops went off to their homes and their Units, although afterwards reformed, were never fit to be taken into action again. It had been a complete victory, in which the fighting qualities of 3RD Battalion, 2ND Punjab Regiment and 6TH Royal Battalion, 13TH Frontier Force Rifles in pushing across the difficult and scrubby country were outstanding.

Sepoy Saudagar Singh and Havildar Natha Singh of 6TH Royal Battalion, 13TH Frontier Force Rifles, fell fighting around Barentu in February, 1941. They were both awarded Indian Order of Merit, posthumously.

East Africa

Keren (1941)

The battle at Keren began on 3RD of February 1941 with both sides exchanging Artillery fire from their dug-in positions. Over 90,000 men in total were engaged in the battle. The Italians, knowing the loss of Keren would mean the loss of their East African empire, were determined to hold their positions, and managed to defend the area for two months of fierce fighting. The battle finally ended on the 27TH March 1941, after the British assaulted and took Mount Sankil, home to an Italian fortress. During the whole battle they used over thirty thousand Infantry and one hundred and forty-four guns. Many of these were fresh troops.

General Frusci in his reports, admitted to having lost three thousand men at Keren, including General Lorenzini. The total Italian losses probably were about ten thousand. He made much of the fact that he had managed to withdraw from Keren the bulk of his Infantry and guns; but the fall of Keren had finally shattered the morale of the Italian Army. At the end of the battle of Keren there were only three Battalions and a few batteries uncommitted between Keren and Asmara. Practically all had been staked on holding Keren. The British and Indian troops had fought hard and won.

The battle was described by General Platt as "a ding-dong battle, a soldier's battle, fought against an enemy infinitely superior in numbers, on ground of his own choosing which gave him every bit of observation against the movement of our troops, the positions of our guns and the approaches of our transport". And it was won by "the tenacity and determination of Commanders and troops, by whole-hearted cooperation of all ranks, whether forward or back, of whatever race or creed, and by the continuous support given to Infantry by the Royal Artillery." The British casualties were not light. Some 500 Officers and 3,000 men had been killed and wounded. The 4TH Indian Division was particularly hard hit. Yet the determination of the British and Indian troops to fight to victory was to leave its mark upon the Italians and to affect their conduct in the subsequent operations. They were never really to stand to fight again in the same spirit. The outcome of the contest in Italian East Africa was no longer in doubt. There were to be more battles and more victories before Italian East Africa was conquered, but Keren had broken the back of Italian resistance and subsequent operations were easier.

The conduct of 4TH and 5TH Indian Divisions won them ready applause from several quarters. "The whole Empire", wrote the British Prime Minister to the Viceroy of India shortly after the victory at Keren, "has been stirred by the achievement of the Indian forces in Eritrea." Lord Wavell found the victory "a fitting climax to the great work in Eritrea of 4TH and 5TH Indian Divisions ably commanded by Major-General N. M. de la Beresford-Peirse and Major-General L. M. Heath respectively". He could now well think of transferring some of the forces from this theatre to the more important areas of War. Eritrea had ceased to present a military threat to the Allies.

East Africa

As Teclesan (1941)

At the fall of Keren, there were still many parties of the enemy in the hills to be collected and brought to the prisoners' camp. The 4TH Indian Division was given the work of mopping up, searching for wounded, burying the dead and collecting booty. The 4TH Indian Division, after two and half months of fighting in this area, went off to gain further laurels in Syria and the Western Desert. From now onwards 5TH Indian Division carried out the campaign alone. It was sad for these two Divisions of the Indian Army thus parted after fighting side by side through this arduous campaign. The Italians had destroyed the road in many places in order to delay the advance and in consequence these operations followed almost a stereotyped form. The mobile troops ran up against the demolition and carried out reconnaissance to discover the extent of the enemy position; the Infantry then arrived and assisted by the Artillery, forced the enemy from the hills on either side; the Sappers and Miners cleared the road block and the tanks and guns went through. There was some hard fighting along the road in which 3RD Battalion, 2ND Punjab, 3RD Battalion, 12TH Frontier Force Regiment and 6TH Royal Battalion, 13TH Frontier Force Rifles particularly distinguished themselves. The Italians were, however, very disorganized and their morale shattered. In the face of these determined attacks, they gave way easily.

Asmara (1941)

When finally 5TH Indian Division broke through, the emissaries came out with white flags. Asmara was declared an open town and was occupied on April 1ST. Thus, after two and a half months intense fighting, the capital Eritrea surrendered; after their long and resolute stand at Keren the Italians had cracked. After the fall of Asmara, 5TH Indian Division was split up. Part went to Massawa; part remained in Asmara sorting out the very difficult problems that arose in taking over this large town, and a small force pursued the Italians down the road towards Addis Ababa. They captured some 2,000 prisoners, who were frequently only too glad to surrender, owing to the activities of the Abyssinian patriots. They secured large dumps of stores and on one occasion captured a complete Battalion in Lorries. The Lorries were turned round and the Battalion moved North under escort.

Massawa (1941)

As the British advanced toward Eritrea, Mario Bonetti, the Italian Commander of the Red Sea Flotilla based at Massawa, realized that his harbour was going to be overrun by the enemy. In the first week of April, 1941, he began to destroy the harbour's facilities and ruin its usefulness to the British. The enemy's resistance increased and was shattered as 4TH Indian Division charged towards Massawa. It then became a race for who would be first into town; a race that was won by 4TH Battalion, 16TH Punjab Regiment. Over 400 Officers, including Admirals and Generals were captured.

East Africa

Amba Alagi (1941)

The Italians decided to defend the area around Amba Alagi in force. In this mountain fortress, the defenders, under command of Amedeo, Duke of Aosta, thought themselves to be impregnable. Major-General Mosley Mayne and the Indian 5TH Infantry Division were given the task of taking Amba Alagi. Mayne was only able to deploy the Indian 29TH Infantry Brigade, for this action. His attacking force was therefore inferior in numbers to the Italian defending force. On 3RD May 1941, Mayne sent in a feint attack from the East while, in the early hours of 4TH May, the main attack was made from the Northwest over the hills. The hills were fiercely defended by the Italians. By 14TH May, Amba Alagi was surrounded. With the arrival of the South Africans, the 7000 Italian troops of Amedeo, Duke of Aosta, were directly attacked by 9000 British troops and more than 20000 Ethiopian irregulars. A final assault was planned for 15TH May, but a fortuitous Artillery shell hit an Italian fuel dump and ruptured a vessel containing oil. This caused oil to flow into the remaining drinking water of the Italian defenders. On 18TH May, Amedeo, Duke of Aosta, surrendered his embattled forces at Amba Alagi. General Mayne agreed to surrender with "full military honours" (allowing the troops to march off the battlefield in formation and then surrender their arms).

Jemadar Aman Singh of 15TH Lancers, Jemadar Amar Singh of 2ND Punjab Regiment, Jemadar Dhera Singh of 3RD Battalion, 2ND Punjab Regiment, Sepoy Saudagar Singh of 6TH Battalion, 13TH Frontier Force Rifles (Posthumous) and Havildar Natha Singh also of 6TH Battalion, 13TH Frontier Force Rifles (Posthumous) were awarded the Indian Order of Merit for their conspicuous gallantry during the East African operations.

Subedar Natha Singh, IDSM, 1ST Punjab Regiment

SOMALILAND 1941

The Italian force attacking British Somaliland in August 1940, numbered about 24,000 soldiers. The British forces in Somaliland numbered about 4,000 soldiers. The force included Sikh soldiers of 3RD Battalion, 15TH Punjab Regiment and the 1ST Battalion, 2ND Punjab Regiment. On 3RD August 1940, the Italian Army crossed the border between Italian East Africa and British Somaliland. At the Italian advance British and Commonwealth forces pulled back towards Tug Argan. By 10TH August, the Italians had closed up on the British positions behind the Tug Argan and made preparations to attack. On 7-8TH August, the British and Commonwealth forces in British Somaliland had received reinforcements with the arrival of 1ST Battalion, 2ND Punjab Regiment and 2ND Battalion Black Watch. The defensive positions of the British Army were centred round six hills overlooking the only road toward Berbera. On 11TH August, one of the Italian Brigades attacked the hill defended by a Company of 3RD Battalion, 15TH Punjab Regiment and captured it, taking heavy casualties. The British launched two unsuccessful counterattacks but fought off Italian attacks on two other hills. The next day, all the British positions were attacked. By evening, Mill Hill had been taken after severe fighting.

Then Italian forces had established themselves in the Assa Hills, dominating the Southern side of the gap through which the road to Berbera ran. On 13TH August, no further positions were taken despite heavy fighting but the Italians continued to improve their position through infiltration. By 14TH August, the defenders' situation started to look critical: the Italians were almost in a position to cut the road and thus the defenders' only line of supply and retreat. On 15TH August, the British forces received orders to withdraw from British Somaliland. Late on 15TH August, the Italians took Observation Hill and after dark the defenders of Tug Argan commenced their withdrawal.

The entire British and Commonwealth contingent withdrew to Berbera with minimal losses and loading of the ships was completed in the early hours of 18TH August. On 19TH August, the Italians took control of Berbera and then moved down the coast to complete their conquest of British Somaliland. The British colony was annexed by Mussolini and the port of Berbera was used by the Italian submarines of the Red Sea Flotilla as a small base in the last months of 1940. British Somaliland remained part of Italian East Africa for a matter of months. On 16TH March 1941, the British executed Operation Appearance, which was staged from Aden; two Battalions from the Indian Army and one Somali Commando detachment were landed on both sides of Berbera. The two Sikh Battalions (which had been part of the defending force evacuated in August 1940), made the first successful Allied landing on an enemy-held beach during World War II. Shortly afterwards the British and Indians re-captured the whole of British Somaliland from its Italian occupiers. The conquest of British Somaliland was the only campaign victory Italy achieved, without the support of German troops, during World War II against the Allies.

NORTH AFRICA

This is titled North Africa instead of Egypt, as the battles also engulfed Libya and Tunisia. On 1ST September, Germany invaded Poland with massive ground and air forces. On 3RD September, Britain declared War on Germany. India got automatically involved in the War and its forces fought in Africa, the Middle East, and Malaya, Italy and in Burma. The situation changed dramatically for the worse with the fall of France and the entry of Italy in the War in June 1940. After the fall of France on 20TH June 1940, French resistance in their colonies in North Africa, Syria and French Somaliland gradually collapsed. The Italians could now concentrate their efforts against the British in North and East Africa. Marshal Grazaini deployed the Tenth Italian Army in Cyrenaica. It's HQ at Tobruk with a motorised group, which had three tank Battalions, plus 72 medium and 30 light tanks and two Libyan Divisions. The Italian XX111 Corps was at Badia with two Metropolitan Divisions and one Black Shirt Division. XX11 Italian Corps with two Divisions was on the line of communication. In the theatre the Italians had a total of 415,000 troops, 215,000 in Libya and 200,000 in East Africa. Wavell, on the other hand, had total of 85,000 men.

The Fourth Indian Division in North Africa contained the Sikh soldiers of the following Units; Royal Indian Engineers, Indian Armoured Corps, 1ST Punjab Regiment, 2ND Royal Battalion, 11TH Sikh Regiment, 3RD Battalion, 12TH Frontier Force Regiment, 3RD Battalion, 14TH Punjab Regiment, and 4TH Battalion, 16TH Punjab Regiment.

In the forward to the history of Fourth Indian Division, General Wavell wrote: "For the fame of this Division will surely go down as one of the greatest fighting formations in military history: to be spoken with such as The Tenth Legion, The Light Division of the Peninsular War, Napoleon's Old Guard."

Nibeiwa, (1940)

After the timorous Italian offensive in September 1940, which took Graziani's troops to Sidi Barrani in Egypt, British General Wavell ordered to General O'Connor, Chief of the "Western Desert Force" to counter attack the Italian troops. On 9TH December 1940, in the morning, 7TH RTR (Royal Tank Regiment) and 4TH Indian Division attacked Nibeiwa camp where was the "Maletti Group", the mobile elements of Graziani's Army. For the Italians, the surprise was total when Matilda tanks crushed barbed wire and entered the camp, firing on all objectives. Having suffered heavy casualties, they could not stand the sight of the bayonet. The bayonet is a terrible weapon in the hands of the men from the plains of Northern India. After some fierce fighting, Nibeiwa was taken; the Italian General was killed and 2,000 prisoners taken.

North Africa

The Tummars, (1940)
The 7TH Royal Tank Regiment and Artillery had softened up Tummars' defences for an hour and as the tanks broke through the perimeter, they were followed by the Infantry. The defenders put up strong opposition but Tummar West was overrun, except for the extreme North East corner. The determination of the Indian soldiers was exemplified by the actions of Havildar Kalyan Singh of 1ST Punjab Regiment. When inside the camp, where there was still much resistance all around, his carrier was set on fire by hand grenade. He wrenched his gun from its mounting, getting badly burnt as he did so, and at once went into action on the ground, silencing an enemy post. Not until his last round had been fired did he think of getting away, and still under fire he saw his men packed into another carrier before finding room for himself. Meanwhile 7TH Armoured Division's 4TH Armoured Brigade, while performing flank defence, had advanced to Azziziya where the garrison of 400 surrendered.

Sidi Barrani, (1940)
On 10TH December, 16TH Infantry Brigade was brought forward from 4TH Indian Division reserve and with elements of 11TH Indian Brigade under command, was sent forward in Lorries to attack Sidi Barrani. Moving forward that morning across exposed ground the force took some casualties but with support from Artillery and 7TH RTR it was in position barring the South and South Western exits to Sidi Barrani by 13.30. At 16.00, supported by the whole of the Division's Artillery, the attack, again with the support of 7TH RTR, went in. The town was captured by nightfall and the remains of the two Libyan Divisions and 4th Blackshirt Division were trapped between 16TH Infantry Brigade and the Selby Force. On 11TH December Selby Force supported by some tanks attacked and secured the surrender of 1ST Libyan Division. In the battle of Sidi Barani 3 Italian Divisions and a mobile group had been dispersed and 20,000 prisoners taken. The Italians were forced back again and again and further and further into Libya. Before what started as a raid was over, the whole of the Tenth Army had been destroyed. Egypt was clear of the enemy on 10TH December when Sidi Omar was captured.

Afrika Korps, (1941)
In early 1941, after the decisive British and Commonwealth victory in Cyrenaica, the military position was soon reversed. Wavell ordered a significant portion of his troops to support Greece. While Wavell was reducing his forces in North Africa, German dictator Adolf Hitler responded to the Italian disaster by ordering the newly formed German "Afrika Korps" as reinforcements to the Italians, to prevent total collapse. The German corps included fresh troops with better equipment and a charismatic Commander, General Erwin Rommel. He quickly defeated the Allied forces at El Agheila on March 24TH. By 15TH April, he had recaptured all of Libya except for Tobruk which was encircled and besieged.

North Africa

Operation Battleaxe, (1941)

Operation Battleaxe was fixed for 15TH June. Tobruk was invested by about two thirds of the enemy forces. The remaining third were strongly entrenched in positions North and West of the Halfaya Pass. They must be defeated before Tobruk could be relieved. Wavell's forces were about equal to Rommel's except in the vital arm, tanks, in which they were markedly inferior in quantity and as it transpired in quality. Operation Battle Axe was a total failure. Seventeen out of eighteen tanks supporting 4TH Indian Division's attack from Halfaya to the sea were ablaze in the first few minutes. The new German tank was the ultimate anti-tank weapon of its day, able to smash the heaviest tank at 2,000 yards. When the British rear was threatened by German Armour, almost intact, while the British had lost in all ninety-six tanks, there was nothing for it but to withdraw to original positions.

The Battle for Omars, (1941)

On 18TH November, Eighth Army launched a surprise attack, advancing West from its base at Mersa Matruh and crossing the Libyan border near Fort Maddalena, some 50 miles (80 km) South of Sidi Omar, and then pushing to the Northwest. Initially all went well for the Allies. 7TH Armoured Division's 7TH Armoured Brigade advanced Northwest towards Tobruk with 22ND Armoured Brigade to their left. XIII Corps and New Zealand Division made its flanking advance with 4TH Armoured Brigade on its left and 4TH Indian Division's 7TH Infantry Brigade on its right flank at Sidi Omar. On the first day no resistance was encountered as Eighth Army closed on the enemy positions. The defences of Libyan Omar and Omar Nuovo had been very well prepared and were sited for all round defence.

Omar Nuovo, (1941)

The Royal Sussex drew Omar Nuovo as their portion and Libyan Omar was allotted to 16TH Punjab Regiment. The 11TH Sikh Regiment was ordered to mask, but not assault, Cove, four miles to the North. The Royal Sussex Regiment surged forward through the trenches and weapon- pits, taking 1,500 prisoners.

Libyan Omar, (1941)

The 4TH Battalion, 16TH Punjab Regiment, with two Tank Squadrons, then passed through Omar Nuovo heading for Libyan Omar. In a few minutes nearly all the tanks were ablaze, immobilized by mines and smashed by the 88s. When the Punjabis debussed and formed up to attack, they had only five tanks instead of thirty. Nevertheless they went in shoulder to shoulder with 1ST Battalion, 1ST Punjab Regiment and 4TH Battalion, 11TH Sikh Regiment. By evening they had 500 prisoners and cleared the Eastern part of the box. Next day, in many Platoon and Company actions, they took a thousand more prisoners and increased their hold to one third of the box.

North Africa

Qineiqina, (1941)
During this battle 4TH Battalion, 11TH Sikh Regiment was staging demonstrations to distract the enemy at Cova. During their demonstrations, Platoons of the Sikh Regiment started off across the open plain to capture a small Italian garrison at Qineiqina. Artillery, mortars, machine guns, and anti-tank guns pinned the Platoons to the ground. There was a minefield round the post and the Sikhs had no supporting fire whatsoever. Ammunition would not last all day and when it was finished the Italians would be able to pick off the prone attackers one by one. It looked as if two Platoons would be wiped out. The only way out of the difficulty was to go forward. With a roar of "Wah Guru ji Ki Fateh" they swept up to the position and within minutes all was over. The Sikhs captured all the heavy guns and accounted for twenty-five of the enemy.

El Gubi, (1941)
The Axis had retreated and formed a defence line running South from the perimeter of Tobruk to El Adem and El Gubi. The next stage was the destruction of the remainder of the Afrika Korps, roaming about the front and the Italian Divisions in the defences of El Gubi, El Adem and round Tobruk. On the morning of 19TH November the advance of 22ND Armoured Brigade was blunted by the Ariete Division at Bir el Gubi that continued to take a major toll of British Armour in the opening phase of the battle. In the Division's centre 7TH Armoured Brigade and 7TH Support Group raced forward and took Sidi Rezegh airfield. Rommel withdrew with expert celerity behind the marshes of El Agheila awaiting the arrival of new tanks and reinforcements. They had not lost many Germans; only tanks which were replaceable and Italians, which were expendable.

Relief of Tobruk, (1941)
It was vital for the Allies' defence of Egypt and the Suez Canal to hold the town with its harbour, as this forced the enemy to bring most of their supplies overland from the port of Tripoli, across 1500 km of desert, as well as diverting troops from their advance. Tobruk was the site of a lengthy confrontation between Axis and Allied forces in North Africa. The siege started on 10TH April 1941, when Tobruk was attacked by an Italian-German force under Lieutenant General Erwin Rommel. The garrison, commanded by Lieutenant General Leslie Morshead, consisted of 9th Division, 18TH Brigade of 7TH Division, along with four Regiments of British Artillery and Indian troops. It was subject to repeated ground assaults and almost constant shelling and bombing, and continued for 240 days, when the Eighth Army relieved it during Operation Crusader.

North Africa

Derna, (1941)

The 7TH Armoured Division moved across to the desert flank of 4TH Indian Division. The hunt was up. These two original desert formations set off in pursuit of Rommel. On 18TH Carmusa was reached. Leaving 4TH Battalion, 16TH Punjabis, to secure the Derna by-pass, the Royal Sussex raced back twelve miles along the road to Martuba. On the way they captured an Italian tank, complete with the crew, one heavy gun, some Italians and Lorries. They threw themselves onto Martuba airfield, destroying three aircraft and securing huge dumps of bombs and stores.

The 4TH Battalion, 11TH Sikhs passed through the Royal Sussex Regiment, and dropped two Companies to block the road against forces retreating from the East, while the Bren carriers and the remainder of the Battalion scrambled down onto the plain. Then the carriers led the charge. The enemy columns were completely unprepared as the carriers and lorrried Infantry swept down upon them shooting up in Wild West fashion. Three hundred prisoners, five 88 mm guns and many vehicles were captured. The carriers poured onto the Derna airfields, and riddled planes, large and small. Transport planes, bombers, fighters, gliders, all were destroyed or captured in the wild scrimmage. In the midst of this action, twelve large JU 52 troop carriers appeared overhead, circled and settled in. The Sikhs, scarcely believing their luck, held their fire until the last plane glided down. Then all opened fire as if on a single word of command. Rifles, machine-gun, mortars, anti-tank guns, field guns and even pistols were used to pour a storm of shot and shell into the Junkers. Eight of these large aircraft were shot to pieces. Two got off the ground but crashed. Out of the dozen only two managed to get away, with the Sikhs hoping that shortage of petrol would account for them also.

The jubilant Sikhs found themselves in possession of tremendous booty. Halfaya and Bardia were being maintained from Derna and no less than 183 enemy aircraft, both sound and damaged, were captured on the landing grounds. Thousands of bombs were stacked round about, as well as large quantities of petrol, wine and food. From contemplation of such an appetising scene the Sikhs tore themselves away with reluctance and by nightfall had reached the edge of the escarpment. On the morning of December 19TH, 4TH Battalion, 11TH Sikhs, disdaining the rather ineffective demolitions on the switchback road down the escarpment, pushed down to Derna and took possession.

North Africa

Benghazi, (1941)

The 4th Indian Division commenced pursuit of the enemy along the coast, while 7th Armoured Division took a short cut across the desert route. By the end of 1941 the Eighth Army had won a famous victory. They had relieved Tobruk, driven the enemy out of Cyrenaica and reduced him from eight Divisions to the equivalent of two. In this victory 4th Indian Division had not played the lead, but a very strong supporting part, proving that the Indian Army of 1941 could fight the best troops that the best Army in the world could put in the field. The Germans took the point. A captured note by a German Staff Officer read, "So long as 7th Armoured Divison and the Indian Division are in the desert, we must watch out. They will be the spearhead of any attack".

Gallantry (1941)

By the end of 1941 the following Sikh Officers and men had been awarded the Indian Order of Merit for their conspicuous gallantry in North Africa; Jemadar Gurbaksh Singh (posthumous) of 4th Battalion, 11th Sikh Regiment; Subedar Fateh Singh (posthumous) and Jemadar Bhagat Singh (posthumous) of 1st Battalion, 1st Punjab Regiment; Jemadar Dhera Singh and Jemadar Amar Singh of 3rd Battalion, 2nd Punjab Regiment; Havildar Natha Singh (posthumous award) and Sepoy Saudagar Singh (posthumous) of 6th Royal Battalion, 13th Frontier Force Rifles, and Jemadar Aman Singh of Indian Armoured Corps.

Rommel attacks, (1942)

On 21st January Afrika Korps mauled the Allied forces, costing them some 110 tanks and other heavy equipment. The Axis forces retook Benghazi and Timimi. The Allies pulled back and commenced building defensive positions at Gazala. The moment the Indian Division crossed this line enemy pressure ended. At once 4th Indian Division began to build defences. But the Division was due for a rest, far overdue. Ever since August 1940, the Division had been constantly in the desert or Eritrea. The casualties had to be replaced, new equipment and vehicles issued, and the whole trained up to the high standards of its predecessors. The 50th Northumbrian Division took over, but it was not until early April that the whole of 4th Indian Division at last reached Delta and comfort.

Gazala, (1942)

Following a lull in the Desert War, this saw the Germans and British reinforce their armies. Rommel suddenly attacked British fortifications on the Northern sector of the British line near Gazala. Pinning down the British in the North and outflanking 1st Free French Brigade, Rommel succeeded in encircling the main British positions, trapping them in what became known as 'The Cauldron.'

North Africa

The Cauldron, (1942)
The only coherent feature of the chaos in the area, known as the Cauldron, was the German Armour, always concentrated, knocked hell out of the British Armour. About 800 British tanks were lost, most to the 88 mm and long-barrelled 50 mm anti-tank guns onto which they were lured by superior tactics. With only 50 cruisers and 20 tanks left, the Infantry were helpless in the open desert. A whole Brigade of 50TH Northumbrian Divison was overrun by Panzers and destroyed, as were 10TH Brigade and half of 9TH Brigade and 5TH Indian Division. Saddest was the fate of 11TH Indian Brigade, which had stormed the Italian camps at Sidi Barani and Cameron Ridge at Keren, chased the enemy from the Jebel Achdar and covered the retreat from Benghazi. It was sent to Tobruk to help to defend the fortress, which no one decided to defend until it was too late. When the Divisional Commander surrendered, 11TH Indian Brigade had to surrender too. Then it was back through Halfaya and Sidi Barani and Mersa Matruh to the place Auchinleck had chosen and prepared for Eighth Army's last stand, El Amein.

El Amein, (1942)
Alamein itself was an insignificant railway station on the coast. The line the British chose to defend stretched between the sea and the Qattara Depression, which meant that Rommel could outflank it only by taking a significant detour to the South and crossing the Sahara Desert. The British Army in Egypt recognized this before the War and had the Eighth Army begin construction of several "boxes" (localities with dug-outs and surrounded by minefields and barbed wire), The British started to construct three defended "boxes". The first and strongest, at El Alamein on the coast, had been partly wired and mined by 1ST South African Division. The Bab el Qattara box, had been dug but had not been wired or mined, while at the Naq Abu Dweis box (on the edge of the Qattara Depression), 34 miles from the coast, very little work had been done. The scattering of X Corps at Mersa Matruh disrupted Auchinleck's plan for occupying the Alamein defences. On 29TH June, he ordered XXX Corps (1st South African, 50TH and 10TH Indian Infantry Divisions) to take the coastal sector on the right of the front and XIII Corps (New Zealand and 5TH Indian Divisions) to be on the left. The remains of 1ST and 7TH Armoured Divisions were to be held as a mobile Army reserve. His intention was the fixed defensive positions should canalize and disorganize the enemy's advance while mobile Units would attack their flanks and rear. On 30TH June, Rommel's Panzer Army Africa approached the Alamein position. The Axis forces were exhausted and under strength. Rommel had driven them forward ruthlessly, being confident that, provided he struck quickly before Eighth Army had time to settle, his momentum would take him through the Alamein position and he could then advance to the Nile with little further opposition.

North Africa

Rommel Attacks, (1942)

On 1ST July, 15TH and 21ST Panzer Divisions were delayed by a sandstorm and then a heavy air attack. By the time they circled round the back of Deir el Abyad they found the feature to the East of it occupied by the Indian 18TH Infantry Brigade. After a hasty journey from Iraq, they had occupied the exposed position just West of Ruweisat Ridge and East of Deir el Abyad at Deir el Shein. On 1ST July, 21ST Panzer Division attacked Deir el Shein. 18TH Indian Infantry Brigade, supported by 23-25-pounder guns, 16 of the new 6-pounder anti-tank guns and 9 Matilda tanks held out the whole day in desperate fighting, but by evening the Germans succeeded in overrunning them. Meanwhile, 1ST Armoured Division had been sent to intervene at Deir el Shein. They ran into 15TH Panzer Division just South of Deir el Shein and drove it West. By the end of the day's fighting the Afrika Korps had 37 tanks left out of its initial compliment of 55, and was forced to dig in. On 2ND July, Rommel ordered the resumption of the offensive. Once again, they failed to make progress so Rommel called the Afrika Korps to abandon its planned sweep Southward and instead join the effort to break through to the coast road by attacking East towards Ruweisat Ridge.

Ruweisat Ridge, (1942)

On 2ND July, Rommel ordered the resumption of the offensive. The British defence of Ruweisat Ridge relied on an improvised formation called Robcol, comprising a Regiment each of Field Artillery and Light Anti-aircraft Artillery and a Company of Infantry. Robcol was able to buy time, and by late afternoon the two British Armoured Brigades joined the battle with 4TH Armoured Brigade engaging 15TH Panzer and 22ND Armoured Brigade 21ST Panzer. They drove back repeated attacks by the Axis Armour, which then withdrew before dusk. The British reinforced Ruweisat on the night of 2ND July. The now enlarged Robcol became Walgroup. The Royal Air Force meanwhile made heavy air attacks on the Axis Units. The next day, 3RD July, Rommel resumed the attack on the Ruweisat ridge. The combination of British Artillery fire and constant air attacks halted the Axis advance.

Tel el Eisa, (1942)

General Ramsden was to capture the low ridges at Tel el Eisa and Tel el Makh Khad and then to push mobile battle groups South towards Deir el Shein. Once more, the Eighth Army had failed to destroy Rommel's forces. For Rommel the situation continued to be grave as, despite successful defensive operations, his Infantry had suffered heavy losses and he reported that "the situation is critical in the extreme". The battle was a stalemate, but it had halted the Axis advance on Alexandria. Eighth Army had suffered over 13,000 casualties in July (including 3,000 in 5TH Indian Infantry Division) but had taken 7,000 prisoners and inflicted heavy damage on Axis men and machines.

North Africa

El Amein, (1942)

Eighth Army counter-offensives during July were unsuccessful and Auchinleck called off all offensive action with a view to rebuilding the Army's strength. In early August, British Prime Minister Winston Churchill visited Cairo and replaced Auchinleck as C-in-C Middle East with General Sir Harold Alexander. Lieutenant-General Bernard Montgomery became Eighth Army Commander. The Second Battle of El Alamein marked a major turning point in the Western Desert Campaign of the Second World War. The battle lasted from 23RD October to 5TH November 1942. During the campaign half of Rommel's 100,000 man army was killed, wounded or taken prisoner. He also lost over 450 tanks and 1,000 guns. The British and Commonwealth forces suffered 13,500 casualties and 500 of their tanks were damaged. However, of these, 350 were repaired and were able to take part in future battles. The allied victory turned the tide in the North African Campaign. It ended Axis hopes of occupying Egypt, taking control of the Suez Canal, and gaining access to the Middle Eastern oil fields. El Alamein was the first great offensive against the Germans in which the Western Allies were victorious. Winston Churchill famously summed up the battle on 10TH November 1942 with the words, "This is not the end, and it is not even the beginning of the end. But it is, perhaps, the end of the beginning." It was Montgomery's greatest triumph; he took the title "Viscount Montgomery of Alamein" when he was raised to the peerage after the War. Rommel, concerned that his Army would be completely enveloped and destroyed if he once again halted to face the Eighth Army, withdrew all the way to Tunisia where the terrain would better suit a defensive action.

Tripoli, (1943)

On 15TH January 1943, General Montgomery launched against Rommel's defences. Weakened by the withdrawal of 21ST Panzer Division to Tunisia, to strengthen von Arnim's Fifth Panzer Army, once again Rommel was forced to conduct a fighting retreat. Tripoli, some 150 miles further on, with its major port facilities, was taken on 23RD January as Rommel continued to withdraw to the French-built Southern defences of Tunisia, the Mareth Line.

Tunisia, (1943)

Rommel was by this time in contact with von Arnim's Fifth Panzer Army, which had been fighting the Tunisia Campaign against the multi-national British First Army. Hitler was determined to retain hold of Tunisia and Rommel finally started to receive replacement men and materials. The Axis now faced a War in Africa on two fronts, with Eighth Army approaching from the East and the British, French and Americans of First Army from the West. Rommel's German-Italian Panzer Army was re-designated Italian First Army under General Giovanni Messe, while Rommel assumed command of the new Army Group Africa, responsible for both fronts.

North Africa

Tunisia, 1943 (Cont.)

Similarly, the two Allied armies were placed under 18TH Army Group with Harold Alexander in command. However, the hope of an early conclusion to the campaign against the Axis forces was thwarted at the Battle of the Kasserine Pass in the second half of February, when Rommel struck a costly blow against the inexperienced U.S. II Corps and destroyed their ability to make an early thrust East to the coast to cut off the Italian First Army's line of supply from Tunis and isolate it from von Arnim's forces in the North.

General Alexander's plan to finish the campaign was for the Americans to take Bizerta and the British First Army to take Tunis from the West; while the Eighth Army attacked from the South. By a quick change of plan 4TH Indian Division and 7TH Armoured were transferred to the First Army, to strengthen the attack on Tunis from the West.

Surrender, (1943)

In the last operation of the War in Africa, 4TH Indian Division, on General Tucker's insistence and despite the misgivings of 4TH British Division on the left, attacked at night. They were supported by such Artillery fire as they had never imagined, and by the morning of 6TH May 1943, they were through with very little loss. There was customary delay in sending through the Armour; for once it did not matter. Five days later Colonel General von Arnim, Commander-in-Chief of all Axis forces in Tunisia, surrendered his own headquarters and Fifth Panzer Armee to Lieutenant Colonel L.C.J. Showers, Commanding 2ND King Edward VII's Own Gorkha Rifles. A few weeks later General Montgomery in a lecture to Officers, made handsome amends for the past: 'I sent First Army my best, 7TH Armoured and 4TH Indian Division (The Red Eagle Division)'.

The 4TH Indian Division came to the end of the long road, which had led from the Western Desert to Eritrea, from Eritrea to Syria, back to the Western Desert and two thousand miles across Africa; while their fame grew from battle to battle until in their last campaign the world came to know them from the lips of the Prime Minister himself, in glowing tribute to the only volunteer Army in this World War. But there is no Officer nor man in the Red Eagle Division who does not regard the fame showered upon him as an equal tribute to other Indian Divisions, who bore the heat and burden of other days and for whom the God of battles had decreed less fortune at the finish.

Gallantry Awards, (1943)

By the end of War in North Africa the following Sikh Officers were awarded the Indian Order of Merit for their conspicuous gallantry; Naik Jagat Singh of 3RD Battalion, 2ND Punjab Regiment, Subedar Major Sohan Singh OBI of 6TH Royal Battalion, 13TH Frontier Force Rifles, Jemadar Kartar Singh (posthumous) of 3RD Battalion, 14TH Punjab Regiment, Havildar Sadhu Singh of 4TH Battalion, 16TH Punjab Regiment and, Havildar Babu Singh (posthumous award) of Indian Engineers.

IRAQ 1941

The events in Iraq in 1941 had crucial strategic consequences. The country's oil reserves were a highly coveted prize for the Axis powers, and its location provided a corridor in the defence of Palestine and the Suez Canal. Had Iraq fallen to the Axis powers, Britain could have lost its foothold in the Middle East and the Mediterranean and risked losing World War II.

The Kingdom of Iraq was governed by the United Kingdom under a League of Nations mandate, the British Mandate of Mesopotamia, until 1932 when Iraq became nominally independent. Before granting independence, the United Kingdom concluded the Anglo-Iraqi Treaty of 1930. This treaty had several conditions, which included permission to establish military bases for British use and provide all facilities for the unrestricted movement of British forces through the country upon request to the Iraqi government. Nuri-al-Said, author of the 1930 treaty was Prime Minister when War broke out. The Premier declared Iraq non belligerent and severed diplomatic relations with Germany.

When Italy entered the War in 1940, however, Nuri-al-Said, then Minister of Foreign Affairs in the cabinet of newly appointed Prime Minister Rashid Ali al-Gaylani was unable to persuade the cabinet to break off diplomatic relations with Italy. The public opinion in Iraq changed radically after France's fall, becoming especially hostile to Britain. Extremists advocated alliance with Germany as the country that would foster independence and unity among Arabs. Leading Army Officers fell under pan-Arab influences and encouraged Rashid Ali to detach Iraq from the British alliance. During 1940 and 1941, Iraqi Officers were unwilling to cooperate with Britain, and the pan-Arab leaders began secret negotiations with the Axis Powers. Britain decided to send reinforcements to Iraq. Rashid Ali, while allowing a small British force to land in 1940, refused further British requests for reinforcements. British contingents entered Iraq from the Persian Gulf and from the Habbaniyah air base in April and May 1941; armed conflict with Iraqi forces followed. On 10TH April, Major-General William Fraser assumed control over Iraq force and the land forces from India headed for Basra. Fraser was given the following instructions: - "The object of his force was to occupy the Basra-Shaiba area in order to ensure the safe disembarkation of further reinforcements and to enable a base to be established in that area". The Indian Forces in Iraq included the Sikh soldiers of the following Regiments, 2ND Royal Battalion, 11TH Sikh Regiment, 3RD Battalion, 11TH Sikh Regiment, and 5TH Battalion, 13TH Frontier Force Rifles.

The battles were fought at Basra, Habbaniyah Airport, Fallujah, and Baghdad. The hostilities lasted 30 days, during which period a few Iraqi leaders, including the regent and Nūrī al-Saīd, fled the country. By the end of May, the Iraqi Army had capitulated.

SYRIA

After the surrender of France in June 1940, the French colonies of Lebanon and Syria passed into the control of the pro-German Vichy French government. The Allied offensive was aimed at preventing Nazi Germany from using the Vichy French-controlled Mandate of Syria and Mandate of Lebanon as springboards for attacks on the Allied stronghold of Egypt, as the Allies fought a campaign against Axis forces further West in North Africa. Although the French had ceded autonomy to Syria in September 1936, they had retained treaty rights to maintain armed forces and two airfields in the territory. The only Indian force engaged was a Brigade of 4TH Indian Division, 5TH Indian Infantry Brigade, with 1ST Battalion, 1ST Punjab Regiment and Bombay Sappers and Miners with their Sikh Companies. 4TH Battalion, 6TH Rajputana Rifles and 7TH Battalion, 11TH Sikh Regiment.

Deraa (1941)

The Brigade Group was ordered to cross the Syrian border from Palestine and take Quneitra and Deraa. The Punjabis crept across the frontier, stalked and destroyed a sentry post, thus leading the invasion. It was hoped that the Vichy forces would not offer any resistance to this advance and in order to give every opportunity for the avoidance of bloodshed, each move was preceded by an emissary carrying a white flag. Next morning a party approached Deraa under cover of white flag. The summons to surrender was rejected and the Regiment opened fire on the town. A column had raced off into the North covering more than 45 miles in the night to reach its debussing point. This area proved to be an enemy outpost zone garrisoned by Infantry and Armoured cars. The Rajputana Rifles immediately attacked and rounded up 4 Officers and 135 men. Unfortunately a trainload of troops from Deraa slipped through before the railway line could be cut. The investment of Deraa was complete. As the attack closed in from all sides, part of the enemy garrison escaped to the East. The Punjabis had taken 250 prisoners, while the Rajputana Rifles rounded up 50 mounted gendarmerie.

Sheikh Meskine (1941)

Sheikh Meskine was the next objective and here again the Vichy forces refused to surrender. A Battalion attack was mounted immediately. The enemy retaliated with heavy machine gun and artillery fire, which held up the frontal approach. A Company was despatched to turn the position by seizure of a ridge to the Northwest of the village. A sharp encounter ensued in which Naik Bhopal Singh of Rajputana Rifles and his Platoon wiped out a series of machine gun nests manned by Foreign Legionaries. Enemy Armoured cars and Artillery joined in the fray but failed to affect the issue. An attack on the village was planned for dawn but when morning broke the garrison was gone.

Syria

Kissoue (1941)

Kissoue was a strong defensive position. East of the road the gardens and houses of the town provided cover for Infantry and tanks, backed by the considerable defence works on the steeply rising Jebel el Kelb and Jebel Abou Atriz behind them. The boulder-strewn country was virtually impassable by wheeled vehicles, except on the road and made progress difficult even on foot. On the evening of June 14TH, Brigadier Lloyd sent an inspiring message to all ranks:

"In the attack on Kissoue I have asked you two Indian Battalions to carry out the impossible. I know you will achieve the impossible and I am confident that only you are able to accomplish this task. Good luck to all!"

The general attack across the river began before dawn on 5TH. The 3RD Battalion, 1ST Punjab Regiment and the Rajputana Rifles facing the Vichy positions had the stiff task of capturing Kissoue itself and Tel Kissoue just behind. The 3RD Battalion, 1ST Punjab moved forward to the attack, and completely surprised the Vichy troops and after some heavy hand-to-hand fighting in the village, captured the whole of it. The impossible had been achieved. Mopping up continued amongst the orchards and little streams, many were six feet deep. After daylight several of the enemy troops were found hiding up to their necks in water and were hunted out.

However, the Punjabis in Kissoue were subjected to much shelling, and shortly after midday it was counter-attacked by a Vichy Battalion with tanks. This attempt was strongly pushed, but failed owing to the Punjabi's excellent marksmanship and clever use of tank-proof cover. Another assault also failed. The two Indian Battalions had not yet finished. They started off Northwest to capture Jebel Medani, 3RD Battalion, 1ST Punjab Regiment directed on the Southern ridge and the Rajputana Rifles on the Northern. The somewhat demoralised enemy did not expect a night attack, or any attack at all so soon after the fall of Kissoue, and by dawn the two Indian Battalions were in full possession of the hill looking forward and down on the city of Damascus itself. Meanwhile on other fronts the situation was much less satisfactory. The Free French on the right flank were hard pressed, while at Quneitra the Royal Fusiliers were in a desperate plight. During June 15TH, the latter's Outpost Company had been driven in and a strong attack launched on them at this important road junction. During the night they were completely invested by a force strong in tanks and artillery. After desperate fighting, during which the one Company which was not surrounded tried without avail to break its way in through the cordon, the Fusiliers ran out of ammunition and had perforce to surrender. On June 17TH, a French Battalion tried to occupy Mouaddamuye, but the woods were found to contain a number of tanks and machine guns, and the attackers were repulsed. The French then occupied Aartouz, and with the help of Bombay Sappers and Miners turned it into a tank-proof locality, although they and the other Battalions were severely bombed.

Syria

Mezze (1941)

On the evening of June 18TH, the two Indian Battalions set forth on what turned out to be one of the most heroic and desperate actions of the War. The Sikh Company of 3RD Battalion, 1ST Punjab Regiment were given the special task of dealing with the fortified hamlet of Medemie, five miles from Mezze on the approaches to Damascus airport. In the orchards surrounding Medemie, the Sikhs encountered intense opposition. Artillery fire searched the road and it was apparent that a strong force blocked the approach to Damascus. Yard by yard the gardens were cleared and a number of enemy tanks destroyed. In this attack Jemadar Bhagat Singh set an example of gallant effort and confident leadership by destroying four strongly held machine gun pill boxes in spite of his Platoon having suffered heavy casualties. In the assault on the fourth pill-box he was killed. Jemadar Bhagat Singh was awarded posthumous Indian Order of Merit.

A charge swept through the village and Medemie was captured by the Sikhs, but with only 27 men of the Company standing. It was then decided to disregard all minor objectives and to march directly on Mezze. The main Brigade column, brushing aside minor opposition along the airfield, approached the South-Eastern outskirts of the village, after twelve hours march across unreconnoitred country. The Infantry immediately deployed and hurried into the assault. The enemy was standing ready and intense fighting developed. For an hour a vicious melee reigned. Two enemy ammunition lorries blew up; their flames revealed a Vichy tank; the Indians stalked it with petrol grenades and destroyed it. Mezze was cleared and 40 prisoners taken.

Meanwhile a Company of the Rajputana Rifles passed around the village and cut the main Damascus Beirut Road, driving away a Cavalry screen. The Rajputs then occupied Mezze House, a large square building surrounded by a wall, where they were surrounded and continuously pounded by Vichy tanks. The remnants of the Company of Rajputana Rifles made a desperate attempt to cut their way out, but it was hopeless and they were compelled to surrender. It had been a fight the like of which can rarely have been seen before, and this gallant defence made possible the capture of Damascus next day.

One and a half Companies of 3RD Battalion, 1ST Punjab Regiment and two Companies of the Battalion de l'Infantrerie de Marine, supported by 1ST Field Regiment was sent to relieve the garrison. They fought their way to the foothills. The gunners advanced their guns with muzzles down and blasted a way through. The charge of 1ST Field Regiment at Damascus, where they always had their guns in line with, sometime even in advance of, the attacking Infantry, is typical of the marvellous spirit of this great Brigade. But when they reached the village, Mezze was silent and deserted. The battered garden walls and the damaged house, the burnt out tanks and the dead bodies were eloquent testimony to the terrific fight.

Syria

Armistice (1941)

While these heroic events were happening on the Palestine border, a force of Indian troops began to advance into Syria from Iraq. The Indian column advanced on Deir - ez - Zor, while the British force moved on Palmyra. The only opposition encountered had been some Vichy armoured cars, which were soon put to flight. The whole force moved rapidly on to Deir - ez - Zor. The surprise was complete. The armoured cars, with the troops and guns following, were able to enter the city with scarcely any opposition. Thereafter very little resistance was encountered by any column and though there were constant bombing and low-flying attacks, yet the casualties suffered were not heavy. The advance continued to Ragga, and although the hostilities were suspended, advanced elements reached the Turkish frontier North of Aleppo. Meanwhile another force had advanced in the North-East of Syria. The first place of importance is the frontier village of Tel Kotehek some 70 miles West of Mosul. The village and station formed an oasis in the middle of the plain and was visible for many miles. Two Companies of 1ST Battalion, 12TH Frontier Force Regiment with Artillery and some armoured cars left Mosul late at night and by daylight were facing the village. The guns were placed in front of the station and a Company sent round each flank. As the object was to secure the village with minimum force, the column Commander went forward to interview the Vichy Commander. At first the latter refused to surrender but on hearing of the large force, which was coming against him, eventually withdrew leaving the village and station undamaged.

The rapid thrust continued at once and by the early morning of the next day the little force was deployed in front of the fort Al Aalo. Again the Vichy Commander refused to surrender, but after a couple of rounds had been fired over the fort, he changed his mind. Three Officers and 130 men were made prisoners. The 4TH Battalion, 13TH Frontier Force Rifles had arrived as reinforcements and a Cavalry post at Kubur el Bid was also captured. Following the capture of Tel Aalo the column was facing the town and fortress of Kamechlie. The Vichy Commander, having declined to surrender, was told that unless the flag was hauled down, the barracks and trenches would be bombarded. Fire was on the point of being opened when a message was received that the town and fortress would be surrendered, if the Commander were allowed to escape with what garrison he could muster. The request was granted and the town and fortress occupied. Much war material, including valuable ordnance and medical stores and many tons of foodstuffs, were captured, but the advance was not delayed. Next day Hasetche, the provincial headquarters, were occupied without opposition. This very rapid thrust had safeguarded the railway and constituted a threat to the rear of the Vichy positions. Subedar Dogar Singh and Jemadar Bhagat Singh of 3RD Battalion, 1ST Punjab Regiment, were awarded the Indian Order of Merit. The Punjabis had 19 Other Ranks killed, 96 wounded and 92 missing presumed dead. Jemadar Mul Singh was mortally wounded.

IRAN

Despite the fact that Iran had declared its neutrality during World War II, Britain and the Soviets started their invasion into Iran. Britain's Minister Reader Bullard and Soviet Ambassador Smirnov handed the Iranian Foreign Office an ultimatum demanding Iran get rid of the Germans or face the consequences. The English had been making preparations by sending Indian troops to Iraq and deploying forces to Iran's South East area. Britain and Russia worked together. A British column marched into Iran from Iraq, while more troops were preparing to land at Bandar Shapour. The Russian Army invaded Iran from Armenia. Indian forces joined the attack from the East on the border of Baluchistan. The British "Persia and Iraq Force" (Paiforce), was made up of 8TH and 10TH Indian Infantry Divisions, 2ND Indian Armoured Brigade, 4TH British Cavalry Brigade and 21ST Indian Infantry Brigade, with the Sikh soldiers of 2ND Royal Battalion, 11TH Sikh Regiment, Indian Engineers, 1ST Battalion, 1ST Punjab Regiment, 4TH Battalion, 11TH Sikh Regiment, 5TH Battalion, 12TH Frontier Force Regiment and 3RD Battalion, 15TH Punjab Regiment. They were opposed by much smaller Iranian forces. The British crossed from Iraq and took control of the richest single oil field in existence. Iran's small sloops were no match for the Royal Navy and Indian troops landed at Bandar Shapour.

Descending from an Army-Officer family, Colonel Reza Khan taking advantage of the chaos in Iran, rode into Tehran at the head of 2,000 Persian Cossacks and took over the country on February 21ST, 1921. The last Qajar King, Ahmad Shah had left the country with an empty treasury for France. Iran had no Army, no roads and was boiling with corruption, ignorance and disease. Reza Shah modernized the Army and restored order, overthrew rebel chieftains, stripped the clerics of their judicial and political powers, drew up a code of civil law, banned child marriage by raising to 15 the age at which a girl might marry, fostered education, set up schools and colleges. He followed the model in Turkey to modernize the country thus improving agriculture, public health, transportation and fomented trade and industry with all his being. He thus got Iran up on its feet. Probably, his greatest accomplishment was the trans-Iranian railroad, which took eleven years to build and runs from the Persian Gulf to the Caspian Sea. On the other hand, he was a fearsome dictator who murdered, tortured, kidnapped, imprisoned all dissidents, turning Iran into a one man corporative state. His greed for power and property made him more enemies than friends.

The Allies sustained light casualties during the invasion. British Forces, suffered 22 killed and just over 40 wounded and sick. Hostilities did not last long because the new Iranian government ordered the Army to cease fighting. Iranian forces surrendered to the British and the Soviets on 29-30TH August. The Shah was deposed and exiled in 1941, and his son, Mohammed Reza Pahlavi, was crowned in his place. A tripartite treaty was concluded between the Soviet Union, the United Kingdom and Iran in January 1942.

GREECE

In late October 1940 Greece was invaded in great force by Italy from Albania. By the year's end the Greek Army, with the help of the Royal Air Force, had thrown back the invasion and occupied one quarter of Albania. The Italians received increasing German help and in March 1941 the Greeks asked for the assistance of a British Expeditionary Force (B.E.F.). This force had scarcely been deployed along a line South of Salonika before, on 6TH April, the Germans invaded Greece in force and compelled the surrender of the Greek Army in Eastern Macedonia and on 10TH April Salonika was occupied. The strong German thrust in the West, coupled with an Italian advance from Albania, threatened to out flank the B.E.F. which withdrew on 14TH April to a line North of Mount Olympus. Again out flanked, the B.E.F. completed by 20TH April a further withdrawal to a line across the peninsula at Thermopylae and the Greek Army to their West also withdrew. But the continued German and Italian attacks on the Greek Army, which had been fighting without respite for sixth months, overwhelmed it on 21st April and the Thermopylae line thus becoming untenable. The B.E.F. started to fall back for evacuation. This withdrawal, without air cover, took place through the Peloponnesus, as the port facilities of Piraeus had earlier been destroyed in an air raid but, despite the difficulties, the Navy had, by 1st June, evacuated 50,000 men (5/6th of the total force) from the Southern Peloponnesus beaches and taken them to Crete or Egypt. On November 25TH, 1942, a combined operation between British Special Forces and the various factions of the Greek Resistance succeeded in blowing up the Gorgopotamos Bridge over the Brallos Pass. Harling was the name given to the 12-man SOE team, under the leadership of Brigadier Eddie Myers that parachuted into Greece in September and October 1942 to coordinate the blowing up of Gorgopotamos Railway Bridge. The purpose was to sever the German supply line South through Greece and onward to North Africa, where Rommel and Montgomery were preparing for their historic rendezvous at El Alamein.

Captain Inderjit Singh Gill* of the Royal Engineers was part of the SOE team that blew up the Gorgopotamos Bridge. He was awarded the Military Cross on 23RD December 1943. Part of the citation of his Military Cross reads; "The successful achievement of this operation was entirely due to his personal gallantry. During the last three months Captain Gill's work has been outstanding. He has constantly worked unsparingly and his work has been inspiration to the team with him." Captain Inderjit Singh Gill transferred to the Indian Army in 1945, and eventually achieved the rank of Lieutenant General.

The progressive liberation of Greece by the Commonwealth Force began on 24TH September 1944 and met with little opposition from the retreating Germans.

* As the Indian Army's Director, Military Operations, Gill, then a Major-General, once again displayed soldierly qualities by planning and executing the defeat of the Pakistani Army in 1971.

ITALY

Three Infantry divisions from the Indian Army participated in the Italian campaign.

4TH Indian Infantry Division

The 4TH Indian Infantry Division arrived in Italy from North Africa on 7TH December 1943. In mid December 1943, it moved to the Potenza area of Italy. On the 9TH January 1944, the Division came under the command of XIII Corps, and moved into the line at Orsogna to relieve the New Zealand Division. In February 1944, it was transferred to the New Zealand Corps and deployed at Cassino. The Division concentrated there by 6TH February. The 7TH Brigade relieved the Americans on 14TH February at Cassino, with the opening attack on 16TH February 1944. The second battle commenced on 15TH March 1944. The Division was withdrawn from Cassino during the 25/26TH March 1944. It was sent back to the Orsogna front. The Division was engaged in operations there and along the line of retreat of the German forces. In July 1944, the Division was involved in the operation in central Italy and the Gothic line battles from August to October. In December 1944, the Division was sent to Greece.

8TH Indian Infantry Division

The 8TH Indian Infantry Division arrived in Italy from Syria via Egypt on 24TH September 1943. The advance party arrived at Taranto on the 3RD September, with the main body arriving on 19TH September. On 19TH October 1943, the Division entered the line at Larino under command of V Corps and on 21ST October 1943, it had its first action in the crossing of the River Biferno. It fought throughout the Italian campaign. Following the Armistice in Europe, the Division embarked for India from Taranto on 25TH and 26TH June 1945.

10TH Indian Infantry Division

The 10TH Indian Infantry Division was formed in Ahmadnagar in India in May 1941. It was sent immediately to Iraq where it took part in the campaign to secure the oilfields in that country. Following the successful conclusion of that campaign, the Division was split up across Iraq, Persia, and Syria. As the situation had deteriorated in Egypt and Libya, the Division was rushed to the desert where it suffered heavy casualties. The Division then moved to Cyprus to refit before moving to Italy in March 1944. At the end of the campaign, it moved to Trieste in May 1945 until August, then moving to Milan before leaving Taranto bound for Italy on 22ND November 1945.

Italy

Three class Units of Sikhs Infantry formed part of the Indian Divisions in Italy. Two Battalions of 11TH Sikh Regiment, 2ND Royal Battalion, and 4TH Battalion, with a Regiment of Nabha Akal Infantry (A Sikh Princely States Unit) Sikhs were, however, largely represented also in 3RD Battalion, 1ST Punjab Regiment, 1ST Battalion, 2ND Punjab Regiment, 3RD Battalion, 8TH Punjab Regiment, 3RD Battalion, 15TH Punjab Regiment, 4TH Battalion, 16TH Punjab Regiment, 1ST Battalion, 12TH Frontier Force Regiment, 4TH and 5TH Battalions, 13TH Frontier Force Rifles, Bombay Engineers, Bengal Engineers and 6TH Lancers, the only Cavalry Regiment to serve in Italy. **They also served in all the supporting services during the Italian campaign.**

Gustav Line, (1943)

Gustav Line was a primary German military fortification in Italy. Gustav Line ran across Italy from just North of where the Garigliano River flows into the Tyrrhenian Sea in the West, through the Apennine Mountains to the mouth of the Sangro River on the Adriatic coast in the East. The centre of the line, where it crossed the main route North to Rome which followed the Liri Valley, was anchored around the mountains behind the town of Cassino, including Monte Cassino, on which was situated an old abbey that dominated the entrance to the Liri Valley (a main route to Rome), and Monte Cairo which gave the defenders clear observation of potential attackers advancing towards the mouth of the Liri Valley. Gustav Line was fortified with gun pits, concrete bunkers, turreted machine gun emplacements, barbed-wire and minefields. It was the strongest of the German defensive lines South of Rome. About 15 German Divisions were employed in the defence. It took the Allies from mid-November 1943 to late May 1944 to fight through all the various elements of the Winter Line, including the well-known battles at Monte Cassino and Anzio.

Trigno, (1943)

On 24TH September 1943, 8TH Indian Division, consisting of 17TH, 19TH, and 21ST Brigades, landed unopposed at Taranto and for 19 months was almost continuously in action, advancing through mountainous country, crossing river after river. The formation later adopted the motto "One more river". The Division concentrated to the East of Taranto and immediately began to follow North in the path of 8TH Army. At Trigno, the Division was committed to its first action in Europe. The 19TH Brigade, with sharp skirmishes against the most skilful and belligerent German formations, took a firm grip on the South bank of the River Trigno through occupation of Monte Mitro and Montefalcone. The Brigade immediately prepared to force the Trigno, in order to seize Tuffilo village and Monte Ferrano on the high ground. The Brigade established a bridgehead over the river Trigno as a result of heavy fighting during the periods 22ND October – 5TH November. A decisive event was the capture of the enemy positions on the San Salvo Ridge, which dominated the area North of the river.

Italy

Tuffilo, (1943)
After crossing the Trigno 4TH Battalion, 13TH Frontier Force Rifles immediately prepared to seize Tuffilo village and Monte Ferrano on the high ground. The Frontiersmen's assault was launched against a typical 'hedgehog' position. All approaches were mined and booby-trapped. A curtain of mortar bombs covered the minefield. Every house held a sniper. Attempts to close were met with a shower of grenades. Quick savage sallies were flung against any ground won. The leading Companies pushed through the barrage and up the hillside under murderous machine gun fire from front and flanks. The 3RD Battalion, 8TH Punjab Regiment joined the Frontiersmen in a new assault upon Tuffilo. The German paratroopers counter-attacked at once, forcing the Punjabis and Frontiersmen back to their start lines. On November $3^{RD}/4^{TH}$, for the third night in succession, the same two gallant Battalions struck for Tuffilo. The recurrent assaults had their effect - the Germans were forced to retire to their main battle positions and the Indians intensified pursuit of the enemy.

Rosello, (1943)
During this advance, 6TH Lancers ferreted deeply in enemy territory. On 13TH November a troop of 'B' Squadron (Sikhs) rushed the village of Rosello four miles behind enemy lines to seize prisoners. The Sikhs stalked it on foot and watched the Germans going about their normal business without a care in the world. Two ventured close to the lurking Sikhs, who grabbed one and shot the other. The Germans, on motorcycles, came charging out with machine guns blazing from side cars. But the Sikhs got away, and their prisoner turned out to be from 1ST Parachute Division, a very significant discovery; the Germans were sending their best to Italy.

Mozzagrogna, (1943)
From Sangro 8TH Indian Division advanced on the fortified village of Mozzagrogna. Corps Artillery concentrated a terrific shoot on the village as 1ST Battalion, 12TH Frontier Force moved forward to attack and capture the place. The bombardment held the enemy garrison in the dugouts and once it lifted, the Germans rushed to their surface posts. The battle resolved into dozens of sudden deadly encounters in cellars, on rooftops, in alleys, and behind the angles of broken walls. In a crypt a number of Germans, who had taken refuge in the wine vats, were dispatched. With the arrival of the British Armour the defences of Mozzagrogna collapsed and essential crossroads to the Northwest of Mozzagrogna were secured. An enemy force, which included flame–throwers, charged the consolidation groups and cut off the Dogra Company. At dawn the Sikh and Dogra Companies of Frontiersmen hurled back the enemy in headlong flight and captured the disabled tanks. One thousand prisoners had been taken and a number of German Units had been decimated. All anchor positions of the Gustav Line were now in British hands.

Italy

Romagnoli, (1943)
To sustain the momentum of the advance, 21ST Indian Brigade turned West from Mozzagrogna along the top of the ridge with Romagnoli. The next objective was a line of trenches concealed behind hedges on the outskirts of the village. Pinning down the defenders, the village was stormed. Three counter–attacks which were shattered in quick succession convinced the enemy that Romagnoli could not be regained.

Lanciano, (1943)
On December 2ND, 6TH Lancers with armoured cars probed until they found a comparatively open road into Lanciano, until they turned a last corner to come face to face with a German tank. The Cavalrymen withdrew hurriedly, but established and held a road block cutting off Lanciano from the West. The town now was closely invested on three sides. That night the enemy made a virtue of necessity, and cleared out. The 3RD Battalion, 15TH Punjab Regiment entered next morning and received a rousing welcome from the liberated civilians.

"Impossible Bridge", (1943)
The next objective was to take Caldari beyond the river Moro. 8TH Indian Division was told to cross the river and capture Caldari as the other two Divisions on the flanks failed to cross the river. It was impossible to build a bridge from the near bank, so it was decided to build it backwards from the enemy's bank. "The Impossible Bridge" over the River Moro came to be a legend in the annals of combat engineering, when the Indian Engineers crossed over to the enemy side and built a bridge in reverse direction, to overcome the technical difficulty arising out of lack of construction space on the home bank. The area surrounding the bridge site was extremely active with German fighting patrols and they reacted violently to this incursion. The Frontiersmen of 1ST Battalion, 12TH Frontier Force cleared the enemy patrols with the bayonet.

Caldari, (1943)
At the opening of the "Impossible Bridge" 8TH Indian Division advanced against Caldari. 1ST Battalion, 12TH Frontier Force Regiment stormed the village after some fierce fighting and seized positions along the road, which ran parallel to the Moro. An enemy tank force, which included flame-throwers, charged the consolidation group and cut off the Dogra Company. At dawn the Sikh Companies of Frontiersmen hurled back the enemy in headlong flight and captured two disabled tanks. The 3RD Battalion, 15TH Punjab Regiment joined the fray and seized fresh positions along the lateral road. The Indians were now firmly embedded in the main German defences.

Italy

Villa Grande, (1943)

There was particularly fierce fighting involving 3RD Battalion, 8TH Punjab Regiment, within the village of Villa Grande itself from 22ND to 28TH December. As high explosive and armour-piercing crashed into the emplacements, the paratroopers bolted into the open. As they ran, machine guns brought them down and the battle for Villa Grande was over. During an attack South of Villa Grande, Sepoy Darshan Singh was commanding a Section. Whilst advancing with his objective in view, another enemy machine gun opened up on his Company position. Realizing that it must be dealt with first, Sepoy Darshan Singh immediately advanced on it single-handed across very difficult ground covered with wire and under heavy enemy fire. In doing so he was wounded in the shoulder but continued on his objective, killing one of the enemy machine gunners and wounding the other. He was largely instrumental in enabling his Company to advance and secure their objective. For his gallantry he was awarded the Indian Order of Merit.

Orsogna, (1944)

Orsogna stood on a high ridge above the river Moro. The town had been fortified to fortress strength, and had thwarted the utmost efforts of the New Zealanders to secure it. When 4TH Indian Division faced this formidable position, it was in anticipation of a stern struggle. After a fortnight's seasoning in the forward positions, during which 4TH Battalion, 16TH Punjab Regiment of 7TH Brigade showed that they had lost nothing of their old art of worrying the enemy. Unfortunately Lieutenant Sukhnandan Singh, in attempting to establish contact with a Platoon got lost in the dark, was taken prisoner. During 16 days in the line the Punjabis had suffered 69 casualties as the cost of taking prisoners and thoroughly stirring up the enemy.

On the night of 18TH/19TH February 1944 Havildar Kuldip Singh IDSM, of 3RD Battalion, 8TH Punjab Regiment, with a fighting patrol of 22 men, was sent to inflict casualties and to take prisoners from the village of Orsogna. The patrol arrived at the outskirts of the village and attacked the first house found to be occupied by the enemy. Havildar Kuldip Singh dashed into the house with two men and surprised the enemy; they captured one prisoner and injured the remainder as they fled. As the main objective of the patrol had been achieved, Havildar Kuldip Singh decided to withdraw. He organized the evacuation of the casualties to the rear. The route was now under heavy fire but Havildar Kuldip Singh remained behind alone and covered the withdrawal by throwing grenades collected from the wounded. Two more men were wounded and, accompanied by one man; he twice went back over the open snow-covered ground and brought them back. A third man was heard calling for help near to the house, and the gallant Havildar went back again, this time alone. Many of the wounded had to be carried back 1,500 yards. Havildar Kuldip Singh was awarded the Military Cross for his conspicuous gallantry and leadership.

Italy

Cassino, (1944)

The Battle of Monte Cassino was a costly series of four assaults by the Allies against the Winter Line in Italy held by the Germans and Italians during World War II. The intention was a breakthrough to Rome. Between 20TH January- 25TH March, Monte Cassino and the Gustav defences were assaulted three times by Allied troops. The Monastery remained out of reach in one of the hardest fought battles of the War in which 4TH Indian Division lost 4,000 men. A gunner Officer expressed the characteristic view: - "There is fierce chagrin that the two best Divisions in the British Army, the New Zealanders and 4TH Indian Division, forming a Corps that seemed a perfect combination, should have achieved nothing."

On 15TH May 1944, 8TH Indian Division and the Polish Corps were brought over from the Adriatic to breach the Gustav Line, to enable British Divisions to pass through. Finally the attack involved twenty Divisions attacking along a twenty-mile front. The German defenders were finally driven from their positions, but at a high cost. On 18TH May the Armour poured through the gap resulting in the final capture of Monte Cassino itself. The 8TH Indian Division cleared the town of Cassino. Lance Naik Rattan Singh of the Indian Signal Corps displayed outstanding bravery when in charge of a cable-laying party during the fighting at Cassino on 15TH and 17TH March 1944. Throughout the rest of battle, until 28TH March, he continued to display outstanding courage and devotion, without thought of personal risk, in maintaining lines of communication with forward Units for which he was awarded the Military Cross.

On 17TH March 1944, a Company commanded by Major Amar Singh of 1ST Battalion, 12TH Frontier Force Regiment, took over a position very close to a strong German position in the Orso area of Cassino. The Company's forward Platoon, situated in a very exposed position in a cave and completely isolated, was particularly an enemy objective. By day no movement was possible and by night it was very difficult. The night after the Company's arrival, the enemy launched an attack on the Platoon in the caves, supported by heavy covering fire. All communications were quickly cut. Major Amar Singh went forward immediately under heavy fire to control the situation, taking an NCO and three soldiers with him. After encouraging his isolated Platoon and taking necessary measures to meet the situation, he returned to his Headquarters and directed the fire of his mortars so successfully that the attack was repulsed with loss. He was the only survivor of the party he took forward with him and had he not acted as he did, his Platoon would have been overrun. During his Company's tenure of this exposed forward position, in close contact throughout with an aggressive enemy, Major Amar Singh set a magnificent example of courage and coolness under fire and of cheerful acceptance of the hardships involved in the appalling winter weather conditions. His offensive spirit and sound leadership quickly resulted in his Company dominating the caves area, a complete reversal of the previous position, for which he was awarded an immediate Military Cross.

Italy

Cassino, (Cont.)

From 9TH March to 23RD March, Jemadar Sardara Singh of 4TH Battalion, 16TH Punjab Regiment, commanded a Platoon, which flanked pt 593 and overlooked Monte Cassino Monastery in Italy. The enemy had excellent observation over the routes, between this Platoon, the next Platoon and the Company Headquarters. Accurate sniping made movement from Company Headquarters to either Platoon impossible by day. Jemadar Sardara Singh, as a senior Viceroys Commissioned Officer commanded both forward Platoons and controlled the defence of this locality, which was of vital importance to the whole Brigade sector.

Jemadar Sardara Singh frequently visited not only his own section posts but also the other Platoon Headquarters to pass orders and instructions and properly coordinate the defence. This he did by crawling behind bushes and rocks and taking advantage of all available cover. Enemy shelling, mortaring and accurate sniping was often concentrated along the area over which he had to pass and to get through unwounded seemed impossible, but he managed to pass through many times to pass his orders. By night the enemy would become more active and in addition to heavy mortaring and shelling, small arms fire and grenades were directed onto the forward positions. Jemadar Sardara Singh showed complete disregard for his own personal safety and moved from post to post encouraging and fostering offensive spirit in his men. The daily casualties reduced the strength of his Platoon severely but Jemadar Sardara Singh appeared to become even more cheerful and confident. Cold nights and rain added to the discomfort of the men but by his personal example and presence whenever the enemy became aggressive his men were inspired to still greater endurance. Thus throughout a period of a fortnight of great strain Jemadar Sardara Singh was responsible for the successful defence of this essential position. Completely undisturbed by the heaviest enemy fire he was able to send back most valuable and accurate information of enemy dispositions and movements. He was responsible for locating hostile batteries and his reports were always prompt and to the point. By his gallantry and devotion to duty he showed leadership of a high order under conditions, which could hardly have been more unpleasant and dangerous for which Jemadar Sardara Singh was awarded an immediate Military Cross. From 30TH March 1944, Jemadar Mehar Singh of the Indian Engineers was in charge of a working party of men, on Mt. Cairo in the vicinity of Mt. Cassino. On the night of April 4TH, six shells fell in the region where his men were mustering to collect the supplies to carry forward. He immediately made arrangements to evacuate his casualties, rallied the remainder of his men and with complete disregard for personal danger led them, continuously under shell fire, up the steep mountain-side and delivered the supplies to the Infantry. He then conducted the party back to Camp through heavy shell and mortar fire. For his excellent presence of mind and outstanding leadership Jemadar Mehar Singh was awarded an immediate Military Cross.

Italy

Orsogna, (1944)

During May 1944, Jemadar Jagit Singh of the Royal Indian Service Corps, was a Troop Commander and took part in the operations before Orsogna in Italy. He was responsible for the maintenance of forward and isolated Infantry Companies. His troop headquarters was often shelled by day and the tracks he had to use by night were known to the enemy and strongly patrolled. On several occasions his mule train clashed with the enemy but his bold and efficient leadership never failed to ensure the arrival of the mules and their loads. In August 1944, he was made acting Indian Adjutant just before the assault crossing of the River Arno began. His increased responsibilities took him into contact with all lower sections of the Company. On many occasions he fearlessly rendered first aid to the wounded drivers, he evacuated wounded animals and organised the salvage of saddlery under most severe conditions. Day after day he walked over the exposed hillsides frequently in full view of the enemy, under mortar and artillery fire, in order to visit forward sections where he inspired the men by his personal bravery and contempt for danger, at the same time he encouraged the muleteers, in spite of fatigue, discomfort, and danger, to take all necessary steps to maintain the condition of their animals and efficiency of their equipment. Throughout this period, under great strain and hazardous circumstances, he maintained the utmost cheerfulness. His was in complete control of every situation, from holding off enemy patrols, to organising a grooming parade, after exhausting nights under fire. Jemadar Jagit Singh was awarded the Military Cross on 24TH February 1945.

Liri Valley, (1944)

15TH Panzer Grenadier Division held the Liri Valley and provided garrisons for the fortifications both of Gustav and Adolf Hitler Lines. As the Sikhs of 3RD Battalion, 8TH Punjab Regiment pushed ahead and locating their first objective charged in abreast line. A few yards short of the close, a belt of wire halted them and four covering machine guns opened at point-blank range. One Platoon, which by impetus of its rush had penetrated the position, was wiped out to a man. They were afterwards found lying under the muzzles of their machine guns. Major Amar Singh MC, who had led his Company in many gallant actions in Italy, was also killed. The 8TH Indian Division relentlessly pushed forward towards Rome. On the day the Frontiersmen attacked Monte Pavone, a commanding feature which covered the approach to Acre, one and a half Companies of German paratroopers stood at bay on the crest of the peak. As Subedar Sadhu Singh's Sikhs closed in on the Germans, they perceived the Indians to be comparatively few in numbers. They sprang to their feet and charged up the hillside. The Sikhs were for an instant astounded by such foolhardiness; as one man they rose with their War cry of "Sat Siri Akal!" and leapt to meet the assailants. It was bayonet to bayonet and the paratroopers were outmatched. They broke and ran. The Sikhs swept forward to seize the enemy positions, capturing a number of prisoners, including a German Officer.

Italy

River Gari, (1944)

The River Gari checked the British advance on San Angelo. It was about forty feet in width, six to eight feet in depth, and swiftly flowing. Major Himmat Singh Sandhu was in command of the Company of 1ST Battalion, 12TH Frontier Force Regiment supplying boatmen for ferrying across personnel during the crossing of the River Gari on the night of $11^{TH}/12^{TH}$ May 1944, where his men were exposed to machine gun and mortar fire from enemy posts. On completion of their task the Company proceeded towards the enemy positions and ran into three machine gun posts. On each occasion, in spite of the continuous fire from the posts, Major Sandhu personally organised and led a series of charges against the posts. Visibility being such that their exact positions could not be located, Major Sandhu was forced to shout his commands and drew much of the fire on himself. His relentless attack on these posts under almost continuous fire from grenades and machine guns and smoke resulted in two enemy posts being withdrawn and the third destroyed. The bridging of the Gari by Indian Sapper and Miners and Royal Canadian Engineers turned the tide of battle. For his conspicuous gallantry and complete indifference to any danger, Major Himmat Singh Sandhu was awarded an immediate Military Cross on 12TH May 1944.

San Angelo, (1944)

As 8TH Army pushed forward, their pressing need was to clean up San Angelo. This stubborn knuckle of resistance blocked further advance. At noon on May 13TH, seven Field Regiments crashed a vicious shoot on the village. After a hurricane of bombardment, the Infantry dashed in. Sixty minutes of deadly fighting followed. No German asked quarter – none was given. In the deep shelters the last fanatical defenders were exterminated. The capture of San Angelo immediately reacted upon adjoining opposition. A German garrison watched the progress of the attack and the deployment of tanks in the open ground beyond the village. Without further resistance this strong point hung out white flags and surrendered in most un-German fashion.

Pignataro, (1944)

To the South of San Angelo, 4TH Battalion, 13TH Frontier Force Rifles was to advance up the valley. As Jemadar Thakur Singh led his Platoon forward, his men spotted four self-propelled guns concealed under the foliage of trees. The tank escorts plastered the site with armour piercing shells. Similarly when German armoured vehicles sallied out to deal with the Indian skirmishers, the tank men saw them first and smashed them. Panaccioni fell to the Frontier Force Rifles on the afternoon of May 13TH. The Frontiersmen, with tank support, attacked Pignataro at twilight. The defenders fought fanatically but by dawn Pignataro was cleared of the enemy. In the four days of fierce fighting, approximately 1,000 Germans had been killed and they had captured the San Angelo-Pignataro - Panaccioni Horseshoe.

Italy

Ortgna, (1944)
On the night of 19TH/20TH May 1944, on the Ortgna front, Jemadar Pritam Singh, when leading a Platoon of 1ST Battalion, 2ND Punjab Regiment, on a night raid, found the initial objectives empty. Without hesitation he chose new objectives and attacked, killing twelve Germans and many others severely handled, and a very valuable prisoner of war taken. He is acknowledged to have killed three Germans in the course of savage close quarter fighting. He engaged the enemy until the wounded got clear and then withdrew his force in full control. For Jemadar Pritam Singh's leadership and personal gallantry he was awarded an immediate Military Cross.

Verlolion, (1944)
Between 30TH May and 2ND June 1944 the Division fought its way from Auce to Alatal. Jemadar Hazura Singh of the Indian Armoured Corps was in almost continuous contact with the enemy, and the advance was greatly accelerated by his gallantry, tactical skill and energy. On 31ST May he was in the leading troop of the Squadron when it encountered a strong enemy rearguard. Here his gallant and skilful leadership enabled his troop to advance two miles against stiff opposition, capturing many prisoners. At Verlolion, 1ST June, the leading element of the Squadron became pinned down by heavy shell and machine gun fire. An enemy counter attack from a flank threatened to overrun them. Jemadar Hazura Singh rapidly appreciated the situation, and on his own initiative, led his troop to a position from which it neutralized this threat, although he was greatly outnumbered. Throughout the campaign in Italy, Jemadar Hazura Singh had shown initiative, outstanding leadership and sound tactical judgment, and personal gallantry for which he was awarded the Military Cross on 19TH April 1945.

Montone, (1944)
On July 6TH, 1ST Battalion, 2ND Punjab Regiment, established contact with the enemy. It was an ideal defensive position, as the tracks to the village from the South and West climbed open spurs, while on the East the summit was protected by a precipitous hillside. The village and a ridge behind it running into the North were held by a Battalion of One Hundred and Fourteenth Jaeger Division. On July 6TH, the Punjabis attacked from the South. Throughout the burning heat of the afternoon Sikhs and Mussalman Companies battled their way forward across the open countryside. As they surged to gain the shelter of the village, blasts of defensive fire caught them. The Germans in a characteristic fashion stuck it out obstinately and several hours of street fighting ensued before Montone was cleared and held. Twenty Germans were killed and sixty-five prisoners taken in return for nineteen British casualties.

Italy

Arezzo, (1944)

On Arezzo sector during the Battalion attack on the Campriano feature on 25TH July 1944, 'C' Company, under the command of Captain Buta Singh Bajwa of 1ST Battalion, 12TH Frontier Force Regiment, was ordered to advance in rear of 'B' Company and capture a Feature. Captain Bajwa infiltrated the Company forward through the enemy defensive fire to a Nullah. Despite the intense fire and increasing casualties Captain Bajwa made no less than three attempts to take his Company forward on to the high ground. He tried first one flank and then another, and on each occasion pressed home the attack with great determination. However owing to mounting casualties his Company was withdrawn and amalgamated with 'B' Company. During the remainder of the night the amalgamated Company was subjected to intense shelling and mortaring. Early in the morning the enemy were preparing to counter attack from the right flank. Captain Bajwa, realizing the seriousness of the situation, reinforced his right Platoon and directed accurate fire on the enemy and completely smashed the impending attack. Throughout this long and difficult action Captain Bajwa, with his unflinching determination to get forward at all costs, his bravery and the skill with which he handled his Company in the dark, set an inspiring example to all, and was in keeping with the finest traditions of the Sikhs. Captain Bajwa was awarded an immediate Military Cross.

Poggio San Giovanni, (1944)

The 2ND Royal Battalion, 11TH Sikh Regiment in the van of 4TH Indian Division, had reached Urbino, 15 miles from the Adriatic coast and due East of Florence. On 4TH September, the Battalion was in action, in an attack on the village of Poggio San Giovanni. Major Harwant Singh's advance was held up by three concealed machine guns, which were sweeping the ridges and gullies across which his men were attacking. Moving about in the open among his forward troops, Major Harwant Singh drew heavy artillery and machine gun fire, and in one burst of machine gun fire, he was wounded in the chest, while every other member of his Company Headquarters was either killed or wounded. However, Major Harwant Singh advanced with his right leading Platoons, and silenced the machine guns, capturing a Spandau and killing its crew. During the attack Major Harwant Singh was wounded in the arm by shellfire. Later he was hit again, and wounded in the leg, but continued to command his Company with complete disregard for his own personal safety. It was only when the position was firmly established, and a direct order had been given by the Battalion Commander, to hand over his Company and come back for treatment that he consented to be removed to the Regimental Aid Post. For his conspicuous gallantry, Major Harwant Singh was awarded an immediate Military Cross.

Italy

Route 71, (1944)
At the beginning of September the Eighth Army had opened a massive offensive on the Adriatic front. The 10TH Indian Division was relieved in the mountains and moved to join in the battle. Wheeler force, which included Nabha Akal Infantry (Sikh Princely States Unit) which had arrived from the Middle East, remained behind to open up Route 71 between Bibbiena and Florence. For the next month this detached column mopped up and harried rearguards in such fashion as to earn encomiums from the Army Commander. At the conclusion of this task the Nabha Akal Infantry rejoined 10TH Indian Division on the Adriatic front.

Monte Paglaiola, (1944)
On the morning of July 10TH, 2ND Royal Battalion, 11TH Sikh Regiment worked forward and after brisk fighting stormed Monte Paglaiola. In this action Sepoy Kartar Singh cleared his Company position single-handed, destroying three machine gun posts before falling severely wounded. Still further to the West, the same afternoon another Company of Sikhs seized Monte Favalto, the highest ground on the front. This summit, nearly eight miles West of Monte San Maria Tiberina, gave source to streams flowing North, South and East. The crest commanded Palazzo di Pero in the loop of the lateral road which joins Arezzo and San Sepolcro.

Florence, (1944)
Fourth German Parachute Division, tough veterans of Crete, Leros and Anzio, held the line of the Mugnone Canal, which encircles the Northern confines of Florence. Self-propelled guns and tanks covered all approaches to the Canal, while along the waterfront Fascist snipers lurked in attics and on the rooftops. All the beautiful Arno bridges had been destroyed except the world famous Ponte Vecchio, which had been blocked by extensive demolitions at either end. Appreciating their advantage, the paratroopers grew belligerent and began to despatch raiding parties across the Arno. On several occasions the Frontier Force Regiment received unwelcome attentions. On August 10TH something like a small battle broke out in Columbaro. After a heavy bombardment paratroopers and Fascist irregulars isolated a Platoon of Frontiersmen. Fierce close-quarter fighting followed, with Canadian tanks lumbering to the rescue in the nick of time. On the next night, a savage shoot again crashed down on the Indian front. When no Infantry attack developed, it was realized that the paratroopers were expending local dumps preparatory to withdrawal. Bit by bit the great city was brought under control, the last enemies extirpated and the public services restored. On August 16TH, 21ST Brigade was relieved in Florence by a British Infantry Brigade and moved back to rest, with the consciousness of a job well done.

Italy

Gothic Line

The Gothic Line followed the Southern slopes of the transverse range from the Carrara massif on the West coast, over the Alpe Apuane, along the broken crests of Tuscany until beyond Florence, where the cross range fuses into the great central spine of the Kingdom. Thereafter the fortifications marched along the basic mountain core into the massive promontory of peaks and ridges which abutted to within a few miles of the Adriatic Coast. The Eastern bulwarks of the defence system were anchored into the easy beaches to the South of Rimini. Both 8TH and 5TH Armies were briefed for the assault upon this great mountain barrier. All Indian Divisions were destined to fight in the new battle. As "D" Day drew near, 4TH Indian Division moved up from Lake Trasimeno, 10TH Indian Division, under 10TH British Corps, waited for the call among the mountains between the Arno and the Tiber. 8TH Indian Division, having cleared Florence, had moved Eastwards to join 13TH Corps in the left hook across the Apennines. In addition, a new Indian formation was closing up for the fray. The 31ST Indian Armoured Division, which had long rusticated in Paiforce and the Middle East, had yielded up 43RD Indian Infantry Brigade to serve as lorried troops.

Monte Calvo, (1944)

On August 30TH, the fifteen miles between the Indians and the Adriatic burst into flame. A thunderous bombardment heralded the assault. By dawn 46TH British Division on the right had broken into strongly fortified and desperately defended positions to a depth of two thousand yards. 4TH Divisional Artillery concentrated on Monte Calvo while fighter bombers swooped with cannon fire against enemy strongpoints. 5TH Brigade passed to the attack with all three Battalions committed. 3RD Battalion, 10TH Baluchis followed by tanks pushed down the crest of the spur in a frontal assault on Monte Calvo, 4TH Battalion, 11TH Sikh Regiment and 1ST Battalion, 9TH Gurkhas worked forward along the Eastern slopes. From folds in the ground and hideouts, enemy riflemen and machine gunners opened fire. A number of British tanks brewed up on mines. On the flanks the advance made rapid headway and the Gurkhas speedily swung into the North, with a view to intercepting any defenders who tried to scuttle at the last moment. In the face of this threat the Germans withdrew to Tavoleto. The Sikhs and Baluchis mopped up Monte Calvo, taking forty prisoners. Leaving the Baluchis in garrison, the Sikhs and Gurkhas pressed on to exploit the gains. The two Battalions battled forward for a mile towards Tavoleto. The enemy stood at bay along the entire front, and began to strike back. As darkness fell on September 1ST, harassing fire searched the Monte Calvo spur and the approaches to Tavoleto. At midnight a sharp counter-attack surged against 1ST Battalion, 9TH Gurkhas, apparently to gain time or in the hope of dislocating the offensive. Some ground was lost, but at dawn the advance was renewed as planned.

Italy

Poggio San Giovanni, (1944)

Throughout September 3RD, the Sappers of the Indian Engineers toiled in the Foglia valley, raising mines, building approaches and smoothing crossings. A Platoon of Sappers was constantly shelled for two hours whilst they were making a road diversion. After each concentration of shells had landed Jemadar Mewa Singh of the Sappers, collected his men and quickly led them back to their task and thus finished the work in the quickest possible time. Mule trains were soon across, followed later in the day by wheeled convoys.

During the same action, Jemadar Kaka Singh of 2ND Battalion, 11TH Sikh Regiment was commanding the left leading Platoon of 'A' Company. The advance was held up by fire from three well-concealed enemy medium machine guns, which were sweeping down the ridges and gullies across which the Company was moving for the attack. Jemadar Kaka Singh, leaving one section in position to engage the enemy's attention, and to disguise his own intention, moved round under cover with his remaining two sections, in order to achieve a position further up the ridge from which he could outflank the enemy's right. While doing so, he was suddenly engaged at a range of 50 yards by a Spandau fire, which had remained silent and un-located up to this time. Taking immediate action, Jemadar Kaka Singh turned on this new danger, collected his two sections, and charged up the hill throwing grenades as he went, killing the German gunners and capturing their machine gun. He quickly consolidated his position and brought his Bren guns into action, silencing the three enemy machine guns that had been holding up the advance of the remainder of his Company. This inspite of the fact that German Artillery, endeavouring to deal with this new threat to their right flank, had brought fire down on his position, on which he had no time to dig in. He kept his guns in action and enabled the advance to go forward, inspite of being exposed in the open and subjected to accurate enemy shellfire. Jemadar Kaka Singh skilfully re-organized his sections, charged the enemy position, and silenced the concealed German machine guns. After some continuous brisk fighting, the village fell to the Sikhs at last light. Jemadar Kaka Singh was awarded an immediate Military Cross for his conspicuous gallantry.

Tavoleto, (1944)

On the night of September 3RD, an unusual sequence of events led to the storming of Tavoleto by troops uncommitted to the assault. 4TH Battalion, 11TH Sikh Regiment and 2ND Camerons had assembled on their start line for attack on the village. The Sikhs and Camerons were waiting for the signal, when the night was shattered by a bedlam of shots, shouts and screams from the village ahead. "What is happening in Tavoleto," reported a Camerons Officer, "is nobody's business." At dawn only dead Germans and gibbering prisoners remained in Tavoleto and less than thirty men of "C" Company were standing.

Italy

Pian di Castello, (1944)

On the night of September $5^{TH}/6^{TH}$, 11TH Brigade launched its attack on Pian di Castello, with 3RD Battalion, 12TH Frontier Force Regiment on the right and the Camerons on the opposite flank. Along the line of the river mortar fire crashed in a continuous curtain. Under the handicaps of rain and mud, the advance became a slow and expensive slogging match. Jemadar Santa Singh was commanding the leading Platoon of 'A' Company of 12TH Frontier Force Regiment. On 6TH September Jemadar Santa Singh was ordered to cooperate with 'D' Company in their attack on Point 419. Posting two of his sections to give covering fire from the low bank, he then led the third section up this drain and rushed an enemy machine gun post in a surprise attack and captured four of the gun crew with their gun. The enemy from the second post panicked and fled leaving their gun behind them. That night, $6^{TH}/7^{TH}$ September, the enemy counter attacked the whole Battalion position with great determination. Jemadar Santa Singh rallied his exhausted Platoon, many of whom were raw recruits and were in battle for the first time, and had been continuously in action for twenty-four hours. Later the same night the Platoon ran short of ammunition. Jemadar Santa Singh distributed the captured German machine guns to them and kept his men firing them until reserve ammunition was brought forward the next morning. Once again the battle hung in the balance until British Armour had skidded and slithered through the valley bottom and had churned up the greasy slopes to support the Infantry in the rush which won home. Jemadar Santa Singh was able very materially to contribute to the success of the whole battle and was awarded an immediate Military Cross.

Gemmano, (1944)

On the night of 12TH September 1944, Jemadar Mewa Singh's Company of 2ND Royal Battalion, 11TH Sikh Regiment was ordered to carry out a night attack on the village of Onverno. The Platoon was heavily mortared and counter attacked by the enemy. The enemy attack was driven off and Onverno was reached and found to be strongly held by the enemy. Inspite of this Jemadar Mewa Singh launched two attacks on the village and throughout the day and night and into the next day, the bitter struggle continued. Only a thin line of Sikhs remained, yet they disdained to yield ground. On September 13TH, with unabated frenzy, the Germans sought to break the assault, counterattacking continually until a final effort pushed the gallant remnants of 2ND Royal Battalion, 11TH Sikh Regiment from the spur. By evening of 13TH the British Divisions had attacked Gemmano eleven times, each time to be thwarted by a desperate defence. Eventually 4TH Indian Division was exclusively committed against this formidable obstacle. With comparatively few casualties Gemmano was stormed and consolidated. For his courageous leadership throughout the night and day and his resourcefulness and initiative Jemadar Mewa Singh was awarded the Military Cross.

Italy

Alpe di Vitigliano, (1944)

General Russell planned to lead off with 21ST Brigade in an assault upon Monte Citerna and Monte Stiletto, two feeder ridges intruding into the Alpe di Vitigliano buttress. At dusk on September 12TH, 3RD Battalion, 15TH Punjab Regiment began their arduous advance. Just before dawn they made contact with the enemy at Point 632, South-West of Monte Citerna. Jemadar Chattar Singh was commanding a Platoon of "B" Company, which had been ordered to capture Alpe di Vitigliano. While the Company was forming up for the attack on a narrow ridge, the enemy brought down heavy artillery fire on the forming up area, causing casualties and considerable confusion in the darkness. In spite of the heavy fire Jemadar Chattar led the assault up an exceptionally steep hillside, covered with thick scrub, and in pitch darkness against strongly prepared enemy positions on the crest of the ridge 350 feet above the forming up place. On reaching the crest, Jemadar Chattar Singh himself led the assault on the enemy trenches. During this assault he saw that one of the enemy, who had been captured, was about to throw a stick grenade; he at once attacked the man, and after a hand-to-hand struggle, overcame and dis-armed him.

Day broke upon a thunderous bombardment which ran for miles along the Apennines, as 13TH and 2ND U.S. Corps moved to the assault. The Punjabis, under Major Nairne, scaled an almost vertical cliff and cut through a belt of wire. Machine gun fire pinned them down on two occasions, but thrusting with splendid dash they swept over Monte Citerna and destroyed the garrison. Without pause the Battalion drove for the central buttress of Alpe di Vitigliano, and shortly after noon, after climbing along the reverse slope of the spur, Lieutenant Colonel Macnamara's men, in a great-hearted effort, routed the garrison on Point 1015, about half-way between Citerna and the main objective. The Punjabis had climbed one thousand feet since dawn and had stormed two positions. They were now halted by concentrated fire from Monte Stiletto on their right rear and Le Scalette on their left front. It was impossible to run the gauntlet of two flanking fires by daylight so the doughty Indians dug in and waited for night. An Officer wrote truly: "The Punjabis have opened with a magnificent innings" After bitter resistance on the lower slopes of Alpe di Vitigliano the Punjabis had spent the day in reorganization. The assault was renewed at 2230 hours that evening. Enemy Artillery and mortar fire searched their line of advance, and when they closed upon their objective at midnight it was in anticipation of a grim struggle. The narrow approach compelled attack on a single Company frontage. As the leading Platoons clambered towards the black skyline they were greeted by heavy small arms fire. Dauntlessly they flung themselves at the crest. A few enemies remained to die in the weapon pits, but more scuttled to safety in the dark. The emplacements were mopped up, and a second bastion of the Gothic Line had fallen. Throughout the action Jemadar Chattar Singh's gallantry and leadership was quite exceptional, for which he was awarded the Military Cross.

Italy

Finnachio, (1944)
On 5TH October 1944, 'C' Company of the Nabha Akal Infantry was ordered to take the high feature of Finnachio. Jemadar Gurdial Singh's Platoon took part in the first wave of the assault. Jemadar Gurdial Singh led the charge up the steep side of the feature in a magnificent manner, taking his place at the head of his assaulting party and shouting encouragement to his men under very heavy Spandau, grenade and mortar fire. On nearing the objective he came upon an enemy trench whose occupants had been giving the advancing troops a great deal of trouble. Seeing that unless this batch of the enemy was quickly neutralized, they would cause many more casualties among the assaulting section, Jemadar Gurdial Singh rushed up to them alone and firing his pistol into their midst and showing outstanding courage under heavy fire, succeeded in killing and wounding all the occupants. Inspired by his brilliant leadership, his assaulting sections stormed and took their objective, causing many casualties to the enemy. On the same day his Company was again employed in another attack in which Jemadar Gurdial Singh again led his men into assault with outstanding bravery, which encouraged his men to carry through the attack with success. Jemadar Gurdial Singh was awarded an immediate Military Cross on 5TH October 1944.

M Di Buffalo, (1944)
During the attack of M Di Buffalo, on 6TH and 7TH October 1944, the Regimental Aid Post, in which Major Gurbaksh Singh of the Indian Medical Service was tending his wounded, came under heavy enemy shelling on many occasions. Twice the Regimental Aid Post was hit, but this Unit Medical Officer continued on imperturbably, with complete disregard of his own personal danger. His only thought was to attend to the casualties and he only moved his Regimental Aid Post on the order of the Commanding Officer. Throughout this action Major Gurbaksh Singh, despite being 47 years of age, with his courage and determination was instrumental in maintaining a very high standard of morale. Major Gurbaksh Singh was awarded an immediate Military Cross followed by the DSO on 21ST November 1944.

Gothic Line, (1944)
In seven days 8TH Indian Division had broken through the Gothic Line. It is no detraction from the superb leadership and outstanding fighting ability of the Indian soldiers to record that the case with which this defensive zone was pierced came as a surprise to everybody. It is difficult to understand why positions of such strength, fortified with such care, should have been entrusted to such meagre garrisons. The German troops did not fight particularly well, but they were much too thin on the ground to make an effective stand against well-mounted attacks.

Italy

Gothic Line, (Cont.)

Captured Officers attributed the disaster to loss of contact between 10TH and 14TH German Armies, which were heavily engaged on both sides of the Indians. Other German prisoners stated that battle reserves were on their way forward and had not arrived. It seems possible that the real answer lay in the paucity of lateral communications and that with the Air completely under Allied control the enemy found it impossible to move reinforcements into the threatened area. The brief, bright record of the assault troops is by no means the full story of 8TH Indian Division's assault on the Gothic Line. Behind the indomitable Infantry that clambered and won the peaks, the entire Division worked in high gear. The smoothness of the Ancillary Services was the yardstick of the speed of the attack. Next to the battle line, both literally and in priority, came the mule trains, the patient animals and the indefatigable drivers who followed wherever the fighting men went. They fetched food, water, ammunition and blankets, and took back litters of wounded. Day by day Indian sappers drove jeep-heads deeper into the hills. Winding up the mountain slopes for mile after mile, the narrow tracks looked like threads of cotton against the brown mountainsides. The Divisional provosts in an unbroken tour of duty policed these routes in order that the traffic might flow steadily and without jam. Signallers laid hundreds of miles of cable; no sooner had the Infantry dug in than the telephones began to buzz. At vehicle-head the stretcher-bearers lifted the wounded from the litter mules and laid them carefully on specially fitted jeeps which edged cautiously down the mountain side. Jemadars Karnail Singh and Chanan Singh of 4TH Battalion, 13TH Frontier Force Rifles, were awarded the Military Cross for their gallantry and leadership in smashing through the Gothic Line.

Pt. 598, (1944)

On 13TH October 1944, 'A' Company of the Nabha Akal Infantry was ordered to attack Pt. 598. Jemadar Sham Singh's Platoon was dispatched to do so. During the assault Jemadar Sham Singh placed himself at the head of the assaulting troops. The whole Platoon came under heavy small arms fire coupled with Artillery and mortar fire, but Jemadar Sham Singh undaunted by this terrific fire led his men in a magnificent charge onto the objective, shouting encouragement to them and having not the slightest regard for his personal safety. It was entirely due to the effort of Jemadar Sham Singh that the assault, which was directed at an extremely strong enemy position, was a success. Again during the same operation Jemadar Sham Singh conducted himself in a magnificent manner during the whole of the enemy attack, exposing himself to the enemy fire many times in his efforts to encourage his Platoon. Owing to Jemadar Sham Singh's gallantry under very heavy fire, his Platoon was able to beat off the enemy counter attack and inflict heavy casualties on him. Jemadar Sham Singh was awarded Military Cross on 13TH October 1944.

Italy

Monte Pianoereno, (1944)

Monte Pianoereno rose to two thousand three hundred feet. On October 17th, a heavy fire was laid down on the approach spur. 3RD Battalion, 15TH Punjab Regiment advanced and after two hours' hard fighting had swept the enemy from Point 711. Two Companies then turned against Croce Daniele; after two repulses, in which serious casualties were sustained, a third furious charge won home. The Germans had had enough and disappeared when darkness fell. For his conspicuous gallantry and leadership during this action Jemadar Dharm Singh of 3RD Battalion, 15TH Punjab Regiment was awarded the Military Cross.

Alberto, (1944)

On 30TH November 1944, Major Inder Singh was in command of 'D' Company of the Nabha Akal Infantry during the attack on Alberto in Italy. Ten minutes before the starting time fresh information compelled him to make urgent alterations to his plan. At the outset of the advance the Company came under heavy enemy Artillery and small arms fire halting the Company. Casualties were heavy including all three Platoon Commanders. Without the slightest hesitation and with complete disregard for his own safety, Major Inder Singh immediately ran forward to carry out a recce. He then moved from Platoon to Platoon, still under very heavy fire, encouraging his men and giving orders to continue the advance. The coolness, courage and leadership displayed by Major Inder Singh were outstanding and undoubtedly ensured the capture of his objective. He displayed a devotion to duty of a very high order and his personal example was an inspiration to the rest of his Company. Major Inder Singh was awarded a Military Cross on 30TH November 1944.

Caterina, (1944)

On 30TH November 1944 in La Podesta area in Italy, Subedar Sudha Singh was in command of a Rifle Company of 1ST Battalion, 2ND Punjab Regiment that was ordered to capture Caterina. Subedar Sudha Singh formed up his Company and personally led them in an extremely difficult advance to the assault over mine-strewn and shell swept country in pitch darkness. After contact, Subedar Sudha Singh so directed his Platoons that the enemy was taken by surprise and a large number of prisoners and booty was captured. Not content with this, Subedar Sudha Singh, after contacting all his Platoons, ordered a Platoon to the right, by which tactics he succeeding in trapping another few Germans who were running away. Despite intense shelling, Subedar Sudha Singh never ceased to visit his Platoons, including the forward sections, and personally organised the consolidating of the positions. It was largely through the gallantry and skill of Subedar Sudha Singh that this Company's attacks were so completely successful. Subedar Sudha Singh was awarded Military Cross on 30TH November 1944.

Italy

Monte Cerere, (1944)

On 12TH December, the German paratroopers reacted with equal vehemence against 4TH Battalion, 13TH Frontier Force Rifles. A determined attack on the Platoon's position was repulsed. For the next three hours, bitter fighting continued, the enemy repeatedly attempting to work their way up to the top. The Platoon lost 6 killed and 13 wounded. Jemadar Balwant Singh was wounded in both hands but continued to command his Platoon skilfully and gallantly. Jemadar Balwant Singh's Platoon undoubtedly inflicted heavy losses on the enemy. The right forward Platoon of the Frontiersmen was overrun, and the Germans burst into the main battle positions. A reserve Company of Frontiersmen doubled into action, and their weight decided the melee; the paratroopers sullenly gave ground. Whereupon the storm troopers who had won ground from the Argylls decided to join the fray. It was their last and worst decision; as they raced from the flank across a hundred yards of open ground, the machine gunners caught them at point blank range. Within seconds the hillside was strewn with dead and dying Germans. Everywhere except on the inner flank of the Argyll position, 19TH Brigade had broken the assault. 1ST British Division picked up a disparing enemy intercept, pleading for reinforcements. This good news stimulated the attackers, who prepared to put paid to the remaining intruders. After a half-hour's bombardment with every available weapon, they charged. Few escaped. Under cover of a Red Cross flag German stretcher bearers moved amongst them, picking up many dead and wounded. For his leadership and gallantry during these operations Jemadar Balwant Singh was awarded the Military Cross.

Molazzana, (1944)

On 31ST December 1944, Risaldar Jagir Singh of the Indian Armoured Corps, was ordered to take a daylight patrol to the commanding village of Molazzana and find out whether it was held, and if possible, obtain identification. While still a mile short of the objective the patrol was heavily fired on from two enemy positions but avoided casualties and continued its advance. The patrol reached the outskirts of Molazzana, capturing a prisoner on the way. Valuable information was gained of enemy mortar and defensive positions. Risaldar Jagir Singh appreciated that he must return by another route, but soon after leaving the village the patrol was heavily fired on again. At the same time an Observation Post was located. The patrol attacked the post and two enemy gunners were captured. Shortly after this the patrol was engaged from several enemy posts by small arms, mortar and grenades and a fire fight ensued in which two Other Ranks were wounded and the prisoners attempted to escape. These were, however, recaptured. The information and identifications gained were of great value and obtained in the face of considerable opposition. Risaldar Jagir Singh showed great gallantry, skill and leadership throughout the operation, for which he was awarded an immediate Military Cross.

Italy

Serchio Valley, (1945)
During the operations in the Serchio Valley in January 1945; 69TH Indian Field Company was called upon to perform a series of bridging operations under accurate enemy fire. Subedar Bhagat Singh was present at all these operations and gave continuous encouragement to his men both by word and by his reassuring presence. In this manner he ensured the earliest construction of the bridges and contributed greatly to the success of ensuing operations. A Senior Officer in the Divisional Engineers, Subedar Bhagat Singh by his sound judgment and advice had also contributed largely to the smooth running and general efficiency in battle of the whole Division of Sappers. Subedar Bhagat Singh was awarded the Military Cross on 13TH September 1945.

Senio, (1945)
Early in February 4TH Battalion, 11TH Sikh Regiment had a bit of luck. Their raiders were closing on an enemy position when a false alarm distracted the German sentries. The submachine guns and spandaus commenced to hose bullets to empty flank, while the Sikhs crept nearer. Undetected the Sikhs sprang upon the engrossed garrison, and destroyed it. In a series of similar bickerings, which imposed a strain upon weakening adversaries, 10TH Division's tour on the river lines wore away. On February 9TH, 3RD Carpathian Division relieved the Indians along the Senio.

Santerno River, (1945)
In the face of strong enemy opposition and continuous counter attacks, 8TH Indian Division established and consolidated shallow bridgeheads over Santerno River in April 1945. Jemadar Dhana Singh commanded the Pioneer Platoon of 1ST Battalion, 12TH Frontier Force Regiment throughout the Italian campaign. During the assault crossing-point of Santerno River, regardless of the heavy shelling and small arms fire, the Platoon cleared and marked a track for personnel and vehicles through the extensive minefields, lifting over one hundred mines, many of which were booby trapped, and thus played a very large part in the success of the operation. Jemadar Dhana Singh was awarded the Military Cross, for his sustained courage throughout the campaign.

On the 11TH April 1945, during the assault across the river, Jemadar Mohinder Singh commanded a Platoon of 'D' Company of 1ST Battalion, 12TH Frontier Force Regiment, and had the task of securing the houses beyond the West flood bank. With speed and determination the Platoon attacked and captured three houses and went on to mop up two further enemy-occupied houses. During this period the Platoon captured between twenty and thirty prisoners and secured the important bridgehead, which enabled the rest of the Company to fan out behind the enemy positions and capture twenty more prisoners. The magnificent skill and quick thinking and aggressive leadership of Jemadar Mohinder Singh earned him the Military Cross.

Italy

Santerno River, (Cont.)

During the assault across the River Santerno, Lieutenant Harbans Singh was Regimental Medical Officer of 1ST Battalion, 12TH Frontier Force Regiment. Having treated and evacuated men wounded in the early stages of the operation, and not satisfied with the speed at which casualties were reaching the Regimental Aid Post, he moved forward to the river bank. There he showed outstanding courage in collecting groups of casualties, dressing them and evacuating them by Jeep. Regardless of heavy shelling and the risk of walking into minefields, which were known to be thickly laid in the area and had not yet been marked, he continued this splendid work throughout the night and into the following day. In this period a hundred and twenty casualties from the Battalion and supporting arms passed through his hands. His outstanding work, far beyond the call of duty earned him the Military Cross. The men of 8TH Indian Division had punched the hole with speed and power which left the enemy reeling; their spearhead had gouged a gaping wound. Many German formations had been destroyed, and upwards of one thousand prisoners taken.

Idice Bridgehead, (1945)

On the afternoon of April 20TH, advanced patrols of 1ST Battalion, 1ST Punjab Regiment reached the Idice, to be confronted with floodbanks thirty feet high, and to find the near bank covered by a wide irrigation ditch at the bottom of the slope. The position was held in force; and for the last time 10TH Division encountered Germans of the type they knew so well. Fanatically brave fighters, skilled in battle, contemptuous of death. The Punjabis moved forward to storm the defences and plunged into its bitterest fighting of the War.

1ST Battalion, 2ND Punjab Regiment, commanded by Subedar Major Daulat Singh, attacked a strong enemy position on the River Idice and suffered very heavy casualties. The towering presence of Subedar Major Daulat Singh in the forward area at a critical period had a marked effect on the course of battle, for which he was awarded the Military Cross.

During the Idice operations Captain Naranjan Singh of Tactical Headquarters was awarded the Military Cross. Part of the citation for the gallantry award reads: "Captain Naranjan Singh has carried out the duties of the battle adjutant in Tactical Headquarters, throughout the period from September 1943 to May 1945. During these operations the personal gallantry, initiative and unswerving devotion to duty of Captain Naranjan Singh have been outstanding, particularly during the operations in Po Valley at the Quaderna and Idice rivers in Italy during April 1945. During these operations, Tactical Headquarters frequently came under severe and accurate enemy shelling. Despite this, Captain Naranjan Singh, with complete disregard for his own safety, organised and kept in operation the Tactical Headquarters, this had far-reaching effects upon the course of the battle".

Italy

Indian Divisions

The 10th Indian Division joined the hunt. The Indians pressed ahead, mopping up scattered pockets of the enemy. Each British soldier and each sepoy was gripped by the exciting knowledge that the end was in sight. 19th Brigade led, passed through the Argenta Gap and struck for Ferrara, city of classical swordsmen, and for the main Po crossings. 3rd Battalion, 8th Punjab Regiment brushed aside light opposition, and at noon on April 22nd closed up on the outskirts of the town. 6th Lancers and Argyll Regiment forged ahead to mop up small groups of Infantry and Armoured cars which sought to delay the pursuit. Prisoners began to be a problem. Along the Po stragglers of hundreds of Units waited disconsolately to be picked up. A motley assembly wearing the insignia of many divisions, they cluttered the roads and overflowed into the fields. Some were shaken and even hysterical, but most sat dumbly with blank faces, their courage and manhood exhausted. Yet such are the fortunes of War that 8th Indian Division was vouchsafed the opportunity of adding a postscript to its great record in the Italian campaign. The Armistice was two days old when Lieutenant Conisbee, with two Sikhs and six Jats, went forward to investigate. He was bluntly informed that the German Commander would only surrender his force if met by an Officer of his own rank. General Russell was far away and an American General close at hand. Yet it was some consolation to know that 8th Indian Division was represented by this small patrol at the capitulation of such formidable adversaries. The Indian forces, though limited to the strength of 4th, 8th and 10th Indian Division, distinguished themselves for courage and tenacity in the battles of the Sangro, Cassino, and the Liri Valley, the Gothic line, the Senio and several other engagements. The Indian soldiers fought in a terrain that was ideally suited for defence and the offensive proceeded against the grain of the country. Yet they fought with unparalleled courage and relentless tenacity.

"The 4th, 8th and 10th Indian Divisions will forever be associated with the fighting for Cassino, the capture of Rome, the Arno Valley, the liberation of Florence and the breaking of the Gothic Line".(The Tiger Triumphs).

Bologna, (1945)

Bologna was captured on 21st April, and here the Poles destroyed the renowned Parachute Division. Axis forces attempted in vain to prevent the juncture of the 5th and 8th Armies, desperately trying to buy time for small detachments of their comrades to escape. But the Allied onslaught, now moving at full speed, quickly swept aside the hasty defences, overwhelming and annihilating numerous Axis rear-guard detachments in the process. Ultimately, over 100,000 Axis troops were forced to surrender in the areas South of the river. The War in this theatre ended on 29th April with the German command signing the Instrument of Surrender.

HONG KONG 1941

As part of a general Pacific campaign, the Japanese launched an assault on Hong Kong on the morning of December 8TH, 1941, just eight hours after the bombing of Pearl Harbour. 52,000 Japanese troops attacked Hong Kong. British, Canadian and Indian forces were outnumbered three to one. The garrison consisted of two British, two Canadian and two Indian Regiments (5TH Battalion, 7TH Rajput and 2ND Battalion, 14TH Punjab Regiment) supported by two batteries of the Hong Kong and Singapore Royal Artillery. The Sikh soldiers bulked in the Hong Kong and Singapore Royal Artillery (HKSRA) and comprised Companies of 2ND Battalion, 14TH Punjab Regiment.

On the first day of the battle, the Japanese wreaked destruction upon Royal Air Force aircraft, achieving immediate air supremacy. The Royal Air Force and Air Unit personnel then fought on as ground troops. On 10TH December, the guns from three batteries of HKSRA supported three British and Indian Infantry Battalions holding a straggling collection of half-finished positions called the Gin Drinker's Line. The Japanese breached the defences of Gin Drinker's Line, causing the evacuation of Kowloon and forcing the allied forces to retreat onto Hong Kong Island. The last to leave the Kowloon peninsula were the Punjabis. Surrounded on Hong Kong Island the gunners were overwhelmed by the much more numerous and experienced Japanese Artillery. HKSRA survivors who had lost their guns were formed into impromptu Infantry Units. The men were untrained in the Infantry tactics and their hobnailed boots foiled all attempts at surprise in the attack on the South of Wong Nei Chong Gap. 30 gunners were killed, and twice that number captured and massacred.

At the outskirts of Tai Po the Punjabis, with their murderous fire, had taken a terrible toll on the advancing Japanese. On 15TH December the Japanese began systematic bombardment of the island's North shore. Two demands for surrender were made on 13TH December and 17TH December. When these were rejected, Japanese forces crossed the harbour on the evening of 18TH December and landed on the island's North-East. That night, approximately 20 gunners were massacred at the Sai Wan Battery after they had surrendered. Fierce fighting continued on Hong Kong Island. Again there was a massacre of prisoners, this time of Medical Staff, in the Silesian Mission on Chai Wan Road. From 20TH December the island became split in two with the British Commonwealth forces still holding out around the Stanley peninsula and in the West of the island. At the same time, water supplies started to run short as the Japanese captured the island's reservoirs. On the morning of 25TH December, Japanese soldiers entered the British Field Hospital at St. Stephen's College, and tortured and killed over 60 injured soldiers, along with the Medical Staff. By the afternoon of 25TH December 1941, it was clear that further resistance would be futile and British Colonial Officials, headed by the Governor of Hong Kong, Sir Mark Aitchison Young, surrendered in person at the Japanese headquarters. The garrison had held out for 17 days. This was the first occasion on which a British Crown Colony had surrendered to an invading force. Most of the Sikh gunners and the Sikh soldiers of the Punjab Regiment had fallen in battle.

MALAYA 1942
Compiled with Lt. Col. Baldev Singh Johl (Retd)

The Battle of Malaya began when the Japanese 25TH Army invaded Malaya, a British Colony then on 8TH December 1941. Japanese troops launched an amphibious assault on the North Eastern coast of Malaya at Kota Bharu and advanced South down the Eastern coast. Simultaneously unopposed landings at Pattani and Songkhla in Thailand enabled the Japanese to proceed South across the Thailand-Malaya border and sweep down the West coast of Malaya to Singapore. In essence, the Japanese thrust to Singapore was along the East coast axis and the West coast axis.

East Coast Axis
Kota Bahru

Battle began shortly after midnight on 8TH December 1941. The Japanese 25TH Army made co-ordinated landings and established 3 beach-heads at Kota Bahru, the capital of the North Eastern state of Kelantan. The lead units of the 18TH Division met stiff resistance and suffered heavy casualties. Sikh gunners of the 9TH Battery of the 1ST HKSRA Regiment struggled to protect landing strips just North of Kota Bahru. Anti-aircraft gunners tried to protect British bombers as they took off to attack Japanese battleships disgorging men and equipment. Three gunners were killed and eight were wounded, but the crews recovered from the initial shock and shot down two Japanese aircraft. Advancing Japanese units, backed by tanks hurled back the British Indian defenders and swung South to capture the township of Kota Bahru. Meanwhile, with most British aircraft lost or out of action, the RAF began to abandon the airfield. Lieutenant Close, the HKSRA Commander, realising that Infantry guarding the airfield had withdrawn without warning, and in the face of Japanese advance ordered his men to withdraw with whatever stores they could muster. Close and a small party stayed behind to destroy the guns and were eventually captured. He later received a Military Cross for his leadership. Remnants of the Battery reached the railway line at Kuala Krai where they took over two 3-inch naval guns. Forced to abandon their positions and fall back with the retreating Infantry, Sikh Gunners found four more 3-inch guns and manned those until British forces abandoned the area.

Kuantan

Kuantan was defended by 22ND Brigade of Indian 9TH Division. The Japanese Takumi Detachment troops were ordered to capture Kuantan, the capital of the state of Pahang, along the Eastern coast. The attack on Kuantan was supported by air attack in and around Kuantan including the main ferry point across the Kuantan River. The attack on the ferry point saw Jemadar Ajit Singh, with some 16 men who were holding out a weak bridge-head. In one skirmish Jemadar Ajit Singh and his men were engaged by Japanese infiltrators. In the contact, Havildar Punjab Singh was killed and Joginder Singh was wounded. Jemadar Ajit Singh flung himself under cover and hurled a grenade at the Japanese.

Malaya 1942

He quickly followed with a second grenade. Simultaneously, one of the section posts opened fire followed by the defences from opposite West bank. Collecting two grenades from Havildar Punjab Singh's haversack and two more from Joginder Singh's, Jemadar Ajit Singh systematically bombed the Japanese. This action stopped the attack and the Japanese withdrew leaving three dead behind. This gallant action of Ajit Singh saved the ferry and thus secured the only line of withdrawal for the defenders. Jemadar Ajit was granted an immediate award of the Indian Order of Merit. Other Japanese units were thrust into the attack on downtown Kuantan. The defenders were eventually ordered to withdraw. The Japanese hurled ferocious attacks on the rearguard of the withdrawing British Indian troops enroute to Jerantut. They also sprung two spectacularly successful ambushes along the withdrawal route trapping the 2ND Battalion, 12TH Frontier Force Regiment. Only 40 Frontiersmen survived.

West Coast Axis

Jitra

Jitra was a strategic border town in North Kedah, a state that bordered Thailand. It stood at the entry point of the Japanese advance along the West axis. Jitra was defended by 5TH Battalion, 11TH Sikh Regiment. On the morning of 11TH December 1941, the observation post, engaged the advancing Japanese with mortar fire. The observation post was detected and attacked by the Japanese Advance Guard. In the ensuing fire fight, Havildar Singh, manning the post was wounded. Another member, L/Naik Tehl Singh ran to and fro from the mortar position to the observation post to observe strikes and adjust fire. His enthusiasm was a great tonic and his skill was enough to silence the Japanese on more than one occasion. The Japanese were pinned down by heavy fire from the Sikhs but eventually the Sikhs suffered heavy casualties and were initially ordered to withdraw. During the night however, the orders were cancelled.

At midnight a patrol of Sikhs took up a position at the Jitra Bridge. At first light the Japanese brought heavy concentration of mortar and artillery fire on the bridge. The initial attack on the bridge was repulsed with grenades, but small groups of Japanese managed to infiltrate between the Sikh and the adjacent Dogra companies. The attacks were repulsed by 'D' Company who re-established the Dogra line. The Japanese barrage then switched to the road axis. The CO of the Battalion then decided to withdraw. "D" Company and was sent back to a covering position. After close fighting the Sikhs broke off combat and withdrew suffering almost 350 casualties. Two British Officers had been killed, two Companies were virtually wiped out and a number of well trained junior leaders killed. The battle was fought at a position from which retreat was to be inevitable. The withdrawal from Jitra to Alor Star was on 12TH December 1941, a day after the initial contact.

Malaya 1942

The battle at Jitra determined the course of the war in Northern Malaya. It was expected to hold out for about 60 days but the battles at Jitra lasted only 2 days. From Jitra, subsequent defending positions were loosely prepared amidst falling morale and positions fell rapidly to the Japanese whose advance picked up momentum against loosely defended positions.

Alor Star

From Jitra, the Japanese advanced to Alor Star, the state capital of Kedah. As the British retreated Southwards from Jitra the Japanese advance swept into the town of Alor Star. The Japanese found the Alor Star airfield virtually intact. Bombs were stacked in neat piles waiting to be loaded. In an adjoining rubber plantation 1000 drums of high octane aviation fuel was left abandoned. In the RAF Officers' mess, porridge, still hot and ready to be served, was left amid the polished silver on the long dining tables. By midday the Japanese began flying their aircraft in from Singora and Patani in South Thailand. In the evening a squadron of Japanese light bombers, fuelled by captured gasoline and bombs, attacked the retreating British forces who, in their haste, even forgot their demolition-before-departure drill.

Penang

From 8TH of December 1941, the Malayan island of Penang was bombed daily by the Japanese. Untenable, the island was abandoned on 17TH December. Again, arms, boats, supplies and a working radio station were left in haste. The evacuation from Penang left the local population at the mercy of the Japanese. The hasty withdrawal caused much embarrassment to the British and alienated them from the locals. Historians judged that "the moral collapse of British rule in Southeast Asia came not at Singapore, but at Penang"

Perak River

The frontline defences at the Perak River, the next line of defence after Penang, were in complete disarray. British Indian troops were exhausted and fatigued and suffered seriously from lack of rest and food. They were rattled by persistent Japanese air attacks and had no answer to the Japanese's' superior ground tactics that highlighted encirclement, infiltration and outflanking moves. Retreating down the Grik road, 3RD Battalion, 2ND Punjab Regiment blunted the Japanese advance briefly with two well engineered ambushes that inflicted heavy casualties on the Japanese. These were the final British actions West of the Perak River. The eventual withdrawal across the Perak River via the Iskandar Bridge was effected with the bridge blown to impede the Japanese advance.

Malaya 1942

Kampar

Kampar was to be the strongest British defence position along the West coast in the campaign and the battle for it ranged from 28TH December 1941 to 2ND January 1942.

The 15TH and 28TH Indian Brigade Groups took up defensive positions around Kampar. General Percival staked much on it to hold and deny the Japanese the central approach. Opposing the British defences were the Imperial Guards, the Okabe Regiment and the Ando Regiment. Patrolling throughout the day by both sides resulted in frequent skirmishes starting from 28th December 1941. Late at night the four-day battle began. British artillery ranged onto Japanese positions. Japanese commanders, suffering some front-line casualties reinforced with fresh troops. The Japanese reached the British Battalions perimeter at 7 pm, 28TH December 1941. Though the Japanese had the advantage of unopposed air and tank support, the terrain around Kampar proved to be ideal for the defending forces. British artillery and mortars caught several Japanese units in the open and inflicted heavy casualties and impeded Japanese manoeuvres. The Argylls especially, North of the town, repulsed attack after attack. Kampar's defences remain firmly in British hands over the next 3 days. Attacks continued but were beaten back. In one attack, a Sikh company of 1ST Battalion, 18TH Punjab Regiment defeated a furious Japanese attack with a classic bayonet charge through massive mortar and machinegun fire. Only 30 members of the Company survived but the position held out.

But disaster soon struck. A message from Changkat Jong, command post located South of Kampar, on the evening of 2ND January 1942 sealed Kampar's fate. The Japanese were directly threatening the main supply route from the South, so an inevitable withdrawal had to be effected. British gunners laid down intense artillery barrages to mask their withdrawal. Fearing a major counter attack by the British, exhausted Japanese commanders, considered retreating. Then to their surprise the British began to retreat towards Slim River village, some 70 kilometres South. Engineers demolished bridges and laid minefields before the withdrawal. Despite this, the Japanese advance by the infantry with light personal equipment and bicycles, found its momentum again soon after and were hot on the tail of the withdrawing forces.

Slim River

The British retreat to prepared positions in the Slim River area intensified with forces withdrawn from the Telok Anson and Bernam River. Japanese tanks spearheaded by troops of the Ando Regiment, pressed down the main North-South trunk route onto British forward defence positions at Trolak. In the heavy fighting several tanks were destroyed. But the advance continued following the arrival of tank reinforcements. This did not last long. Fearful of losses, Scottish defenders retreated further. A communications breakdown prevented British rear defences from receiving updated reports of the Japanese thrust. Confusion set in.

Malaya 1942

The Slim River road bridge fell to the Japanese intact and trapped the Indian 11TH Division's 12TH and 28TH Brigades. About 3,200 soldiers, surrendered to the Japanese along with 23 heavy artillery pieces, six aircraft guns, 50 armoured cars, 550 other motor vehicles and large quantities of food, ammunition and medical supplies. The victorious Japanese delightedly proclaim the battle spoils "Churchill Supplies." The Slim River debacle blasted away all hopes of saving central Malaya.

Kluang

On January 30TH, 1942, a Sikh Battalion sprung an ambush on a strong Japanese party North of Kluang, Johor, state just North of Singapore. The Japanese were surprised with a bayonet charge by the Sikhs. Sikhs launched a charge on Japanese positions and captured 250 motor cycles and 150 bicycles and machine gun posts. Two small field guns and many mortars which were tied on the bicycles and Tommy-guns were also destroyed. About 400 Japanese casualties were inflicted.

Niyor

On January 24TH, 5TH Sikhs advanced from Kluang to join the Brigade at Niyor. The Battalion had covered 11 miles and was within 2 miles of Niyor, when they came under Japanese fire. The forward platoon of the advance guard commanded by Jemadar Nagindar Singh out-flanked the road block and engaged the enemy. Jemadar Nagindar Singh dropped 12 Japanese beyond the road block and engaged other enemy, in shallow trenches on the crest beyond. Jemadar Nagindar Singh received a burst of Japanese fire on his shoulder. His Platoon Havildar Dalip Singh was mortally hit about a minute later. The immediate seizure of the ground had fore-stalled the enemy, who ceased their fire and withdrew. Jemadar Nagindar Singh was awarded the Indian Order of Merit. He later died as a Prisoner of War. On January 25TH the Japanese offensive commenced again. A counter attack on the Japanese was ordered preceded by artillery and mortar concentration. A Sikh Company swept forward with Havildar Lehna Singh well to the fore. The attack was met by a somewhat ragged Japanese fire. With shouts of "Sat Siri Akal", Sikhs charged the crest. The Japanese hastily left their positions some of them throwing away their arms in an effort to escape, the rest were bayoneted. On January 28TH during a grim fight, Subedar Sampuran Singh and Jemadar Ajit Singh claimed to have hit about 80 Japanese, while the remainder bolted into the jungle. Many gallant deeds were performed during the fight. Sepoy Basta Singh had already displayed marked courage and leadership in the defence of the ferry at Kuantan on 31ST December. He was badly wounded in the knee, and was left lying in a position exposed to Japanese fire. From his position he observed two Japanese in a tree top some 200 yards away. He shouted to a Light Machine Gunner 10 yards away to bring him his light machine gun. The latter refused.

Malaya 1942

Thereupon Basta Singh, despite his shattered knee, crawled over to the light machine gun and took possession of the gun and shot down both Japanese. Later in the fight, two men were wounded in an effort to get to evacuate him. He shouted to his Platoon Commander not to send any one else but to shoot him before they left.

The Brigadier now decided to march through the jungle to make contact with 8TH Brigade in the vicinity of Sedenak. The suffering of the wounded during this nightmare march was unspeakable. The stoicism and heroism was beyond comment. Five of the Sikhs died during the march. Many of them had reached the limit of their endurance. Not many troops in this campaign had endured so much and fought so hard and so successfully. Owing to the complete exhaustion of the remnants of the Brigade, 5TH Battalion, 11TH Sikh Regiment decided to capitulate.

The Causeway

The British forces finally made their way to Johore Bahru, from where the planned move across the causeway to Singapore was made. They managed to keep transport bottlenecks to a minimum. The planned spoiling Japanese action from the West failed to materialise and as darkness descended, the retreat across the Causeway began unopposed. Under the silent moonlight 3RD Corps, the original Northern defenders, departed without incident. Gradually through the night, the forces crossed the causeway to their new positions in Singapore. At 8.15 am the following morning, Indian sappers blasted a 70-foot wide gap in the Causeway. Malaya was lost.

1ST Battalion, 13TH Frontier Force Rifles

The 1ST Battalion, 13TH Frontier Force Rifles' role in the Malaya Campaign was a nostalgic experience. At the start of the campaign, the Battalion landed at Penang, and carried out reconnaissance in Perak, Selangor, Negri Semblan and other vulnerable points. It then proceeded to support the troops holding the Kota Bahru aerodrome. As they reached the aerodrome, it was in flames as the retiring gunners had set fire to the petrol dumps making all movements plainly visible. Heavy fighting for control of the aerodrome took place and the Battalion slowly withdrew pursued by the Japanese. On the 26TH January 1942, as the Frontiersmen continued their retreat, they came into contact with the Japanese. A fierce encounter took place and the Sikh Company with the cry of "Sat Siri Akal" charged home with bayonets, turning the table on the Japanese. Some thirty Japanese were killed, and a small mortar and a number of light automatics captured. The Battalion continued its retreat and reached Kulai, twenty miles North of Johore Bahru. On 1ST February the Frontiersmen crossed the Johore Bahru causeway to Singapore. The battle for Singapore ensued.

SINGAPORE

Singapore, an island at the Southern end of the Malay Peninsula, was considered a vital part of the British Empire and supposedly impregnable as a fortress. The Japanese onslaught through the Malay Peninsula took everybody by surprise. Speed was of the essence for the Japanese, never allowing the British forces time to re-group. This was the first time British forces had come up against a full-scale attack by the Japanese. To stop the Japanese advance, Singapore had a garrison of 90,000 men, British, Indian and Australian troops. On 8TH February, the Japanese landed in the North-West of the island and within six days they were on the outskirts of Singapore city, which was also under constant air attack. The Japanese prepared for the invasion of Singapore with a heavy bombardment. They began their amphibious landings on the North-West of the island, where the Strait of Johore is narrowest. Twenty-four hours later a second Japanese landing force struck between the Causeway and the mouth of the Kranji River. The Australian, British and Indian troops tried to hold the Japanese at various defensive lines but after two days many of their dreadfully depleted Battalions had to be reorganised into composite units. A counter-attack on 10TH and 11TH February failed and by 13TH February the Japanese were within five kilometres of the Singapore waterfront. The entire city was now within range of Japanese artillery. Official evacuations from Singapore had begun in late January and continued until almost the last moment. By 14TH February the Japanese had captured Singapore's reservoirs and pumping stations. The bombing, fighting and heavy shelling continued; many of the troops, separated from their units, wandered around aimlessly and the hospitals were crowded and overflowing. Some troops were deserting and others had become separated from their units. Hard fighting continued but on 15TH February Lieutenant General Arthur Percival, the British Commander in Singapore, called for a ceasefire and made the difficult decision to surrender. He signed the surrender document that evening at the Ford Factory on Bukit Timah Road. After days of desperate fighting, British Empire troops laid down their arms at 8.30 that night. More than 100,000 troops became prisoners of war together with hundreds of European civilians who were interned.

Reformatory Road

On the morning of 11TH February 1942 in the action on Reformatory Road on Singapore Island where a Company of 1ST Punjab Regiment held the forward position of the Brigade. The Company was being subjected to heavy shelling; continuous mortar and light machine gun fire, sustaining heavy casualties to its forward Platoons. Subedar Jaswant Singh immediately commenced to rally the Company, got up reinforcements, reorganized the position, and had casualties removed, he continually encouraged and heightened the morale of his Company. For his gallant behavior, leadership and disregard of personal danger he was awarded the Military Cross on 19TH December 1942.

Singapore

Mount Pleasant
On 13TH February 1942, Jemadar Amar Singh of the Hong Kong and Singapore Royal Artillery, was in command of a 40 mm gun. This particular position was subjected to persistent and repeated bombing and machine gun attacks by low flying aircraft throughout the day. Jemadar Amar Singh fought with his gun in the coolest possible manner, never failing to engage a suitable target and bringing down at least one Japanese aircraft and certainly damaging others. This action was an inspiration to neighboring units and was an outstanding feature of the day's fighting. For his outstanding courage and tenacity, Jemadar Amar Singh was awarded the Military Cross in 1942.

Captain Pritam Singh
Captain Pritam Singh of 16TH Punjab Regiment was wounded during the battle of Singapore, and taken prisoner by the Japanese. He escaped from the notorious Nee Soon Prisoner of War Camp and made his way through Malaya, Thailand, Burma, reaching India after over six months of life-threatening experiences. In so doing he travelled thousands of kilometers through enemy territory on foot, boat and train. Captain Pritam Singh was awarded the coveted Military Cross for exemplary courage and resolve. Pritam Singh later served in the Army of Independent India and retired with the rank of Brigadier.

Lieutenant Colonel Gurbaksh Singh
Throughout the operations in Malaya, Lieutenant Colonel Gurbaksh Singh commanded a Battalion, which was responsible for the defence of two main aerodromes in Singapore. These areas were regularly and heavily bombed, and later dive-bombed and machine-gunned. Lieutenant Colonel Gurbaksh Singh was most successful in avoiding heavy casualties in his unit by skilful dispositions of his troops and effective command. He maintained a very high standard of morale and efficiency, for which his own gallant bearing under fire and his determined personality were responsible. In the later stages of the fighting when the forward troops withdrew in the Tengah area, leaving the flanks of the aerodrome unprotected, the Battalion defended their position on 10TH and 11TH February with commendable tenacity, inflicting heavy casualties on the Japanese. The Battalion eventually withdrew in good order, having suffered considerable losses after the action of which an Indian State Force Unit should well be proud. Subsequently Lieutenant Colonel Gurbaksh Singh took a prominent part in the defence of the outskirts of Singapore, where he again displayed a high degree of courage and leadership under continuous shelling and mortar machine gun fire. Lieutenant Colonel Gurbaksh Singh was awarded the DSO on 13TH December 1945. For his outstanding loyalty, leadership and personal example whilst in captivity in Singapore Lieutenant Colonel Gurbaksh Singh was awarded the OBE. Gurbaksh Singh later served in the Army of Independent India and retired with the rank of Lieutenant General.

BURMA

Burma had been administered from India until April, 1937. After separation the country had achieved a degree of self-government though was still effectively controlled by the British through the Governor. The Government of Burma was responsible for the defence of the country and for financing the armed forces and acquiring stores and equipment from the British War Office.

The strategic significance of Burma for the defence of the region was not lost on British senior Commanders and from 1937 onwards it was argued that forces in Burma should be controlled by the Commander-in-Chief in India. This was finally decided on 11TH December, 1941 by Prime Minister Churchill and the Chiefs of Staff. After separation from India in April 1937, responsibility for the defence of Burma lay with the Government of Burma. The Burma Army became a small, independent military command formed by the transfer of Units from the Indian Army. The first Commander of the Burma Army was Major General D.K. McLeod. The separation resulted in the transfer of 'The Burma Rifles' (Sikhs, Punjabis, and Gurkhas) and six Battalions of the Burma Military Police which became the 'Burma Frontier Force' (Sikhs, Punjabis, and Gurkhas) administered by the Defence Department and under the command of the GOC, Burma Army. The Burma Rifles were expanded, their strength being doubled, as was the Burma Frontier Force. In April 1941, 13TH Indian Infantry Brigade arrived in Burma from India and was stationed initially in Mandalay. The three Brigade groups in the country were formed into 1ST Burma Division in July 1941, with divisional HQ at Taungoo, under the command of Major General J Bruce Scott. At the end of November, 16TH Indian Infantry Brigade began arriving from Calcutta and was placed under the direct command of Burma Army HQ. The Brigade was the last reinforcement to arrive before the Japanese invasion.

At various times, 5TH Indian Division, 7TH Indian Division, 14TH Indian Division, 17TH Indian Division, 19TH Indian Division, 20TH Indian Divison, 23RD Indian Division, 25TH Indian Division, 26TH Indian Division Campaign and 1ST Burma Brigade, fought in Burma.

Japanese Invasion, (1941)

Within a week of their initial attacks across Southeast Asia on 8TH December 1941, the Japanese had reached Burma, and after air raids on the Burmese capital, Rangoon, they began invading from Siam early in 1942. The Indian, British and Burmese troops were forced to commence a long withdrawal. By 9TH March, the Japanese had captured Rangoon. In April, they crushed the Chinese, in May they pushed the Allied British and Indian forces back into India. By the end of 1942, the Japanese had consolidated their position in Burma. One of the most difficult places on earth to fight with its thick jungles, razorback mountains, steep wild valleys and a plethora of debilitating and deadly tropical diseases. Recapturing the country would take the Allies 14TH Army, known with bitterly realistic humour as the 'Forgotten Army', three years of desperate fighting, predominately by the Indian Army, with the Sikh soldier in the vanguard.

Burma

Rangoon, (1942)

Japanese troops appeared at Rangoon's doorsteps toward the end of February 1942. The British 7TH Armored Brigade attempted to counterattack the Japanese troops marching from the direction of the Sittang River, but failed. On 6TH March, Japanese troops reached the city and the final evacuation order was given by British Officers on the next day.

The Retreat, (1942)

The remaining forces retreated into India. Japanese forces captured the entire country of Burma, including the important airfields in Myitkyina near the Chinese border. All but two of the Burma Rifles' Battalions came apart; many of the soldiers deserted, fearing for their family's safety at the mercy of the Japanese. The most steadfast soldiers in the Burma Rifles were Sikhs, the Punjabis and Gurkhas. The Burma Army had carried out the longest withdrawal in the history of the British Army, 1,100 miles under the most testing conditions. Outnumbered, lacking air superiority, and with the majority of the soldiers badly trained, they had learned and learned fast. Elements of the retreating Burma Army began arriving at Tamu, India during May 1942. The 17TH Indian Division was retained at Imphal to reform with 48TH and 16TH Brigades while 63RD Brigade was centered on Kohima protecting the lines of communications and tracks from the Naga Hills. The 1ST Burma Division, "Burdiv", and its Brigades were now dispersed, later to be redesignated and organised as 39TH Indian Division. The 1ST Burma Brigade became 106TH Indian Infantry Brigade in June 1942 and with 113TH (formerly 13TH) Indian Infantry Brigade, came under command of 39TH Division. Practically all units and headquarters of the Burma Army were disbanded during May 1942.

General Situation (1942)

Before proceeding with a detailed account of the forthcoming Sikh soldier's gallantry, it might prove convenient to explain very briefly the general situation at that time. The British intention was to advance as soon as preparations were complete, and make a combined land and sea attack on Akyab. Akyab had been the objective of the earlier and unsuccessful Arakan campaign, and it would prove a valuable acquisition, as the only sea-port of any importance in the Arakan. Accordingly, when 5TH Indian Division arrived, it moved into the coastal sector North of Maungdaw, while 7TH Indian Divison crossed the Mayu Range into the country to the East. Initial operations in the early winter took the form of small advances with the intention of closing on the Japanese forward positions North of the Maungdaw-Buthidaung road.

Burma

Akyab, (1943)

General Wavell, Theatre Commander for Burma, decided to take some offensive action. He saw that the small Burmese port of Akyab was only lightly garrisoned. On an island and with an airfield, it would be a very useful place to posses and should be easy to hold and defend. In January 1943, Indian troops were given the task of advancing along the Burmese coast to Akyab. This was done by 14TH Indian Division. They found only light Japanese resistance and many Japanese posts were manned by just a few soldiers.

The real problem for the Allies was the environment. Burma was criss-crossed with jungle, mountains, rivers and mangrove swamps. Moving equipment was a nightmare across such hazardous terrain and worse was the constant threat of disease. Malaria was a very real problem. Where the Japanese were stationed, they had dug themselves in. This made attacking them difficult as their bunkers had been well constructed and well camouflaged. Most could only be destroyed by heavy artillery and moving such equipment about in Burma was extremely difficult. Combined with the well-placed and well-built bunkers, was the fighting spirit of the Japanese, who fought until death. Inspite of persistent efforts the British could make little progress on the Donbaik front of Akyab. Earlier Captain Ujagar Singh Dhillon of 'A' Company of 2ND Battalion, 1ST Punjab Regiment had been killed leading his men.

Meanwhile, the 'D' Company had advanced with great gallantry on the right. The Company, under the command of Captain Budh Singh, advanced over the open and bullet-swept country and captured its objective. At that moment both its flanks lay open, owing to the Japanese–occupied position on its left and the momentary absence of the Enniskillen Fusiliers on the right. Terrific fire on the front and flanks took a heavy toll on the attackers. Captain Budh Singh realized that all that he could do now was to withdraw across the open to his original position. This he did with cool courage, collecting as many of the wounded men as he could on his way back. The Company strength was reduced to forty-four through casualties, including Jemadar Surjan Singh and Havildar Major Indar Singh, both Platoon Commanders wounded. For his gallantry during this engagement Captain Budh Singh was awarded the Military Cross. The attack had cost 2ND Battalion 131 casualties. The 14TH Indian Division, after six weeks, had to pull back as a result of a Japanese counter-attack.

In March, 1943, Major Sarbjit Singh Kalha took over the command of 2ND Battalion, 1ST Punjab Regiment. He was the first Indian to command a Battalion of the Regiment.

Donbaik, (1943)

On January 6TH, 1943, near the Japanese-occupied village of Donbaik, Havildar Parkash Singh of 5TH Battalion, 8TH Punjab Regiment, was a 28 year old serving in the Bren Gun Carrier. His Battalion was engaged in fighting against Japanese forces, when the following deed took place, for which he was awarded the VC.

Burma

Hitzwe, (1943)

On March 8TH 1943, 2ND Battalion, 1ST Punjab Regiment, moved upto the front line at Hitzwe. "D" Company commanded by Captain Budh Singh, was the first to experience the momentum of the Japanese offensive. Six successive waves of Japanese assaulted in vain against the Battalion, which repulsed the enemy with heavy casualties, estimated at about 100 killed and many wounded. Soon after, the Battalion was told to take up another rearward position, where "D" Company was again the first to be attacked. Just before dawn on 14TH, about 300 Japanese attacked Jemadar Kalyan Singh's Platoon, guarding the left flank of the Battalion headquarters. Captain Budh Singh, hastened with reinforcements to his Platoon, took charge of the situation and repulsed the assailants, who left seventy three dead around the position. Captain Budh Singh was awarded a bar to his Military Cross for his valiant leadership of "D" Company during this action. But the Japanese managed to infiltrate into the Company's camp in the rear, where they killed or captured most of the occupants. In a successful counter attack the Japanese were badly shaken and started running away across open paddy-fields, where they were caught by guns, mortars and light automatics. Altogether, 103 dead Japanese were counted. Subedar Surjit Singh was awarded the Military Cross for his exceptional leadership in mounting the counter attack with very young and raw men.

Tiddim, (1943)

In late September the Japanese showed signs of activity in the Chin Hills. Alarmed by the Japanese build up, it was decided to concentrate the whole of 17TH Division at Tiddim. The 1ST Battalion, 16TH Punjab Regiment was loaned to 17TH Division and was ordered to move to Tiddim by forced marches, arriving there on 1ST November. The Battalion occupied the Milestone 52 position on 2ND November. Shortly afterwards dust was seen in the valley to the North. It was suspected that the Japanese might be building a track on a similar spur to the one occupied by the Battalion, which ran into the road at Milestone 54. On 9TH November, Major Lawford led a strong fighting patrol to ambush the Japanese road building parties. Moving by night the patrol ran into a Japanese position overlooking the Khwe Lui crossing. In a night of sharp action, both sides suffered casualties, the patrol withdrawing with 6 wounded and 2 missing. This action showed that the Japanese had been considerably re-inforced. Events now moved fast. On 12TH November in bright moonlight a Japanese Company attacked the "B" Company Platoon on point 6531. The Platoon under Jemadar Ishar Singh shot steadily and well, repelling repeated Japanese attacks. Jemadar Ishar Singh was awarded and I.D.S.M. for his fine leadership.

Burma

Kalapanzin Valley, (1944

On 5TH February 1944 Lance Naik Kernail Singh of 1ST Battalion, 11TH Sikh Regiment, was a Section Commander in a Platoon ordered to attack the enemy in a position in a hill feature near Linbali in the Kalalpanzin Valley. The Platoon penetrated into the enemy position and preparatory to making the final assault, had reached a point about 50 yards from the top of the feature, when they came under extremely heavy light machine gun, grenade and rifle fire. Very soon only nine men were left unwounded. The Company Commander, who was present and wounded, decided that the Platoon was insufficiently strong to overcome the enemy's resistance and ordered a withdrawal. The Company Havildar Major, with Lance Naik Kernail Singh and one Sepoy, continued to advance with the intention of covering the withdrawal of the Platoon, which was hampered by the presence of many wounded men. The Company Havildar Major was killed almost immediately and the Sepoy wounded, whereupon, Lance Naik Kernail Singh, his Tommy gun out of action, seized a light machine gun and continued alone. He was last seen advancing on the enemy position firing the machine gun from the hip. This act of gallantry and self-sacrifice on the part of Lance Naik Kernail Singh caused a diversion sufficient to enable the remainder of the Platoon, with its casualties, to withdraw without further loss. His body was found lying across a trench in which there were three dead Japanese, in the heart of the enemy position. He was awarded posthumous Indian Order of Merit.

Ngakyedauk Pass, (1944)

From 7TH to 10TH February 1944, between Kreingyaug and East of Ngakyedauk Pass, during repeated attacks on the gun position, Jemadar Kartar Singh of the Indian Artillery, showed great initiative and complete disregard for his own safety. For his gallant leadership, Jemadar Kartar Singh was awarded an immediate Military Cross on 10TH February 1944. On 10TH February 1944, while advancing to its objective, 2ND Battalion, 1ST Punjab Regiment, was held up by the Japanese in a strongly entrenched position, the Commanding Officer was killed almost immediately. Subadar Gurbachan Singh carried on and silenced the post by courageously crawling forward and throwing grenades at the post. Five Other Ranks were killed and seven Other Ranks wounded. As no further progress could be made, Subadar Gurbachan Singh, with the dead and wounded withdrew on the following morning. For his gallant conduct and leadership Subedar Gurbachan Singh was awarded the Military Cross.

During the operations in the Ngakyedauk pass, a Sikh Platoon in 'A' Company, of 2ND Battalion, 1ST Punjab Regiment commanded by Subedar Munsha Singh, successfully attacked Pt.1070. Next day the Platoon, with a bayonet charge, drove the enemy from his positions. Again fighting in the Litan area the Sikhs were conspicuous for their excellent work. Subedar Munsha Singh was severely wounded leading a counter attack on a strongly held Japanese position. For his courage and determination, Subedar Munsha Singh was strongly recommended for and awarded the Military Cross on 12TH March 1944.

Burma

Mayu Range, (1944)

Subedar Mangal Singh commanded No. 6 Platoon of 'D' Company, 2nd Battalion, 1st Punjab Regiment on the Mayu Range front in Burma. On 19th February 1944, this Company was ordered to attack and capture the feature 391523, the only approach to which was over a very narrow knife-edge, covered the whole way by enemy medium machine guns. The Platoon successfully captured the enemy's forward post, destroyed a medium machine gun, and a section of seven enemies at very small loss to itself. Soon afterwards another pocket of enemy was spotted about 30 yards away, and Subedar Mangal Singh charged at them with his two sections, but unfortunately came under a shower of grenades from two previously undiscovered enemy positions, and half the force became casualties, he himself being wounded in the left arm. He successfully brought all his casualties back and to reach the seriously wounded, he had to creep right forward, while doing so another grenade blew most of his right toe off but this did not deter this daring and fearless leader, who carried the wounded man back to his trenches and continued to command his Platoon until relieved later. Subedar Mangal Singh, during this action and throughout the previous and present campaign had shown the finest example of gallantry, daring and leadership and had earned the praise of all ranks. He was strongly recommended for and awarded the Military Cross on 25th February 1944.

Sikh Hill, (1944)

On 20th February 1944, in Burma, Subedar Gulcharan Singh commanded a Platoon of 1st Battalion, 11th Sikh Regiment, which had been ordered to carry out an attack on an enemy position. When the Platoon had reached its rendezvous two of his men were wounded by enemy mortar fire (one fatally) and the Platoon came under light machine gun fire from the hill feature. Disregarding these mishaps, the Platoon advanced below the feature called Sikh Hill. When the covering fire ceased the attacking Platoon was within 50 yards of the enemy's positions. A shower of grenades and light machine gun fire some 20 yards from the enemy halted the forward section, three men having been wounded and one killed. Covered by a few mortar bombs from the rear and grenades from the leading section, the Platoon now attacked from the right. This attack was also checked when three men were wounded. A third attack was then made on the left, again being halted after one man had been killed and one wounded. So far the Platoon had suffered two men killed and seven wounded. Subedar Gulcharan Singh's Platoon was now in a semi circle about 15 yards from the enemy, who was in a strong entrenched position. Headquarters had now reinforced the Platoon with three sections, two of which were covering the right flank. A general attack was then made, during which some of the enemy left their trenches and ran away. Other Japanese stuck it out; Jemadar Gulcharan Singh personally shot one and bayoneted another.

Burma

Sikh Hill, (Cont.)

The remainder were bombed out. He now took a patrol forward to search the Southern and Western slopes of Sikh Hill. He moved two parties along two parallel spurs. About 30 yards from the main position he saw a party of seven Japanese in a Nullah between the two spurs and was immediately attacked. Three were killed from a burst by a light machine gun and as the other four were trying to escape, Jemadar Gulcharan Singh ordered the rest of his patrol on the other side to get forward. This they did, sighting the Japanese and killing them all with rifle and light machine gun fire. From the moment that the orders for the attack were issued until the last Japanese was killed, Jemadar Gulcharan Singh was an inspiration to his men and to the whole Company. Jemadar Gulcharan Singh was awarded the Military Cross on 22ND February 1944.

Buthidaung, (1944)

The Japanese had attempted an invasion of India, beginning in the coastal strip of Arakan. There, a Platoon of 1ST Battalion, 11TH Sikh Regiment was sent to observe a Japanese post and seize it if possible, which they did. They then fought off violent counter-attacks, after which the position was surrounded, preventing re-supply. Asked by radio how long they could hold out, the Platoon commandeer replied: "Without food for six more days; without ammunition, as long as you like, we have the bayonets." It was no idle boast, as the Sikhs repeatedly proved.

Nat Taung, (1944)

At Nat Taung, Kabaw Valley, on 11TH March 1944, Jemadar Bahadur Singh of 2ND Battalion, 13TH Frontier Force Rifles, was in command of a Platoon, which furnished observations and listening posts in the area. On the night of 11TH March the Platoon had been attacked by the enemy. These enemy attacks were all broken up with heavy losses. Jemadar Bahadur Singh continued to repulse and the enemy was severely mauled during these actions. Throughout these engagements Jemadar Bahadur Singh displayed skill, judgment and courage of the highest order for which he was awarded the Indian Order of Merit.

Sikh soldiers during the Burma campaign, 1944.

Burma

Ngakyedauk Pass, (1944)

On the night of 24TH/25TH March 1944, East of the Ngakyedauk Pass in Arakan, a party of the enemy, estimated about one Company, infiltrated behind the forward positions and occupied a ridge overlooking the East Gate of the Administrative Base. It was of vital importance that this ridge should be captured without delay, in order that the road to the Administrative Base could be opened. Jemadar Didar Singh of 1ST Battalion, 11TH Sikh Regiment was ordered to take his Platoon and attack and capture the end of the ridge overlooking the main road. The leading section of the Jemadar's Platoon came under heavy enemy fire as it approached the top of the ridge and was held up. He dashed forward and led the section on, under heavy fire, to capture the forward line of trenches of his objective. The Platoon was again held up on this line by heavy fire from the second line of enemy trenches. In spite of this fire at point blank range, Jemadar Didar Singh got up and bombarded the enemy with hand grenades. This forced the enemy to withdraw further along the ridge to their main positions and enabled the Jemadar to capture and secure the whole of his objective. Twelve of the enemy were killed while withdrawing along the ridge.

The enemy main position was to be attacked from the other end of the ridge to that which Jemadar Didar Singh had captured. In this attack Didar Singh was instructed to give covering fire to the attacking Platoons and to destroy any enemy trying to make their escape. Although these attacks made considerable initial progress, they were held up before reaching their final objective by four light machine guns located some 100 yards in front of his position. As soon as Jemadar Didar Singh saw that the covering fire had not silenced these machine guns and the attack could make no further progress, he led a patrol and tried to destroy the machine guns with grenades. This involved a difficult advance along a knife-edge ridge under considerable fire. Jemadar Didar Singh got his patrol forward with great skill and dash, and succeeded in throwing a number of grenades on the enemy guns. He was, however, hit by enemy grenades in the chest and killed while in the act of throwing a further grenade on the enemy. Jemadar Didar Singh was awarded a posthumous Military Cross.

Sikh platoon in Burma including Naik Nand Singh VC

Burma

Maungdaw-Buthidaung, (1944)

In Arakan, Burma, whilst engaged on operations for the capture of the Westraji Tunnel on the Maungdaw-Buthidaung road on 26th March 1944, Jemadar Nand Singh of the Indian Engineers was in charge of his section erecting an S.B.G. Bridge, over a bridge which had been demolished by the enemy. The work was carried out under fire from enemy snipers. He organised the whole of this task, which was not finished until the following morning. During the night there were Japanese in close proximity and the Section was sniped and mortared. As soon as the bridge was finished, this enabled tanks to get up to the mouth of the Tunnel and to clear the enemy. Later in the operations in the Eastern Tunnel, with some of his section, he lifted enemy mines laid on the road near the Tunnel and carried out a reconnaissance into the enemy territory. During the whole period his keenness, despite the danger from enemy action, set a high example to his men which inspired them with confidence, and by his leadership enabled them to carry out their duties in a highly efficient manner, for which Jemadar Nand Singh was awarded the Military Cross on 26TH October 1944.

Buthidaung, (1944)

On 1ST April 1944, Subedar Sham Singh of 5TH Battalion, 16TH Punjab Regiment was in command of a recce patrol, on a position Southwest of Buthidaung, which was ambushed and encircled by jungle set on fire by the enemy. Subedar Sham Singh kept complete control of his patrol and fought his way out of the ambush, wiping out an enemy light machine gun and killing at least four of the enemy. In this action Subedar Sham Singh was wounded but refused to leave his Company. On the following day Subedar Sham Singh led another patrol against the enemy. After personal recce of a route used by the enemy, he set up an ambush in which 25 Japanese were killed and injuries inflicted on the ones fleeing the ambush. Again on 3RD April, Subedar Sham Singh led a patrol of two sections to the South of Comma position where they encountered the enemy in superior strength. With great dash and gallantry the Subedar personally lead his Patrol in a charge. In the ensuing hand-to-hand fighting six of the enemy were killed with the bayonet, ten by rifle fire and at least fifteen more badly wounded with the loss of only two killed to the patrol. Then Subedar Sham Singh skilfully extricated his patrol under heavy Mortar and light machine gun fire, bringing back an enemy body and enemy weapons for identification. He was the last to withdraw after ensuring that his own dead were recovered. In all these actions the Platoon's casualties were extremely light. The success obtained by the patrols in these actions was entirely due to the cool-headedness, clear planning and complete disregard for his own safety of Subedar Sham Singh, who throughout by his leadership, example and determination to close with the enemy was an inspiration to his men, for which Subedar Sham Singh was awarded an immediate Military Cross.

Burma

Wilugyaung, (1944)

On 9TH April, 1944, at Wilugyaung in Burma, Captain Piara Singh of 7TH Battalion, 16TH Punjab Regiment, was sent to the aid and recovery of three Patrols that were cut off by the enemy. After seven days without food and most of his ammunition exhausted, Captain Piara Singh returned through the enemy lines with these Patrols. On 21ST April 1944, at Khomwei a superior Japanese force attacked his position. He drove them back and chased them some two miles across a plain, inflicting severe casualty on them. On 27TH April, at Laukai, where identification of the enemy was required, he captured two Japanese soldiers as a result of a skilful ambush. For his leadership and high standard of courage Captain Piara Singh was strongly recommend for and awarded the Military Cross on 1ST August 1944.

Sanjing, (1944)

On the night of 18TH April 1944, when the Company of 1ST Patiala Rajindra Infantry, under the command of Lieutenant Baldev Singh was occupying an isolated position in Burma; a superior enemy force took up a position close to the Company. On the morning of 19TH April, Lieutenant Baldev Singh was ordered to keep this enemy force occupied, in order to prevent it digging in before the main force arrived to attack the position in the afternoon. Lieutenant Baldev Singh therefore organised constant "Jitter" parties around the enemy position, he himself leading one of these parties in order to raise the moral and self-confidence of his Company. By his bold action and personal example he successfully prevented the enemy digging more than one foot in ten hours. This greatly assisted the main force in capturing the position and saved many casualties. Subsequently, on 28TH April, he led a party of twenty strong on a special mission lasting four days. This party operated in a radius of ten miles from the main base, behind the strong enemy position at Sanjing. In carrying out this mission Lieutenant Baldev Singh's party was for seventy-two hours on the main Japanese line of control, during which time he laid three successful ambushes against superior enemy forces. As a result of these ambushes, 29 of the enemy were killed; three of them by Lieutenant Baldev Singh, and in addition much valuable information obtained. His casualties were one man wounded. The success of this mission was due to the personal gallantry and leadership of Lieutenant Baldev Singh. Lieutenant Baldev Singh's determination, devotion to duty and disregard of personal safety had been noticeable in previous operations in which he had taken part. Lieutenant Baldev Singh was awarded the Military Cross on 15TH August 1944.

Burma

Imphal-Ukhrul Road, (1944)

On 19TH April 1944, a strong enemy force occupied a position between Jemadar Amir Singh's Company and the Imphal-Ukhrul road in Burma. Jemadar Amir Singh of 1ST Patiala Rajindra Infantry was therefore given the task of harassing this enemy force in order to prevent him from digging in before the arrival of the rest of the Battalion. Jemadar Amir Singh led a section, which operated on the enemy's flank and continuously harassed the enemy to great effect. When he was due to be relieved he again volunteered to lead another section, as he considered that his knowledge of the area would be of great assistance. He was eventually recalled for further operations. During the whole of the period he successfully kept the enemy occupied and inflicted a number of casualties on them. Later in the same day Jemadar Amir Singh was commanding a leading Platoon in an attack on a hill feature covering the main enemy position. Under heavy enemy fire, he led his Platoon with such dash and determination that the enemy was forced to beat a hasty retreat. Subsequently another Platoon passed through his position; he then repulsed the enemy counter attack on the flank of the other Platoon, inflicting heavy casualties. Again on 29TH April he commanded a party of 20, which was sent out, with the task of conducting Guerrilla operations on the enemy in the Samshak area. His party operated continuously for 18 hours on the Japanese line of control, and laid several successful ambushes, with the result that at least 12 Japanese were killed, and valuable identifications obtained, without any loss to his party. Throughout these operations Jemadar Amir Singh led his Platoon with skill and determination, for which he was awarded the Military Cross on 16TH August 1944.

Sakpao, (1944)

During April, 1ST Patiala Rajindra Infantry was ordered to take the village of Sokpao. Very careful recce were made on the morning of 19TH for the main attack, which was to go in up a spur just West of the main road. The "D" Company rose up at the start line and rushed forward, shouting the Patiala battle cry, "Sat Sri Akal." The Japanese, taken by surprise, were overwhelmed and in nine minutes the position had been captured. The fight had only begun. Six minutes later, when "D" Company was still hastily reorganizing, the Japanese came from the East and hurled themselves on the rear of the Company. There was no time to take up fire positions; the Company Commander charged with his reserve at the oncoming Japanese; he fell in the hand-to-hand grapple, but his action checked the enemy for the moment. Five minutes later the Japanese came again, a little father down the ridge and was held by "B" Company, but he was not yet spent; a nine-minute interval and he came a third time between "B" Company and Battalion H.Q. Colonel Balwant Singh did not hesitate; as one of his Officers had done a few minutes earlier, he charged magnificently into the fray at the head of his H.Q. The Japanese were halted at last.

Burma

Sakpao, (Cont.)

The Patiala account of these tremendous affairs runs: "Balance of the battle from 1425 to 1455 hours simply hanged round the gutts, it was anybody's battle during this time." The day cost the Patialas sixty six casualties. On 19TH April 1944, during an attack on Sakpao, Jemadar Rakha Singh of 1ST Patiala Rajindra Infantry was ordered to capture a steep hill overlooking Sakpao. The enemy had established himself on this hill but Jemadar Rakha Singh, by skilful use of the ground, completely surprised the enemy and carried the position at the point of the bayonet, making the enemy withdraw hurriedly and in disorder. Later, when his Company Commander was killed and he was severely wounded, he with great determination and disregard of his own safety took over the command of the Company and reorganized his defences and met a second counter attack successfully. He refused to be evacuated and remained in command till the arrival of the Company Commander. For his leadership, determination and gallantry Jemadar Rakha Singh was awarded the Military Cross on 21ST May 1944.

Kalalpanzin Valley, (1944)

On the night of $6^{TH}/7^{TH}$ May 1944 Jemadar Mehar Singh of 1ST Battalion, 11TH Sikh Regiment was Commanding the leading Platoon in an attack on an important hill feature in Kalalpanzin Valley. He led his Platoon under the heavy artillery barrage with such dash and determination that the enemy was forced to make a hasty retreat from their covering positions. On 12TH March 1944, Jemadar Mehar Singh's Platoon was ordered to recapture a hill feature overlooking the Maungdaw-Buthidaung road, on to which the enemy had infiltrated during the night. The enemy had constructed deep foxholes and trenches along the top of the knife-edged ridge of the feature. The Jemadar personally led his Platoon on the steep slope of the hill with great determination and dash, under heavy enemy grenade and machine gun fire. He was wounded early on and his Platoon temporarily held up. With complete disregard for his own safety he reorganized his Platoon and led them forward to capture the objective and completely annihilate the enemy Platoon. Jemadar Mehar Singh's brilliant leadership and great bravery enabled his men to kill thirty-three of the enemy and capture all their arms and equipment. The recapture of this hill feature was of vital importance and was held by a very determined enemy. Jemadar Mehar Singh was awarded the Indian Order Merit for his gallant leadership.

Burma

Seitpudaung, (1944)

On 11TH May at Seitpudaung in Burma, Jemadar Kesar Singh of 1ST Battalion, 15TH Punjab Regiment was in command of a fighting Patrol, which suddenly encountered the Japanese in considerably great strength. The Patrol came under heavy fire from Japanese automatic fire and four of the Platoon was wounded immediately, including Jemadar Kesar Singh. As a large party of the enemy moved round the right flank, ignoring his own wounds Jemadar Kesar Singh fought back, inflicting losses on them and by skilful disposition and his own example of steadiness under fire, extricated his Platoon, taking his casualties to Paddaukon Village. The Japanese in greatly superior numbers again attacked and attempted to surround him, but Jemadar Kesar Singh again fought back hard, inflicting casualties and skilfully extricating his Platoon again. He made repeated contact with the enemy and finding all routes blocked by superior numbers of the enemy took up a defensive position for the night.

Next day he continued to encounter superior numbers of Japanese and continued to fight back stoutly, inflicting more casualties on the enemy and succeeding in safeguarding his own increasing casualties. By ignoring his own wounds and by his cheerfulness and personal example, the Jemadar heartened the wounded so that they too made light of their wounds. On the third day Jemadar Kesar Singh, although in pain, so inspired his Platoon that they continued in excellent fighting spirit, fought their way back to their Company line and brought in all their wounded and identifications of enemy killed. The Platoon had been out for 56 hours surrounded by enemy, and, though short of food, had covered many miles in thick jungle and fought with conspicuous success, inflicting many casualties on the enemy. For Jemadar Kesar Singh's high standard of military skill and leadership, his complete disregard of personal safety, his steadiness, and determination he was awarded the Military Cross.

Kanglatongbi (1944)

On 16TH May 1944, at Kangla Tonbi in Burma, two Companies of 2ND Battalion, 2ND Punjab Regiment clashed with the Japanese. Both Companies engaged suffered considerable losses. Among the killed was Subedar Dhera Singh, having twice been awarded the I.O.M. in the Western Desert. Another contact with the Japanese on 14TH September resulted in a short but fierce action, which cost the Punjabis six killed and six wounded. The killed included the then Company Commander, Ram Singh. Also Subedar Pritam Singh, whose gallant conduct on that day was followed by a posthumous award of the Indian Order of Merit. For his gallantry in these actions Subedar Ram Singh was awarded the Military Cross.

Burma

Kohima, (1944)
In Kohima area in Burma on 28TH May 1944, Jemadar Didar Singh of the Burma Regiment led his Platoon in a counter-attack on a position recently captured by the enemy and succeeded in capturing his objective, destroying 2 light machine gun posts and 2 other automatic gun posts, inflicting several casualties on the enemy. For his great coolness and clever leadership, Jemadar Didar Singh was awarded the Military Cross on 15TH October 1944.

Imphal (1944)
At the Imphal Area in Burma, on 28TH May 1944, Subedar Gurdas Singh of 1ST Battalion, 16TH Punjab Regiment was Second in Command of his Company. The Japanese shelled the Battalion position for some three hours, particularly concentrating on his Company's position. The fire was extremely accurate and came mainly from 105 mm guns. These shells in many cases pierced the head cover of the bunkers and the Company suffered heavy casualties. Subedar Gurdas Singh moved from bunker to bunker while the shells were exploding. He bandaged up the wounded in bunkers and encouraged the remainder to stand firm. While moving from bunker to bunker, he was wounded by a bursting shell. Unable to move he refused to leave the Company position until the Company Commander ordered his stretcher-bearers to carry him out. The fearless example displayed by Subedar Gurdas Singh inspired the whole Company with the resolution to hold on at all costs, and undoubtedly contributed to the firmness with which his Company beat off subsequent Japanese attacks. Subedar Gurdas Singh was awarded the Military Cross on 3RD July 1944.

Modhung, (1944)
Lieutenant Pritam Singh of 1ST Battalion, 11TH Sikh was in command of the Mortar Platoon during operations in Burma. The Mortar Platoon was subjected to prolonged enemy attack throughout the whole of a night in May. The Platoon maintained its mortars in action in spite of artillery, mortar, grenade and medium machine gun fire at very close range both on the mortar position and Observation Point. Although the enemy was threatening the mortar position on several occasions the Mortar Platoon fired continuously throughout the action and assisted in no small way in repulsing the enemy with great loss. Lieutenant Pritam Singh carried out difficult patrols behind the enemy lines with great courage and determination. Lieutenant Pritam Singh gave a fine example of this on 30TH May when the enemy commenced shelling his Observation Post while covering an attack near the village of Modhung. He continued to direct the fire of his mortars inspite of shells falling all around him. He brought down such accurate and effective concentrations on the enemy that the leading Platoon was able to get on to its first objective with little loss. He stayed at his Observation Post directing fire of his mortars until he was badly wounded and became too weak to observe fire. For his gallant leadership he was awarded the Military Cross on 6TH October 1944.

Burma

Kanglatongbi, (1944)
In June 1944 a Company of 1ST Battalion, 11TH Sikh Regiment was operating behind the enemy lines North of Kanglatongbi. On one occasion in these operations over seventy Japanese launched a fanatical attack against a Platoon and overran the leading section. Subedar Bishan Singh was wounded early in the action, but he refused to be evacuated and remained with his Platoon. It was partly due to his leadership and determination that the operation was successfully accomplished. Subedar Bishan Singh had been present with the Battalion throughout the Burma campaign and he had at all times displayed outstanding leadership and gallantry. He had been in the forefront of some of the fiercest fighting seen by the Battalion and had been wounded no less than four different occasions when leading his men against the Japanese. He was awarded the Military Cross on 20TH March 1946.

Sirurukhong, (1944)
At Sirurukhong in Burma on 14TH June 1944, Lieutenant Mehar Singh of the Indian Artillery was Forward Observation Officer with a Company, which was attacking the village. Owing to the conformation of the ground and to the number of buildings in the village, observation was very limited; clear fields of view of over thirty yards were rarely available. Lieutenant Mehar Singh accompanied the leading Platoon of the Company in the initial assault onto the forward edge of the village. Immediately on entering the village the Platoon was held up by heavy rifle and light machine gun fire to their front. From the Platoon's position Lieutenant Mehar Singh was unable to pin point accurately the position of the Japanese. Accordingly, he crawled forward until, from a distance of thirty yards, he was able to see the enemy weapon pits. Giving his fire orders from behind a very shallow bund, he brought down fire from the Mountain Battery onto these positions and eliminated them. The Platoon advanced and Lieutenant Mehar Singh accompanied it, moving with the leading section. He was constantly on the alert for targets, and once sighted, engaged them without hesitation and with great accuracy. Lieutenant Mehar Singh displayed complete contempt for personal safety and on several occasions carried out reconnaissance of his targets from forty or fifty yards distance, under persistent and heavy, light and medium machine gun fire. His personal bravery and keenness were exceptional and throughout this action he displayed initiative and dash of a high order in engaging surprise targets. The success of the attacks was, in a large measure, due to the excellent control of the Mountain Battery by Lieutenant Mehar Singh. Lieutenant Mehar Singh was awarded the Military Cross on 12TH August 1944.

Burma

Satthagyen, (1944)

On the night of 5TH July, Jemadar Bhag Singh of 1ST Battalion, 11TH Sikh Regiment was in command of an isolated Platoon in the village of Satthagyen in Burma. The total strength of the Platoon numbered 22 men. Approximately 150 Japanese heavily attacked the Platoon's position. The telephone line was cut and owing to the heavy rain the wireless ceased to function and all communication with the Battalion was lost, so that no defensive fire could be given from supporting arms. A determined enemy under cover of heavy mortar, grenade discharger and automatic fire, heavily attacked the Platoon throughout the night. Jemadar Bhag Singh moved continuously from trench to trench cheering and encouraging his men and the Platoon succeeded in beating off all enemy attacks. On the morning of 4TH July an attack was launched to relieve the Platoon, but it was not until later that the contact was established. When relieved the Platoon had less than 5 rounds of ammunition per man and 29 enemy bodies were found on the wire surrounding the position. The inability of the enemy to take the village largely contributed to holding off the offensive by Jemadar Bhag Singh. Again at Abya on the night of 7TH July Jemadar Bhag Singh was commanding his Platoon in an attack on a very strongly fortified Japanese position and was severely wounded in the arm. Despite his wounds he continued to lead his Platoon with the greatest gallantry and resolution. After the attack, owing to the shortage of Viceroy's Commissioned Officers, Jemadar Bhag Singh refused to be evacuated. In the five days hard, bitter fighting, the conduct of Jemadar Bhag Singh was beyond praise. His gallantry and tenacity were an inspiration to all ranks of the Battalion and he richly deserved the award of the Military Cross.

Ukhrul, (1944)

During May, June and July 1944, Major Mohinder Singh of the Indian Artillery commanded his Battery with conspicuous success throughout the operations on the Assam-Burma borders. His technical efficiency, disregard of his own safety under fire and personal encouragement to his subordinates were responsible for the success of such Artillery support that was asked for by the Infantry at Kohima, Kidena and Ukhrul. During the arduous march to Ukhrul his initiative, energy and the example he set to men played a major part in the surmounting by his Battery of obstacles of the utmost severity. Throughout these operations Major Mohinder Singh had on all occasions displayed the highest qualities of leadership, devotion to duty, and courage, for which he was awarded the Military Cross on 5TH April 1945.

Burma

Chepu, (1944)

On 7TH July 1944, at Chepu in Burma, 3RD Mountain Battery of the Indian Artillery was across the lines of withdrawal of a large party of Japanese, who attacked desperately all day in an effort to breakthrough. Jemadar Budh Singh, with about twenty men of his Battery, took over a sector of the position just below a ridge whence the main strength of the enemy attacks developed. When a party on his flank was driven back, Jemadar Budh Singh's party held their ground and continued successfully to engage the enemy at a range of a few yards, though their flank was temporarily left open. Jemadar Budh Singh, though wounded, continued to carry out his duties, for which he was awarded an immediate Military Cross.

On 8TH July 1944, a Japanese force of some 500 strong, attacked positions in the village of Chepu in Burma held by 4TH Battalion, 12TH Frontier Force Regiment. The Japanese managed to occupy the North and higher end of a hill feature overlooking the village, thus dominating the positions below with medium machine guns. The troops in the lower positions were very exposed, but it was essential to the success of the operation that these positions should continue to be held. Major Kehar Singh Rai was ordered to take his Company forward into these positions to reinforce the Company already there. On arrival in the positions, Major Rai found that both the Company Commander and the Company Officer of this Company had been killed and that the Company had suffered heavy casualties. He at once rallied the men and reorganized the defence of the area. Later in the afternoon, two Platoons of another Company were despatched to strengthen Major Rai's position. The Company Commander was seriously wounded immediately after arrival in the position. Major Rai at once took command of these men and personally led them to their positions, despite heavy fire from medium machine guns. His personal gallantry and determination and the infliction of very heavy casualties upon the Japanese earned Major Kehar Singh Rai the Military Cross on 7TH August 1944.

Ralph Hill, (1944)

On 24TH July 1944, Subedar Ajmer Singh of 1ST Patiala Rajindra Infantry was commanding the forward Platoon, when his Company was ordered to capture Ralph Hill, a prominent feature covering the enemy line of control on Tamu road in Burma. His forward Sections were held up by heavy enemy fire. His Platoon was now in a position overlooked by the enemy. There was no other approach to the enemy's position. Subedar Ajmer Singh at once went forward encouraging his men and with complete disregard for his own safety, he personally led his Platoon up the steep slopes of the hill with great determination and dash, completely annihilating the enemy Platoon. Subedar Ajmer Singh's brilliant leadership and bravery enabled his men to kill 17 of the enemy and capture all their arms and equipment. On 27TH July 1944, he led a very successful fighting patrol at Lockhao River, killing many Japanese who wanted to escape that way.

Burma

Ralph Hill (Cont.)

And from 27TH July to 31ST July, when the Company had succeeded in establishing itself in the rear of the enemy's position, he successfully led many small Jittering parties the whole day, to stop the enemy from strengthening their positions before the final attack. Throughout the bitter fighting at Sakpao and subsequent operations, Subedar Ajmer Singh set a magnificent example of gallantry, for which he was awarded the Military Cross on 12TH October 1944. On 25TH July 1944, at Ralph Hill, after the capture of an enemy position, a Platoon under the command of Subedar Darbara Singh of 1ST Patiala Rajindra Infantry was sent to clear a road to 1ST Seaforths Highlanders' position about two miles away. His scouts saw an enemy party in position in their front, covering a gun withdrawal, which was escorted by one Company. Subedar Darbara Singh, who was moving with the leading section, at once led the charge, without waiting for the rest of the Platoon to come up. He succeeded in capturing the position after killing all seven Japanese occupants. He then advanced further and with his whole Platoon captured a feature overlooking the road. He again inflicted heavy casualties on the enemy's main party including two gun mules. Later, when the enemy counter attacked in superior force to regain the feature, he repulsed the attack with heavy losses to the enemy, with the result that the enemy had to leave all gun ammunition and vital parts of the gun on the spot. Subedar Darbara Singh's dauntless courage, self sacrifice and bold leadership earned him the Military Cross, which was awarded to him on 16TH November 1944.

Palel-Taku, (1944)

Shortly after dark on 27TH July 1944, "A" Company of 1ST Battalion, 16TH Punjab Regiment, after a long and arduous flank march of fourteen hours through thick jungle, reached the road Palel-Taku, in Burma. The Company had been ordered to lay an ambush astride the road in this area. The road at this point was completely overlooked by the enemy in great strength. Subedar Narinjan Singh was ordered to attack the hill and drive off the enemy. The ground, over which the attack was to be made, and the exact positions and the strength of the enemy were unknown. Despite this and all the other difficulties inherent in a night attack over un-reconnoitred ground, Subedar Narinjan Singh resolutely led his Platoon towards the enemy position. When advancing some distance the Platoon came under fire from automatic rifles. Making an accurate and rapid appreciation of the situation, Subedar Narinjan Singh ordered his Platoon to attack. He led the attack to capture the position at the point of the bayonet, driving out the enemy, who fled, leaving a quantity of automatic weapons, rifles and other equipment. By his resolution, courage and skilful handling of his Platoon, Subedar Narinjan Singh was responsible for capturing, under very difficult conditions a feature, which was essential for the further advance of the Brigade. For his personal courage and outstanding leadership, throughout the operation, Subedar Narinjan Singh was awarded the Military Cross on 11TH August 1944.

Burma

Chamol, (1944)

During an advance of the enemy in Chamol area in Burma, on 14TH July 1944, Jemadar Sarwan Singh of the Patiala Rajindra Infantry, was Commander of a forward Platoon and established himself on the bound after pushing back a small enemy party to a hill beyond. Another Platoon ordered to leapfrog through, had not yet arrived, when Jemadar Sarwan Singh saw two enemy Platoons advancing towards the targeted position. Realizing that the enemy position would become very strong on arrival of the reinforcements, Jemadar Sarwan Singh at once, without waiting for orders, led a charge on the advancing enemy. When his forward section was held up by heavy light machine gun fire from the front and the bunker position on his right, he put his 2 inch Mortar and reserve section to neutralize the right position and without hesitation, and shouting at the top of his voice "Patiala Will Not Be Held Up By The Japanese" and with complete disregard for his safety, personally led the forward sections into uphill charges. After a stiff fight in which many enemy soldiers were killed, he succeeded in capturing both enemy positions before the arrival of his reinforcements.

The enemy soon put up a counter attack on their lost positions. Again quite regardless of his own safety, he moved between his three sections, first to ensure that fire was held until the enemy were within forty yards and later to exhort the men under his command during the actual attack. The enemy was forced to retreat in disorder, abandoning four of their dead comrades on the field. From the noise in the Nullah nearby it appeared that considerable damage was done to the enemy. By his very fine personal example and leadership, under almost intolerable weather conditions, he captured the position, which if allowed to be reinforced would have resulted in a major operation and many casualties. Earlier when in occupation of a defensive position near Chamsol, he exhibited remarkable qualities of leadership and personal gallantry in beating off all enemy attacks. Although wounded during the four attacks, he refused to be evacuated until ordered by his Company Commander next morning. On 25TH July 1944, when his Company was boxing-in the enemy position in Chamsol area, he again proved himself most resourceful in preventing all his efforts to escape. Jemadar Sarwan Singh's dash throughout these operations was of a very high order, he showed most outstanding power of leadership under most difficult conditions, while his personal bravery and relentless determination to close with the enemy can seldom have been surpassed. Jemadar Sarwan Singh was awarded the Military Cross on 12TH October 1944.

Burma

Maungdaw, (1944)

On 9TH October 1944, in the area South of Maungdaw, one of the sections of 4TH Battalion, 12TH Frontier Force Regiment was preparing to take up position on the Sausage feature, when it came under concentrated Artillery fire from a Japanese 75m.m. gun. One of the Sepoys was badly wounded and Subedar Karam Singh, Commander of the Platoon, ran out into the open and brought him back into a trench. In the afternoon of the same day, one of his Sections was giving a supporting fire on to a feature, when its guns came under direct fire from an enemy 75m.m. gun, but the Section maintained its concentrated fire. The Platoon thus neutralized the enemy's small arms fire and enabled the operation to be carried out successfully with few casualties. For a further month until its withdrawal in November, the Platoon with great courage under constant enemy shell-fire carried out successful attacks against the enemy. For his gallant leadership Subedar Karam Singh was awarded the Military Cross on 26TH December 1944.

Mamgheng Ridge, (1944)

On 14TH October 1944, Jemadar Ujagar Singh of 4TH Battalion, 14TH Punjab Regiment was in command of a fighting Patrol of 25 men, which had arrived on the Mamgheng ridge in the Chin Hills in Burma. Early in the morning the Patrol encountered an enemy force of over 500. The battle which ensued lasted for over three hours and many casualties were inflicted upon the enemy. During these operations Jemadar Ujagar Singh commanded his Patrol with marked ability and courage and though opposed by overwhelming odds, kept up the battle until casualties and lack of ammunition compelled him to disengage. Jemadar Ujagar Singh was strongly recommended for and awarded the Military Cross on 28TH February 1945.

Chaukggyin, (1944)

At Chaukggyin in Burma on 26TH November 1944, Risaldar Hazara Singh of the Armoured Corps was in command of a troop of tanks leading the advance. The enemy permitted the troop and its escorting Infantry Platoon to advance right up to his positions before opening heavy automatic and grenade fire on the Infantry and mortars and artillery fire on the tanks. The tanks quickly neutralized the enemy fire then switched accurate fire on to the other enemy positions, enabling the Infantry Platoon to assault the forward enemy posts. Throughout the action, which lasted some two hours, Risaldar Hazara Singh displayed great coolness; skill and initiative in engaging enemy positions, maintaining contact with his Infantry Platoon and in sending back clear and accurate information by wireless. He withdrew only on orders from the Infantry Brigade Commander. The success of this action, during which considerable casualties were inflicted on the enemy, was very largely due to the skill, leadership and courage of Risaldar Hazara Singh. Risaldar Hazara Singh was awarded the Military Cross on 22ND March 1945.

Burma

Ngapyin Bridgehead, (1945)

Jemadar Kapur Singh's Platoon of 1ST Battalion, 15TH Punjab Regiment was heavily attacked by the enemy on several occasions and in particular on the night of 23RD January 1945 in the Ngapyin Bridgehead. One section was completely disabled having 4 men killed and 2 wounded. With a composite section drawn from his Platoon Headquarters and the remaining two sections, he continued to deny the ground to the enemy until he was reinforced. The attacks continued throughout the night and Jemadar Kapur Singh, under heavy fire, moved amongst his section posts, exhorting his men with complete disregard for his own safety. In an action a few days later Jemadar Kapur Singh was wounded while leading his Platoon. For his courage and determination, throughout the operation, Jemadar Kapur Singh was awarded the Military Cross on 28TH August 1945. Subedar Hari Singh was a Platoon Commander of "A" Company, 1ST Battalion, 15TH Punjab Regiment. On 25TH January at the Ngapyin Bridgehead, as his Bren gun section moved forward the enemy opened fire and the No 1 of the Bren gun was killed. At the same time fire was opened on the Subedar from his right and front. Hari Singh ordered his Platoon Havildar to man the right hand Bren gun and engage the enemy's light machine guns. Four enemies were killed but the light machine guns were not silenced. Simultaneously a party of about 20 Japanese charged the Platoon position and was engaged by the left hand section, 7 enemies being killed. On several previous occasions Subedar Hari Singh's Platoon had borne the brunt of strong enemy attacks during the establishment of the Bridgeheads. The excellent control and personal example displayed by Subedar Hari Singh enabled the Platoon to inflict many casualties on the enemy, with little loss to the Platoon and earned him the Military Cross, which was awarded to him on 25TH June 1945.

Singu, (1945)

At Singu in Burma on 11TH February 1945, Jemadar Lal Singh of the Armoured Corps was Commander of one of the leading tanks, which came under heavy and accurate automatic and close range anti tank gunfire. His tank received multiple hits and the petrol tank began to leak. In spite of the grave risk of fire, Jemadar Lall Singh remained in action returning the fire of the guns and making calm and accurate reports to his troop leader. Later while still engaging the gun, which had not yet been silenced, his tank was again penetrated frontally. Jemadar Lall Singh unperturbed reported the position of the flash, which he could now see and with the help of other tanks silenced it. Although his tank had received 13 direct hits, of which 3 penetrated, he kept his tank in action until assaulting troops reached the objective and only then halted when all his petrol had expired. For his skill, dogged determination and splendid courage, which were an inspiration to the remainder of the Squadron; Jemadar Lal Singh was awarded the Military Cross on 24TH April 1945.

Burma

Meiktilla, (1945)

On 2ND March 1945 in the Field, Lieutenant Avtar Singh was detailed as Field Operations Officer with the leading Company "A" of 4TH Battalion, 11TH Sikh Regiment during the operations, which led to the capture of Meiktilla in Burma. The enemy had mined the town very thoroughly and numerous snipers were active. An enemy gun opened fire as they neared the railway crossing and knocked out one Sherman tank. Lieutenant Avtar Singh brought down a concentration of fire, which temporarily neutralized the gun. When later the gun opened fire again, in spite of the heavy sniping, light machine gun and maxi machine gun fire and bursting mines, Lieutenant Avtar Singh climbed up into an adjoining house and brought down another concentration of fire on the area where the gun flash was seen. This enabled the Tank Squadron Commander who was near him, to move to a position from which the gun could be engaged directly with fire from the Tank's 75mm gun, and the enemy gun was finally silenced. By his initiative, disregard of danger, appreciation of the urgency of the situation and accurate shooting he definitely aided the "Cleaning up" operation and very materially speeded up the conclusion of the battle of Meiktilla. Lieutenant Avtar Singh was awarded the Military Cross for his conspicuous bravery in action.

On 2ND March 1945, Jemadar Phaga Singh was a Platoon Commander in 'A' Company of 4TH Battalion, 12TH Frontier Force Regiment, which was part of an attacking force ordered to capture and clear the area of Meiktilla town. Shortly after crossing the starting line, Jemadar Phaga Singh's Platoon came under very heavy automatic, mortar, grenade and rifle fire, and was pinned to the ground, suffering casualties. The whole area was a mass of bunkers and foxholes, and infested with cunningly concealed snipers. Without hesitation Jemadar Phaga Singh ran forward to his leading Sections, pin-pointed the opposition in front of each, and then rushed back to the tanks, giving them instructions, led them up to positions from which they could bring fire to bear on the enemy. Throughout the action he was under heavy fire, and his complete disregard for his own life, and the devotion with which he calmly directed the fire of the tanks, thus enabling his men to advance and mop up, was beyond praise and an inspiration not only to his own men, but to the tank crews in addition. He was greatly to the fore in the evacuation of his casualties. His indomitable courage and determination to exterminate every Japanese soldier, throughout eight gruelling hours of stiff hand-to-hand fighting was worthy of the highest standards of the Indian Army, and his personal count of enemy dead was considerable. As part of the same operations, Jemadar Phaga Singh's Platoon was ordered to form part of the Road Block on the Mandalay Road. On the morning of 14TH March the enemy attacked the position, but was driven off with heavy casualties. Thereafter supported by armoured cars, Jemadar Phaga Singh's Platoon was ordered to go forward and capture a Japanese gun that had been located the previous day. Upon hearing the advance the enemy opened up with concentrated fire, and made determined attempts to destroy the armoured cars with magnetic mines.

Burma

In this they were frustrated, but the cars were forced to withdraw to a safer distance. Jemadar Phaga Singh then went in to the attack, and under his inspiring leadership the Frontiersmen overran the enemy position, killing 20 Japanese in hand-to-hand fighting and completely routed the enemy force, considerably superior in numbers to their own. In the two actions detailed above Jemadar Phaga Singh showed the highest qualities of courage and true leadership, and the great success achieved against determined enemy are due to the outstanding qualities as a great leader in the Field. Jemadar Phaga Singh was awarded an immediate Military Cross at the conclusion of the above fighting.

Sadaung, (1945)

On 8TH March 1945, Major Virk, in command of "C" Company of 4TH Battalion, 12TH Frontier Force Regiment, with Royal Deccan Horse in support, was ordered to attack and capture the village of Sadaung in Burma, which was known to contain a strong force of the enemy with 75mm guns, medium machine guns and mortars. Inspite of heavy enemy fire, he secured a firm base well inside the village. However, his Company was held up by heavy mortar fire from South of the village, and very accurate medium machine gun fire from the front and a pagoda to the left flank. Discharger grenades were also being showered in to his position. He left the Platoon in what cover was available, and extricated his other two Platoons, with the object of putting in an attack from the Eastern Flank. The country here was very boggy and two tanks at once sank into the mud, but relying on swift and decisive action to achieve success he ordered the tanks away to high ground on the left to give covering fire. Major Harbans Singh Virk formed his men for the attack and with a great shout to his men, dashed into the centre of the enemy position, which was quickly overrun. He then led his men in a further magnificent charge, to clear the Southern portion of the village and finally reported that the enemy was beaten and running. The tanks then came into their own and demoralized the running Japanese. The enemy killed by Major Virk and his Company on this afternoon, amounted to over one hundred and the booty included two 75mm guns, five medium machine guns, two 81 mm mortars and quantities of small arms and equipment, at the cost of comparatively light casualties to the Company. This victory was solely due to the high courage and initiative of this lion-hearted Officer. Throughout the action, under extremely heavy fire, he was ubiquitous, climbing on to the tanks to give orders under a hail of bullets. He so inspired his men with his indomitable spirit, that when he gave the order for the charge, they followed him with the utmost dash and the battle was won. This Officer showed the highest qualities of courage and leadership throughout these operations, and led and inspired his men onto victory on several previous occasions. It was the faith in their leader, inspired and bred from previous actions, which gave the great impetus to the Company to achieve what they did on this day. His personal count of dead Japanese had been considerable. Major Harbans Singh Virk was awarded an immediate Military Cross followed by the DSO on 27TH May 1945.

Burma

Meiktila-Mahlaing, (1945)

On 10TH March 1945, Jemadar Udham Singh of 4TH Battalion, 12TH Frontier Force Regiment was the Platoon Commander of No.3 Platoon, 'A' Company, detailed to attack and clear up an enemy position astride the road Meiktila-Mahlaing in Burma. A troop of tanks was operating in support of his Platoon. The Platoon deployed and went into action with the tanks on the left of the road and at once came up against fanatical Japanese resistance. Jemadar Udham Singh, however, led his men in this close and difficult country, into action at 25 strong and after magnificent fighting on the part of all, he had only 12 men left, the remainder either being killed or wounded. The troop of tanks then went off leaving his small force to carry on without them, and surrounded by snipers on all sides. This situation, however, merely goaded this gallant leader to redouble his efforts, rallying his men he went forward again, clearing up trench after trench, and inflicting great slaughter amongst the enemy. It was not until 1400 hours that a fresh Company supported by tanks could be sent forward to relieve him on the ground to carry on the fight. Jemadar Udham Singh had killed many Japanese both with grenades and Sten gun, and it was his gallantry and inspiring leadership that spurred on the remnants of his gallant band of men to fight with frenzy, until finally ordered to withdraw and reorganize. Jemadar Udham Singh was awarded an immediate Military Cross on 10TH March 1945.

Okshithon, (1945)

On 21ST March Subedar Basant Singh was commanding his Platoon of the Sikh Light Infantry in the area of Okshithon near Meiktilla, Central Burma, when enemy were seen in scrubland on their flank. Subadar Basant Singh immediately organized and led an attack against the enemy, who were discovered to be in a dug-out position with light machine guns and grenade dischargers. The enemy strength was 56, which was considerably larger than Subadar Basant Singh's Platoon. In a series of sharp encounters and section charges, all led personally by this very gallant Officer, forty enemies were killed in hand-to-hand fighting. The Japanese who fled were quickly killed by reinforcements, who had by then arrived. This Officer's leadership, bravery and personal example were undoubtedly the cause of such a fine victory. He further distinguished himself in many patrol actions between March 20TH and April 2ND while the Battalion was on a detached ambush role. On 6TH April 1945, when the Battalion was preparing their night camp under heavy sniping fire after the successful attack on Thabebyn village, Subadar Basant Singh was wounded in the left thigh at the same time as his Company Commander was mortally wounded. Subadar Basant Singh paid no attention to his own wound and at once assumed command of his Company and organized them on the perimeter for the night. The next morning this intrepid Officer led out a fighting patrol and routed out and killed five Japanese snipers.

Burma

On 9TH April, in the attack on Mingladon Monastery, when Subadar Basant Singh's Company Commander was wounded, this Officer again assumed command of the Company and led the successful final assault, which resulted in the capture of the Monastery. On 8TH May 1945 Subadar Basant Singh took out a small patrol of two sections to search a village near Penwagon in South Burma where Japanese had been reported. The patrol found approximately 100 Japanese in a Nullah near the village. Instead of keeping them under observation and reporting back, this gallant leader at once decided to attack the enemy himself. This he did to such good effect that seven enemy were killed, fifteen wounded, and the remainder fled in confusion. Subadar Basant Singh acted throughout the South Burma campaign with great distinction, for which he was awarded the Indian Order of Merit.

Taungup Road, (1945)

On 6TH April 1945, 'A' Company of 2ND Battalion, 13TH Frontier Force Rifles was in position on the summit of a high steep feature, East of Taungup Road in Burma. The summit was divided into two knolls of equal height separated from each other by a bare narrow ridge about hundred yards long and five yards wide. The enemy about thirty to forty strong, were dug in on the Eastern Knoll. Jemadar Santa Singh led his Platoon along the ridge with supporting fire from tanks and medium machine guns on the South and North flanks respectively. When supporting fire ceased he led his Platoon straight in on the enemy positions. Although wounded in the first rush he charged on, inflicting heavy casualties on the enemy with his Sten gun. The attack and subsequent consolidation were successful, the enemy medium machine gun was captured, and heavy casualties inflicted on the enemy, sixteen bodies being recovered, including that of an Officer. With this attack the enemy resistance on Point 370, which had been the scene of bitter fighting for two days, ceased. For his gallant leadership Jemadar Santa Singh was awarded an immediate Military Cross.

Pyawbwe, (1945)

During the attack of Pyawbwe in Burma, on 10TH April 1945, Jemadar Gurbachan Singh of the Indian Armoured Corps was commanding a troop of tanks leading the attack. With superlative dash and vigour, and in order to give the maximum support to the attacking Infantry, he led his troop unscathed through a heavily mined area onto the enemy position, where he found himself almost on top of two enemy light machine gun posts. Disdaining to reverse his tank, and leaning far out of his turret, he succeeded in throwing grenades into and destroying both positions. He then engaged and destroyed a 70 mm gun, a 37 mm gun and a light machine gun position, and forced a 75 mm gun to be pulled out of action that was later found abandoned. He was of great assistance in the capture of the position, which caused the enemy to withdraw that night. Jemadar Gurbachan Singh was awarded the Military Cross on 24TH May 1945.

Burma

Pyawbwe-Meiktila, (1945)

On 10TH April 1945, Jemadar Narain Singh of 4TH Battalion, 12TH Frontier Force Regiment was a Platoon Commander of 'B' Company, when the Battalion was ordered to attack and consolidate the Frontier Force lines area of the main Pyawbwe-Meiktila road in Burma, as there was a strong enemy presence there. The 'B' Company had to advance across 1000 yards of bullet-swept, open country. Jemadar Narain Singh was in the vanguard of the advance, which was an inspiration to the remainder of the Battalion, who were privileged to witness his determined progress. Jemadar Narain Singh kept the Platoon under perfect control inspite of casualties from the enemy's light machine guns. On arrival it was found that contrary to reports, the Frontier Force lines area was very strongly held by the enemy. The attack went in on a two Company fronts, with 'B' Company on the right. Jemadar Narain Singh's Platoon at once came under heavy mortar and automatic fire, and the Platoon suffered casualties. Holding his ground, however, Jemadar Narain Singh arranged, at great personal risk to himself, the evacuation of his wounded and then personally directed the Artillery fire, preliminary to his further advance. He then led his Platoon forward, but the enemy once again replied with everything he had and the attacking Platoon suffered more casualties. Time was precious however, and without further ado, Jemadar Narain Singh led the charge and rushed in at their head to capture the first objective. Inspired by his leadership his men fought magnificently and the area was soon under control. There remained the wooded area, round the church and up to the railway line to be captured. Again 'B' Company was on the right, and Jemadar Narain Singh urgently requested that his Platoon lead the attack. His request was granted and the men went in at the head of the tanks. The enemy fought back bravely and tenaciously, as the Platoon cleared the whole area yard-by-yard.

Throughout this day, Jemadar Narain Singh led his men with utmost gallantry. His fierce cries of 'Sat Siri Akal', and the encouragement he gave his men, going from section to section and personally directing the attack, were an inspiration to all and his imperturbability under the heaviest fire was beyond praise. On this day, Jemadar Narain Singh personally killed six Japanese and his Platoon added another 133 to the very substantial Battalion total. Within the Company he had earned for himself the name of 'Sher' (Lion)". Jemadar Narain Singh was awarded an immediate Military Cross on the 10TH April 1945.

Burma

Pozut, (1945)

At Pozut in Burma, on 25TH April 1945, Jemadar Lall Singh of the Indian Armoured Corps encountered a party of Japanese in strongly defended positions. As he was unable to depress the guns of his tank sufficiently to fire at the enemy, he threw grenades from the turret of his tank. The enemy returned fire and wounded him in the shoulder. Undeterred, he dismounted from his tank and by throwing more grenades killed four of the enemy. Unable to dislodge the remainder he returned to the Squadron Commander, to report the situation and although suffering from his wound, led a section of attached Infantry back to the position, where under his leadership the remaining enemy was completely destroyed. For outstanding services and continuous gallantry in action, Jemadar Lall Singh was awarded an immediate Bar to his Military Cross.

Pegu, (1945)

Jemadar Pritam Singh had fought in all the actions in which a Squadron of Indian Armoured Corps had been engaged, from the period between crossing the Irrawaddy until the capture of Pegu in Burma. Throughout this campaign, he commanded his tank with extreme competence and effect, and his conduct was deserving of very high praise. He had twice been wounded, and once burnt, when his tank was destroyed by an enemy action on 28TH April 1945. He always showed tremendous keenness to close with the enemy and fought with his tank with an efficiency and relish for action, which called for the highest praise. His conduct throughout had been a constant source of inspiration to the men under his command, and the object of confidence and admiration of his Squadron Commander. Jemadar Pritam Singh was awarded the Military Cross on 5TH November 1945.

Mondaing, (1945)

On 3RD of May 1945, a Platoon of 1ST Battalion, 11TH Sikh Regiment was detailed to contact and destroy an enemy party in the village of Mondaing in Burma. The Platoon made contact with the enemy, killing a Japanese Officer and three men without loss to the Platoon. In addition the Sikhs captured and destroyed an enemy truck with much ammunition. On the night of 10TH May an ambush party, which while returning to the Battalion area came on to the 'B' Echelon transport of a large enemy force attacking the Battalion position. Without hesitation the Platoon attacked and inflicted a great number of casualties on the enemy and damage to his transport. The Sikhs continued to harass the enemy from the rear until the Japanese force stopped its attacks and retreated from the front of the Battalion position. Subedar Naranjan Singh showed himself to be an outstanding Platoon Commander during all the Burma Campaigns from 1942 to 1945, having seen a great deal of heavy fighting. For his outstanding performance at Mondaing Subedar Naranjan Singh was awarded the Military Cross. .

Burma

Skanemtkyi, (1945)

At Skanemtkyi in Burma on 6TH May 1945, Subedar Bachan Singh was the Senior Officer of the advance guard Companies of 1ST Battalion, 11TH Sikh Regiment, who spotted a party of fifteen Japanese bathing in the Pani Chaung by Kaemgngegy. They were immediately attacked, some were killed and the remainder chased across the Nullah into the village. Once reaching the village the Platoon came under very heavy rifle and medium machine gun fire. The Japanese held the village in great strength and the attackers suffered a number of casualties. Subedar Bachan Singh then led his men forward in an endeavour to silence the enemy trench. Under heavy fire this party crawled forward to within ten yards of the enemy trench and endeavoured to throw grenades over a fence into the enemy trench. They became an easy target for the enemy and the men were rapidly killed, leaving Subedar Bachan Singh as the sole survivor. He crawled back collected another section and again endeavoured to close in with the enemy strong point from another direction. Subedar Bachan Singh realizing that further attacks on this strong point would only result in further casualties, ordered two men to give covering fire while he crawled forward and dragged six wounded men back into the cover of a nearby trench, then under cover of mortar fire he led the third and successful attack, which succeeded in capturing the village and liquidating the enemy of approximately a 100 strong, who after their first surprise fought with dogged courage. The courage, self sacrifice and devotion to duty of Subedar Bachan Singh was of the highest order and far exceeded the call of duty. Subedar Bachan Singh was awarded an immediate Military Cross 6TH May 1945.

Race to Rangoon, (1945)

Officers and men of 2ND Battalion, 1ST Punjab Regiment in Burma in their race for Rangoon performed many daring and gallant deeds. On May 16TH, Subedar Chaiju Singh's fighting patrol contacted a party of thirty Japanese dug in on a small feature. Despite his numerical inferiority, the Subedar led a direct attack against the Japanese machine gun post and personally killed a Japanese Officer in close combat, while his patrol accounted for ten others; the remaining Japanese took to their heels. Subedar Chaiju Singh was awarded the Military Cross for his conspicuous gallantry and leadership.

On the dash for Rangoon 2ND Battalion, 1ST Punjab Regiment had to mop up many Japanese Companies on the way. Subedar Sewa Singh took a reconnaissance patrol forward through dense jungle, directed Artillery fire on the Japanese bunker holding up the advance and personally led a small party which drove the Japanese from their positions, killing three of them. For his gallantry and leadership Subedar Sewa Singh was awarded the Military Cross on 17TH August 1945.

Burma

Kama Bridgehead, (1945)

Lieutenant Sucha Singh was commanding "D" Company, 4TH Battalion, 15TH Punjab Regiment during the Kama Bridgehead operations near Prome in Burma. On 27TH May 1945, the Company was ordered to move its position to the right in order to close up with the next Company and block a possible escape route of the Japanese in the Bridgehead. Owing to late receipt of the orders, only two Platoons of the Company had reached the new position and were not dug in when the Japanese put in their first attack. This was repulsed with heavy loss to the enemy. The third Platoon came up before dusk and the defensive position was dug, but not wired, as none could be brought up. A further attack by the Japanese was also beaten off. During the night seven attacks were put in by the Japanese on this position, which proved that it lay across an important Japanese escape route. Twice during these attacks, the direction of which was from three sides, the Japanese penetrated the position but were driven out by grenades and the bayonet. Throughout the engagement Lieutenant Sucha Singh directed the defence with utmost coolness and determination, encouraging the Company with cheering remarks. During one attack he killed a Japanese soldier who was creeping up unnoticed along a covered approach. His communications throughout the night was only by a 48 set to the next Company, and his N.C.O.'s set did not work. Nevertheless he passed all orders through his set with complete coolness and caused most accurate Artillery defensive fire to be brought down in front of his position. The Company counted forty-eight dead Japanese bodies around the position the next morning and the Company had suffered four killed and seven wounded. The leadership of Lieutenant Sucha Singh throughout the whole engagement was of the highest order and contributed very largely to the successful defence of the position and the blocking of one important Japanese escape route. In view of the fact that the Officer was a Subaltern commanding a Company for the first time in action, his performance is considered especially outstanding. Lieutenant Sucha Singh was awarded an immediate Military Cross.

Pagan, (1945)

At Pagan, Burma, in 1945, Subedar Jogindar Singh was 2ND I/C of the 'B' Company 1ST Battalion, 11TH Sikh Regiment, which with tank support was attacking an enemy position. A party of the enemy about 150 strong slipped behind the Company cutting them off from their base. The Company was pinned down to the ground by very heavy fire in open country and was in a critical position. The Company Commander was seriously wounded. Subedar Jogindar Singh took command of the Company and under heavy machine gun fire, rapidly reorganized his Company, and then moved to the tanks, which had been singled out a special target by the enemy and coolly directed their fire on the enemy concentrations and strong points. Only due to his great gallantry, coolness and initiative, a very critical situation was converted to an overwhelming victory. Subedar Jogindar Singh was awarded an immediate Military Cross on 25TH May 1945.

Burma

Kandaung, (1945)
During the period Major Amrik Singh was in command, he proved himself to be a brave and skilful Commander. He fought and led his Company of 4TH Battalion, 12TH Frontier Force Regiment, with great distinction at Meiktilla in Burma. On the second day of the attack on the town, though wounded himself in the shoulder, he refused to be evacuated, and by evening had cleared the enemy from the whole of the built-up area from North to South. A few days later he organised a most successful roadblock on the Mandalay Road, when his Company killed 40 Japanese and captured several guns. Again on the Meiktilla–Mahlaing road he led his Company in to attack and capture the high ground, against numerically superior enemy forces over most difficult and broken country, thickly entrenched and bunkered. In two days fighting the Infantry with the Tanks in support, and despite their own heavy casualties, killed over 200 of the enemy. Major Amrik Singh distinguished himself again at Kandaung and at the battle of Pyawbwe; numerous Japanese being killed and much equipment captured on both occasions. Finally it was Major Amrik Singh and his Company, which after a day and night of tough, close quarter fighting, secured the bridgehead over the Pegu River, thus enabling the Division to continue its advance Southwards. Despite very heavy casualties amongst his command, he maintained a magnificent fighting spirit in his Company. The Company bears the proud record of never having failed to win all objectives given to them. For his gallant leadership, Major Amrik Singh was awarded the Military Cross on 15TH May 1945.

Atya, (1945)
On 6TH July 1945 at Atya in Burma, Subedar Gurbachan Singh was the Senior Officer of 'A' Company, 1ST Battalion, 11TH Sikh Regiment, which was detailed to attack a strongly fortified Japanese position, situated in an isolated Pagoda in the centre of flooded paddy fields. The attack was across 300 yards of open flooded paddy fields often waist deep in water and swept by shell and machine gun fire. The Company Commander was seriously wounded and the Company Officer Lieut. Jogindar Singh was killed while moving forward to take over command of the Company. Subedar Gurbachan Singh at once took command and endeavoured to lead two Platoons round in a flank attack, under the covering fire of the leading Platoon which was already pinned to the ground by the enemy fire. Heavy casualties were suffered and to save further loss of life the Company was ordered to withdraw. It took Subedar Gurbachan Singh twenty four hours to extricate his Company together with all their wounded, arms and ammunition and throughout this time he was always to be seen where the fire was hottest and the situation most critical. Subedar Gurbachan Singh was awarded an immediate Military Cross.

Burma

Ngemplak area, (1945)

On 23RD November 1945, during an attack in Ngemplak area of Sourabaya in Burma, two sections of the leading Platoon of Subedar Kartar Singh's Company, of 2ND Battalion, 2ND Punjab Regiment, of which he was Second in Command, were pinned down to the ground by enemy automatic fire from two strong concrete bunkers. Subedar Kartar Singh dashed forward from Company Headquarters under very heavy fire to take charge of the situation. He then, at very great risk to himself, carried out a personal reconnaissance before leading the third section of the Platoon in an outflanking movement, which culminated in a magnificent charge onto the enemy position. While leading this extremely gallant charge Subedar Kartar Singh fell severely wounded in the stomach. From where he lay, he continued to shout words of encouragement to his men until they had over-run the position. He refused to be evacuated until he was certain the Platoon could continue its advance without him. Subedar Kartar Singh's outstanding leadership and utter disregard for his own safety were superb examples of courage and devotion to duty and inspiration to all. Subedar Kartar Singh was awarded an immediate Military Cross on 23RD November 1945.

Kandaingbauk, (1945)

In 1945, Subedar Mohinder Singh was Second in Command of 'B' Company, Sikh Light Infantry. The Company was ordered to capture the village of Kandaingbauk in Meiktilla area of Central Burma. Within the first five minutes of the advance, the Company Commander was killed and all the Platoon Commanders wounded. Subedar Mohinder Singh was severely wounded in the leg. Despite his wound he took command of the Company and continued the advance until the Company was pinned down, by accurate medium machine gun, light machine gun and mortar fire. Subedar Mohinder Singh re-organised the Company under fire and withdrew them to a more favourable position. He was the last man to withdraw and refused to have his wound dressed until all his men had been treated. The Company had suffered heavy casualties; 25 killed and 53 wounded including all Officers and Platoon Havildars, yet this young Officer, though in considerable pain, showed his powers of leadership and command and extricated his Company skilfully. When his wound had been dressed, he asked permission to attack again. Throughout the action Subedar Mohinder Singh displayed outstanding instigative drive and courage in the best traditions of the Sikhs. Subedar Mohinder Singh was awarded the Military Cross.

End of the War in Burma

The War in the Far East finally ended with the dropping of atomic bombs on the Japanese cities of Hiroshima and Nagasaki in August 1945.

Burma

Excerpted from the "History of the Indian Air Force"
By Mr. Pushpinder Singh

Indian Air Force

The infant, and tiny Indian Air Force first "cut its teeth' in operations on the North West Frontier in 1938 and then also gained its first gallantry award. A bombing attack was to be carried out by Flt.Lt. Peter Haynes, with Hawai Sepoy 1st Class Kartar Singh Tounque as air gunner / bombardier. Kartar Singh was given the trade "Fitter Armourer" but soon qualified as an air gunner as well, and went with 'A' Flight to Peshawar in 1936. September 1938 saw the entry of the last batch of Indian cadets to RAF Cranwell with Arjan Singh, and Prithpal Singh joining the College in September 1938. Arjan Singh and Prithpal Singh completed their training by 22ND December 1939, the course having been shortened by six months because, in September 1939, War had been declared against Germany. Air vice Marshal John Baldwin who was Commandant of the RAF College during this period, was mightily impressed by these Indian Flight Cadets who would, soon enough, prove their mettle in action during War operations, hardly three years from the time they left Cranwell. In India, the IAF was being expanded to seven Squadrons and modernized with Hurricane fighters and Vengeance dive bombers. No.3 Squadron IAF, commanded by Sqn. Ldr. Prithpal Singh and flying Hurricane II fighter bombers from September 1943 to January 1945 became mainstay of the North West Frontier Watch and Ward duties. Nos. 3 and 4 Squadrons were re-equipped with the Hurricane IIC in January and June 1943 respectively but the third IAF formation to fly Hurricanes was No.6 Squadron under redoubtable Sqn.Ldr.Mehar Singh who was its Commanding Officer for over two years. No.6 Squadron's efficiency, enthusiasm and excellent performance evoked numerous messages of praise which was to result, in November 1943, in its selection for the coming campaign in Burma, the first Squadron of the newly equipped Indian Air Force to go to War of the Second Arakan Campaign, achieving great distinction and earning the sobriquet "Eyes of the XIV Army". Before the 1943 winter campaign began, in which Air Chief Marshal Sir Richard Peirse had "ordained" that the Indian Air Force was to go into battle with their new Hurricanes and Vengeances, he called a meeting of the seven IAF Squadron Commanders in New Delhi, four of which were ready to go into the front line, the others then converting to their new aircraft. Interestingly, of these seven Squadron Commanders of the Indian Air Force, five were Sikhs: Sqn Ldr Arjan Singh (No.1 Squadron), Sqn Ldr Surjit Singh Majithia (No.2 Squadron), Sqn Ldr Prithipal Singh (No.3 Squadron), Sqn Ldr Dalip Singh Majithia (No.4 Squadron) and Sqn Ldr Mehar Singh (No.6 Squadron). The C.O.s were ordered to fly in their own aircraft from wherever they happened to be and report at Air H.Q. for the opening of the conference by the AOC-in-C. All got the signal in ample time to act on it, except for Sqn. Ldr. Mehar Singh, Commanding No.6 Squadron.

Burma

Indian Air Force

As recorded, "He was taking his boys to the front at the time and had only received the signal at nine o'clock on the night before he was supposed to report to Delhi. He took off at lO p.m., on a moonless night to fly alone and without wireless aids to Delhi. He flew at fourteen thousand feet, landed at Allahabad to refuel and reached Willingdon airport, nine hundred miles from his starting point at 4 a.m. He was at the opening session of the conference that morning with all the others, as if nothing had happened. It was a magnificent flight. Sir Richard described it later, as "a feat of which any air force in the world would be proud". In his classic account of the War in Burma "Defeat into Victory", Field Marshal Sir William Slim describes his visit to No.6 Squadron and its C.O. Sqn.Ldr.Mehar Singh who were keeping up steady patrols with Tactical-Reconnaissance Hurricanes: "I was impressed by the conduct of a recce Squadron of the Indian Air Force. Flying in pairs, the Indian pilots in their outmoded Hurricanes went out, time and again, in the face of overwhelming enemy fighter superiority. I looked in on the Squadron just at a time when news had come in that the last patrol had run into a bunch of Oscars and had been shot down. The Sikh Squadron Leader, an old friend of mine, at once took out the next patrol himself and completed the mission. His methods, rumour had it, were a little unorthodox. It was said that if any of his young pilots made a bad landing he would take them behind a basha and beat them! Whatever he did, it was effective; they were a happy, efficient and very gallant Squadron".

In April 1944, No.6 Squadron notched a scorching 620 hours of operational flying, when the Kaladan and Mayu valleys received increased attention. Flt.Lt. Mohinder Singh Pujji, one of the Flight Commanders who had earlier been with the RAF over France and the Middle East, flew as many as six sorties a day, clocking 61 operational flying hours in one month. At the beginning of June, after an incredible operational tour, No. 6 was withdrawn from the front. Squadron Leader Mehar Singh was awarded the only DSO to an Indian of the Air Force. "Meher Baba" remains perhaps the greatest legend of the Indian Air Force. No. 1 Squadron of the Indian Air Force was to be in the thick of the vital battles of 1944, returning to War and glory under command of Sqn. Ldr. Arjan Singh. The "Tigers" had earlier been based at Kohat, operating Hawker Hurricane IIBs when during December 1943; the C-in-C Indian Army Field Marshal Sir Claude Auchinleck visited the RAF Station and also inspected No. 1 Squadron. He was most impressed by its standard and spirit and when Sqn. Ldr. Arjan Singh advocated the intense desire of No. 1 Squadron to go back into battle, keenly supported by the RAF Station Commander, he gave his acquiescence. Within a week of this request, No. 1 Squadron was ordered to move immediately to Imphal on the Manipur front where massive build-ups were taking place on both sides of the Assam Burma border.

Burma

Indian Air Force

The next fifteen months were to be breathless with action and epoch marking in the already chequered history of the Tiger Squadron. No. 1 Squadron reached Imphal (Main) on 3RD February 1944 and were thereafter to remain in action for a record 14 months, taking vital part in the fateful siege of Imphal followed by the trans-Chindwin and trans-Irrawaddy offences. Once again, No. 1 Squadron IAF shared the base with their old colleagues-in-arms, No.28 Squadron RAF, both being Tactical Reconnaissance Units (Tac/R), cooperating closely with the Army. No.1 Squadron under Sqn. Ldr. Arjan Singh commenced operational flying immediately, with sector reconnaissance flown on 5TH February, carrying out offensive, tactical and photographic sorties to observe Japanese movements on the Chindwin, beyond Tiddim, and as far East as the Myitkyina-Mandalay railway, much valuable information being obtained by the Squadron.

The siege of Imphal was finally broken and the Japanese 15TH and 31ST Divisions began to disintegrate and while still resisting, were definitely on the retreat. However, in the Palel area and the area South of Imphal, the Japanese 33RD Division hung on grimly to their positions but on 2ND July, the Japanese actually discontinued their Imphal operations, and concentrated on forming defensive lines to check the Allied advance. Following opening of the Imphal-Kohima road, No. 1 Squadron's Hurricanes were involved, in addition to the tasks referred to, in reconnoitring the Japanese lines of communication in use by the retreating troops and attacking them. Sqn. Ldr. Arjan Singh's leadership had a distinct style: quiet courage, no flamboyance, firmness but with a ready smile. After the Japanese had been thrown back, in a great and signal honour to Arjan Singh and indeed the Indian Air Force, the Supreme Commander Lord Louis Mountbatten, personally flew into Imphal and in the presence of Air Chief Marshal Sir Richard Peirse and the assembled Squadron at the airfield, pinned the Distinguished Flying Cross on Arjan Singh's tunic. In the few words of the Supreme Commander "He had done a great job". Twenty years later, Arjan Singh was to be appointed Chief of Air Staff and led the Indian Air Force during the September 1965 War. After retiring in 1969, he served as India's ambassador in several countries and became Lt. Governor of Delhi. Most active on the Golf Course, he is still regarded by nearly all as simply "The Chief".

Squadron Leader Arjan Singh was awarded the Distinguished Flying Cross (DFC) in 1944 for his services in Burma.

Squadron Leader 'Baba' Mehar Singh was awarded the Distinguished Service Order (DSO) in 1944 for his services in Burma.

Squadron Leader Mohinder Singh Pujji was awarded the Distinguished Flying Cross (DFC) in 1944 for his services in Burma.

Warrant Officer Harjinder Singh, an engineering genius, was awarded Most Excellent Order of the British Empire (MBE) for his services in Burma; eventually he was promoted to the rank of Air Vice Marshal in the Indian Air Force.

JAVA

A class Regiment of Sikhs 1ST Patiala Infantry, and Sikh Companies of PAVO Cavalry (FF), 1ST Battalion, 16TH Punjabis and two Battalions of 1ST Punjab Regiment served in the Java debacle.

A few days before their surrender the Japanese had formed a government of their Javanese collaborators. These hoodlums had proceeded to treat with extreme brutality several thousand Dutch internees. The men and the boys had been taken from the internment camps and thrown into prison, the women and girls left to the mercy of the Indonesian Youth Army and the mob who, on the Japanese surrender, acquired most of their arms. On 25TH October 49TH Brigade arrived at Sourabaya, charged with succouring the Dutch internees, disarming and evacuating the Japanese, and keeping the peace. The city was in chaos, with road blocks and machine gun posts manned by every kind of thug. On 28TH October a 49TH Brigade convey was attacked; eleven Officers and fifty Other Ranks were captured and shot out of hand. Another convoy of Dutch women and children being brought down to the docks was also attacked; most of the Lorries burnt, the Dutch and their small Indian escort hacked to pieces. In three days 49TH Brigade had lost eighteen Officers and 374 men. The 5TH Indian Division arrived to carry out the tasks which had proved beyond 49TH Brigade. First to disembark was the PAVO Cavalry Regiment with Stuart tanks, and were invaluable for escorting convoys of Dutch refugees from their camp inland to the docks for evacuation. In some of these operations the PAVO was assisted by Japanese troops who had not been disarmed. They brought over 6,000 women and children past mobs screaming for their blood and threatening every obscenity and barbarity. Any Dutch, British or Indian who fell into their hands were mutilated, raped and dismembered in public. Eventually the city had to be cleared by a methodical advance of 123RD Brigade. The battle lasted nineteen days. Many fine soldiers died in this quarrel which had nothing to do with them, the men who had fought in East Africa, the Desert, the Arakan, Assam and Burma. Among these was one of the finest soldiers in the Indian Army, Lieutenant Colonel Sarbjit Singh Kalha, DSO and Bar, 2ND Battalion, 1ST Punjab Regiment, just the sort of an Officer that his country now most needed.* *Excerpted from the ' The Indian Army' by Trench.*

"It was tragic the last action of any importance in which 2ND Battalion, 1ST Punjab Regiment were engaged should have been the most disastrous, in that Colonel Kalha lost his life. He had been at the Staff College and had served with the Battalion off and on from the first day it went into action. Calm and unruffled in battle, fearless and with delightful manners, he had won D.S.O. and Bar. His remarkable ability included that of commanding both British and Indian Officers, and there was no one in his Battalion or in the Division who did not hold him in the highest regard. He was one of those senior Indian Army Officers whom India could least afford to lose." * *Excerpted from the 'Ball of Fire' by Antony Brett-James.* For the Indians the War ended when they were relieved by Netherlands Marines early in 1946.

INDO-PAK WAR, 1947

Sikh Soldier

When India was partitioned in 1947, the exodus of Muslim troops resulted in the raising of the proportion of Sikhs in the Army dramatically to 30 percent. This predominance irked those in the ruling party who inherited the mantle of the Raj. The home minister Sardar Vallabhbhai Patel vowed to cut down the Sikhs strength in the Army in line with their population. Patel is also believed to have decreed that no Sikh shall be appointed Chief of the Army Staff. There is no denying the fact that, despite five decades of republican democracy, India has had several outstanding Sikh Generals but never a be-turbaned Chief of Army Staff, until General Joginder Jaswant Singh assumed charge of the Indian Army, as the 22ND Chief of Army Staff, on 31ST January 2005, followed by General Bikram Singh on 31ST May 2012.

Indo-Pak War, (1947)

The first War between India and Pakistan began in October 1947 and ended in December 1948. The origins of the first War between India and Pakistan can be traced to the final status of Kashmir, following the establishment of an independent India and Pakistan on August 15TH, 1947. Kashmir was strategically located between India and Pakistan and though it was led by a Hindu Maharaja, Muslims made up the majority of the population. Sikhs and Hindus made up the other major ethnicities. Though required to choose between India and Pakistan, the Maharaja was unable to decide which state to join. Tensions between Pakistan and the government of Kashmir grew as the Maharaja's indecision frustrated Pakistan and pro-Pakistani factions within Kashmir. Hostilities began in early October 1947 when a tribal rebellion broke out in Poonch in Southwest Kashmir. By October 20TH the Pakistani Army entered the conflict in support of the tribal forces. Tribal and Pakistani forces experienced significant successes in the opening days of the conflict as they were able to take Domel on the first day and overpowered a Kashmir Government Battalion at Muzaffarabad by October 23RD. On October 26TH, 1947, after four days, they were in the vicinity of Srinagar. Kashmir State Forces seemed to have been beaten. The Maharaja had already fled his capital, Srinagar, to seek the comparative safety of Jammu. Tribal and Pakistani forces met fierce resistance at Uri, where Kashmiri Government forces, despite the desertion of many of its Muslim troops, were able to delay the Pakistani forces for two days until it was destroyed. Retreating Kashmiri forces were able to destroy a key bridge thus delaying Pakistani forces for an additional day.

The Maharaja, facing near certain defeat, asked India for military support. India agreed to help, provided that Kashmir acceded to India and that the Prime Minister of Kashmir agreed to the accession. Both the Maharaja and the Prime Minister agreed to these terms and on October 26TH the Maharaja signed the Instrument of Accession.

Indo-Pak War 1947

Defence of the Valley
The strength of the Indian troops in the Valley comprised of 161 Infantry Brigade, with the Sikh soldiers of 1ST Patiala Infantry, 1ST Battalion, The Sikh Regiment, 7TH Battalion, The Sikh Regiment, The Armoured Corps, Indian Artillery, and Sikh Commanders of various Infantry Regiments.

Shalateng, (1947)
On November 7TH, 1 Sikh along with 1 (Para) Kumaon and 4 Kumaon fought the battle of Shalateng, which broke the back of the raider's column advancing towards Srinagar. Baramula was retaken by the Sikhs on November 8TH. The Battalion then moved towards Uri and retook it from the raiders. The Pakistanis made a number of attempts to capture this piquet but were foiled. In the defence of one of the attempts, Naik Chand Singh of 1 Sikh earned a posthumous Mahavir Chakra.

Srinagar-Baramula Road, (1947)
The 1 Sikh was in position on the Srinagar-Baramula Road and fought an action against the Pakistani raiders. Several of the raiders were killed as the rest fled from the attacking Sikhs. Lance Naik Ram Singh and Sepoy Arjan Singh were awarded the Vir Chakra for their conspicuous gallantry.

Uri, (1947)
During the Indo-Pakistani War of 1947, some 4,000-6,000 raiders had entered the Uri sector of Jammu and Kashmir. On December 12TH, 1 Sikh marched out from Uri to remove this threat. They quickly overcame the opposition on the way and reached the main enemy position, where they encountered a strong enemy force and a fierce hand-to-hand fight ensued. In this encounter, "B" and "D" Companies suffered heavy casualties and were ordered to withdraw.

Battle of Chamb, (1947)
On 7TH December, 1ST Patiala was ordered to recapture Chhamb which had fallen into Pakistani hands, and hold the banks of Manawar Tawi at all costs. On 8TH December the Patialas reached the Northern banks of Manawar Tawi and opened fire, giving the impression to the raiders that a frontal attack was imminent. Two Rifle Companies crossed the Tawi four Kilometres upstream and descended on the surprised raiders and captured 35 Pakistani raiders/soldiers. Brigadier (later Lieutenant General) Lakhinder Singh, the local formation Commander, joined the Patialas by late evening. By nightfall the raiders set up bonfires all around the Patiala camp. They were sure that they would eventually overwhelm Patiala troops. Some four to five thousand raiders then got into Chhamb Village, beating drums, and started firing intensely. The CO of the Patialas, Brigadier Bikram Dev Singh, DSO, issued quick but simple orders "Fight to the last man". The Patialas cleared the Chhamb village killing or wounding scores of enemy soldiers. The Patialas had fought heroically at Chhamb earning two Vir Chakra (VrC): Lance Havildar Phuman Singh VrC and Havildar Seva Singh VrC.

Indo-Pak War 1947

Battle of Tithwal, (1947)

163 Infantry Brigade was given the task of advancing towards Tithwal, clearing enemy opposition enroute, and recapturing lost territory, including the strategic town of Tithwal. The Brigade commenced operations from Handwara on 18TH May, and by 20TH May, had taken Chowkibal. The next day, Nastachun Pass had been captured, and by 23RD May, Tithwal was in Indian hands. A galaxy of Sikh soldiers of 1 Sikh was awarded the Vir Chakra at the capture of Tithwal, and the pursuit of the fleeing enemy. Major Sardara Singh VrC, Sepoy Zail Singh VrC (Posthumous), Sepoy Maghar Singh VrC, Sepoy Shingara Singh VrC, Sepoy Gurbachan Singh VrC, Sepoy Ujagar Singh VrC, Sepoy Sarwan Singh VrC (Posthumous), and Major Kehar Singh VrC.

Naushera, (1947)

On 31ST December, 1ST Patiala moved to Naushera where it formed part of 'Z' Brigade. Till 7TH January 1948 the Patialas were in various local actions against the enemy, who were trying to capture positions of tactical advantage to launching an attack on Naushera. During January and February the Battalion must have made 11 to 12 trips between Jammu-Naushera for clearing the areas of raiders. On 1ST March the Patialas were involved in some more offensive actions and on 2ND March the Unit fought heroically earning two awards posthumously: Subedar Gurdial Singh MVC (Posthumous) and Havildar Gurdial Singh VrC (Posthumous). Other Regiments were also involved in fighting in the vicinity of Naushera. The soldiers of these Regiments were awarded gallantry awards for their conspicuous bravery against the enemy: Lance Naik Sham Singh VrC of 2ND Battalion, 2ND Punjab (1 Guards), Havildar Gurdial Singh VrC of 'The Punjab Regiment', Major Piara Singh VrC of 'The Rajput Regiment', Lieutenant Colonel Inderjit Singh Butalia MVC of 'The Dogra Regiment', Lieutenant Colonel Harbans Singh Virk MVC of the '3RD (Para) Maratha Light Infantry', and Major Piara Singh VrC of 'The Rajput Regiment'.

The Sikh Regiment

For fighting in Handwara area, Tarehgam village, the following Sikh soldiers of 1 Sikh were awarded gallantry medals for their gallantry against the enemy: Sepoy Dyal Singh VrC, Sepoy Kabal Singh VrC (Posthumous), Jemadar Karnail Singh VrC, Captain Jagir Singh Kokri VrC, and Naik Sowarn Singh VrC (Posthumous).

"During 1947-1948 Indo-Pakistani conflict, Lieutenant Kartar Singh Sandhu was a Forward Observation Officer attached to 4TH Battalion, The Dogra Regiment during the Rajauri operations. In spite of being exposed to heavy enemy fire during the battle, which decided the fate of Rajauri, he continued pounding the enemy with accurate Artillery fire and thereby completely demoralized them. Lieutenant Sandhu showed exemplary courage and devotion to duty." Lieutenant Kartar Singh Sandhu was awarded VrC for his exemplary courage.

Indo-Pak War 1947

Jhangar, (1948)

The 1ST Patiala also played a prominent role in the recapture of Jhangar on 16/17TH March 1948. The battle of Jhangar and its subsequent recapture resulted in securing lines of communication to troops in that sector, thereby paving the way for the liberation of Rajauri and subsequently towards breaking the siege of Punch. In this theatre the Patialas also earned a number of honours and awards: Sepoy Hari Singh MVC, Major Joginder Singh VrC, Naik Mehar Singh VrC, and Naik Naurang Singh VrC.

Chhamb- Jaurian (1948)

On 2ND February 1948, a patrol of 7 Rajput was ambushed by the enemy in the Chhamb- Jaurian sector in Jammu and Kashmir. Jemadar Kartar Singh, who was leading the patrol of the 7 Light Cavalry, showed great presence of mind and ordered his men to surround the enemy. His action was so successful that the patrol was able to capture about 20-25 of the enemy and about 15 rifles, for which he was awarded the Vir Chakra. On 1ST November 1948, Jemadar Kartar Singh was in command of the leading troop, which entered Gumri though constantly under heavy enemy fire; he continuously kept his head out of the turret and engaged targets, which were difficult to see through the periscope due to poor visibility. By this bold action he destroyed a number of enemy bunkers and created confusion in enemy ranks, for which he was awarded Bar to his Vir Chakra on 1ST November 1948.

Zoji La, (1948)

Zoji La had been seized by Pakistani raiders in 1948 in their campaign to capture Ladakh. The pass was captured by Indian Forces on 1ST November in a daring assault, which achieved success primarily due to the surprise use of Armour, then the highest altitude at which Armour had operated in combat in the world. Initially, an unsuccessful attack was launched by 77 Parachute Brigade to capture Zojila. M5 Stuart light tanks of 7 Light Cavalry were moved in dismantled condition through Srinagar and winched across bridges; while two Field Companies of the Madras Sappers converted the mule track from Baltal up the Zoji La to Gumriinto to a jeep track. The attack on 1ST November by the Brigade saw the Pakistanis being surprised. The pass was forced and the raider column pushed back to Matayan and later Dras.

1ST Patiala

The Patialas had early shown their mettle in the battles of Chhamb, Naushera and Jhangar prior to the battle of Zojila, and had established an enviable record during this War. It won a total tally of 8 MVCs, 18 VrC's and various other awards as well, including the coveted Battle Honour, 'Zojila'. This is an unparalleled record to have established by a Battalion during any War in the history of the Indian Army.

Indo-Pak War 1947

Zojila, (1948)

The following Sikh Officers and men of 1ST Patiala were awarded the Mahavir Chakra for their outstanding bravery in battle at Zojila: JCO Lal Singh MVC, Jemadar Hardev Singh MVC, Sepoy Amar Singh MVC, Naik Pritam Singh MVC, and Jemadar Sapuran Singh MVC. Among the VrC's awardees were: Jemadar Sant Singh VrC (Posthumous), Subedar Balwant Singh VrC, Havildar Mukand Singh VrC, Naik Sajjan Singh VrC, Sepoy Teja Singh VrC (Posthumous), Sepoy Hazura Singh VrC (Posthumous), Sepoy Gajjan Singh VrC (Posthumous) Lance Naik Chand Singh VrC, Sepoy Zaila Singh VrC, and Sepoy Bachan Singh VrC.

Jammu and Kashmir

Innumerable deeds of outstanding gallantry were performed by the Sikh soldiers against the Pakistani Army and the tribal raiders during the Jammu and Kashmir operations. Classic examples are the cases of the following stalwarts; Major Sardar Malkiat Singh Brar MVC (Posthumous) Commanding 'B' Company of 1 (Para) Kumaon was killed in action while saying "Well done 'B' Company. Get down, I am all right." For his ultimate sacrifice he was awarded a posthumous Mahavir Chakra. Throughout the advance from Skanpur to Baingdangdo, Captain Kartar Singh of the Army Medical Corps, kept up with the forward line. It was entirely due to the courage and resourcefulness of Captain Kartar Singh that the wounded were given immediate treatment; thereby saving them from much loss of blood and life. He constantly dressed the wounded and evacuated them to safety. Captain Kartar Singh was awarded the well deserved VrC. Major H.S. Bolinas, leading a Company of 4 Kumaon, got within 25 yards of the enemy and was held up. Major Bolina then very cleverly manoeuvred his Platoon behind the enemy and captured Pt.7760. Major Bolina's courageous, cool and clever handling of a very hard attack over extremely difficult ground in a heavy thunderstorm earned him the VrC. Lance Naik Sohan Singh 2 Punjab (1 Guards) was mainly responsible during the night of 16th April for repulsing the enemy attack, which followed shortly after heavy 3-inch mortar shelling. Throughout the battle, Lance Naik Sohan Singh stood up at his post and fought with determination and zeal, for which he was awarded the VrC. On 25TH November 1948, Lance Naik Gian Singh of 11 Jammu & Kashmir Light Infantry was in the foremost section of a column, advancing to capture a hill feature in Poonch. With complete disregard for his personal safety, Gian Singh jumped forward and took a position right in front of the enemy's gun, despite the shower of bullets, and with lightning speed he opened fire, silencing the enemy. The spontaneous act of great courage enabled the column to pierce the enemy's defences. Lance Naik Gian Singh displayed gallantry of a high order in this action and was awarded the VrC.

Indo-Pak War 1947

Indian Armoured Corps

The 7 Light Cavalry was the first Regiment of Indian Armour ordered to join 161 Infantry Brigade for service in Jammu and Kashmir in October 1947. A month earlier Lieutenant Colonel, later Major General, Rajinder Singh had taken over the command of the Regiment from Lieutenant Colonel, later Major General, Tara Singh Bal. On 1ST November 'B' Squadron proceeded from Ambala to Srinagar, while the rest of the Regiment concentrated at Jammu. 'B' Squadron reached Srinagar airport on 5TH November 1947. Successful defence of the airport included outflanking maneuvers by the Indian Armour. The defeated tribal forces were pursued as far as Shalateng. The ensuing battle of Shalateng was a major disaster for the enemy, who lost 600 killed in the battle and pursuit; abandoning all their vehicles and load carriers, which had brought them from the North West Frontier almost upto the gates of Srinagar. Baramula was retaken the next day and this was followed by the recapture of Uri on 13TH December, thus ensuring the safety of Srinagar. Subsequently the Squadron successfully continued to perform various tasks like patrolling, escort duties and supporting Infantry operations, often under enemy sniping and fire.

Naushera (1948)

With the enemy forces building up at Asar Kadala for an attack on Naushera, it was decided to make a surprise strike on this area from Chhamb, and Cheetah Force was to assemble in secrecy without any hint of what their task was to be. Lt. Col. Rajinder Singh was appointed Force Commander and the Force moved out on 25TH January 1948. Resistance was met from small parties of the enemy on the way, but leaving detachments to deal with these; the Force pushed on at full speed and caught the enemy completely by surprise. Three hundred casualties were inflicted; damage to enemy equipment and stores also being heavy. This swiftly executed attack was a telling blow and completely destroyed the enemy base at Asar Kadala for the planned thrust to Naushera. The Squadron continued to play an important role in the operations in Naushera area, being actively engaged in patrolling the roads, and in harassing the enemy's build up with repeated raids on his positions around Naushera. On 6TH February, some five thousand tribals led by Pakistani Officers put in simultaneous attacks on Taindhar, Kot and Kangora features in a desperate attempt to break through the outposts, but were repulsed with devastating fire from the armoured cars and mortars, suffering heavy casualties. The enemy began to withdraw, but the Squadron pursued them and continued to inflict casualties. The Squadron distinguished itself by its dogged determination and courage during this phase of the operations.

Indo-Pak War 1947

Indian Armoured Corps

Jhangar (1948)

The recapture of Jhangar was a massive and well planned operation codenamed 'Vijay'. Jhangar was an important centre of communications and so located that its capture was essential. At that time, an enemy force estimated at Brigade strength was deployed along the Naushera–Jhangar road. Planning for this operation commenced in earnest, and to maintain secrecy the tanks were camouflaged to look like lorries, moving only by night. The column of 7 Light Cavalry commanded by Lt, Col. Rajinder Singh, advanced on 17TH March and despite encountering stiff enemy resistance, Jhangar was recaptured on 18TH March.

Uri Sector, (1948)

As the ridge overlooking Uri was still partly occupied by the enemy, 1 Sikh was ordered to clear the main ridge on 12TH December. It supported the 1 Sikh attack on the village of Bhatgiran on which the enemy was reported to be based. The Infantry attack did not go as planned, as the Sikhs overshot the objectives, and on seeking to retrace their steps found that the alert Pathans had quickly cut off their retreat. The Battalion had to fight its way back and inflicted heavy casualties on the enemy. In the process however they, themselves, took over one hundred casualties in dead and wounded, including the famous Jemadar Nand Singh, VC. Nevertheless, the two separate actions fought that day by Armour and Infantry, once and for all cleared Uri of the threat posed by the raiders, especially because the armoured cars had effectively neutralized their efforts to harass movement of men and vehicles at the entrance to Uri.

Indian Artillery

Lieutenant General Prem Singh Gyani was the first Indian Director of Artillery from 1947 to 1950.

Participation of Indian Artillery in Jammu and Kashmir operations during 1947-48 commenced with the first flights of civil and Royal Indian Air Force Dakotas, which transported 1 Sikh to Srinagar on the morning of 27TH October 1947. Personnel of 2 Field Regiment (SP) and 13 Field Regiment donned uniform of 1 Sikh and proceeded as a composite Company of the Battalion of 13 Field Regiment. It operated as Infantry till the first week of November 1947 when four 3.7 inch howitzers reached the area. Thereafter they took over the guns and assisted the Infantry to drive out the infiltrators along Srinagar - Baramula road. Later Artillery proved to be a battle winning factor in defence of Srinagar airfield and subsequent route of Pakistani tribesmen in Jammu region and Kashmir Valley. Artillery played a dominant role in the recapture of Poonch, Rajauri, Thangdar, Tithwal, Dras and Kargil during 1947-48.

Indo-Pak War 1947

Indian Air Force

The only all weather road link to the Kashmir Valley was through Rawalpindi and Murre in West Punjab and fair weather road link was through Rajauri, Punch and Uri after passing through the Haji Pir pass, portions of which were already under control of militiamen. The road link through Banihal was bad. Induction of the Army by road would have taken a long time and not served the purpose of saving Srinagar from the fast advancing militiamen. The only viable option was to airlift troops to Srinagar before the militiamen over ran the Airfield.

Srinagar, (1947)

The airstrips at Jammu and Srinagar were made for the small light personal aircraft of the Maharaja and were short and unpaved. There were no navigational aids, landing aids, fire fighting facilities or proper refuelling facilities available either at Jammu or at Srinagar. The high mountain ranges of the Himalayas were often covered with clouds and had to be negotiated by the Dakota aircraft with limited ceiling and negligible navigational aids. Each take off and landing would raise a cloud of dust from the unpaved airstrip and reduce the visibility further. The airlift requirements demanded landing and take off of aircraft in quick succession, leaving hardly any time for the dust to settle.

The First Sorties, (1947)

The Government wasn't sure if the airfield at Srinagar was occupied by the militiamen or not. The mission order had an unusual rider attached to it i.e. "To reconnoitre from the air and return to Jammu if the raiders have occupied the airstrip". The first three Dakotas of No 12 Sqn RIAF took off from Willingdon (Safdarjung) airfield at 0500h on 27TH October 1947 with troops of 1 Sikh. The first aircraft touched down at 0830h, within hours of the signing of the Instrument of Accession and just in time to save the Srinagar airstrip and the city from being overrun by the militiamen.

Infantry Brigade

An Infantry Brigade was to be airlifted to Srinagar. The Dakotas did the transportation while Tempests, Spitfires and even Harvards provided the necessary Close Air Support to the Army. Even help of Airlines, their pilots and ground crew was requisitioned and they rose to the occasion and did a magnificent job. Air Commodore Mehar Singh, AOC Operational Group, with his professional acumen, accomplished the uphill task in the record time of five days. Lord Mountbatten acknowledged this achievement of RIAF saying that in all his experience of South East Asia Command and Over the Hump Flights to China, he had never known such an airlift being effected at such short notice.

Indo-Pak War 1947

Indian Air Force

Air Bridge to Poonch, (1947)

In the Poonch Sector along the Pakistan-Kashmir border, the Indian troops had taken up tactical positions in the important towns along the Jammu-Srinagar Highway at Sunderbani, Naushera, Borripatam, Bhimber, Mirpur, Kothi, Rajauri and Poonch. They were constantly being troubled by the invaders who had entrenched themselves in the hills. With the road link to Jammu under threat of being cut off, the only option was an air bridge to Poonch but there was no landing ground there. A decision was taken to construct an emergency airstrip at Poonch. Six thousand refugees worked day and night and constructed an airstrip within a record time of one week. AVM Subroto Mukherjee and Air Commodore Mehar Singh landed the first aircraft on the newly constructed airstrip at Poonch on 8TH December 1947. The landing and take off at Poonch was not easy as the Airstrip was surrounded by streams from three sides and the approach was extremely steep. Despite these difficulties and against heavy odds, Air Commodore Mehar Singh created a sort of record by landing a Dakota with three tons of load against normal rated load of one ton. In a span of six days, No 12 Sqn RIAF carried out 73 sorties, averaging more than two sorties per aircraft per day, carrying more than 210 tons of supplies to Poonch and evacuating thousands of refugees during the return journey. The air bridge to Poonch was maintained for one year till the declaration of ceasefire on 1ST January 1950.

Spitfire Fighter Operations, (1947)

Spitfires from the Advanced Flying School Ambala were inducted at Srinagar on 30TH October 1947 and were soon engaged in strafing of intruders beyond Pattan. During the first week of November 1947, the enemy was able to close in undetected as much as upto half a mile from the Srinagar airfield, when the fighters spotted the enemy concentration. After that the enemy was strafed so thoroughly that it broke the backbone of their resistance. This engagement was the turning point as it removed the immediate threat to Srinagar airfield and brought a successful close to the first phase of the campaign. Notable among the Spitfire Pilots was Fg Offr Dilbag Singh, who subsequently rose to the rank of Air Chief Marshal and retired as the Chief of Air Staff.

Fighter Bomber Operations

Within a week of the commencement of air operations, Tempests of No 7 Squadron RIAF ex-Ambala were playing a decisive role in the battle of Shelatang checking the advance of militiamen. The Tempests were involved in repeated attacks and tactical recce missions over Naushera, Poonch, Rajauri, Jhangar and Handover areas causing heavy damage to enemy strongholds. The strikes over vital enemy strongholds at Pilandri, Domel and Kishan Ganga Bridge had effectively stopped the enemy troop movements and literally paralysed them.

Indo-Pak War 1947

Indian Air Force

Air Bridge to Leh, (1948)

The District of Ladakh with HQ at Leh is a high altitude desert with stark barren land East of Kashmir. There were small villages along the river Indus. During the spring of 1948, the invaders captured Skardu Fort and cut off the road link from Srinagar to Leh. The garrison at Leh was too weak in numbers and armament stores to offer any meaningful resistance to the invaders and was poised to be overrun. Major General K.S. Thimmaya, GOC 19 Div had realised that the only way to save Leh was to augment supplies through the air. Landing a low ceiling aircraft like Dakota at such high altitude after negotiating Himalayan mountain ranges was the greatest challenge any Pilot could have thought of. 24TH May 1948 was a historic day in the history of the Indian Air Force when Air Commodore Mehar Singh, with Major General Thimmaya as passenger, led a flight of Six Dakotas of 12 Squadron RIAF across the high mountain ranges of the Himalayas, towering up to 24,000 feet, negotiating the Zojila and Fatula Passes and landed at an improvised sandy airstrip next to the Indus river at a height of 11,540 feet. Air Commodore Mehar Singh in his ancient Dakota didn't have the luxury of de-icing equipment, cabin pressurisation or route maps. A big airlift was called for to save Leh but the weather wouldn't co-operate and no airlift could take place for the next three days. From 28TH May 1948 onwards, braving all odds, No 12 Sqn flew in soldiers armed with arms and ammunition, food supplies, tentage equipment and medical stores before the enemy arrived i.e. after three days. No 12 Squadron flew 700 sorties and airlifted 1000 tons of stores during the air bridge operations to Leh from Srinagar.

A Tribute

The large scale operations in Jammu and Kashmir were planned, directed and conducted almost entirely by Indian Officers. The few British Officers still holding some senior appointments in India gave some advice and assistance only in the first few months of the operations. The Indian Officers of whom Cariappa was the senior most, had till then little experience in the higher planning and conduct of War. It is a remarkable evidence of their high calibre and professional competence that they managed so well the long campaign which took place in exceptionally difficult circumstances. As already related, there had been no previous planning at all for any military action in Jammu and Kashmir. The first troops were flown to Srinagar with hardly a couple of days planning and preparation. During the long campaign, the small RIAF lost a total of 32 Officers and men who laid down their lives for the nation during these operations. In this roll of honour, there were no less than 9 Officers. The enemy casualties were definitely many times the total of Indian Army and RIAF casualties, and one estimate concluded that the enemy suffered 20,000 casualties, including 6,000 killed.

Indo-Pak War 1947

Indian Air Force

RIAFs contribution to the success of the Jammu & Kashmir operations cannot be over emphasised and it was the one weapon to which the enemy had no answer. Only the impromptu air lift to Srinagar in October 1947 saved the Kashmir Valley. A hundred planes landed every day on the improvised airfield at Srinagar, bringing in troops, ammunition and supplies and evacuating casualties and the refugees. The Air Force and civilian pilots of these Dakotas defied the mountains, the weather, and fatigue to continue the airlift till the valley was saved. Leh and the entire Ladakh region were saved by Air Commodore Mehar Singh and his gallant boys; Mehar Singh himself landing the first Dakota at the hastily prepared and untested air strip at Leh. Flight Lieutenant D.E. Pushong similarly landed the first Dakota at Punch, and made almost a hundred landings thereafter, bringing in, often under enemy shelling, the urgently needed 25 Pounder gun and essential supplies. Sqn Ldr V.P. Hegde, Flight Lieutenant L.S. Grewal and Flight Lieutenant D.N. Ghadiok were among the many other transport pilots who supplied the hard-pressed garrisons in Punch, Tithwal, Dras, Kargil, Leh etc. in innumerable sorties, in spite of getting hit many times by enemy ground fire. They all received the Vir Chakra award for their skill, dedication and gallantry. In the close support role, intrepid Fighter Pilots accurately and repeatedly attacked enemy positions at Gurais, Zoji La, Pindras, Rajauri etc., winning many Vir Chakra awards. One can well imagine the skill and courage required to hit pin-point targets, among high hills and deep valleys, in the face of heavy machine gun fire. Though Skardu could not be maintained by air supply and fell after six months of siege, when ammunition was totally exhausted, and tough inclement weather over the high hills sometimes kept the planes grounded, the overall performance of the RIAF was superb indeed. Air Commodore Mehar Singh, the AOC of No. 1 Group RIAF controlling all the air operations in Jammu & Kashmir, was honoured with the MVC for this superb performance and his vitally important contribution to it.

During the Indian thrust towards Shakargarh Sector, Captain Gurmeet Singh Punia was ordered to register targets deep inside the enemy defences. Despite enemy small arms and Artillery fire directed at him, he remained airborne directing the Artillery fire on enemy targets. During this mission, he spotted three enemy Sabre aircraft in the area. Undeterred, he remained airborne to complete his task. When attacked by enemy aircraft, he displayed great presence of mind and kept flying with great skill, evading the initial attack. The enemy ultimately shot his aircraft. Though badly burnt, he nursed his aircraft back to base and was awarded the VrC.

In all, 1,500 soldiers died on each side during the Indo-Pak War of 1947. Pakistan was able to acquire roughly two-fifths of Kashmir which it established as Azad (free) Kashmir.

HYDERABAD

The State of Hyderabad comprised most of the Deccan Plateau. It was like many other princely states where a Hindu majority was ruled over by a Muslim ruler, called the Nizam. In 1947 the Nizam of Hyderabad, dreaming of an independent state, sought Dominion status from the British only to be rebuffed by Lord Mountbatten. This only emboldened the Razakars, a militant organization led by Kasim Rizvi. Helped by the manipulations of the Nizam and his men, the Razakars let loose an orgy of violence. There was an orgy of political murders and Hindu villages were razed. Since the trouble began the Razakars had attacked about 70 villages in the state, 150 attacks outside the state, killing, raping and looting. The Nizam was given a last Warning to rein in the Razakars. India decided to mount a military operation to annexe Hyderabad to the Union territory.

Hyderabad Army

Hyderabad had a large Army with a tradition of hiring mercenary forces. This included Arabs, Rohillas, UP Muslims and Pathans. The State Army consisted of 3 Armoured Regiments, a horsed Cavalry Regiment, 11 Infantry Battalions and Artillery. These were supplemented by irregular Units with a horse Cavalry, four Infantry Battalions and a garrison Battalion for a total of 22,000 men. Finally there were the Home Guards and Razakars. They were commanded by Major General El Edroos, an Arab. The Razakars totalled about 200,000 although only 25 percent were armed with modern small arms and the rest with muzzleloaders and swords.

Jalkot, (1948)

The first obstacle was the Naldurg fort, which stood on the Sholapur - Secunderbad road about 19 km from the state border. Behind it was the Bori River with a bridge vital for the passage of Indian Armour. The fort was defended by 1 Hyderabad Infantry, some irregulars and two 25-pounder guns. The task of capturing the bridge was given to 7 Brigade consisting of 2 Sikh, 3 Grenadiers and a Battery from 34 Anti-tank Regiment, a detachment from Armoured Reconnaissance and some Engineers. Achieving complete surprise the bridge was secured intact. The main column, led by 1 Armoured Brigade, brushing aside the odd sniping and the occasional Artillery volley, linked up with 7 Brigade. Meanwhile 2 Sikh made a dash for Jalkot. Havildar Bachittar Singh Commanding a Platoon saw 2 vehicles coming from Naldurg. In spite of the withering fire he ran forward and succeeded in capturing the vehicles with their escorts. Later during the day an entrenched Hyderabad position opened up with Bren guns. Bachittar Singh led a skilful charge. 25 metres from the post he was hit on the thigh. Still he crawled forward and silenced the post with 2 grenades. Refusing to allow any medical help he kept encouraging his men till the end. He was awarded the Ashok Chakra.

Hyderabad

Umarge, (1948)

The Armoured columns of 1 Armoured Brigade now reached Jalkot. The 3RD column was ordered to pass through and continue advancing. The column, commanded by Lieutenant Colonel Ram Singh, brushing aside the resistance, made it to Umarge where the Razakars were quickly overpowered. The 4TH column was in charge of clearing the Northern flank of the main advance. Its task was to capture Tuljapur. This straddled the Sholapur Osmanabad road and connected to Naldurg by road. The column advanced from Barsi; crossing the border it isolated Tuljapur by stationing a Company each on the Tuljapur Osmanabad road and Tuljapur Naldurg road. A ridge commanding the plateau below was held by 200 Razakars and 1 Hyderabad Infantry; the ridge was captured against a stubborn resistance lasting for 2 hours.

Aurangabad, (1948)

Major General D.S.Brar was given the task of taking Aurangabad. An important military and civil centre, its early capture was essential. A column comprising 3/5 Gorkha Rifles, 2 Companies of 17 Sikh, a Squadron of Stuarts and Armoured cars from Armoured Corps School, 20 Field Battery and Engineers and Ancillary was tasked with taking the city. Moving along the Nangaon - Aurangabad axis, it brushed aside the odd opposition and entered Daulatabad fort by the afternoon. As the column reached the city outskirts the civil administration came out to surrender. A column consisting of 3 Sikh, a Company of 2 Jodhpur and some tanks from 18 Cavalry marched to Jalna. Here the Hyderabad forces resisted stubbornly before giving up.

Bidar, (1948)

After the fall of Homanabad, the column led by Ram Singh advanced towards Zahirabad to capture the junction where the road from Bidar met the Sholapur - Hyderabad road. The Armoured column was slowed down by a mine field which was cleared in due time. All along the route there was sporadic resistance by Hyderabad forces and by nightfall Ram Singh's men were a few km short of Bidar. On September 17TH, in the early hours, the Indian Army entered Bidar. With the Nizam forces being routed from all directions, the Government resigned. The next day General Chaudhari rode at the head of an armoured column to Secunderbad and the Hyderabad Army represented by Major General El Edroos surrendered. The Indian Army suffered 66 killed and 97 wounded. The Hyderabad State forces had 490 killed and 122 wounded. The Razakars suffered even more. The State of Hyderabad was annexed to the Union territory.

GOA

Goa was originally a Portuguese colony after the British left India. The Portuguese refused to give up their colonies, in spite of repeated requests from India. Even though the Portuguese assumed that India had renounced the use of force both the Prime Minister, Jawaharlal Nehru, as well as the Defence Minister, Krishna Menon, made it clear that India would not fail to resort to force as an option, if all diplomatic efforts to make the Portuguese give up Goa failed. After years of negotiation, in late 1961, the Government decided to deploy the Armed Forces in an effort to evict the Portuguese out of Goa and other Enclaves.

Operations

On 11TH December 1961, 17TH Infantry Division and attached troops were ordered to advance into Goa to capture Panjim and Marmagao. On December 18TH, the 50 Para Brigade Group moved into Goa in three columns. The Western column, 2 Sikh Light Infantry Group marched on the Dodamarg-Tivim-Betim-Panjim axis, the central column 1 (Para) Punjab on the Benastarim-Panjim axis and the Eastern column 2 (Para) Maratha on the Dodamarg-Usgao-Ponda axis. The first 2 competed in the race for Panjim.

The Western column led by Armour moved out at 0630 hrs. The Armour reached Betim shortly after 1700 hrs without encountering any opposition. The 2 Sikh Light Infantry joined it by 2100 hrs, crossing over mines and demolished bridges en-route. Panjim now lay only 549 metres away. In the absence of orders from above, the Unit stayed at Betim for the night. The same night Major Sidhu of the 7 Cavalry was killed when Portuguese guards fired on an unsuspecting Indian rescue party at Aguada Fort. On December 19TH, 2 Sikh LI received permission to cross over to Panjim and the two Rifle Companies landed there at 0735 hrs. The race to Panjim was won.

The central column of 1 (Para) Punjab crossed the border at 0600 hrs. Up to Bicholim it moved as the Eastern column but from there it turned on the Benastarim-Panjim axis. It reached Benastarim at 1730 hrs but was held up there on account of the broken bridge. On December 18TH, the water obstacle was negotiated and the column reached Panjim by 0830 hrs, 55 minutes after the Sikhs. The Eastern most columns 2 (Para) Maratha moved on the Northern route on the Sanquelim-Usgao-Ponda axis. It reached Ponda at 1345 hours and brought order to the town. The Eastern column conducted patrolling in the Ponda-Benastarim sector and established contact with the rear elements of 1 Para on December 19TH. The 63 Indian Inf. Bde, moved into Goa from Anmond in two columns. The right column, 2 Bihar, moved through a track whereas the left column, 3 Sikh, moved down the existing road. Both columns linked up at Mollem and then moved on to Ponda taking separate routes. 3 Sikh could not go beyond Darbandora on December 18TH. 2 Bihar went further to settle at Candeapar for the night. Meanwhile the 4 Sikh, the rear Battalion, reached Candeapar River crossing at midnight. At 0600 hrs on December 19TH, the 4 Sikh crossed Candeapar by wading through chest high water and by mid-day rolled into Margao.

Goa

Operations

It then marched on to Dabolim through Verna where a number of Portuguese surrendered at 1530 hrs. Finally it moved to Vasco Da Gama where the Portuguese formally surrendered at 2030 hrs. With 4 Sikh in the lead, 2 Bihar also pressed on in the direction of Margao. But finding the Sikhs well set on the outskirts of the town it advanced on Verna. The enemy stronghold was attacked on both flanks and their resistance collapsed. The swift action of 2 Bihar at Verna enabled 4 Sikh to press on to Dabolim and Marmagao unhindered. The 3 Sikh was put on reserve on December 19TH. From here it marched on to Margao and beyond in two columns. Some 400 Portuguese soldiers surrendered before it on December 20TH. A diversionary move was made from South along the Majali-Canacon-Margao axis, in Company strength. It was meant to mislead the Portuguese about the direction of the main Indian thrust. The Southern column marched up to Margao overcoming road blocks, mines and broken bridges and helped in restoring order there. The 17 Division ended more than four centuries of Portuguese rule over Goa in just 40 hours. The IAF also played a useful role as its Canberra aircraft twice bombed the Dabolim airfield, whereas Hunters bombed Bambolim wireless station.

The Indian Air Force

The Indian Air Force was requested to provide support elements to this massive ground force. The AOC-in-C of the Western Air Command, Air vice Marshal Erlic Pinto, was appointed Theatre Commander of all Air Forces in the Goan Operations. Air Commodore Shivdev Singh conducted operations in conjunction with HQ 17 Division.

The first use of air power occurred on December 18TH. No.35 Squadron sent in a massive wave of 12 Canberras led by the CO, Wing Commander N.B. Menon to attack Dabolim. The Canberras dropped 63,000 lbs. of bombs within minutes, on the runway. A second raid by eight Canberras of 16 Squadron led by Wing Commander Surinder Singh dropped more bombs on the runway area. However the Portuguese pilots of these aircraft proved to be both foolhardy but brave. During nightfall, they managed to take off the aircraft from the still damaged airfield and made their getaway to Portugal. Meanwhile six Hunters of.17 Sqn led by the CO, Squadron Leader Jayawant Singh, took off from Sambre and attacked the Wireless station at Bambolim. Attacking with a mixture of rockets and gun cannon ammunition, the station was soon left a smouldering wreck.

The Portuguese Governor, Manuel Anonia Vassalo De Silva, signed the surrender document on December 19TH and 3306 Portuguese troops of European origin laid down their arms. They were repatriated to Portugal after a few months.

Air Commodore Shivdev Singh became AOC-in-C Eastern Command and later Western Command. He retired as the Vice-Chief of Air Staff.

INDO-CHINA WAR

After its independence in 1947, India not only inherited Britain's occupation of parts of Chinese territories, but also further encroached Northwards and pushed its borderline to the McMahon Line in 1953, and as a result, invaded and occupied 90,000 square kms of Chinese territory.

In 1959, India voiced its claim to the Aksai Chin, a Uygur Autonomous Region of China. In April 1960, Chinese Premier Zhou Enlai went to New Delhi to hold talks with Indian Prime Minister Nehru, no agreements were reached and ensuing meetings between the officials of the two countries also produced no results. Unable to reach political accommodation on disputed territory along the Himalayan border, the Chinese attacked India on October 20TH, 1962.

At the time, nine Divisions from the Eastern and Western commands were deployed along the Himalayan border with China. None of these Divisions was up to its full troop strength, and all were short of Artillery, tanks, equipment, and even adequate articles of clothing. In Ladakh the Chinese attacked South of the Karakoram Pass at the Northwest end of the Aksai Chin Plateau and in the Pangong Lake area. The defending Indian forces were easily ejected from their posts in the area of the Karakoram Pass and from most posts near Pangong Lake. However, they put up spirited resistance at the key posts of Daulat Beg Oldi and Chushul (located immediately South of Pangong Lake and at the head of the vital supply road to Leh, a major town and location of an Air Force base in Ladakh). Other Chinese forces attacked near Demchok and rapidly overran the Demchok and the Jara La posts. In the Eastern Sector, in Assam, the Chinese forces advanced easily despite Indian efforts at resistance.

On the first day of the fighting, Indian forces stationed at the Tsang Le post on the Northern side of the Namka Chu, the Khinzemane post, and near Dhola were overrun. On the Western side of the North-East Frontier Agency, Tsang Dar fell on October 22ND, Bum La on October 23RD, and Tawang, the headquarters of the 7 Infantry Brigade, on October 24TH. The Chinese made an offer to negotiate on October 24TH. The Indian Government promptly rejected this offer. With a lull in the fighting, the Indian Military desperately sought to regroup its forces. Specifically, the Army attempted to strengthen its defensive positions in the North-East Frontier Agency and Ladakh and to prepare against possible Chinese attacks through Sikkim and Bhutan. Army Units were moved from Calcutta, Bihar, Nagaland, and the Punjab to guard the Northern frontiers of West Bengal and Assam. Three Brigades were hastily positioned in the Western part of the North-East Frontier Agency, and two other Brigades were moved into Sikkim and near the West Bengal border with Bhutan to face the Chinese. Light Stuart tanks were drawn from the Eastern Command headquarters at Calcutta to bolster these deployments. In the Western Sector, a Divisional organization was established in Leh; several Battalions of Infantry, a Battery of twenty-five-Pounder guns, and two troops of AMX light tanks were airlifted into the Chushul area from the Punjab.

Indo-China War 1962

The reinforcements and redeployments in Ladakh proved sufficient to defend the Chushul perimeter despite repeated Chinese attacks. However, the more remote posts at Rezang La and Gurung Hill and the four posts at Spanggur Lake area fell to the Chinese. In the North-East Frontier Agency, the situation proved to be quite different. Indian forces counterattacked on November 13TH and captured a hill Northwest of the town of Walong. Concerted Chinese attacks dislodged them from this hard-won position, and the nearby garrison had to retreat down the Lohit Valley. In another important section of the Eastern Sector, the Kameng Frontier Division, six Chinese Brigades attacked across the Tawang Chu near Jang and advanced some sixteen kilometres to the Southeast to attack Indian positions at Nurang, near Se La, on November 17TH. Despite the Indian attempt to regroup their forces at Se La, the Chinese continued their onslaught, wiping out virtually all Indian resistance in Kameng. By November 18TH, the Chinese had penetrated close to the outskirts of Tezpur, Assam, a major frontier town nearly fifty kilometres from the Assam-North-East Frontier Agency border. The Chinese did not advance further and on November 21ST declared a unilateral cease-fire. They had accomplished all of their territorial objectives, and any attempt to press further into the plains of Assam would have stretched their logistical capabilities and their lines of communication to a breaking point. By the time the fighting stopped, each side had lost 500 troops. After administering a blistering defeat in 1962, the Chinese forces withdrew 20 km behind the McMahon Line, which China called "the 1959 line of actual control" in the Eastern Sector, and 20 km behind the line of its latest position in Ladakh, which was further identified with the "1959 line of actual control" in the Western Sector.

Twang Sector

During the 1962 Indo-China War, Subedar Joginder Singh commanded a Platoon of 1 Sikh in the Tawang sector of NEFA (North East Frontier Agency). While holding a defensive position on a ridge in Tongpeng La area on Bum La axis, the Platoon noticed heavy Chinese concentrations opposite Bum La across the McMohan Line on October 20TH. On October 23RD, the Chinese launched a heavy attack on the Bum La axis. The intention was to achieve a breakthrough to Tawang. The Chinese attacked the ridge in three waves, each about 200 strong. The attack was supported by Artillery and mortar fire, besides other weapons. The fierce resistance of the Sikh Platoon, however, compelled the Chinese to fall back with heavy losses. But they regrouped quickly and launched a fresh attack under the cover of an Artillery barrage. Subedar Joginder Singh and his Platoon stood firm like a rock before the advancing enemy. In this fierce action, the Platoon lost half of its men but not the will to fight. Subedar Joginder Singh, despite a thigh wound, refused evacuation. His Platoon also refused to yield any ground to the Chinese. The last wave of the Chinese attack, which was more determined and more forceful, followed next.

Indo-China War

Subedar Joginder Singh, therefore, manned a light machine gun and killed a large number of enemies, about 52 men. But he could not stem the tide of the Chinese advance single-handedly. The Chinese Army continued advancing with little concern for the casualties. By now all ammunition with the Platoon had been exhausted. When the situation became desperate, Subedar Joginder Singh and his men emerged from their position with fixed bayonets, shouting the Sikh battle cry, "Wahe Guruji ka Khalsa, Wahe Guruji ki Fateh." They fell upon the advancing Chinese and bayoneted many to death. Finally better weapons and numerical superiority of the Chinese prevailed and Subedar Singh was captured after this epic battle. He died from his wounds and frostbite as a POW in Chinese custody. For his inspiring leadership, steadfast courage and devotion to duty beyond all odds, Subedar Joginder Singh was awarded the highest Wartime Gallantry medal, the Param Vir Chakra, posthumously.

The Sikh Soldier

Two Battalions of The Sikh Regiment fought in this War, 1 Sikh, in the Towang sector and 4 Sikh, in the Walong sector. The Sikh Light Infantry Regiment was rushed to Arunachal Pradesh. Neither the tough harsh unknown terrain, nor the bad weather, nor the inadequate weapons and equipment nor the challenges of the enemy deterred them from performing with excellence. The Regiment sacrificed 151 all ranks during the operation. A bronze plaque with the names of the brave 'Sikh Light Infantry' Soldiers who made the supreme sacrifice in the operation has been fixed in the War Memorial at Tawang.

A number of citations and recommendations for gallantry were ignored by the "higher ups" under the ostensible gloom and despondency that enveloped the politicians after the debacle. However, the outstanding gallantry displayed by the Sikhs earned them the following gallantry awards: Major Sardul Singh Randhawa MVC, Major Gurdial Singh MVC, Major Sher Pratap Singh Shrikent MVC, Major Ajit Singh MVC, Sepoy Kewal Singh MVC, and Havildar Malkiat Singh VrC.

A classic example of the Sikh gallantry during 1962 battle:-

"During the 1962 Indo-China War, the 14 Jammu and Kashmir Militia was deployed in the Ladakh sector. Havildar Sarup Singh was the Second-in-Command at the post at Bhujang. The Chinese, armed with automatic weapons and mortars, mounted a massive attack on the post on the night of 19TH October. The few Indian defenders of this post were ill equipped to resist this furious Chinese onslaught. The Chinese came in waves and seemed unstoppable, but, inspired by the Havildar, the Indians fought gallantly, inflicting heavy casualties on the enemy. The Havildar was finally overpowered and killed." For his act of courage and supreme gallantry Havildar Sarup Singh was posthumously honoured with the Mahavir Chakra.

INDO-PAK WAR 1965

The second Indo-Pakistani conflict was also fought over Kashmir and started without a formal Declaration of War. The War began in August 5TH, 1965 and was ended September 22ND, 1965. The War was initiated by Pakistan, who since the defeat of India by China in 1962, had come to believe that Indian Military would be unable or unwilling to defend against a quick military campaign in Kashmir, and because the Pakistani Government was becoming increasingly alarmed by Indian efforts to integrate Kashmir within India. There was also a perception that there was widespread popular support within Kashmir.

After Pakistan was successful in the Rann of Kutch earlier in 1965, Ayub Khan was pressured by the Army to infiltrate the ceasefire line in Kashmir. The action was based on the incorrect premise that indigenous resistance could be ignited by a few saboteurs. On August 5TH, 1965 between 26,000 and 33,000 Pakistani soldiers crossed the Line of Control dressed as Kashmiri locals headed for various areas within Kashmir. Indian forces, tipped off by the local populace, crossed the cease fire line on August 15TH. The initial battles between India and Pakistan were contained within Kashmir, involving both Infantry and Armour Units with each country's Air Force playing major roles. It was not until early September when Pakistani forces attacked Akhnur that the Indians escalated the conflict by attacking targets within Pakistan itself, forcing the Pakistani forces to disengage from Akhnur to counter Indian attacks.

The largest engagement of the War occurred in the Sialkot region where some 400 to 600 tanks squared off. Unfortunately the battle was indecisive. By September 22ND both sides had agreed to a UN mandated cease-fire, ending the War that had by that point reached a stalemate. Overall, the War was militarily inconclusive; each side held prisoners and some territory belonging to the other. Losses were relatively heavy on the Pakistani side, twenty aircraft, 200 tanks, and 3,800 troops. Pakistan's Army had been able to withstand Indian pressure, but a continuation of the fighting would only have led to further losses and ultimate defeat for Pakistan. With declining stockpiles of ammunition, Pakistani leaders feared the War tilting in India's favor. Therefore, they quickly accepted the ceasefire in Tashkent.[1] Despite strong opposition from Indian Military leaders, India bowed to growing international diplomatic pressure and accepted the ceasefire On 22ND September, the United Nations Security Council unanimously passed a resolution that called for an unconditional ceasefire from both nations. The War ended the following day.

India's Prime Minister, Shastri, suffered a fatal heart attack soon after the declaration of the ceasefire.

During the War Lieutenant General Harbakhsh Singh had refused orders to retreat, annihilated the Pakistani attacking force and saved the Punjab falling into Pakistani hands.

Indo-Pak War 1965

"Sikh War with Pakistan!"

I have read in the recent past some Indian journalist calling 1965 the "Sikh War with Pakistan." I always wondered why this respected journalist called it a Sikh War and not India's War. If analyzed, this War was wholly fought by Sikh Generals. Almost all Senior Commanders in the Western Sector and the Punjab Sector were Sikhs. Lieutenant General Harbakhsh Singh, with his Chief of Staff, Major-General Joginder Singh, commanded the entire Western zone and was, as such, the principal architect of India's victory. Involved with planning at the Army headquarters was another Sikh General, Major-General Narinder Singh. Lieutenant General Joginder Singh Dhillon, a brilliant tactician, with Brigadier Parkash Singh Grewal, and Artillery Commander, Brigadier S.S. Kalha, commanded the troops operating in the Punjab and parts of Rajasthan. Major-General Niranjan Prasad was replaced midbattle by Major-General Mohindar Singh as Division Commander in the Amritsar sector, the other Division Commander, in the Khem Karan sector, being Major-General Gurbaksh Singh. North of the Ravi, Major-General Rajinder Singh 'Sparrow', Commanding an Armoured Division in a lightning push into Pakistan, his Centurion tanks humbled Pakistan's prestigious American gifted Pattons and Chaffees. The Khem Karan sector, too, was turned into what came to be known as the graveyard of the Pakistani Patton tanks. South of the Satluj, Brigadier Bant Singh, Commanding an independent Sikh Brigade Group, defended stoutly an extensive border covering the entire Ferozepore and Ganga Nagar districts. To the North in Kashmir Major Ranjit Singh Dayal, later Lieutenant General - led his troops up the impenetrable Haji Pir Pass and captured it, inflicting a devastating blow on the enemy control in the area. Both at Hussainiwala and Fazilka, Sikh Battalion Commanders held fast to their positions despite intensely heavy shelling by Pakistan Artillery.

The Indian Air Force, with many heroic Sikh pilots under the command of the Sikh Air Chief Marshal, Arjan Singh, made devastating strikes and surprised military experts the world over by decisively outpacing a far superior, i.e. better equipped, Pakistani Air force.

Armoured Corps

The spectacular success of Indian Armour during the 1965 Indo-Pakistan War was due to the Squadron Commanders, Troop Leaders and above all Tank Crews, who have gone unnamed but who, apprehensive as they were about being pitted against a technically superior tank, faced them with stout heart, high morale and with quiet confidence in their own superior training. They inflicted such crushing blows on the enemy that he had to abandon his ambitious attempt to conquer half the Punjab. (Sandhu).

Indo-Pak War 1965

Armoured Corps

Major Bhupinder Singh, MVC

During the 1965 Indo-Pakistani War. Major Bhupinder Singh commanded the 'B' Squadron of 4 Horse. On 11TH September he successfully led his Squadron in cutting off the enemy retreat along the Gadgor-Phillora road. In the battle of Sadoke that followed, Major Singh took over the command of the Regiment after the Commander was forced to abandon his tank. Inspired by this gallantry, the Regiment fought valiantly and destroyed several enemy tanks. Nine days later the Major led his men in the battle of Sodreke. His tank, targeted by the enemy, caught fire after it was struck several times. The Major continued fighting even when all but two of his tanks were disabled. However, he sustained severe burns when he was finally compelled to abandon his burning vehicle, and died soon after. He was posthumously honoured with the Mahavir Chakra for his awe-inspiring courage and gallantry.

Second Lieutenant Har Iqbal Singh Dhaliwal, VrC

During the 1965 Indo-Pakistani War, on 8TH September, Second Lieutenant Har Iqbal Singh Dhaliwal of 17 Horse was leading the advance of his troop in Sialkot Sector in Pakistan. His first contact was made with five Pakistani Patton tanks on the North of Phillora crossroads. As he ordered his troops into firing positions, his tank was hit by direct fire from enemy tanks and burst into flames. He baled out with his crew and led them to the safety of a ditch. He saw that his driver had fallen down near the burning tank and was badly injured. With complete disregard of his personal safety, Lieutenant Dhaliwal ran forward under direct enemy fire, picked up the driver and brought him to safety. Then he led his full crew back to the rear of the Squadron position. In this action, Lieutenant Dhaliwal displayed exceptional courage and presence of mind and was a source of inspiration to all men under his command. Lieutenant Dhaliwal was awarded the Vir Chakra on 8TH September 1965.

The Regiment of Artillery

Prior to the Indo-Pakistan War of 1965 Indian Artillery was called upon to thwart Pakistani designs in the Rann of Kutch. During this operation 11 Field Regiment, 17 Para Field Regiment and Air Observation Post did the Regiment proud. These actions were followed by Artillery actions to prevent large scale Pakistani infiltrations during August 1965. Haji Pir Pass in Kashmir was considered to be a strategically and tactically vital feature. This pass was captured after heavy fighting due to support of 164 Field Regiment, a Battery from 7 Field Regiment, a medium and a mountain Battery. Thereafter gunners excelled in all operations from the frozen deserts of Ladakh to Gujrat to the West. Air defence Artillery, locators and air observation posts all rose to the occasion whenever they were called to support.

Indo-Pak War 1965

The Regiment of Artillery

Major Sarvjit Singh Ratra, VrC

During the 1965 Indo-Pakistani War, Major Sarvjit Singh Ratra performed the duties of Air Observation Post in Lahore Sector of the Punjab. In order to gain vital information and direct accurate fire on the Pakistani tank concentrations, bridges and crossing sites over the Lchhogil Canal, he had to undertake a number of flights over enemy piquets. With great courage, he carried out these extremely dangerous missions in an unarmed aircraft. Based on his information, Indian aircraft destroyed an important enemy bridge and thus cut off the enemy's Armour exit route. He was responsible for the destruction of five enemy tanks and several vehicles. His daring performance and willingness to face grave risks was a shining example to all his men. Major Sarvjit Singh Ratra was awarded the Vir Chakra on 15TH September 1965.

Second Lieutenant Arjun Singh Khanna, VrC

During the 1965 Indo-Pakistani War, Second Lieutenant Arjun Singh Khanna was the Artillery Forward Observation Officer of a Parachute Field Regiment at Biar Bet during the operations against Pakistani intruders in the Kutch area. On 15TH April 1965, the intruders attacked Biar Bet, supported by Artillery and tanks. Lieutenant Khanna engaged the intruders with accurate Artillery fire and repulsed the attack. The intruders launched a fresh and determined attack with Infantry, overwhelmingly superior in numbers, supported by Artillery and tanks. Despite accurate shelling and direct fire from tanks, Lieutenant Khanna continued to direct effective fire towards the intruders and slowed down their advance. At one stage, when a shell fired from a tank demolished the overhead cover of his bunker, he shifted to a nearby trench and stuck to his duties until ordered to withdraw. In this action he had directed heavy Artillery fire, which inflicted heavy casualties on the intruders. Under his Artillery protection the troops were able to withdraw without leaving a single man or any equipment behind. Second Lieutenant Arjun Singh Khanna was awarded the Vir Chakra in April 1965.

Major Jagdish Singh, VrC

During the 1965 Indo-Pakistani War, Major Jagdish Singh of Regiment of Artillery was Battery Commander with an Infantry Company, which launched an attack on an objective in the Poonch Sector. The Company came under heavy enemy fire and Major Jagdish Singh was wounded. Undaunted, he accompanied the Battalion Commander right up to the objective and personally directed Artillery fire accurately. He was thus able to reduce the number of casualties of the troops. Throughout Major Jagdish Singh displayed exemplary courage and determination for which he was awarded the Vir Chakra on 5TH September 1965. He retired with the rank of a Lieutenant General.

Indo-Pak War 1965

Arjan Singh, Marshal of the Air, DFC, Padma Vibhushan

Marshal of the Indian Air Force Arjan Singh, DFC, was one Pilot who grew up in the annals of the Air Force as the first Chief for leading the force into War. He was Chief of Air Staff when the Indian Air Force saw action in its first combat of the modern age in 1965. He was hardly 44 years of age when entrusted with the responsibility of leading the Indian Air Force. A responsibility he carried with considerable flamboyance and élan. Arjan Singh was born on 15TH April 1919, in Lyallpur, completing his education at Montgomery. He was still in college in 1938, 19 years of age, when he was selected for the Empire Pilot training course at RAF Cranwell. His first posting on being commissioned was flying Westland Wapiti biplanes in the North Western Frontier Province as a member of the No.1 IAF Squadron. Arjan Singh flew against the tribal forces, before he was transferred for a brief stint with the newly formed No.2 IAF Squadron. Later he moved back to No.1 as a Flying Officer, when the Squadron re-equipped with the Hawker Hurricane. Promoted to Squadron Leader in 1944, Arjan Singh led the Squadron against the Japanese during the Arakan Campaign. Flying close support during the crucial Imphal Campaign and later assisting the advance of the Allied Forces to Rangoon, Burma. For his role in successfully leading the Squadron in combat, Arjan Singh received the Distinguished Flying Cross (DFC) in 1944. He was given command of the IAF Display Flight, flying Hawker Hurricanes after the War, which toured India giving demonstrations. On 15TH August 1947, he had the unique honour of leading the fly-past of over a hundred IAF aircraft over Delhi, over the red fort. Promoted to Wing Commander, he attended Staff College at UK, and immediately after Indian independence became the AOC, Ambala in the rank of Group Captain. In 1949, promoted to Air Commodore, Arjan Singh took over the Air Officer Commanding of Operational Command, which later came to be known as Western Air Command. Arjan Singh had the distinction of having the longest tenure as the AOC of Operational Command, from 1949-1952 and again from 1957-1961. Promoted to Air Vice Marshal, he was the AOC-in-C of Operational Command. Towards the end of the 1962 War, he was appointed the DCAS and became the VCAS by 1963. He was the overall Commander of the joint air training exercises "Shiksha" held between the IAF, RAF and RAAF. On 1ST August 1964, Arjan Singh took over as the Chief of Air Staff in the rank of Air Marshal, which became the pinnacle of his career. Arjan Singh was the first Air Chief who kept his flying category till his CAS rank. Having flown over 60 different types of aircraft from Pre-WW-2 era biplanes to the more contemporary, Gnats & Vampires, he also had flown in transports like the Super Constellation. Arjan Singh's testing time came in September 1965, when the subcontinent was plunged into War. When Pakistan launched its Operation Grand Slam, in which an armoured thrust targeted the vital town of Akhnur, he was summoned into the Defence Minister's office with a request for air support. With a characteristic nonchalance, he replied "...in an hour."

Indo-Pak War 1965

Arjan Singh, Marshal of the Air, DFC, Padma Vibhushan (Cont.)

And true enough, the Air Force struck the Pakistani offensive in an hour. He led the Air Force through the War showing successful leadership and effort. Though at a certain level, mistakes were made and planning could have been better, in all fairness, it must be said that the credit for thwarting Ayub Khan's grandiose plans to capture Kashmir is shared by the Indian Army and the Indian Air Force, and Arjan Singh for leading the Air Force through the War. Arjan Singh was awarded the Padma Vibhushan for his leadership of the Air Force, and subsequently in recognition of the Air Force's contribution in the War, the rank of the CAS was upgraded to that of Air Chief Marshal and Arjan Singh became the first Air Chief Marshal of the Indian Air Force. He retired in August 1969, thereupon accepting ambassadorship to Switzerland. He remained a flyer to the end of his tenure in the IAF, visiting forward Squadrons & Units and flying with them. Arjan Singh was a source of inspiration to a generation of Indians and Officers. In recognition of his services, the Government of India conferred the rank of the Marshal of the Air Force onto Arjan Singh in January 2002 making him the first and the only 'Five Star' rank Officer with the Indian Air Force.

Indian Air Force

In 1965, Pakistan launched a surprise invasion into India. This was the first time the Indian Air Force actively engaged an enemy air force. However, instead of providing close air support to the Indian Army, the Indian Air Force carried out independent raids against Pakistan Air Force bases. These bases were situated deep inside Pakistani territory, making Indian Air Force fighters vulnerable to anti-aircraft fire. During the course of the conflict, the PAF enjoyed technological superiority over the Indian Air Force and had achieved substantial strategic and tactical advantage due to their sudden attack. The Indian Air Force was restrained by the Government from retaliating to Pakistan Air Force attacks in the Eastern Sector while a substantive part of its combat force was deployed there and could not be transferred to the Western Sector, against the possibility of Chinese intervention. Moreover, international (UN) stipulations and norms did not permit military force to be introduced into the Indian state of Jammu & Kashmir beyond what was agreed during the 1949 ceasefire. Despite this, the IAF was able to prevent the Pakistan Air Force from gaining air superiority over conflict zones. The small and nimble Indian Air Force Folland Gnats proved effective against the F-86 Sabres of the Pakistan Air Force earning it the nickname "Sabre Slayers".

Indo-Pak War 1965

Indian Air Force

Air Vice Marshal Prem Pal Singh, MVC

During the 1965 Indo-Pakistani War, Wing Commander Prem Pal Singh was the Commanding Officer of an operational Bomber Squadron. He undertook six major offensive and tactical close-support operations which included: reconnaissance over the Sargodha Airfield complex; Dab, Akwal and Murid Airfields; marking of Peshawar Airfield; and bombing of Pakistan troop and Armour concentrations in various sectors. Disregarding personal safety in these very dangerous operations in the face of heavy enemy anti-aircraft fire, he led a number of bombing and reconnaissance missions with courage, determination and tenacity. Throughout the operations, Wing Commander Singh displayed a high sense of duty, professional skill and gallantry in the best traditions of the Indian Air Force, for which he was awarded the Mahavir Chakra.

Squadron Leader Tej Prakash Singh Gill, VrC

During the 1965 Indo-Pakistani War, Squadron Leader Tej Prakash Singh Gill led missions in support of the ground forces in the Sialkot, Chhamb, Lahore and Kasur Sectors. He took part in as many as 21 ground attacks. On 21ST September 1965, he encountered a very heavy barrage of anti-aircraft fire. Instead of breaking off the attack he pressed it home defiantly in utter disregard for his personal safety and destroyed a considerable number of enemy Armour and field guns.

Squadron Leader Jasbeer Singh, VrC

During the 1965 Indo-Pakistani War, Squadron Leader Jasbeer Singh was a Flight Commander in a Fighter Squadron operating in the Western Sector during the operations against Pakistan. On 7TH September 1965, he led a strike mission against a high-powered Pakistani radar Unit near the Gujranwala airfield, which was greatly hampering air operations. As his formation was about to attack, he observed four enemy Sabre jets approaching in their flying formation. He immediately warned the formation but undaunted by the intercepting enemy aircraft of superior performance and intense ground fire, he pressed home his attack and inflicted severe damage to the radar station. In this final attack, when he had to approach the target very low, his aircraft was hit by ground fire and crashed near the target. He was awarded the Vir Chakra on 7TH September 1965.

The following Sikh Indian Air Force Officers were also awarded the Vir Chakra for their conspicuous gallantry during the 1965 Indo-Pakistan War:-

Squadron Leader Tej Prakash Singh Gill VrC, Squadron Leader Ajit Singh Lamba VrC, Squadron Leader Inderjeet Singh Parmar VrC, Squadron Leader Amar Jit Singh Sandhu VrC, and Flight Lieutenant Amarjeet Singh Kullar VrC.

INDO- PAK WAR 1971

Liberation of Bangladesh

The Indo-Pakistani conflict was sparked by the Bangladesh Liberation War, a conflict between the traditionally dominant West Pakistanis and the majority East Pakistanis. The Bangladesh Liberation War was ignited after the 1970 Pakistani election, in which the East Pakistani Awami League won 167 of 169 seats in East Pakistan and secured a simple majority in the 313-seat lower house of the Majlis-e-Shoora (Parliament of Pakistan). Awami League leader Sheikh Mujibur Rahman presented his credentials to the President of Pakistan and claimed the right to form the Government. After the leader of the Pakistan Peoples Party, Zulfikar Ali Bhutto, refused to yield the premiership of Pakistan to Mujibur Rahman, President Yahya Khan called the military, dominated by West Pakistanis, to suppress dissent. Wary of the growing involvement of India, the Pakistan Air Force (PAF) launched a pre-emptive strike on India. The attack was modelled on the Israeli Air Force's Operation Focus during the Six-Day War. However, the plan failed to achieve the desired success and was seen as an open act of unprovoked aggression against the Indians. Indian Prime Minister Indira Gandhi declared War on Pakistan in aid of the Mukti Bahini (Bengal Liberation Army); she ordered an immediate mobilisation of troops and launched the full-scale invasion of East Pakistan. This marked the official start of the Indo-Pakistani War. Three Indian Corps were involved in the invasion of East Pakistan. They were supported by nearly three Brigades of Mukti Bahini fighting alongside them, and many more fighting irregularly. This was far superior to the Pakistani Army of three divisions. The Indians quickly overran the country, bypassing heavily defended strongholds. Pakistani forces were unable to effectively counter the Indian attack, as they had been deployed in small Units around the border to counter guerrilla attacks by the Mukti Bahini. Unable to defend Dhaka, the Pakistanis surrendered on 16TH December 1971.The Instrument of Surrender was signed at Ramna Race Course in Dhaka on December 16TH, 1971, by Lieutenant General Jagjit Singh Arora, General Officer Commander in Chief of Eastern Command of the Indian Army and Lieutenant General A.A.K. Niazi, Commander of Pakistani forces, as the formal act of surrender of all Pakistani forces.

Lieutenant General Jagjit Singh Arora

Indo- Pak War 1971

Liberation of Bangla Desh

Lieutenant General Jagjit Singh Aurora, PVSM, PV

In 1971, Jagjit Singh Aurora was Commander of Indian Forces in the East, and he was responsible for hostilities in East Pakistan. In less than two weeks, months of guerrilla Warfare were ended and Pakistan split in two, losing 55,000 square miles of its territory and 70 million of its people, in an operation meticulously prepared months in advance by Aurora and others. Aurora had also been closely involved in training and equipping the Mukti Bahini, a ragtag group of freedom fighters who were transformed into an effective guerrilla force that harassed and demoralised the Pakistanis. This softened up the Pakistanis in readiness for India's strike, which was launched after Pakistan carried out bombing raids on several Indian airfields on December 3RD; 1971.These had been preceded by several Pakistani attacks on Mukhti Bahini camps inside India. War was now inevitable. Aurora had helped to oversee the logistical preparations for the coming battles, including the improvement of roads, communications and bridges, as well as the movement of 30,000 tons of supplies close to the border of East Pakistan. Even so, the Indian Army could never have anticipated how quickly the Pakistanis would be routed. Instead of attacking Pakistani positions head-on, Aurora ordered his troops to bypass them wherever possible and head straight for Dhaka. The key breakthrough came when thousands of forces succeeded in crossing the Meghna River, which the Pakistanis had left unguarded, having blown up the only bridge. Local people ferried the Indian troops across in huge numbers of small boats under cover of darkness: "That was the turning point," Aurora later recalled. On December 16TH, 1971, a day familiar to every Bangladeshi, Aurora accepted the surrender of Pakistani forces led by General Niazi. After signing the document at about 4.30pm, the Pakistani Commander handed over his Personal Pistol and Lanyard to General Aurora and removed his badges of rank. Earlier Lieutenant General Aurora inspected a combined Guard of Honour offered by local Pakistani troops, as well as the Indian Army troops which had come into Dacca. This was the first time such an event had occurred in History. Lieutenant General Aurora was accompanied by his wife.

The signing of the document ended the War, and led to the formation of Bangla Desh, the name of the new country was used in the instrument of surrender, which declared: "The Pakistan Eastern Command agree to surrender all Pakistan armed forces in Bangla Desh to Lieutenant-General Jagjit Singh Aurora, General Officer Commanding-in-Chief of the Indian and Bangla Desh forces in the Eastern Theatre." Aurora accepted the surrender without a word, while thousands cheered. He was hoisted on soldiers' shoulders amid shouts of jai Bangla (victory to Bangla).In honour of his contribution to Bangladesh liberation; he was awarded the 'Bir Pratik' Gallantry Award by the newly formed Bangladesh nation.

Indo- Pak War 1971

Liberation of Bangla Desh

Lieutenant General Inderjit Singh Gill PVSM, MC

As the Indian Army's Director, Military Operations, Gill, then a Major-General, once again displayed the same soldierly qualities and blunt reasonableness by planning and executing the defeat of the Pakistani Army in 1971. He never left his Operational Headquarters for the fortnight-long War that ended with the capture of over 91,000 Pakistani soldiers and the formation of Bangladesh.

Major General Shabeg Singh, AVSM, PVSM

When the Eastern Sector of India was becoming deeply involved in Naga anti-insurgency operations, Shabeg Singh was posted as Deputy GOC of the largest Indian Division, 8 Mountain Division which had nearly 50,000 troops under command. With his leadership qualities and employment of daredevil tactics, he was greatly successful in handling the counter-insurgency operations in that region. In 1971, when the political turmoil in East Pakistan (now Bangladesh) started and the Bengalis declared their intention to separate, the Yahya Khan Government cracked down on the Bengalis, forcing them to flee to neighbouring Indian States. India decided to intervene and in 1971 started the clandestine insurgency operations in East Pakistan. The Indian Army Chief Field Marshal Manekshaw specially selected Shabeg Singh, then a Brigadier, and put him in-charge of Delta Sector with lead Quarters at Aggartala. He was given the responsibility of planning, organizing and directing insurgency operations in the whole of Central and East Bangladesh. Under his command were placed all the Bangladesh Officers that had deserted from the Pakistan Army. These included Colonel Osmani, as adviser, Major Zia-Ur-Rehman and Mohammad Mustaq. Zia Ur Rehman later became the President of Bangladesh while Mustaq Mohammed became Bangladesh's Army Chief. Starting from about January to October 1971, the insurgency operations gradually grew to such intensity that by the time War started, the Pakistan Army in East Bengal had completely lost their will to resist. The Indian Government did not want the world to know that the Indian Army was training and directing the Bengali insurgents, so all activities were very secret. Shabeg was so thoroughly involved in these clandestine operations that for five months from December 1970 to April 1971, his family had no news about his whereabouts. The Pakistani Army got so widely dispersed in trying to contain the 'Mukti Bahini' that when the Indian Army launched its operations in November, 1971, they were able to walk through to Dacca, virtually unopposed. Over one hundred thousand enemy troops with the complete General Staff surrendered, leading to the emergence of Bangladesh. The credit for this great achievement was mainly due to the efforts of Shabeg Singh, who spent day and night organizing, motivating and training young Bengali youth to fight for their land.

Indo- Pak War 1971
Liberation of Bangla Desh
Major General Shabeg Singh
Guerrilla strikes were launched on five star hotels and on ships in Chittagong harbour to show the extent of power which the Mukti Bahini wielded. Strategic bridges were destroyed, factories closed and movement within Bangladesh restricted, resulting in a paralysis of the economy. No doubt it was a cakewalk for the Indian Army when the actual operations were launched. The Indian Government promoted Shabeg Singh to the post of Major General and awarded him the Param Vishist Sewa Medal in recognition of his Services. He had earlier been awarded the Ati Vishist Sewa Medal also. The Jaya Pyakash Narayan movement had started during 1972-73 and became a serious threat to the Indira Government. Police were sympathetic with JP and his followers, so the Government decided to use the Army. General Shabeg was asked to arrest JP and take some harsh measures against his followers but he refused saying this was not his job. . The vindictiveness of the Indian Government and the Army Chief was made obvious, when one day prior to General Shabeg's retirement, on April 30TH, 1976 the hero of Mukti Bahini, a highly decorated General with PVSM and AVSM, who had been actively involved in every operation that the Indian Army had fought since his joining Service and who spent the major portion of his life in field areas was dismissed from the Army. Such was the treatment meted out to a brave Soldier and an outstanding General, a leader of men, whom the Indian Government and some senior Army Officers in 1984, after Operation Blue Star, dubbed as 'disgruntled' and frustrated because he was loyal to his community and fought for its honour and to protect the Golden Temple against the Army attack. He died protecting the Golden Temple.

Major General Dalbir Singh, PVSM
Major General Dalbir Singh had the honour of forming and commanding 9 Infantry Division, in the 1971 War. On December 6TH, Dalbir Singh's Division was given the task of advancing along the axis of Bojra-Jessore-Khulna to capture Jessore and Khulna. The former was not only heavily fortified and well defended by a brigade-size force but it also housed Headquarters 9 Infantry Division of the enemy, commanded by Major General Idris. Expecting stiff resistance from the enemy, the General planned to punch a hole through Jessore's defences at Durgabati, 15 km West of the former. The Indian Division moved so swiftly that by December 8TH, Jessore was captured. This brought to Dalbir Singh the title of the "Hero of Jessore". Thereafter, the enemy fell back in great confusion to Khulna, 40 km South-East of Jessore. Moving on the heels of the enemy, 9 Infantry Division captured Khulna on December 16TH and on December 17TH, the Pakistani Brigade Commander surrendered to Major General Dalbir Singh. Major General Dalbir Singh's action in the Bangladesh War brought him the Param Vashisht Seva Medal (PVSM).

Indo-Pak War 1971

Liberation of Bangla Desh

Brigadier Sant Singh, MVC and Bar

Brigadier Sant Singh was a much-distinguished soldier decorated with the Mahavir Chakra during the 1965 Indo-Pak War. During the 1971 Indo-Pakistani War, Brigadier Sant Singh, while commanding a sector on the Eastern Front, achieved spectacular results with a mixed force, having one regular Battalion, advancing 38 miles almost on foot, to secure Mymensingh and Madhopur in eight days. During the advance, in spite of stiff opposition from the enemy, he cleared heavily defended positions at several places. Throughout these actions, Brigadier Sant Singh personally led and directed the troops, exposing himself to enemy medium machine gun fire and shelling. His personal gallantry, leadership, skilful handling of meagre resources, audacity, improvisation and maximum use of local resources were responsible for the successful and rapid advance against much stronger enemy in well prepared defensive positions. Throughout Brigadier Sant Singh displayed conspicuous gallantry and inspiring leadership for which he was awarded a Bar to his Mahavir Chakra.

Brigadier Joginder Singh Bakshi, MVC

During the 1971 Indo-Pakistani War, Brigadier Joginder Singh Bakshi was commanding a Mountain Brigade during the operations against Pakistan on the Eastern front. The Brigade, under his leadership, launched a series of successful attacks and captured a number of well-prepared enemy localities, culminating in the capture of Bogra. Brigadier Bakshi displayed professional competence of a high order and by his daring execution outwitted the opposing forces, breaking their resistance and capturing a large number of men and equipment, including the Commander of 205 Brigade of the Pakistan Army. Throughout the operations Brigadier Bakshi displayed conspicuous gallantry, determination and skill for which he was honoured with Mahavir Chakra.

Brigadier Hardev Singh Kler, MVC

Brigadier Hardev Singh Kler commanded a Mountain Brigade during the 1971 Indo-Pakistani War. The Brigade had to move along the Kamalpur-Turang River and clear enemy positions at several places on the way, including Kamalpur, Bakshigunj, Jamalpur, Tangail and Turang. The Brigadier led the advance from the front, directing the operations with great skill, disregarding the dangers to his life. It was at the battle of Jamalpur that he proved his mettle. The inspiring presence of the Brigadier helped his troops lay siege behind the enemy positions South of Jamalpur. The enemy was successfully halted; even their subsequent efforts to recapture the position were foiled by the Brigadier's astute strategy. The Pakistanis suffered heavy losses and a heavy cache of arms and ammunition fell into Indian hands. Brigadier Kler was decorated with the Mahavir Chakra for his inspiring leadership and gallantry. (Later Major General).

Indo- Pak War 1971
Liberation of Bangla Desh
Brigadier Joginder Singh Gharaya, MVC
During the 1971 Indo-Pakistani War, Brigadier J.S.Gharaya was commanding an Infantry Brigade in the Eastern Front in the Jessore Sector. His Brigade was attacked on four successive occasions and despite heavy casualties, his troops stood their ground, due largely to his excellent tactical handling, outstanding courage, constant presence and guidance. During the subsequent offensive operations, Brigadier Gharaya was with the leading troops when he was severely wounded. He refused to be evacuated till he had seen the attack through. Throughout this operation, Brigadier Gharaya conducted himself with extraordinary courage and through his personal example inspired such spirit and confidence among troops that led to the complete success of the difficult operations. For his extraordinary courage and leadership he was awarded the Mahavir Chakra.

Lieutenant Colonel K. S. Pannu, MVC
During the 1971 Indo-Pakistani War, Lieutenant Colonel K. S. Pannu was Commanding 2 Para (Maratha) Regiment. Lieutenant Colonel Pannu is most famous for having led the 2 Para in the famous Tangail Airdrop to capture the Poongli Bridge over the River Jamuna on 11TH December 1971, during the Bangladesh Liberation War. The Battalion was airdropped near Tangail (now in Bangladesh) and tasked to cut off 93 Brigade of the Pakistani Army which was retreating from the North to defend Dacca and its approaches. For his conspicuous gallantry and leadership, Lt. Col. Pannu was awarded the Mahavir Chakra.

Lieutenant Colonel Amarjeet Singh Brar, VrC
During the 1971 Indo-Pakistani War, Lieutenant Colonel Amarjeet Singh Brar, was Commanding a Battalion of Rajputana Rifles, and was given the task of capturing an important enemy position in Eastern Sector. Against heavy odds the attack was successfully carried out and the position held against fierce enemy counter-attacks. On 6TH December, the Battalion surprised the enemy and captured all their troops without firing a single round, enabling the neighbouring formation to occupy that position. Again on 9TH December, Lieutenant Colonel Amarjeet Singh Brar led the Battalion and captured the formidable Mynamati defences and held on against fierce enemy counter-attacks which were supported by tanks. Lieutenant Colonel Amarjeet Singh Brar was awarded the Vir Chakra in December 1971.

Indo-Pak War 1971

Liberation of Bangla Desh

Lieutenant Colonel Kuldip Singh Brar, VrC

During the 1971 Indo-Pakistani War, Lieutenant Colonel Kuldip Singh Brar was commanding a Battalion of Maratha Light Infantry during the operation on the Eastern Front. His Battalion was in the lead from 4TH to 16TH December 1971 and took a major part in the liberation of Jamalpur. During the attack on Jamalpur on the night of 10TH December, Lieutenant Colonel Kuldip Singh Brar inspired his men to capture the objective. In the subsequent counter-attacks, he moved from one Company locality to another, unmindful of his personal safety, encouraging his men to stand fast and beat back the enemy attacks. The enemy attacked six times but all these attacks were repulsed with heavy losses to the enemy in men and equipment. Lieutenant Colonel Kuldip Singh Brar was awarded the Vir Chakra on 11TH December 1971.

The following Sikh soldiers were awarded gallantry awards for their conspicuous gallantry against the enemy during the liberation of Bangla Desh: Second Lieutenant Samsher Singh Samra MVC, Subedar Malkiat Singh MVC, Major Davinder Pal Singh VrC, Second Lieutenant Baljit Singh Gill VrC, and Naib Subedar Gurcharan Singh VrC.

Western Sector

Unable to deter India's activities in the Eastern Sector, on December 3RD, 1971, Pakistan launched an air attack in the Western Sector on a number of Indian airfields, including Ambala in Haryana, Amritsar in the Punjab, and Udhampur in Jammu and Kashmir. The attacks did not succeed in inflicting substantial damage. The Indian Air Force retaliated the next day and quickly achieved air superiority. Action in the Western Sector was divided into four segments, from the cease-fire line in Jammu and Kashmir to the marshes of the Rann of Kutch in Northwester Gujarat. On the evening of December 3RD, the Pakistani Army launched ground operations in Kashmir and the Punjab. It also started an armoured operation in Rajasthan. In Kashmir, the operations were concentrated on two key points, Punch and Chhamb. The Chhamb area witnessed a particularly intense battle where the Pakistanis forced the Indians to withdraw from their positions. In other parts of Kashmir, the Indians made some small gains along the cease-fire line. The major Indian counteroffensive came in the Sialkot-Shakargarh area South and West of Chhamb. There, two Pakistani tank Regiments, equipped with United States-made Patton tanks, confronted the Indian First Armoured Corps, which had British Centurion tanks. In what proved to be the largest tank battle of the War, both sides suffered considerable casualties.

Indo- Pak War 1971

Western Sector

Lieutenant General Jaswant Singh, PVSM, VSM

As a Major General, Jaswant Singh commanded 10 Infantry Division in the strategically important Chhamb Sector during the 1971 Indo-Pakistan War and was responsible for thwarting what was the biggest Pakistani offensive of that War, despite the last minute orders to cancel their offensive plan, and lack of air support in the first three critical days of the War. The importance of this offensive to Pakistan can be gauged from the fact that Pakistan employed much more Artillery guns to support this thrust towards Jammu, than it had in support of its entire Eastern Command in East Pakistan! In fact Prime Minister Mrs. Indira Gandhi, in a meeting with General Jaswant shortly after the War, acknowledged it to be the "toughest battle" of the War. It is also noteworthy, that during the 1971 Indo-Pakistan War, six persons from the same family, four of whom were brothers, were fighting for the nation on the Western and Eastern fronts i.e. Jaswant was a Division Commander, Harbhajan was a Brigade Commander, Upkar was a Battalion Commander, Mohinder was a Flight Commander, Ardaman Jit was an OP Officer and Sarabjit was an Engineer Platoon Commander!.

Lieutenant General Jaswant Singh became a Lieutenant General at a very young age of 50 years. He served as the Deputy Chief of the Indian Army, and also commanded 1 Corps. He was also the 'Colonel' of the Punjab Regiment. Later, he was promoted as Vice Chief of Army Staff of the Indian Army, wherein he died in harness on 30TH March 1980 at the age of 55 years. Had his life not been cut short abruptly, he had a very good chance of becoming the first Sikh Chief of the Indian Army. During his long and very Distinguished Service, Lt. General Jaswant Singh was awarded the Param Vishist Seva Medal, the Vishisht Seva Medal as well as the C-in-C's Commendation Card.

Lieutenant Colonel Narinder Singh Sandhu, MVC

During the 1971 Indo-Pakistani War, the Pakistani Army held the vitally strategic bridge over the River Ravi at Dhera Baba in the Punjab. Lieutenant Colonel Narinder Singh Sandhu was asked to lead the 10 Battalion, The Dogra Regiment to secure the Eastern end of the bridge. In readiness, however, Pakistanis had already set in place several fortified shelters and machine gun positions. As Lieutenant Colonel Sandhu began his attack his tanks immediately got stuck in the marshes bordering the river. His men then dismounted and began the five-kilometre march to the bridge. When they were 15 metres away from the bridge, they sprang out at the enemy with the cry "Durga Mata Ki Jay". Lieutenant Colonel Sandhu remained in the forefront all through this fierce engagement, despite being wounded in the leg. His mere presence inspired his men and they emerged victorious. Lieutenant Colonel Sandhu was decorated with the Mahavir Chakra for his gallantry and skilful leadership.

Indo- Pak War 1971

Western Sector

Lieutenant General Sartaj Singh, Padma Bhushan

In the 1971 War, India was under the impression that Pakistan had only one Brigade earmarked for the Chhamb-Jaurian sector, whereas during the operations, it was discovered that there were five Brigades under the Pakistani 23 Infantry Division operating against the Indians. Pakistan started its offensive on the night of December 3RD. After a fierce battle in the Chhamb sector, in which both sides suffered heavy casualties, the Indians had to withdraw to the East of Manawar Tawi on the night of December 6TH. The Pakistanis then started their operations East of the Tawi in a bid to capture Akhnur. It was on the night of December 9TH that the enemy launched a determined attack to dislodge the Indians from East of the Tawi. Reacting to this, the GOC of Indian Division started considering the withdrawal of two Brigades to the depth positions. It was at this time that the late Lt-Gen Sartaj Singh, the then GOC 15 Corps, flew into the sector, rejected the plan of withdrawal, assumed control of the sector, reorganised the forces and ordered a counter-attack, which met with success. Thus General Sartaj Singh saved the Honour of the Country. General Sartaj Singh, known to be one of the most determined Field Commanders of his time, retired as GOC-in-C Southern Command in 1974.

Major Kuldip Singh Chandpuri, MVC

Major Kuldip Singh Chandpuri, with his small band of men of the Punjab Regiment, held fast to the Indian base at Longewala, despite several Pakistani attacks to dislodge them. The Battle of Longewala was one of the first major engagements during the Indo-Pakistani War of 1971, fought between assaulting Pakistani forces and Indian defenders at the Indian border post of Longewala, in the Thar Desert of the Rajasthan state in India. The Battle goes down in the annals of military history as a classic case of human resolve and motivation in the face of extremely heavy odds. In this battle a handful of troops, numbering approximately 100 of the Punjab Regiment, not only faced a Brigade attack supported by a Regiment and a Squadron of tanks but successfully stalled the same after incurring heavy losses on the enemy at the cost of negligible casualty to the defenders. In addition, as a result of the subsequent combined Army-Air Force effort, the enemy suffered more casualties thereby turning the tides against the superior force of the attackers during the battle. Major Chandpuri's men had completely destroyed 12 enemy tanks and the Indian Air Force accounted for 25 tanks and a railway train. The Pakistani retreating force was seen moving with only eight functional tanks out of a total of 59 tanks All through the operations the Major kept up his men's morale, moving from bunker to bunker, urging them to hold on and fight back. His dynamic leadership and gallantry won Major Kuldip Singh Chandpuri the Mahavir Chakra.

Indo- Pak War 1971

Western Sector
Subedar Mohinder Singh, MVC

During the 1971 Indo-Pakistani War, 21 Battalion, Punjab Regiment, including Subedar Mohinder Singh, was deployed at the Kargil sector in the North overlooking the critically vital Srinagar-Leh highway. The deployment was to prevent Pakistani encroachments in the area. Close by lay the heavily fortified enemy position at Hathi Matha, from where, it was believed, that further Pakistani offensives would commence. To prevent this, 21 Battalion was asked to capture Brachil pass, as it was an important vantage point. The attack commenced early on 7TH December, and in a short while they had reached the left shoulder of the pass where they were held up by heavy enemy fire. Subedar Mohinder Singh, commanding a Platoon, charged forward and engaged the enemy in close combat. His men, inspired by his daring, fought ferociously and forced the Pakistanis to retreat. This victory was a morale-booster and led to many other successes in this area. For his gallantry and leadership Subedar Mohinder Singh was awarded the Mahavir Chakra.

Subedar Gurdial Singh, MVC

In the 1971 Indo-Pak War the East Pakistan towns of Khulna, Chaugacha, Durinda, Makapur and Siramani were the scenes of battle victories by the Sikhs. In the Western Sector, in the battle of Chhamb, 27 men of 5 Sikh laid down their lives as they withstood three well-coordinated enemy attacks with tanks and earned the Regiment a crucial time of 30 hours. Subedar Gurdial Singh of 5 Sikh was awarded the Mahavir Chakra for his astute leadership and gallantry at the battle of Chhamb.

Major Jasbir Singh, MVC

The Sikh Regiment was deployed in Chhamb sector on the Western front. Major Jasbir Singh's Company was in possession of the crucial Phagia Ridge position. The enemy began the first of its offensives to dislodge the Indian forces there. The first attack was successfully repulsed, but the Pakistani troops returned with a stronger force the next day. They broke through the Indian defence and soon bitter hand-to-hand fighting ensued in which the Pakistanis were hurled back for the second time with a loss of twelve lives. The fighting was at its fiercest on December 5TH. The Sikh Company suffered heavy casualties, but led by a determined Major Jasbir Singh; they not only repulsed the advance but also recaptured a post on the Ridge lost earlier. Major Jasbir Singh was awarded the Mahavir Chakra for his exemplary leadership.

Indo- Pak War 1971

Western Sector
Lance Naik Shangara Singh, MVC

In 1971, during the attack on Pun Kanjiri by The Sikh Regiment, enemy fire had pinned down the Platoon in which Lance Naik Shangara Singh was Second in Command. In utter disregard for personal safety, Lance Naik Shangara Singh made a dash through the minefield towards the first machine gun post and hurled a grenade inside the bunker successfully silencing the gun. Then he charged the second machine gun post, leapt over the loophole and succeeded in physically snatching the gun. In doing so, he received a burst of fire in his abdomen, but undeterred he continued to hold the machine gun. The enemy was completely unnerved and fled from the bunker leaving the machine gun in Lance Naik Shangara Singh's hands. In this heroic action, Lance Naik Shangara Singh displayed conspicuous gallantry and exemplary dedication to duty in the face of the enemy and made the supreme sacrifice in the highest traditions of the Army. Naik Shangara Singh was posthumously honoured with the Mahavir Chakra.

The following Sikh Officers and men were awarded the Vir Chakra in the Western Sector: Major Harpal Singh Grewal VrC ,Major Hardev Singh Grewal VrC (Posthumous) Major Sarlejeet Singh Ahluwalia VrC, Major Daljeet Singh Sra VrC, Major Devinderjit Singh Pannu VrC (Posthumous), Lieutenant Mohan Singh VrC, Major Amrik Singh VrC, Havildar Dilbag Singha VrC (Posthumous), Havildar Piara Singh VrC, Havildar Piara Singh VrC, Subedar Pritam Singh VrC, Naik Gurjant Singh VrC (Posthumous) Naik Naib Singh VrC (Posthumous), Sepoy Sampuran Singh VrC, Sepoy Mohan Singh VrC, Sepoy Rachhpal Singh VrC, Sepoy Boota Singh VrC, Sepoy Karnail Singh VrC (Posthumous), Sepoy Swaran Singh VrC, Sepoy Jagjit Singh VrC (Posthumous), Sepoy Avtar Singh VrC (Posthumous), and Naik Chanan Singh VrC.

Regiment of Artillery

The 1971 Indo-Pakistan War was more challenging for the Regiment of Artillery than ever before. It was the first time that the Indian Army was fighting full fledged War on two fronts. In the Eastern Sector, Artillery had to improvise extensively to get guns, ammunition and vehicles across various major and minor rivers. It ensured that not once did the Infantry or the Armour have to look over their shoulders for Artillery support. During these operations 49 Para Field Battery took part in a para drop with 2 Para to capture Poongli Bridge on Lohaganj River near Tangail, which expedited surrender by the Pakistani Army in East Pakistan. 2 Para was first to enter Dacca around 11.30am on 16TH December 1971 followed by 851 Light Battery. Soon 563 Mountain Battery also entered Dacca. With this a new nation was born. In the Western Sector, Artillery played a major role in the capture of important Pakistani piquets in Ladakh, Kashmir, Rajauri, Jammu, the Punjab and Rajasthan. It was also instrumental in defeating Pakistani designs to capture large Indian territories in the Western Sector Rajasthan.

Indo- Pak War 1971

Regiment of Artillery

Lieutenant Colonel Gurbaksh Singh Sihota, VrC, VSM, AVSM, PVSM

Gurbaksh Singh Sihota was commissioned into the Regiment of Artillery on 30TH June 1963, and got his baptism of fire as a Forward Observation Officer with 1 Sikh in the Tithwal sector of Kashmir during the 1965 War while serving with 7 Field Regiment (Gazala). His services were recognised by his being 'Mentioned in Despatches'. The 1971 War found him flying a Chetak helicopter (Alouette III) with 659 AOP Squadron in the victorious offensive in Bangladesh. In addition to taking shoots with the Artillery, he flew communications sorties and operational reconnaissance many of which were with General Sagat Singh, the audacious Commander IV Corps. On December 9TH, he flew General Ben Gonsalves, GOC 57 Division, and other Officers to reconnoitre landing sites for taking troops across the mighty Meghna River. Penetrating deep into enemy held territory his helicopter was hit by ground fire, his passengers having a lucky escape. Landing at a forward helipad he took off again after evacuating two soldiers in need of urgent medical attention. That afternoon, flying the same damaged Chetak he led the first wave of the Heliborne operation on the road to Dhaka, guiding the force to the designated landing spot. The Meghna Heli-Bridge was one of the most bold operations of the campaign and succeeded because of the "can do" spirit of all concerned. For his actions on that day and the resourcefulness, courage and professional skills displayed by him, Sihota was awarded the Vir Chakra to add to the Vayu Sena Medal already bestowed upon him for his earlier flying in the operations. This Officer was later awarded the Ati Vishisht Sewa Medal and Param Vishisht Sewa Medal. He retired as Southern Army Commander in 2004, and now heads the War Decorated India Organisation.

The citation for Vir Chakra awarded to him on 9TH December 1971 read.....

"On 09 December 1971 Captain Gurbaksh Singh Sihota was ordered to carry a reconnaissance party for the selection of a suitable landing site for helicopter borne operations in the Eastern Sector. Skilfully piloting his helicopter, he penetrated deep behind enemy occupied territory. During this reconnaissance, the helicopter was fired upon and hit by enemy small arms fire. Captain Sihota, however, brought the damaged aircraft safely back to a forward helipad. Although his helicopter was damaged, he undertook a mission to evacuate two serious casualties. Later, the same afternoon and in the same damaged helicopter, he led the first wave of the helicopter-borne operations and directed other helicopters to a safe landing. Throughout, Captain Sihota displayed courage, initiative and professional skill of a high order".

Indo- Pak War 1971

Regiment of Artillery

Major Manjit Singh Dugal, VrC

During the 1971 Indo-Pakistani War, Major Manjit Singh Dugal was a Battery Commander attached to The Dogra Regiment during the operations in the Eastern Sector. Throughout the operations, he provided effective Artillery support and repeatedly exposed himself to enemy small arms and mortar fire to direct Artillery fire on enemy targets. His conduct was a source of inspiration to others and was instrumental in the success of the operations undertaken by The Dogra Regiment. In this action, Major Dugal displayed gallantry, determination and leadership of a high order. Major Manjit Singh Dugal was awarded the Vir Chakra on 7TH December 1971.

Major Atma Singh Hansra, VrC

During the 1971 Indo-Pakistani War, on 5TH December, the enemy attacked Longewala in the Rajasthan Sector in overwhelming strength with Armour and Infantry. During the battle, which lasted up to 11TH December, Major Atma Singh Hansra of an Air Observation Post Flight, unmindful of the enemy fire, was continuously in the air spotting enemy moves and concentration of troops and Armour and directing own Artillery fire against them. He also brought back valuable information. During one of the flights when he had to force land, he brought the aircraft to a safe area, got it repaired and was on vigilance mission again. Major Atma Singh was awarded the Vir Chakra on 5TH December 1971.

Captain Sukhwant Singh Gill, VrC

During the 1971 Indo-Pakistani War, Captain Sukhwant Singh Gill was Battery Commander attached to The Sikh Regiment in the Chhamb Sector. The Pakistanis launched a series of massive attacks supported by Armour, Artillery and mortar fire on the Indian positions. Captain Gill's accurate and effective control of the Artillery fire was responsible to a large extent in inflicting heavy casualties and breaking up the enemy assault. On 6TH December as the Sikhs counter-attacked, Captain Gill, acting also as the Observation Post Officer, brought down heavy Artillery and automatic fire on the enemy. Undeterred by heavy enemy Artillery and automatic fire, he came out in the open to observe and direct the Artillery fire, thereby contributing to the success of the attack. Captain Sukhwant Singh Gill was awarded the Vir Chakra on 6TH December 1971.

Indo- Pak War 1971

Regiment of Artillery

Captain Harbant Singh Kahlon, VrC

During the 1971 Indo-Pakistani War, Captain Harbant Singh Kahlon was the Observation Post Officer with the Ranian position in the Western Sector. The Pakistanis launched seven attacks on this position between 3RD and 4TH December in overwhelming strength under heavy Artillery support. Captain Kahlon, with complete disregard for his personal safety, moved from one position to another despite heavy shelling, observing and directing fire on enemy concentrations. With exceptional competence, he brought down own Artillery fire as close as twenty yards from his own position to break up the enemy assault. The defensive battle of Ranian is attributable largely to Captain Kahlon's tireless, determined and bold efforts. Captain Harbant Singh Kahlon was awarded the Vir Chakra on 3RD December 1971.

Captain Surjit Singh Parmar, VrC

During the 1971 Indo-Pakistani War, on 13TH December 1971, Captain Surjit Singh Parmar was Observation Post Officer with a Company of 11 Battalion, Gorkha Rifles, which was assigned the task of attacking enemy entrenchments in the Eastern Sector. As the attack progressed, the enemy brought down accurate and effective machine gun and Artillery fire. During the assault, Captain Parma's radio operator was wounded. Undaunted by this, he took over the radio set and carrying it himself continued to direct fire most effectively. Though hit by a bullet in the arm and by a splinter in the neck, he remained with the troops till the objective was captured. Captain Surjit Singh Parmar was awarded the Vir Chakra on 13TH December 1971.

Captain Prithvi Pal Singh Sangha, VrC

During the 1971 Indo-Pakistani War, on 5TH December, the enemy attacked Longewala in the Rajasthan Sector with Armour and Infantry in overwhelming strength. Captain Sangha of an Air Observation Post Flight was ordered to be airborne to direct tank and Artillery fires against enemy tanks and troop concentrations. Throughout, this action from 5TH to 11TH December with complete disregard for his personal safety, he spent most of the time carrying out airborne missions of observing enemy movements and sending back valuable information and directing attacks. Captain Prithvi Pal Sangha was awarded the Vir Chakra on 5TH December 1971.

The following gunners were also awarded the VrC during the Indo-Pak War of 1971: Captain Gurbaksh Singh Sihota was awarded on 9TH December 1971. Second Lieutenant Gurjeet Singh Bajwa was awarded on 9TH December 1971. Havildar Ajmer Singh was awarded on 5TH December 1971 and Gunner Ajit Singh was awarded the Vir Chakra on 8TH December 1971.

Indo- Pak War 1971

Armoured Corps
The Pakistani Armour deployed in Bangladesh consisted of M-24 Chaffee tanks and a few PT-76 light amphibious tanks. These elements were quite easily overpowered and made ineffective by Indian Armour. In the West the military campaign for India was merely a holding operation as West Pakistan tried to open a second front and occupy territory to take the pressure off their beleaguered forces in the East. Even though the micro relief was unfavorable, the combination of the superior firepower of T-55 medium tanks and the superior mobility of PT-76 light amphibious tanks allowed a certain degree of freedom to the Indian Armour. A very significant contribution was made by the Armour troops of the Indian Army who took part in the Liberation War of Bangladesh in 1971. The mixture of amphibious and medium tanks proved to be very effective in breaking through the obstacle-ridden territory. The terrain of Bangladesh, with water obstacles spread all over, was more suitable for the defenders than the invaders.

Lieutenant Colonel Sukhjit Singh, MVC
During the 1971 Indo-Pakistani War, 14 Horse, commanded by Lieutenant Colonel Sukhjit Singh, crossed into enemy territory and established itself near Nainakot. On 10TH December, Pakistani forces made a powerful armoured attack to dislodge the Indians from this position. Lieutenant Colonel Sukhjit put up a determined resistance. Leading from the front, he directed his tanks with great skill and courage. The enemy, having lost one of its tanks, retreated. The next day he led an operation to capture enemy tanks at Malakpur. During this move his forces came under heavy Artillery and mortar fire, but an unruffled Lieutenant Colonel surged ahead. In the ensuing operation, eight tanks and some Pakistani Officers were captured. Not only did the Lieutenant Colonel win a Mahavir Chakra for his inspirational leadership, his Regiment earned several Battle Honours for its exceptional courage.

Major Amarjit Singh Bal, MVC
During the 1971 Indo-Pakistani War, Major Amarjit Singh Bal of the Armoured Corps was in command of a Squadron at Jarpal, overlooking the Basant River. It was a position most vulnerable to enemy attack. Sure enough, the Pakistani forces began shelling the area heavily. The Indian troops foiled these attempts repeatedly, killing several enemy troops. The Pakistanis persisted and launched several counter-attacks over the next two days. The Indians were heavily outnumbered, but Major Amarjit Singh
Bal was able to inspire his men to repel several enemy attacks. As many as 27 Pakistani M-48 tanks were destroyed. For his inspirational leadership and able manoeuvring of his troops in battle, Major Bal was awarded the Mahavir Chakra.

Indo- Pak War 1971

Armoured Corps

Major Malvinder Singh Shergill, VrC
During the 1971 Indo-Pakistani War, Major Malvinder Singh Shergill was commanding a Squadron of 7 Light Cavalry in the Shakargarh Sector. On 8TH December 1971, he was ordered to capture a railhead, which was held in strength by enemy Infantry and Armour. During the assault, he moved swiftly and captured the railhead, despite heavy opposition and continued to hold the same till the Infantry Battalion moved forward and occupied it. During the period 7TH to 12TH December he led two missions against enemy Armour and destroyed two tanks. On 13TH December, his Squadron was instrumental in throwing back elements of 20 Lancers and 33 Cavalry of the Pakistani forces. Major Malvinder Singh Shergill was awarded the Vir Chakra on 13TH December 1971.

Lieutenant Rajvinder Singh Cheema, VrC
During the 1971 Indo-Pakistani War, Lieutenant Rajvinder Singh Cheema led his troop of the Armoured Corps for the capture of certain areas in the Western Sector. He showed great skill and determination in crossing a bund and, undeterred by enemy fire, captured an enemy post. Even when isolated at night, he stuck to his position and repulsed enemy counter-attacks. Lieutenant Rajvinder Singh Cheema was awarded the Vir Chakra on 6TH December 1971.

Second Lieutenant Kanwarjit Singh, VrC
During the 1971 Indo-Pakistani War, Second Lieutenant Kanwarjit Singh was commanding troops of 14 Horse in the Shakargarh Sector. The Squadron was ordered to attack the enemy holding Chakra crossing near the river Bein. Second Lieutenant Kanwarjit Singh closed in with the enemy positions despite stiff opposition and accurate anti-tank and Artillery fire. In the fight he manoeuvred and handled his troop effectively and thus enabled the rest the Squadron to locate and engage the enemy, inflicting considerable damage. He personally engaged and knocked out two enemy emplacements and a tank missile-launching site. While leading his troop, his tank became the target of concentrated fire. Undaunted, he remained in the open cupola of his tank directing operations and correcting the fire of his own tank when he was mortally wounded. Lieutenant Kanwarjit Singh was awarded the Vir Chakra on 12TH December 1971.

The following Sikh soldiers of the Armoured Corps were also awarded the Vir Chakra during the Indo-Pakistan War of 1971; Naib Risaldar Basta Singh VrC, Naib Risaldar Mohan Singh VrC, Naib Risaldar Dyal Singh VrC, and Sowar Mohan Singh VrC.

Indo- Pak War 1971

Indian Air Force

In East Pakistan, the overwhelmingly superior Indian Air Force was able to attain total air supremacy within 48 hours of the commencement of War with daringly innovative daylight bombing attacks by newly-acquired MiG-21 supersonic fighters, pulverizing Pakistan Air Force bases at Kurmitola and Tezgaon; and in the process, effectively grounding the Pakistan Air Force for the entire duration of the War.

While India's grip on what had been East Pakistan tightened, the Indian Air Force continued to press home attacks against Pakistan itself. The campaign settled down to a series of daylight anti-airfield, anti-radar and close-support attacks by fighters, with night attacks against airfields and strategic targets by B-57s and C-130 (Pakistan), and Canberras and An-12s (India). The Pakistan Air Force's F-6s were employed mainly on defensive combat air patrols over their own bases, but without air superiority the Pakistan Air Force was unable to conduct effective offensive operations, and its attacks were largely ineffective. Sporadic raids by the IAF continued against Pakistan's forward air bases in the West until the end of the War.

Air Chief Marshal Dilbagh Singh, PVSM, AVSM, VM

At the outbreak of the 1971 War, Dilbagh Singh was under Central Air Command, as Air Officer Commanding of Lohegaon AFB, near Pune. From his base, No.35 Squadron flying Canberras struck Karachi Oil Tanks and Harbour Installations. Dilbagh's responsibilities included providing facilities to aircraft of the maritime air operations.

Air Marshal Shivdev Singh

Air Marshal Shivdev Singh had fought in the "Battle of Britain". He was rushed back home when the Japanese conquered Burma and flew the Hurricanes in the Arakan within Burma. One of the pioneers of the Indian Air Force, Shivdev Singh, was responsible for the evacuation of his Squadron from Kohat to Chaklala at the time of Partition in 1947. He later moved to Agra to found the Transport Squadron. Besides flying the political leaders of the day, Shivdev and his men organized the massive airlift to Srinagar in time to save the Kashmir Valley from Pakistani raiders. What makes his contribution to the IAF unique is that he was perhaps the most operationally experienced Commander. He was in charge of the IAF's role in "Operation Vijay" in the liberation of Goa. The IAF Fighter Pilots played no major role in the 1962 Sino-Indian conflict. The crowning glory was his role as the Vice-Chief, when he master-minded the entire Air Operations in the 1971 Indo-Pak War. Although the Chief, P.C. Lal, was given the credit publically, the man at the head of the operation table was Shivdev Singh.

Indo- Pak War 1971

Indian Air Force

Flying Officer Nirmal Jit Singh Sekhon, PVC

Fg. Off. Nirmal Jit Singh Sekhon was commissioned into the Indian Air Force on 4TH June 1967. During the 1971 Indo-Pak conflict, Fg. Off. Sekhon was with 18 "Flying Bullets" Squadron flying the Folland Gnat Fighter based at Srinagar, In accordance with the international agreement dating back to 1948, no air defence aircraft were based at Srinagar. This changed with the outbreak of hostilities with Pakistan in 1971. Fg. Off. Sekhon was, therefore, unfamiliar with the terrain and was not acclimatized to the altitude of Srinagar, especially with the bitter cold and biting winds of the Kashmir winter. Nevertheless, from the onset of the War, he and his colleagues fought successive waves of intruding Pakistani aircraft with valour and determination, maintaining the high reputation of the Gnat aircraft.

On 14TH December 1971, Srinagar Airfield was attacked by a wave of six enemy Sabre aircraft. Flying Officer Sekhon was on readiness duty at the time. However, he could not take off at once because of the clouds of dust raised by another aircraft which had just taken off. By the time the runway was fit for take-off, no fewer than six enemy aircraft were overhead, and strafing of the airfield was in progress. In spite of the mortal danger of attempting to take off during an attack, and in spite of the odds against him, Flying Officer Sekhon took off and immediately engaged a pair of the attacking Sabres. In the fight that followed, at tree top height, he all but held his own, but was eventually overcome by sheer weight of numbers. His aircraft crashed and he was killed. In thus, sacrificing himself for the defence of Srinagar, Flying Officer Sekhon achieved his object, for the enemy aircraft fled from the scene of the battle without pressing home their attack against the town and the airfield. The sublime heroism, supreme gallantry, flying skill and determination, above and beyond the call of duty, displayed by Flying Officer Sekhon in the face of certain death, set new heights to Air Force traditions.

Nirmal Jit Singh Sekhon is the only Officer of the Indian Air Force to be awarded the Param Vir Chakra.

Folland Gnat Fighters

Indo- Pak War 1971

Indian Air Force

Air Marshal Man Mohan Singh, VrC

Air Marshal Man Mohan Singh, after a stint on the staff of HQ Western Air Command, took over 15 Squadron operating Gnats from Bagdogra. In the pre-December phase of the campaign the Unit conducted air patrols to protect "own territory" as well as discreet incursions into what was then East Pakistan to provide air cover for Mukti Bahini and covert Indian operations. At this stage M.M. Singh was approved for promotion to the next rank and warned about a fresh posting. However the Gallant Air Warrior preferred to defer his promotion and stay with his Squadron to take them to war. The Squadron conducted its first strikes on enemy positions held by 4 Frontier Force at Hilli. According to the Army after two strikes by four aircraft each from the 'Fighting Fifteen' the Pakistan Army vacated their defences in the area. The Unit continued to provide close air support in the Northern Bangladesh sector thereafter. Moving to Dum Dum on 8TH December, the Squadron provided close air support to the Army at Khulna, as well as conducting offensive strikes against river shipping, sinking two 10,000 tonnes capacity vessels at Chalna port. The Flying Lances achieved the distinction of operating thereafter from Agartala (from 13th of December to be exact) till then considered unsuitable for fighter operations because of its short runway, a considerable feat in professional terms. The Squadron supported 57 Mountain Division's successful heliborne crossing of the Meghna by providing air cover and fire support. The Flying Lances fully lived up to their motto 'Nihantavya Shtravaha' meaning 'annihilate the enemy'. Overall the fighting fifteen flew a total of 250 sorties during the War without losing a single aircraft or suffering any damage, with M.M. Singh himself flying 20 missions.

Air Marshal Manjit Singh Sekhon, PVSM, VrC, SC, VM

During the 1971 Indo-Pakistani War, as a Flight Lieutenant, Manjit Singh Sekhon was commanding a detachment of a frontline Fighter Squadron. He flew 14 missions at low height in very difficult terrain of Jammu and Kashmir and caused extensive damage to several enemy bunkers, vehicles, guns mortar position, petrol and ammunition dumps. He carried out these missions in the face of heavy ground fire. He substantially contributed to the success of the ground forces in Kargil, Tithwal, Poonch, and Uri Sectors. Flight Lieutenant Manjit Singh Sekhon was awarded Vir Chakra on 13TH December 1971.

Indo- Pak War 1971

Indian Air Force

Group Captain Man Mohan Bir Singh Talwar, MVC

During the 1971 Indo-Pakistani War, Wing Commander Talwar, Commanding Officer of a Bomber Squadron, led five day and night-bombing missions against very heavily defended enemy targets within the first 10 days of operations. He inflicted severe damage to the Pakistani Air Force installations at Sargodha. In a daylight mission in the Chhamb area, in support of the Army, he attacked four heavily defended gun positions near the Munawar Tawi River and effectively silenced three of them, facilitating the advance of troops in difficult terrain. The bold leadership, tenacity of purpose, flying skill and conspicuous gallantry displayed by Wing Commander Talwar were largely responsible for the many successes of his Squadron, for which he was awarded the Mahavir Chakra."

Wing Commander Harcharan Singh Mangat, MVC

During the 1971 Indo-Pakistani War, Wing Commander Harcharan Singh Mangat, who commanded a Fighter-bomber Squadron on an airfield at the Western front, swiftly retaliated against Pakistani raids into Indian Territory. On 4TH December, his Squadron took off to attack enemy targets. The Wing Commander led a formation of four aircraft, and his aircraft was hit three times, but continued on his way unperturbed, 200 kilometres deep into enemy territory. As another aircraft suffered a direct hit and was badly damaged, Wing Commander Mangat immediately ordered a pull out and with some adroit manoeuvring led it back to base, despite the damage sustained by the aircraft. Wing Commander Mangat continued with his missions into Pakistan inflicting immense damage to their forces. Wing Commander Harcharan Singh was awarded the Mahavir Chakra for his gallant actions against the enemy.

Wing Commander Harser Singh Gill, VrC

During the 1971 Indo-Pakistani War, Wing Commander Harser Singh Gill led several operational missions on air defence, close support, and counter air operations during the period from 3RD to 13TH December. His Squadron shot down one enemy F-194 aircraft over Jamnagar and hit another F 104 on 12TH December. Disregarding his personal safety, and with great courage and skill, he undertook strike missions over the Badin Signals Unit complex in the face of intense enemy anti-aircraft fire. On 13TH December, he undertook another strike mission on the same target. During this attack his aircraft was shot down by enemy fire. Wing Commander Harser Singh Gill was awarded the Vir Chakra on 13TH December 1971.

Indo- Pak War 1971

Indian Air Force

Wing Commander Manmohan Singh, VrC

During the 1971 Indo-Pakistani War, Wing Commander Manmohan Singh was in command of an operational Fighter Squadron in the Eastern Sector. He personally led 19 sorties and successfully engaged enemy defence positions, gunboats and ships despite heavy ground fire. His Squadron provided very effective air cover for the successful completion of the task. In addition the Squadron provided close support to the Army. Wing Commander Manmohan Singh was awarded the Vir Chakra on 5TH December 1971.

Squadron Leader Jasbir Singh, VrC

During the 1971 Indo-Pakistani War, Squadron Leader Jasbir Singh was a Senior Pilot of a Fighter-bomber Squadron. On 6TH December, he carried out a tactical reconnaissance mission deep behind the enemy lines in the Longewala area and brought back exhaustive information of vital importance, which altered the course of the battle in the area to advantage. Later on the same day he destroyed a tank and a large number of support vehicles in that area. Again on 9TH December, after carrying out another tactical reconnaissance, he attacked and destroyed four tanks despite heavy ground fire. His mission contributed significantly in neutralizing the enemy thrust in the area. Squadron Leader Jasbir Singh was awarded the Vir Chakra on 6TH September 1971.

Squadron Leader Preet Pal Singh Gill, VrC

During the 1971 Indo-Pakistani War, Squadron Leader Preet Pal Singh Gill carried out a number of successful night bombing missions over vital and heavily defended targets deep inside enemy territory, and caused severe damage to enemy installations notwithstanding heavy enemy opposition. Squadron Leader Preet Pal Singh Gill was awarded the Vir Chakra on 17TH December 1971.

The following Sikh Officers of Indian Air Force were awarded the gallantry award Vir Chakra for their conspicuous gallantry during the Indo-Pakistan War of 1971: Squadron Leader Gursaran Singh Ahluwalia VrC, Squadron Leader Iqbal Singh Bindra VrC, Squadron Leader Charanjit Singh VrC, Squadron Leader Jiwa Singh VrC (Posthumous), Squadron Leader Kirpal Singh VrC, Squadron Leader Jasjit Singh VrC, Flight Lieutenant Apramjeet Singh VrC, Lieutenant Shivinder Singh Bains VrC, Flight Lieutenant Manjit Singh Dhillon VrC, Flying Officer Sukhdev Singh Dhillon VrC, Flight Lieutenant Perminder Singh Harbans VrC, Flight Lieutenant Parminder Paul Singh Kwatra VrC, Flight Lieutenant Hamir Singh Mangat VrC, Flight Lieutenant Manbir Singh VrC, Flight Lieutenant Gurdev Singh Rai VrC (Posthumous), Flight Lieutenant Kuldeep Singh Sahota VrC, Flight Lieutenant Charanjit Singh Sandhu VrC, and Flight Lieutenant Trilochan Singh VrC.

Indo- Pak War 1971

Squadron Leader Mohinder Singh Sandhu, VrC

In his own words!

"I was commissioned on 18TH November 1963 in the IAF and was posted to a Fighter Squadron and then to a Bomber Squadron. When I became fully operational I was posted to the most prestigious Canberra Squadron in November 1968. I did a number of missions before, during and after the 1971 War with Pakistan. A real crisis was faced by one of the Bomber Squadrons on the second day of the War and that was on 4TH December. Two Pilots of this Squadron reported sick and the Commanding Officer of this Squadron in great panic came to my CO and requested a Pilot to fly a bombing mission to Sargodha. I happened to be next to my CO and I volunteered to carry out Sargodha bombing mission on 4TH December on the Canberra aircraft which I had last flown in November 1968. For this mission, fuel was very marginal and we had to stick to the flight plan to save every single pound of fuel. At the take off point at Agra we were told to hold take off due to air raid warning. I volunteered to take off without runway light which was finally permitted by Chief Operation Officer. Close to Pakistan airspace we descended to 300 feet and navigated low level for Sargodha. As per plan we accelerated near Sargodha and climbed to our bombing height, which was 7000 feet. During pull up and passing 5000 feet I spotted the runway and aligned the aircraft nose towards intersection of cross runway, and then my navigator took over and carried out precision tracking and released the bombs at the intersection of the runway. As the first two 1000 pounds bombs exploded there was heavy anti aircraft fire and which were reaching to our height. My navigator shouted Sandy get down and I just said Dicky shut up. I wanted to avoid anti aircraft guns firing range, and also I was 100 percent confident that since anti aircraft guns had opened fire and thus there would be no Combat Air Patrol over Sargodha airfield. As we went out of firing range we immediately descended to our escape height and entered our territory. As per intelligence report received subsequently this was the most successful mission that night. As far as my family is concerned my father was with the British Army and was mentioned in dispatches during World War 1, and his citation was signed by Sir Winston Churchill (then Secretary for War). Three brothers were in the Indian Army and we all fought in the 1971 War. The eldest (Lt Gen Jaswant Singh) became Vice Chief of Army and died in harness on 30TH March 1980, while the younger two (Harbhajan and Upkar) rose to the rank of Brigadier. Jaswant Singh's son Capt (later Major General) A.J.S. Sandhu and Harbhajan's son Capt Sarbjit also fought in the same War, making it six from the same family!" The citation for the award of VrC to Squadron Leader Mohinder Singh Sandhu reads: "During the 1971 Indo-Pak War, Flight Lieutenant Mohinder Singh Sandhu flew a number of operational reconnaissance missions over enemy territory. On 4TH December he was detailed for an air mission over Sargodha at night. He carried out this mission successfully, causing extensive damage to enemy installations".

Indo- Pak War 1971

Indian Navy

The Indo-Pak War of 1971 has many firsts to its credit for the Indian Navy. It was the first major War in which the Indian Navy was fully involved and the role it played tilted the balance of power in favour of India. The Aircraft Carrier INS Vikrant was strategically employed in the Eastern theatre to launch offensive operations against Pakistani ports and Units in East Pakistan. The luring and sinking of the Pakistani submarine PNS Ghazi by an innovative combination of deception and manoeuvre marked the high point of operational art. Action in the Bay of Bengal led to the total isolation of East Pakistan from any possible reinforcements. On a sadder note, the Indian Navy lost one of its Frigates, INS Khukri and part of her crew in the attack by the Pakistani submarine PNS Hangor. The Navy's innovative employment of Missile Boats INS Nirghat, INS Nipat & INS Veer to carry out lightning strikes on Karachi led to destroying not just her Men-of-War and merchant ships but also her national will and morale to fight. The daredevil missile attack on the night of December 4TH on Karachi harbour, called Operation Trident, is celebrated every year as the Navy Day.

This operation was closely followed by another successful attack on Karachi, codenamed Operation Python four days later.

Commander Rajinder Singh Grewal, VrC

During the 1971 Indo-Pakistani War, Commander Rajinder Singh Grewal was the Commander in Charge of all flying operations from INS Vikrant. The wind off Bangladesh during these operations was such that it made the taking off of aircraft from the Vikrant very difficult. Commander Grewal, however, continued to fly fighter-bombers and anti-submarine aircraft from this ship regularly. It was largely due to him that the two aircraft shot down by the enemy were recovered despite the fact that the wind conditions for recovery were extremely hazardous. Commander Rajinder Singh Grewal was awarded Vir Chakra on 4TH December 1971.

Lieutenant Raminder Singh Sodhi, VrC

During the 1971 Indo-Pakistani War Lieutenant Raminder Singh Sodhi was the Pilot of an Indian Naval Aircraft, which carried out repeated strikes on enemy ports in Bangladesh. He carried out eight strikes on the heavily defended ports of Chittagong, Khulna and Mongla. Although his aircraft was hit by enemy fire he continued his attack and led his section until one enemy ship and port oil installations were set on fire. On 11TH December he was with the force, which attacked Chittagong harbour. Despite heavy enemy anti-aircraft fire, he destroyed two oil tanks and shore installations. Lieutenant Raminder Singh Sodhi was awarded Vir Chakra on 6TH December 1971.

Indo- Pak War 1971

Sikh soldier's ultimate Sacrifice

Maj. Gen. Fazal Muqeem Khan, author of book "Pakistan's Crisis of Leadership" "The major reason for our defeat is Sikhs. We are simply unable to do anything before them despite our best efforts. They are very daring people and are fond of martyrdom. They fight courageously and are capable of defeating an Army much bigger than them. On 3RD December 1971 we fiercely and vigorously attacked the Indian Army with Infantry Brigade near Hussainiwala border. This Brigade included Pakistan Army's Punjab Regiment together with the Baluch Regiment. Within minutes we pushed the Indian Army quite far back. Their defence posts fell under our control. The Indian Army was retreating back very fast and the Pakistani Army was going forward with great speed. Our Army reached near Kausre-Hind post (Kausre). There was small segment of Indian Army appointed to defend that post and their soldiers belonged to the Sikh Regiment. A few number of the Sikh Regiment stopped our way forward like an iron wall. They greeted us with the ovation (Slogan) of 'Bolé-so-Nihal' and attacked us like bloodthirsty, hungry lions and hawks. All these soldiers were Sikhs. There was even a dreadful hand-to-hand battle. The sky filled with roars of 'Yaa Ali and Sat Sri Akal'. Even in this hand-to-hand fighting the Sikhs fought so bravely that all our desires, aspirations and dreams were shattered. In this War Lt. Col. Gulab Hussain was killed. With him Maj. Mohammed Zaeef and Capt. Arif Alim also died. It was difficult to count the number of soldiers who got killed. We were astonished to see the courage of those, handful of Sikh soldiers. When we seized the possession of the three-story defence post of concrete, the Sikh soldiers went onto the roof and kept on persistently opposing us. The whole night they kept on showering fires on us and continued shouting the loud ovation of 'Sat Sri Akal'. These Sikh soldiers kept on the encounter till next day. Next day the Pakistani tanks surrounded this post and bombed it with guns. Those, handful of Sikhs got martyred in this encounter while resisting us, but other Sikh soldiers then destroyed our tanks with the help of their Artillery. Fighting with great bravery they kept on marching forward and thus our Army lost its foothold. Alas! A handful of Sikhs converted our great victory into big defeat and shattered our confidence and courage. The same thing happened with us in Dhaka, Bangladesh. In the battle of Jassur, the Singhs opposed the Pakistan Army so fiercely that our backbone and our foothold were lost. This became the main important reason of our defeat; and Sikhs' strength, safety and honour of the country, became the sole cause of their victory."

SRI LANKA

The Indian Peace Keeping Force (IPKF) was the Indian military contingent performing a peacekeeping operation in Sri Lanka between 1987 and 1990. It was formed under the mandate of the Indo-Sri Lankan Accord signed between India and Sri Lanka in 1987 that aimed to end the Sri Lankan Civil War between militant Sri Lankan Tamil nationalists such as the Liberation Tigers of Tamil Eelam (LTTE) and the Sri Lankan military. The main task of the IPKF was to disarm the different militant groups, not just the LTTE. It was to be quickly followed by the formation of an Interim Administrative Council. These were as per the terms of the accord signed between India and Sri Lanka, at the behest of Rajiv Gandhi, then Prime Minister of India. Given the escalating level of the conflict in Sri Lanka, and with the pouring of refugees into India, Rajiv Gandhi took the decisive step to push this accord through. The IPKF was inducted into Sri Lanka on the request of then-Sri Lankan president J. R. Jayewardene under the terms of the Indo-Sri Lanka Accord. The force was initially not expected to be involved in any significant combat by the Indian High Command. However, within a few months, the IPKF became embroiled in battle with the LTTE to enforce peace. The differences started with LTTE trying to dominate the Interim Administrative Council, and also refusing to disarm, which was a pre-condition to enforce peace on the island. Soon, these differences led to the LTTE attacking the IPKF, at which point the IPKF decided to disarm the LTTE militants, by force if required. In the two years it was in Northern Sri Lanka, the IPKF launched a number of combat operations aimed at destroying the LTTE-led insurgency. Given LTTE's tactics in guerrilla Warfare and using women and child soldiers to fight battles, it soon escalated into repeated skirmishes between the IPKF and LTTE. At its peak the Indian Peace Keeping Force (IPKF) in Northern and Eastern Sri Lanka numbered nearly 100,000 men and comprised four Infantry Divisions (4, 36, 54, and 57) plus supporting arms and services, as well as paramilitary forces. The IPKF began withdrawing from Sri Lanka in 1989, on the request of the newly elected Sri Lankan President Ranasinghe Premadasa. The last IPKF contingents left Sri Lanka in March 1990.

Brigadier Manjit Singh, MVC

In October 1987, Brigadier Manjit Singh assumed command of 41 Infantry Brigade, deployed in Sri Lanka as part of India's peacekeeping forces. One of the Brigade's first tasks was to clear the Jaffna terrorist stronghold, and to establish a link with the Maratha Light Infantry in Jaffna port. All the approach roads were heavily mined and the Brigadier, on arriving at Palali Airfield, found several Indian troops facing stiff resistance at Anna Collai and Manipal. Brigadier Manjit Singh by deploying just two Companies of the Rajasthan Rifles was able to break the militant cordon and secure a link with forces at Jaffna fort. Brigadier Singh was honoured with Mahavir Chakra for his leadership.

Sri Lanka

Lieutenant Colonel Inderbal Singh Bawa MVC (Posthumous)

Lieutenant Colonel Inderbal Singh Bawa commanded 4 Battalion, 5 Gorkha Rifles during operations in Sri Lanka in 1988. The Battalion was entrusted with the task of clearing the enemy in the axis of Vasavilan, Urgmpurai and Jaffna Fort. These were well-defended militant strongholds. Lieutenant Colonel Bawa inflicted heavy casualties on the enemy along the way to capture these strongholds. In early October by marching through heavily fortified enemy territory Lieutenant Colonel Bawa successfully extricated stranded Indian soldiers from the militant's strongholds. Towards the end of the operations, a suicide squad sprayed him with bullets, killing him instantly. Lieutenant Colonel Inderbal Singh Bawa was posthumously honoured with Mahavir Chakra for his supreme sacrifice.

Lieutenant Colonel Abjit Singh Sekhon, VrC (Posthumous)

Lieutenant Colonel Abjit Singh Sekhon, Commanding Officer 7 Madras, was deployed in Sri Lanka as part of the Indian Peace Keeping Force. On 13TH April 1988, he received information about the location of an arms cache at a place called Vannerkulam and also the presence of some hard-core militants. He exercised imagination and calculated risk and approached the target areas in vehicles along a hitherto unmapped and sparsely used tract. He reached his target areas undetected and completely surprised the militants. In this action, Lieutenant Colonel Sekhon who was guiding the column killed two hard-core militants, one of whom was found to be the Area Leader. Again on 21ST April 1988, when information was received about the presence of 10 to 14 militants in the village of Urithirapuran, he gathered two Platoons and along with another Officer, personally led the column to the site of the militants. The party came under intense fire from the militants. He jumped out of his vehicle and despite intense militant fire, organised his party and returned the fire. He personally shot dead one militant and wounded another. It was at this stage of encounter that Lieutenant Colonel Sekhon was hit by a militant's bullet through the chest and died on spot. Lieutenant Colonel Abjit Singh Sekhon was awarded posthumous Vir Chakra on 26TH January 1990.

Lieutenant Colonel Manoranjan Singh, VrC

Lieutenant Colonel Manoranjan Singh, Commanding 8 Mahar, as part of the Indian Peace Keeping Force in Sri Lanka, was tasked to capture Kopia North, a citadel of the militants from 13TH October onwards. His Battalion made repeated attempts to capture this strongly held fortified militant position, but met with strong resistance. Undaunted by the odds against him, Lieutenant Colonel Singh personally led the attack by his Battalion on 18TH October 1987 and, after a prolonged and bloody encounter, captured the prestigious stronghold. The Battalion also captured intact a factory of the militants for making explosive devices; 1000 Kilos of explosives were also seized.

Sri Lanka

Captain Ravinder Singh Chopra, VrC

During the operations in Sri Lanka in 1988, on 21ST April, Captain Ravinder Singh Chopra of 5 Madras volunteered to accompany his Commanding Officer to intercept the militants at Urithirapuram. As they and their two Platoons neared the target area, the militants fired upon them. In order to cover the move of his column, and also to pre-empt any attempt by the militants to escape, Captain Chopra, along with his party, manoeuvred to a flank in the face of intense automatic fire. He spotted a militant firing at the troops and with an accurate aim shot the militant dead. At this moment, the Commanding Officer was hit and collapsed, Captain Chopra rushed to the help of his Commanding Officer and in the process was himself hit by three or four bullets in his thighs, a graze across the chin and also a direct hit on his right hand, which shattered his right thumb and detached it from the hand. He also sustained two punctures on the front portion of his chest. Despite these injuries, he continued to fire from his own weapon and to pass orders to the Platoon Commanders directing their fire and movement. The militants eventually broke off action and withdrew. Captain Ravinder Singh Chopra reorganized his Platoons and returned to the base, from where he was evacuated to hospital. Captain Ravinder Singh Chopra was awarded the Vir Chaka on 26TH January 1990.

Second Lieutenant Ranjeev Singh Sandhu, MVC (Posthumous)

During the operations in Sri Lanka in 1988, as Second Lieutenant Sandhu of 4 Assam was leading a convoy back from Mangani, militants launched a sudden attack on the convoy and Sandhu was grievously wounded. Though bleeding heavily he crawled out, carbine in hand to prevent the militants from capturing the jeep's weapons and ammunition. As a militant approached the jeep, Lieutenant Sandhu sprayed him with bullets, instantly killing Kumaran, a prominent militant leader. Sandhu continued firing till his very last breath, thwarting all militant attempts to approach the jeep. For his supreme sacrifice, Second Lieutenant Sandhu was posthumously awarded the Mahavir Chakra.

The following Sikh soldiers were awarded the Vir Chakra in Sri Lanka: Second Lieutenant Amardeep Singh Bedi VrC (posthumous), Subedar Sampuran Singh VrC (Posthumous), Subedar Sampuran Singh VrC (Posthumous), Lance Naik Mohinder Singh VrC (Posthumous), Sepoy Gurdip Singh VrC (posthumous), Sepoy Dayal Singh VrC, Sepoy Kuldip Singh VrC (Posthumous), Sepoy Sukhwant Singh VrC (Posthumous), and Sepoy Bachittar Singh VrC (Posthumous).

Sri Lanka

Sikh Light Infantry

The 1, 7, 13 and 14 Battalions of Sikh Light Infantry were deployed for peacekeeping in Sri Lanka. 14 Sikh Light Infantry was the first Battalion to land at Palali airfield on 30TH July 1987. It was later moved to the Elephant Pass area, where it effectively dominated its area of operations, till it was de-inducted in January 1989. 13 Sikh Light Infantry was airlifted from Gwalior to Palali airfield in Northern Sri Lanka on 11TH October 1987. With snags developing in the aircrafts, only the Battalion Headquarters with two depleted Companies (a total of 7 Officers, 9 JCOs and 240 Other Ranks) could land at Palali. That same day the Battalion was tasked to capture the LTTE fortress of Jaffna University, at Kokkuvil, in a heliborne operation. Jaffna University was the military headquarters of the Liberation Tigers of Tamil Eelam (LTTE). Pathfinders of 10 Para (Commando) were tasked to secure the helipad and landing zone and 13 Sikh Light Infantry was to follow in five helicopters. At about 0100 hours on 12TH October two helicopters carrying a Platoon of 'D' Company led by Major Birender Singh took off. They had a fiery reception at the landing zone, landing amidst heavy and accurate fire. Three remaining helicopters, already airborne, with the remainder of 'D' Company were ordered to return to Palali due to the effective LTTE fire. Subsequent landings were aborted and this brave Platoon could neither be reinforced nor extricated. Amidst the confusion prevailing, the Battalion was ordered to advance on vehicles to link up with the beleaguered Platoon. All communication had snapped. The last transmission from Major Birendra Singh was "Not to worry, we'll hold on". This gallant Platoon fought to the last, despite overwhelming odds, losing all but one of its men. It was probably the only action in modern times when men bayonet charged the enemy and created dread in their hearts. A quote from 'The Hindu' dated 21ST October 1987 stated, "The fact that 29 of them died and only one taken prisoner indicates the tenacity of their action". It was only on 24TH October 1987 that 13 Sikh Light Infantry could reach Jaffna University, by land, and capture the campus the same day. This is perhaps the only incident in modern War of troops fighting to the last man and last round. The action earned four Vir Chakras and nine Sena Medals, all posthumous, for the Battalion. 1 Sikh Light Infantry, moved from Jammu to Sri Lanka in January 1989. The Battalion was deployed in the Point Pedro area and was involved in the conduct of patrols and ambushes against the LTTE. 7 Sikh Light Infantry was deployed in the Trincomalee sector from November 1988 till March 1990. It had significant success on 6TH February 1990, when the LTTE attacked an ENDLF camp on the coast, very close to the Battalion post at Murgapuri. The alertness of the sentry and the quick reaction resulted in repulsing the attack and the killing of 21 militants. Two fibreglass boats, fitted with outboard motors along with a large amount of weapons were also captured. 7 Sikh Light Infantry was the last Indian Army Battalion to leave the island.

Sri Lanka

Indian Air Force

For almost three years, from 29TH July 1987 to 24TH March 1990, a period of 32 months, the Indian Air Force was engaged in continuous support of the largest expeditionary armed force in the country's history. A number of Indian Air Force tactical transport and helicopter Squadrons were used in support of the land and Naval forces in the four divisional sectors while the recently established Army Aviation Corps `cut its teeth' in central Sri Lanka, and the Naval Air Arm committed aircraft on maritime patrol and logistics.

Squadron Leader Rajbir Singh, VrC

Squadron Leader Rajbir Singh was with the Indian Air Force of the Indian Peace Keeping Force in Sri Lanka. On 3RD November 1987, Squadron Leader Singh was detailed to strike the militant's strongholds, which were impeding the advance of a Para Commando Regiment towards Mulai. On reaching the area he was directed to attack a stronghold, which was heavily defended with heavy machine guns. In spite of heavy ground fire, he carried out repeated front gun attacks with deadly accuracy. During this third attack on a machine gun nest, the aircraft was hit by ground fire. After pulling out of the attack, he noticed that the left engine was damaged and had a heavy oil leak. He immediately switched off the left engine and established flight on a single engine to avoid engine fire. Though the aircraft was heavily loaded with ammunition he decided not to jettison the much-needed armament stores. Squadron Leader Rajbir Singh realised that he was flying over a very hostile area and a forced landing would result in capture by the militants. He kept absolutely calm, and nursed the aircraft back in a very professional manner. He tried to contact base Radio Telephony but the radio set also had been damaged by ground fire. In spite of heavy traffic over the base, he landed the aircraft on a single engine, without causing any damage to the aircraft. Squadron Leader Rajbir Singh was awarded the Vir Chakra on 3RD November 1987.

Group Captain PS Bhagat and Flight Lieutenant Amarinder Singh Gill was awarded the Yudh Seva Medal for their Wartime services in Sri Lanka in 1987.

Yudh Seva Medal

(Yudh Seva Medal is India's highest Wartime Distinguished Service decoration. It is awarded for the highest degree of distinguished services in an operational context. "Operational context" include times of War, conflict, or hostilities.)

SIACHEN

Prior to the 1980s, neither India nor Pakistan maintained any permanent military presence in the Siachen region. However, Pakistan began conducting and allowing a series of mountaineering expeditions to the glacier beginning in the 1950s. By the early 1980s, the Government of Pakistan was granting special expedition permits to mountaineers and United States Army maps deliberately showed Siachen as a part of Pakistan. India, possibly irked by these developments, launched a military operation in April 1984. The entire Kumaon Regiment of the Indian Army was airlifted to the glacier. Pakistani forces responded quickly and clashes between the two followed. The Indian Army secured the strategic Sia La and Bilafond La Mountain passes and by 1985, more than 1,000 square miles (2,600 km) of territory, 'claimed' by Pakistan, was under Indian control. The Indian Army continues to control all of the Siachen Glacier and its tributary glaciers. Pakistan made several unsuccessful attempts to regain control over Siachen. In late 1987, Pakistan mobilised about 8,000 troops and garrisoned them near Khapalu, aiming to capture Bilafond La. However, they were repulsed by Indian Army personnel guarding Bilafond. During the battle, about 23 Indian soldiers lost their lives while more than 150 Pakistani troops perished. Further unsuccessful attempts to reclaim positions were launched by Pakistan in 1990, 1995, 1996.

Major Varinder Singh, VrC

The adversary, taking advantage of bad weather during the middle of April, 1987, established themselves on a dominating feature, 'Left Shoulder', in the Siachen Glacier area and started firing with machine guns and rocket launchers, preventing maintenance both by surface and air of Indian posts in Bilafondla. This created an adverse tactical position. On the night of 23RD June, 1987, the assault team of 8 JAK LI, under Major Varinder Singh managed to make an approach adopting the most difficult route to the 700 feet high vertical ice-wall on the Saltore Ridge and next night negotiated the ice wall and reached just 200 metres from the top. The advance was resumed at 2100 hours on 25TH June 1987 and under intense fire his party managed to capture the bunker after lobbing grenades at 0200 hours on 26TH June 1987. It was their third night in the open sub-zero temperature. By 0500 hours, Major Varinder Singh's assault team captured the second bunker after firing twenty rounds of 84 M M Rocket Launcher. He pressed on the attack, providing supporting fire cover while a small party led by Naib Subedar Bana Singh crawled to the last bunker and after a ferocious charge captured it. While mopping up operations were in progress, there was heavy Artillery shelling by the adversary's troops in which the Officer was badly wounded. Undeterred by his wounds, Major Varinder Singh assumed control of the Area Top by 1600 hours on 26TH June 1987, thus regaining tactical superiority over the adversary. Major Varinder Singh displayed conspicuous courage and valiant leadership in the face of the adversary. Major Varinder Singh was awarded the Vir Chakra on 26TH January 1988.

Siachen

Naib Subedar Bana Singh, PVC

Naib Subedar (Later Subedar Major & Honorary Captain) Bana Singh, PVC was born on 3RD January 1949 into a Sikh family, at Kadyal in Jammu and Kashmir. He enrolled in the Indian Army on 6TH January 1969 into the Jammu and Kashmir Light Infantry (JAK LI). He was trained at the High Altitude Warfare School in Gulmarg (in Kashmir) and also at another school at Sonamarg. He was awarded the Param Vir Chakra, the highest Wartime Gallantry Medal in India. During June 1987, 8 Battalion, Jammu & Kashmir Light Infantry was deployed in the Siachen area. It was then found that a large number of Pakistani infiltrators had intruded over the Siachen Glacier. The ejection of these infiltrators was considered difficult but necessary and a special task force was constituted for the purpose. Naib Subedar Singh volunteered to join this force. The Pakistani intrusion had taken place at a height of 6500 metres, the highest peak in the Siachen Glacier area. From this feature the Pakistanis could snipe at Indian Army positions since the height gave a clear view of the entire saltoro range and Siachen glacier. The Pakistanis called this post 'Quaid post' after their founder Quaid-e-Azam Md Ali Jinnah. The enemy post was virtually an impregnable glacier fortress with ice walls, 457 metres high, on either side. Naib Subedar Bana Singh led his men through an extremely difficult and hazardous route. He and his men crawled and closed in on the adversary. Lobbing hand grenades, charging with a bayonet and moving from trench to trench, he cleared the post of all intruders. A total of 62 people participated in the final operation. Two Officers, 3 JCO and 57 jawans were selected. The operation was conducted in three phases on June 23RD, June 25TH and June 26TH, 1987. A first Platoon was sent under Major Varinder Singh on 23RD June but unfortunately they had to come back. Two soldiers were killed. The second Platoon led by Subedar Harnam Singh with 10 jawans made an attempt on June 25TH. At that time, there was no problem with the rope, but due to a communication gap, the mission had to be aborted. The next day, on 26TH, Bana Singh and his team were told that they were to try another attack and capture the Post from the enemy that day. A message was passed from the Major General who was the Task Force Commander and they got the green light. The assault was in daylight and there was a heavy snowfall. There was a single bunker on the top. At the end, a total of six Pakistanis were killed. Their bodies were brought back and were later handed over to the Pakistani authorities during a flag meeting in Kargil. The entire operation was completed by 5 pm. Naib Subedar Bana Singh was awarded the Param Vir Chakra, the highest Wartime Gallantry Medal in India, for conspicuous bravery and leadership under most adverse conditions on January 26TH, 1988. The peak which he captured was renamed Bana Top in his honour. At the time of the Kargil War, he was the only PVC awardee who was still serving in the Army.

KARGIL

Pakistani paramilitary forces and Kashmiri insurgents in mid-1999 captured the deserted, but strategic, Himalayan heights in the Kargil district of India. These had been vacated by the Indian Army during the onset of the inhospitable winter and were supposed to be re-occupied in spring. The regular Pakistani troops who took control of these areas received important support, both in the form of arms and supplies, from Pakistan. Once the scale of the Pakistani incursion was realised, the Indian Army quickly mobilised about 200,000 troops and Operation Meghdoot was launched. Two months into the conflict, Indian troops had slowly retaken most of the ridges they had previously abandoned. The Indian Army launched its final attacks in the last week of July; as soon as the Drass sub sector had been cleared of Pakistani forces, the fighting ceased on 26TH July. By the end of the War, India had resumed control of all territory South and East of the Line of Control, as was established in July 1972 per the Shimla Accord.

Captain Gurjinder Singh Suri, MVC (Posthumous)

Captain Gurjinder Singh Suri commanded a military Post at Faulad situated at a height of 11,200 ft in the Gulmarg sector of Jammu and Kashmir. On November 9TH 1999, the enemy launched an attack on the post, which was successfully repulsed. Captain Gurjinder Singh Suri immediately set out to clear the enemy bunkers, one by one. He killed two enemy soldiers and silenced a machine gun. However, he got a burst in his left arm in the process. Unmindful of his injury, he continued to lead his men. He then lobbed two hand-grenades into another bunker and entered inside spraying bullets, and killed one enemy soldier. At this point, he was hit by a rocket-propelled grenade and was critically wounded. He refused to be evacuated and continued to exhort his men till he breathed his last. Captain Suri displayed extraordinary leadership, inspired by which the Ghataks (Platoon) fell upon the enemy with vengeance and annihilated them. Captain Gurjinder Singh Suri thus displayed conspicuous bravery and leadership of the highest order in the face of the enemy, and made the supreme sacrifice in the highest traditions of the Indian Army. Captain Gurjinder Singh Suri was posthumously honoured with the Mahavir Chakra.

Colonel Umesh Singh Bawa, VrC

During "Operation Vijay" 17 Jat was tasked to capture Pimple complex, part of Point 4875, a most dominating feature in the Mushkoh Valley. Colonel Umesh Singh Bawa, the Commanding Officer of the Unit, led the attack. Under heavy enemy Artillery, mortar and small arm fire, he supervised capture of four enemy positions that led to the crumbling of enemy defences. The Unit also successfully repulsed the enemy counter attacks on Pimple Two. The Unit also recovered thirty-five weapons and twenty-two enemy dead bodies, including that of an Officer. For his exemplary courage Colonel Umesh Singh Bawa was awarded the Vir Chakra.

Kargil

Subedar Nirmal Singh, VrC (Posthumous)
On 5TH July 1999, Subedar Nirmal Singh of 8 Sikh was leading a small team to establish a foothold on an objective in Drass sub-sector as part of 'Operation Vijay'. While advancing, Subedar Singh noticed enemy movement. Before the enemy could react, he directed fire on the enemy and inflicted heavy casualties. The enemy was forced to retreat. Subedar Karnail Singh quickly reached the objective and captured it. The rest of the Company followed up next day and reorganized defences. Subedar Nirmal Singh was mortally wounded on the slope of Helmet and made the supreme sacrifice for the nation. Subedar Nirmal Singh was awarded a posthumous Vir Chakra in 1999.

Naib Subedar Karnail Singh, VrC (Posthumous)
During 'Operation Vijay' Naib Subedar Karnail Singh, and five soldiers of 8 Sikh, was deployed on the reverse slope of area Helmet in the Kargil Sector. The enemy opened heavy fire and then attacked the position held by the Sikhs. Naib Subedar Karnail Singh fought the enemy in the hand-to-hand fighting and the attack was repulsed. Karnail Singh was seriously wounded during the fighting. Soon the enemy launched a counter-attack with 40 to 50 men. Despite being seriously wounded Naib Subedar Karnail Singh charged at them with his men, inflicting heavy casualties on them in close combat. He killed four enemy soldiers and injured many more, forcing them to flee. He, along with his men, kept the enemy at bay till they all succumbed to their fatal injuries. Displaying conspicuous courage, bravery and exceptional devotion to duty, Naib Subedar Karnail Singh made the supreme sacrifice of his life. Naib Subedar Karnail Singh was awarded posthumous Vir Chakra in 1999.

Sepoy Satpal Singh VrC, (Posthumous)
Sepoy Satpal Singh of 8 Sikh, along with his section, was deployed in the Drass sector during 'Operation Vijay' on 6TH July 1999. The enemy launched an attack and intense fire fighting ensued between Sepoy Satpal Singh and the intruders. While repulsing the attack, Sepoy Satpal Singh got seriously wounded. He did not allow the enemy to come closer and beat back the counter attack. The enemy launched a second counter attack with 40 to 45 intruders. He boldly confronted them again. Though suffering from multiple gunshot wounds, he kept engaging the intruders and killed four of them. Many more intruders were injured and this finally forced the enemy to flee. He held on to his post and kept motivating his comrades to fight till the last. Displaying extreme bravery and courage, Sepoy Satpal Singh single handedly took on the enemy face-to-face at close quarters, which motivated the troops around him and subsequently repulsed the fierce counter attack. Sepoy Satpal Singh was mortally wounded during the fighting and succumbed to his injuries. Sepoy Satpal Singh was awarded posthumous Vir Chakra in 1999.

AMERICAN SIKH SOLDIERS

Bhagat Singh Thind

India Bhagat Singh Thind was born on October 3RD, 1892, in the village of Taragarh in the state of the Punjab, India. He went to the United States in 1913 to pursue higher education in an American university. However, on July 22ND, 1918, he was recruited by the US Army to fight in World War One. A few months later, on November 8TH, 1918, Bhagat Singh was promoted to the rank of an Acting Sergeant. He received an honorable discharge on December 16TH, 1918, with his character designated as "excellent". After the War he sought the right to become a naturalized citizen, following a legal ruling that Caucasians had access to such rights. In 1923, a crucial Supreme Court case United States v. Bhagat Singh Thind was decided in favor of the United States, retroactively denying all Indians citizenship for not being Caucasian in "the common man's understanding of the term". However, Thind remained in the U.S., completed his PhD, and delivered lectures in metaphysics. Thind applied for and received U.S. citizenship, however, the Immigration and Naturalization Service appealed and the court revoked his citizenship. Finally he received his citizenship certificate on December 9TH, 1918, wearing military uniform as he was still serving in the U.S. Army. However, the Immigration and Naturalization Service did not agree with the district court granting the citizenship. Thind's citizenship was revoked in four days, on December 13TH, 1918, on the grounds that he was not a "free white man". Thind applied for citizenship again from the neighboring state, Oregon, on May 6TH, 1919. The same Immigration and Naturalization Service official who got Thind's citizenship revoked first time, tried to convince the judge to refuse citizenship. The judge took all arguments and Thind's military record into consideration and declined to agree with the INS. Thus, Thind received US citizenship for the second time on November 18TH, 1920. Thind's citizenship was revoked and the INS issued a certificate in 1926 canceling his citizenship for a second time. In 1935, the 74th congress passed a law allowing citizenship to U.S. veterans of World War I, even those from the barred zones. Thind received his U.S. citizenship through the state of New York in 1936, taking the oath for the third time to become an American citizen. Thind, who had earned a PhD, became a writer and was respected as a spiritual guide. Thind was working on some books when he died on September 15TH, 1967.

The following American Sikhs served in the American Armed Forces with their articles of faith intact: Colonel Gopal Singh Khalsa (from 1976 to 2004), Colonel Arjinderpal Singh Sekhon (from 1984 to 2009), and Colonel G.B. Singh (from 1979 to 2007).

Major Kamaljeet Singh Kalsi, Captain Tejdeep Singh Rattan and Corporal Simran Preet Singh Lamba are the only three Sikhs serving in the U.S. Army currently (2013). Having shattered stereotypes, the three have won awards and commendations for their service, including postings in Afghanistan.

Sikhs have a historic military culture and have long kept their articles of faith in the militaries of Britain, Canada, Malaysia, Singapore, Kenya, and India.

American Sikh Soldier
The Purple Heart
The Purple Heart is a United States military decoration awarded in the name of the President to those who have been wounded or killed while serving on or after April 5TH 1917 with the U.S. military. The National Purple Heart Hall of Honor is located in New Windsor, New York.

Bronze Star
Bronze Star, a United States military decoration was awarded to personnel who had distinguished themselves by heroic or meritorious military achievements.

Sergeant Uday Singh Taunque, MOPH, BSM
Sergeant Uday Singh Taunque (1982-2003) was the first soldier of Indian origin to die fighting in the Iraq War as part of US Army. He was born in Jaipur, India on 23RD April 1982. In June 2000 he left for the US with his father and sister and decided to join the US Army. Uday enlisted in the US Army on 28TH August 2000 and on termination of initial training at Fort Knox was assigned to Charlie Company 1ST Battalion, 34TH Armor Regiment, based at Fort Riley, Kansas, USA. Uday's Unit was deployed to Iraq in September 2003. On 1ST December, Uday was in the lead Humvee of his Platoon as a gunner while out on reconnaissance in Habbaniyah, when the Platoon came under fire. Uday was the first to return fire, and kept the insurgents pinned down until reinforcements arrived. However, in the continuing fire fight he was hit with a gunshot to his head and subsequently died whilst being transported to the hospital. The mission led to the capture of a number of terrorists and large cache of weapons. Uday was awarded with the Bronze Star and Purple Heart for his bravery and ultimate sacrifice. Uday's ashes are buried at Arlington National Cemetery, Arlington (near Washington D.C.) Section 60 Gravesite No 8122. Also, a memorial for perpetuating his memory is established at his home in Chandigarh, Illinois General Assembly also paid homage to Sergeant Uday's bravery and martyrdom by passing a Senate Resolution. It is also noteworthy that Sergeant Uday was a fourth generation soldier from a distinguished military family.

American Sikh Soldier
Sergeant Uday Singh Taunque, MOPH, BSM (Cont.)

In what was the first time a foreign Army held a funeral ceremony in India, for a young U.S. Army Sergeant who died in Iraq. He was accorded full US honours in a solemn ceremony in his home town Chandigarh on 11TH December 2003. The coffin draped in the US flag was brought out from the vehicle and a group of U.S. soldiers folded the American flag into a triangle. Lt Gen James Campbell, the Commander of the U.S. Army in the Pacific, who had flown in especially from Hawaii, handed over the flag to Uday's father after laying a wreath on the coffin. The U.S. soldiers then presented a guard of honour to Uday, whose body was draped in "Class A" uniform, by firing a volley of shots. It wasn't the tricolour that the body was draped in, but the stars and stripes. It wasn't The Last Post that was played, but Taps, its U.S. Army equivalent. And both India and the US mourned the loss of Uday Singh, the 21-year-old U.S. Army sergeant of Indian origin - an American hero and an Indian son. Later, the funeral pyre was lit by Uday's father Preet Mohinder Singh, a former Indian Army Officer, in the presence of grieving relatives and friends. Addressing Udai Singh's family and the gathering of their relations and friends, Campbell said: "Sergeant Uday Singh was and always will be an American soldier. He always placed the mission first. He never accepted defeat and he never quit. He is our hero. Today, we stand tall as a nation and an Army, and in our grieving take enormous pride in saluting Sergeant Uday Singh for his noble stance to make the world safer, his sense of honour and commitment and his loyal and faithful service to our country." Playing glowing tributes to "a brother in arms and India's son", the U.S. General said: "Today, two great democratic nations pause and mourn the loss of this courageous young man who chose the life of a soldier."

The following Sikh soldiers of the Indian Army were awarded the American gallantry awards, while serving alongside the American Army during the Italian campaign of the Second World War.

Jemadar Gurnam Singh, of 12TH Frontier Force Regiment was awarded the 'Silver Star' for gallantry in action in Italy on 11TH April 1945.

Lance Naik Harnam Singh, of 2ND Punjab Regiment was awarded the 'Silver Star' for gallantry in action in Italy on 20TH April 1945.

Sapper Atma Singh, of Bengal Sappers and Miners was awarded the 'Bronze Star' for Meritorious Service in Italy in 1944.

Sepoy Bishan Singh, of 15TH Punjab Regiment was awarded the 'Bronze Star' in Italy on 15TH September 1944

Lance Naik Mehr Singh, of Indian Service Corps was awarded the 'Bronze Star' during the early part of the Cassino operations.

MALAYSIAN SIKH SOLDIERS
Compiled with Lt. Col Baldev Singh Johl (Retd)

Malaysian Sikhs have played a great part in the history of the Malaysian Armed Forces. The early Sikhs, that joined the Malaysian Armed Forces (then Malayan Army), can be traced to the early 1950s, when General Sir Gerald Templer's twelve selected local cadets were sent to the Royal Military Academy, Sandhurst, United Kingdom for Officer Training. The first Sikh Officer selected was Lakhbir Singh Gill, who formed part of the famous Templer's twelve. From then on there was a gradual recruitment of Sikhs into the Malaysian Armed Forces to this day. Sikhs were part of Units and establishments in which they held key appointments and partook in missions/assignments to defeat threats to the country or accomplish set missions. True to the traditions of their forefathers, Malaysian Armed Forces Sikhs served their country unconditionally. Only four Sikh Officers are on record, to have earned some form of Award for Gallantry.

Dara Singh, Brigadier-General

In 1939, when 4,000 Chinese from Malaya volunteered for service in China, Dara Singh went along with them. "I was the only Indian in the party, but then I knew Chinese." As a Chinese speaking Sikh, called Dara Ah-Leng, in the Kuomintang Army, he succeeded and rose from Sergeant to Colonel in two years and then was personally promoted to Brigadier-General by Chiang Kai Shek in 1943. Later he served with the American forces in Burma and worked closely with General Joseph W. Stillwell, who was Commanding Chinese troops against the Japanese. Here he was the General's aide, bodyguard, and interpreter, making good use of the language skills he had nurtured in Malaya and China. He spoke fluent Hokkien and six other Chinese dialects, Malay, English, Hindi, Tamil, Punjabi, and Burmese. Working with General Stillwell then provided the opportunity to work with Lord Louis Mountbatten, the World War Two Allied Chief of Combined Operations, and South East Asia. It was during this period that he rescued Lord Louis from a jeep crash. He had been struck in the eye with bamboo while driving and lost control of the vehicle. Prompt first aid from Dara and then a fast trip to a field hospital with him saved Mountbatten's sight, something acknowledged publicly by Lord Louis at a reception in Malaysia in 1967. When he finally returned to Taiping after the War, the Chinese gave him a hero's welcome and for one year, everything was given free to him and his family as a thank you for what he had done. Free food, accommodation, clothes and more, everything was free! Appointed as Protector of Aborigines (Orang Asli) he made friends with them and their children by handing out used tennis balls no longer required by the clubs. When he left the post he was crowned by the Aborigines "Tata (grandfather) of all Aborigines". He turned down the post of Ambassador to an African country, offered by the Prime Minister Tun Abdul Razak, preferring to stay in Malaysia and live a simple life, working hard, without any form of pension, to ensure his children were educated.

Malaysian Sikh Soldiers

Rajbans Singh Gill, Brigadier General

Brigadier General Rajbans Singh Gill joined the Army in February 1953. He was trained at Eaton Hall, UK in May 1953 and was commissioned on 5TH September 1953. He was posted to 1ST Federation Regiment. He was awarded *"Mention in Despatch"* on 19TH June, 1959, while serving with the UN in the Congo. He commanded 3RD Royal Ranger Regiment May 1970 to January 1971. He was promoted to Brigadier General on 1ST December 1979 (the first Sikh to attain the General rank) and commanded Rejang Area Security Command (RASCOM), a Brigade Group Organization, from January 1980 to February 1981, in the Rejang area of Sarawak. He served as the Chief of Staff General Branch, Army Corps HQ from March 1981 to December 1982 and commanded 10TH Brigade in 1983 to 1985.

Baljit Singh, Brigadier General

Brigadier General Baljit Singh joined the Army on 2ND February 1953. He first trained at Eaton Hall, UK from 29TH August 1953 to 17th December 1953 and later at RMA Sandhurst from 10th March 1954 to 27TH July 1955. He was commissioned on 28TH July 1955 and was posted to 1ST Federation Regiment. He served with the Malayan Special Force Congo Group (UN) from November 1961 to August 1962. He was awarded *"Mention in Despatch"* for actions in the Congo. He later commanded 1ST Royal Ranger Regiment from April 1971 to January 1973 and Commandant of the Malaysian Army Combat Training Centre from 1ST January 1981 to 31ST December 1981. He was promoted to Brigadier General on 1ST January 1982 (the second Sikh Officer to be promoted to that rank in the Malaysian Army) and commanded 1ST Malaysian Infantry Brigade from January 1982 to December 1983. He also commanded 10TH Malaysian Infantry Brigade from January 1984 to October 1985. He later was the Commandant of the Malaysian Armed Forces Defence College from November 1985 to April 1986.

Ranjit Singh Ramday, Brigadier General

Brigadier General Ranjit Singh Ramday was commissioned in the Army on 31ST October 1974. He was posted to 3RD Royal Ranger Regiment. Having served in various appointments in the early years, he volunteered to join 8TH Royal Ranger Regiment, the newly formed Malaysian Parachute Infantry Battalion. He served in the Regiment as a Company Commander, Second-in-Command and finally commanded the Regiment from June 1996 until June 1999. He also served with the UN HQ (MONUC) in the Democratic Republic of the Congo from May 2004 to June 2005. He was Directing Staff at the Malaysian Armed Forces Staff College from January 2000 to January 2003 and later at the Malaysian Armed Forces Defence College from July 2007 to February 2011. On 28TH February 2011, he was posted to the Army Training Command as Chief of Staff and was promoted to Brigadier General.

Malaysian Sikh Soldiers

*Ranjit Singh Gill, Brigadier General Dato**

Brigadier General Ranjit Singh Gill joined the Royal Military College in February 1968 and was commissioned Pilot Officer in September 1968. He got his "Wings" in January 1970. He was an active Helicopter Pilot supporting ground missions against the Malayan Communist Party in the border regions with Indonesia and Thailand. He rose to become a Pilot Examiner and a Category 'A' Instructor. He had a short stint as a Fixed Wing Pilot flying the Twin-Engine Cessna 402B Transport Aircraft. He commanded the Training Base at Kluang, Johor from 1992 to 1995 and later the Operational Base at Subang, Selangor in 1996 and 1997. He served as the Chief of Staff in No. 2 Air Division in Subang and shortly after set up and commanded the Air Force's Safety, Standards, and Readiness (SSR) Department, which carried out examinations of all Pilots and Cabin Crew. This included the examination and assessment of the Operational Readiness Inspections (ORI) of all RMAF Units. Ranjit had the distinction of being the first Sikh General in the Air Force and the third in the Malaysian Armed Forces (MAF) after Brigadier General Rajbans Singh and Brigadier General Baljit Singh. Before his retirement in 2003, he was bestowed with the title of "Dato"[1] by His Royal Highness, The Sultan of Pahang, and the first Sikh in the Malaysian Armed Forces to be granted such an award.

Baldev Singh Johl, Lieutenant Colonel

Lieutenant Colonel Baldev Singh Johl was trained at the Royal Military College, Kuala Lumpur from April 1969 to April 1971. He was posted into the Royal Ranger Regiment and held several appointments in the various Units he served in. In 1974, as the Unit Intelligence Officer of 7TH Royal Ranger Regiment, his analysis led to an ambush operation that resulted in the elimination of 5 communist terrorist (CT) of the MCP within a day of execution. In 1977, in a similar ambush operation, a subunit of his Company eliminated 2 CTs in the Malaysia/Thailand border region. He commanded 6TH Royal Ranger Regiment from 1991 to December 1993, during which time the Regiment was involved in a humanitarian effort to rescue the victims of a massive Highland Tower collapse. Later in 1999, while serving with the UN Military Observer group in East Timor, he intervened in a militia raid on refugees, escaping into the UN HQ in Dili. Lieutenant Colonel Baldev Singh Johl retired on 28TH April 2004, after a good 35 years service.

---

* **'Dato'** is the highest state title conferred by the Ruler on the most deserving recipients who have contributed greatly to the nation or state.

Malaysian Sikh Soldiers

Harchan Singh, Colonel
Colonel Harchan Singh was trained at Eaton Hall, UK from 24TH April 1953 to 22ND August 1953 and at the RMA Sandhurst from 9TH September 1953. He was commissioned on 3RD March 1955 and posted to 1ST Federation Regiment. He served with the Malayan Special Force Congo (UN) from September 1961 to December 1962. He was awarded the *"Mention in Despatch"* in September 1965. He commanded 2ND, 4TH, 5TH, and 9TH Royal Ranger Regiments at various times. He was appointed as Defence Attaché to Vietnam from December 1976 to January 1979. He retired in April 1985 leaving behind the legacy of his command and leadership.

Lakhbir Singh Gill, Major
Major Lakhbir Singh Gill was one of the twelve potential Officers selected personally by General Sir Gerald Templer, the High Commissioner for the Federation of Malaya, in July 1952, to attend Officer Training at the RMA Sandhurst. The basis for his selection, as Platoon Commander, was to form the first multi-racial Battalion (1ST Federation Regiment) for Malaya. It was part of the effort to unite the Malayan people in the fight against the Malaysian Communist Party and to prepare for Malaya's independence. Major Lakhbir was trained from 10TH September 1953 and was commissioned on 3RD February 1955. He was posted to 1ST Federation Regiment. He held various appointments in the Army and was a model Officer for young Sikhs in the Army.

Wing Commander Jaswant Singh
Jaswant Singh was born in Kuala Lumpur, where he lived all his life. In 1951 he joined the Auxiliary Air Force as a Cadet Officer. Thus began an 18-year flying career that would see him become the first local Pilot of the Malayan Auxiliary Air Force, and a pioneer Member of the Royal Malayan Air Force. By April 1955 he had done 470 hours flying and clocked the magic 500 hours two months later as the only local Pilot in the fly past on the 2ND anniversary of the coronation of Elizabeth II. During the communist insurgency, all through the mid-1950s to mid-60s, Jaswant flew relief and supply missions to Police and Military jungle forts, often putting down his Single Pioneer on postage-stamp sized grass landing strips, earning Mention in Dispatches for Distinguished Service in difficult and dangerous conditions, which saw some of his brave friends, perish. In 1965, Squadron Leader Jaswant became the first Commander of the now Royal Malaysian Air Force's Labuan base off Borneo, where he also served as Senior RMAF Officer for the newly incorporated states of East Malaysia.

With British RAF personnel still holding top positions in the RMAF, Jaswant returned to the peninsula in 1966, and now as Wing Commander, becoming Deputy Commandant of the main Air Force base in Kuala Lumpur, ending there, in December 1969, his Air Force career, at the same place where it all began.

SIKH MOTOR MUSCLE

The Sikhs, once fierce adversaries of the British during the two bitterly contested Anglo-Sikh Wars in the Punjab during the mid-19TH century, played a disproportionately large role, given their numbers, as part of the British Empire's forces in the First World War. Although accounting for just 2% of the population of British India at the time, the Sikhs made up more than 20% of the British Indian Army at the outbreak of hostilities. By the end of the War around 130,000 Sikhs saw active service. They fought on most of the War's major fronts, from the Somme to Gallipoli, and across Africa and the Middle East. They went on to have a major impact in terms of campaigns fought, medals and commendations won and the widespread respect and reputation they gained as fighters.

The First World War was a seminal event in modern history, touching every continent and involving millions of civilians and soldiers throughout the British Empire. The 130,000 Sikhs, who served on various fronts, taking heavy casualties, played a crucial role.

The role of Sikhs in the Great War is a largely unknown but fascinating part of the story of the Allied War effort is the participation of the Sikh soldiers in the Dominium forces of Australia and Canada.

Australia

It appears that the first Sikhs arrived in Australia, somewhere in the late 1830s. The Sikhs came from an agrarian background in India, and thus fulfilled their tasks as farm labourers on cane fields and shepherds on sheep stations. Sikhs were recorded as being present on the gold fields of Victoria during the time of the Victorian gold rush of the 1850s and '60s. Seven Sikhs were part of the Australian Armed Forces during the First World War, which fought in Europe. Six of these soldiers returned safely after the War ended in 1918, but one of them (Sarn Singh) died in action in the bitter fighting in France and Flanders.

Canada

Sikhs have been in Canada since at least 1887. One of the first Sikh soldiers arrived in Canada following Queen Victoria's Diamond Jubilee. Sikhs were one of the few Asian immigrant communities who were loyal members of the British Empire. Sikhs found employment in laying the tracks of the Canadian Pacific Railway, in lumber mills and mines. At a time when Sikhs were actively prevented from immigrating to Canada and were denied Canadian citizenship, they still joined with other Canadians to fight in Europe. Eight of the ten Sikhs served in England and France. One man who enlisted never left Canada. Three were wounded, two more than once, two were killed in action, and one died of his injuries and tuberculosis after his return to Canada.

AUSTRALIAN SIKH SOLDIERS

Private Ganessa Singh

Private Ganessa Singh was born in the Punjab, India, and enlisted in 10TH Battalion on 11TH September 1916. He was a 37 year old farmer. The 10TH Battalion was an Infantry Battalion of the Australian Army, which served as part of the Australian Imperial Force during World War I, together with 9TH, 11TH and 12TH Battalions; it formed part of 3RD Brigade, 1ST Division. It served at Gallipoli from April to December 1915, before being transferred to the Western Front in France in March 1916 where it took part in bitter trench Warfare until the Armistice in 1918. The last detachment of men from 10TH Battalion returned to Australia in September 1919.

Trooper Desanda Singh and Trooper Sirdar Singh

Trooper Desanda Singh was born in the Punjab, India; he was 38 years old and enlisted in 3RD Light Horse on 1ST November, 1917. Trooper Sirdar Singh was born in the Punjab, India; he was 39 years old and enlisted in 3RD Light Horse on 8^{TH,} October, 1917. The Regiment had arrived in Egypt in the second week of December, 1914. The Regiment was deployed in Gallipoli and landed there on 12Th May 1915. It left Gallipoli on 14TH December 1915. Back in Egypt; the Regiment was deployed to protect the Nile valley from bands of pro-Turkish Senussi Arabs. In Egypt it joined the forces defending the Suez Canal, and played a significant role in turning back the Turkish advance on the canal at the battle of Romani on 4TH August. The 3RD Light Horse joined the Allied advance across the Sinai in November and was subsequently involved in the fighting to secure the Turkish outposts on the Palestine frontier - Magdhaba on 23RD December 1916 and Rafa on 9TH January 1917. The Regiment's next major engagement was the abortive second battle of Gaza on 19TH April. Gaza finally fell on 7TH November. With the capture of Gaza, the Turkish position in Southern Palestine collapsed. The 3RD Light Horse Regiment participated in the advance to Jaffa that followed, and was then committed to operations to clear and occupy the West bank of the Jordan River. It was involved in the Amman (24TH-27TH February) and Es Salt (30TH April-4TH May) raids and the repulse of a major German and Turkish attack on 14TH July 1918.The final British offensive of the campaign was launched along the Mediterranean coast on 19TH September 1918, with the ANZAC Mounted Division taking part in a subsidiary effort East of the Jordan aimed at Amman. Turkey surrendered on 30TH October 1918. The 3RD Light Horse Regiment sailed for Australia on 16TH March 1919, where the troopers Desanda Singh and Sirdar Singh were demobilized.

Australian Sikh Soldiers

Private Gurbachan Singh

Private Gurbachan Singh was born in the Punjab, India, and on immigrating to Australia he enlisted in 56TH Battalion on 5TH April, 1916. He was 43 years old. Arriving in France on 30TH June 1916, the Battalion entered the frontline trenches for the first time on 12TH July and fought its first major battle at Fromelles a week later. After a freezing winter manning trenches in the Somme Valley, in early 1917, 56TH Battalion participated in the advance that followed the German retreat to the Hindenburg Line. Later in the year, 56TH's major battle here was at Polygon Wood on 26TH September. The 56TH fought its last major battle of the War, St Quentin Canal, between 29TH September and 2ND October 1918. It was resting out of the line when the Armistice was declared on 11TH November. Soon after, members of the Battalion began to be returned to Australia for discharge.

Private Davy Singh

Private Davy Singh was born in the Punjab, India, and on immigrating to Australia; he enlisted in 33RD Battalion on 12TH February 1916. He was 34 years old. The 33RD Battalion became part of 9TH Brigade of 3RD Australian Division. It left Sydney, bound for the United Kingdom in May 1916. Arriving there in early July, the Battalion spent the next four months training. It crossed to France in late November, and moved into the trenches of the Western Front for the first time on 27TH November, just in time for the onset of the terrible winter of 1916-17. The Battalion had to wait until the emphasis of British and Dominion operations switched to the Ypres Sector of Belgium in mid-1917 to take part in its first major battle; this was the battle of Messines, launched on 7TH June. The Battalion held the ground captured during the battle for several days afterwards and was subjected to intense Artillery bombardment. One soldier wrote that holding the line at Messines was far worse than taking it. The Battalion's next major battle was around Passchendale on 12TH October. The battlefield, though, had been deluged with rain, and thick mud tugged at the advancing troops and fouled their weapons. The battle ended in a disastrous defeat. For the next five months the 33RD alternated between periods of rest, training, labouring, and service in the line. When the German Army launched its last great offensive in the spring of 1918, the Battalion was part of the force deployed to defend the approaches to Amiens around Villers-Bretonneux. It took part in a counter-attack at Hangard Wood on 30TH March, and helped to defeat a major drive on Villers-Bretonneux on 4TH April. Later in 1918, 33RD also played a role in the Allies' own offensive. It fought at the battle of Amiens on 8TH August, during the rapid advance that followed, and in the operation that breached the Hindenburg Line at the end of September, thus sealing Germany's defeat. The 33RD Battalion disbanded in May 1919.

Australian Sikh Soldiers

Private Hazara Singh

Private Hazara Singh was born in the Punjab, India, and on immigrating to Australia he enlisted in 13TH Battalion on 28TH December 1915. He was 33 years old. He had previously served in 32ND Sikh Pioneers during the Northwest Frontier operations, before immigrating to Australia. The 13TH Battalion with 14TH, 15TH and 16TH Battalions formed 4TH Brigade. The Brigade proceeded to Egypt, arriving in early February 1915. The 4th Brigade landed at Anzac Cove in Gallipoli in the afternoon of 25TH April 1915. From May to August, the Battalion was heavily involved in establishing and defending the Anzac front line. In August, 4th Brigade attacked Hill 971. The hill was taken at great cost, although Turkish reinforcements forced the Australians to withdraw. The 13th also suffered casualties during the attack on Hill 60 on 27TH August. The Battalion served at Anzac until the evacuation in December. After the withdrawal from Gallipoli, the Battalion returned to Egypt. While in Egypt the Australian Imperial Force was expanded and was reorganised. The 13TH Battalion was split and provided experienced soldiers for 45TH Battalion. The 4TH Brigade was combined with 12TH and 13TH Brigades to form 4TH Australian Division. In June 1916, 13TH sailed for France and the Western Front. From then until 1918, the Battalion took part in bloody trench Warfare. Its first major action in France was at Pozières in August. In February 1917, Captain W. H. Murray, who had transferred to 13TH from 16TH Battalion, earned the Victoria Cross for his actions during an attack near Gueudecourt. He became one of the most highly decorated Officers in the AIF. The 13TH Battalion, along with most of 4TH Brigade, suffered heavy losses at Bullecourt in April when the Brigade attacked strong German positions without the promised tank support. The Battalion spent much of the remainder of 1917 in Belgium advancing to the Hindenburg Line. In March and April 1918, the Battalion helped to stop the German spring offensive. It subsequently played a role in the great allied offensive of 1918, fighting near Amiens on 8TH August 1918. This advance by British and empire troops was the greatest success in a single day on the Western Front, one that German General Erich Ludendorff described as ".the black day of the German Army in this War...".The 4TH Brigade continued operations until late September 1918. On 18TH September Maurice Buckley, serving as Sergeant Gerald Sexton, was awarded the Victoria Cross for valour near Le Verguier. At 11 am on 11TH November 1918, the guns fell silent. In November 1918 members of the AIF began to return to Australia for demobilisation and discharge.

Australian Sikh Soldiers

Private Sarn Singh

Private Sarn Singh was born in the Punjab, India, and on immigrating to Australia; he enlisted in 43RD Battalion on 15TH May 1916. He was 33 years old. The Battalion embarked in June 1916 and, after landing briefly in Egypt, went on to Britain for further training. The Battalion arrived on the Western Front in late December. The 43RD Battalion spent 1917 bogged in bloody trench Warfare in Flanders. In June the Battalion took part in the battle of Messines in which Private Sarn Singh was killed.

The Battalion spent much of 1918 fighting in the Somme valley. In April they helped stop the German Spring offensive at Villers-Bretonneux. In July the Battalion was part of General Monash's attack at Hamel. In August and September the Battalion helped drive the Germans back to the Hindenburg Line. The 43RD joined the advance that followed 2ND Division's victory at Mont St Quentin. At 11 am on 11TH November 1918, the guns fell silent on the Western Front. The November Armistice was followed by the Treaty of Versailles signed on 28TH June 1919. Through 1919 the men of the 43RD Battalion returned to Australia for demobilizations and discharge having 386 of their comrades killed in the blood drenched fields of Flanders.

Roll of Honour - Sarn Singh

Service Number: 2255

Rank: Private

Unit: 43rd Battalion (Infantry)

Service: Australian Army

Conflict: First World War, 1914-1918

Date of death: 10TH June 1917

Place of death: Belgium

Place of association: Maggea South Australia, Australia

Cemetery or memorial details: Ypres (Menim Gate) Memorial, Belgium

Source: AWM145 Roll of Honour cards, 1914-1918 War, Army

Location on the Roll of Honour

Sarn Singh's name is located at panel 137 in the Commemorative Area at the Australian War Memorialin at Australia's capital, Canberra.

CANADIAN SIKH SOLDIERS

Compiled with David R. Gray

From the early 1900s to 1908, when restrictions on immigration from India were imposed, about 5,000 men, mostly Sikhs from the Punjab region, emigrated from India to Canada. Despite being denied Canadian citizenship, a handful of these immigrant Sikhs enlisted in the Canadian Army and fought for their adopted country during World War One. They were among some 250 men born in India who enlisted in Canada during the "Great War." Most of the 250 men were of British origin. Only twelve of the men who enlisted were of Indian descent. Of these twelve, one was Muslim, one probably Hindu and the ten others, most with the surname Singh, were Sikhs. The story of these ten Sikh men, as found in their Canadian military records, and through a series of wonderful links and remarkable connections, is a unique story of service, discipline and cultural clash set against the tragic background of the First World War. The Canadian Sikhs joined individually; in different localities, or at different times. Their attestation papers show no sign of any of them joining up together. Five of the ten men had served previously in the Indian Army. Their motivation for joining the Army may have been influenced by the concept of serving the same King, King George V, who was India's reigning monarch as well as Canada's. Eight of the ten Sikhs served in England and France. One man who enlisted never left Canada. Three were wounded, two more than once, two were killed in action, and one died of his injuries and tuberculosis after his return to Canada. The following information on the ten soldiers is based on research for the 2012 award-winning documentary film: *Canadian Soldier Sikhs: A Little Story in a Big War*, produced for OMNI TV.

Sunta Gouger Singh (Goojar Singh, Sunta Gougersingh)

Sunta Gouger Singh, born in Lahore, Punjab, in 1881, enlisted in Montreal in January 1915 at the age of 32. His father and wife lived in Phillaur, Punjab, India. He had served for three years in 32ND Punjab Rifles of the Indian Army. He joined 24TH Battalion (the Quebec Regiment) and sailed from Montreal to England on the S.S. *Cameronia* in May 1915. The Battalion arrived in Boulogne, France in September 1915. A month later he became the first casualty of the ten Canadian Soldier Sikhs. Sunta Gouger Singh was killed in action early in the War, on October 19TH, 1915, in the trenches near Kemmel, Belgium, just South of Ypres. At the time of his death, the Battalion working parties were in the front line trenches day and night, under heavy Artillery bombardment. Gouger Singh's gravestone is in the La Laiterie Military Cemetery, near Kemmel. His grave is among those of 197 other Canadians, all from three Infantry Battalions, all buried together. Strangely, Gouger Singh's gravestone does not have the expected Canadian Maple Leaf, though his Canadian Battalion number is noted. The inscription is very unusual for a Canadian gravestone. The script is in the Gurmukhi language and reads: "God is one" and "Victory is to God."

Canadian Sikh Soldiers

Buckam Singh (Bukkam, Buk Am, Bukkan)

At 22 years old, Buckam Singh he was the youngest of the ten men who enlisted. Born in India in 1893, he was from Mahilpur, India, where his parents and wife lived. Buckam Singh had come to Canada in 1907 and worked in both British Columbia and Ontario. He enlisted in Smith Falls, Ontario in April 1915, and went to England in September, then to France. He was originally attached to 59TH Battalion, and then transferred to 20TH and later 28TH Battalion. Buckam Singh was the first of the Canadian Sikh soldiers to be wounded. In June 1916 he suffered a scalp wound as a result of being hit by shrapnel at Vimy Ridge, and a month later, at St. Eloe, a bullet fractured his leg just below the knee. He was sent to hospital in France, then England after both incidents. Though he returned to action twice after recovering from his wounds in British hospitals, in early 1917 he became ill with tuberculosis and was sent back to England, travelling on a cross-channel steamer turned hospital ship. Buckam Singh was the first of the Sikh soldiers to return to Canada. In April 1917 he was repatriated to Canada. Seriously ill, he was transported from the hospital to the hospital ship on a stretcher. He travelled back to Canada on the hospital ship *Letitia* in April 1917. With the other stretcher cases, Buckam Singh would have been housed in the expanded hospital on the stern of the former passenger liner. Buckam Singh was demobilized in August 1918 in London, Ontario. He was sent to the Freeport Sanatorium in Kitchener, where he died a year later of his War-induced illness. He was buried in the Mount Hope Cemetery in Kitchener, Ontario. In November 2007 we visited Buckam Singh's grave, perhaps for the first time in almost 90 years. It is likely the only Canadian Sikh soldier's grave in Canada. In the same year, a remarkable set of circumstances brought Buckam Singh's War medal back to his community. A Canadian Sikh collector and historian, Sandeep Singh Brar, purchased his War medal, not knowing it belonged to a Canadian soldier. Following the discovery of Buckam Singh's War medal, Sandeep has created an excellent website on the life of this Canadian Sikh soldier, and founded an annual Remembrance Day ceremony at the soldier's gravesite.

Sewa Singh

Sewa Singh, born in June 1890 in Dinjutah, India, was a widower, with two sons living in India. He had served in 14TH Sikhs for 3 years in India. At the time of his enlistment in Vancouver, in June 1918, Sewa Singh worked in a Vancouver sawmill. Sewa Singh joined the Canadian Army in June 1918, only six months before the War's end, and he served in the 1ST Canadian Reserve Battalion in England, but did not see action in France. He arrived back in Canada on the liner *Aquitania* in late June 1919, and was discharged in Vancouver, British Columbia, a week later.

Canadian Sikh Soldiers

Harnom Singh

Harnom Singh, a sawyer or sawmill worker, enlisted in Vancouver in October 1916, under a false name, Harry Robson. His attestation paper also states that he was born in Mexico in 1888, though his parents were from India and he had a wife in Raipur, India. On enlistment he joined 47TH Battalion, and then served in 143RD Battalion, the Railway Construction Battalion. Harnom Singh sailed to Britain in April 1917 on the S.S. *Saxonia* and arrived in France in early January 1918. Two weeks later, he was wounded in action in France during the fighting of January 1918, but he remained on duty in the Railway Construction Battalion in spite of his wound. It was only after this incident that he declared his real name, in August 1918. He returned to Canada in May 1919, on the troopship S.S. *Celtic*, and was demobilized in Vancouver. He became a farmer in Chilliwack, BC.

Hari Singh

Hari Singh, a caretaker for the *Canadian Courier* magazine, was 33 years old when he enlisted in Toronto in July 1915. His personal identification mark was a scar from a wolf bite on his left shoulder. Hari served in 5TH Bombay Cavalry Sindhars for 3 years in India. Hari Singh travelled to England on a famous Atlantic liner, the *Empress of Britain*, in April 1916. He arrived in France in August 1916. His Canadian military service included time with 75TH Battalion and 198TH Battalion in1917, and 3RD Reserve Battalion in 1918, before joining the Royal Canadian Dragoons. Hari Singh was the second of the four Canadian Sikh soldiers wounded at Vimy Ridge. He was wounded in the back by an exploding shell at the front line at Vimy Ridge on April 1ST, 1917. He was awarded a good conduct stripe in July 1917. He returned to duty on the front lines in France after six months in British hospitals. He was again sent to hospital due to severe back pain in June 1918 after receiving a blow in the back from a sandbag. After spending time in six different hospitals, he returned to Canada on the hospital ship *Neuralia* in November 1918. Hari was discharged as medically unfit in February 1919, in Toronto. After the War, Hari worked for many years at Toronto Carpet Manufacturers and then for a short time with the Canadian Corps of Commissionaires. Though he had a wife and children in India near Amritsar, it seems he did not return to India, and died in Toronto on April 8TH, 1953.

Ram Singh

Born in the Punjab in December 1888, Ram Singh was a labourer in Grand Forks, British Columbia, possibly at the Riverside Nursery where his uncle, Ralla Singh, worked. He enlisted in 11TH Battalion (BC Regiment) in Vancouver, BC, in December 1917, but apparently never joined his Regiment. He was only officially demobilized in February 1919.

Canadian Sikh Soldiers

John Baboo (John Baboo Singh)
Born in the Punjab in 1888, John Baboo immigrated to Canada in 1902 and was living in Winnipeg, Manitoba, at the beginning of the War. He was married to an Irish woman from the USA and had a daughter who was born in the USA. He formerly served for 4 years with 28TH Calvary Madras in India. He enlisted in Winnipeg at the end of January 1916. When he enlisted, it was noted that he had his name tattooed on his arm. He joined 144TH Battalion, and then transferred to 44TH Battalion in January 1917. He left Canada on the troopship H.M.T. *Olympic* in September 1916 from Halifax, and arrived in France in January 1917. A month after his arrival, he was sent to hospital at Le Havre, suffering from the mumps. He spent several weeks there before he could rejoin his Unit in March 1917, just in time to go into action at Vimy Ridge. John Baboo was wounded by a shell which broke his right leg at Vimy Ridge on April 7TH, 1917. He travelled across the English Channel on the hospital ship *Panama* to England in April 1917. He underwent several operations at military hospitals. As a result of the compound fracture, his leg was shortened and he required a cane to walk. No longer fit for duty, he was returned to Canada on the troopship *Saxonia* in November 1917.John was discharged as "medically unfit" in January 1918 and moved to Victoria, BC, were he lived with his family, until his death in July 1948 at the Veteran's Hospital.

John Singh
John Singh, farm labourer, enlisted in Winnipeg in January 1916 (the day before John Baboo enlisted). He was born in 1880 in India. He walked with a limp due to an old fracture, and was the oldest of the ten soldiers at 35 years. John Singh's military will, written in November 1916, bequeathed all his personal estate to the Second Avenue Sikh Temple in Vancouver. In 1916, his next of kin was given as Sidodo S. of Fraser Mills, B.C., though he also had a brother in Lahore, Punjab, India. John Singh travelled to Britain in September 1916, with 5000 other soldiers, on the *Olympic*, sister ship of the ill-fated *Titanic*. John Singh and John Baboo were on the same troopship voyage. His military Units included 108TH Overseas Battalion, 2nd Labour Battalion, and 73RD Canadian Forestry Corps. In January 17TH, 1918 he donated part of his pay to the Halifax Relief Fund after the Halifax Explosion of December 1916.John contracted pneumonia in November 1918, which brought an end to his active service. He returned to Canada in 1919 on the troopship *Canada*. He seems to have returned to Winnipeg in March 1919 and was demobilization in April 1919, in Winnipeg. John Singh's name appears in the Winnipeg city directories between 1942 and 1959, as retired and living in a boarding house.

Canadian Sikh Soldiers

Waryam Singh

Waryam Singh, farmer and labourer, belonged to the Sikh Temple in Vancouver. He was born in the Punjab in January 1883 and his family lived in Kapurthala. He enlisted in Barriesfield, Ontario in May 1915 and served in 59TH and 38TH Battalions (Eastern Ontario Regiment). He served in Canada for 5 months, in Bermuda for 10 months, and England for 2 months before arriving in France in August 1916. When he wrote letters home from France to India in 1916, three of his letters were intercepted by the censor of the Indian Army mails. His translated letters are at the British Library in London, England, along with thousands of letters from soldiers in the Indian Army. His letters described both military action and more personal aspects of the War. Two letters describe events during the Battle of the Somme. In one of the letters to his father Wazir Singh in Kapurthala, India, in November 1916, Waryam wrote: *"On 4TH of November there was a big fight, and much hand to hand fighting took place and many prisoners were taken... When we took the trenches some of the enemy escaped and some were taken. The dead were countless. The bravery which we showed that day was the admiration of the British soldiers. After the fight they asked me how it was that I was so utterly regardless of danger."* Four months after his last intercepted letter home, his Battalion had moved north to take part in the capture of Vimy Ridge. There, in late April 1917, Waryam Singh was wounded in the shoulder. He remained on duty despite his wound, but then he also got "trench fever" and pneumonia and spent almost eight months in hospitals in France and England. He also underwent an operation on his shoulder because the wound had not healed, and a piece of shrapnel had to be removed. Waryam Singh was the third soldier to return to Canada. He was invalided to Canada and travelled on the hospital ship *Braemar Castle* in December 1917, still suffering from his wounded left shoulder. Waryam was discharged in Vancouver in March 1918, still with impaired functioning of his shoulder.

Lashman Singh (Loal Singh, Laal Singh)

Lashman Singh, labourer, was born in the Punjab in January 1885. His brother lived in Bulowall near Hoshiarpur, India. He enlisted in Smiths Falls, Ontario, in September 1915. His name was variously given as Loal and Laal Singh in his military records. His initial Unit was 80TH Battalion of 1ST Canadian Regiment. Lashman left Canada in May 1916 and served in 42ND Regiment and 74TH Battalion, before being transferred to 75TH in July 1916. He arrived in France in August 1916 and soon saw action in the trenches. The 75TH Battalion took part in the Battle of the Somme in 1916. Lashman was temporarily attached to 182ND Canadian Tunnelling Company in December 1916. The 75th Battalion moved to Vimy Ridge and took part in the battle to capture the Ridge in April 1917.

Canadian Sikh Soldiers

Lashman Singh (Cont.)

After a brief leave in Paris in October 1917, Lashman and 75TH Battalion moved through Ypres and Zonnebeke and then into the trenches at Passchendale in November 1917. Following that action, the Battalion moved south into France for a time of recuperation. A small part of the story of Lashman Singh's War service is preserved in a database of WW1 court martial in Canada's national archives. At the end of November 1917 Lashman was accused of striking a Superior Officer, apparently after that Officer accused him of stealing money. In the court martial record of January 19TH, 1918, we find Lashman's own words in his defence, through a translator: *"I came to France with the Battalion in August 1916 and have always tried to be a good soldier and to do my best. Since coming to France I have had only two minor charges against me and had none before that... I produce my discharge certificate from the Indian Army where I served for three years and three months and was discharged with a very good character."* The Court Martial found Lashman Singh guilty of striking a superior Officer and he was given ninety days in detention. Suffering from a "Very sore face" while in detention, he was sent to hospital and spent two months in the General Military Hospital in France. He returned to 75TH Battalion on 12TH August 1918. With 75TH Battalion, Lashman would have taken part in several important actions including the crossing of the Canal du Nord and the fighting for Cambrai. He was killed in action late in the War, on October 24TH, 1918, at or near the town of Bellaing, France, where the Canadians were driving back the German Army with a ferocious, but costly, success that soon brought the War to an end. A book, *The Dead of the 75TH Battalion* (Vance, 2004), suggested it was very likely that Lashman Singh was killed with four others from his Battalion when they were retreating from a night raid into German-held territory on the East side of the Canal de l'Escaut. Five men were drowned on October 25TH, when they were entangled in barbed wire as they tried to swim back while under fire. However, a detailed search of the death and burial records of all the men who were killed that day showed that Lashman was not one of the five.

Because the death records of all Canadian soldiers with surnames beginning with the letters "Sim" to "Z..." are missing in the Canadian archives, we have no information on how or exactly where he died. Lashman Singh was first buried in the churchyard at Bellaing, about 7 km West of Valenciennes, along with another Canadian soldier, Joseph Nadeau (of 87TH Battalion), who died of a shrapnel wound at Raismes, about 7 km Northwest of Bellaing in an isolated incident, the day before Lashman died. Though they did not die together, the two Canadian soldiers were reburied side by side in the Arras Road British Cemetery, near Roclincourt, France, along with over one thousand other First World War commonwealth soldiers.

Canadian Sikh Soldiers

Lashman Singh (Cont.)

In 2010, while searching for any sign of Lashman's first grave in Bellaing, we discovered in the town square, a forgotten WWI memorial bearing the names of the two Canadian soldiers, Lashman Singh and Joseph Nadeau, who died as the Canadians liberated the area.

The text of memorial:

SOLDATS CANADIENS
TOMBES POUR LA
REPRISE DU VILLAGE

J. NADEAU
23-10-18

L. SINGH
24-10-18

Gurmit Singh of Toronto, a collector of Indian Army medals, discovered in 2008 that Lashman Singh's World War One Canadian War medal had survived and turned up in Birmingham, England. Sadly, before he could contact the owner, the rim of the medal with Singh's name and service (219222 Pte L Singh Canadian Infantry) had been erased by a jeweller at the owner's request.

Sources:

Canadian Soldier Sikhs: A Little Story in a Big War. 2012. Documentary Film. Director: David R. Gray. Film Website: www.canadiansoldiersikhs.ca

www.sikhmuseum.com/buckam

Contact

David R. Gray

Grayhound Information Services
3107 8th Line Road, Metcalfe, Ontario
Canada, K0A 2P0   Tel: 613-821-2640
Email: grayhound@xplornet.com

Possible photos and captions for David Gray's article

1. Canadian soldier Lashman Singh's grave at the Arras Road Military Cemetery in France. March 2011. Photo by David R. Gray. Copyright Grayhound Information Services (vertical)

2. Canadian soldier Lashman Singh's grave at the Arras Road Military Cemetery in France. March 2011. Photo by David R. Gray. Copyright Grayhound Information Services   (horizontal)

3. Historian David Gray at Canadian soldier Lashman Singh's grave at the Arras Road Military Cemetery in France. March 2011. Photo by Emily Campbell. Copyright Grayhound Information Services

4. WWI memorial at Bellaing, France, with Lashman Singh's name. March 2011. Photo by David R. Gray. Copyright Grayhound Information Services (vertical)

5. WWI memorial at Bellaing, France, with Lashman Singh's name. March 2011. Photo by David R. Gray. Copyright Grayhound Information Services (close-up)

6. Canadian soldier Sunta Gouger Singh's (Goojar Singh) grave at La Laiterie Military Cemetery, Kemmel, Belgium. March 2011. Photo by David R. Gray. Copyright Grayhound Information Services. (Inscription)

7. Kiara (student from Alberta) placing poppy and flags at Sunta Gouger Singh's grave at La Laiterie Military Cemetery, Kemmel, Belgium. March 2011. Photo by David R.Gray. Copyright Grayhound Information Services. (Vertical)

8. Kiara (student from Alberta) placing poppy and flags at Sunta Gouger Singh's grave at La Laiterie Military Cemetery, Kemmel, Belgium. March 2011. Photo by David R. Gray. Copyright Grayhound Information Services. (Horizontal)

9. La Laiterie Military Cemetery, Kemmel, Belgium. March 2011. Photo by David R. Gray. Copyright Grayhound Information Services.

10. WWI postcard of entrance to La Laiterie Military Cemetery, Kemmel, Belgium. Grayhound Information Services.

11. WWI postcard of hospital ship HMHS *Letitia* "lying in Southampton Water with wounded Indians aboard," 1915. This is the ship that brought Buckam Singh back to Canada in 1917. Grayhound Information Services.

APPENDIX

Sikh Misls 1748

1 The Ahluwalia Misl — Approximately 10,000 horsemen
2 The Bhangi Misl — Approximately 10,000 horsemen
3 The Dallewalia Misl — Approximately 5,000 horsemen
4 The Singhpuria Misl — Approximately 5,000 horsemen.
5 The Kanhaiya Misl — Approximately 5,000 horsemen.
6 The Karorasinghia Misl — Approximately 10,000 horsemen
7 The Nakai Misl — Approximately 7,000 horsemen.
8 The Nishanvalia Misl — Approximately 2,000 horsemen
9 The Ramgharia Misl — Approximately 5,000 horsemen
10 The Shahid Misl — Approximately 5,000 horsemen.
11 The Sukarchakia Mils — Approximately 5,000 horsemen.

The Khalsa 1845

The Fauj-e-Ain
62 Infantry Battalions, 49,000 Soldiers
13 Cavalry Regiments, 7,800 Troopers
32 Artillery Batteries
General Avitabile's Brigade
4 Infantry Battalions
1 Cavalry Regiment
10 Guns Horse Artillery
8 Heavy Field Guns
General MS Majithia's Brigade
4 Infantry Battalions
1 Cavalry Regiment
12 Guns, Horse Artillery
General Paovindia's Brigade
3 Infantry Battalions
14 Guns, Horse Artillery
Raja Suchet Singh's Brigade
2 Infantry Battalions
1 Cavalry Regiment
10 Heavy Garrison Guns
4 Guns, Horse Artillery
General Calcuttawalia's Brigade
4 Infantry Battalions
1 Cavalry Regiment
16 Guns, Horse Artillery

The Fauj-e-Khas
4 Infantry Battalions
2 Cavalry Regiments
Jagirdari Cavalry Squadron
34 Guns (Artillery)
General Kahn Singh's Brigade
4 Infantry Battalions
10 Guns, Horse Artillery
General Tej Singh's Brigade
4 Infantry Battalions
1 Cavalry Regiment
10 Guns, Horse Artillery
General Jawala Singh's Brigade
2 Infantry Battalions
4 Guns, Horse Artillery
General LS Majithia's Brigade
2 Infantry Battalions
2 Heavy Garrison Guns
3 Heavy Field Guns
10 Guns, Horse Artillery
General Bishan Singh's Brigade
2 Infantry Battalions
2 Guns, Horse Artillery
General GS Majithia's Brigade
1 Infantry Battalion
8 Artillery Guns

Appendix

General Court's Brigade
1 Infantry Battalion
10 Guns, Horse Artillery
General Donkal's Brigade
2 Infantry Battalions
General Courtland's Brigade
2 Infantry Battalions
10 Guns, Horse Artillery
Raja Heera Singh's Brigade
2 Infantry Battalions
1 Cavalry Regiment
3 Heavy Garrison Guns
6 Guns, Horse Artillery
Ghulam Mohi-ud-din's Brigade
1 Infantry Battalion
8 Heavy Field Guns
6 Guns, Horse Artillery

Sardar NS Ahluwalia's Brigade
1 Infantry Battalion
11 Heavy Field Guns
4 Guns, Horse Artillery
Dewan Sawan Mull's Brigade
3 Infantry Battalions
40 Heavy Garrison Guns
6 Guns, Horse Artillery
Raja Pratap Singh's Brigade
3 Infantry Battalions
Raja Gulab Singh's Brigade
3 Infantry Battalions
40 Heavy Garrison Guns
15 Guns, Horse Artillery
Imam-ud-din's Brigade
3 Infantry Battalions
4 Guns, Horse Artillery

The Nihangs – also known as Akalis

The Nihangs were self-appointed guardians of the faith and the state. At times of war or major conflict, they allied themselves to the Khalsa, in four mounted Jathas called Changri; a total of 5,000 warriors.

Gallantry Awards

Victoria Cross

The Victoria Cross (VC) is the highest recognition for valour "in the face of the enemy" that can be awarded to Members of the British and some Commonwealth Armed Forces (British Empire personnel prior to the Commonwealth). In 1911 King George V extended this to include Officers and men of the Indian Army. Previously the equivalent award for which these soldiers were eligible was the Indian Order of Merit.

Indian Order of Merit

The East India Company first introduced this medal in 1837 and it was proposed for "conspicuous gallantry in the field". The Indian Order of Merit was the highest gallantry award available to Indian soldiers between 1837 and 1911, when the eligibility for the Victoria Cross was extended to Indian Officers and men. The Indian Order of Merit ranks high among the oldest and most venerable of decorations for bravery, pre-dating the Victoria Cross by nineteen years and the United State's Medal of Honour by twenty-four years. The order was removed when India became independent in 1947.

Appendix

Military Cross

The Military Cross is awarded to commissioned Officers of the substantive rank of Captain or below or Warrant Officers for distinguished and meritorious services in battle. "…gallantry during active operations against the enemy."

Indian Distinguished Service Medal

Instituted in 1907, the Indian Distinguished Service Medal was awarded for distinguished services in the field.

Croix de Guerre (France)

The Croix de Guerre is bestowed on individuals who distinguish themselves by acts of heroism involving combat with enemy forces.

Cross of St. George (Russia)

Established in the Russian Empire in 1807, being Imperial Russia's highest military award for gallantry in the face of enemy, it held the same value and honour as the British Victoria Cross, US Medal of Honor, French Legion of Honor, and Indian Param Vir Chakra.

Silver Star

The Silver Star is the third highest award given for valour that can be awarded to a member of any branch of the United States Armed Forces. It is awarded to any person who distinguishes him or herself by extraordinary heroism in action against an enemy of the United States.

Bronze Star

The Bronze Star Medal was awarded to personnel, male or female, serving in any capacity with the United States Armed Forces who shall have distinguished themselves by heroic or meritorious military achievements, or service in connection with military operations.'

Param Vir Chakra

The Param Vir Chakra (PVC) is the highest gallantry award given to the Indian Armed Forces, for the highest degree of valour in the presence of the enemy. The PVC is the post-Independence equivalent of the Victoria Cross. Since Independence only 21 awards were made, as many as 14 of these are posthumous awards.

Mahavir Chakra

The Mahavir Chakra is the second highest military decoration in India and is awarded for acts of conspicuous gallantry in the presence of the enemy.

Vir Chakra

Vir Chakra is a gallantry award presented for acts of bravery in the battlefield. It is third in precedence in the Wartime gallantry awards and comes after the Param Vir Chakra and Mahavir Chakra.

Appendix
The Punjab Frontier Force

Following the Sikh Wars the British annexed the frontier territory which was to become the North West Frontier Province in 1901. To maintain the peace of the border a special force was raised, which consisted of 5 Regiments of Cavalry, the Corps of Guides, 5 Regiments of Infantry, 3 Light Field Batteries, 2 Garrison Batteries, 2 Companies of Sappers and Miners, from the disbanded soldiers of the Khalsa.

In 1903 the four Sikh Infantry Regiments were brought into the new Indian Army Line by adding fifty to their original numbers:-

51ST Sikhs (Frontier Force)
52ND Sikhs (Frontier Force)
53RD Sikhs (Frontier Force)
54TH Sikhs (Frontier Force)

The five remaining Regiments of Punjab Infantry were consecutively renumbered in the same sequence to become:-

55TH Coke's Rifles (Frontier Force)
56TH Punjabi Rifles (Frontier Force)
57TH Wilde's Rifles (Frontier Force)
58TH Vaughan's Rifles (Frontier Force)
59TH Scinde Rifles (Frontier Force)

In 1903 the four mountain batteries were re-numbered from twenty-one, and the former *Piffer* batteries were thus:-

21ST Kohat Mountain Battery (Frontier Force)
22ND Derajat Mountain Battery (Frontier Force)
23RD Peshawar Mountain Battery (Frontier Force)
24TH Hazara Mountain Battery (Frontier Force)

During peacetime the Force was under the direct control of the Lt.-Governor of the Punjab, but in war it came under the Commander-in-Chief, India. After the three Presidency armies, it was the most important military force at the Governor-General's disposal. Deployed and engaged in numerous border expeditions, it became the most experienced body of fighting troops in India. Most of the force saw action during the Second Afghan War. The designation The Punjab Frontier Force was dropped in 1901, but with the Kitchener Reforms of the British Indian Army two years later, the former distinction was restored to the newly re-numbered Regiments in the form of the subsidiary title Frontier Force.

During the continuing military operations on the frontier the following Sikh soldiers were awarded the Indian Order of Merit for their conspicuous gallantry:- Corps of Guides:- Subedar Kor Singh and Sowar Dul Singh (1853) at Borer Valley. 2ND Punjab Infantry: - Sepoy Bux Singh and Sepoy Jawhir Singh (1857) at Khan Band

Appendix

Appendix
Gallantry Awards, Sikh soldier, 1857-1918

Sepoy Mutiny 1857
231 Indian Order of Merit

Bhutan Dewangiri 1865
5 Indian Order of Merit

Abyssinia Expedition
5 Indian Order of Merit

North –West Frontier 1866-1885
8 Indian Order of Merit

Second Afghan War 1878-1880
96 Indian Order of Merit

Burma 1889
5 Indian Order of Merit

Somaliland 1890
1 Indian Order of Merit

North –West Frontier 1891-1895
42 Indian Order of Merit

British Central Africa 1891-1895
15 Indian Order of Merit

Burma 1893
10 Indian Order of Merit

North –West Frontier 1897
92 Indian Order of Merit

East Africa 1897-1898
10 Indian Order of Merit

Appendix

China 1900
2 Indian Order of Merit

Ashanti (Ghana) 1900
1 Indian Order of Merit

North –West Frontier 1902
8 Indian Order of Merit

Tibet 1904
8 Indian Order of Merit

North –West Frontier 1908
10 Indian Order of Merit

India 1907
The Indian Distinguished Service Medal was instituted by Royal Warrant of 25TH June 1907 and immediate award of 10 medals were made to the Sikh soldiers.

WW 1
290 Indian Order of Merit
774 The Indian Distinguished Service
21 Military Cross
13 Croix de Guerre (France)
15 Cross of St.George (Russia)

Appendix

Sepoy (Later Captain) Ishar Singh VC

"In 1922, Sepoy Ishar Singh earned a unique 'peacetime' Victoria Cross, making him an even more exclusive soldier than his peers, who earned theirs in the heat of overseas campaigns during wartime. It was the first Victoria Cross awarded to a Sikh soldier. Along the rugged, barren, mountainous Northwest Frontier of India lived truculent peoples of various clans who were a law unto themselves. Fanatically religious and incited by their Mullahs, they often declared 'holy war' on the infidel. These well armed, blood thirsty marauders, ready to kill torture and mutilate, constantly raided the British territories and attacked the military posts and their supply convoys of camels laden with food, weapons and ammunition. On the 10TH April 1921, near Haidari Kach (Waziristan), when his convoy protection troop was attacked, Ishar Singh was leading a Lewis Gun section. Early in the action he had received a very severe gunshot wound in the chest, and had fallen beside his Lewis Gun. During the ensuing hand-to-hand fighting, the British and Indian Officers of his Company were either killed or wounded, and Ishar Singh's Lewis Gun was captured. Calling up two other men, he got up, charged the attackers, killing two of them and chasing away a third, and recovered the Lewis Gun. Although bleeding profusely, he again got the gun into action. His Jemadar took the gun from Ishar Singh and ordered him to go back and have his wounds dressed. Instead of doing this Ishar Singh went to the Medical Officer and was of great assistance in pointing out where the wounded were and in carrying water to them. He made innumerable journeys to the river and back for this purpose. On one occasion he stood in front of the Medical Officer who was dressing a wounded man, thus shielding him from the gunfire with his own body. It was over three hours before he finally submitted to be evacuated, being then too weak from loss of blood to object. His gallantry and devotion to duty were beyond praise. His conduct inspired all that saw him and earned him the Victoria Cross."

In 1947 Ishar Singh was transferred to The Sikh Regiment and retired with the rank of Captain.

Gallantry Awards- Iraq 1920

The 45TH Rattray's Sikhs were awarded a cluster of Indian Orders of Merit medals, for conspicuous gallantry during the violent fighting in Iraq during 1920.

Havildar Tara Singh IOM

"During an attack on a column, Havildar Tara Singh was often exposed to heavy enemy fire, but repeatedly established his signalling stations. On reaching the most forward position, he twice climbed up a telegraph pole under fire in order to 'Tap in'. He displayed great gallantry and initiative."

Appendix

Sepoy Ram Singh IOM
"During an attack on a position, Sepoy Ram Singh was one of a Lewis Gun team. By the accuracy of his fire, he materially assisted the advance of the line. He was severely wounded, but refused to leave his gun. His determination and courage were a splendid example to all."

Sepoy Chanan Singh IOM
"During an attack, when the firing line was unable to advance, Sepoy Chanan Singh ran back fifty yards under heavy fire and brought up a Lewis Gun. Though wounded, he managed to get the gun into action, and his courage and coolness were beyond all praise. This gallant Sepoy succumbed to his wounds."

Sepoy Mahna Singh IOM
"Sepoy Mahna Singh was awarded the IOM for conspicuous gallantry on July 7th 1920, in Mesopotamia, in rescuing wounded, who were lying within 100 yards of the enemy's position. He displayed marked courage and initiative under fire in locating snipers, who were effectively enfilading the stretcher bearers. Two of them he killed and the remainder fled."

Havildar Ganga Singh IOM
"Havildar Ganga Singh was awarded the IOM for conspicuous gallantry and devotion to duty on July 22ND 1920. When the rear guard was heavily attacked and driven back, on his own initiative he took up a position, and brought such an effective fire to bear on the enemy that the latter were unable to advance. By his bravery and coolness, he so inspired the men under him, that the line was restored and the enemy had been driven back."

Havildar Hardit Singh IOM
"Havildar Hardit Singh was awarded the IOM for conspicuous gallantry and devotion to duty on July 22ND 1920. During an attack on a position his Platoon Commander was wounded. He at once took command, and by his skilful leading drove back the enemy. Later when the rear guard was driven in, on his own initiative he took up a position on the flank, and by his accurate fire materially assisted in stopping the rush."

Gallantry Awards- Anatolia 1920

Naik Bhag Singh IOM
"Naik Bhag Singh was awarded the Indian Order of Merit for conspicuous gallantry and devotion to duty on 15TH June 1920. Although severely wounded, he continued to lead his section and direct his Lewis Guns under heavy Machine Gun fire. He set a splendid example to his men."

Appendix

Lance Naik Kehr Singh IOM

"Lance Naik Kehr Singh was awarded the Indian Order of Merit for conspicuous gallantry and devotion to duty on 15TH June 1920. Although severely wounded he continued to fire his Lewis Gun under heavy Machine Gun fire from three directions. He was afterwards carried back, but retained his Lewis Gun which he brought into action in another position."

Gallantry Awards – World War 11

Havildar Parkash Singh VC

"In Burma on January 6TH, 1943, near the Japanese-occupied village of Donbaik, the enemy hurled a salvo of grenades at the leading armoured troop carrier. Havildar Parkash Singh's Superior Officer, Captain Bert Causey, was immediately wounded. Parkash took command while Causey retired. He saw that further forward two other carriers were bogged down and under heavy fire from the advancing Japanese. With his Bren gunner wounded, he drove forward with one hand, firing the Bren with the other. He charged into the ranks of the astonished Japanese, scattering them and continued into their fixed positions causing such consternation that they fled. He then returned to pick up the stranded men. Despite a hail of fire from a fresh Japanese attack, all eight men embarked and crouched, shaking, on the floor with rifle and machine-gun fire hammering against the casing all the way back to the British/Indian lines.

On January 19TH the carriers were ordered to advance along the beach and draw the enemy's fire. They were greeted by a burst of anti-tank gunfire against the lightly armoured carriers. Several were wrecked, including Causey's, whose driver had both legs shot off. Dragging his terrified driver out of a trench, Parkash guided his carrier down to the beach again, through a hail of small and large calibre gunfire. He discovered that Causey and his driver were too badly injured to be moved. Ignoring Causey's pleas to retreat and save himself, Parkash rigged up a makeshift tow-chain, exposing himself to enemy fire as he scuttled between the two vehicles. Causey was too weak from his wounds to put his vehicle in neutral and Parkash vaulted from one vehicle to the other to free the jammed lever. One of the more hair-raising tows in vehicular history then took place; over rough ground with anti-tank rounds ripping through the hulls of both carriers. For the last hundred yards, in a gesture of admirable bravado, Parkash sat on top of his vehicle, a splendid, be-turbaned figure with arms folded, impassively ignoring the Japanese bullets whistling around his ears. As they came into their own lines one observer said presciently "There's a fellow winning a VC."

In 1947 Parkash Singh was transferred to the Sikh Regiment, retiring with the rank of Major in 1968.

Born at Sharikar, Lyallpur District, Punjab, India, 31ST March 1913.

Died in London, 23RD March 1991 aged 78.

Appendix

Naik Nand Singh VC

The Japanese had taken Burma and were poised for the invasion of India. 1ST Battalion, 11TH Sikh Regiment became part of 7TH Indian Division formed for the re-conquest of Burma and the destruction of the Japanese forces. The Japanese would not surrender; and had to be killed one by one. On the night of March 11TH/12TH, 1944, a Japanese platoon about 40 strong, with medium and light machine guns and a grenade discharger, infiltrated into the Battalion's position covering the main Maungdaw-Buthidaung road. They occupied a dominating position where they dug foxholes and trenches on the precipitous sides of the hill, threatening to hold up the main advance. A Platoon was ordered to capture the position at all costs. Naik Nand Singh, a Section Commander, led his men on a narrow path up to the top of a very steep knife-edged ridge. This necessitated proceeding in single file under heavy machine gun and rifle fire. Shouting the Sikh battle cry, "Sat Siri Akal", Nand Singh led the attack. Although wounded in the thigh, he rushed ahead of his section and captured the first enemy trench. He then crawled forward alone under heavy fire. Although wounded again in the face and shoulder by a grenade that burst one yard in front of him, he took the second trench at the point of his bayonet. Shortly afterwards, when all his section had been either killed or wounded, Naik Nand Singh dragged himself out of the trench and captured a third trench, killing all the occupants with his bayonet. Due to the capture of these three trenches the remainder of the Platoon were able to seize the top of the hill and deal with the remaining Japanese. During these operations Nand Singh personally killed seven of the enemy.

Owing to his determination, outstanding spirit, and magnificent courage, the dominating position was won back from the enemy and he was awarded the Victoria Cross.

In the 1947 conflict over Kashmir, Nand Singh was mortally wounded while leading a bayonet attack on the enemy. For his supreme sacrifice in this action Nand Singh was awarded MVC (Mahavir Chakra), the second highest military award for valour in India. Nand Singh is the only Indian soldier to have been awarded both the VC and MVC.

Lieutenant Karamjeet Singh Judge VC

In Burma on 18TH March 1945, Lieutenant Karamjeet Singh Judge was ordered to capture the Cotton Mill area on the outskirts of Myingyan. Up to the last moment Lieut. Karamjeet Singh Judge dominated the entire battlefield by his numerous and successive acts of superb gallantry. Although cover around the tanks was non-existent, Lieutenant Karamjeet Singh Judge remained with the tanks, regardless not only of heavy small-arms fire directed at him but also of extremely heavy shelling directed at the tanks. Lieut. Karamjeet Singh Judge succeeded in recalling the tanks and personally indicated the bunkers for the tanks to deal with, thus allowing the Infantry to advance. In every case Lieutenant Karamjeet Singh Judge personally led the Infantry charges against the bunkers and was invariably the first to arrive.

Appendix

In this way, this brilliant and courageous Officer eliminated ten bunkers. On one occasion, as he was going into attack, two Japanese with fixed bayonets suddenly rushed at him from a small Nullah at a distance of only ten yards. He killed both. About fifteen minutes before the battle finished, a last nest of three bunkers was located in a position that was difficult for the tanks to approach. An enemy light machine gun was firing from one of them and holding the advance of the Infantry. Undaunted and at great personal risk, Lieutenant Karamjeet Singh Judge directed one tank to within 20 yards of the bunkers, and then threw a smoke grenade as a marker. After some minutes firing from the tank, he asked the Commander to cease firing whilst he went in with a few men to mop up. He then went forward and got within 10 yards of the bunker, when the machine gun opened fire again, mortally wounding him in the chest. By this time, however, the remaining men of the section were able to storm this strong point and so complete the long and arduous task. During this battle, Lieutenant Karamjeet Singh Judge was an example of cool and calculated bravery. In three previous and similar actions, this young Officer had already proved himself an outstanding leader of matchless courage. In his last action, Lieut. Karamjeet Singh Judge gave a superb demonstration of inspiring leadership and outstanding courage.

Naik (Later Subedar Major) Gian Singh VC

In Burma, on March 2ND 1945, the Japanese were holding a strong position astride the Kamye-Myingyan road. As all water supply points were within the enemy's position, it was vital that he should be dislodged. The attack on the first objective was successful and one Platoon was ordered to attack a village to the right. This Platoon's attack, with the aid of tanks, advanced very slowly under very heavy enemy fire. Naik Gian Singh was in command of the leading section. The enemy was well concealed along the cacti hedges but Naik Gian Singh soon observed enemy foxholes some 20 yards ahead. Ordering his light machine gunner to cover him, he rushed the enemy foxholes alone, firing his Tommy gun. He was met by a hail of fire and wounded in the arm. In spite of this he continued his advance alone, hurling grenades. He killed several Japanese including four in one of the enemy main weapon pits. By this time a troop of British tanks moved in support and came under fire from a cleverly concealed enemy anti-tank gun. Naik Gian Singh quickly saw the threat to the tanks, and ignoring the danger to himself and in spite of his wounds, he again rushed forward, capturing the gun and killing the crew single-handed. His section followed him, and he then led them down a lane of cacti hedges, clearing all enemy positions, which were being firmly held. Some 20 enemy bodies were found in this area, the majority of which fell to Naik Gian Singh and his section. After this action, Naik Gian Singh was ordered to the Regimental First Aid Post but, in spite of his wounds, requested permission to lead his section until the whole action had been completed. This was granted.

Appendix

There is no doubt that many casualties to Naik Gian Singh's Platoon were prevented by his acts of supreme gallantry. They enabled the whole operation to be carried out successfully with severe losses to the enemy. Although wounded, the magnificent gallantry, devotion to duty and leadership of Gian Singh throughout this action could not have been surpassed.

At the division of the Indian Army in 1947 Gian Singh was posted to The Sikh Regiment. During the Indo-China War of 1962, Subedar Major Gian Singh was again decorated, on this occasion with the Indian MC.

During the WW11 the Sikh soldiers were awarded the following gallantry awards:-
4 Victoria Cross medals, 30 Indian Order of Merit medals, 108 Military Cross medals, 225 Indian Distinguished Service medals, 269 Military medals, 14 Burma Gallantry medals, 5 George Cross medals, 2 Distinguished Flying Cross medals, 5 The Distinguished Service Order medals, 9 British Empire Medal medals, and American gallantry awards; 2 Silver Star medals and 3 Bronze Star medals.

Indo-Pak War 1947

Lieutenant General Kalwant Singh

On 8TH September 1947, Jammu and Kashmir forces Headquarters was set up in Jammu under the command of Major General Kalwant Singh. In April 1948 the forces in Jammu and Kashmir were re-organized and Major General Kalwant Singh was appointed Chief of Staff of the Corps. India airlifted troops and equipment to Srinagar, where they reinforced the Princely State Forces, established a defence perimeter and defeated the tribal forces on the outskirts of the city. The towns of Baramula and Uri were recaptured. The Indians held onto Jhangar against numerous counterattacks, which were increasingly supported by regular Pakistani Forces. In the Kashmir Valley the Indians attacked, recapturing Tithwal. During this time the front began to settle down. The siege of Poonch continued. An attack was launched to capture Zojila La pass. Stuart light tanks of 7TH Cavalry were moved in dismantled condition through Srinagar and winched across bridges, while two Field Companies of the Madras Sappers converted the mule track across Zojila La into a jeep track. The surprise attack on 1ST November by the Brigade with Armour supported by two Regiments of 25 pounders and a Regiment of 3.7 inch guns, forced the pass and pushed the tribal/Pakistani forces back to Matayan and later Dras. The Brigade linked up on 24TH November at Kargil with Indian troops advancing from Leh, while their opponents eventually withdrew northwards toward Iskardu. The Indians now started to get the upper hand in all sectors. Poonch was finally relieved after a siege of over a year. The Indians pursued the Pakistanis as far as Kargil before being forced to halt due to supply problems. The Zojila La pass was forced by using tanks and Dras was recaptured.

Appendix

At this stage Indian Prime Minister Jawaharlal Nehru decided to ask the UN to intervene. A UN cease-fire was arranged for 31ST December 1948. A few days before the cease-fire the Pakistanis launched a counter attack, which cut the road between Uri and Poonch. After protracted negotiations a cease-fire was agreed to by both countries, which came into effect. General Kalwant Singh was not in favour of cease-fire. Nehru ignored his request to capture Muzaffarabad. Both differed on Kashmir policy. Kalwant Singh retired as Lieutenant General from the Army and was the first Sikh Officer to be bypassed and superseded. He was senior to next Army Chief General J.N. Chaudhary. His last posting was as General Officer Commanding Western Command.

Atma Singh, Major General

Major General Atma Singh, after receiving his commission from Officer Training at Sandhurst, joined the 2ND Battalion, 1ST Punjab Regiment. He was involved in extensive military operations on the North-West Frontier Province and Waziristan. With the outbreak of the Second World War, many raiding gangs, at the instigation of the Faqir of Ipi, said to be subsidized by Germany and Italy, became active in Waziristan and all military traffic had to be strongly escorted. During the Second World War, with surprising rapidity and masterly skill, the Japanese had pushed back the Allied Forces in Burma to the Indian border. It was not only essential to stop the Japanese from invading India, but also imperative to regain Burma. The 2ND Battalion was mobilized in February, 1942 as a part of 47TH Brigade and joined 14TH Indian Division on April 5TH. In October, 1942, 14TH Division mounted offensive operations against the Japanese in the first Arakan campaign and captured Donbaik and Hitzwe. Atma Singh, with the Battalion, was in the vanguard of defeating the Japanese in Burma. He ended the war as a Lieutenant Colonel. Immediately after the Independence of India he was rushed to Jammu and Kashmir, to contain the Pakistani aggression. At the partition of the Indian Subcontinent, Kashmir being a Muslim-dominant state was considered a natural part of Pakistan, which had made Islam the basis of its modern nationality. The Army Headquarters of Pakistan planned the main invasion plan, code-named Operation Gulmarg. According to Operation Gulmarg, every Pathan tribe was required to enlist at least one Lashkar of 1,000 tribesmen. These Lashkars were to be concentrated at Baftnu, Wana, Peshawar, Kohat, Thal and Nowshera by the first week of September 1947. The Brigade Commanders at these places were to issue arms, ammunition and some essential clothing items. Each Lashkar was also to be provided with a Major, a Captain and ten JCOs of the regular Pakistan Army. The entire force was to be commanded by Major General Akbar Khan, who was given the code name Tariq. When the first wave of tribal warriors from Pakistan invaded the Kashmir Valley on 22ND October 1947, the kingdom of Jammu and Kashmir had not acceded to either Pakistan or India.

Appendix

Therefore, taking the plea that it was an internal matter, India refused to send in its troops to the Valley. However, when Maharaja Hari Singh signed the Instrument of Accession with the Indian Government on the evening of 26TH October 1947, Jammu and Kashmir became an integral part of the Indian Dominion legally, morally and constitutionally. Now was the time to react to the tribal invasion, which India did commendably, considering the short notice given to its Military Commanders. On October 27TH, 1947, the Indian Army entered Kashmir to flush out the intruders from Kashmir. Nearly one hundred planes were pressed into service to bring troops and arms in Leh and Ladakh. The Indian soldiers fought the war at the height of 23900 feet. Lieutenant General Kalwant Singh was in overall command and ordered, now Major General Atma Singh, to the relief of Poonch. Operation Easy was aimed at establishing the final link-up with Poonch, which had proved to be difficult throughout most of 1948. An attempt to link up with Poonch could be made either from the South, namely, via Thana Mandi or Rajauri, or from the North via the Haji Pir Pass. Major General Atma Singh was ordered to plan for a link-up accordingly. Major General Atma Singh was further ordered to carry out Phase I (secure Pir Badesar) by October 8TH; commence Phase II (demonstrate North of Thana Mandi) by October 10TH; and concentrate in Rajauri the required force for Operation Easy by October 116TH. On October 9TH, Major General Atma Singh finalised and implemented his orders. The main operation was to commence on about October 19TH with 5TH Brigade advancing from Rajauri and securing Pir Kalewa ridge. Lieutenant Colonel Jagjit Singh's Column was then to pass through, moving from South of Thana Mandi to secure a firm base in the area around. Major General Atma Singh now detailed 19TH Brigade Group to capture Point 5732 with a view to exploit Jhhika Gali, an enemy stronghold barring the way to Mendhar and also captured its objective at 0620 hours. Then the exploitation began. The link-up with Poonch in November 1948 was a notable performance. The enemy ring round Poonch was broken and attempts to force the Poonch garrison to surrender were finally frustrated. Operation Easy resulted in the capture of 800 square miles of territory. Large numbers of refugees, including 10,000 Muslims were able to get away and obtain relief from the State Administration. India brought the matter before the United Nations. Under the supervision of the United Nations, the cease-fire was implemented on January 1ST, 1949.

Atma Singh retired from the Army with the rank of Major General.

Appendix

Harbakhsh Singh, Brigadier

Harbakhsh Singh was commissioned into 5TH Sikh Regiment in 1935. He was a Graduate of the first course at the Indian Military Academy. He had a year's attachment with a British Battalion, The Argyll and Sutherland Highlanders, wherein he saw active service on the North-west frontier. He commanded a Company of 5TH Sikhs in 1942 in Malaya against the Japanese. Severely wounded in the head, a steel plate, which he carried to his last day, was a constant reminder. He was in a Military Hospital when General A.E. Percival, Allied Field Commander, surrendered to the Japanese. He spent three years of a miserable existence, in a Japanese Prisoner of War camp. Released at the end of the war in 1945, he remained in a military hospital for some months. Posted as Second-in-Command of 4TH Sikh Regiment on release from hospital, he was perhaps the only Deputy ever to ride a horse on parade in an Infantry Battalion, as he was too weak to march. We now come to three episodes in his brilliant military career which make him stand out as one of the outstanding Commanders in modern Indian history. India became independent on 15TH August 1947, and Pakistani-backed regulars, irregulars and tribesmen crossed into the state of Jammu and Kashmir on October 22ND In spite of a determined effort by the Jammu and Kashmir State Forces and by the initially inducted Indian troops, the enemy reached the outskirts of Srinagar on November 20TH and the fall of the capital city was imminent. On November 21ST, reports came in of a concentration of around 3,000 enemy troops on the outskirts of Srinagar at Shalateng, just 4 miles from the city centre, preparing to attack the city. Colonel Harbakhsh Singh, then Second-in-Command of the newly inducted 161ST Brigade was given the task of conducting the battle. He attacked Shalateng on November 22ND with two Infantry Battalions, 1ST Sikh and 1ST (Para) Kumaon with a troop of armoured cars of 7TH Cavalry and, in a brilliantly planned and executed operation, routed the enemy leaving 472 enemy dead on the field. He was promoted to command 163RD Brigade, on 17TH May 1948, to clear the enemy out of the Jhelum Valley, up to Muzaffarabad and Domel. While 161ST Brigade was held up near Uri, Brigadier Harbakhsh Singh's offensive, as discussed by General Birdwood in his book; 'A Continent Decides' was a triumph.

"Pakistan's situation was now grim, and had India only used air supply more aggressively to maintain the impetus of this outflanking success, her forces would so severely have threatened Muzaffarabad as to force a Pakistani withdrawal from the whole of the Northern sector. Luckily for Pakistan, they paused." Tithwal fell on May $23^{RD.}$ In six days, Brigadier Harbakhsh Singh had in a lightning move secured all territory starting from Handwara to the Kishanganga over the Nasta Chun Pass and Tithwal after fighting aggressive battles.

Appendix

Brigadier Pritam Singh, 'Saviour of Poonch'

The City of Poonch was surrounded by high hills from all four sides in the year 1947. All the surrounding heights of Poonch city were under the control of the Pakistan army and tribal raiders. Beside the local population of the city of Poonch there were about 40000 refugees in the city as they were forced to leave the areas captured by the tribal raiders and Pakistan army. In 1947-48 Brigadier Pritam Singh was commanding 1 Kumaon (PARA) in the operations in Kashmir. He successfully led the unit in the Battle of Shalltang near Srinagar, crushing all the hopes of raiders of conquering Srinagar. After the successful battle of Shalltang, 1 Kumaon (PARA) was directed to save Poonch as a part of Poonch Brigade. The Brigade column was ambushed and divided into two parts. The major chunk of the Brigade went back to Uri whereas Lieutenant Colonel Pritam Singh headed to Poonch against all the odds. In November 21ST, 1947, Brigadier Pritam Singh (Lt. Col. at that time) leading only 419 soldiers of 1 Kumaon Para Battalion entered Poonch to write a history of sacrifice, gallantry and heroism. He had to do the impossible job of saving dying refugees, maintaining law and order and fighting with well equipped enemy sitting all around. At that time there was no link between Poonch and rest of country. Under the exemplary leadership of Brigadier Pritam Singh, Advance Landing Ground (ALG) was constructed with the volunteer civil cooperation in record time to set up a link. But for this historic Air Strip (ALG) the fate of Poonch could have been different. In the second week of December, 1947, the Air Force started landing Dakotas at Poonch. A large number of peoples were air lifted to Jammu and other parts of the country as resources at Poonch were inadequate to accommodate such a large population at that time. Brigadier Pritam Singh reorganized the resources he had and led daring attacks on the enemy posts and succeeded in uprooting the settled enemy locations. The operation lasted for almost one long year to bring peace back in Poonch.

Jemadar Nand Singh, VC, MVC

At this juncture, Jemadar Nand Singh was commanding a forward Platoon of "D" Company. He led his Platoon into the attack like a band of Trojans. The enemy's intense fire, however, brought down many Sikhs. Nand Singh pressed on despite an injured leg. His men, shouting cries of 'Jo Bole So Nihal, Sat Sri Akal', closed in on the enemy. In the hand-to-hand fighting that followed, Jemadar Nand Singh was the first to draw his bayonet and killed five enemy soldiers. His men now were inspired to frenzy and, acting like fiends, bayoneted the enemy right and left. The enemy broke and tried to flee, but not many escaped. Jemadar Nand Singh had done his duty and captured the objective, but as he stood on top of the bunker, a burst of light machine gun fire hit him in the chest, killing him on the spot. This extraordinary performance won him Mahavir Chakra, posthumously. Jemadar Nand Singh is the only Indian soldier to have the combination of Mahavir Chakra and the Victoria Cross gallantry awards.

Appendix

Rajinder Singh 'Sparrow', Lieutenant Colonel

Rajinder Singh was commissioned in the Army in 1937. He saw service in the North West Frontier Province for a year with a British Unit. After that he joined 7TH Light Cavalry and subsequently became its Commander. When India became independent on 15TH August 1947, Pakistani-backed regulars, irregulars and tribesmen invaded the state of Jammu and Kashmir on October 22ND. Hopelessly outnumbered the Indian troops had to withdraw to Naushera, and Jhangar was occupied by the Pakistanis. In May 1948, as the Pakistanis were poised to attack Naushera, Lieutenant Colonel Rajinder Singh, leading a force named "Chita Force" attacked Asar Kadala, the Pakistani base for operations against Naushera, and completely annihilated the enemy. During the battle for recapture of Jhangar in March 1948, Rajinder Singh was commanding two Squadrons of light tanks. The main road from Naushera to Jhangar is of an extremely poor class and completely dominated and flanked by precipitous hills. Twelve days of incessant rain had literally turned the Naushera Jhangar valley into a bog. The enemy, previous to the rain, had carried out extensive mining of the routes leading up to Jhangar. These mines had got completely covered and camouflaged when the rains ceased. Lieutenant Colonel Rajinder Singh led his tanks with great dash and élan, without regard to his personal safety. One tank was blown up over approximately three mines and rendered completely useless. It was a hazardous task removing this tank from the route; it was completely blocking the only passage and the area was under heavy fire from the enemy. Undaunted by innumerable difficulties, Rajinder Singh led his armour onwards. His selfless devotion to duty and his untiring zeal were one of the major factors, which made 7TH Light Cavalry enter Jhangar ahead of all other troops, and thus led to the successful finish of this battle. In the battle of Jhangar Rajinder Singh was awarded the most coveted Gallantry Award, the Mahavir Chakra. Rajinder Singh was the first soldier to receive the Mahavir Chakra non–posthumously. He made Armour history at the Battle of Zojila November 1ST, 1947, when he led 7 Stuart tanks to support an attack by 77TH Parachute Brigade. His Stuarts were brought from Srinagar using deception, across bridges that were too light to support the tanks. The last part of the journey was over a mule track that was hastily improved. The Zojila Pass lies at an altitude of 3900-metres. The assault began on November 1ST and the bewildered Pakistanis were hunted down and decimated. Until then nobody could have imagined that tanks could be deployed at such a high altitude. He then led the tanks and cleared the road to Ladakh. He was credited with the most spectacular success against the Pakistan Army and is also responsible for destroying the largest number of Pakistani Patton tanks and other equipment, and making the deepest salient into Pakistani territory.

Appendix
Gallantry Awards, Indo-Pakistan War 1947

Lance Naik Karam Singh

"During the Jammu and Kashmir operations against the Pakistan Army in the summer of 1948, the Indian Army made substantial gains in the Tithwal sector. This led to the capture of Tithwal on 23RD May 1948. The battle of Tithwal went on for months. The enemy could not, however, make a dent on the Indian defences. On October 13TH, they launched a desperate attack in Brigade strength to evict the Indian Army from their strongly held positions. The objective was to recapture Richmar Gali to the South of Tithwal and to outflank the Indian Army by marching on to Nastachur Pass to the East of Tithwal. Both attempts failed. During this attack, some bitter fighting took place in the Richmar Gali area on the night of October 13TH. The attack commenced with heavy shelling of guns and mortar. The fire was so devastating that nearly all bunkers in the Platoon's area were damaged. In this action the 1ST Battalion, Sikh Regiment played a very important role in beating back the enemy onslaught. Lance Naik Karam Singh was commanding a forward outpost when the enemy, in vastly superior strength, attacked his post eight times. The Sikhs repulsed the enemy every time. When ammunition ran short, Lance Naik Karam Singh joined the main Company position, knowing full well that due to the heavy enemy shelling, no help would be forthcoming. Although wounded, he brought back two injured comrades with the help of a third Jawan. Ringed by enemy fire, it was almost impossible for them to break out. Ignoring all dangers, he crawled from place to place encouraging his men to keep up the fight. Often he beat back the enemy with grenades. Twice wounded, he refused evacuation and continued to hold on to the first-line trenches. The fifth enemy attack was very intense. Two enemy soldiers came so close to his position that he could not engage them without hitting his men. Lance Naik Karam Singh jumped out of his trench and bayoneted the two intruders to death. This bold action so demoralized the enemy that they broke off the attack. Karam Singh and his men also repulsed three more enemy attacks." Lance Naik Karam Singh was honoured with the highest wartime gallantry medal, Param Vir Chakra, for his outstanding role in the battle of Tithwal.

Total Gallantry Awards, Sikh soldier, Indo-Pak War 1947

1 Param Vir Chakra medal,

12 Mahavir Chakra medals,

45 Vir Chakra medals

Appendix
Indo-China War 1962

Subedar Joginder Singh, PVC

The citation for the Param Vir Chakra awarded Subedar Joginder Singh reads: "Subedar Joginder Singh was the Commander of a Platoon of the Sikh Regiment holding a defensive position at a ridge near Tongpeng La in NEFA. At 0530 hours on 23RD October 1962, the Chinese opened a very heavy attack on the Bumla axis with the intention of breaking through to Towang. The leading Battalion of the enemy attacked the ridge in three waves, each about 200 strong. Subedar Joginder Singh and his men mowed down the first wave, and the enemy was temporarily halted by the heavy losses it suffered. Within a few minutes, a second wave came over and was dealt with similarly. But the Platoon had, by then, lost half its men. Subedar Joginder Singh was wounded in the thigh but refused to be evacuated. Under his inspiring leadership the Platoon stubbornly held its ground and would not withdraw. Meanwhile the position was attacked for the third time. Subedar Joginder Singh himself manned a light machine gun and shot down a number of the enemy. The Chinese however continued to advance despite heavy losses. When the situation became untenable, Subedar Joginder Singh and the few men that were left in the position fixed bayonets and charged the advancing Chinese, bayoneting a number of them before he and his comrades were overpowered. Throughout this action, Subedar Joginder Singh displayed devotion to duty, inspiring leadership and bravery of the highest order."

Brigadier General Harbaksh Singh

The outstanding Commander of the 1947 Indo-Pak war, Brigadier General Harbaksh Singh finally commanded 5TH Division and 4TH Corps for a while, during the Chinese Operations of 1962. Many soldiers believe that had he been allowed to command the Corps during the second phase of the battle by the Chinese, which started on November 20TH, the situation would have been quite different in NEFA. Sadly for the Corps, their old GOC, Lt. General B.M. Kaul, was sent back to command, from a sick bed in Delhi, by Krishna Menon, the then Defence Minister. Lieutenant General Harbakhsh Singh was then given command of 33RD Corps at Siliguri and he finally took over as the Western Army Commander in November 1964

Total Gallantry awards, Sikh soldier, Indo-China War 1962

A number of citations and recommendations for gallantry were ignored by the "higher ups" under the ostensible gloom and despondency that enveloped the politicians after the debacle. However, the outstanding gallantry displayed by the Sikh soldiers earned them the following gallantry awards:-

1 Param Vir Chakra medal
6 Mahavir Chakra medals
8 Vir Chakra medals

Appendix
Gallantry Awards, Indo-Pakistan War 1965

Major General Mohinder Singh
"During the 1965 Indo-Pakistani War, 115TH Infantry Division was deployed in the Lahore area of the Punjab. Major General Mohinder Singh assumed command of the Division on 15TH of September. Commissioned in the Army in 1940, the Major General was already a decorated soldier. He had been awarded the Military Cross for bravery during the Second World War. As head of the Infantry Division, one of the first responsibilities he was entrusted with was the capture of Ichhogil Canal. Major General Singh planned the operation well. As the assault commenced, disregarding the risk to his own life, he moved from one formation to the other, exhorting and inspiring his men to their best. The bridge was successfully captured. For his able leadership and sound operational planning, he was decorated with the Mahavir Chakra."

Major General Gurbaksh Singh
"During the 1965 Indo-Pakistani War, Gurbaksh Singh, General Officer Commanding a Mountain Division was responsible for operations against Pakistan in the Khem Karan Sector. His formation captured its initial objectives on the first day but was forced to fall back to better tactical positions owing to attacks by an overwhelmingly superior enemy armoured force. Three enemy armoured groups, followed by an Infantry Division, later launched an attack. Although the enemy force was numerically superior, the troops under the command of Gurbaksh Singh not only held their position, but also practically eliminated one-and-a-half enemy Tank Regiments. Early next morning the remnants of this attacking tank force were forced to surrender. By personal example he inspired his troops to face overwhelming odds successfully and inflict heavy losses on a well-equipped enemy force for which he was awarded the Mahavir Chakra."

Subedar Ajit Singh
"During the 1965 Indo-Pakistani War, 4TH Battalion, The Sikh Regiment was assigned the task of capturing the village of Barkhi in Pakistan. As Subedar Ajit Singh and his section launched their assault on Barkhi, a well-positioned Pakistani machine gun held up their advance. Subedar Ajit Singh was given the responsibility for destroying the gun. As he charged at the enemy position, a burst of machine gun fire wounded him in the chest. He carried on defiantly and went near enough to throw a grenade that effectively silenced the gun. His gallantry inspired his comrades and they routed the enemy but the Subedar succumbed to his injuries." He was posthumously honoured with the Mahavir Chakra.

Total Gallantry Awards, Sikh soldier, Indo-Pakistan War 1965
16 Mahavir Chakra medals
33 Vir Chakra medals

Appendix

Total Gallantry Awards, Sikh soldier, Indo-Pakistan War 1971

1 Param Vir Chakra
19 Mahavir Chakra
75 Vir Chakra

Siachen Glacier, 1987

Naib Subedar Bana Singh

Naib Subedar Bana Singh was born in Kadyal, Jammu on 6TH January 1949. He was enrolled in the Indian Army on 6TH January 1969 into the Jammu and Kashmir Light Infantry (Jak Li). During June 1987, 8TH Jak Li was deployed in the Siachen area. It was found that a large number of Pakistani infiltrators had intruded in the Siachen Glacier. The ejection of these infiltrators was considered difficult but necessary and a special task force was constituted for the purpose. Naib Subedar Singh volunteered to join this force.

His award citation states:

"Naib Subedar Bana Singh volunteered to be a member of a task force constituted in June 1987 to clear an intrusion by an adversary in the Siachen Glacier area at an altitude of 21,000 feet. The post was virtually an impregnable glacier fortress with ice walls, 1,500 feet high, on both sides. Naib Subedar Bana Singh led his men through an extremely difficult and hazardous route. He inspired them by his indomitable courage and leadership. The brave Naib Subedar and his men crawled and closed in on the adversary. Moving from trench to trench, lobbing hand grenades, and charging with the bayonet, he cleared the post of all intruders." Naib Subedar Bana Singh was awarded the Param Vir Chakra, the highest wartime gallantry medal, for conspicuous bravery and leadership under most adverse conditions.

Sri Lanka 1988

Second Lieutenant Ranjeev Singh Sandhu

"During the operations in Sri Lanka in 1988, as Second Lieutenant Sandhu was leading a convoy back from Mangani, militants launched a sudden attack on the convoy and Sandhu was grievously wounded. Though bleeding heavily he crawled out, carbine in hand to prevent the militants from capturing the jeep's weapons and ammunition. As a militant approached the jeep, Lieutenant Sandhu sprayed him with bullets, instantly killing Kumaran, a prominent militant leader. Sandhu continued firing till his very last breath, thwarting all militant attempts to approach the jeep." For his supreme sacrifice, Second Lieutenant Sandhu was posthumously awarded the Mahavir Chakra.

Total Gallantry Awards, Sikh soldier, Sri Lanka 1988

1 Mahavir Chakra medal
8 Vir Chakra medals

SOURCES

Allen, Charles. (2004) *Duel in the Snow*. John Murray: London.
<http://cyberraja.com/index.php?option=com_content&view=article&id=464:swo-amar-singh-military-police-training-schools-new-co&catid=77&Itemid=583>
<http://worldWar2daybyday.blogspot.co.uk/2010/08/day-352-august-17-1940.html> (accessed 11 May 2012)
<http://www.sikhcybermuseum.org.uk/history/IndianMutiny1857.htm> (accessed 25 April 2012)
<http://www.sikhcybermuseum.org.uk/history/SikhRegiments1859-1914.htm> (accessed 25 April 2012)
<http://www.sikhiwiki.org/index.php/The_Sepoy_Mutiny_-_1857> (accessed 25 April 2012)
<http://www.trenchfighter.com/40117/165201.html> (accessed 11 May 2012)
Andrews, C. F. and Pearson W. W. (1918) *Indian Indentured Labour in Fiji*. Colour type Press: Perth.
Anon. (compiled by various Officers). (1938) *History of the Guides 1846 – 1922*. Gale and Polden: Aldershot.
Beachey, Ray. (1990) *The Warrior Mullah, The Horn Aflame*. Bellow Publishing: London.
Bhagat Singh. (1990) *Maharaja Ranjit Singh and His Times,* Delhi.
Bhangu, Ratan Singh. (1962) *Prachin Panth Prakash* [Reprint]. Amritsar.
Bickers, Robert. (2003) *Empire Made Me*. Allen Lane: London.
Birdwood, F. T. (1950) *The Sikh Regiment in the Second World War*. Jarrod & Sons: Norwich.
Caroe, Olaf. (1964) *The Pathans*. Macmillan and Co. Ltd: London.
Chhabra, G. S. (2005) *Advanced Study in the History of Modern India (Volume 2 1813 - 1920)*. Lotus Press: New Delhi.
Chupia, B.R. (1969) *Kingdom of the Punjab*, Hoshiarpur.
Churchill, Winston. (1908) *My African Journey*. Hodder & Stoughton: London.
Cook, H.C.B. *The Sikh Wars: British Army in the Punjab*, 1845-49. London: Leo Cooper, 1975
Cunningham, Joseph Davy. *A History of the Sikhs: From origin of the Nation to the Battle of the Sutlej*. Delhi: Chand & Co. 1966.
Deol, G.S. (1972) *Banda Bahadur*. Jalandhar.
Duckers, Peter. (1999) *Reward of Valour, I.O.M.* Jade Publishing Ltd.: Lancashire.
F. Yeats-Brown (19454) Martial India, Eyre & Spottiswoode, London.
Ferndale, Sir Martin. (1988) *History of the Royal Regiment of Artillery: The Forgotten Fronts and the Home Base*. Royal Artillery Institution: London.
Fleming, P. (1961) *Bayonets to Lhasa*. Rupert Hart-Davis: London
Foran, W. R. (1936) *Cuckoo in Kenya*. Hutchinson: London.
Gale, W. D. (1958) *Zambezi Sunrise*. Howard. B .Timmin: Cape Town.
Gaylor J.(1992) *Sons of John Company,* Spellmount Publishers, Staplehurst.
General Staff, Army Headquarters, India. (1921) *Operations in Waziristan, 1919-1920*. Superintendent Government Printing: Calcutta.

Sources

Gopal Singh. (1979) *A History of the Sikh People*. Delhi.
Government of India. (1942) *The Tiger Strikes*. Government of India: Calcutta.
Government of India. (1944).*The Tiger Kills*. HMSO: London.
Government of India. (1946) *The Tiger Triumphs*. HMSO: London.
Grant, Sir James Hope. (1875) *Incidents in the China War of 1860*. Blackwood and Sons: London.
Griffin, Lepel. (1909) *Chiefs and Families of Note in the Punjab*, Lahore.
Griffin, Lepel. (1977) *The Rajas of the Punjab*. Delhi.
Griffin, Sir Lepel. (1890) *The Punjab Chiefs*. Lahore.
Gupta, Hari Ram. (1979) *History of the Sikhs, vol. III*. Delhi.
Gupta, Hari Ram. (1982) *History of the Sikhs, vol. IV*. Delhi.
Harbans Singh. (1980) *Maharaja Ranjit Singh*. Delhi.
Harbans Singh. (1983) *The Heritage of the Sikhs*. Delhi.
Harbans Singh. (1995) *The Encyclopaedia of Sikhism*, Patiala.
Heath, I. (1999) *The North East Frontier*. Osprey Publishing Ltd.: Oxford.
Heathcote TA (1974) *The Indian Army,* David & Charles, Newton Abbot.
Herbert, Christopher. (1978) *The Great Mutiny*. Allan Lane: London.
India Army Intelligence Branch (2006) *Frontier and Overseas Expeditions from India* (Vol.V1). The Naval and Military Press Ltd.: Uckfield.
Irvine, W. (1922) *Later Mughals*. London.
J.D. Cunningham. (1849) *A History of the Sikhs*, John Murray.
Kaur, Arunajeet. (2003) *Sikhs in the Policing of British Malaya and Straits Settlements*. VDM Verlag Dr, Muller: Germany.
Khoo, Gilbert. (1982) *SINGA, The Lion of Malaya*. Eastview Productions: Malaysia.
Khushwant Singh. (1962) *Ranjit Singh: Maharajah of the Punjab* 1780-1839. Bombay.
Khushwant Singh. (1963) *A History of the Sikhs*, vol. I. Princeton.
Khoo, Gilbert. (1982) *SINGA, The Lion of Malaya*. Eastview Productions: Malaysia.
Latif, Syed Muhammad. (1961) *History of the Panjab*. Delhi.
Lopo, Malkiat Singh. (1979) *Sikhs in Malaysia Series (Volume Two)*. Lope Ghar Publication: Penang, Malaysia.
Mackenzie, Compton. (1951) *Eastern Epic*. Chatto and Windus: London.
Macmunn, Sir George. (1936) *The History of the Sikh Pioneers*. Sampson Low, Marston and Co. Ltd.: London.
Magor, R. B. (1993) *African General Service Medals*. The Naval and Military Press: London.
Major General Gurcharan Singh Sandhu (1981), *The Indian Cavalry,* Vision Books, Delhi.
Major General Gurcharan Singh Sandhu (1987), *The Indian Armour,* Vision Books, Delhi.

Sources

Metcalf, Thomas, R. (2008) *Imperial Connections*. University of California Press: London.
Moyse-Bartlett, H. (2002) *The King's African Rifles* (reprint). Naval and Military Press: London.
Mollo, Boris, (1981) *The Indian Army,* Blandford Press, Dorset
Neville, H. L. (2005) *Campaigns on the North–West Frontier*. The Naval and Military Press: Uckfield.
Nutting, Anthony. (1994) *Scramble for Africa*. Constable & Co.: London.
Page, Malcolm. (1998) *K.A.R. A history of The Kings African Rifle*. Leo Cooper: South Yorkshire.
The Punjabis.sg. (2012) *SWO Amar Singh Military Police Training School's new CO* (www document)
Qureshi, Mohammed Ibrahim. (1958) *The First Punjabis*. Gale & Polden: Aldershot.
Renfrew, Barry. (2009) *Forgotten Regiments*. Terrier Press: Amersham.
Robson, Brian. (1986) *The Road To Kabul*. Arms and Armour Press: London.
Rollo, Dennis. (1991) *The Guns & Gunners of Hong Kong*. Gunner's Roll of Hong Kong: Hong Kong.
Rutter, Owen. (1922) *British North Borneo*. Constable and Co Ltd.: London.
S. S. Gandhi (2006) *Portraits of Valour: India's Highest Gallantry Awards and their recipients,* Defence Review, Delhi
Saul, David. (2002) *The Indian Mutiny*. Viking: London.
Sharma, Gautam. (1989) *Valour, and Sacrifice*. Allied Publishers Ltd.: New Delhi. **390**
Shorey, Anil. (2005) *A Legendary Force: 1st Patiala*. Manas Publications: New Delhi.
Sikh Cyber Museum (2003) *The Indian Mutiny - 1857* [www document]
SikhiWiki. (2009) *The Sepoy Mutiny – 1857*. [www document]
Singh, Amarinder. (2010) *The Last Sunset*. Roli Books: New Delhi.
Singh, Harbans. (2004) *The Encyclopaedia of Sikhs*. Punjabi University: Patiala.
Singh, Inder. (1965) *History of Malay States Guides*. Cathay Printers Ltd.: Penang.
Singh, Karam. (2009) *The Police Contingent*. Lorong Pisang Bat: Singapore.
Sinha, N.K. (1933) *Ranjit Singh*. Calcutta.
Smyth, G. Carmichael. (1970) *A History of the Reigning Family of Lahore*. Patiala.
Soldiers Burden (undated) *Smutts: East Africa Dispatches* (www document)
Swann, Alfred, J. (1910) *Fighting the Slave Hunters in Central Africa*. Frank Cass and Co. Ltd.: London.
WW11 AT 70, (2010) World War II Day-By-Day: Day 352 August 17, 1940 (www document)
Younghusband, G. J. (1896) *The Relief of Chitral*. Macmillan & Co: London.
Merewether & Smith, (1919) *The Indian Corps in France,* John Murray, London.

INDEX

Abyssinia 106, 177
Adina Beg Khan 53
Afghan Invasions 51
Agordat 180
Ahluwalia Jassa Singh 57
Ahluwalia Fateh Singh 60
Ahmadabad 150
Ahmed Khel 89
Ahmed Shah Abdali 51
Air Marshal Dilbag Singh 310
Air Marshal Man Mohan Singh 312
Air Marshal MS Sekhon 312
AJS Sandhu Maj. Gen. 2, 8
Akyab 236
Alberto 220
Alexander of Macedon 15
Alkali Phula Singh 59
Alkali Sadhu Singh 59
Alor Star 227
Alpe di Vitigliano 217
Amara 142
Amba Alagi 183
Ambela 85
American Sikh soldiers 327
Anatolia 175
Angoni Rebellion 112
Annenkovo 156
Arezzo 212
Armentieres 120
Aryans 13
As Teclesan 182
Asmara 182
Atma Singh 359
Attock 15, 66
Atya 263
Aurangabad 281
Australian Sikh soldiers 335
Baba Deep Singh Shahid 47
Badhowal 49
Baghdad 145
Baghel Singh 44
Bairam Ali 155

Baldev Singh Johl Lt. Col. 8,233
Bana Singh PVC 367
Banda Bahadur 34
Bant Singh Brig. 288
Barentu 180
Barjisiya 141
BS Dhillon Maj.Gen. 1, 8
Basra 140
Battle for Omars 186
Battle of Aliwal 77
Battle of Beersheba 136
Battle of Chhamb 270
Battle of Chillianwala 81
Battle of Ferozeshah 76
Battle of Gamburu 116
Battle of Gujrat 82
Battle of Jidbali 116
Battle of Mudki 75
Battle of Ramnagar 80
Battle of Sobraon 78
Battle of Tithwal 271
Battle of Tofrek 107
Benghazi 190
Bhangi Misl 43
Bhimbar 64
Bidar 281
Bir-En-Nuss 131
Bologna 224
Boxer Rebellion 104
BS Dhaliwal, Lt. Gen. 1, 3
Bukoba 160
Burma Mounted Rifles 150,151
Bushire 152
Buthidaung 240
Caldari 205
Canadian Sikh soldiers 339
Caspian Sea 13
Caterina 220
Chakdara Fort 94
Chamol 252
Charasiah 87
Chaukggyin 253

Index

Chepu 250
Chhota Ghallughara 40
China 102
Ctesiphon 143
Dal Khalsa 39
Dalbir Singh Maj. Gen. 297
Dallewalia Misl 43
Dargai 95
David R. Gray 8, 339
Dehbid 148
Deraa 196
Derna 189
Dilwar 152
Donbaik 236
Dujailah 143
Dushak 156
El Amein 193
El Gubi 188
Fao 140
Faqir of Ipi 169
Faridkot 50
Festubert 122
Finnachio 218
First Battle of Gaza 135
Firuzabad 151
Florence 213
Fort Gulistan 91
Gallabat 179
Gazala 190
Gazi 159
Gemmano 216
General Littler 75
Genghis Khan 20
Ghausa Khan 59
Ghilzais 89
Gian Singh VC 357
Givenchy 124
Gothic Line 214
Gough General 76
Gulab Singh Dogra 78
Gulistan 91
Gumun 149
Guptas Dynasty 18

Gurbaksh Singh Maj. Gen. 266
Gurdas Nangal 38
Gurkhas 63
Guru 100
Guru Amar Das 22
Guru Angad Dev 22
Guru Arjan 22
Guru Gobind Singh 27
Guru Har Gobind 23
Guru Har Rai 25
Guru Nanak Dev Ji 21
Guru Ram Das 22
Guru Tegh Bahadur 26
Gustav Line 203
Haidari Kach 253
Haidaru 66
Halazin 134
Hannah 144
Hardev Singh Kler Brig. 298
Harjit Singh Sajjan Lt. Col. 3, 8
Hari Singh Nalua 59, 66, 72
Hazara 67
Hitzwe 237
Hukam Singh Chimni 59
Hunza-Nagar 90
Inderjit Singh Gill Lt. Gen. 201
Imphal 247
Indo-Bactrian kingdom 16
Ishar Singh VC 353
Jagjit Singh Arora Lt. Gen. 295
Islamic Invasions 19
Jalkot 280
Jammu 300
Jamrud 72
Jandola Fort 167
Jassa Singh Ramgharia 63
Jaswant Singh Lt. Gen. 301
Jassin 159
Java 268
Jebel Hamlin 146
Jerusalem 137
Jhangar 272
Jind 48

Index

Jitra 226
Joginder Singh PVC 286
Joginder Singh Bakshi Brig. 298
Joginder Singh Gharaya 299
Jordan Valley 137
Jowaki Afridis 85
Judean Hills 137
Kaahka 155
Kabul Residency 87
Kachin 164
Kaithal 49
Kalalpanzin Valley 238
Kalsia 50
Kalwant Singh Lt. Gen. 358
Kampar 228
Kandahar 89
Kandaingbauk 264
Kandaung 263
Kanglatongbi 246
Kanhaiya Misl 44
Kapurthala 49
Karam Singh PVC 364
Karamjeet Singh Judge VC 256
Kargil 326
Karola 101
Karora Singhia Misl 44
Keren 179
Khan Baghdadi 146
Khwaja Jamali 149
Kilimanjaro 160
King Vardhana 18
Kisangire 161
Kissoue 197
Kluang 230
Kohima 247
Koragh 92
Kota Bahru 226
Krithia 132
Kuantan 230
Kulu valley 65
Kurdistan 147
Kushans 17
Kut-Al-Amara 142
La Bassée 120
Ladwa 51
Lahaj 130
Lal Singh 74
Lanciano 205
Bangla Desh 295
Liri Valley 209
Lohgarh 35
Longido 159
Loos 129
M Di Buffalo 218
Magdhaba 135
Mahmud of Ghazni 19
Maiwand 89
Maizar 92
Malakand 93
Malay States Guides 105
Malaya 105, 226
Malaysian Sikh soldiers 330
Mashileh 153
Massawa 182
Maungdaw 253
Maurya Empire 16
Mayu Range 239
Mbuyuni 160
Meiktilla 255
Mezze 198
Modhung 247
Mohinder Singh Maj. Gen. 366
Molazzana 221
Mondaing 260
Monte Calvo 214
Monte Cassino 207
Monte Paglaiola 213
Monte Pianoereno 220
Montone 211
Mosul 199
Mozzagrogna 204
Mughal Empire 30
Mu'in-ul-Mulk 52
Multan 61
Nabha 48
Nadir Shah 51

Index

Nand Singh VC 356
Nasiriyah 142
Nat Taung 240
Niazi Lt. Gen. 295
Naushera 271
Neuve Chapelle 122
Ngakyedauk pass 238
Ngapyin Bridgehead 254
Ngemplak 264
Nibeiwa 185
Nihangs 348
Nirmal Jit Singh Sekhon PVC 311
Nishananvali Misl 45
Niyor 230
Okshithon 257
Omar Nuovo 187
Orsogna 206
Ortgna 211
Pagan 262
Palel-Taku 251
Parkash Singh VC 236
Parthian Empire 17
Patiala 48
Pegu 260
Peiwar Kotal 87
Peking 103
Perak River 228
Perim 130
Persians 14
Peshawar 69
Phulkian Misls 48
Pian di Castello 216
Pignataro 210
Poggio San Giovanni 212
Porus 14
Pozut 260
Prince Nau Nihal Singh 73
Prome 262
Pyawbwe 258
Qashqais 149
Qurna 141
Rafah 135
Ramgharia Misl 46
Rangoon 235
Ranjodh Singh Majithia 51
River Gari 210
Romagnoli 205
Romani 135
Rosello 204
Ruweisat Ridge 192
Sadaung 256
Sadhaura 35
Sahib Singh Bedi 59
Sahiwal 64
Samana 35
San Angelo 210
Sanjing 243
Sannaiyat 144
Santerno River 222
Sarbat Khalsa 39
Sham Singh Attariwala 78
Sargarhi 93
Sartaj Singh Lt. Gen. 302
Sarhind 27
Satthagyen 249
Scythians 17
Second Battle of Gaza 136
Seitpudaung 246
Senio 222
Sepoy Mutiny 84
Serapeum 131
Serchio Valley 222
Shabeg Singh Maj. Gen. 296
Shabkadr fort 94
Shah Alam 44
Shah Zaman 57
Shahanchi Khan 58
Shahid Misl 47
Shahur Tangi 169
Shaiba 141
Shaikh Said 130
Shalateng 270
Sheikh Meskine 196
Shimber Berris 163

Index

Shivdev Singh 283
Siachen 323
Sidi Barani 191
Sikh Hill 238
Singhpuria Misl 42
Singu 254
Sinho 103
Sir Harry Smith 51
Sirurukhong 248
Skanemtkyi 261
Slim River 229
Sokpao 244
Spinkai Ghash 168
Sri Lanka 318
Srinagar 358
Sukkarchakkia Misl 47
Tamerlane 20
Tarakai 168
Tara Singh Ghaiba 43
Tarlochan Singh Marwaha, 3, 8
Tej Singh 74
Tel El Eisa 192
The Ashanti Campaign 113
The Delhi Sultanate 19
The Huns 18
The Khalsa 34
The Mughals 20
The Tummars 186
Third Battle of Gaza 136
Tibet 98
Tiddim 237
Tirah 95
Tori Khel 169
Trans-Caspia 157
Trigno 203
Tripoli 138
Tsavo River 158
Tsingtao 165
Tuffilo 204
Tunisia 193
Umarge 281
Utman Khel 86
Vadda Ghallughara 55

Verlolion 211
Vice Admiral Harindar Singh 8, 9
Villa Grande 206
Wadi Majid 134
Wadi Senab 133
Wana 91
Wilugyaung 243
Yahiya Khan 40
Ypres 119
Zakariya Khan 39
Ziarat 150
Zoji La 272
1 Sikh 170
1 Sikh Light Infantry 321
1ST Sikh Cavalry 102
1ST Sikh Infantry Regiment 92
1ST Patiala 272
1ST Patiala Rajindra Infantry 131
1ST Punjab Cavalry 89
1ST Punjab Regiment, 178
2ND Lancers 118
2ND Mountain Battery 95
2nd Punjab Infantry 83
2ND Punjab Regiment 184
2ND Sikh Infantry 88
2ND Sikhs, 115
2 Sikh 280
2 Sikh Light Infantry 282
3 Sikh 282
3RD Sikh Infantry 89
3RD Sappers and Miners 140
3RD Horse, 166
4 Sikh 282
4TH Bombay Rifles 109
4TH Cavalry-118
4TH Punjab Cavalry 89
4TH Sikh Infantry 89
5TH Punjab Infantry 89
5TH Punjab Cavalry 88
6TH King Edward's Own Cavalry-118
7 Sikh 170
8TH Mountain Battery 95
9TH Bengal Cavalry 108

Index

9TH Hodson's Horse-118	31ST Lancers,166
11TH Bengal Lancers 94	31ST Punjabis, 139
11TH Sikh Regiment 179	32ND Sikh Pioneers.85
12TH Bengal Cavalry 87	33RD Cavalry 141
12TH Frontier Force Regiment, 178	3RD Cavalry 141
13 Sikh Light Infantry 321	33RD Punjabis, 158
13TH Bengal Lancers 94	34TH Signal Company 142
13TH Frontier Force Rifles, 178	34TH Sikh Pioneers 118
14 Sikh Light Infantry 321	35TH Sikhs 93
14TH Ferozepore Sikhs 85	36TH Mountain Battery 154
14TH Punjab Regiment, 178	36TH Sikhs 165
14TH Punjabis.177	38TH Central India Horse-118
14TH Sikhs, 152	39TH Central India Horse 118
15TH Lancers, 152	45TH Rattray's Sikhs 93
15TH Ludhiana Sikhs 95	47TH Sikhs, 118
15TH Punjab (Patiala) Battalion 98	51ST Sikhs 92
15TH Punjab Regiment 184	53RD Sikhs 144
16TH Cavalry, 142	56TH Sikhs 143
16TH Punjab Regiment. 185	57TH, Rifles 118
17 Sikh 281	58TH Sikhs 136
18TH King George's Own Lancers118	58TH, Rifles 118
18TH Punjab Regiment 229	59TH Rifles 118
19TH Bengal Lancers 89	66TH Punjabis 141
19TH Punjabis 154	67TH Punjabis, 139
20TH Deccan Horse-118	69TH, Punjabis, 118
20TH Punjab Regiment 102	76TH Punjabis 141
20TH Punjabis 140	84TH Punjabis, 139
21ST (Kohat) Mountain Battery 132	89TH Punjabis 131
22ND Punjabis.152	92ND Punjabis 131
23RD Sikh Pioneers. 85	Burma Mounted Rifles 149
24TH Punjab Infantry 104	Central African Rifles 111
24TH Punjabis 141	East African Rifles 109
24TH Hazara Mountain Battery 158	Fane's Horse 102
25TH Punjabis, 139	Faridkot Sappers and Miners, 158
25TH Cavalry (Frontier Force), 158	Jind Infantry, 158
26TH (Jacob's) Mountain Battery 132	Kapurthala Infantry, 158
27TH Punjabis, 118	Lahore Mountain Battery.115
27TH Mountain Battery, 158	Malay States Guides 105
27TH Punjab Infantry.102	Mounted Infantry 100
29TH Lancers-118	Nabha Akal Infantry 203
29TH Punjabis 91	Patiala Lancers 131
30TH Lancers-118	Sikh light Infantry 257
30TH Punjabis, 158	Somaliland Camel Corps 115
	Uganda Rifles 109

THIS BOOK

In this, his fifth and final full volume, Narindar Singh Dhesi charts once more the course of Sikh martial prowess through the ages. After the success of his previous books dealing with gallantry awards, battle honours, military leaders and the policing of the British Empire, Mr Dhesi turns his attention to the broad sweep of conflicts into which the Sikh fighter has thrown himself. From the rise of the first Punjabi people, through Mughal tyranny, the flowering of Sikh independence under Maharajah Ranjit Singh, British occupation and Empire, supreme sacrifice in the World Wars, the painful birth of India and Pakistan, to the situation today where Sikhs lead and fight in the armed forces of countries from Canada to Singapore, Mr Dhesi, with his customary thoroughness, leads us through the Sikh soldier's contribution. From the great movements of peoples and wars, to the point of the bayonet in man-on-man skirmishes in a Burmese jungle, Mr Dhesi mixes the big picture with the small detail to create another compelling portrait of the valour of the fighting men from the Punjab.

Narindar Singh Dhesi was born in 1940 at Eldoret in Kenya, where his father had migrated from the Punjab. He moved to England in 1957 and joined the British Army. After leaving the armed forces in 1964, he worked in the building and construction industry. He is married with four children and living in retirement at Southend on Sea, England. He is the author of five books on Sikh Soldier i.e. *Sikh Soldier: Battle Honours (ISBN 978184574891) Sikh Soldier: Gallantry Awards (ISBN 9781845749057) Sikh Soldier: Policing the Empire (ISBN 9781781519851)* and *Sikh Soldier: Warriors and Generals (ISBN 978783310234) and Sikh Soldier: At War.*
They are available from the Naval and Military Press.

www.ingramcontent.com/pod-product-compliance
Lightning Source LLC
Chambersburg PA
CBHW071811230426
43670CB00013B/2421